T0142350

Communications in Computer and Information Science 1811

Rationale

The CCIS series is devoted to the publication of proceedings of computer science conferences. Its aim is to efficiently disseminate original research results in informatics in printed and electronic form. While the focus is on publication of peer-reviewed full papers presenting mature work, inclusion of reviewed short papers reporting on work in progress is welcome, too. Besides globally relevant meetings with internationally representative program committees guaranteeing a strict peer-reviewing and paper selection process, conferences run by societies or of high regional or national relevance are also considered for publication.

Topics

The topical scope of CCIS spans the entire spectrum of informatics ranging from foundational topics in the theory of computing to information and communications science and technology and a broad variety of interdisciplinary application fields.

Information for Volume Editors and Authors

Publication in CCIS is free of charge. No royalties are paid, however, we offer registered conference participants temporary free access to the online version of the conference proceedings on SpringerLink (http://link.springer.com) by means of an http referrer from the conference website and/or a number of complimentary printed copies, as specified in the official acceptance email of the event.

CCIS proceedings can be published in time for distribution at conferences or as post-proceedings, and delivered in the form of printed books and/or electronically as USBs and/or e-content licenses for accessing proceedings at SpringerLink. Furthermore, CCIS proceedings are included in the CCIS electronic book series hosted in the SpringerLink digital library at http://link.springer.com/bookseries/7899. Conferences publishing in CCIS are allowed to use Online Conference Service (OCS) for managing the whole proceedings lifecycle (from submission and reviewing to preparing for publication) free of charge.

Publication process

The language of publication is exclusively English. Authors publishing in CCIS have to sign the Springer CCIS copyright transfer form, however, they are free to use their material published in CCIS for substantially changed, more elaborate subsequent publications elsewhere. For the preparation of the camera-ready papers/files, authors have to strictly adhere to the Springer CCIS Authors' Instructions and are strongly encouraged to use the CCIS LaTeX style files or templates.

Abstracting/Indexing

CCIS is abstracted/indexed in DBLP, Google Scholar, EI-Compendex, Mathematical Reviews, SCImago, Scopus. CCIS volumes are also submitted for the inclusion in ISI Proceedings.

How to start

To start the evaluation of your proposal for inclusion in the CCIS series, please send an e-mail to ccis@springer.com.

Communications
in Computer and Information Science   1811

Rationale

The CCIS series is devoted to the publication of proceedings of computer science conferences. Its aim is to efficiently disseminate original research results in informatics in printed and electronic form. While the focus is on publication of peer-reviewed full papers presenting mature work, inclusion of reviewed short papers reporting on work in progress is welcome, too. Besides globally relevant meetings with internationally representative program committees guaranteeing a strict peer-reviewing and paper selection process, conferences run by societies or of high regional or national relevance are also considered for publication.

Topics

The topical scope of CCIS spans the entire spectrum of informatics ranging from foundational topics in the theory of computing to information and communications science and technology and a broad variety of interdisciplinary application fields.

Information for Volume Editors and Authors

Publication in CCIS is free of charge. No royalties are paid, however, we offer registered conference participants temporary free access to the online version of the conference proceedings on SpringerLink (http://link.springer.com) by means of an http referrer from the conference website and/or a number of complimentary printed copies, as specified in the official acceptance email of the event.

CCIS proceedings can be published in time for distribution at conferences or as post-proceedings, and delivered in the form of printed books and/or electronically as USBs and/or e-content licenses for accessing proceedings at SpringerLink. Furthermore, CCIS proceedings are included in the CCIS electronic book series hosted in the SpringerLink digital library at http://link.springer.com/bookseries/7899. Conferences publishing in CCIS are allowed to use Online Conference Service (OCS) for managing the whole proceedings lifecycle (from submission and reviewing to preparing for publication) free of charge.

Publication process

The language of publication is exclusively English. Authors publishing in CCIS have to sign the Springer CCIS copyright transfer form, however, they are free to use their material published in CCIS for substantially changed, more elaborate subsequent publications elsewhere. For the preparation of the camera-ready papers/files, authors have to strictly adhere to the Springer CCIS Authors' Instructions and are strongly encouraged to use the CCIS LaTeX style files or templates.

Abstracting/Indexing

CCIS is abstracted/indexed in DBLP, Google Scholar, EI-Compendex, Mathematical Reviews, SCImago, Scopus. CCIS volumes are also submitted for the inclusion in ISI Proceedings.

How to start

To start the evaluation of your proposal for inclusion in the CCIS series, please send an e-mail to ccis@springer.com.

Wenxing Hong · Yang Weng

Editors

Computer Science and Education

17th International Conference, ICCSE 2022
Ningbo, China, August 18–21, 2022
Revised Selected Papers, Part I

Editors
Wenxing Hong 🆔
Xiamen University
Xiamen, China

Yang Weng 🆔
Sichuan University
Chengdu, China

ISSN 1865-0929   ISSN 1865-0937 (electronic)
Communications in Computer and Information Science
ISBN 978-981-99-2442-4   ISBN 978-981-99-2443-1 (eBook)
https://doi.org/10.1007/978-981-99-2443-1

This Springer imprint is published by the registered company Springer Nature Singapore Pte Ltd.
The registered company address is: 152 Beach Road, #21-01/04 Gateway East, Singapore 189721, Singapore

Preface

We are pleased to introduce the proceedings of the 17th International Conference on Computer Science and Education (ICCSE 2022), which was held online and offline at NingboTech University in Zhejiang, China, during August 18–21, 2022.

Organized by the China Research Council of Computer Education in Colleges & Universities (CRC-CE) with the technical sponsorship of IEEE Education Society, the conference served as an international forum for presenting state-of-the-art research in the fields of computer science education, engineering, and advanced technology. Focused on rapidly evolving digital literacy and skills, as well as their applications in education practices and digital areas, professors, experts, professionals, and researchers from universities, research institutes, and related industries came together to exchange new research results, ideas, and novel perspectives on a wide range of computer science, especially AI, data science, and engineering, and technology-based education, by addressing frontier technical and business issues essential to the applications of data science in both higher education and advancing e-Society.

We were honored to have three renowned speakers share their latest research works: Ben M. Chen from The Chinese University of Hong Kong, China; Shimin Hu from Tsinghua University, China; and Shihua Li from Southeast University, China. Additionally, ICCSE this year received 510 submissions, of which 168 high-quality manuscripts were accepted in the proceedings. Submissions with the topics of computer science, data science, educational technology, and e-Society or smart society were carefully evaluated through a rigorous double-blind peer-review process (three reviews per submission) by an esteemed panel of international reviewers, comprising the organizing and advisory committee members, as well as other experts in the field from across the world. We express our gratitude to all the authors for their valuable contributions to the conference and their commitment to advancing the field, and to all the reviewers.

Finally, we would like to express gratitude to the program chairs for their wise advice and suggestions on organizing the conference technical program. We are also indebted to the conference organizing committee members, who have all worked extremely hard on the details and activities of this conference.

We sincerely hope that you will find these proceedings instructive and inspiring for further research.

March 2023

Wenxing Hong
Yang Weng

Organization

Honorary Chairs

Clarence de Silva	University of British Columbia, Canada
Hu Zhengyu	NingboTech University, China
Li Maoqing	Xiamen University, China

General Chair

Hu Jie	NingboTech University, China

Organizing Chairs

Hong Wenxing	Xiamen University, China
Lu Dongming	NingboTech University, China
Tang Dandan	Ningbo Association for Science and Technology, China

Program Chairs

Li Xin	Louisiana State University, USA
Luo Shijian	NingboTech University, China
Marcin Kilarski	Adam Mickiewicz University, Poland
Pang Chaoyi	NingboTech University, China
Weng Yang	Sichuan University, China

Publications Chairs

Wang Qing	Tianjin University, China
Xia Min	Lancaster University, UK
Yang Fan	Xiamen University, China
Zhang Bailing	NingboTech University, China
Zheng Tongtao	Xiamen Institute of Software Technology, China

Industry Chairs

Hu Changxing	NingboTech University, China
Li Chao	Tsinghua University, China
Wu Dazhuan	NingboTech University, China

Regional Chairs

Cui Binyue	Hebei University of Economics & Business, China
Cai Liang	NingboTech University, China
Lang Haoxiang	Ontario Tech University, Canada
Li Jingyue	Norwegian University of Science and Technology, Norway

Program Committee

Ben M. Chen	Chinese University of Hong Kong, China
Cen Gang	Zhejiang University of Science and Technology, China
Chen Zhibo	Beijing Forestry University, China
Chen Zhiguo	Henan University, China
Ching-Shoei Chiang	Soochow University, Taiwan
Deng Zhigang	University of Houston, USA
Ding Yu	Netease Fuxi AI Lab, China
Dong Zhicheng	Xizang University, China
Farbod Khoshnoud	California State Polytechnic University, Pomona, USA
He Li	Software Guide Magazine, China
He Liang	East China Normal University, China
Hiroki Takada	University of Fukui, Japan
Hiromu Ishio	Fukuyama City University, Japan
Huang Jie	Chinese University of Hong Kong, China
Jiang Qingshan	Shenzhen Institutes of Advanced Technology, CAS, China
Jin Dawei	Zhongnan University of Economics and Law, China
Jonathan Li	University of Waterloo, Canada
Koliya Pulasinghe	Sri Lanka Institute of Information Technology (SLIIT), Sri Lanka

Lang Haoxiang	Ontario Tech University, Canada
Li Taoshen	Nanning University, China
Li Teng	University of British Columbia, Canada
Li Xiaohong	Tianjin University, China
Lin Xianke	Ontario Tech University, Canada
Lin Zongli	University of Virginia, USA
Liu Renren	Xiangtan University, China
Liu Tao	Anhui University of Engineering, China
Liu Tenghong	Zhongnan University of Economics and Law, China
Peng Yonghong	Manchester Metropolitan University, UK
Peter Liu	Carleton University, Ottawa
Qiang Yan	Taiyuan University of Technology, China
Qiao Baojun	Henan University, China
Sena Seneviratne	Melbourne University, Australia
Shao Haidong	Hunan University, China
Shen Xiajiong	Henan University, China
Tom Worthington	Australian National University, Australia
Wang Chunzhi	Hubei University of Technology, China
Wang Jiangqing	South-Central University for Nationalities, China
Wang Ming	Lishui University, China
Wang Yang	Southwest Petroleum University, China
Wang Ying	Xiamen University, China
Wang Zidong	Brunel University, UK
Wei Shikui	Beijing Jiaotong University, China
Wen Lifang	China Machine Press/Huazhang Co., China
Wu Xinda	Neusoft Institute Guangdong, China
Xi Bin	Xiamen University, China
Xi Chunyan	Computer Education Press, China
Xiangjian (Sean) He	University of Technology Sydney (UTS), Australia
Xiao Huimin	Henan University of Finance and Economics, China
Xie Lihua	Nanyang Technological University, Singapore
Xu Li	Fujian Normal University, China
Xu Zhoubo	Guilin University of Electronic Technology, China
Xue Jingfeng	Beijing Institute of Technology, China
Yang Li	Hubei Second Normal College, China
Yu Yuanlong	Fuzhou University, China
Zhang Yunfei	VIWISTAR Technologies Ltd., Canada
Zhao Huan	Hunan University, China
Zheng Li	Tsinghua University, China

Zhou Qifeng   Xiamen University, China
Zhou Wei   Beijing Jiaotong University, China
Zhu Shunzhi   Xiamen University of Technology, China

Contents – Part I

Contents – Part II

Teaching Innovations in Computer Education Research

Contents – Part III

Innovative Studies on Technology-Enhanced Teaching and Learning

Intelligent Technology in Education and Data Analysis

SATCN: An Improved Temporal Convolutional Neural Network with Self Attention Mechanism for Knowledge Tracing

Ruixin Ma[1,2], Hongyan Zhang[1,2], Biao Mei[1,2], Guangyue Lv[1,2], and Liang Zhao[1,2(✉)]

[1] Dalian University of Technology, Dalian 116600, China
liangzhao@dlut.edu.cn
[2] The Key Laboratory for Ubiquitous Network and Service Software of Liaoning Province, Dalian, China

Abstract. With the rapid expansion of E-education, knowledge tracing (KT) has become a fundamental mission which traces the formation of learners' knowledge states and predicts their performance in future learnng activates. Knowledge states of each learner are simulated by estimating their behavior in historical learning activities. There are often numerous questions in online education systems while researches in the past fails to involve massive data together with negative historical data problems, which is mainly limited by data sparsity issues and models. From the model perspective, previous models can hardly capture the long-term dependency of learner historical exercises, and model the individual learning behavior in a consistent manner is also hard to accomplish. Therefore, in this paper, we develop an Improved Temporal Convolutional Neural Network with Self Attention Mechanism for Knowledge Tracing (SATCN). It can take the historical exercises of each learner as input and model the individual learning in a consistent manner that means it can realize personalized knowledge tracking prediction without extra manipulations. Moreover, with the self attention mechanism our model can adjust weights adaptively, thus to intelligently weaken the influence of those negative historical data, and highlight those historical data that have greater impact on the prediction results. We also take attempt count and answer time two features into account, considering proficiency and forgetting of the learners to enrich the input features. Empirical experiments on three widely used real-world public datasets clearly demonstrate that our framework outperforms the presented state-of-the-art models.

Keywords: Knowledge Tracing · Temporal Convolutional Neural Network · Self Attention Mechanism

1 Introduction

Knowledge Tracing(KT) is a foremost task of on-line education, which propose to trace learners' knowledge states based on their historical learning trajectories. The success of knowledge tracing can benefit both personalized learning

W. Hong and Y. Weng (Eds.): ICCSE 2022, CCIS 1811, pp. 3–17, 2023.
https://doi.org/10.1007/978-981-99-2443-1_1

and adaptive learning so that has attracted prodigious attention over the past decades [1–3].

The KT task can be defined as a supervised sequential sequence learning task: according to learners' historical exercise interactions $X = \{x_1, x_2, ..., x_t\}$, predicting their future interaction x_{t+1} [4]. In the question-answering system, the tth interaction is expressed as a tuple $x_t = (q_t, a_t)$, where q_t is the label of exercise that the learner attempts at a certain timestamp t and a_t is the correctness of the learner's answer about q_t. $a_t \in \{0, 1\}$, where correct answer is recorded as 1 and incorrect answer is recorded as 0. The purpose is predicting the probability of learners will be able to answer the future exercise correctly, i.e., predicting $p(a_{t+1}|q_{t+1}, X_t)$.

In the previous studies, many efforts have been made towards knowledge tracing. Among them, Bayesian Knowledge Tracing (BKT) is one of the most representative early works [2]. However, BKT is a highly restricted structured model. Recent years, benefit from the high capacity and effective representation learning of deep neural networks, the first KT model based on deep learning named Deep Knowledge Tracing (DKT) [4] has become BKT's alternative model, and its excellent performance boost leads us to inspect limitations of BKT. DKT is the first KT method based on deep learning that utilizes Long Short-term Memory (LSTM) [5] which is an excellent variant of recurrent neural networks (RNNs) to trace learners' knowledge states. The latest progress in deep learning has developed a series of deep KT models. Two representative deep KT models are Dynamic Key-Value Memory Networks (DKVMN) [6] and Sequential Key-Value Memory Networks (SKVMN) [7], which leverages Memory-Augmented Neural Networks (MANNs) [8] and hop-LSTM respectively to solve knowledge tracing.

For the purpose of learning high-quality KT models, a substantial amount of comprehensive data is inevitably required for ensuring the stability of neural networks during training. However, the practical educational scenes usually encounter negative historical data problem, which is ubiquitous in learning process. To be more specific, as shown in Fig. 1, a learner want to solve an exercise on "Quadratic equation" (e_5) which belongs to the knowledge concept "Equations". We can see that there are four exercises have been finished, and they are linear equations (e_1), arithmetic (e_2), plane geometry (e_3), and solid geometry (e_4) respectively. The goal of prediction is whether quadratic equation(e_5) can be done right. Obviously, the correctness of the first two exercises should have greater impact on the prediction result than the last two exercises. However, the impact of each exercise is often treated equally, which is apparently irrational. In addition, if the correctness of the latest two exercises (e_3, e_4) is not optimistic, then they would become negative historical data for prediction results.

Therefore, in this paper, we conduct principled studies on above issues, and propose an Improved Temporal Convolution Neural Network with Self-Attention Mechanism for Knowledge Tracing (SATCN). Firstly, SATCN can accomplish the time series prediction task while capturing long term dependency, which can take full advantage of time information in learning data. In addition, the input

Fig. 1. Left sunfigure shows sequence of exercises that one learner attempted in a timestep and right sunfigure demonstrates knowledge concept corresponding to each exercise.

sequence is each learner's exercises they finished instead of treating all learners as a whole or taking much fewer skills as input like previous models, which eases the problem of data sparsity to a certain extent. This is because lots of questions only correspond to much fewer skills. This is also why our model can achieve personalization without additional processing by training and testing each learner's exercise sequence in a consistent manner. We also consider the attempt count and answer time to simulate learners' proficiency and forgetting to enrich the input features. It can be observed from the original data that learners often give correct answer in the first attempt if they have already mastered related knowledge, while questions they tried many times are rarely answered correctly. Thus, we can speculate that learners haven't mastered the relevant knowledge but want to guess the correct answer. Answer time is the time interval between learners start answering questions and submitting answer. It reflects learners' proficiency in the relevant knowledge to a certain extent. As we all known, the more proficient in the relevant knowledge, the more likely they answer the questions correctly and harder to forget. We build a self-attention layer between the input layer and the hidden layer to enable the model can adjust weights adaptively, then it is able to deal with a series of problems caused by negative historical data, so as to achieve more accurate predictions.

Our main contributions are summarized as follows:

(1) The KT task is creatively described as a time series forecasting task and an Improved Temporal Convolutional Neural Network with Self Attention Mechanism for Knowledge Tracing (SATCN) is proposed by improving DeepTCN architecture, which can better simulate the learning process of learners.
(2) By designing a novel data processing and training method, our model can relieve the problem of data sparseness and can model learning process in a consistent manner. At the same time, it can achieve personalized prediction without requiring other operations.
(3) Our model can automatically discover and reduce the influence of negative data on prediction results by accomplished with Self Attention Mechanism. Simultaneously, by considering the characteristics of data we take proficiency and forgetting into consideration to enrich the input features and bring a performance boost of our model.

2   Related Work

2.1   Knowledge Tracing

KT is a necessary task in Intelligent Education System (ITS) [9]. The current knowledge tracing methods can be roughly divided into three categories: the first is KT methods based on probability graph, then KT methods based on logistic regression and KT methods based on deep learning. We mainly study the last KT methods in this paper.

KT methods based on probability graph mainly refer to Bayesian Knowledge Tracing (BKT) [2]. BKT is a Hidden Markov Model (HMM) with hidden variables. Subsequential works include contextualization of slip and guess probability estimation [10], problem difficulty [11], and personalization [12,13]. The most commonly used KT methods based on logistic regression are Item Response Theory (IRT) [14] and Performance Factors Analysis (PFA) [15]. The main idea of IRT is to estimate the probability that learners can answer questions correctly base on their learning ability and item's difficulty. While PFA expands the static knowledge assumption, and it can model multiple features simultaneously with its basic structure.

In 2015, Chris Piech et.al. firstly applied RNNs in KT models which increased the AUC by 25%. The appearance of DKT [4] subverts BKT's transcendent status in KT area. Since then, KT models based on deep learning have attracted the attention of large number researchers. Apart from enriching model features, subsequent improvement works further rely on more powerful neural networks. For example, DKVMN [6] has one static matrix called key and the other dynamic matrix called value, which unlike standard memory-augmented neural networks only supports a single memory matrix or two static memory matrices. Therefore, DKVMN can solve the problem that existing methods fail to accurately determine which concepts learners are good at or unfamiliar with when modeling the knowledge state of each predefined concept. SAKT [16] is the first model uses the attention mechanism, which can solve the problem that other models can't generalize well when dealing with sparse data. SAINT [17] imitates the encoder-decoder structure of Transformer [18], and inputs exercise and response separately, where the exercise sequence is fed into encoder, the outputs of encoder and response sequence are fed into decoder. Several works [19,20] try to introduce graph structure into knowledge tracking, so that KT models can process non-Euclidean data. GKT [19] uses graph neural network [21] to transform the KT task into a time-series node-level classification mission in graph structure. While GIKT [20] utilizes three-layer Graph Convolutional Network (GCN) [22] to generalize the high-order relationship between problems and skills before training.

However, all of the above models face the same data sparsity problem with few features, and don't make full use of the temporal information in the data. Negative historical data problems are ignored in these models, and they can't model the individual learning behavior in a consistent manner. In this paper, our model alleviates the data sparseness from two perspectives: data processing and feature enrichment, which enable our model simulates proficiency and forgetting while simulating interactions. The network architecture that can make full use of implicit time information for training would be used, at the same time, it can adjust weights adaptively to solve negative historical data problems with self-attention mechanism.

2.2   Deep Temporal Convolutional Neural Network

DeepTCN [23] is a probabilistic forecasting framework based on convolutional neural network (CNN) [24] for multiple related time series forecasting. This framework consists of stacked residual blocks based on dilated causal convolutional nets with encoder-decoder structure, which are constructed to capture the temporal dependencies of input series with expansive receptive field and to capture long-range temporal dependencies with fewer number of layers. DeepTCN has powerful representation learning capabilities, so that it is capable of learning complex patterns like regularity, internal and inter-date influence, and to exploit those patterns for more accurate forecasts. When exercises data is sparse or unavailable this capability will show its powerful ability which is common in our study.

A general probabilistic forecasting problem for multiple related time series can be described as follows: Given a set of time series $y_{1:t} = \{y_{1:t}^{(i)}\}_{i=1}^{N}$, the future time series are $y_{(t+1):(t+\Omega)} = \{y_{(t+1):(t+\Omega)}^{(i)}\}_{i=1}^{N}$, where N is the number of series, t is the length of the historical observations and Ω is the length of the forecasting horizon. Therefore, prediction results and be described as:

$$P(y_{(t+1):(t+\Omega)}|y_{1:t}) = \prod_{\omega=1}^{\Omega} p(y_{t+\Omega}|y_{1:t}, X_{t+\omega}^{(i)}, i = 1, ..., N) \qquad (1)$$

Our primary motivation for using DeepTCN is the success of CNNs and adaptability of DeepTCN in this task. DeepTCN is a non-autoregressive probability prediction framework for great quantity correlated time series, which can learn the latent correlations among sequences and model their interactions. Specially, it is able to handle data sparsity and cold start problems that are common in complex real-world forecasting situations, and has high scalability and extensibility. Extensive empirical researches show that DeepTCN outperforms the state-of-the-art methods in both point prediction and probability prediction tasks. By using this framework, our model can capture long-term dependencies with expansive receptive field, and it can excavate temporal information in data automatically. Especially, it's able to deal with historical data sparse or unavailable problem well which is ubiquitous in KT task.

3   Proposed Method

3.1   Input Representation

Our model is used to predict whether learners will be able to answer the future exercise x_{t+1} correctly based on their historical interactions $X = \{x_1, x_2, ..., x_t\}$.

The architecture of SATCN is shown in Fig. 2, the interaction tuple x_t is a quintuple tuple, and the meaning of each notation is presented in Table 1.

Table 1. Notations

Notations	Description
s_t	the tth learner in all learners
e_t	the tth exercise solved by the learner
a_t	the correctness of e_t
ac_t	the attempt count of e_t
at_t	the amount of time that a learner spent on e_t

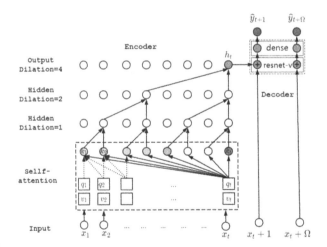

Fig. 2. The architecture of SATCN.

The embedding layer in SATCN maps each input vector x_i to latent space to generate its embedding vector. Specifically, it maps all the five features of x_i to high-dimensional vector space, then the connection operation is performed, which aims to turn the vector x_i into an embedding vector with a fixed dimension of 512. At each timestamp $t + 1$, embedding layer uses Exercise embedding to embed the exercise that the learner is currently trying to solve into the query space to obtain the corresponding query q_i, and uses Interaction embedding to embed historical interactions x_t into the key and value space to obtain the corresponding k_i and v_i (see Fig. 3).

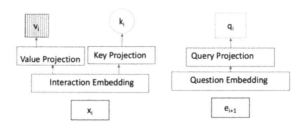

Fig. 3. Embedding layer.

3.2 Self-attention Layer

The purpose of self-attention layer is to acquire the query, key, and value corresponding to the input from the embedding layer, and calculate the attention weight. We use Q_{in}, K_{in} and V_{in} represent the sequence of query, key and value respectively. The multi-head attention network utilizes different projection matrices to perform h different projections on the same input sequence to maps Q_{in}, K_{in} and V_{in} into the latent space, which can be described as:

$$Q_i = [q_1^i, ..., q_k^i] = Q_{in} W_i^Q \tag{2}$$

$$K_i = [k_1^i, ..., k_k^i] = K_{in} W_i^K \tag{3}$$

$$V_i = [v_1^i, ..., v_k^i] = V_{in} W_i^V \tag{4}$$

Herein, q, k, v represent projected queries, keys and values respectively. We employ scaled dot-product attention mechanism. The correlation between value and given query is determined by the dot product between query and the key corresponding to the value.

There are total 8 attention heads and each of them($head_i$) is the product of matrix $\frac{Q_i K_i^t}{\sqrt{d}}$ after Softmax operation and values V_i.

$$head_i = Softmax(\frac{Q_i K_i^t}{\sqrt{d}})V_i \tag{5}$$

where d is the dimension of query and key, which is used to scale.

The 8 attention heads multiply by W^O after connection to aggregate the output of different attention heads, which is the final output of multi-head attention network, i.e., attention weights.

$$MultiHead(Q_{in}, K_{in}, V_{in}) = Concat(head_1, ..., head_h)W^O \tag{6}$$

3.3 Encoder: Dilated Causal Convolutions

In the encoder part, stacked dilated causal convolutions are constructed to simulate the stochastic process of historical observation and output $h_t^{(i)}$. Causal convolutions refer to the convolutions that the output at time can only be obtained from the input, similar to the Mask mechanism in Transformer. Dilated causal convolutions allow the application of filters in a range of more than its length by skipping input value with a certain step. In the situation of univariate series, given the one-dimension input series x, the output of dilated convolutions at location t with kernel ω is feature map s,which can be described as:

$$s(t) = (x *_d \omega)(t) = \sum_{k=0}^{K-1} \omega(k)x(t - d \cdot k) \tag{7}$$

where d is the dilation factor, and K is the kernel size. The network can retain very broad receptive field by stacking more than one dilated convolution, and capture long-term temporal dependencies with less layers. As shown in Fig. 2, there are dilated causal convolutions with dilation factors $d = \{1, 2, 3\}$ in the left, and the size of the kernel $K = 2$. The receptive field with a size of 8 is constructed by stacking three layers.

The details of each layer in encoder are shown in Fig. 4, where there are two dilated convolution modules in each layer, and they are exactly the same(with same kernel size K and dilation factor d). Every two layers of dilated causal convolutions assemble a residual block. Each layer of dilated causal convolutions is followed by batch normalization and rectified nonlinear unit (ReLU). The difference is that the output of the batch normalization which at the location of the second dilated causal convolution layer would be used as the input of the residual block, then the second ReLU. In the case of capturing long-term dependencies, the residual block helps train the network more stable and efficient. At the same time, the rectified nonlinear unit (ReLU) is corrected to obtain better prediction accuracy.

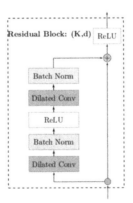

Fig. 4. Encoder module.

3.4   Decoder: Residual Neural Network

The decoder module is composed of Resnet-v and a dense layer. The Resnet-v module is the variant of residual neural network, which is used to capture the information of two inputs (one is hidden outputs and the other is exogenous variables) from the encoder. It can be described as:

$$\delta_{t+\omega}^{(i)} = R(X_{t+\omega}^{(i)}) + h_t^{(i)} \tag{8}$$

In which $h_t^{(i)}$ is hidden outputs, $X_{t+\omega}^{(i)}$ is exogenous variables, and the hidden outputs of resnet-v is $\delta_{t+\omega}^{(i)}$. $R(\bullet)$ is the residual function acting on exogenous variables. It explains the residuals between the predict value and the true value, and plays the role of transfer function at the same time. Simply speaking, resnet-v combines hidden outputs $h_t^{(i)}$ and exogenous variables $X_{t+\omega}^{(i)}$ processed by residual function, and generates new hidden outputs.

Figure 5 shows the detailed structure of the decoder. The first dense layer and batch normalization are used to project the exogenous variables $X_{t+\omega}^{(i)}$, then ReLU is used for activation. There are the second dense layer and batch normalization subsequently. All of them construct the residual function $R(X_{t+\omega}^{(i)})$ acting on exogenous variables $X_{t+\omega}^{(i)}$. At last, use a dense layer to map the hidden outputs $\delta_{t+\omega}^{(i)}$ that generated by Resnet-v to obtain the predicted probability.

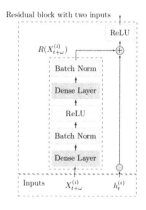

Fig. 5. Decoder module.

3.5   Network Training

The model is trained by minimizing the quantile loss $L_q(y, \hat{y}^q)$. For a specific quantile q, the true value and predicted value is y and $\hat{y}^q$ respectively, and its loss function can be described as:

$$L_q(y, \hat{y}^q) = q(y - \hat{y}^q)^+ + (1 - q)(\hat{y}^q - y)^+ \tag{9}$$

where $(y)^+ = max(0, y)$ and $q \in (0, 1)$. Given a set of quantile levels $Q = \{q_1, ..., q_m\}$, the objective of training is to minimize the total quantile loss L_Q:

$$L_Q = \sum_{j=1}^{m} L_{qj}(y, \hat{y}^{qj}) \tag{10}$$

4 Experiments

4.1 Datasets

ASSIST2009: This dataset is collected from ASSITments in 2009 $\sim$ 2010 school year which is an online education platform. We screen learners on the condition of each learner's exercise sequence no less than 400, and then intercept the first 400 as the historical exercise sequence of each learner.

ASSIST2012: This dataset is also collected from ASSITments, which contains learning data in 2012 $\sim$ 2013 school year. We select exercise sequence of each learner in case of sequence length no less than 400.

Junyi Academy: This dataset is collected from Junyi Academy in 2015, which is an online education website provides learning materials and practice platform about various science subjects. We totally choose 800 learners and their exercise sequence length no less than 800.

The statistical data of all datasets are shown in Table 2.

Table 2. The statistical data of all datasets

	ASSIST2009	ASSIST2012	Junyi Academy
Student Number	876	800	800
Question Number	24879	31689	616
Exercise Number	400	400	800
Attempt Count	400	29	333
Answer Time(ms)	173301	11864	262582

4.2 Baseline Models

The Baseline Models we compared are:

DKT [4]: Deep Knowledge Tracing (DKT) is the first KT model based on deep learning, which utilizes LSTM of recurrent neural network to process KT task.

DKT+ [25]: This model is the variant of DKT, which introduce regularization terms corresponding to reconstruction and waviness into the loss function of DKT to robust the consistency of prediction.

DKVMN [6]: This model improves MANN by using Dynamic Key-Value Memory to construct Dynamic Key-Value Memory Network, which is been recognized as an excellent KT improvement model based on deep learning.

SAKT [16]: Inspired by Transformer, it is the first KT model use self-attention mechanism.

4.3   Implementation Details

We take the correctness of each question as the main element, and the remaining four data (learner id, question id, attempt count and answer time) are embed as covariates. Suppose the exercise sequence length of each learner is Q, then the input data is a $Q * 5$ matrix, and each column represents learner id, question id, correctness, attempt count and answer time respectively. The input data will become a vector with 512 dimensions after embedding layer, and we train and test for every single learner. We uniformly set the last 30 exercise sequence as test datasets, and the other $Q - 30$ exercise sequence as train datasets.

We set LR as 0.001, and keep the dropout rate as 0.1 to avoid overfitting. The performance of all models evaluate by calculating the area under the ROC curve (AUC) and its standard deviation. We randomly choose 10 consecutive epochs from the result after the model converged and report the mean and standard deviation of AUC.

4.4   Results and Analysis

The area under the ROC curve(AUC) demonstrate every model's prediction performance: AUC with high value means high prediction accuracy and better prediction performance, and the standard deviation of AUC reflects model's stability: the smaller the standard deviation, the better the stability. We compare our model with standard DKT, DKT+, DKVMN and SAKT model, and the overall performance of all models is shown in Table 3.

Table 3. Test AUC for all datasets

Datasets	ASSIST2009		ASSIST2012		Junyi Academy	
Model	mean	std	mean	std	mean	std
DKT [4]	0.797	0.0099	0.669	0.0082	0.855	0.0246
DKT+ [25]	0.787	0.0089	\	\	\	\
DKVMN [6]	0.672	0.0214	0.682	0.0014	0.574	0.0524
SAKT [16]	0.704	0.0117	0.718	0.0106	0.795	0.0611
SATCN[our]	**0.811**	**0.0005**	**0.800**	**0.0011**	**0.874**	**0.0003**

In ASSIST09, the average AUC of DKT can reach 0.797, but its variant model DKT+ only reaches 0.787. DKVMN and SAKT reach 0.672, 0.704 respectively, and SATCN reaches the best average AUC with 0.811. Comparing with DKT, DKT+, DKVMN and SAKT, SATCN improves by 1.76%, 3.05%, 20.68% and 15.20%. At the same time, DKVMN shows the most obvious fluctuation with the maximum standard deviation. The other 3 baseline models' stability is better but still inferior to SATCN. Our SATCN model surpasses previous models both in accuracy and stability at this data set.

In ASSIST12, the performance of DKT is severely degraded and its AUC only reaches 0.669, while the performance and stability of DKVMN and SAKT have lightly improved, and their AUC reach 0.682 and 0.718 respectively. Our model reaches 0.800 that improve by 19.58%, 17.30% and 14.42% comparing with DKT, DKVMN and SAKT. Meanwhile the stability of SATCN reaches the best performance.

In JunyiAcademy, DKT and SAKT represent good AUC with 0.855 and 0.795, which means they show the best model performance. But DKVMN displays poor AUC with 0.574, and all baseline models exhibit the worst stability. While our model shows the best AUC with 0.874, and the best stability simultaneously. Comparing with DKT, DKVMN and SAKT, SATCN improves by 2.22%, 52.26% and 9.94%, respectively.

Restricted by devices, memory space and computing power DKT+ model need in ASSIT12 and JunyiAcademy can't be satisfied, so we couldn't get the result.

We can summarize from the experimental results in Table 3 that DKT, SAKT and SATCN reach the best performance in JunyiAcademy which contains the longest interaction sequence and the minimal question type, and they show poorer performance in ASSIST09 and ASSIST12 which include shorter interaction sequence and more question type. We find that the more question type involved under the same length of interaction sequence length, the worse the performance, while DKVMN shows the opposite effect.

We think longer interaction sequence and less question type means more frequent interactions in each question, and neural network is good at capturing these interactions. Meanwhile the more question type involved under the same length of interaction sequence length means many questions would be answer only once and their interaction is not obvious. Therefore, more details about the above experimental results are revealed in Table 3. The original work of DKVMN [6] also find that it will achieve better performance when there are large number of different questions. We think it's involved with external memory, because it can capture low-frequent interactions better than neural network. Even if the neural network captures low-frequent interactions, it also has great probability of forgetting and dropout.

To conclude, the performance of SATCN in all datasets outperform other baseline models, especially in JunyiAcademy which contains more frequent interactions about each exercise. The experimental results indicate that our model can capture exercise interactions better and make more accurate prediction.

4.5   Ablation Studies

To explore the influence of answer time and attempt count about experimental results, we conduct ablation studies at the four variants of SATCN,SATCN-AC,SATCN-AT, SATCN-BA, and their detail settings are shown as bellow. Their performance is shown in Table 4. For SATCN-AC, we remove attempt count related to each exercise. For SATCN-AT, we remove answer time related to each exercise. For SATCN-BA, we remove both attempt count and answer time related to each exercise.

Table 4. Effect of Ablation Models

Datasets	ASSIST2009		ASSIST2012		Junyi Academy	
Models	mean	std	mean	std	mean	std
SATCN-BA	0.765	0.0007	0.740	0.0041	0.840	0.0007
SATCN-AC	0.758	0.0017	0.745	0.0014	0.851	0.0005
SATCN-AT	**0.839**	0.0007	0.797	0.0012	0.853	0.0030
SATCN	0.811	**0.0005**	**0.800**	**0.0011**	**0.874**	**0.0003**

From above results, we can see that SATCN-BA shows the most significant performance degradation, which remove both attempt count and answer time. Both attempt count and answer time show a certain positive effect on the improvement of performance. We can also seen that compared with answer time, attempt count has greater impact on experimental results. This result proves our conjecture: answer time can model learner's proficiency, combined with attempt count our model can accurately simulate the knowledge state of a learner come to understand whether they has mastered or not and their proficiency. This level of proficiency is also can be used to simulate forgetting, thereby improving the performance of our model.

5   Conclusions and Future Work

In this paper, we propose a new learning framework named SATCN from the perspective of temporal sequence prediction to deal with KT task. Our model can be used in actual education scenarios to help tutors and learners to improve teaching and learning efficiency. SATCN not only outperforms the state-of-the-art models with the same type, but also solves ubiquitous problem of negative historical data. In future work, we will make efforts to improve model interpretability and performance by utilizing graph structure and more robust neural networks.

References

1. Khajah, M., Lindsey, R.V., Mozer, M.C.: How Deep is Knowledge Tracing?. In Proceedings of the 9th International Conference on Educational Data Mining, (EDM), Raleigh, North Carolina, USA, June 29 - July 2 (2016)
2. Corbett, A.T., Anderson, J.R.: Knowledge tracing: Modeling the acquisition of procedural knowledge. User Modeling and User-Adapted Interaction **4**(4), (1994), 253–278 (1994)
3. Kuh, G.D., Kinzie, J., Buckley, J.A., Bridges, B.K., Hayek, J.C: Piecing together the student success puzzle: research, propositions, and recommendations: ASHE Higher Education Report. Vol. 116. John Wiley & Sons (2011)
4. Piech, C., Spencer, J., Huang, J., et al.: Deep knowledge tracing. arXiv preprint arXiv:1506.05908 (2015)
5. Hochreiter, S., Schmidhuber, J.: Long short-term memory. Neural Comput. **9**(8), 1735–1780 (1997)
6. Zhang, J., Shi, X., King, I., Yeung, D.Y.: Dynamic key-value memory networks for knowledge tracing. In: Proceedings of the 26th International Conference on World Wide Web, pp. 765–774 (2017)
7. Abdelrahman, G., Wang, Q.: Knowledge tracing with sequential key-value memory networks. In: Proceedings of the 42nd International ACM SIGIR Conference on Research and Development in Information Retrieval, 175–184 (2019)
8. Santoro, A., Bartunov, S., Botvinick, M., et al.: Meta-learning with memory-augmented neural networks. In: International Conference on Machine Learning. PMLR, pp.1842–1850 (2016)
9. Polson, M.C., Richardson, J.J.: Foundations of intelligent tutoring systems. Psychology Press (2013)
10. Baker, R.S.J., Corbett, A.T., Aleven, V.: More accurate student modeling through contextual estimation of slip and guess probabilities in bayesian knowledge tracing. In: Woolf, B.P., Aïmeur, E., Nkambou, R., Lajoie, S. (eds.) ITS 2008. LNCS, vol. 5091, pp. 406–415. Springer, Heidelberg (2008). https://doi.org/10.1007/978-3-540-69132-7_44
11. Pardos, Z.A., Heffernan, N.T.: KT-IDEM: introducing item difficulty to the knowledge tracing model. In: Konstan, J.A., Conejo, R., Marzo, J.L., Oliver, N. (eds.) UMAP 2011. LNCS, vol. 6787, pp. 243–254. Springer, Heidelberg (2011). https://doi.org/10.1007/978-3-642-22362-4_21
12. Pardos, Z.A., Heffernan, N.T.: Modeling individualization in a bayesian networks implementation of knowledge tracing. In: De Bra, P., Kobsa, A., Chin, D. (eds.) UMAP 2010. LNCS, vol. 6075, pp. 255–266. Springer, Heidelberg (2010). https://doi.org/10.1007/978-3-642-13470-8_24
13. Yudelson, M.V., Koedinger, K.R., Gordon, G.J.: Individualized bayesian knowledge tracing models. In: Lane, H.C., Yacef, K., Mostow, J., Pavlik, P. (eds.) AIED 2013. LNCS (LNAI), vol. 7926, pp. 171–180. Springer, Heidelberg (2013). https://doi.org/10.1007/978-3-642-39112-5_18
14. Ebbinghaus, H.: Memory: a contribution to experimental psychology. Ann. Neurosci. **20**(4), 155 (2013)
15. Pavlik Jr, P.I., Cen, H., Koedinger, K.R.: Performance factors analysis-a new alternative to knowledge tracing. Online Submission (2009)
16. Pandey, S., Karypis, G.: A Self-Attentive model for Knowledge Tracing. ArXiv preprint arXiv:1907.06837 (2019)

17. Choi, Y.: Towards an Appropriate Query, Key, and Value Computation for Knowledge Tracing. ArXiv preprint arXiv:2002.07033 (2020)
18. Vaswani, A., et al.: Attention is all you need. In: Advances in Neural Information Processing Systems, pp. 5998–6008 (2017)
19. Nakagawa , H., Iwasawa, Y., Matsuo, Y.:Graph-based knowledge tracing: modeling student proficiency using graph neural network. In: 2019 IEEE/WIC/ACM International Conference On Web Intelligence (WI). IEEE, 2019: 156–163 (2019)
20. Yang, Y., Shen, J., Qu, Y., et al.: GIKT: A Graph-based Interaction Model for Knowledge Tracing (2020)
21. Gori, M., Monfardini, M., Scarselli, F.: A new model for learning in graph domains. In Neural Networks, 2005. In: IJCNN'05. Proceedings 2005 IEEE International Joint Conference on, Vol. 2. IEEE, 729–734 (2005)
22. Kipf, T.N., Welling, M.: Semi-supervised classification with graph convolutional networks. arXiv preprint arXiv:1609.02907 (2016)
23. Kang, Y., Chen, Y., Chen, Y., et al.: Probabilistic forecasting with temporal convolutional neural network. Neurocomputing **399**, 491–501 (2020)
24. Krizhevsky, A., Sutskever, I., Hinton, G.E.: Imagenet classification with deep convolutional neural networks. In: Advances in Neural Information Processing Systems, pp. 1097–1105 (2012)
25. Yeung, C.K., Yeung, D.Y.: Addressing two problems in deep knowledge tracing via prediction-consistent regularization. In: Proceedings of the Fifth Annual ACM Conference on Learning at Scale, pp. 1–10 (2018)

Design of Smart Mistake Notebook Based on AI and Big Data

Zeyi Yu⬤, Gang Cen(✉)⬤, Linhao Zhao⬤, and Chenjie Zhu⬤

Zhejiang University of Science and Technology, 318 Liuhe Road, Xihu, Hangzhou, Zhejiang, China
gcen@163.com

Abstract. Under the general direction of information technology in education, traditional teaching methods are gradually integrating with intelligent technology. The notebook used for recording past mistakes on exams or exercises will be referred to as the "mistake notebook", which has been proved to be an effective learning tool in practice, but due to its difficulty in recording, retrieval and low efficiency, it also needs to be transformed into intelligent and electronic. The research group has proposed and designed a smart mistake notebook based on AI and big data. By automatically collating and analysing students' mistakes, it will help students to use the mistake notebook more efficiently and review more effectively and accurately to improve their academic performance.

Keywords: Big data · AI · Mistake analysis · Question recommendation

1 Introduction

At present, Chinese students in junior and senior high schools often use their notebooks to collect and collate questions that were done wrong, to learn from their mistakes and understand weakness in knowledge. In the teaching process, teachers also suggest students to gather mistakes to better understand the reasons and avoid making them repeatedly. The mistake notebook uses the educational concept of the shortcoming detection, which often has a good effect on improving grades. However, as collecting, summarising and transcribing mistakes is tedious and takes a long time, students often find it difficult to record their mistakes in time and insist on using the mistake notebook. In addition, it is difficult to retrieve and categorise the mistakes in paper mistake notebooks, which makes it inconvenient for students to look at the mistakes and greatly reduces their willingness to use the mistake notebook and learning efficiency.

With the advancement of technology, education is moving towards informatization and digitization. The Action Plan for Education Informatization 2.0,

W. Hong and Y. Weng (Eds.): ICCSE 2022, CCIS 1811, pp. 18–28, 2023.
https://doi.org/10.1007/978-981-99-2443-1_2

officially proposed by the Ministry of Education of the People's Republic of China on 13 April 2018 [1], calls for the comprehensive promotion of education modernization with education informatization and the opening of education in the smart era [2]. The integration of big data analysis, artificial intelligence and education will promote the formation of a personalised education system to teach students according to their abilities. The idea of a "smart mistake notebook" is based on the current problems students have in recording their mistakes. The transformation of the paper mistake notebook from manual to intelligent has a crucial role to play in the education industry.

2   Proposal of Smart Mistake Notebook System

According to the survey, a Chinese high school student's exam papers and assignments stacked together for three years are at a height of more than two metres, but they contained many repetitive and ineffective questions. Students repeatedly work on questions that they have already mastered or that are beyond their knowledge and ability. As it is difficult to carry out personalised education for students in general teaching, especially in the homework assignment and exam papers, students can only follow a uniform teaching requirement and waste time on repetitive and ineffective topics.

As the mistake notebook reflects the students' individual revision status, it helps them to analyse mistakes, accumulate knowledge and further strengthen their memory of knowledge, so many high-achieving students have the habit of making their personal mistake notebooks and teachers strongly promote this behaviour. However, in the traditional learning environment, students spend a great deal of time and effort in recording their mistakes, and there are various problems in the recording and utilization of the mistakes, such as:

– The students blindly transcribe questions that were done wrong in their notebooks, but they don't really master them.
– After recording all questions, the workload becomes too heavy to finish.
– It is difficult to categorise the questions, resulting in a disorganised notebook.
......

In response to these problems, the research group uses big data, machine learning and modern information technology to create the "Smart Mistake Notebook Based on AI and Big Data" with smartphone and Web as the carrier to help students focus their limited study time on areas that will improve their performance. The smart mistake notebook is a way of information-based education [3], which is close to the actual learning scenario of students and will become a powerful assistant for students' learning in the era of information technology in education, effectively improving students' enthusiasm and efficiency in learning.

3   Design of Equipment Management System

3.1   Overall Design

Based on big data and machine learning technologies, the smart mistake note-book goes a step further by automatically collating students' mistakes. On the one hand, it classifies questions based on different subject and provides analysis of questions that were done wrong. On the other hand, it personalises learning content and recommends similar new questions for students to practice based on their ability, considering dimensions such as key points, syllabus, etc. The system consists of a mistake entry module, a customised test paper generation module, a mistake analysis module, a smart question recommendation module, a statistical analysis module and a revision plan module. The overall functional design is shown in Fig. 1.

3.2   System Usage Process

Mistake Entry Module. The smart mistake notebook allows users to enter questions into the question bank by taking photos or importing test paper, and selects categories, labels, reasons for mistakes and degree of mastery for the questions when importing them, automatically categorising them by subject and type of question, and clearly displays all the imported questions.

Customised Test Paper Generation Module. By selecting the questions, users can quickly create a set of test papers and the corresponding QR code from the existing question bank, which users can print and export. After completing the exercise, scan the QR code to correct the test paper and update the question bank.

Mistake Analysis Module. The system applies OCR technology to identify the imported questions that were done wrong. Based on the content of the questions and the wrong answers entered by the user, it uses artificial intelligence and big data analysis technology to deeply analyse the key points, and automatically classifies the questions according to the reasons for the mistakes: wrong examination, wrong thinking, carelessness, ambiguous concepts, etc., and provides knowledge cards for the questions to show the problem-solving methods.

After OCR pre-processing and segmentation, features are first extracted by convolution, then downsampled to retain more important features, and after further convolution and downsampling, the features obtained from the last layer of downsampling are transported to the fully connected layer for processing and final output of the probability distribution, and finally the current text is determined [4].

The mistake analysis function uses data mining techniques, combined with the learning model of the policy-based network, to systematically and iteratively add a trajectory dataset of content and use this dataset to train the model.

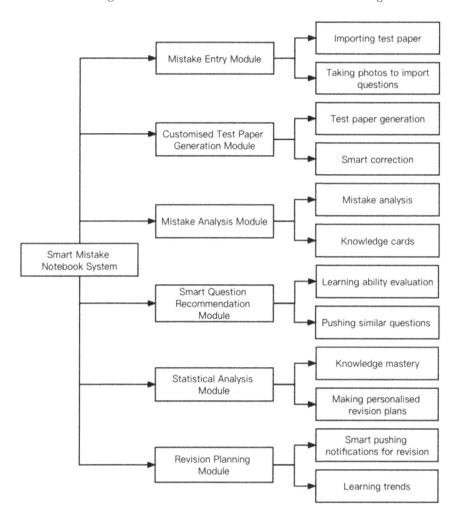

Fig. 1. Main functions of the system

The model is then trained on this dataset, additional trajectory information is collected using the model and assembled into this dataset, and the two steps are alternately used for reinforcement learning, ultimately finding the cause of the user's mistakes. The process of data mining is shown in Fig. 2.

The knowledge cards are displayed by using a focused crawler to query the local question bank, parse out the knowledge of the questions and find similar questions within the question bank.

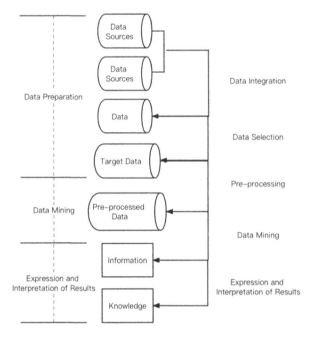

Fig. 2. Data mining process

Smart Question Recommendation Module. Through big data, the user's learning ability are considered comprehensively, and questions like the past mistakes are searched automatically. Questions matching the user's ability and knowledge needs are provided and to strengthen the consolidation of the same type of questions.

The user's learning ability evaluation builds a student model by establishing a BP neural network of learning ability, including three parts: output layer, implicit layer, and input layer [5], using the student's relevant ability as the input to the BP neural network. The student model is the basis and key to the implementation of individualised teaching. The model should be able to reflect the essential features and states in the students' learning behaviour in a timely and correct manner and reflect the students' mastery and understanding of a certain learning content and the learning styles, habits and learning abilities contained in their learning behaviour [6]. The classification of student models is shown in Fig. 3.

The model design process starts from the design of the BP neural network to the training of the BP modelling, and finally the BP network prediction. The system is calculated by a highly optimised L-M algorithm, which in turn forms a BP neural network model. The resulting student model can objectively represent the cognitive ability of the student and has good reasoning ability about what the student is going to learn [7]. The BP neural network learning evaluation training process is shown in Fig. 4.

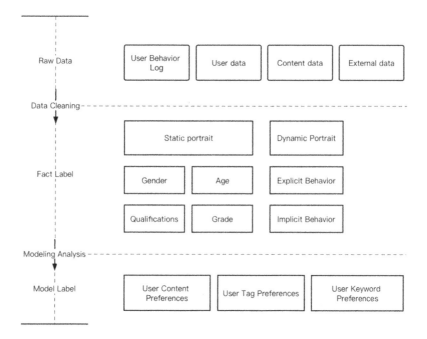

Fig. 3. Classification of student models

Push similar questions function in order to improve the correlation with the questions that were done wrong, will be through the machine learning to constantly understand questions, and finally achieve the analysis of the key points. Then, according to the key points, it will intelligently match the questions with the same key points in the question bank and push these courses and exercises.

Statistical Analysis Module. The system relies on artificial intelligence technology and big data to dynamically analyse the user's learning situation and generate a learning analysis report based on the mistakes and revision. After a comprehensive analysis of students' learning shortcomings in each subject, the system can accurately analyse students' learning trends and pinpoint their weak points.

Revision Planning Module. The system plans the most optimal revision route for each user based on the answer situation and customises the revision plan for each user for precise consolidation and improvement. It will improve the accuracy of notification content based on a range of algorithms, combined with cloud computing and big data technologies, including subjects, question type, key points, to give users greater clarity in their revision.

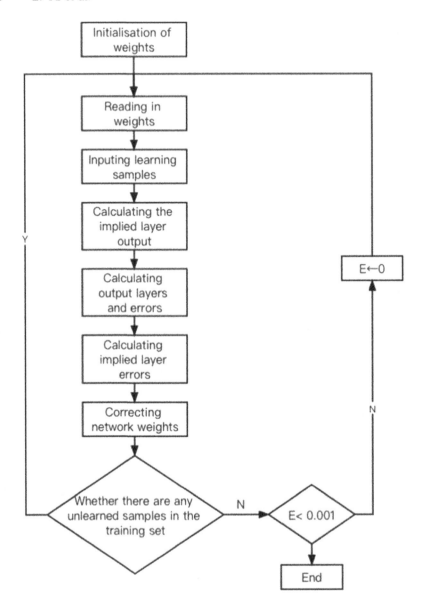

Fig. 4. BP neural network learning evaluation training process

4   Design of Smart Mistake Notebook System

4.1   Architecture Design

The front-end and back-end of the system are separated, with the front-end adopting MVVM (Model-View-ViewModel) architecture and the back-end adopting MVC (Model-View-Controller) architecture. The front-end node service directly accesses the Java API interface service, the API interface finally accesses the database to complete the data query and finally returns to the node layer, and it renders the response data to the front-end. For the synchronization of session information, a middleware Redis cache database is used to solve the problem of synchronising information between the node on the front-end and the API on the back-end.

The system uses a RESTful architecture, which is simple, low-coupling and stateless, so that there is no need to consider the contextual flow or state when invoking the interface [8]. In addition, it makes full use of several HTTP actions, which allows the browser or middleware to determine whether data has changed and decide whether to cache the data based on the actions.

4.2 Technology Selection

Front-end. The front-end uses Vue, a lightweight MVVM framework for front-end interface rendering, to provide a view layer driver for complex web applications [9]. Element UI is used at the interaction level to rapidly shape the user interface and shorten the development cycle of the platform. Data exchange is developed using the Axios plugin to facilitate cross-domain requests. Synchronous transfer combined with asynchronous transfer is used for data interaction with the server side. Synchronous transfer has the advantage of fast transfer speed, while asynchronous transfer has the advantage of good interactivity and is combined with ESLint to control the quality and improve the readability of the code. The main Web interface is shown in Fig. 5.

The client is developed using the Kotlin language, with less code and faster development speed. It is compatible with a large library of resources, adaptable to all types of mobile devices and platforms. The declarative UI has a data-driven view to improve development efficiency, while using component-based development and responsive layout to improve user experience. The main client interface is shown in Fig. 6.

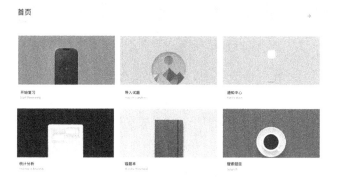

Fig. 5. Main Web interface

Back-end. The server side uses a microservice architecture system, with Spring-CloudAlibaba at its core, to provide a one-stop solution for microservice development. The system is divided into isolated, non-dependent subsystems that communicate through well-defined protocols [10]. Each subsystem service is built around a specific business and can be deployed independently to a production environment.

Artificial intelligence models are developed using the pytorch framework and accelerated in the aistudio cloud computing platform. Based on the training results, the algorithms generate new models or readjust pre-trained models for specific applications and help the models learn their parameters. In the inference phase, new data is predicted and decisions are made based on the learned parameters.

The massive amount of questions in the question bank is crawled through the web crawling and collection frameworks such as Pyspider and Cola, using a parallel crawling work method to increase the crawling speed, crawling in the major open question banks, according to certain web analysis algorithms, after analysis, filtering, to build the index and the questions are stored in the system question bank.

Fig. 6. Main client interface

5   Characteristics of Smart Mistake Notebook

This system combines mistake notebooks with intelligence to create a personalised, trackable, full process smart mistake notebook system on the premise of completing the automatic collation of mistakes.

5.1   Personalisation

In response to the difficulty of traditional learning software in providing content that meets the needs of different users, the system enables personalised teaching and learning with the help of artificial intelligence. Users are provided with personalised learning content and targeted practice of mistakes based on data analysis, which greatly reduces the amount of review and eliminates the inefficient way of learning by doing a lot of exercises. In addition, the system's unique user model based on students' learning style and level fully satisfies personalised learning needs.

5.2   Trackable

Once the user model is established, the system is constantly optimised and learnt based on each use, in order to establish an accurate assessment of the user's learning ability to better recommend subsequent learning content. In addition, a learning curve is created by recording each review of the user and showing the weakness in knowledge at different stages. Users can view their learning trace at any time, including statistical analysis reports of each previous session and the completion of revision.

5.3   Full Process

Learning consists of three stages: preparation stage, practice stage and effect stage. The system covers a complete learning process from uploading questions that were done wrong, analysing the causes of mistakes, recommending similar questions, making revision plan, generating test paper to statistical analysis of the learning situation, solving the lack of revision after learning and the lack of relevance during revision, so that all aspects and steps in the learning process can be optimised for the users, thus greatly improving efficiency.

6   Trial Operation Results

The results of a trial of the smart mistake notebook in a local school showed a significant improvement in the performance of the class using the smart mistake notebook compared to the unused control class, as well as an increase in students' enthusiasm for learning and efficiency, proving that the system meets students' needs for efficiency and personalisation in collating their mistakes.

7   Conclusion

The research group designed the "Smart Mistake Notebook Based on AI and Big Data" according to the current direction of education informatization and the learning needs of students. The system is based on artificial intelligence, big data and other technologies to help users learn efficiently and effectively. The smart mistake notebook greatly improves the efficiency of students' learning and solves the complicated transcription and sorting work of the traditional paper mistake notebook. It provides a personalised platform for users to collate their mistakes by establishing a user learning evaluation model, intelligently analysing the causes of mistakes and recommending similar questions, thus promoting the transformation of education into intelligence.

Acknowledgements. This research was supported by the Humanities and Social Science Research Fund Project of the Ministry of Education of China in 2017 (No. 17YJA880004) and the National College Student Innovation and Entrepreneurship Training Program in 2021 (No. 202111057015).

References

1. The State Council issued the Development Plan for the New Generation of Artificial Intelligence. China Standardization. **503**(15), 28 (2017)
2. Chaozi, L.: Comprehensively promoting education modernization with education informatization to open a new journey of education in the intelligent era. People's Educ. **2**, 40–43 (2019)
3. Shun, Z., Libin, H.: AI technology helps to establish and apply practical research on students' error books. China Modern Educ. Equip. **16**, 7–8 (2019)
4. Meng, W.: Research on natural scene text detection and recognition method based on deep learning. Guangdong University of Technology (2019)
5. Wen, S.: Research on induction motor fault diagnosis method based on deep learning model. Nanjing Southeast University (2017)
6. Chunming, W., Jiansheng, W.: Student model design of intelligent teaching system based on neural network. Intell. Comput. Appl. **1**(6), 52–53 (2011)
7. Guoqiang, H., Lizhen, L., Chao, D.: Design of student models for intelligent learning systems. Comput. Eng. Design. **30**(10), 2554–2557 (2009)
8. Chuanqi, W.: Research and implementation of RESTful-based mobile teaching aid system. Network Security Technology and Application (2009)
9. Wenshui, M.: Research on the application of MVVM framework in Web front-end. Network Secur. Technol. Appl. **196**(4), 64 (2017)
10. Yanan, C.: Research and application of microservices-based software architecture design method. Beijing University of Posts and Telecommunications (2019)

The Research on the Challenges Confronted by the Combination of Virtual Reality Technology and Educational Games

Yang Kuang$^{(\boxtimes)}$ ⓘ, Shan Yang ⓘ, and Jie Jiang ⓘ

The college of education, Jiang Xi Science and Technology Normal University,
Nanchang 330038, Jiangxi, China
23490954@qq.com

Abstract. As one of the key technologies of the 21st century, virtual reality technology has been widely used in the field of education, and educational games based on this technology are becoming increasingly mature. This article adopts a case study approach to investigate examples of combining virtual reality technology with educational games. The article focuses on the advantages, necessity and development of virtual reality technology in the field of educational games as well as its characteristics, and presents the problems and challenges in the process of combining virtual reality technology with educational games to provide reference and reference for empirical research in this field.

Keywords: Virtual reality · Educational games · Challenges

1 Introduction

The 14th Five-Year Plan clearly proposes to take the innovation of learning resources in the mode of information technology as a grasp [1]. With the advent of the Internet era, virtual reality technology has been gradually applied to primary and secondary school courses, university courses and vocational training and other teaching and training fields. Studies have shown that virtual reality technology can stimulate learners' interest and motivation in learning. Applying virtual reality technology to educational games can not only enhance the sense of game experience, but also better maintain learners' motivation in learning. Therefore, it is a pressing issue for technology developers and educational researchers to explore the integration of virtual reality technology with educational games and apply it to students" learning environments to achieve the desired educational outcomes.

This work is supported by Research on the Construction of Embodied Cognitive Learning Approach Supported by Virtual Reality Technology in the Humanities and Social Sciences of Jiangxi Province in 2020 (Project No. JY20106).

2   Research Status of the Combination of VR Technology and Education

2.1   Concept

Virtual reality (VR) technology is regarded as one of the key modern technologies in the 21st century. It is generally accepted that virtual technology has the following important characteristics: immersion, interaction, and imagination. The immersive nature makes the device practical and operable. It can help disconnect the users' multiple senses from the outside world through sensors, so that users can be completely immersed in an interactive atmosphere. Imagination means that VR technology brings people a new way and means of understanding the world, full of fantasy and triggering new associations.

2.2   Research Status of the Combination of VR Technology and Education

Foreign Research Status. In 2020, the Association for The Informatization of Higher Education in The United States released the 2020 EDUCAUSE Horizon Report: Teaching and Learning Edition, predicting that the application of VR would become the development trend of future education [2]. Research has shown that over 100 colleges and universities in the US have built virtual environments for teaching and research in Second Life, while 80% of universities in the UK are using Second Life [3]. At present, VR theory and technology are improving in western countries represented by the United States [4]. In addition, there are many foreign game companies developing educational games and VR educational games. For example, at the 2019 ED Games Expo hosted by the US Department of Education, there were more than 100 educational Games on display, and about one-fifth of them were VR-related. Half of the winning works in the same year were created based on VR and AR technologies.

Domestic Research Status. In 2018, Article 25 of the "40 Higher Education in the New Era" issued by the Ministry of Education proposed to vigorously promote the construction of virtual simulation laboratories and the application of virtual reality and other modern technologies in education [5]. The Laboratory Management Branch of China Association of Higher Education has carried out many large-scale virtual simulation experimental teaching research activities in various provinces and cities across China, promoting the educational application of virtual reality technology [6].

3   The Combination of VR Technology and Educational Games

Schell Games is the largest full-service educational and entertainment game development company in the United States. The VR educational games developed by the company have won many awards. The author takes the successful game "Hololab-Champions" (hololab) developed by the company as an example (as shown in Fig. 1) to analyze the advantages of combining VR technology with educational games.

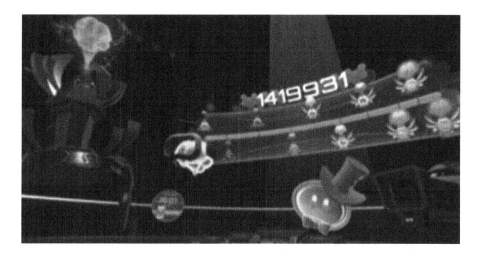

Fig. 1. "Hololab Champions " game scene

3.1   Advantages of VR Technology in the Field of Education

Hololab is a VR educational game designed to improve students' familiarity with laboratory equipment, procedures and chemistry course content. Its game mechanism is to guide students to learn chemical knowledge to participate in the challenge to obtain trophies. The game features holographic hosts and camera robot partners who guide students through the layers of mini-lab challenges to meet the final lab challenge. The game also features a practice mode that allows students to train for challenges in a free environment to hone accuracy, precision and timing skills. Due to the immersive and interactive nature of VR technology, compared with traditional teaching classes, users have a stronger subjectivity in this game, where they can immerse themselves in personalized services to achieve immersive effects. VR immersion is also reflected in various educational practices, such as learning about red culture in VR Red Memorial Hall [7]. The interactive nature of VR education can also be seen in other VR educational instances, such as shooting the correct phrase in Alphabet Kingdom game and some technical skills in vocational education. The model of the relationship between VR technology features and learning motivation factors is shown in Fig. 2. As a new modern technology, VR technology can also break through the limitations of time and space to assist distance education and further promote educational equity. In some specific scenarios, such as fire drills, the virtual training ground can guarantee the safety of teachers and students.

Both in foreign countries and in China, its application in the field of education has made certain achievements [8].

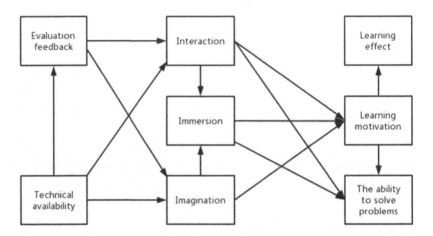

Fig. 2. The relationship model between VR technology characteristics and learning motivation factors

3.2   The Combination of VR Technology and Educational Games

There are many tools available for creating game engines. The two most representative are unity3D and 3dsMax. Unity3D has a very powerful editor engine, which is the most widely used game engine at present. Many models created by 3D modeling software can be easily imported into unity3D, C# or JavaScript is used as programming language to write program components and assign them to virtual objects. 3dsMax can model complex objects, and the two can be used together to develop games in a short period of time. And the steam VR tools to jointly complete visual programming development and delivery of VR education games used in VR equipment. The specific development flow chart is shown in Fig. 3.

VR technology and integrated education play game productions attract the attention of education researchers. For example, Guo Xuechun created a VR educational game called "island rescue plan" (as shown in Fig. 4) according to grade seven geography curriculum "continents and ocean", with the control experiment, test to prove her game can help students consolidate knowledge to some extent, and help middle-level students in geography learning to achieve good progress [9]. Wang Yulin developed and designed a VR educational game named "In Order To Dr." , as shown in Fig. 5. After a two-week controlled experiment, he concluded that English teaching in junior middle school based on VR educational games had a moderate positive impact on students' academic performance [10]. VR technology is not just a tool for display, observation and experience, but a

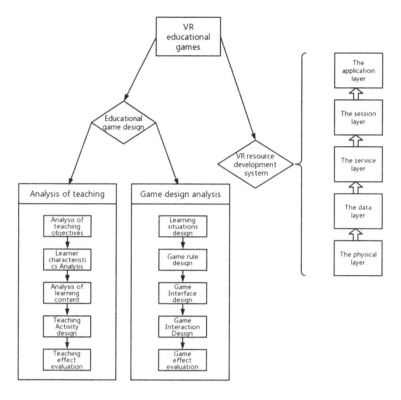

Fig. 3. Design system diagram of VR educational game development process

learning application that can help learners practice and construct their learning content more deeply. The use of VR technology can facilitate the interaction between students' body and environment in the learning process, and gamified design can promote a mind-flow experience.

4   Challenges Faced by the Combination of VR Technology and Educational Games

Due to the current VR technology still has some problems, there are also many doubts about the application of educational games. VR technology and educational games combined in both game development and teaching mode have some drawbacks. Through the analysis of case games, practical application and extensive reading of literature, the author concluded that the integration of VR technology and educational games still faces the following challenges.

Fig. 4. game scene of "Island Rescue"   **Fig. 5.** game scene of "In Order To Dr."

4.1 Challenges Faced by VR Technology Itself

There are three types of virtual reality technology: the first is desktop based virtual reality, the second is laser-controlled virtual reality, and the third is stereo virtual reality based on head-mounted devices. As the first two kinds of immersion are not strong, head-mounted devices are generally used for teaching at present.

Problems with Head-Mounted Display Devices.

1). Although VR devices have gone through three generations of development, the quality of head-mounted displays is still uneven. Mainstream players in the market, such as Samsung Gear VR, Google Cardboard, and HTC Vive, are facing technological challenges with low resolution. To a large extent, the user's immersion experience is worse, and some users may even feel dizzy after wearing it, which has not been solved yet.

2). The weight and volume of head-mounted display devices are often too large, and most of the educational objects are underage learners, who cannot bear to wear them for a long time.

3). The power supply and data transmission of the head-mounted display device require a cable connection, which makes the user's experience much less enjoyable, without truly immersive experience and with hidden security problems. At the same time, it also needs strong network equipment and adequate environmental facilities.

4). The equipment is relatively expensive. The average price of VR equipment on the market is expensive and temporarily unable to meet the needs of every student in every region.

Lack of Visual or Tactile Feedback. In some areas with more developed economic levels, VR education applications have been implemented into the teaching field. Practice shows that due to the immersive nature of VR technology devices, when students put on VR headsets, they cannot simultaneously observe the real world and follow the instructions of others, so actions like communicating with teachers and stopping the game in time are more difficult to do in a timely manner.

4.2 Challenges in the Development of Combining VR and Educational Games

Challenge 1: Teaching design combining VR technology and educational games.

The development of VR technology and educational games can help learners build a VR game environment. How to build an effective VR game environment is the most important thing that designers and developers need to consider. Schank and Kass [11]summarized three elements of an effective learning environment: first, a goal that motivates learners; second, placing learners in an authentic learning environment; and finally, setting learners Finally, the learner is given tasks that require independent learning to complete. Adequate pedagogical design must be developed before teaching games can be developed. At the moment, virtual technology is still in its infancy and there is a huge lack of quality teaching resources, making teaching design and development even more challenging.

Challenge 2: Experimental data on combining VR and educational games.

Educational experiment is a common method to study the learning effect. The influence of different control variables on learning effect was studied through control experiment [12]. The experimental group can be set as one group or multiple groups, and multiple groups can further explore the impact of VR specific technology application type, degree or feedback degree on the learning effect. The types of techniques introduced previously, whether the combination of physical movement and cooperative learning can be used as variables for future research. At present, the application of VR educational games is still in its infancy. After consulting the data, the author found that there is not a large amount of rigorous experimental data to support it.

Challenge 3: The development cost of combining VR and educational games.

The development of games based on VR technology involves a number of technical as well as pedagogical conceptual challenges, and it is difficult for teachers to design and develop VR games as easily as they can design courseware. The design of VR educational games involves technical support in other areas such as UI design, programming development, and animation and pedagogical content integration design, meaning that realizing such development requires a great deal of effort, time and money, and also requires collaboration between educational researchers and researchers from different fields.

Challenge 4: Learning effects of VR combined with educational games.

Research has shown that when active in a virtual environment, the overload of features and richly simulated scenarios of the virtual world can distract learners from important content and make it difficult for learners to focus on the learning activity. The ultimate goal of creating educational games is to promote learner effectiveness, but VR technology differs from traditional teaching methods in that learners interact directly with the game platform and educators cannot intuitively and effectively judge learner effectiveness through traditional means, which requires games to provide adequate measurement and proper evaluation. The current challenge is that although VR learning systems can record data about students' learning processes, there is no mature solution for how to use this data to effectively monitor learning behavior and evaluate learning outcomes.

Developing educational games involves setting up game scenes and creating game characters according to the target knowledge. And carry out experimental research to explore the learning effects of students. Although some studies have proved that VR technology can improve students' learning effect to a certain extent, these studies tend to focus more on data such as questionnaire survey, but lack of experimental validation, and controls [13]. In future studies, the effects need to be measured through rigorous variable studies and experiments.

4.3   The Challenge of Teaching by Combining VR with Educational Games

Challenge 1: VR educational environment.

According to the constructivist learning theory, only by ensuring the authenticity of the internal environment of VR games can the teaching effect be effectively guaranteed. Learners' identity in VR environment is realized through virtual roles, and learners' behaviors in VR environment may be different from those in real environment. In the traditional classroom environment, teachers can usually judge students' personality characteristics and behavior habits according to the long-term accumulated cognition, and choose appropriate teaching methods and educational attitudes according to the judgment. In contrast, in a virtual learning environment, learners' receptiveness and interests are different, and learners' learning behavior as well as their learning performance may shift.

Challenge 2: Identity transformation in VR educational games classroom.

In the practice of VR games, the classroom is transformed into a student-centered, teacher-led teaching mode, where the teacher is no longer the sole transmitter of knowledge, but plays a more guiding and supporting role; both teachers and students should be aware of the shift in teaching and learning identities. However, as VR games do not fully occupy all classrooms, the transition between the student-centered teaching model of VR games and the traditional teaching model of the classroom needs to be further addressed.

Challenge 3: The dependence on VR educational games.

It is obvious that educational games involving VR technology are more likely to attract students' interest. However, improper and excessive applications are likely to make learners dependent. Ding Nan suggests that when the authenticity of the virtual world is guaranteed, it will stimulate the best mind-flow experience for the users [14]. Users will empathize with things that are part of their role in the virtual world, such as in-game objects and social relationships, which are inherently tied to the subject by the VR device, and when the user is a mentally immature group of students, this can lead to technology addiction and even the development of a "second personality".

Challenge 4: Teacher training for VR education.

Ma Xinyan's study shows the problems of insufficient integration, weak innovation and professional development of information literacy development of primary and secondary school teachers in China [15]. In a virtual gaming environment, teachers without relevant knowledge of VR technology are less likely to carry out the teaching work of leading students to learn and to identify whether students are focused on learning in the virtual world. At present, teachers have varying levels of modern information technology and little knowledge of VR, which will undoubtedly limit the effective use of VR games in their teaching work. Educators should look at the duality of the integration of virtual technology and educational games, dissipate their negative effects, promote the positive impact of educational games and properly play their role in helping students.

5   Strategies for Combining Virtual Reality Technology and Educational Games

Solution 1: Challenges of virtual reality technology itself.

The development and equipment of virtual reality technical educational games is a complicated and delicate work. In order to avoid poor reusability and high difficulty in secondary development, technical standards of the industry need to be established. At the same time, we should explore the sharing mechanism to realize the sharing of data and resources between schools. Gradually improve the quality of campus network, popularize 5G network, timely update equipment functions, and ensure the effectiveness and synchronization of data transmission. Strengthen independent research and development, promote school-enterprise cooperation, and gradually promote the popularization and application of VR equipment in schools. According to "Virtual Reality Industry Development White Paper (2021)", games as the main application scene of VR market, several star products appeared this year, no matter in the picture performance, as well as the degree of scene interaction, freedom and other aspects, have achieved breakthrough innovation. This also means that VR technology itself is constantly innovative and convenient.

Solution 2: Challenges of the development in virtual reality technology education game combination.

The development of educational games needs to build game scenes and create game characters according to the target knowledge. And carry out experimental research to explore the learning effect of students. This requires the support of a large number of experts and scholars, and cannot be achieved without the support of policies. It requires the government to strengthen the construction of virtual reality educational game resources and encourage enterprises to develop VR educational games that meet the conditions. At the same time, schools should also cooperate, strengthen the awareness of independent development and strengthen educational experiment research, and help to explore the effect of VR educational games on learning effect. Although some studies have proved that virtual reality technology can improve students' learning effect to a certain extent, these studies tend to pay more attention to data such as questionnaires, but lack experimental verification and comparison, which to some extent reduces the persuasiveness of its teaching effect [16]. In future studies, more strict data control and variable research can be used to measure the learning effect from multiple angles through various methods, so as to better demonstrate the teaching effect of virtual reality [17].

Solution 3: Challenges of virtual reality games in the teaching process.

As far as authenticity is concerned, teachers are required to carry out inquiry learning, strengthen the awareness of modern information technology education, and master the characteristics of students' behavior in the virtual environment. As far as identity change is concerned, students need reasonable guidance in key teaching links to carry out effective learning activities in VR environment, which cannot be separated from the guidance of teachers, who are still the dominant player in the classroom. Teachers should strengthen the study of virtual reality technology related knowledge, reduce the difficulty of using technology, and ensure the quality of the classroom. In the aspect of teaching research, it is necessary to carry out strict experimental control and select effective effect pointer to carry out empirical research on the teaching effect of virtual reality technology. Educators should see the duality of the integration of virtual technology and educational games, dispel its negative effects, promote the positive effects of educational games, and correctly play its role in education.

Solution 4: Increased effectiveness of virtual reality games.

Educational games have been widely used in basic education, vocational education and safety education, because they can provide users with a safe and reliable environment. Kim and Ke investigated students' performance in learning math through VR educational games. The results show that using VR educational games to provide real-life scenarios can engage users and encourage them to learn math. In fact, scholars have analyzed and studied the teaching effectiveness, learning performance, immersion and other factors of VR educational games from different perspectives. Merchant et al. conducted a meta-analysis in which they assessed the effectiveness of VR-based instruction in three areas: virtual worlds, games, and simulation environments. The results showed that games were more effective at increasing knowledge benefits in virtual reality environments compared to virtual worlds. However, educational games are not designed to simply play games. Unlike ordinary games, which are random and have no definite goals, students' behaviors are impromptu. Therefore, VR educational games should focus on the teaching goals of the country and the school, and the game content should be closely combined with the teaching content. Therefore, VR educational games not only need to match the game levels with the key and difficult points of teaching, be playable and attract players strongly, but also need to balance the game and education, keep the game screen friendly and improve the sense of immersion. While following these principles, teaching difficulties and key points in the process of teaching are solved in the game, so that students can acquire real knowledge, improve learning ability, cultivate learning interest and improve classroom participation.

Solution 5: Strengthen experimental research on the application of VR in educational games.

In the current literature on the application of VR in the teaching of educational games, there are few experimental studies on the learning effect. In addition, the relevant effect evaluation is still measured by questionnaires, tests or recorded learning behaviors, and analyzed by quantitative data processing. However, due to the lack of reliability and validity test in questionnaires, tests and behavior records, the construct validity of research results cannot be estimated. Moreover, part of the research process lacks experimental verification and comparison, which reduces the persuasiveness of teaching effect to some extent. Therefore, diversified research methods should be adopted to strengthen this type of research and explore a better entry point.

Solution 6: Focus on the integration of VR technology and humanistic care.

The application of VR technology in educational games is to help improve the teaching effect, and the center and soul of education is the students, the development of technology and the development of students should not be generalized, in the design and development of VR educational game resources, we should pay attention to the cultivation of humanistic quality and humanistic care. In the classroom design, the teacher, as the leader of the classroom, should pay attention to the people-oriented concept. The teacher should strengthen the learning of virtual reality technology related knowledge, reduce the difficulty in using technology, ensure the high quality of the classroom, but also pay attention to the humanistic care of learners, and promote the comprehensive development of their comprehensive quality.

6   Conclusion

To sum up, due to its unique characteristics and advantages, VR technology combined with educational games is bound to create a brand-new teaching experience for teachers and students, so as to promote the enthusiasm of learners and improve the improvement of education quality. Although educational games and virtual technology have their own different development rules and tracks, VR and educational games are facing various challenges, but the cooperation between the two will greatly promote the progress of technology and the development of education.

References

1. The Opinions of the Ministry of Education on strengthening and Improving the Basic education teaching and Research work in the New Era. Bulletin of The State Council of the People's Republic of China, 2020(08), 69–72
2. Geping, L., Xing, W.: Virtual reality reshaping online education: learning resources, teaching organization and system platform. China Electron. Educ. **92–101**, 92–101 (2020)
3. Wang, H., Burton, K.: Second life in education: A review of publications from its launch to 2011. Br. J. Edu. Technol. **3**, 357–371 (2013)
4. Gao, S., Zhao, F., Liu, X.: Problems and enlightenment of foreign virtual reality (VR) education research. China E-Educ. **2018**(03), 19–23+73 (2018)
5. Opinions of the Ministry of Education on Accelerating the Construction of High-level Undergraduate Education and Comprehensively Improving talent Cultivation Ability. Bulletin of the Ministry of Education of the People's Republic of China,19–25,19–25 (2018)
6. Ping, L.: Promoting the Application of virtual reality technology to Improve the quality of college education and teaching. Lab. Res. Exploration **37**(01), 1–4 (2018)
7. Hongjiang, W., Yike, G.: Research and implementation of VR system for university red culture exhibition hall. J. Shenyang Inst. Eng. (Soc. Sci. Ed.) **67–71**, 67–71 (2020)
8. Zhang, T., Yang, Y., Yang, Q., Chai, C.: Laboratory Research and Exploration, vol. 201,40(07), pp. 305–308
9. Guo, X.: Development and application of Educational games based on VR in geography teaching of junior middle school . Jiangxi normal university of science and technology (2021). 10.27751/,dc nki. GJXKJ. 2021.000216
10. Wang. Y.: For the application of VR education in junior middle school English teaching game. Liaoning normal university (2020). 10.27212/, dc nki. Glnsu. 2020.000480
11. Schank Roger, C.: Kass Alex. A Goal-Based Scen. High School Commun. ACM **39**(4), 28–29 (1996)
12. Wang, C., Li, H., Shang, J.: Application and Development prospect of educational games based on virtual reality and augmented reality. China Electron. Educ. **2017**(08), 99–107 (2017)
13. Gao, Y., Liu, D., Huang, Z., Huang, R.: Research of e-education, vol. 37(10), pp. 77–87+103 (2016)
14. Nan, D., Yamein, W.: Application of virtual reality in education: advantages and challenges. Mod. Educ. Technol. **2**, 19–25 (2017)

15. Ma, X.: Research on Information Literacy of Primary and Secondary School Teachers. East China Normal University (2019)
16. Gao, Y., Liu, D., Huang, Z., Huang, R.: The core elements and challenges of virtual reality technology in promoting learning. Res. E-Educ., 37(10), 77–87+103 (2016)
17. Xiangtong, L., Xiangtong, L.: Bear aid country; Cao Qiuxiang, Some Problems and development Prospect of virtual reality technology. Water Sci. Technol. Econ. **59–62**, 59–62 (2006)

Design and Development of the Intelligent Parking Management System for Urban E-bikes

Linhao Zhao, Yuefeng Cen(✉), Zeyi Yu, Chenjie Zhu, Lingchao Wang, and Zhiqi Jin

School of Information and Electronic Engineering,
Zhejiang University of Science & Technology, Hangzhou, China
cyf@zust.edu.cn

Abstract. Under the general direction of information technology in education, traditional teaching methods are gradually integrating with intelligent technology. The notebook used for recording past mistakes on exams or exercises will be referred to as the "mistake notebook", which has been proved to be an effective learning tool in practice, but due to its difficulty in recording, retrieval and low efficiency, it also needs to be transformed into intelligent and electronic. The research group has proposed and designed a smart mistake notebook based on AI and big data. By automatically collating and analysing students' mistakes, it will help students to use the mistake notebook more efficiently and review more effectively and accurately to improve their academic performance.

Keywords: AI · IoT · E-bike parking management · Image processing

1 Introduction

China plans to adopt strong policies and measures to peak CO_2 emissions by 2030 and achieve carbon neutrality by 2060 [1]. In this social context, the state strongly advocates the use of non-motorised vehicles instead of motor vehicles for daily travel, of which e-bikes have become an important means of transport for people by virtue of their lightness, flexibility, low price and ease of driving. According to national statistics, China has nearly 300 million e-bikes, with annual production ranking first in the world [2]. While the e-bikes has created huge economic benefits and convenience for the country and its citizens, various social and safety issues have arisen as their numbers have grown. The lack of planning for e-bike parking areas on city roads, the lack of enforcement of e-bike laws and the weak awareness of traffic regulations among drivers have made the problem of chaotic parking of e-bikes one of the "persistent problems" of urban management [3]. At the same time, due to the special characteristics of the structure of e-bikes, unattended e-bikes are prone to significant safety hazards such as aging wiring, short circuits and excessive temperatures in the

W. Hong and Y. Weng (Eds.): ICCSE 2022, CCIS 1811, pp. 42–52, 2023.
https://doi.org/10.1007/978-981-99-2443-1_4

process of parking, resulting in huge economic losses and even threatening the personal safety of others [4]. In addition, because a perfect registration system for the identity of e-bikes has not yet been established, resulting in repeated cases of theft of e-bike batteries, which not only causes losses to the owner's property, but also brings enormous pressure on the public security system. This time-consuming and laborious management method not only makes it difficult to fundamentally solve the problem of e-bike parking, but also causes a great waste of social human resources and further increases management costs.

In view of the obstinacy of the e-bike parking problem, there has been relevant research on the solution to the e-bike parking problem in China. Sun Jinhua and Zhou Yan designed a new three-dimensional e-bike parking device, hoping to maximize the utilization of parking space [5]. Lu Yao attempted to derive the design of non-motorized parking barrier as part of the urban public landscape and proposed a conceptual model [6]. And as technologies such as AI and the IoT are combined with traditional industries and commercialised on a large scale, they also bring new development opportunities for the creation of smart parking [7]. With the goal of "unattended" parking, the YouFuLinLi company has developed a smart parking system for non-motorised vehicles, but it requires the construction of a separate smart parking lot, and its practical applicability is still to be considered. The Laureii company uses infrared thermal imaging technology to automatically track and alert e-bikes to high-temperature spots, but its functions are relatively simple, and it only monitors e-bikes in the charging state, which is not comprehensive enough. At the same time, the equipment maintenance is expensive, so its popularization is poor.

The research of others provides important reference for the application development of this paper. The group decided to make use of the research results of image recognition, infrared thermal sensors and other related fields to apply them reasonably in the management of e-bike parking and proposed the "Intelligent Parking Management System for Urban E-bikes". The core of the system is the use of CNN (Convolutional Neural Networks) combined with camera module equipment to process picture information in real time and the use of infrared thermal camera module to monitor the temperature of the parking area, to achieve e-bike license plate recognition, face recognition, parking management, fire warning and other functions. The system is also designed with a WeChat mini program client and a Web back-stage management terminals to establish a visual e-bike management system, realising a series of management and security functions during parking. It aims to continuously optimise the original downtime e-bike parking management model for efficient, low-cost and standardised management.

2   The Technical Architecture of System

2.1   Architecture Design

The system is built by separating the front-end and back-end. The front-end and the back-end interact with each other through RESTful interface and JSON as the data format. After the separation of front-end and back-end, the development mode of front-end and back-end has changed from serial to parallel, the development efficiency has been significantly improved, there is no coupling between modules, and the developers at each end perform their respective duties, which not only greatly reduces the development cost, but also facilitates the various expansion of applications in the later stage [8].

The system adopts the distributed application development mode. The client, server and data are independent of each other, and each terminal operates based on the cluster mode. The client and server control the server group composed of multiple physical machines through gateway and load balancing service to realise the forwarding processing of requests. The data cluster is composed of multiple MySQL relational servers and non-relational server Redis, in which MySQL stores business data as a persistent layer and ensures the integrity of data through master-slave backup; Redis, as a data buffer layer, stores timely business data to reduce the number of accesses to the database by the client and server, avoid cache breakdown and cache avalanche, reduce the burden on the database server and improve the operation efficiency of the system.

2.2   Technology Selection

Front-end. The client takes the Taro framework as the solution for WeChat mini program , uses the Taro UI to design and develop the interactive interface, and provides good robustness for the system in the form of Typescript, SCSS and Cloud development. In the data interaction layer, the system adopts the RESTful mode, which reduces the unpacking operation of traditional requests and has a clear structure. When calling an interface (accessing and operating resources), the context and current state can be ignored, which greatly reduces the complexity of development [9]. The Web management terminal uses React framework to render the front-end interface, which provides view layer drivers for complex web applications, and uses Ant Design, echarts, etc. at the interactive level. The management terminal uses synchronous transmission combined with asynchronous transmission to exchange data with the server, and process the asynchronous task queue through the JS engine to avoid the blocking effect caused by single synchronization and other behaviours affecting performance. The combination of the two greatly improves the work efficiency of the system administrator.

Back-end. The development of the server adopts the MVC design mode and adheres to the ideas of high cohesion and low coupling, which greatly increases the independence of the module and greatly improves the scalability and maintainability of the system [10]. In order to speed up the development process, the server adopts the lightweight framework Springboot based on Java EE for development, which makes the code much more maintainable and scalable. At the same time, the encapsulation, polymorphism and inheritance of Java language ensure the efficiency and security of the server. Based on Spring Cloud technology, the server adopts the idea of microservice, divides projects with functional modules, deploys various service suites independently, and improves the concurrency and stability of the platform.

The research group uses TensorFlow framework to train the deep learning AI models and uses CNN (Convolutional Neural Network) to realise the functions of subject recognition and face recognition. AI models are trained on Baidu's cloud computing platform and are continuously adjusted and optimised based on the training results. After completing the initial training, the model will be exported and directly deployed to the IoT devices (Raspberry Pie 4B Visual Development Module Hardware Equipment). The model will dynamically correct itself by using real-time data to achieve the purpose of real-time training.

3   The Design and Implementation of System

The system consists of four parts: client, management terminal, server and IoT terminal. In order to avoid a series of tedious processes such as software download and user registration, and to obtain better convenience, the client is designed as a WeChat mini program, which provides parking guidance, message notification, e-bike centre, user centre and other functions to restrict users' parking behaviour and ensure e-bike safety. It also provides peripheral functions such as second-hand trading platform and online communication platform to enrich the user experience. The Web management terminal provides data visualization management function in the form of charts, etc., which is convenient for the system administrator to manage relevant information and maximise the management efficiency. Based on AI, the server provides functions such as subject recognition, face recognition and license plate recognition, and provides data support for the system, as well as the daily maintenance function of the administrator. The deployment of IoT devices near the parking area is not only an important carrier to undertake the AI model of the service terminal, but also an important part of the system to obtain regional real-time information. The main functions of the platform are shown in Fig. 1.

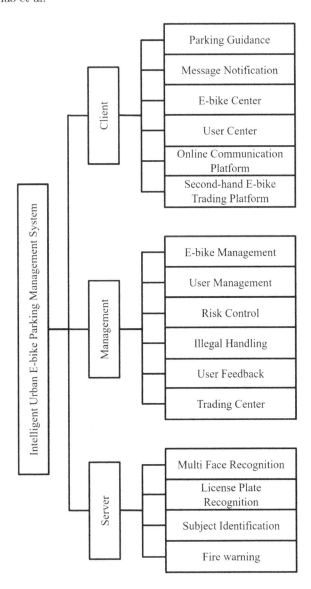

Fig. 1. Main functions of the system.

3.1 Client

Parking Guidance. After the user enters the destination, the system automatically sets the free parking area closest to the destination as the target parking area. If the user is not satisfied with the parking area automatically selected by the system, he can also manually select a legal free parking area as the target parking area. The system is also equipped with electronic map and navigation system. After the user determines the target parking area, the navigation system will be automatically turned on to help the user quickly reach the target parking area for parking.formation. The GUI of parking guidance are shown in Fig. 2.

Message Notification. When the system identifies user violations or risk events, the system will select the corresponding level of alert method to notify the user according to the level of hazard, from low level to high level: mini program notification, SMS notification and phone notification respectively. When the hazard level is too high, the system will send a warning to all users with e-bikes parked in the area, and notify the administrator to carry out emergency action quickly to minimise the loss.

E-bike Centre. On this page, users can edit their personal e-bike information (license plate, color, model, etc.), view their personal parking records, service life of e-bike battery, self-inspection manuals, repair shops, etc.

User Centre. On this page, users can edit personal information, enter or modify face information, view violation records, view user credit score and redeem points, etc. The system uses the credit score as a reference for judging whether the user's behaviour is good or not, and the credit score will be deducted from the user's violation, When the user's credit score is too low, the system will automatically issue a ticket. If the user's credit score remains at a high level for a long time, it can be exchanged for certain points. The points obtained can be used to exchange corresponding rewards, including physical or virtual rewards.

Online Communication Platform. In the "online communication platform", users can not only give feedback on problems with the system and provide optimisation suggestions, but also share with other users some interesting stories and beautiful scenery they have encountered during their rides to improve the user experience.

Second-hand E-bike Trading Platform. In order to facilitate users to deal with old and idle e-bikes, the system has built a second-hand e-bike trading platform to provide the most authentic information on the transfer, purchase and sale of second-hand e-bikes to maximise the value of e-bikes.

Fig. 2. Parking Guidance.

3.2 Management Terminal

The GUI of management terminal are shown in Fig. 3.

E-bike Management. Manage e-bike information, including registration, modification, cancellation and other operations. Administrator can also batch import or export data reports for easy aggregation and statistics. A one-click reminder function is set up to urge users who have not yet registered e-bikes in the database to register as soon as possible.

User Management. Manage the administrator and registered user accounts. It includes editing user roles, assigning user permissions, viewing user operation logs and other functions. The system will automatically monitor user behaviour and locks out accounts for illegal users.

Risk Management. All parking areas are automatically managed and monitored throughout the day, including the temperature monitoring of the parking area of each parking lot, e-bike anti-theft monitoring, health status monitoring of IoT devices parking area management and other functions. The monitoring data is displayed in the form of charts for visual management.

Illegal Handling. Administrator can view details of the violation records of all users and the judgment certificate of violations captured by the system corresponding to each record (generally in the form of pictures). In addition, if users have doubts about the violations automatically judged by the system, they can also apply for manual review to reduce the risk of misjudgements and to ensure that every violation record is justified and traceable.

User Feedback. Display the system bugs and optimization suggestions reported by users, which is convenient for technicians to deal with and ensure the stability of the system.

Trading Centre. Display the transaction records of the second-hand e-bike trading, handle transaction disputes and ensure the legitimacy and fairness of the transaction. Administrator can put the products on sale and edit them in the trading centre.

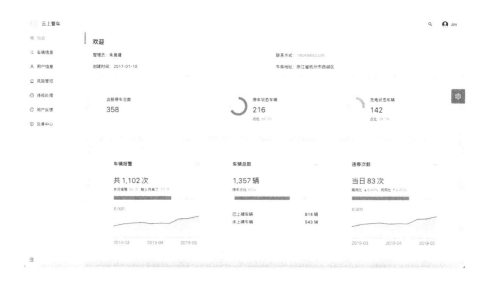

Fig. 3. Management Terminal.

3.3 Server

Multi-face Recognition. In order to effectively identify the user's identity information, the research group integrates face recognition technology into the system and adopts MTCNN (Multi-task convolutional neural network) algorithm to efficiently complete the tasks of multi-face detection and alignment. In addition, in the face recognition algorithm, the research group selected the

ArcFace Loss function with more strict requirements for classification to replace the traditional Triplet Loss function to train the network, which can obtain the depth features with higher recognition accuracy and ensure the detection speed and accuracy in the practical application environment.

License Plate Recognition. As the only identification information of e-bikes, the ability to quickly and accurately identify the number plate information is the key to the normal operation of the system. After acquiring the image information from the IoT devices, the system will first segment the possible license plate areas by "yellow + edge", use CNN classification to remove the areas that are not number plates, then greyscale the detected plates and obtain the maximum projection angle through Randon transformation to rotate the image for correction. The image is then denoised and the top and bottom borders and rivets are removed by the jump count method and vertical projection method, then the characters on the plate are segmented and finally the segmented images of the individual characters are recognised and recombined to achieve accurate plate recognition.

Subject Identification. In order to detect whether the parking of e-bikes is standardised, the research group uses the R-CNN (Region-CNN) target detection algorithm to detect the coordinate positions of multiple subjects in the image captured by IOT devices, and gives the classification label of the subject, the confidence score of the label and the location information of the detection frame of the target subject (determined by four parameters: left, top, width and height). After filtering out irrelevant subjects, by comparing the position information of the detection frame of the e-bike with the position information of the legal parking area designated by the system, judge whether the parking of the e-bike is standardized. It is also combined with the plate recognition function, by comparing the location information of the identified plate with the location information of the detection frame of the main body of the e-bike, in order to achieve accurate positioning of the identity of the e-bike.

When the e-bike moves or falls, the position information of the detection frame of the e-bike often changes greatly. When the system detects abnormal changes, it sends a warning to the owner. The specific workflow is shown in Fig. 4.

Fire Warning. The research group uses several infrared thermal sensors deployed in the parking area to transmit the temperature of the parking lot as a numerical value to the IoT devices. The IoT devices compares with a preset temperature, distinguishes the color according to the threshold, and transmits the data to the management terminal through the WiFi module. When the temperature in an area is detected to be too high, the system will automatically send a warning to the administrator. The administrator can also judge whether there is a fire hazard in the parking lot by observing the color of the Web interface.

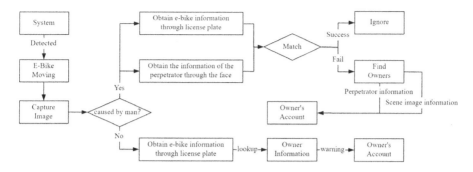

Fig. 4. Flowchart of the System Detecting Illegal E-bike Movement.

4   The Advantages of System

The intelligent parking management system for urban e-bikes mainly has the following system advantages.

4.1   Visual Management

The management terminal provides data visualization management in the form of charts and other forms, which facilitates administrators to deal with all kinds of information more intuitively and greatly improves their work efficiency.

4.2   One-stop Service

In addition to the main functions of e-bike parking management, the system also includes a series of functions such as e-bike purchase, licensing, maintenance and transfer, providing a one-stop service around the relevant needs of users.

4.3   Effectively Guarantee E-bike Safety

By processing the images and data captured by the IoT devices deployed in the parking area, the system can provide real-time feedback on the status of parked e-bikes to the administrator and relevant users, providing a strong guarantee for e-bike safety. At the same time, with the increase of training data, the system can continuously improve the recognition accuracy in the process of use, reducing the occurrence of misjudgment situations.

4.4   Humanized Design

The interface is simple in design and easy to operate, enabling users to quickly familiarise themselves with the system. If users are dissatisfied with the punishment result, they can raise objections to the system. The system will arrange the administrator to conduct manual review and inform the review results at the first time to protect the legitimate rights and interests of users from being infringed.

4.5   Voice Broadcast Feedback

Considering the elderly group as the representative of users who do not carry smartphones, when the system detects a violation, the IoT device will remind the user to correct it in time through voice broadcast to expand the user group.

5   Conclusion

The research group designed and developed the "Intelligent Parking Management System for Urban E-bikes" by using cutting-edge technologies such as AI and the IoT, aiming at some pain points in the parking management of e-bikes. It provides a relatively perfect solution for the problems existing in e-bikes, such as disorderly parking and placement, frequent safety accidents, weak normative awareness of e-bike owners, and difficult management, and has achieved some results in practical application. Although there are still some problems and deficiencies in the current system design, with the development of technology and the enrichment of scientific research resources in the future, the research group will further improve the system and optimize the user experience in the follow-up research and development.

Acknowledgements. This research was supported by the Humanities and Social Science Research Fund Project of the Ministry of Education of China in 2017 (No. 17YJA880004) and the National College Student Innovation and Entrepreneurship Training Program (No. 202111057015) in 2021.

References

1. Yuanyu, T., Yingyun, Q., Yongning, Z.: Construction of green emission reduction system under carbon neutrality constraint. Chem. Progr. **41**(02), 1078–1084 (2022)
2. Jianxin, T.: Brief analysis of the current situation and development of the electric vehicle industry. Fortune Times, pp. 28–29 (2021)
3. Nubxyab, D., Ying, L., Jiayi, L., Shibin, C.: Optimization of non-motorized vehicle systems in small and medium-sized cities. Enterprise Science and Technology and Development, pp. 33–35 (2020)
4. Xuesong Y.: RAnalysis of the current situation of electric vehicle fires and measures to solve them. China Science and Technology Information, pp. 38–39 (2021)
5. Jinhua, S., Yan, Z.: Analysis and design of non-motorized parking device. Science and Technology and Innovation, pp. 38–39 (2018)
6. Yao, L.: Design of non-motorized landscaped parking in machine-office segregation zone **42**(11), 19–21 (2014)
7. Yuanyuan, H.: Research on intelligent parking under Internet of things, artificial intelligence and big data. Intelligent Building, pp. 38–39 (2020)
8. Xiangshuang, M.: Research on front and back-end separated WEB application development. Electronic components and information technology, pp. 40–43 (2019)
9. Shaojing, Z., Ying, J., Hongbin, P., Jian, H., Zhengyuan, Y.: Research on the application of RESTful architecture. Netw. Digital Technol. Appl. **36**(05), 59–60 (2018)
10. Li, L.: Research on the application of MVC design pattern in JavaWeb development. Information Communication, pp. 104–106 (2020)

Asian Games Service Intelligent System Based on Privacy-Preserving Recommendation

Zifan Zhang[1], Yuefeng Cen[1(✉)], Xujun Che[2], Zeping Yang[1],
Lingchao Wang[1], and Xuanyu Lin[1]

[1] School of Information and Electronic Engineering,
Zhejiang University of Science and Technology, Hangzhou, China
cyf@zust.edu.cn
[2] School of Science, Zhejiang University of Science and Technology, Hangzhou, China

Abstract. As the Hangzhou Asian Games is approaching, the research group has designed and implemented an intelligent system for Asian Games services with privacy-preserving recommendation system, aiming to solve the problem that people cannot obtain personalized Asian Games information. The system adopts Term Frequency Inverse Document Frequency (TF-IDF) and the privacy enhanced matrix factorization to realize the multi-criteria privacy-preserving recommendation. The system can meet the individuals' needs to obtain sports event information with the protection of user privacy. It improves the users' experiences, meanwhile, conduce to the spread of Hangzhou and the Asian Games.

Keywords: Asian Games · intelligent recommendation · privacy protection

1 Introduction

The 2008 Beijing Olympic Games was successfully held, which brought a wave of national sports. The continuous and stable development of China's economy and the increasing improvement of people's living standards have made people's material and spiritual life have a high pursuit [1]. And sports can just meet people's growing spiritual needs, which creates a strong atmosphere for the holding of large-scale comprehensive games. The rich content contained in large-scale comprehensive games is attractive to people. Sports meeting has gradually become the focus of people's close attention [2]. This was perfectly reflected in the Beijing Winter Olympics that just passed. According to statistics, the Beijing Winter Olympics has become the Winter Olympics with the highest ratings so far [3]. The enthusiasm of the domestic masses to participate in ice and snow sports is high, and the vision of "driving 300 million people to participate in ice and snow sports" has been successfully realized.

The large-scale comprehensive gamesalso playe a huge role in promoting the development of the economy, transportation, infrastructure construction, tourism and the transformation as well as upgrading of the industrial structure. The Guangzhou Asian Games has promoted the urban development of Guangzhou. The regional GDP brought by the Asian Games city investment is about 100 billion yuan, and the tertiary industry has also been fully developed, accounting for more than 60%. This makes Guangzhou's exhibition economy and modern service industry to flourish [4]. The Olympic venue, the Olympic Park during the Beijing Olympics, has now become a new urban public activity center. With convenient transportation and perfect infrastructure, it has attracted many tourists and promoted the development of tourism [5]. It is precisely the successful holding of these large-scale international multi-sport games, which provides a wealth of experience for Hangzhou to host the Asian Games.

Now, Hangzhou will usher in the 19th Asian Games in 2022, which is a rare opportunity for development in this century. As an ancient city with a long history and culture, it must use the stage of the Asian Games to show its unique charm. After the successful bid to host the Asian Games, the mayor of Hangzhou said that only with the participation and joint efforts of all the people can the concept of the Asian Games be truly practiced and an unforgettable Asian Games be held [6]. Hangzhou takes "China's New Era Hangzhou New Asian Games" as its orientation, "Chinese characteristics, Zhejiang style, Hangzhou charm, and splendidness" as its goal. The Hangzhou Asian Games is a historical choice and an inevitable development.

With the rapid development of modern technology, users can obtain information anytime and anywhere on smart devices such as smartphones and laptops [7]. Under the background of modern society with information explosion, the cost of acquiring information is gradually decreasing, even approaching zero indefinitely, but in the face of massive information, it is difficult to filter out the information we are interested in [8]. Information grows exponentially, but there is very little information that can meet users' needs [9]. When people receive too much repetitive information or information they don't want to read, the efficiency of the users' receiving information will be greatly reduced, and the users' experience will be very bad. Based on the above situation, how to extract and filter out the information that users are interested from the massive information has become an urgent problem to be solved by this research group.

2 System Design

2.1 The Proposition of the Intelligent System of Asian Games Service

With the arrival of the Hangzhou Asian Games, to reduce the ineffective dissemination of information about the Hangzhou Asian Games and serve the public, the research group designed an intelligent Asian Games service system that integrates intelligent recommendation, information, events and dynamics. The system not only uses an intelligent recommendation algorithm to avoid invalid information as much as possible, and greatly reduces the phenomenon of information waste, but also sets up functions such as navigation, dynamic sharing, and quiz, which comprehensively connects events and users, further shortens the distance between the public and the Asian Games and implements the concept of the Asian Games of "all people participating and benefiting the whole people".

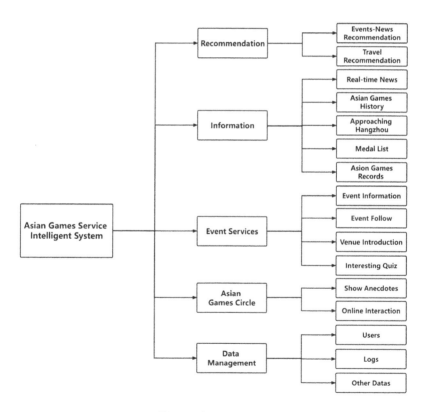

Fig. 1. Architecture

2.2   Architecture

The overall design of the Asian Games service intelligent recommendation system is shown in Fig. 1. The system consists of five modules: recommendation, information, event services, Asian Games circle, and data management.

2.3   Main Functional Modules

Recommendation. This module includes several functions such as events-news recommendation, travel recommendation (as shown in Fig. 2).

– Events-News recommendation: According to the tags of interest selected by the users and the users' browsing records, likes and collections and so on, the system provides privacy-preserving recommendation. Based on users' behaviors and news portraits, it realizes the recommendation of events and news while protecting the users' privacy.

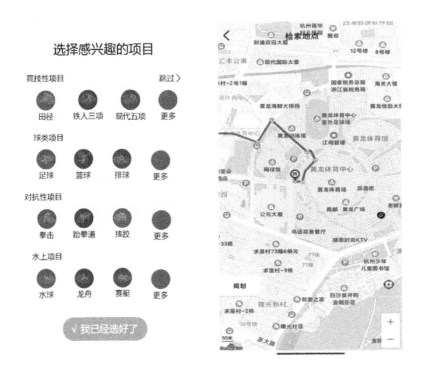

Fig. 2. Events-News And Travel Recommendation

– Travel recommendation: The online map is introduced. Meanwhile, according to the users' geographic location, integrate elements such as time, distance, traffic mode, weather, recommend the optimal travel mode for the users.

Information. An information bulletin module that includes the news information of various Asian Games competitions, the history of the Asian Games, Hangzhou culture, and real-time medal standings.

– Real-time News: Push news of the games, post-game analysis, event introduction, off-court news during the Asian Games.
– Asian Games History: Introduce overview of each Asian Games since the first New Delhi Games.
– Approaching Hangzhou: Take users to "tour" Hangzhou, show Hangzhou's special food, cultural tourist attractions. Enjoy the profound cultural heritage and customs of Hangzhou.
– Medal List: Sort by the number of gold, silver and bronze medals of each country's national team, according to the number of gold medals as the main keyword, silver as the secondary keyword, and bronze as the third keyword.
– Asian Games Records: The Asian Games records of previous events, including the highest scores of the events that have been completed this year, with special notes on the events and results those broke records Fig.2 and Fig. 3.

Fig. 3. Home Page

Event Services. Focus on specific sports competitions and create the ultimate Asian Games feast for users.

- Event Information: Schedule information of all Asian Games competitions, including time, venues, participating teams, etc., and provide online viewing methods and channels.
- Venue Introduction: Details of the competition venue, including brief introduction, history, traffic information, and comprehensive introduction of the competitions or theatrical performances it has hosted.
- Interesting Quiz: Provide a platform to quiz the results of the game, and reward users with points for successful quizzes. When the points reach a certain value, they can get the corresponding title.

Asian Games Circle. Online communication and interaction platform, users can share the anecdotes around the Asian Games and publish their own news on the platform. At the same time, users can also like and comment on the dynamics posted by others, and express their own opinions.

Fig. 4. Asian Games Circle

Data Management. Manage system users and administrators control users' permissions and view users' logs. The system will intelligently detect abnormal risks and lock illegal users. The users can also change the interest items selected when logging in for the first time. At the same time, manage user-followed event information and favorite news, and remind users by means of message push one hour before the game starts to prevent users from missing the game.

3   System Technology

The system adopts the development mode of front-end and back-end separation, applies tools such as Android Studio and IntelliJ IDEA to realize them, and uses TF-IDF model and privacy enhanced matrix factorization to realize intelligent recommendation.

3.1   Client

Development Environment. Based on the Android system, the research group adopts native application, develops this system in the native environment and uses the Kotlin language to develop on Android Studio, which is efficient and fast. The native application runs based on the local operating system, so its compatibility and access capabilities are better. Meanwhile, it has the best users' experience, the best interactive interface, and the overall users' experience are good.

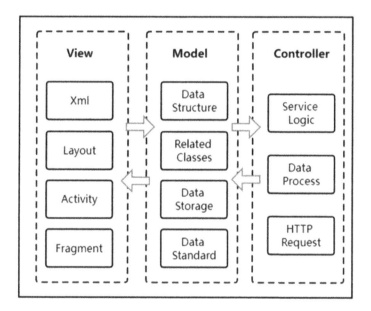

Fig. 5. Android Framework

Front-end. The research group selected the MVC (model-view-controller) framework as the main front-end framework, and used the method of separating the MVC framework function module and data module to organize the code. Among them, the view layer uses XML, Layout, Activity, Fragment and other files to describe the interface, and is responsible for displaying interface data and interacting with users. The model layer establishes relevant classes and data structures for business models, and realizes data storage and specification. The control layer mainly performs business logic, data processing, and network request work, as shown in Fig. 5. Using the MVC framework, the structure is concise, the division of responsibilities is clear, the degree of code differentiation is improved, and the degree of coupling is reduced,which is conducive to software engineering management [10].

3.2   Server

Development Environment. Using Java language as the main development language, IntelliJ IDEA as the main development tool, Tomcat as the web container, Postman as the interface calling tool, MySQL and Redis as the database cluster, and with Navicat Premium database management tool, you can easily and quickly Data transfer between various database systems makes it more convenient to manage different types of data such as tag data and users' information.

Back-end. This system is developed based on the Spring Boot framework and adopts the Spring Cloud microservice design concept. It realizes business decoupling and improve the efficiency of development and deployment. On the one hand, it uses the Hibernate framework to interact with the MySQL database, and implements data caching based on Redis to improve system interface performance. On the other hand, it builds a Swagger server to manage and control all APIs, update code, make API documents automatically update, improve the efficiency of developing and maintaining interfaces, use RESTful style to implement different CRUD operations, unify the interfaces for data operations, and implement standardized management ofAPIs.

3.3   Core Technology

Privacy-preserving Recommendation. In terms of recommendation algorithm, the research group uses Python language to implement functions. The TF-IDF model is built through the jieba Chinese word segmentation framework, and the words in the news are vectorized and given corresponding weights to extract news keywords. The research group built a multi-criteria privacy-preserving recommendation system, as shown in Fig. 6. The system calculates the users' comprehensive rating of the news based on the tags that the users are interested in, the news that the users have viewed, and the keywords corresponding to the news. The privacy-enhanced matrix decomposition algorithm

[11], which satisfies local differential privacy (LDP), is then used to factorize the users rating matrix into users profiles and news profiles while protecting users' privacy, enabling flexible and easily scalable recommendation prediction in multiple scenarios, such as home page news recommendation based on matrix completion, similar news recommendation based on news profiles, etc.

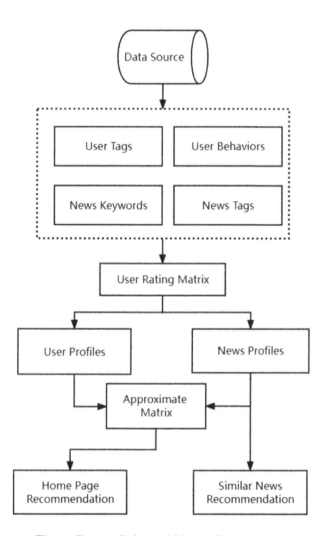

Fig. 6. Privacy Enhanced Matrix Factorization

User Security Verification. After the users log in successfully, the system will generate a Token for it based on the JWT, return this Token to the users, and store it in the database. When users want to access other pages, the Token will be carried, and the Token will be verified in the system. If the Token is not within the validity period or the Token is invalid, this access will fail. If the background verifies that Token is valid, and the corresponding users' identities are parsed through the Token, then the system will go to the database to obtain the corresponding permissions according to the users' identities, so that the API services that meet the identity permissions can be accessed. Users can access the APP within the validity period of the Token, and do not need to log in again. Every time you access the APP, the system will automatically refresh the validity period of the Token, and at the same time return the new Token to the users and store it in the database. When the token expires, the users need to re-enter the account password to log in. As shown in Fig. 7.

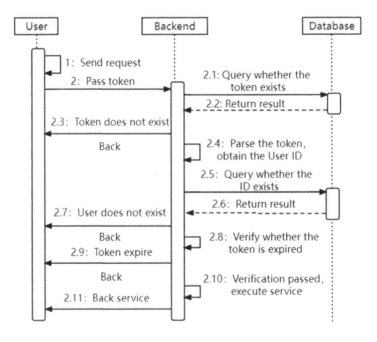

Fig. 7. Privacy Enhanced Matrix Factorization

4   System Features

4.1   Personalized Recommendations

Sports applications are combined with personalized recommendations. Among the 40 major items and 61 subitems of the Hangzhou Asian Games, users can actively select tags with different preferences, so that they can receive recommended content more in line with their personal preferences which help users to get the information they like quickly and efficiently. At the same time, the system will also give weights to each behavior according to the users' browsing records, hobbies, collections and other behaviors. Extracting keywords to label the news can display the keywords corresponding to the news in the recommendation results, which is helpful for users to understand the recommendation results. What's more, keywords have strong stability in capturing the interests of users, which is conducive to accurate recommendation and improves the degree of personalization.

4.2   Diversified Services

Compared with traditional sports applications, the intelligent recommendation system for Asian Games events not only pushes sports event information, but also adds several services about events such as "Approaching Hangzhou", "Asian Games Circle" and "Interesting Quiz" . These services have rendered the Asian Games a casual and cheerful atmosphere. The diversified users' experience are also convenient for faster integration into the Hangzhou Asian Games.

4.3   Privacy Protection

In the process of news recommendation, the system adopts an algorithm that satisfies LDP constraints, which effectively avoids inference attacks from adversaries, increases the difficulty for attackers to identify users' personal information, prevent the leakage of users' private data. What's more, the system has strengthened the protection of users' privacy, so that users can use the system with peace of mind.

5   Conclusion

The Asian Games service intelligence system with privacy-preserving recommendation adopts TF-IDF, privacy enhanced matrix factorization technologies. It's a new design idea for the mobile terminal design of the Hangzhou Asian Games. It effectively solves the problem that users cannot obtain valid information in the face of massive information, and strengthens the protection of users privacy. It is conducive to serve the Asian Games and promote the Asian Games and Hangzhou. However, the system at present still has certain limitations about cross-platform development compatibility and support and maintenance for all versions, and further optimization is required. It is believed that with the unremitting efforts of the research group, the system will be continuously updated and improved, and finally presented to the public in a perfect manner.

Acknowledgment. This work was supported by the Humanities and Social Sciences Research Program Fund of the Ministry of Education of China (No. 17YJA880004); The grants from Zhejiang Xinmiao Talents Program (No.2021R415026).

References

1. China's economy to grow by 8.1% in 2021. XIANDAIQIYE. **50**(2), 6 (2022)
2. Zhang, Y.: On the Influence of Beijing Olympic Games on China's Sports Development. Contemp. Sports Technol. **37**(04), 249+251 (2017)
3. Sunlei, L.: Technological innovation and digital communication of the 2022 Beijing Winter Olympics. Omnimedia Exploration. **Z1**, 4–9 (2022)
4. Cheng, G., Yuyong, H.: Sports Events and Urban Development: an empirical study using the guangzhou asian games as an example. Sports Sci. **34**(4), 33–38+53 (2013)
5. Hu, H., Qi, F.: Research on the influence of the Olympic Games on the development of urban space-Taking the Beijing Olympic Games as an example. Econ. Res. Guid. **28**, 168–172 (2012)
6. The Asian Games will surely become a new dynamism and new driving force for the development of Hangzhou - Hangzhou Mayor Zhang Hongming accepts an exclusive interview with the media after Shen Ya's success. Gazette of the Peoples Government of Hangzhou Municipality. **9**, 49 (2015)
7. Zhangjin, Y., Wang, L.: The influence of ubiquitous knowledge environment on user information demand behavior. Sci. Technol. Inform. **14**, 106 (2013)
8. Wu, N.: Technology wind. Internet Inform. Screen. **8**, 92 (2017)
9. Baoke, M.: Talking about the construction of information resources under the network environment. Inner Mongolia Sci. Technol. Econ. **21**, 75–76 (2021)
10. Zhouzi, J., Peng, Y.: Application research and practice of MVC framework in android development. Comput. Programm. Skills Maintenance. **5**, 59–61 (2021)
11. Shin, H., Kim, S., Shin, J., Xiao, X.: Privacy enhanced matrix factorization for recommendation with local differential privacy. IEEE Trans. Knowl. Data Eng. **30**(9), 1770–1782 (2018)

Intelligent Chinese Speech Learning Correction System

Keying Zhu, Yuefeng Cen(✉), and Jiaming Gu

School of Information and Electronic Engineering, Zhejiang University of Science and Technology, Hangzhou, China
cyf@zust.edu.cn

Abstract. In order to meet the learning needs of Chinese learners and help them correct the nonstandard pronunciation of Mandarin, the project team applies intelligent speech technology to Chinese learning, designs and develops a intelligent Chinese speech learning correction system. The system realizes Chinese learning and speech correction for all users through the combination of intelligent mobile terminal and Web background management terminal. Users improve their oral communication skills in Chinese through intensive listening and follow-up reading, correct pronunciation errors in spoken language with the help of the system's audio-video dual-modal algorithm, improve their understanding of Chinese characters through writing training, and practice Chinese ability in community communication. After the application test, the system can effectively improve the learners' Chinese oral expression ability.

Keywords: Chinese learning · assessment · speech correction

1 Introduction

At present, China has established 541 Confucius Institutes and 1,170 Confucius Classrooms in 162 countries or regions. A total of 75 countries around the world have incorporated Chinese into their national education systems. More than 4,000 foreign universities have offered Chinese courses, and they are learning Chinese outside of China. The number of people is about 25 million, and it is gradually increasing with a good trend [1]. From 2016 to 2020, more than 40 million people took Chinese proficiency tests(HSK) and YCT which is Chinese Test for Primary and Secondary Schools [2]. thus it can be seen that more and more people are learning Mandarin Chinese internationally, and at the same time, the demand for excellent Mandarin teachers abroad is also showing a significant growth trend. The penetration and influence of information technology on education has become increasingly prominent, So the integration of Chinese learning and information technology has become one of the important driving forces for the reform of Chinese education [3]. Since the beginning of the 21st century, with the development of technologies such as 5G, artificial intelligence,

W. Hong and Y. Weng (Eds.): ICCSE 2022, CCIS 1811, pp. 65–76, 2023.
https://doi.org/10.1007/978-981-99-2443-1_6

big data, and cloud computing, smart education empowered by technology has gradually come to fruition from the previous concept.

Under the new situation of normalization of online teaching, international Chinese education must adapt to the needs of the intelligent era, and use intelligent technology to reform the teaching environment, teaching mode, teaching content, teaching organization, teaching evaluation, etc., to provide learners with more personalized and Accurate Chinese wisdom education can solve the major problem that the sustainable development of international Chinese education cannot be achieved by offline communication at home and abroad [4]. In China, due to the heavier local accents in some regions, the Mandarin of Chinese people is not standard. In the process of interpersonal communication in daily life, people usually have many misunderstandings due to non-standard pronunciation, which deepens the difficulty of communication between the two parties, and also brings a lot of inconvenience in life. How to effectively improve the quality of Chinese people's Mandarin has become a major difficulty in people's thinking [5]. To this end, under the background of Chinese smart education at home and abroad, based on the computer-aided environment to improve the accuracy of learners' pronunciation, an intelligent Chinese phonetic learning system is built to assist Chinese teachers, help domestic people to improve their Mandarin level, and help foreign friends. Learning Mandarin Chinese also plays a role in deepening the feelings of friends at home and abroad. Compared with software such as Yinshu, Rehabilitation Cloud, and Dr.Qiyin, which require payment, this system is free for learners and has the function of speech correction.

2   The Research and Design of the System

2.1   The Proposal of the System

The project team found that the global educational mobility continued to weaken, while the number of people learning Mandarin Chinese continued to grow, which greatly affected the learning of Chinese. In the actual spoken Mandarin teaching in China, everyone's learning habits are different, and the materials for oral Chinese learning are scattered, while the traditional online oral language learning software has a very high personal abandonment rate due to the boring and lonely learning process.

Based on the current background of the times, the project team starts with the needs of domestic and foreign friends for oral Mandarin learning, alleviates the social status quo of the serious lack of online Mandarin personalized education, and fills the gap in the online Chinese phonetic learning correction software on the market, so that Mandarin learners do not have to Get high-quality spoken language learning and pronunciation error correction while worrying about cost [6]. To this end, the project team proposed and designed and developed the system, which is a new dual-modal intelligent Chinese speech correction platform developed under the background of the current shortage of Chinese speech learning and correction resources in the market. Targeting at home and abroad

Chinese learners and different learning scenarios, it helps to more comprehensively implement the core concept of "internationalization at home".

2.2   The Design of the System

This system is mainly aimed at Chinese people with non-standard Mandarin and foreign friends who have Chinese learning needs, helping domestic and foreign learners to learn spoken Chinese efficiently. The overall structure of the system is shown in Fig. 1. It is mainly divided into modules such as intensive listening, follow-up reading, speech correction, learning assessment, writing training, book reading, and community communication. Each module is independent and complementary to each other, ensuring the stable operation of the system and the hierarchical learning of users. In the wave of "Mandarin fever", the system builds up the application of Chinese learning and speech correction through the Internet. In order to meet the user's learning of Chinese spoken language, the project team constructs the intelligent Chinese speech learning correction system.

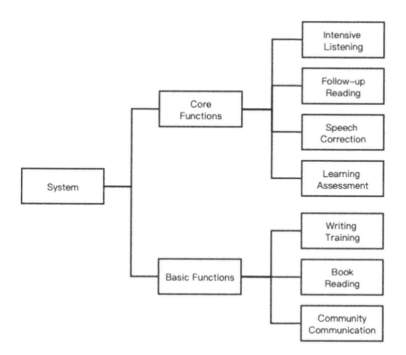

Fig. 1. The overall structure of the system.

This system assists teachers in teaching by "seeing, listening, practicing, commenting, writing, and discussing", and provides users with a new channel to quickly improve their oral Chinese learning. This system concretizes the way of oral language learning into three core learning functions: intensive listening, follow-up reading and speech correction. Each function has a corresponding scoring mechanism, and finally a comprehensive learning evaluation score is obtained based on the three scoring results, allowing users to clarify their own Chinese speaking learning level. In terms of basic functions, users can exercise their writing ability through the writing training, and at the same time, they can watch the books they are interested in through the book reading. The system also provides a community communication function to help users consolidate and strengthen the practical application ability of spoken Chinese.

2.3   Each Functional Module

The following is a detailed description of the functions of each module of the system and its architecture.

Intensive Listening. The system collects a large number of high-quality movie and video clips, which are classified according to types such as suspense, history, military, romance, science fiction, etc., which enriches users' application requirements for spoken Chinese in various scenarios and facilitates users to search for oral Chinese learning materials. Users can choose their favorite categories and then select videos for listening practice. Users can also listen carefully through browsing history and favorites. Users can listen to Chinese carefully by choosing to open subtitles and close subtitles, which can gradually strengthen their learning of spoken Chinese. After listening to Chinese intensively, users need to rate their own listening, and give their own clear assessment of this listening exercise, which is helpful for users to improve their Mandarin level in the process of self-evaluation and comparison. This self-rating result It also serves as the basis for the system to evaluate the user's comprehensive learning.

Follow-up Reading. While improving Chinese listening ability, users can use the follow-up reading function to perform follow-up reading according to the high-quality movie and video clips provided by the system, so as to improve their oral Chinese communication ability. The system only records the user's audio under the follow-up reading function. The user can choose to follow the sentence by sentence or read the whole article, and after the system records the user's follow-up voice, the user can compare it with the original audio to find out his own shortcomings. At the same time, the system will mark the text with different pronunciation from the original audio in red to attract users' attention to the text with non-standard pronunciation. The user can repeat the follow-up exercise. After the user has recorded the entire follow-up reading, the system will give the score based on the last follow-up reading result.

Speech Correction. Under the follow-up reading function, the film and video clips that the user has completed follow-up will appear under the speech correction module. The speech correction function can help users correct the pronunciation of sentences that have always been non-standard during follow-up reading. Users need to record their own audio and video under the speech correction function. Under the movie video clips, the user reads the sentences marked in red in turn, and the system first determines whether they are accurate or not. If some of the text is still marked in red, the system will cut and analyze the audio and video during the just follow-up process according to the audio-video dual-modal algorithm. According to the video mode, it identifies and corrects the movement details such as the pronunciation action of the lips and the zooming position of the front and rear nasal sounds. According to the audio mode, it identifies and corrects the sound problems such as the front and rear nasal sounds and tonal pronunciation of the content read aloud by the user. Finally, the results of the cutting analysis are fused and summarized. The system will give a spoken pronunciation video of word-by-word pronunciation and a text description suggestion for the pronunciation of the word, helping users to more accurately correct the spoken pronunciation by watching the video and reading the text. The user can repeat the follow-up correction repeatedly. After the user's last follow-up recording and correction is completed, the system will give a score for improving the follow-up accuracy through voice correction. For example, if the score is 80 points after the follow-up reading, and the score is 90 points after correction by the speech correction function, the speech correction score of the movie video clip is $(90-80)/(100-80)$)*100=50 points.

Learning Assessment. The user's comprehensive learning situation is presented in scores, ranging from 0 to 100. The system averages the user's self-score after each intensive listening, and the average value will be used as the user's intensive listening score. Similarly, the system takes an average of the scores of each follow-up reading of the user, and the average value will be used as the score of the user's follow-up reading. The system also averages the scores of each speech correction of the user, and the average value will be used as the score of the user's speech correction. However, if a certain movie video segment under the speech correction module is not full score, and the correction has not started, it will be processed with 0 points; Finally, the scores of intensive listening, follow-up reading and speech correction are weighted and averaged according to the weights of 0.2, 0.35 and 0.45 respectively, and this value is used as the user's current learning evaluation result.

Writing Training. Chinese characters have the characteristics of being figurative, and only a better understanding of the characters can have a better writing training effect. After the learner has determined the writing content of interest, the system provides the user with a relevant video containing the text, including other relevant introductions such as the origin and evolution of the text. After watching the video, users will have a deeper understanding and mastery of the text to be written. The user takes a picture of the written Chinese character and uploads it, and the system provides accurate and effective Chinese character modification suggestions and scores for the user's writing result through the feature extraction algorithm and semantic analysis algorithm of artificial intelligence.

Book Reading. While learning spoken Chinese, users can use the book reading function to watch books they are interested in, and add books to the bookshelf to read books that have not been read or have no time to read for the time being, making it easier for users to find the book. Users can choose to read the book or listen to the book to read the book. If they encounter difficult reading, they can also click to query. The text that can be queried usually appears in the form of phrase pairs, and the user can know the pronunciation of the word and its Chinese meaning. The book reading function further strengthens the user's mastery of spoken language, deepens the user's understanding of Chinese, and sublimates the user's love for Chinese culture.

Community Communication. Users can communicate in the community, which is open to all registered users. Users can share their learning experience of spoken Chinese and recent life anecdotes in the community by sending text, pictures and short videos. Users can search for interesting content through the search bar. Based on the collaborative filtering algorithm, the system pushes high-rated dynamic content that users are interested in according to their preferences. Users can like, comment, favorite and rate the updates sent by others, and users can also see other users' comments and like the comments under the same update. Users can start chatting by clicking on their avatars. There are various chat methods. Users can choose text input, or send short voice messages. They can also send emoticons, photos and videos to strengthen their communication skills through practical exercises. The user can also follow the person he likes, and the user can conveniently and timely receive the immediate dynamic of the person he has followed through the follow. It is conducive to establishing friendly communication between users, narrowing the distance between people who learn spoken Chinese at home and abroad, and enhancing the feelings between international friends.

3   Technology Route

3.1   Technology Framework

In order to make the system available to all users who need to learn spoken Chinese, the project team adopts both iOS and Android development, and also develops a background management website as the management terminal. The system is developed using the Flutter framework and introduces Redux-middlewar to handle more complex business [7]. Realize a set of code, multi-end generation, and realize complex and flexible interface design through composable space combination and rich animation library.

The client uses Dart as the programming language for development. Dart is one of the few languages that supports both JIT (just-in-time compilation) and AOT (compile-before-running), so it also shows the characteristics of fast running speed and good execution performance during the development and running process.

In server-side development, we use SpringBoot as the framework, MVC as the main architecture, and MyBatis as the persistence layer framework. In terms of performance optimization, we introduce Kafka as a message middleware to process message queues in the state of large amounts of data, and use it as push processing for streaming media and learner forums. In addition, we use Redis distributed caching technology to safely back up user data, and also widely used in operations such as displaying, deleting and filtering lists [8]. Finally, we use Nginx-based Ip-Hash strategy to bind clients and servers to achieve one-to-one, and optimize Nginx's reverse proxy and load balancing .

SpringBoot combines MVC architecture as a backend framework This model is used for layered development of programs. We use the SpringBoot framework to greatly facilitate the plug-in deployment process and simplify the initial construction and development process of the application. Using the Controller as a proxy for the connection, the View and Model are easily connected, allowing multiple Views to share a Model.

MyBatis is a semi-automatic persistence layer framework that encapsulates the process of JDBC operating the database. We only need to focus on SQL itself, which uses simple XML and annotations for configuration and original mapping, allowing us to use the use of object oriented programming method (OOP) to operate the database.

Redis is an in-memory database, which not only improves user access speed, but also saves data space and reduces database pressure while ensuring data integrity in the process of data caching. We use its own hash data structure to realize the data storage of the learning forum, and finally use the master-slave data backup mode to cache messages, set the expiration time according to the key, and automatically delete it to improve the security of user data backup.

Kafka is a distributed, partition-supported messaging system that uses its batch processing mechanism to meet the needs of large data volume transmission processing and low latency.

The Ip Hash strategy is a built-in strategy. The front-end access IP is hashed first, and then requests are allocated to different back-end nodes according to the results. Through Nginx implementation, each front-end access IP will access a back-end node fixedly, which can avoid the problem of session sharing.

3.2   Core Technology

Speech Correction Technology. The user records audio and video through the interactive interface, and inputs the audio and video into the system, the system will automatically convert the video in mp4 format into audio part and video part, and the video part will be automatically decoded and cut into a picture sequence, one frame by one picture. The system chooses 24 frames as the unified input metric of the model to achieve two balanced effects of no loss of information and as small a model input as possible. In order to improve the robustness of the model, and considering that users speak at different times on each word, the system uses multiple copying operations starting at random starting points to replace the method of re-copying at fixed positions. At the same time, the system adds the processing methods of random frame loss and random movement of pictures. Random frame loss occurs when the number of samples is greater than a specified specific value, and the lips of a series of pictures are not in the same position, so as to enhance the generalization ability of the model.

In terms of feature extraction, in terms of video, the face-alignment toolkit of the dlib library in Python is used to extract the face feature points of the face part of the video picture sequence. In practical situations, it is difficult to predict the shape of the face by using features with high confidence, and to ensure the accuracy of the features extracted from the shape of the face [9]. To solve this problem, the system uses an iterative approximation method to extract the sample features based on the current predicted shape, and then uses the extracted features to update the vector when predicting the shape. This process is repeated several times until convergence. Finally, the corresponding 20 lip key point positions are obtained through the lip key point number, and the relative radian between the key points is used as a feature [10]. Subsequently, all the features of the entire video sequence are combined into a 2D tensor.

In terms of audio, the user's input is evaluated by using the characteristics of different frequencies, and the two feature tensors are respectively sent to the bidirectional long-short-term memory network Bi-LSTM for judgment. The overlapping segments of the two sequences have lower confidence. That is, the mispronunciation fragment. After the audio data entered by the user is processed by audio segmentation, the audio of a single word is sent to the trained lstm model for evaluation and scoring.

Based on the large-scale Chinese data set dedicated to the pronunciation of cloud port language, the system can effectively train and establish a high-accuracy spoken language recognition model. Finally, the two features of audio and video are input into the multi-modal deep neural network. Finally, the system performs comprehensive evaluation and scoring according to the scores obtained from video processing and audio, and provides users with accurate pronunciation of each text with non-standard pronunciation according to the output results of the network. Video suggestions and text suggestions for speaking improvement.

Writing Recognition Technology. Based on the current mainstream image text recognition model, a text recognition model based on attention mechanism is proposed, and its framework is shown in Fig. 2.

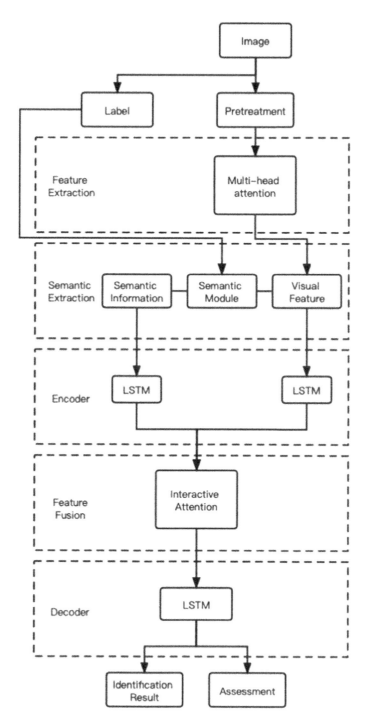

Fig. 2. Text recognition model framework based on attention mechanism.

The user uploads the written text in the form of a photo. After the image is uploaded, the system preprocesses it to eliminate irrelevant information as much as possible, highlight useful real information, and then perform grayscale processing.

The model is mainly composed of five functional modules: feature extraction, semantic extraction, encoder, feature fusion and decoder. The feature extraction module uses the multi-head attention mechanism to extract the deep visual feature information of the image. In the specific implementation, the number of heads is set to 8. Q, K, and V are fixed single values and are input to 8 Linear layers, so as to "focus" on the input values from 8 angles. The obtained 8 single-head attention features are used for feature fusion, and then the multi-head attention value of the input information is obtained through the full-connection neural network for advanced conversion, so as to realize the deep feature extraction of the input information. In order to make up for the fact that the current image text recognition model ignores the semantic information of the text to cause text recognition errors, the semantic information features of the image text are extracted in the image text recognition to strengthen the role of the semantic information in the image text recognition. Then, the visual feature information and semantic feature information are encoded through a two-layer bidirectional Long Short Term Memory Networks (LSTM). In order to effectively fuse image visual information with text semantic information and retrograde, a feature fusion method based on interactive attention mechanism is adopted, that is, visual features interact with semantics to obtain image recognition features that are more critical and accurate for the current recognition task. Achieve efficient fusion of visual features and semantic features. Finally, a bidirectional long-short-term memory neural network is used to decode the fused features to generate text recognition results.

4   The Implementation and Highlights of the System

4.1   The Implementation of the System

After the completion of the development of the system, each sub-function can run normally. The home page nterface and speech correction interface are shown in Fig. 3. Through the practical application of the system by the surrounding students, the results show that the users can effectively improve the spoken Chinese expression ability.

4.2   The Highlights of the System

This system provides a six-in-one all-round teaching method for Chinese teaching, which greatly meets the needs of all kinds of Chinese learners at home and abroad. The speech correction function helps learners to separate and decode the input audio and video, conduct in-depth analysis of lip movements and pronunciation, and finally give more accurate suggestions for improving the spoken

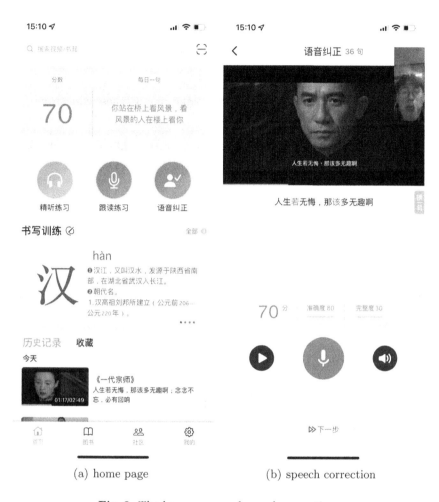

(a) home page   (b) speech correction

Fig. 3. The home page and speech correction.

language of the user's non-standard pronunciation. Compared with the blurred text image, the writing training function can also more accurately identify the text and image features uploaded by the learners, and efficiently integrate the visual features and semantic features to give the recognition results and evaluation results. Learners in different regions can also conduct real-time cross-regional real-time communication through community communication, improve oral language and improve interpersonal communication skills, and shorten the distance between each other.

5 Conclusion

The project team designed and implemented the intelligent Chinese speech learning correction system. The system combines intelligent speech technology and

Chinese language learning to provide solutions for problems such as non-standard Mandarin pronunciation and high demand and limited resources for Chinese learning. The system has been tested on a small scale in the university community, and has achieved good results. Some teachers have clearly proposed that the design concept of the system meets the needs of Chinese learning in the current era and promotes the implementation of international Chinese education.

Acknowledgment. This research is supported by the general planning fund for Humanities and Social Sciences Research of the Ministry of Education (No.17YJA880004) in 2017.

References

1. Niu, N., Li, D.: Take the Confucius Institute of Traditional Chinese Medicine at the University of Pecs as an Example. J. North China Univ. Sci. Technol. (Social Science Edition) **21**, 147–741 (2021)
2. Huang, F.L., Wu, J.Y.: Study and implementation of intelligent e-learning system for modern spoken Chinese. Int. Conf. Mach. Learn. Cybern. **5** 2968–2974 (2009)
3. Ho, W.Y.J: Coming here you should speak Chinese. The multimodal construction of interculturality in YouTube videos, Language and Intercultural Communication, pp. 1–19 (2022)
4. Zhan, H., Cheng, H.: The role of technology in teaching and learning Chinese characters. Int. J. Technol. Teach. Learn. **10**(2), 147 (2014)
5. Qinming, C., Jun, L.: Analysis of Teaching Treatment Strategy of Foreign Students Majoring in Overseas Chinese Education. In: International Conference on Education Technology and Economic Management(ICETEM 2019), pp. 806–811 (2019)
6. Su, Y.: A Study of Curriculum Learning Experience and influence Factors od International Doctoral Students Studying in China under the BackGround of "the Belt and Road". In: International and Comparative Education, 9rd, pp. 8–26+35 (2019)
7. Huang, H.: Design and Implementation of a College English Listening Learning System Based on Android Platform. Int. J. Emerg. Technol. Learn. **13**(7), 43 (2018)
8. Zheng, Z., Cheng, J., Peng, J.: Design and implementation of teaching system for mobile cross-platform. Int. J. Multimed. Ubiquitous Eng. **10**(2), 287–296 (2015)
9. Lan, Y., Theobald, B.J., Harvey, R., Ong, E.J., Bowden, R.: Improving visual features for lip-reading. In: Auditory-Visual Speech Processing (2010)
10. Adeel, A., Gogate, M., Hussain, A., Whitmer, W.M.: Lip-reading driven deep learning approach for speech enhancement. IEEE Trans. Emerg. Topics Comput. Intell. **5**(3), 481–490 (2019)
11. Rodriguez, P., Velazquez, D., Cucurull, G., Gonfaus, J.M., Roca, F.X., Gonzalez, J.: Pay attention to the activations: a modular attention mechanism for fine-grained image recognition. IEEE Trans. Multimedia **22**(2), 502–514 (2019)

Overview of Infrared and Visible Image Fusion Based on Deep Learning

Haixia Zhao, Xia Chang$^{(\boxtimes)}$, and Yuelin Gao

Ningxia Key Laboratory of Intelligent Information and Big Data Processing School of Math and Information Science, North Minzu University, Yinchuan, China
changxia0104@163.com

Abstract. Deep learning can extract image features automatically and then fuse them under the constraint of loss function by training multi-layer and deep neural networks, which is more intelligent, and has been successfully applied to the field of infrared and visible image fusion. This paper gives an overview of infrared and visible image fusion methods, followed by a detailed analysis of the deep learning based infrared and visible image fusion framework and loss function, and points out the existing problems of infrared and visible image fusion methods and the development prospects.

Keywords: Deep learning · Loss function · Convolutional neural · Generative adversarial network · Auto-encoder

1 Introduction

The key of image fusion is to gain the useful feature information from images obtained from multiple source sensors and combine them according to a series of specific rules to generate a fused image [1]. This fused image can provide clearer target information and richer scene information, which is favorable to the subsequent target recognition and image understanding.

Infrared sensors are sensitive to heat source radiation and based on this, the infrared images are obtained by measuring the heat radiation emitted from objects. They work well at night or in hazy weather, but their resolution is low and visual effect is blurred. In contrast, visible sensors obtain visible images by light reflection imaging. They have high resolution and clear scene texture, but they are susceptible to environmental conditions. Especially in low light conditions, their have serious loss of information. By combining these two types of information through certain rules, the fused image has both the target of infrared images and the content of visible images, which can effectively improve the reliability and accuracy of the information.

Existing infrared and visible image fusion methods can be broadly classified into two categories, the traditional methods and deep learning based methods. Among the traditional methods, the most representative schemes are multi-scale decomposition (MSD) [2], sparse representation (SR) [3], methods based on hybrid transformation [4]. The main steps of these methods are to decompose the source images and then fuse them using specific strategies, and finally to reconstruct the result using inverse transformation to get the fused image. For both images meaningful information representation, due to the different imaging mechanisms between infrared and visible sensors, infrared images characterize their meaningful target features in terms of pixel brightness, while visible images characterize their meaningful scene texture in terms of edges and gradients. In order to capture important information effectively, these fusion methods adopt more and more complex feature extraction strategies, which increases the difficulty of feature extraction and makes the fusion task more time consuming. Deep learning based models utilize the unique structure of convolutional neural network to extract deep features from images, which have strong capabilities in feature extraction and data representation, and do not require the design of complex feature extraction ways and fusion methods. For the image fusion, deep learning based methods construct and train deep neural networks which are capable of modeling complex relationships between data set and automatically extracting useful information from input images and then fusing them [5]. Deep learning-based methods are generally used in the areas of infrared and visible image fusion and have obtained favorable results in the most cases.

The advantages of deep learning for infrared and visible image fusion are mainly including [6]:

(1) The deep learning model can extract deep abstract features automatically from infrared and visible image datasets without the need to design complex feature extraction strategies manually.
(2) Deep learning models can capture intrinsic and targeted representations in images and can effectively describe complex relationships between input and output images.
(3) Large and publicly available deep learning databases facilitate the study of infrared and visible image fusion problems.

Therefore, deep learning based methods occupie an important position in the computer vision, and become the most promising direction in image fusion, especially in the infrared and visible image fusion and is a hot topic of current research.

2   Infrared and Visible Image Fusion Framework

2.1   Fusion Framework Based on Convolutional Neural Network

With the increasing maturity of deep learning and convolutional neural network technology, researchers are beginning to apply this powerful self-learning algorithm in infrared and visible image fusion recognition technology. In 2017, Liu Yu et al. [7] firstly adopted convolutional neura network for multi-focus image fusion tasks, which solved the problem that traditional image fusion methods required manual design of activity level measurement and fusion rules. However, the method only achieved good results in multifocus image fusion results. Since traditional CNNs adopt average fusion rule for the base layer and the features extracted by CNNs are relatively large, details of fused images are lost and contrasts are decreased. To overcome these problems, Yan et al. [8] designed a remarkably effective image fusion framework combination of visual saliency weight map (VSWM) and CNN. In this image framework, the VSWM is applied in the image fusion framework for the first time to enhance the contrast information of the considered images. Next, multiresolution singular value decomposition (MSVD) was used to preserve more details of the image before further processing by CNN. For the sake of make the most of the feature information of infrared and visible images, a fusion framework of infrared and visible images based on supervised convolutional neural network was proposed in literature [9]. The network is composed of encoding layer, fusion layer, decoding layer and output layer. It adopts the fusion results obtained from the existing fusion framework proposed in the essay as its training label, and optimizes the loss function. The fused image is gained by weighted fusion of the trained infrared image, the visible image and the feature image (Fig. 1).

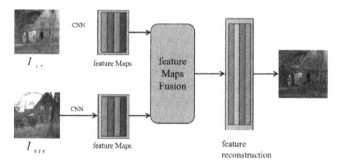

Fig. 1. The framework of CNN.

Since there are no standard fusion reference images. Most supervised-based deep learning methods must be pre-trained on other labeled large datasets. These supervised-based networks are complicated to implement, and the generalization ability of the obtained fusion models is poor because infrared and visible source images are not participate in network training. Point at above problems, literature [5] proposed an image fusion method based on unsupervised convolutional neural network. In this network structure of this fusion framework, the authors use a densely linked convolutional neural network (DenseNet) as a subnetwork for feature extraction and reconstruction so that the fused images retain more information of the source images. Perceptual loss is applied into the loss function and together with the structural similarity loss to constrain the updating of the weight parameters during back propagation of the network training, which is helpful to effectively improve the visual information fidelity of fused images. To overcome the problems of limited training dataset and misalignment of multi-source images, literature [10] proposed an end-to-end image fusion framework. This model not only requires less training dataset, but also more robust to two images that are not precisely aligned.

In end-to-end model, the fusion problem is solved by depending on ideal fusion image and specifically designed metrics. Nevertheless, ideal fusion image and Specially designed metrics for most computer vision tasks do not exist, and these problems became a major obstacles for model unification and supervised or unsupervised learning applications. In order to address different image fusion problems, literature [11] proposed a innovative unified fusion network named U2Fusion. Feature extraction and information calculation are used in this method, U2Fusion voluntarily calculate the significance of the two kinds of input images and proposes an adaptive useful information retention degree algorithm [11]. It avoids the loss of original fusion ability by continuously training a unified model for all kinds of tasks, and obtain a unified model suitable for different fusion mission. In reference [12], densely connected convolutional layers was introduced in the fusion framework, with short straightforward connections are established between every and all layers use feed-forward manner, which can solve the problem of gradient disappearance and enhance the feature transfer while significantly decreasing the number of parameters in this network. Li et al. used the image decomposition method in the literature [14] to firstly decompose input images into base part and detail content. Then the weighted average method is used to merge the base part, and for the detail content, a deep learning network (VGG-19 Network) is used to calculate multilayer features in order to retain as much detail as possible [15]. Literature [16] proposed a unified unsupervised densely connected network (FusionDN), using a block of weights to get two weights as the degree of retention of feature information from different input images. The similarity loss of these weights is applied to unsupervised learning. In addition, the elastic weight consolidation is adopted in this paper, instead of training single model for each fusion task or joint training task roughly, which solve the problem that the features extracted from the previous layers are forgotten by the later tasks due to the multi-layer task of training at once in this way, a unified image fusion model is constructed that is suitable for different image fusion tasks.

In conclusion, CNN has strong feature extraction and data representation capability without the need to set fusion rules manually. Meanwhile, convolutional neural networks can model the intricate relationships between various signals, which is suitable for fusion between images obtained from sensors with large differences.

2.2 Fusion Framework Based on Generative Adversarial Network

Generative Adversarial Network (GAN) was proposed by Goodfellow et al. [19] in 2014. It gradually improves the forgery or discrimination ability of each by establishing an adversarial relationship that allows the generator and discriminator to boost each other during multiple iterations of training. When the distance between the two distributions they construct is small enough, that is the discriminator is unable to distinguish the real data from the forged data. At this point, we obtain a trained GAN that can be used for the fusion task. In 2019, Ma et al. [20] applied GAN to infrared and visible image fusion task for the first time. Existing fusion methods based on deep learning usually rely on CNN approaches, but this case usually requires the provision of standard fused images, which can be avoided by GAN. GAN consists of the generator and the discriminator. The GAN based approach is to set up an adversarial game between the merged images and the input images, and train the generator until the generated image contains sufficient feature information of the input images (Fig. 2).

The fused image generated by FusionGAN can retain the detail information well, but the extraction of small target details and sharpness of entire image need to be improved.

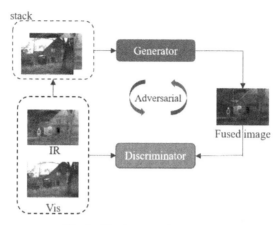

Fig. 2. The framework of GAN.

Based on the above problems, literature [21] proposed a new end-to-end network framework named U-GAN for image fusion. The author used U-net [22] for image segmentation as part of feature extraction to fully extract the contour information of targets present in the infrared image and the background and details present in the visible image, which is beneficial for the recognition of diminutive target in image, and the eventual fused image is gained by using a antagonistic idea of generator and discriminator. The U-net feature extraction model in the paper aims to increase the gradient information, so that objects in final fused image are more viewable and the background texture is more prominent.

Literature [23] proposed a image fusion method based on a texture conditional generative adversarial network (TCGAN). The TC-GAN is constructed to generate a jointed texture map for obtaining the gradient conversions in the process of fusion [23]. The network framework of the generator in this network is an encoding and decoding structure, and such a structure is more conducive to fully extracting detailed information, this framework also uses a squeeze and extraction module to enhance the weight of texture information in this texture map, the design of two kinds of loss make the texture information present in input image are better preserved. However, designing only one discriminator perhaps drop some details present in the infrared images and some contrast features present in the visible images. For this reason, Li et al. [24] proposed a two-discriminator generative adversarial network named D2WGAN, which is a structure in which the network is designed to have two discriminators acting together. The first discriminator is used to obtain the contrast information in the infrared image, and the second discriminator is designed to retain the texture details in the visible image. Moreover, in order to ameliorate the performance of D2WGAN, authors designed a GAN with Wasserstein distance, in addition, a new LBP (Local binary pattern) loss is defined to let the final combined image preserve more useful information in the texture feature maps.

Literature [25] proposed a practical image fusion method named RCGAN, in this framework, coupled generative adversarial network was introduced to image fusion.

Moreover, the authors apply a effective relativistic discriminator to the network structure, which makes the network converge faster, at the same time, it can effectively preserving the contrast of target and texture details in the input images. Similarly, literature [1] proposed a generative adversarial network with multiclassification constraints (GANMcC) that shift image fusion into a multi-distribution meanwhile estimation task to merge two kinds of images. In addition, the authors put forward creatively a special loss, the main and auxiliary losses are introduced into the loss function, which enables the generator in a complementary way to get more important feature information from the input image.

Ma et al. [26] came up with a fresh end-to-end image fusion framework, called dual-discriminator conditional Generative Adversarial network (DDcGAN). This network constructs an adversarial game between one generator and two discriminators. The dual discriminator structure allows the generator to be more fully trained and avoids information loss due to introducing a discriminator on only one type of input images. The method shows better performance in multiresolution source image fusion due to the use of the trainable deconvolution layers and the content constraint.

2.3   Fusion Methods Based on Auto-encoders

Autoencoder is an artificial neural network capable of learning efficient representation of input data through unsupervised learning. In 1986, Rumelhart proposed the concept of autoencoder and applied it to high-dimensional complex data processing, which promoted the development of neural networks (Fig. 3).

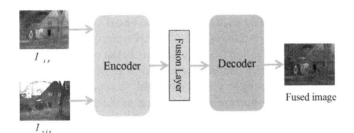

Fig. 3. Autoencoder

2017, Prabhakar et al. [27] proposed a simple convolute ion neural network architecture composed of two encoding layers and three decoding layers, but the network was too simple and used only the last layer of the network for computation, which resulted in the extracted salient features were not accurate enough and lost too much useful information from the middle layers. Based on this, Li et al. [28] put forward an end-to-end multi-loss function (EMF) based deep learning mode for image fusion. The image fusion algorithm is implemented by using improved pseudo-twin feature extraction mechanism and multi-loss function weighting model mechanism. The network is mainly divided into encoder, fusion layer and decoder. The residual block is used as the basic unit of the network to avoid the effect of vanishing gradient when the features are transmitted forward in small datasets. For the sake of improve the training speed of this network and increase the nonlinear expression ability of the model, BN and Relu operations are performed after each convolution. This algorithm avoids the influence of human factors in traditional algorithms, and the details and saliency information of fused images are richer, which has good prospects for application. In literature [29], the deep residual learning module was introduced to further improve the information flow in each layer.

In the generator network architecture of the literature [26], the authors introduced two deconvolution layers, an encoder network and a corresponding decoder network, The feature extraction and feature fusion are carried out together in the encoder, and the final result are obtained as the output. These results are then fed into the decoder to reconstruct final fusion result. Such a design can retain significant and valuable information and also gain the most or approximate most feature from the input image. In reference [23], the authors designed the generator as a codec structure that extracts more detailed texture information, and applied a squeeze-andexcitation module to this codec framework to enhance the weight of important texture information, and then generate a more detailed combined texture map. In reference [30], the authors proposed a new network architecture with dense blocks that not only improves the flow and gradient of information through the network, but also facilitates the training of the network. Due to the regularization effect of the dense connection method in this network, the overfitting problem caused by too many parameters can be reduced.

Li et al. [31] combined the convolutional layers, fusion layers and dense blocks to form a coding network, and connected the outputs of each layer. Using this structure, the coding process can obtain more useful features from the input images. Then adopted two fusion strategy to fuse obtained features, named the additive fusion strategy and the 1-norm strategy. Finally, a decoder is used to reconstruct the final fused image.

2.4 Other Image Fusion Methods

Recently, convolutional neural networks have obtained a remarkable success in multi-focused image fusion. However, limited by the local acceptance domain of the convolution operator, CNN always fails to capture enough recognition features, which limits the performance of most current methods based on CNN. Focus on the problem, Guo et al. [32] proposed Siamese self-attention network (SSAN) for multifocus image fusion. In detail, two SA (self-attention) modules (position SA (PSA) and channel SA (CSA)) are used to establish the dependence relationship between focusing and defocusing regions in multi-focus image fusion, so as to alleviate the limitation of convolution computation on local acceptance domain in CNN. Similarly, in literature [7], Liu et al. came up with a fusion method based on Siamese convolutional network, in which the output is a weight graph use on the final decision. Literature [33] proposed an fusion method based on deep learning. Firstly, the input infrared image is divided into a foreground part and a background part, where the foreground part is fused to keep the salient information of the target and the background fusion focuses more on the texture detail information in the background. An image fusion network based on neural style migration algorithm is constructed by segmenting the foreground and background of the input image. After that, the fusion of foreground and background is controlled using foreground loss and background loss respectively. Finally, the two parts are combined to reconstruct the fused image. Literature [34] combined convolutional neural network with NSST used to realize the fusion of infrared and visible images, which improved the contrast of fused image, enriched background information, and was more conducive to human eyes recognition.

For the problems of missing edge information and blurred details in previous image fusion algorithms, literature [35] put forward a image fusion algorithm based on convolutional neural network combined with guided filtering in latent low rank representation framework. The algorithm adopts the latent low-rank representation to decompose the input image into the low-rank component and significant component of the source image. Then, based on the feature information of source image, the convolutional neural network is used to get the weight map, and the edge sharpening of the weight map is performed by the guided filtering algorithm. After that, the weight graph is fused with the low-rank component and significant component to obtain the low-rank component and significant component of the output image. Finally, the two components are superimposed to obtain the final fused image. In accordance with this principle, literature [36] proposed a new multi-level decomposition method (MDLatLRR) as a part of image fusion framework. In this structure, the authors use MDLatLRR to decompose the input image in order to get the significant detail information and base part. The detail part is reconstructed using an adaptive reconstruction operator, and the base part is merged by average merge strategy. Ultimately, the detail parts are combined with the base parts to reconstruct the fusion image.

3   Loss Function

In recent years, network architecture, activation function and loss function have been innovated in the area of image fusion. The field of infrared and visible image fusion has also emerged a large number of related articles. The loss functions reflect the differences between the fusion images and the labels, which acts a key part in the performance of the model. Selecting a suitable loss function can also help the model convergence faster. The choice of different loss functions results in different contrast and detail information richness of the original image contained in the fused image.

For the sake of reconstruct the image more accurately, loss function minimization is adopted in literature [31] to train the encoder and decoder of the proposed model. The total loss function consists of pixel loss and structural similarity loss.

$$L = \lambda L_{SSIM} + L_p \tag{1}$$

$$L_p = \|O - I\|_2 \tag{2}$$

$$L_{SSIM} = 1 - SSIM(O, I) \tag{3}$$

where, O represents the fused image and I represents the source image.

The loss function in the literature [11] is defined as follows:

$$L(\theta, D) = L_{sim}(\theta, D) + \lambda L_{ewc}(\theta, D) \tag{4}$$

where, θ represents the parameter in DenseNet, D is the training dataset.

For the first term in Eq. (4), although *SSIM* pay attention to the variation of structure, it has weak constraints in terms of intensity distribution [11]. Minimizing the mean square error loss function directly gives good resolution results, but it is difficult to avoid blurring in details. The authors combined the two items and control the tradeoff through α. The formula is as follows:

$$L_{sim}(\theta, D) = L_{SSIM}(\theta, D) + \alpha L_{mse}(\theta, D) \tag{5}$$

$$L_{SSIM}(\theta, D) = E[\omega_1.(1 - S_{I_f,I_1}) + \omega_2.(1 - S_{I_f,I_2})] \tag{6}$$

$$L_{mse}(\theta, D) = E[\omega_1.MSE_{I_f,I_1} + \omega_2.MSE_{I_f,I_2}] \tag{7}$$

The second item in Eq. (5) is designed for continual learning and is defined as follows:

$$L_{mse}(\theta, D) = \frac{1}{2} \sum_i \mu_i(\theta_i - \theta_i^*)^2 \tag{8}$$

$$\mu_i = E[(-\frac{\partial}{\partial \theta_i^*} L(\theta^*, D^*))^2 | \theta^*] \tag{9}$$

where, θ^* is the data from the previous task. For details, see literature [11].

Similar to literature [31], literature [9] introduced structural similarity loss on the basis of square loss, which ensures the overall brightness of the fused image while preserving as much detail as possible. The specific formula is as follows:

$$\begin{aligned} L &= \lambda L_P + L_S \\ &= \lambda(L_{PIR} + L_{PVIS} + L_{PFU}) + L_{SIR} + L_{SVIS} + L_{SFU} \end{aligned} \tag{10}$$

$$L_P = \sum_{i=1}^n (\|X_i - Y_{IRi}\|_2 + \|X_i - Y_{VISi}\|_2 + \|X_i - Y_{FUi}\|_2) \tag{11}$$

$$\begin{aligned} L_S &= \sum_{i=1}^n [1 - SSIM(X_i - Y_{IRi})] + \sum_{i=1}^n [1 - SSIM(X_i - Y_{VISi})] \\ &+ \sum_{i=1}^n [1 - SSIM(X_i - Y_{FUi})] \end{aligned} \tag{12}$$

where, L_p is square loss, L_s is structural similarity loss, Y_{IRi}, Y_{VISi} and Y_{FUi} respectively represent the infrared fusion images, visible fusing images and feature fusion images in the group i, and X_i represents the label in group i.

The fusion image obtained using the loss in pixel space are blurred in detail and have poor visual effects. Based on this, some scholars introduced perceptual loss, and the fusion results obtained by this method are rich in detail and have better visual effects. Foe the sake of objectively enhance the quality of the merged image and guarantee that the input image is sufficiently similar to the final fused image. Literature [5] introduced perceptual loss into the image fusion, jointed with architecture similarity loss, and under its constraint makes the input and output optimum. The specific definition is as follows:

$$L = g_1 L_{per} + g_2 L_{SSIM} \tag{13}$$

where, L_{Per} is perceptual loss, L_{SSIM} is structural similarity loss, g_1 and g_2 are ratios that are progressively revised during training.

$$L_{Per}(Y_I, Y_F) = \frac{1}{C_j H_j W_j} \left\| \varphi_j(Y_I) - \varphi_j(Y_F) \right\|_2^2 \tag{14}$$

$$L_{SSIM} = 1 - (w.SSIM(I, F) + (1 - w).SSIM(V, F)) \tag{15}$$

where, φ is the network of VGG-16, Y_I is the incorporation of infrared feature image、visible feature image and fusion feature image, Y_F is the fusion results of the three feature maps, $C_j H_j W_j$ is the feature graph C_j of the j th layer and the size of feature map, $\varphi_j(Y_I)$ and $\varphi_j(Y_F)$ respectively represent the feature graph generated by the j th layer of VGG-16 network, and ω is the weight [5]. Obviously, the perceptual loss has the same form as the L_2 loss, except that the computational space is shifted to the feature space.

In literature [16], pre-trained VGG-16 was used as a feature extractor. However, for perceptual loss, the feature images extracted from the higher levels of VGG-16 can not reconstruct detailed information such as texture and shape, but only reconstruct content and overall spatial structure. In order to make the appearance of fused image clearer, the authors introduced gradient loss to constrain the gradient difference. The total loss is expressed as follows:

$$L = L_{SSIM} + \alpha L_{Per} + \beta L_{gra} \tag{16}$$

where, L_{SSIM} represents structural similarity loss, L_{Per} represents perceptual loss, L_{gra} represents gradient loss, α and β are used to control trade-offs, and the specific definitions are as follows:

$$L_{SSIM} = \omega_1(1 - SSIM_{I_f, I_1}) + \omega_1(1 - SSIM_{I_f, I_2}) \tag{17}$$

$$L_{Per} = \omega_1 L_{Per}(I_f, I_1) + \omega_2 L_{Per}(I_f, I_2) \tag{18}$$

$$L_{gra} = \omega_1 L_{gar}(I_f, I_1) + \omega_2 L_{gar}(I_f, I_2) \tag{19}$$

$$L_{gra}(x, y) = \frac{1}{HW} \left\| \nabla x - \nabla y \right\|_F^2 \tag{20}$$

where, L_{SSIM} and L_{Per} are calculated as shown above, and the gradient loss is calculated by the square of the frobenius norm between the gradient changes of the image x and y. In the training stage of reference [13], the encoder and decoder can obtain the final weight parameters through the constraint of loss function. The loss function is also composed of structural similarity loss and pixel loss (square loss mentioned above).

For generative adversarial networks, in order to obtain different effects, various loss functions can be added to constrain the network. In reference [24], the author came up with a generative adversarial network with two discriminators for fusion task. In this network, the loss function includes the generator loss and the discriminator loss. Generator loss is indicated as follows:

$$L = L_{adverse}(G) + \lambda_1 L_{content} \tag{21}$$

It is composed of adversarial loss $L_{advers}(G)$ and content loss $L_{content}$. In order to capture more meaningful information, the content loss is used in this paper, formula is as follows:

$$L_{content} = \frac{1}{HW} (\mu \| I_f - I_r \|_F^2 + \gamma \| LBP(I_f) - LBP(I_v) \|_F^2) \tag{22}$$

the first item compels the merged image (I_f) to retain the intensity information of the infrared image (I_r). The second item uses LBP to calculate the texture similarity of the merged image and the visible image, as present in Eq. (23). LBP is an operator defined to describe local feature information of images, and it is calculated as follows:

$$LBP(x_c, y_c) = \sum_{p=0}^{p-1} 2^p s(i_p - i_c) \tag{23}$$

where, (x_c, y_c) represents the pixel in the center of the i_c, i_p represents the luminance value of the adjacent pixels, p represents the p th pixel of the adjacent pixels, and s is the sign function. The total loss function is as shown in Eq. (24),

$$L_{advers}(G) = - \sum_{i=1}^{N} E_{z \sim p_g} [D_i(z)] \tag{24}$$

where, z represents generated data and N represents the number of discriminators.

When there is one adversarial game between the merged images and the input images only, the fused image maybe lose the intensity information present in the infrared image and the capacity to retain texture details present in the visible image is weakened. The design of the two discriminators enables the final fused image to retain more details from both infrared and visible input images. So the loss functions are defined as:

$$L_{D_{ir}} = -E_{x \sim p_{ir}} [D_{ir}(x)] + E_{z \sim p_g} [D_{ir}(z)]$$
$$+ \lambda_2 E_{\tilde{x}} [(\| \nabla_{\tilde{x}} D_{ir}(\tilde{x}) \|_2 - 1)] \tag{25}$$

$$L_{D_{vis}} = -E_{x \sim p_{vis}} [D_{vis}(x)] + E_{z \sim p_g} [D_{vis}(z)]$$
$$+ \lambda_3 E_{\tilde{x}} [(\| \nabla_{\tilde{x}} D_{vis}(\tilde{x}) \|_2 - 1)] \tag{26}$$

among them, the first two items are Wasserstein distance estimation. The last item represent gradient penalty used for network regularization. P_g is distribution of the generated data, p_{ir} and p_{vis} represent infrared image data distribution and visible image data distribution respectively, λ_2 and λ_3 are constant weighting parameters.

Initially, GANs was considered unstable training that often leads to artifacts or noise in the fused image, and a possible solution to this problem is to introduce content loss.

In literature [26], Ma et al. adopted a loss function similar to [13], and the total loss is still as shown above, the corresponding content loss and adversarial loss are designed as follows:

$$L_{con} = E[\|\psi G(v, i) - i\|_F^2 + \eta \|G(v, i) - v\|_{TV}] \tag{27}$$

$$
\begin{aligned}
L_G^{adv} &= E[\log(1 - D_v(G(v, i)))] \\
&+ E[\log(1 - D_i(\psi G(v, i)))]
\end{aligned}
\tag{28}
$$

where, the TV norm in the regularization term is used to constrain the fused image so that the final merged image has the similar gradient variation to the source visible image. Compared with the $\ell 0$ norm, the TV norm can efficaciously resolve the uncertainty polynomial time hard issue. The fusion framework of DDcGAN proposed in this paper is still a dual discriminators structure, and its discriminator loss function is defined as follows:

$$L_{D_v} = E[\log D_v(v)] + E[-\log(1 - D_v(G(v, i)))] \tag{29}$$

$$L_{D_i} = E[\log D_i(i)] + E[-\log(1 - D_i(\psi G(v, i)))] \tag{30}$$

In the same year, Ma et al. [1] put forward a new generative adversarial network with multiclassification constraints (GANMcC). In this paper, the authors designed a very unusual content loss to restraint generators. The loss function to guide generator optimization includes content loss $L_{G_{con}}$ used to constrain the effective extraction of information and adversarial loss $L_{G_{adv}}$ used to constrain the information balance. The specific form is as follows:

$$L_G = \gamma L_{G_{con}} + L_{G_{adv}} \tag{31}$$

$$
\begin{aligned}
L_{G_{con}} &= \beta_1 L_{int_{main}} + \beta_2 L_{grad_{main}} + \beta_3 L_{grad_{aux}} + \beta_4 L_{int_{aux}} \\
&= \beta_1 \|I_{fused} - I_{ir}\|_F^2 + \beta_2 \|\nabla I_{fused} - \nabla I_{vis}\|_F^2 \\
&+ \beta_3 \|\nabla I_{fused} - \nabla I_{ir}\|_F^2 + \beta_4 \|I_{fused} - I_{vis}\|_F^2
\end{aligned}
\tag{32}
$$

$$L_{G_{adv}} = (D(I_{fused}^n)[1] - d)^2 + (D(I_{fused}^n)[2] - d)^2 \tag{33}$$

where, I_{ir}, I_{vis} and I_{fused} represent source infrared image, source visible image and fusion image respectively, and ∇ is a second-order gradient operator. Since some texture detail is also presented in the infrared image, similarly, the visible image has the available contrast as well [1]. Therefore, the idea of auxiliary loss is proposed, that is, the auxiliary gradient loss $L_{grad_{aux}}$ is constructed between the fusion image and the infrared image, and an auxiliary intensity loss $L_{int_{aux}}$ is constructed between the fusion image and the visible image. In adversarial loss, d is the probability label of the fused image determined by the discriminator. Since the discriminator is a multi-classifier, the output of discriminator is a 1×2 probability vector. $D(\cdot)$ [1] is the first item, which represents the possibility that the merged image is a visible image. At the same time, $D(\cdot)$ [2] is the second item, which represent the possibility that the merged image is an infrared image. The loss function of discriminator is given below, and the total loss of discriminator is as follows:

$$L_D = L_{D_{vis}} + L_{D_{ir}} + L_{D_{fused}} \tag{34}$$

$$L_{D_{vis}} = \frac{1}{2N} \sum_{i=1}^{N} ((P_{vis}(I_{vis}^n) - a_1)^2 + (P_{ir}(I_{vis}^n) - a_2)^2) \tag{35}$$

$$L_{D_{ir}} = \frac{1}{2N} \sum_{i=1}^{N} ((P_{vis}(I_{ir}^n) - b_1)^2 + (P_{ir}(I_{ir}^n) - b_2)^2) \tag{36}$$

$$L_{D_{fused}} = \frac{1}{2N} \sum_{i=1}^{N} ((P_{vis}(I_{fused}^n) - c)^2 + (P_{ir}(I_{fused}^n) - c)^2) \tag{37}$$

where, a_1 and a_2 are probability labels. a_1 is taken as 1, a_2 is taken as 0, In detail, when the input is a visible image, the discriminator has a very high probability of determining it as a visible image and the discriminator has a very low probability of determining it as a infrared image. Similarly, b_1 is set to 0 and b_2 is set to 1. c is the probability label of the merged image determined by the discriminator Finally, in order to achieve an informative balance, the same label c was used by the authors for two results, in detail, for discriminator, the merged image is a false visible image and a false infrared image to the similar extent.

4　Conclusions

In this paper, we present a detailed comparison and analysis of existing frameworks for deep learning-based fusion of infrared and visible image fusion. In the fusion of infrared and visible images, the methods based on deep learning still need to solve the visible image detail information loss and the high time complexity. Among them, visible image detail information loss may directly lead to the failure of image fusion task. Real-time performance is crucial for image fusion applied to military survey. With the development of deep learning, various network models with better performance have emerged. At present, unsupervised models of infrared and visible image fusion are relatively few. Further research can be carried out in the future around the following two aspects:

(1) Setting of fusion rules. If the network can learn the fusion rules adaptively, the efficiency of image fusion will be greatly improved and the real end-to-end image fusion will be realized.

(2) Design of the perceptual loss. The depth of perceptual loss network is generally deep, and the extracted feature maps can be output in shallow layers, intermediate or high layers. Subsequently, the feature outputs of multiple perceptual layers can be used to jointly calculate the perceptual loss as a way to better constrain the fusion process.

Acknowledgements. This work is supported by the Ningxia Natural Science Foundation (No. 2022AAC03236), by the National Natural Science Foundation of China (No. 11961001, No. 61907012), by the First-Class Disciplines Foundation of Ningxia (No. NXYLXK2017B09), and by the Special project of North Minzu University (No. FWNX01), and by the Master Degree Candidate Innovation Program (No. YCX22106).

References

1. Ma, J., Zhang, H., et al.: GANMcC: a generative adversarial network with multiclassifification constraints for infrared and visible image fusion. IEEE Trans. Instrument. Measurm. **70**, 1–14 (2021)
2. Chen, C., Meng, X., et al.: Infrared and visible image fusion method based on multiscale low-rank decomposition. Acta Optica Sinica, J. **40**(11), 72–80 (2020)
3. Chen, G., Chen, Y., et al.: Infrared and visible image fusion based on discrete nonseparables-hearlet transform and convolutional sparse representation. J. Jilin Univ. (Eng. Technol. Ed,), J. **51**(03), 996–1010 (2021)
4. Liu, Y., Liu, S., et al.: A general framework for image fusion based on multi-scale transform and sparse representation. Inf. Fusion **24**, 147–164 (2015)
5. Xu, D., Wang, Y., et al.: Infrared and visible image fusion using a deep unsupervised framework with perceptual loss. IEEE Access, 206445–206458 (2020)
6. Liu, Y., Chen, X., et al.: Deep learning for pixel-level image fusion: Recent advances and future prospects. Inf. Fusion **42**, 158–173 (2018)
7. Liu, Y., Chen, X., et al.: Multi-focus image fusion with a deep convolutional neural network. Inf. Fusion **36**, 191–207 (2017)
8. Yan, L., Cao, J., Rizvi, S., et al.: Improving the performance of image fusion based on visual saliency weightMap combined with CNN. IEEE Access, 59976–59986 (2020)
9. An, W., Wang, H.: Infrared and visible image fusion with supervised convolutional neural network. Optik **219**, 165–120 (2020)
10. Li, L., Xia, Z., et al.: Infrared and visible image fusion using a shallow CNN and structural similarity constraint. IET image Proc. J. **14**(14), 3562–3571 (2020)
11. Han, X., Ma, J., et al.: U2Fusion: a unified unsupervised imagefusion network. IEEE Trans. Pattern Anal. Mach. Intell. J. **44**(1), 502–518 (2020)
12. Xie, C., Li, X.: Infrared and visible image fusion: a regionbased deep learning method. Intell. Robotics Appli. **11744**, 604–615 (2019)
13. Raza, A., Liu, J., et al.: IRMSDNet: infrared and visible image fusion based on infrared features and multiscale dense network. IEEE J. Selected Topics Appli. Earth Observations Remote Sens. **14**, 3426–3437 (2021)
14. Li, S., Hu, J.: Image fusion with guided fifiltering. IEEE Trans. Image Process. **22**(7), 2864–2875 (2013)
15. Li, H., Wu, X., et al.: Infrared and visible image fusion using a deep learning framework. In: 14th International Conference on Pattern Recognition, ICPR, pp. 2705–2710 (2018)
16. Han, X., Ma, J., et al.: FusionDN: a unifified densely connected network for image fusion. In: AAAI Conference on Artificial Intelligence. Journal **34**(7), 12484–12491 (2020)
17. Bin, S., Wen, Y., et al.: Infrared and visible image fusion based on convolutional neural network. Infrared Technol. J. **42**(7), 660–669 (2020)
18. Shen, Y., Chen, X.: Infrared and visible image fusion based on a latent low-rank representation decomposition and VGG Net. J. Beijing Univ. Aeronaut. Astron. **47**(06), 1105–1114 (2021)
19. Goodfellow, I., Pougetabadie, J., Mirza, M., et al.: Generative adversarial nets. In: Advances in Neural Information Processing Systems, pp. 2672–2680 (2014)

20. Ma, J., Wei, Y., et al.: FusionGAN: A generative adversarial network for infrared and visible image fusion. Inf. Fusion **48**, 11–26 (2018)
21. Chen, Z., Fang, M., et al.: U-GAN model for infrared and visible images fusion. J. Northwestern Polytechnical Univ. **38**(4), 904–912 (2020)
22. Ronneberger, O., Fischer, P., Brox, T.: U-net: convolutional networks for biomedical image segmentation. In: International Conference on Medical Image Computing and Computer-Assisted Intervention, pp. 234–241 (2015)
23. Yang, Y., Xiang, J., et al.: Infrared and visible image fusion via texture conditional generative adversarial network. IEEE Trans. Circ. Syst. Video Technol. J. **31**(12), 4771–4783 (2021)
24. Li, J., Huo, H., et al.: Infrared and visible image fusion using dual discriminators generative adversarial networks with wasserstein distance. Inf. Sci. **529**, 28–41 (2020)
25. Li, Q., Li, Z., et al.: Coupled GAN with relativistic discriminators for infrared and visible images fusion. IEEE Sensors J. **21**(6), 7458–7467 (2019)
26. Jiayi Ma, X., Han, J.J., et al.: DDcGAN: a dual-discriminator conditional generative adversarial network for multi-resolution image fusion. IEEE Trans. Image Process. **29**, 4980–4995 (2020)
27. Ram Prabhakar, K., Sai Srikar, V., Venkatesh Babu, R.: DeepFuse: a deep unsupervised approach for exposure fusion with exreme exposure image pairs. In: IEEE International Conference on Computer Vision, pp. 4724–4732 (2017)
28. Li, C., Sun, T., Xie, J.: EMF Deep learning based infrared and visible image fusion algorithm. Foreign Electronic Measurem. Technol. J. **39**(10), 25–32 (2020)
29. K He, X Zhang, S Ren, J Sun. Deep residual learning for image recognition, pp. 770–778. IEEE (2016)
30. Huang, G., Liu, Z., Van Der Maatenet, L., et al.: Densely connected convolutional networks. In: IEEE Conference on Computer Vision and Pattern Recognition, pp. 2261–2269 (2017)
31. Li, H., Xiaojun, W.: DenseFuse: a fusion approach to infrared and visible images. IEEE Trans. Image Process. J. **28**(5), 2614–2623 (2019)
32. Guo, X., Meng, L., Mei, L., et al.: Multi-focus image fusion with Siamese self attention network. IET Image Process. J. **14**(7), 1339–1446 (2020)
33. Xie, C., Jian, X., et al.: Infrared and visible image fusion method based on deep learning. Command Inf. Syst. Technol. J. **11**(2), 16–38 (2020)
34. Huan, K., Li, X., et al.: Infrared and visible image fusion with convolutional neural network and NSST. Infrared Laser Eng. J. **51**(3), 512–519 (2022)
35. Lou, X., Feng, X.: Infrared and visible image fusion in latent low rank representation framework based on convolution neural network and guided filtering. Acta Photonica Sinica J. **50**(3), 188–201 (2021)
36. Li, H., Wu, X., Kittler, J.: MDLatLRR: a novel decomposition method for infrared and visible image fusion. IEEE Trans. Image Process. **29**, 4733–4746 (2020)
37. Xu, X.: Infrared and Visible Image Fusion Method Based on Sparse Representation. University of Electronic Science and Technology of China, Sichuan (2017)
38. Sun, C., Zhang, C., Xiong, N.: Infrared and visible image fusion techniques based on deep learning: A Review. Electronics **9**(12), 2162 (2020)
39. Xu, S.: Research on Image Fusion Methods Based on Deep Learning. Jiangnan University, Jiangsu (2020)
40. Wang, J., Ke, C., Liu, M., et al.: Overview of infrared and visible image fusion algorithms based on neural network framework. Laser J. **41**(7), 7–12 (2020)
41. Xiong, M.: Research on image fusion method based on deep neural network. Jiangnan University, Jiangsu (2019)

Topic Term Clustering Based on Semi-supervised Co-occurrence Graph and Its Application in Chinese Judgement Documents

Xin Yang[1], Yang Weng[1], and Baogui Chen[2(✉)]

[1] College of Mathematics, Sichuan University, Chengdu, China
wengyang@scu.edu.cn

[2] Data Management Department, Information Center of Supreme People's Court of P.R.C., Beijing, China
9322135@qq.com

Abstract. With the continuous progress of society and the improvement of people's awareness of law, the number of cases accepted by the people's court of China continues to run at a high level in recent years. In the increasingly severe situation of the contradiction of "many cases but few people", how to ensure judicial justice and improve the efficiency of the trial has become an urgent problem to be solved. Under the new litigation system, courts organize debates around controversial issues, which are the core of the conflicts between the parties in the case. Similar controversial issues play an important role in identifying similar cases. Similar cases also play an important role in improving judges' trial efficiency, promoting similar cases to be judged similarly, and ensuring the uniformity of law application. However, in the process of identifying controversial issues, it is not only affected by the uncertainty of law and facts, but also affected by the judge's discretion and factors outside the case. So it is difficult to format controversial issues and inappropriate to judge the similarity by the consistency of controversial issues. Meanwhile, controversial issues data is subject to power law distribution, and its types are hard to be exhausted, which further aggravates the difficulty of manual annotation. Machine learning is an appropriate method to identify similar groups in the case of huge amount of controversial issues data. In this paper, a semi-supervised short text clustering algorithm is proposed to identify the homogeneous groups in controversial issues. In this algorithm, a graph model is constructed to discover the closely connected term groups, which are used as the clustering topics, and controversial issues are classified according to the topic term groups. In addition, the algorithm incorporates prior knowledge of law to improve the performance of the algorithm. This algorithm can capture semantic similarity in controversial issues, automatically induce the topic term

This work was partly supported by National Key R&D Program of China under Grant 2020YFC0832400. This work was partly supported by Key R&D Program of Sichuan Province under Grant 2021YFS0397.

groups of controversial issues' categories, flexibly adjust the number of categories, and quickly get the clustering result, so as to promote the identification and retrieval of the similar case.

Keywords: controversial issues · semi-supervised short text clustering · power law distribution · topic term

1   Introduction

With the continuous development of Chinese society and the continuous improvement of people's living standards, people's demand for a better life is also more comprehensive. Under the background of the continuous construction of law-based society, people's legal awareness is constantly improved and more attention is paid to the protection of individual legal rights. On the one hand, the number of cases accepted by Chinese courts at all levels has been high in recent years. People are more willing to protect their rights through legal means and have more convenient access. On the other hand, from the perspective of judicial fairness and openness, to protect people's right to know, participate and supervise, and to better exercise restraint and supervision of power, under the environment of rapid development of information technology, the release of judgement documents on the internet has been a decisive measure. By March this year, more than 130 million documents had been posted on the website, with more than 83 billion visits. Under the increasingly severe situation, how to improve the efficiency of trials and ensure judicial justice has become an urgent problem to be solved.

Judicial process is the application process of law, and the most intuitive way to measure judicial justice is the unification of legal application criteria, that is, similar cases get the same trial results, and the trial results of different cases are coordinated. Because judges are independent individuals with self-thoughts and feelings, coupled with the differences in areas, trial level, trial experience and other aspects, the situation of different judgments in similar cases often occurs. This phenomenon seriously affects the fairness of the judiciary, and in the long run, it will certainly affect the authority of the judiciary and the credibility of the judiciary among the public. The acquisition of similar cases is an important step in realizing same judgment in similar cases. Judges can select the level of court, date of judgment, case type (e.g., criminal case, civil case, administrative case), cause of action and other formatted information to search, but these pieces of information are either not relevant to the case content, or the scope is too large to be accurate to a small number of cases with high similarity. Judging the similarity of a large number of cases leads to the low efficiency of the judges in obtaining similar cases and affects the trial efficiency. Admittedly, it can also be searched by keyword matching, but some cases can not be summarized by individual key words. With the continuous progress of judicial reform, courts organize debates between the disputing parties around controversial issues [1], which are the core of the conflict between the disputing parties and mainly exists in civil cases, commonly in administrative cases, and rarely in criminal cases. The contents of the judgment documents include the legal argumentation process of sorting out controversial issues, organizing investigation and debating. Controversial issues play a crucial role in the trial of the case, the recovery of the trial site and the judge's trial logic. So the information in controversial issues plays an important role in the identification of the similar cases, the retrieval of the similar cases, and the promotion of same judgment in similar cases.

A natural idea of using controversial issues to facilitate similar cases retrieval is to divide the controversial issues into homogeneous groups, so that the contents expressed by the controversial issues belonging to the same group are semantically similar. Because cases with similar controversial issues may have higher similarity, the judge can greatly reduce the search scope and achieve faster and more accurate similar cases' retrieval by selecting the controversial issues' category that the case to be retrieved belongs to. However, the summary of the controversial issues is a process that reflects the judge's ability to determine the facts of the case by using law and court rules and the verbal interaction of various parties. This process is not only affected by the fact and legal uncertainty in the case, but also by the judge's discretionary power and factors outside the case, so it is difficult to form accurate and formatted expression. Therefore, similar controversial issues are expressed in different ways, and it is not appropriate to judge similar controversial issues based on whether the controversial issues are same. It is laborious for experts to manually judge and classify the similarity of controversial issues. Controversial issues follow the power-law distribution [2], so it is difficult to continue and coordinate the work under the condition that the data volume of controversial issues is huge and the categories are inexhaustible, which greatly wastes professional human resources. Therefore, it is very important to use machine learning methods to identify the controversial issues groups with different expression forms but similar semantic content on the legal level, and to further refine the retrieval structure of judgment documents as the basis of the case retrieval based on the controversial issues.

In machine learning, algorithms for identifying homogeneous groups in data can be roughly divided into two categories: classification and clustering. The main difference of them is whether to use labeled data. Classification belongs to supervised learning, which trains classifiers according to labeled data with category information, and then applies the trained classifiers to unlabeled data for category recognition. The effect of the classification algorithm largely depends on the label data. So the quality of the labeled data has a great impact on the classification results. Due to the noise of data and randomness of data extraction, it is difficult to ensure the quality of a small amount of labeled data, and it is difficult to label a large number of data. Moreover, the data of controversial issues is huge, its categories are difficult to exhaust, and its structure is complex, which makes it difficult to use labeled data to run the classification algorithm in controversial issues. Clustering is a kind of unsupervised learning in machine learning. This kind of algorithm is to identify the structure of the data and divide the similar data into a category, so that the similarity between the data of the same category is larger, and the data varies widely between categories. Because clustering algorithm does not require prior category information, manual labeling can be omitted. So it is more suitable for the identification of homogeneous groups of controversial issues in the absence of sufficient labeled data. Therefore, this paper adopts the idea of model-based short text clustering algorithm. And based on TRTD [3] method, we put forward a clustering method for controversial issues – topic word clustering based on semi-supervised co-occurrence graph, abbreviated as SCG.

The main contributions of this paper are as follows: First, the SCG method proposes a semi-supervised co-occurrence graph model to overcome the sparsity of short text to capture semantic information in controversial issues, and uses the form of seed term and affiliated terms to extract topic term groups, then obtains closely connected term groups as the basis of category allocation. Secondly, the phenomenon that clustering and topic extraction are separated or there is no topic in previous controversial issues clustering work [4] [5] is eliminated. The clustering method with topics is more conducive to the searchers and maintainers' selection and improvement of the categories of controversial issues in the actual situation, and has better intuitiveness, interpretation and readability. Third, we extract the controversial issues in real the judgment documents, and label the category information, build a standard controversial issues data sets. SCG is tested on the real controversial issues under multiple cases, and the result of clustering is better, which plays an important role in identifying the homogeneous controversial issues groups.

The rest of this paper is structured as follows: The second chapter introduces some relevant methods and the SCG method proposed in this paper; the third chapter introduces the experimental data and results; the fourth chapter summarizes this paper.

2   Model and Method

Short text clustering methods can be roughly divided into representation-based methods and model-based methods. Representation-based methods focus on learning effective representation vectors for short texts and exploiting traditional clustering methods such as K-Means [6] for clustering. Model-based methods focus on designing new clustering strategies for short texts. The method of this paper mainly adopts the idea of model-based methods.

TermCut [7] bisect one subgraph (one cluster) at a time based on whether the text contains a core term that meets the minimum RMcut value in the subgraph. This core term can be seen as a thematic distinction between the two clusters that have been bisected. However, the bisecting in which order in multiple categories has different clustering effects under some stop criteria, and it may not be appropriate to bisect only based on a single term, but also ignore the importance of term frequency. WordCom [8] also ignored the term frequency information, which is a very important information in the data at controversial issues, and represents the probability of the occurrence of the corresponding topic in this corpus.

TRTD is a model-based clustering method. Its advantages are that it does not need word embedding and can better avoid sparsity and high dimension of text data, which are very serious in short text data (controversial issues are also short texts). At the same time, TRTD has a good interpretation of the results of clustering. Its category allocation is carried out according to the topic terms, and the topic terms are frequently appeared in the cluster and closely linked with each other, so these terms can be regarded as the topic of a cluster to explain the content. A similar algorithm is LDA(Latent Dirichlet Allocation) [9]. However, as an algorithm based on Bayes' theorem, LDA is a model with high computational cost in the implementation process, and the number of clusters K needs to be determined in advance, so the calculation cost of changing the number of clusters is high. TRTD is fast in calculation, and the recalculation cost for changing the number of clusters is almost zero. It can also be realized quickly for large sample data.

Based on TRTD, the SCG method in this paper combines the characteristics of controversial issues and uses a small amount of labeled data for semi-supervised improvement. The idea of clustering is similar to most graph model-based clustering methods, which is to find closely connected subgraphs in graph model. The improvement of the algorithm in this paper can be roughly divided into three aspects: first, similar to most clustering algorithms requiring word segmentation, the method in this paper also needs to delete stop terms, but it cannot only use a preset universal stop terms list to identify and eliminate stop terms, because controversial issues belong to a special field. In addition to the general stop terms, there are also domain-special stop terms. We use the labeled data to identify and delete them in a semi-supervised way, and realize the integration of prior information and algorithm. Second, because the number of each category of controversial issues obey power-law distribution, a small number of categories may contain most of the data. However, the judgment of seed terms in TRTD has its own defects and does not adapt to power law distribution data, which leads to terms in the categories with large amount of data are identified as seed terms, and the phenomenon of excessive topic term groups in the clustering results appears. In this paper, the recognition of seed terms is modified to make the algorithm suitable for power-law distribution, and some good properties of the original method are maintained, such as the weight of seed terms in the graph model is higher than most of the affiliated terms. Thirdly, in the actual data of controversial issues, different categories may contain terms that can represent their topics in common. Because the frequency of these terms in each category is not low, and there is more than one category, it is easy to lead to the high frequency of these terms and be identified as seed terms. As a result, similar but different categories will be identified as one category, and if the number of controversial issues in these categories is large, the final clustering effect will not be applicable in the actual situation. To solve this problem, SCG uses a small amount of labeled data to subdivide the frequent and important

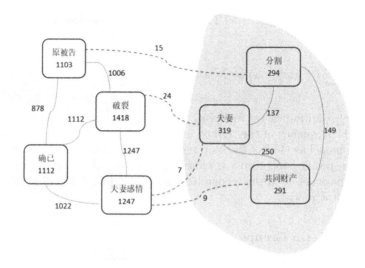

Fig. 1. Graph structure

topic term groups after preliminarily identifying the topic term group of each category. If it is identified that a topic term group may contain more than one category, it will be divided. Through the combination of automatic recognition and supervised subdivision, the final topic term group can be obtained by s a semi-supervised way. SCG methods in this paper can be roughly divided into three steps :(1) graph model construction; (2) topic term groups extraction; (3) controversial issues category allocation.

2.1 Graph Model Construction

Suppose that the corpus is $D = (d_1, \ldots, d_n)$, containing n controversial issues data, with labeled data for $D^l = (D_1{}^l, \ldots, D_m{}^l)$, in which each $D_i{}^l$ represents all labeled data of a category, and $D_i{}^l \subseteq D$. Terms in the controversial issue d is d $=(w_1, \ldots, w_s)$. Because a controversial issue is a sentence that describes the core of the conflict between the two sides of the dispute, s is a smaller value, which is also a common feature of the short text.

We construct a semi-supervised co-occurrence graph, denoting $G = (V, E)$, in which the node $v \in V$ represents a term, the weight $f(V)$ represents the frequency of the corresponding term appearing in corpus D, and the edge $e \in E$ between the two nodes w and v represents the co-occurrence of the two terms w, v in all controversial issues in D. Its weight $f(w, v)$ is the sum of the co-occurrence frequency of the terms w, v in D, and each time the two terms appear in a controversial issue at the same time. Graph structure is shown in Fig. 1.

We use a common stop terms list to identify general stop terms, use labeled data to identify domain-specific stop terms, and remove all corresponding nodes and edges from the graph model. The rule for identifying stop terms using labeled data is *Rule 1*:

$$\sum_{i=1}^{i=m} I(f_i^l(w) > \alpha) > \beta \quad \text{and} \quad Max(f_i^l(w))/Min(f_i^l(w)) < \gamma \qquad (1)$$

where $I(x)$ is an indicative function, that is, when $f_i^l(w) > \alpha$ is 1, otherwise 0, $f_i^l(w)$ is the frequency of the term w in $D_1{}^L$ in the labeled data. We still denote the graph model as G after the stop terms are removed. Because the recognition of domain-specific stop terms is closely related to labeled data, we manually select the parameters in the recognition process and do not give much attention to them in the model.

2.2   Topic Term Groups Extraction

Most of the graph-based clustering methods are to find closely connected subgraphs for clustering, and this paper is no exception. As shown in Fig. 1, the yellow and green areas are closely connected internally, but the connection between the two areas is weak, which can be clearly identified as two clusters. How to identify two closely connected subgraphs varies in different clustering algorithms. The idea in this paper is similar to the TRTD method, which identifies seed terms (central terms) and combines closely linked terms together as a term cluster (subgraph). Since controversial issues follow the power-law distribution, that is, fewer categories contain more data, while more categories contain less data, we pay more attention to the terms that occur more frequently, so this paper will identify the seed terms according to the term frequency from high to low. We identify the term with the highest frequency as a seed term first. TRTD considers that a term with a weight greater than the neighboring point is a seed term, so the term with the highest frequency in the graph model must be a seed term and the terms closely connected with the seed term can be considered as the affiliated terms of the seed term, and the seed term with the affiliated terms together constitute a topic term group. The rule for distinguishing v as an affiliated term of w is *Rule 2*:

$$f(v)/f(w) > \theta \quad \text{and} \quad f(v,w)/f(w) > \sigma \qquad (2)$$

That is, terms with similar frequency to the seed term and high co-occurrence are affiliated terms of seed term. Taking the term with the highest frequency in the graph model as the seed term, and finding affiliated terms of the seed term as a topic term group according to the above rule, the first topic term group can be obtained. Then, the extracted terms in the topic term group were marked as non-candidate terms of seed term, and the term with the highest frequency were found as a seed term in the nodes not marked as non-candidate terms of seed term in the graph model. The affiliated terms searched according to rule 2, and the above process was repeated to find all the topic term groups $(T_1, \ldots, T_k)$.

In order to avoid the fact that similar but not identical categories are divided into the same cluster, based on a small amount of labeled data, this paper semi-supervised to determine whether a topic term group need to be divided. Let $A_i = (j|f_j(S_i)/|D_j| > \omega, 0 \leq j \leq m)$, Where$|D_j|$ and $f_j(S_i)$ are the number of controversial issues in labeled data D_j and the frequency of S_i in D_j respectively. Then, the dividing rule is *Rule3*:

$$\mathbf{a_j} = \{t \mid t \in T_i \, , \, f_j(t)/|D_j| > \omega\} \text{ ,where } j \in A_i \tag{3}$$

Then all $\mathbf{a_j}, j \in A_i$ constitute an overlapping partition of T_i, and replace T_i as new topic term groups to obtain the final topic term groups. We still denote all the resulting topic term groups as $(T_1, \ldots, T_k)$.

2.3   Controversial Issues Category Allocation

The category assignment is based on the number of overlapping terms between controversial issues and topic term groups, also based on the number of terms in topic term groups. The category p of the controversial issue d should satisfy *Rule 4*:

$$|T_p| = min\{|T_i| \mid i \in \{j \mid \arg\max_j |d \cap T_j|\}\} \tag{4}$$

where $|T_i|$ is the number of terms in T_i, $|d \cap T_i|$ is the number of overlapping terms between the controversial issue d and topic term group T_i. The overall process of SCG is presented in Algorithm 1. CountFrequency is a function that records the occurrence of data in multiple sets and calculates the frequency of the data.

Algorithm 1. *SCG*

Input: Corpus D, labeled data D^l and parameter γ, θ, σ.
Output: Set of topic term groups $(T_1, \ldots, T_p)$ and categories list L.
1: // *step 1: graph model construction*
2: Initialize multisets V',E' as $\emptyset$.
3: **for** d in D **do**
4:     $V' = V' \cup \{w \mid w \in d\}$.
5:     $E' = E' \cup \{(w,v) \mid w, v \in d, w \neq v\}$.
6: **end for**
7: $[V, f(w)] \leftarrow CountFrequency(V')$.
8: $[E, f(w,v)] \leftarrow CountFrequency(E')$.
9: Construct graph model based on $[V, f(w)]$ and $[E, f(w,v)]$.
10: According to Rule 1, label data is used to identify and delete the high frequency words.
11: //*step 2: topic term groups extraction*
12: Initialize set of topic term groups T as $\emptyset$.
13: Sort points in V in descending order according to f(w), still denoted as $[V, f(w)]$.
14: **for** term w in the node set $[V, f(w)]$ **do**

15:     **if** the term w does not appear in the extracted topic term groups T **then**
16:         Construct an empty set C_w to store the seed term w and its affiliated terms, and the recognition rule of affiliated terms is Rule 2.
17:             **if** C_w needs subdivision according to Rule 3 **then**
18:                 Use *rule 3* to subdivide C_w.
19:             **end if**
20:             Add C_w to collection T.
21:     **end if**
22: **end for**
23: *//step 3: Controversial issues category allocation*
24: Create an empty list L to record the categories of controversial issues.
25: **for** d in D **do.**
26:     Assign d category according to set T and Rule 4, and add category to the end of list L.
27: **end for**
28: **return** T,L.

3   Data and Experiments

3.1   Data

Controversial issues are recorded in the judgment documents, but not in all documents, nor in the standard and formatted form, so they need to be extracted from the original documents. In order to reduce the cost of manual annotation, the method of regular expression is adopted for the extraction of controversial issues. We extract controversial issues of all cases obtained online and stored them according to the cause of the case. After the extraction of controversial issues, we use manual annotation to label categories of them. Then we adopted the controversial issues under the two causes of action to conduct the experiment. The detailed information is shown in Table 1.

3.2   Experiments

Firstly, we preprocess the data to remove punctuation marks, digits and special characters in the text data. Because the text in Chinese is not composed of words,

Table 1. Some information of two causes of action

cause of action	labour dispute	divorce dispute
The number of controversial issues	5521	2735
The number of categories	1295	567
Average length of controversial issues	27.83	23.89
Maximum category size	859	605
Minimum category size	1	1

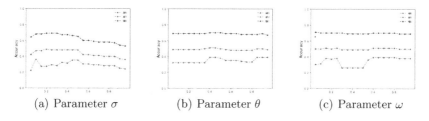

(a) Parameter σ (b) Parameter θ (c) Parameter ω

Fig. 2. Parameter analysis for the cause of labor dispute

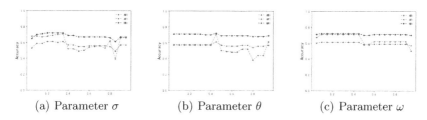

(a) Parameter σ (b) Parameter θ (c) Parameter ω

Fig. 3. Parameter analysis for the cause of divorce dispute

so word segmentation is needed for the experiments. In the experiment of this paper, the common *jieba* segmentation is mainly used. After word segmentation, we used *baidu stop terms list* to remove common stop terms.

As controversial issues data include ground truth cluster labels, we adopt three popular external metrics: Adjusted Rand Index (ARI) [10], Adjusted Mutual Information (AMI) [10] and Normalized Mutual Information (NMI) [11] to evaluate the clustering accuracy.

In the experiment, the seed terms' frequency must be greater than 10 (we can adjust the number of clusters by changing this threshold), and we optimized and analyzed the three main parameters σ, θ, ω in the model. In order to reduce the calculation of parameter optimization, we set the step size to 0.05 according to the approximate value range (0,1) of the three parameters, and optimize the parameters within the value range according to evaluation metrics. Parameter analysis is shown in Fig. 2 and Fig. 3. In the analysis of a single parameter, the other parameters are always fixed as the optimal value. It can be seen from the analysis diagram of σ, the parameter controlling co-occurrence frequency, under the two causes of action that the values of the three evaluation metrics are different, but the general trend is the same, and each metric almost reaches the maximum value at the same point, indicating that the three evaluation metrics are consistent in measuring the clustering effect. As the parameter value of σ and θ increases from the minimum value, the evaluation index value increases and then decreases after reaching the peak value. The parameters σ and θ are mutually constrained, and the optimization direction is intuitively consistent. In both of two causes of action, the change of the evaluation metrics for parameter ω is relatively stable around optimal value, which indicates that the topics of controversial issues in the top several categories are relatively obvious, that is,

Table 2. Clustering accuracy comparison

Methods	Metrics	Labour dispute	Divorce dispute
SCG	AMI	**0.51**	**0.61**
	ARI	**0.39**	**0.71**
	NMI	**0.70**	**0.72**
TRTD	AMI	0.34	0.55
	ARI	0.18	0.60
	NMI	0.50	0.65
LDA	AMI	0.43	0.46
	ARI	0.33	0.30
	NMI	0.62	0.60

The maximum value of the evaluation metrics under each causes of action is shown in bold.

Table 3. A topic term group and sample controversial issues in corresponding category

topic term group: couple, division, joint property
1. How should the joint property be divided.
2. Whether the division of marital joint property and debt by the original trial court is appropriate.
3. The division of joint property.
4. Whether the original judgment is appropriate for the division of the couple's joint property.

the frequency difference between the high-frequency topic terms and the non-topic terms is significant, which can clearly distinguish the two. In order to evaluate whether the proposed method can achieve better clustering effect on controversial issues, we compare it with two methods: TRTD and LDA. The settings of parameters δ and θ in TRTD are consistent with θ and σ in SCG, and the parameter K of total clusters in LDA is consistent with the number of clusters in SCG. The results are compared in Table 2.

In addition, a main feature of the algorithm in this paper is the extraction of topic term groups. The final category allocation process is also based on the topic term groups. For example, Table 3 shows a topic term group and several dispute focus sample in the corresponding category in the divorce dispute cause of action. It can be seen that terms in the topic term group can indeed represent the main common semantics of the controversial issues.

4   Conclusion

Based on TRTD algorithm, this paper improves it and proposes a semi-supervised algorithm SCG. First of all, SCG follows some characteristics of TRTD: with better interpretation, faster computing speed, easy to intuitively adjust the number of clusters, and better solve the high-dimension and sparsity of short-text clustering. Secondly, because high-frequency terms have a great influence on the clustering algorithm, some high-frequency terms are stop terms, which have poor resolution for text data and need to be deleted. TRTD uses the list of common stop terms to delete stop terms, but as controversial issues belong to the field of law, the list of common stop terms cannot meet this situation. This paper uses prior knowledge to identify stop terms under specific causes to optimize the graph model. Thirdly, according to the characteristics of power law distribution of controversial issues, SCG improves the extraction of the seed terms in TRTD, and determines the seed term and affiliated terms in a more intuitive way. Then, semi-supervised learning is used to adapt the phenomenon that controversial issues in a few categories have high similarity and are easily divided into the same category in the clustering process, which makes the algorithm more suitable for the actual situation. Finally, the method, which simply uses the number of overlapping terms between topic term groups and controversial issues to cluster, is improved in SCG. It is more reasonable in the case of the contents of different categories of data may contain each other. Using the method in this paper, the clustering effect can be improved by a small amount of labeled data under the condition that the calculation rate of TRTD is hardly changed. After obtaining the clustering results, we associate the category information of controversial issues with cases and integrate it into the retrieval system. In the retrieval process, in addition to the conventional retrieval options, the searcher can also select the category of controversial issue of the retrieved case to retrieve. The short text data for this particular field achieves better clustering effect and further promotes similar cases' retrieval.

References

1. Chen, G.M.: Issues concerning several relations in the design of pretrial preliminary procedure. Polit. Sci. Law Tribure **4**(11), 9–15 (2004)
2. Clauset, A., Shalizi, C.R., Newman, M.E.J.: Power-law distributions in empirical data. SIAM Rev. **51**(4), 661–703 (2009)
3. Yang, S., Huang, G., Cai, B.: Discovering topic representative terms for short text clustering. IEEE Access **7**, 92037–92047 (2019)
4. Fang, Y., et al.: Few-shot learning for Chinese legal controversial issues classification. IEEE Access **8**, 75022–75034 (2020)
5. Tian, X., et al.: K-means clustering for controversial issues merging in Chinese legal texts. In: Legal Knowledge and Information Systems, vol. 313 (2018)
6. Jain, A.K.: Data clustering: 50 years beyond K-means. Pattern Recogn. Lett. **31**(8), 651–666 (2010)
7. Ni, X., et al.: Short text clustering by finding core terms. Knowl. Inf. Syst. **27**(3), 345–365 (2011)

8. Jia, C., et al.: Concept decompositions for short text clustering by identifying word communities. Pattern Recogn. **76**, 691–703 (2018)
9. Blei, D.M., Ng, A.Y., Jordan, M.I.: Latent Dirichlet allocation. J. Mach. Learn. Res. **3**, 993–1022 (2003)
10. Yan, X., et al.: A biterm topic model for short texts. In: Proceedings of the 22nd International Conference on World Wide Web, pp. 1445–1456 (2013)
11. Vinh, N.X., Epps, J., Bailey, J.: Information theoretic measures for clusterings comparison: variants, properties, normalization and correction for chance. J. Mach. Learn. Res. **11**, 2837–2854 (2010)

Facial Expression Image Classification Based on Multi-scale Feature Fusion Residual Network

Yuxi Zhao[1], Chunzhi Wang[1(✉)], Xianjing Zhou[2], and Hu Liu[2]

[1] School of Computer Science, Hubei University of Technology, Wuhan, China
chunzhiwang@vip.163.com
[2] Wuhan Zall Information Technology Co., Ltd., Wuhan, China

Abstract. Due to the peculiar subtlety and complexity of facial expressions, only using the depth features of the network will ignore the complementarity between the multi-layer features, resulting in the loss of effective information. A facial expression image classification model based on a multi-scale feature fusion residual network is proposed to aim at these problems. Firstly, the ResNet-50 network structure is selected for improvement, with the dilated convolutional extraction introduced to extract the multi-scale features in the neural network; design a new two-branch multi-scale feature fusion module, using multiple deep features to fuse shallow features in parallel to obtain finer-scale abstract information, showing the advantages of high-performance model training while having efficient inference speed; the 3-time full connection and classifier have been packed to strengthen the consistency of feature map and category and enhance model generalization. The improved network model is trained in RAF-DB, JAFFE, and Oulu-CASIA datasets. According to the experimental results, the network obtains an accuracy of 85.79%, 96.65%, and 97.29% in the classification of facial expression images, respectively, which is higher than other advanced methods and can serve as a reference for how to conduct facial expression image classification.

Keywords: Facial expression recognition · Residual network · Image classification · Dilated convolution · Feature fusion

1 Introduction

Facial expressions are the core of affective computing systems, and emotions are intuitively displayed by facial expressions [1]. The key to image classification is to use neural networks for feature extraction, use different classifiers for a category or directly use neural networks for recognition. Convolutional neural networks (CNN) have become the highlight of image processing.

The traditional image classification algorithms select and extract features from the image. Still, the extraction method based on traditional manual design wastes resources and incomplete feature extraction. Therefore, the facial expression images in this paper focus on the following features: (1) The facial features of different people vary in size and are easily affected by sunglasses, masks, and other occlusions, resulting in significant differences in the size of the features. It is required to consider the effect of convolution kernel size and different scale features when image classification. (2) The differences between the five facial forms are subtle and difficult to distinguish when doing expression transformation. Many training samples and flexible screening of effective features are needed to achieve feature fusion. (3) There are grayscale images, color images, and different sizes of images, which require the influence of pixels to be fully considered when classifying.

This paper proposes a multi-scale feature fusion residual network for the facial expression image classification model to address the above problems. And the main improvements include the following three aspects:

- Changing the output of the residual network by using dilated convolution with different dilated rates to achieve an increased perceptual field without reducing the resolution of the feature map and to obtain contextual information.
- Designing a simple but powerful two-branch multiscale fusion module consisting of upsampling, convolutional layers, and batch normalization operations to reduce the loss of information in each layer of the network and effectively utilize in-depth features containing rich semantic information and shallow features with texture information.
- The design of Linear Regression + ReLU activation function + Dropout is used several times in the fully connected layer to reduce the parameter operations so that the network has better anti-overfitting performance.

2 Related Work

The feature extraction method is an essential component of facial expression recognition that determines the algorithm's accuracy. Traditional feature extraction methods are based on the features of the image itself, mainly including local binary patterns (LBP) [2], haar-like features [3], Gabor wavelet transforms [4], histogram of oriented gradients (HOG), and scale-invariant feature transform (SIFT). However, traditional expression recognition algorithms cannot efficiently solve the nonlinear facial appearance variations caused by pose differences, occlusions, etc. It is still difficult to improve the classification level effectively. On the other hand, deep learning methods automatically train a feature classifier to distinguish images based on samples. Therefore, research scholars have used convolutional neural networks such as AlexNet, VGG, GoogleNet, ResNet, etc., in the field of facial expression recognition. Xie [5] et al. introduced an attention mechanism to obtain feature vectors through multiple connections before classification. Chen et al. proposed to combine local window self-attention with convolution to bring the information features between windows, and finally fused and sent to a feedforward network to get the output features. Many current advanced methods are adding attention mechanisms. Although focusing on the expression focus region, this method will ignore the local detail information while emphasizing the facial expression integrity. Yang et al. mainly used a spatial pyramid to extract four different scales of features and thus obtained the multi-scale feature set while assisting the high-scale features for computation.

The overly deep network is prone to gradient explosion or disappearance. The deep residual network proposed by Kaiming He [6] et al. scholars solves the problem that the classification performance no longer improves after the number of network layers reaches a certain depth. Therefore, this paper chooses the ResNet-50 network for improvement. Figure 1 shows the structure of the ResNet-50 network. The input part consists of a 7*7 convolutional kernel and maximum pooling; the middle convolutional part introduces the residual block to achieve feature extraction; the output part goes through global adaptive smoothing pooling and a fully connected layer. The residual block divides the input data into two parts. One part goes through a 3*3 convolution layer. The other part goes through a shortcut. 4 residual blocks are stacked 3, 4, 6, and 3 times in this order.

layer name	50-layer
conv1	7×7, 64, stride 2
	3×3 max pool , stride 2
conv2_x	$\begin{bmatrix} 1×1, & 64 \\ 3×3, & 64 \\ 1×1, & 256 \end{bmatrix} ×3$
conv3_x	$\begin{bmatrix} 1×1, & 128 \\ 3×3, & 128 \\ 1×1, & 512 \end{bmatrix} ×4$
conv4_x	$\begin{bmatrix} 1×1, & 256 \\ 3×3, & 256 \\ 1×1, & 1024 \end{bmatrix} ×6$
conv5_x	$\begin{bmatrix} 1×1, & 512 \\ 3×3, & 512 \\ 1×1, & 2048 \end{bmatrix} ×3$
output	average pool , softmax

Fig. 1. ResNet-50 structure diagram

However, the number of training parameters in this method is still large. The residual network does not consider the influence of the interrelationship between features on recognition, resulting in the loss of effective features. Some studies extracted convolutional layers to realize visualization and found that the low layer of the convolutional neural network learns to focus on texture features, and the high layer learns semantic features. Combining multi-layer feature information can get more suitable features for facial expression recognition and improve recognition accuracy. Therefore, this paper improves the existing classical network structure by performing multi-scale feature extraction and deep and shallow layer feature fusion operations. The features at different levels complement each other.

3 Image Classification Model Based on Multi-scale Feature Fusion Residual Network

3.1 Overall Network Structure

The network structure studied in this paper prefers to share the task evenly rather than leaving some nodes idle. The branch of the residual network combined with the idea of dilated convolution is introduced to extract detailed features at different scales fully; a new deep and shallow layer feature fusion module is designed; the fully connected layer is improved to output the best classification effect. The overall network structure is designed as shown in Fig. 2.

Input the facial expression pictures (224, 224, 3) into ResNet-50, and the average pooling and fully connected layers of ResNet-50 are removed to bring more possibilities to the network rather than stacking along a straight line. Since the shallow convolutional layers extract similar information points, which can negatively affect infusion, no operation is performed on conv1_x. The last three layers of the proposed residual network are used as the output feature layers of the backbone network. The null convolution with expansion rates of 8, 4, and 2 is introduced in the feature layers with feature output channel numbers (28, 28, 512), (14, 14, 1024) (7, 7, 2048), and the output channel numbers (44, 44, 32), (22, 22, 32), (11, 11, 32) are the new layer2, layer3, and layer4 of the residual network, respectively. layer4 layers for the next operation. Based on the principle that deeper features are more important, layer2, layer3, layer4 are utilized 1, 2, 3 times in the feature fusion part, layer3 network features are integrated into layer4 (red region), layer2 network features are integrated into layers3 and 4 (purple region), up-sampling and feature replication stitching are taken to restore the resolution of the image, and the branching structure can better utilize the complementarity between features to achieve deep and shallow layer feature fusion. The final feature map (1, 7) is used for image classification with improved fully connected and Softmax layers.

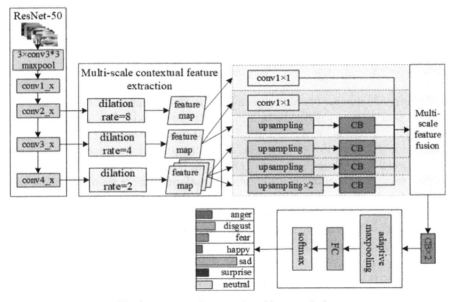

Fig. 2. The overall network architecture design

3.2 Residual Network Layer Combined with Dilated Convolution

As the number of layers of the residual network increases, it causes the feature map to keep decreasing due to the increase in computation [7]. And the feature map resolution is reduced to 1/8, 1/16, and 1/32 of the original in the last three stages of ResNet-50, respectively. To avoid reducing the resolution of the feature map while losing the detailed features of facial expressions, this paper compensates for its computational weakness by adding a dilated convolution to the residual network structure, as shown in Fig. 3.

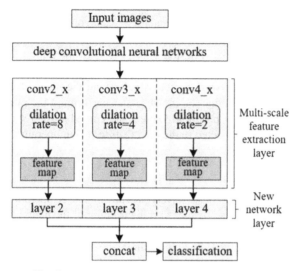

Fig. 3. Multi-scale feature extraction layer design

Dilated convolution [8] fills the convolution kernel with zero elements by setting different dilation rates to expand it to the corresponding size. The dilation rate determines the interval at which the convolution kernel processes the data to expand the perceptual field of the convolution kernel. The dilated convolutional perceptual field is calculated as follows: let the input layer be $L^{Win*Hin*Din}$, the dilated rate be d, the number of convolution kernels be k, the size of convolution kernels be $m \times n$, the step size be s, the padding value be p, and the output layer be $L^{Wout*Hout*Dout}$. After the dilated convolution operation, the relationship between the input layer and the output layer is:

$$m_0 = (m - 1)*(d - 1)+m \tag{1}$$

$$n_0 = (n - 1) * (d - 1) + n \tag{2}$$

$$W_{out} = \frac{Win + 2p - m_0}{s} + 1 \tag{3}$$

$$H_{out} = \frac{Hin + 2p - n_0}{s} + 1 \tag{4}$$

$$D_{out} = k \tag{5}$$

Because the shallower the layers are, the more the perceptual field needs to be expanded. Therefore, the dilated convolution with expansion rates of 8, 4, and 2 is used in the output layers of conv2_x, conv3_x, and conv4_x of the residual network, respectively, without adding any parameters. After calculation, the size of the convolution kernel with stride $= 1$ becomes 5×5, 9×9, 17×17, respectively, after passing the number of output channels of the residual network with 512, 1024, 2048 through the empty block, and the perceptual field size of the feature map expands 7×7, 15×15, 31×31 times compared to the perceptual field of the standard 3*3 convolution kernel. The number of output channels after passing the empty block all Compared with the features extracted by the ResNet-50 backbone network, the sensory field of the output unit is increased, which improves the network's ability to extract feature information at different scales of the image, enabling the network to better understand the image, form an enhanced residual network layer, and refine the image. After performing the multi-scale feature extraction operation, the most profound features are copied into three copies. The new network layer obtained is subjected to the next feature fusion operation.

3.3 Merge Conv+BN

The network layers are prone to slow convergence and increased operations of the parameters when adding more layers. To speed up the training of the neural network, the CB operation, i.e., merging conv3×3+BN [9], is applied several times. The formula before and after fusion is shown in the following formula, the output of the convolutional layer neuron is x_i, the output after the BN layer is y_i, μ is the mean within a Batch, σ^2 is the standard deviation within a Batch, $\in$ is a very Small constant, γ and β are a learnable parameter, w is the weight, and b is the bias.

Before fusion:

$$x_i = w * x_{i-1} + b \tag{6}$$

$$y_i = \frac{x_i - \mu}{\sqrt{\sigma^2 + \in}} \gamma + \beta \tag{7}$$

where, et

$$\mu_6 \leftarrow \frac{1}{m} \sum_{i=1}^{m} x_i \ , \ \sigma_6^2 \leftarrow \frac{1}{m} \sum_{i=1}^{m} (x_i - \mu_6)^2, \ \hat{x}_I \leftarrow \frac{x_i - \mu_6}{\sqrt{\sigma_6^2 + \in}}$$

After fusion:

$$y_i = \frac{\omega * \gamma}{\sqrt{\sigma^2 + \in}} \cdot x + \left(\frac{b - \mu}{\sqrt{\sigma^2 + \in}} \cdot \gamma + \beta \right) \tag{8}$$

$$w_{new} = \frac{\omega * \gamma}{\sqrt{\sigma^2 + \in}}, \ b_{new} = \left(\frac{b - \mu}{\sqrt{\sigma^2 + \in}} \cdot \gamma + \beta \right) \tag{9}$$

The normalization layer is viewed as a convolutional operation with a convolutional kernel of 1*1. The BN is incorporated into its upper convolutional layer during the experiment, which turns the two-step operation into a one-step one and also achieves the acceleration purpose. In deep learning, we choose to merge the conv and BN layers. From the perspective of mathematical computation, the essence of merging is changing the weights and biases of the convolutional layers. Since they are both linear operations, merging them is equivalent to less computation of the BN layer, and merging the layers to reduce the parameters can improve the network performance. In this paper, after using the convolution +BN layer fusion operation, the error of the output before and after the fusion is one part per billion, which is equivalent to the equivalent replacement, and the computation speed is increased by about 6% after the fusion, which almost does not affect the performance.

3.4   Two-Branch Multi-scale Feature Fusion Module

Although the deep neural network structure ensures that the features involved in the fusion have low correlation and avoid introducing too much redundancy, the deepening of the network reduces the feature map, resulting in the loss of relevant detail information, and often contains only a small amount of information when reaching the last layer. The goal of feature fusion is to achieve complementarity between multiple features and better classification performance. To solve this problem, this paper proposes a strategy of multi-scale feature fusion. By widening the network structure and establishing relationships to enhance the feature transfer between the network layers, the problem of information loss in the deep network during training is alleviated. This module uses the concatenation of deep and shallow features in the convolutional layer. Concatenation means that the number of features describing the image itself is increased and is stitched in the channel dimension. The specific network structure is shown in Fig. 4.

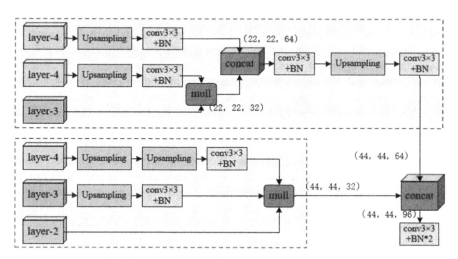

Fig. 4. Two-branch multi-scale feature fusion module

RepVGG [10] is a one-way minimalist architecture that replicates VGG with structural reparameterization, converting all network layers to conv3*3 through a fusion strategy without adding attention mechanisms and various novel activation functions. It is a minimalist but powerful neural network structure that achieves high accuracy while accelerating the deployment of the network. A more accurate model usually requires a more complex module and a wider or deeper network structure. However, such models are always too heavy to deploy, especially in limited hardware performance, and just-in-time inference is required. Considering efficiency, smaller, more compact, and faster models are naturally preferred. Models such as FCN and U-Net in semantic segmentation, FPN, DSSD, and YOLOV3 in target detection are used to fuse low and high level abstract semantic information by Hourglass structure for enhanced effect, and upsampling is exactly the method to fuse to enlarge the high-level feature map to the same level as the bottom level feature map. This paper designs a new two-branch multi-scale feature fusion module to deploy this model using only upsampling, CB operation, mull (feature multiplication), and concat.

The outputs of layer-2, layer-3, and layer-4 in the feature extraction module are used as inputs for lateral connectivity to equivalently convert the multi-branch model into a single-way model for feature fusion. The first stage first upsamples the in-depth features of both layer-4 after upsampling and CB operations and upsamples the features to the desired spatial dimensions after bilinear interpolation. One of the first outputs the number of channels (22, 22, 32) after feature multiplication with layer-3 and then outputs the number of channels (22, 22, 64) after concatenating these three operations. This stage operation is used to fuse layer-3 and layer-4 features. The fused features are subjected to successive CB operations, upsampling operations, and CB operations to output the number of channels (44, 44, 64). The purpose of this operation is to make the feature map length and width can become consistent with the array to be fused afterward, to merge the features of each channel again instead of just feature superposition, and to use them as the input for the next feature fusion. In the second stage, layer-4 is firstly subjected to two consecutive upsampling operations followed by a CB operation, layer-3 is subjected to one upsampling operation, and CB operation, and then the features of layer-4, layer-3, and layer-2 are multiplied to output the number of channels (44, 44, 32), and this stage operation is used to fuse the features of layers 2, 3 and 4. Finally, after concatenating the results of the two stages, the number of channels (44, 44, 96) is output, and two more CB operations are performed to enhance the feature extraction further. The deep features of layer-4 are the most important in this module, which are used 3 times in total, and the shallow features of layer-3 and layer-2 are used 2 times and 1 time, respectively.

The model uses only up-sampling and CB operation of constant connection reconstruction, taking two branches to fuse deep and shallow features jointly. The key to the model in the form of multi-branch construction and transformation method, making full use of the multi-scale information of each layer, reducing the loss of effective information in each layer of the network, in order to improve the accuracy of recognition of feature map details.

3.5 Pooling Layer and Fully Connected Layer Improvements

Usually, neural networks add fully connected layers to reduce the impact of feature location on classification [10]. However, the face is located in the center of the image and occupies most of the pixels, and the location information is not essential. Therefore, we first use the max-pooling layer to directly sum the spatial information to achieve dimensionality reduction and reduce the network parameters.

Each layer in the fully connected layer is composed of many neurons, and its primary role is to achieve classification. Using more than two fully connected layers can solve the nonlinear problem. That is, sub-features of facial expressions are found, and neurons are activated. These features are obtained from the previous convolutional layers, upsampling.

In this paper, we design 3-layer fully connected network module to package with a classifier. The structure of the fully connected layer is shown in Fig. 5. First, the modules are added to successive containers in the order passed in the constructor. After the first fully connected layer, the input data is expanded into a one-dimensional array with 512 nodes in the connected layer, followed by a layer of ReLU activation function and Dropout deactivation of some neurons to reduce overfitting, with a default ratio of 0.5 for forwarding propagation only. A second fully connected layer is defined with 256 nodes, followed by another layer of ReLU activation function and Dropout to destroy the close interaction between feature information. The last fully-connected layer outputs the number of classification classes as 7. This fully connected module dramatically reduces the influence of feature location on classification and strengthens the consistency of feature map and category. It enables the network not to rely too much on certain local features, enhances model generalization, and prevents overfitting. Finally, the Softmax function is used as the output layer.

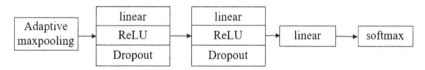

Fig. 5. The fully connected layer structure

4 Experimental Results and Analysis

4.1 Experimental Environment and Parameter Settings

This experiment is based on Windows 10 operating system, using the Pytorch deep learning framework for experiments, the Python version is 3.7.0, and the graphics card used in the experiment is NVIDIA GeForce GTX1070 8G with memory is 16G. The learning rate in the experiment is set to 0.005, the batch scale is set to 32, the momentum is set to 0.9, and the number of iterative rounds was set to 300.

4.2 Experimental Datasets and Pre-processing

Three face expression datasets are taken to verify the validity of the model, namely, RAF-DB, JAFFE, and Oulu-CASIA datasets.

- The RAF-DB dataset includes 29672 diverse face images, each with about 40 individual tags, and the expression images in the database compound the features of real-life expression images. 16489 images with expression labels are selected for the experiments, of which 13307 are used as training samples, and 3182 are used as test samples.

- The JAFFE dataset contains 213 images, and each of the 10 Japanese female students made 7 expressions, with an average of about 4 expressions per person. The JAFFE dataset images were rotated clockwise and counterclockwise and then expanded the dataset by mirroring and flipping, and a total of 852 images were expanded by adding black boxes to some of the eyes and mouths to simulate the realistic occlusion situation. Of these, 680 were used as training samples, and 172 were used as test samples.
- The Oulu-CASIA dataset consists of six basic expressions from 80 individuals, and the experiments were selected from the strong light image set under the visible light imaging system and selected the last five peak frames in each sequence to form a total of 2400 images. 1920 were used as training samples and 480 as test samples.

4.3 Mainstream Method Comparison Experiment

This model first obtained the accuracy of the dataset on the ResNet-50 network with 82.83%, 92.50%, and 88.05% respectively. Table 1 shows the comparison results of the classification accuracies of different methods on three datasets, RAF-DB, JAFFE, and Oulu-CASIA. The experimental results show that the classification accuracy of this model is better than the basic classification model and other advanced models.

Table 1. Performance comparison of different face expression classification methods.

Dataset	Method	Accuracy
RAF-DB	SP_ResNet18_CA	84.42 (+1.37)
	gACNN	85.07 (+0.72)
	LDL_ALSG	85.53 (+0.26)
	Ours	**85.79**
JAFFE	DCMA-CNNS	94.75 (+1.90)
	DFR	96.25 (+0.40)
	DMFA-ResNet	96.30 (+0.35)
	Ours	**96.65**
Oulu-CASIA	IDFERM	88.25 (+9.04)
	Fram2seq	91.67 (+5.72)
	DMFA-ResNet	92.57 (+4.70)
	Ours	**97.29**

The classification accuracy of this model on the three datasets is 85.79%, 96.65%, and 97.29%, which is 2.96%, 4.15%, and 9.04% higher than the basic model ResNet-50. The experimental results indicate that the classification enhancement effect of introducing an attention mechanism is not obvious, and the ability to change the classification accuracy should start from the perspective of retaining more detailed features and fusing features within the model, and the importance of different features needs to be given different weights, which in turn improves the representation ability of the model features. In this paper, the JAFFE dataset is added with some images under black frame occlusion during data preprocessing, and the experimental results still maintain high classification accuracy, which indicates that the model is sufficient to capture the detailed features in facial expressions for recognition and is also applicable to image classification studies with occluded expressions. The accuracy improvement of this model on the Oulu-CASIA dataset is more obvious than in the other two datasets. This dataset is characterized by the selection of images of facial expressions under strong light, the light has important expressiveness in the camera, and the difference between strong and weak light will affect the subject's sense of emotion, indicating that this model is more suitable for recognition of expression images under strong light.

4.4   Ablation Experiments

In this paper, ablation experiments are used to compare the improvement effect of different methods on the model. The experiments are conducted without introducing dilated convolution, feature fusion, and improved fully connected layers, and this method is denoted as Base. PF (Pooling and FC) indicates the addition of enhanced pooling and fully connected layers, DC (Dilated Convolution) suggests the introduction of dilated convolution for feature extraction, and SP (Second Process) indicates the fusion of channels by double branching for channel splicing fusion. The evaluation metric used for the experiments is the percentage of model classification accuracy, and the experimental results are shown in Table 2.

Table 2. Comparison of ablation experiments.

PF	FE	SP	RAF-DB	JAFFE	Oulu-CASIA
×	×	×	82.83	92.50	88.05
√	×	×	84.13	93.75	94.68
×	√	×	85.09	94.37	95.66
×	×	√	85.13	95.83	95.98
√	√	×	85.29	96.25	96.45
√	√	√	85.79	96.25	97.29

To explore more precisely the performance capability of this model under different expressions, the confusion matrices of the three datasets on the method of this paper are plotted in (a), (b), and (c) in Fig. 6. The confusion matrix details the recognition accuracy of each expression and the proportion of misclassified as other expressions, where the data on the diagonal line indicates the recognition accuracy of each expression.

From Table 2 above, it can be seen that the different improvement strategies used in this paper have all improved the classification accuracy of the model to some extent compared with the original ResNet-50. The analysis shows that when the cavity convolution is introduced on the Base method, the classification accuracy on the three datasets

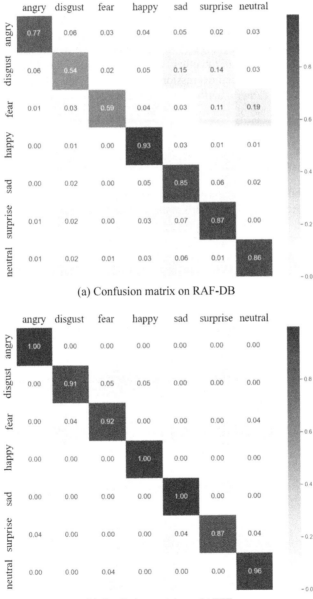

(a) Confusion matrix on RAF-DB

(b) Confusion matrix on JAFFE

Fig. 6. Confusion matrix diagram

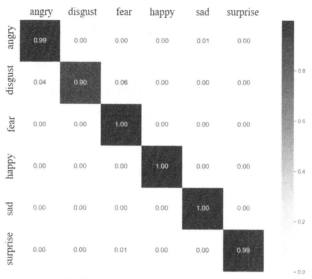

(c) Confusion matrix on Oulu-CASIA

Fig. 6. (*continued*)

is 85.09%, 94.37%, and 95.66%, respectively, with an increase of 0.96%, 0.62%, and 0.98%, thus proving the effectiveness of introducing cavity convolution for facial expression recognition; when the multi-scale feature fusion module is added, the classification accuracy rises by 0.5%, 0.4%, and 0.84%, respectively, thus demonstrating the effectiveness of multiple deep and shallow feature fusions for facial expression recognition tasks.

As can be seen from the figure, the three datasets have the highest recognition rate of happy expressions, all reaching over 90%. The exaggerated facial features and large motion amplitude of the happy faces are the easiest to recognize among all categories of expressions. For the RAF-DB dataset, disgust and fear have the smallest sample size and the highest recognition error rate. The highest recognition error rate for disgust is for sad and surprised expressions. The highest recognition rate for fear is for natural expressions because these expressions have similar appearance features. And the expression recognition rates were higher in the two datasets JAFFE and Oulu-CASIA. And a certain degree of masking of expressions in JAFFE may have a more significant impact on the extraction of surprised eye features and mouth features, causing instability. For the Oulu-CASIA dataset, the aversion recognition error rate is the highest for fear and anger expressions because they all have pulled-back lips and frown features. The performance of the confusion matrix of the model on the three datasets is similar.

5   Conclusion

An improved model of image classification with a multi-scale feature fusion residual network is proposed for the facial expression image classification problem. First, we change the output method based on the residual network and add dilated convolution to obtain multi-scale feature information of facial expressions; and design a new two-branch multi-scale feature fusion module to get finer-scale abstract information by using multiple in-depth features fusion of shallow features in parallel; and improve the pooling method and fully connected layer to prevent overfitting. The effectiveness of the proposed method is verified by conducting experiments on three datasets respectively. By comparing with other classical algorithms, the classification effect is higher than that of traditional convolutional neural networks, further verifying the excellence of the method.

Acknowledgment. This work is funded by the National Natural Science Foundation of China under Grant No. 61772180, the Key R & D plan of Hubei Province (2020BHB004, 2020BAB012).

References

1. Ben, X., Ren, Y., Zhang, J.: Video-based facial micro-expression analysis: a survey of datasets, features and algorithms. IEEE Trans. Pattern Anal. Mach. Intell. **44**(9), 5826–5846 (2021)
2. Ding, Y., Zhao, Q., Li, B.: Facial expression recognition from image sequence based on LBP and Taylor expansion. IEEE Access **5**, 19409–19419 (2017)
3. Whitehill, J., Omlin, C.W.: HAAR features for FACS AU recognition, pp. 5–101. IEEE, UK (2016)
4. Bartlett, M.S., Littlewort, G., Frank, M.: Recognizing facial expression: machine learning and application to spontaneous behavior, pp. 568–573. IEEE (2005)
5. Xie, S., Hu, H., Wu, Y.: Deep multi-path convolutional neural network joint with salient region attention for facial expression recognition. Pattern Recog., 177–191 (2019)
6. Yu, F.S., Yu, J., Lu, Y.: Gender classification of iris image based on residual network. Laser Optoelectron. Prog. **58**(16), 1610022 (2021)
7. Fang, T., Chen, Z., Fu, Y.: Face recognition method based on neural network multi-layer feature information fusion. J. Intell. Syst. **16**(02), 279–285 (2021)
8. Lai, Z.Y., Chen, R.H., Qian, Y.R.: Real-time microexpression recognition algorithm based on atrous convolutions for CNN. Appl. Res. Comput., 3777–3780 (2020)
9. Zhang, P., Kong, W., Teng, J.: Face expression recognition based on multi-scale feature attention mechanism. Comput. Eng. Appl., 182–189 (2022)
10. Ding, X., Zhang, X., Ma, N.: RepVGG: Making VGG-style ConvNets Great Again (2021)

Privacy-Preserving Educational Credentials Sharing Based on Blockchain and Proxy Re-Encryption

Dongkun Hou[✉], Jieming Ma, Zitian Peng, Jie Zhang, and Xiaohui Zhu

School of Advanced Technology, Xi'an Jiaotong-Liverpool University, Suzhou, China
{Dongkun.Hou20,Zitian.Peng20}@student.xjtlu.edu.cn,
{Jieming.Ma,Jie.Zhang01,Xiaohui.Zhu}@xjtlu.edu.cn

Abstract. The educational credential is an important reference for enterprises to screen students. However, the educational credentials are normally stored in a centralized cloud server with improper maintenance and inadequate supervision, and students' credentials are easily tampered with by server administrators. In addition, students' credentials are also sensitive information and therefore need to be encrypted and stored in the cloud server, but traditional encryption schemes face challenges because of private key sharing. The paper designs a privacy-preserving educational credentials sharing scheme based on blockchain and proxy re-encryption. The proposed approach addresses the problems of centralized storage and encryption sharing. Students' sensitive information is encrypted and stored in a cloud server, and the hash index is stored in a blockchain. Enterprise is able to match students' public information and request private credentials by proxy re-encryption. We also realize the prototype of the system and evaluate the performance of the encryption scheme.

Keywords: Educational Credential · Data Sharing · Privacy Preservation · Blockchain · Proxy Re-Encryption

1 Introduction

The educational credential is the proof of a student's educational background, which is referred to as a candidate criterion of enterprise or university, so current education institutions set up a centralized server to keep electronic educational

This research is supported by the National Natural Science Foundation of China under (Grant No. 62002296), the Natural Science Foundation of Jiangsu Province under (Grant No. BK20200250), the Suzhou Science and Technology Project-Key Industrial Technology Innovation (Grant No. SYG202006, SYG202122), the Future Network Scientific Research Fund Project (Grant No. FNSRFP-2021-YB-41), the XJTLU Key Programme Special Fund under (Grant No. KSF-E-54, KSF-E-65), the XJTLU Research Development Fund (Grant No. RDF-17-02-04), the XJTLU AI University Research Centre and Jiangsu Provincial Data Science and Cognitive Computational Engineering Research Centre at XJTLU.

credentials. In this way, students can share their electronic credentials with an enterprise or university, and the receivers can validate the electronic credentials by looking up an identification number in the education server. However, a centralized server does not guarantee educational credentials' authenticity [5]. For example, server administrators are able to easily tamper with students' credentials due to a lack of supervision. In addition, students' sensitive information (e.g., ID number, home address, phone number, etc.) is occasionally leaked if the cloud server is attacked.

Blockchain is a decentralized ledger maintained by many managers nodes. In the literature, many researchers used the immutability and security of blockchain to develop a reliable educational sharing platform with transparency and trust. In [1,2,7,13], blockchain was employed to provide a secure and tamper-resistant platform for students to store and share their educational credentials with external institutions. Besides, students' course credits were recorded in the blockchain for sharing educational credits between different educational institutions to facilitate student exchange, and educational mobility [10,11]. Although the use of blockchain in education protects the integrity and authenticity of educational credentials, students' sensitive information can still be compromised, given that all nodes are able to access the information on the blockchain.

In order to overcome the issue of privacy protection for educational credentials sharing, many papers employed encryption algorithms to the educational credentials in the blockchain. [6] designed a blockchain-based electronic academic record system with two encryption structures, but the records were stored in a cloud database, which may cause privacy leakage by the database manager. [8] also developed a educational credentials sharing scheme based on a consortium blockchain that educational institutions control the blockchain network and upload the encrypted students' credentials into the blockchain; however, the design only was secure and credible using permissioned blockchain. Besides, in [9], students used the requester's public key to encrypt educational credentials and upload the ciphertext to the blockchain, but students may upload fake educational credentials to get admission to the institution. Moreover, educational credentials were easily lost if they only were stored on the students' devices.

To address these challenges, we develop a privacy-preserving educational credentials sharing scheme based on blockchain and proxy re-encryption. The hash index of educational credentials is stored in the blockchain to protect data security, and a proxy re-encryption scheme is employed against students' privacy leakage. We also analyze the time cost of proxy re-encryption compared with the no encryption approach and evaluate the performance of blockchain for our smart contract transaction.

The remainder of this paper is structured as follows. Section 2 provides the preliminary knowledge of blockchain and proxy re-encryption. Section 3 explains the proposed approach and implementation. The experimental results are illustrated in Sect. 4. Finally, Sect. 5 concludes this paper.

2   Preliminary

This section introduces the blockchain and proxy re-encryption.

2.1   Blockchain

Blockchain technology is an emerging technology abstracted from the underlying Bitcoin. It is a distributed ledger maintained by many miners nodes across the network. Blockchain transactions are stored in miners nodes avoiding single-point failure and tampering maliciously with the data. In addition, each block keeps the hash value of the previous block, so the modification to the transaction information will cause the change of the previous hash value. Blockchain is a decentralized network that does not require a trusted third party to regulate and control it. The corresponding functions are accomplished through distributed consensus protocols and smart contract technology.

Current blockchain systems can be divided into three types: public blockchain, consortium blockchain private blockchain. A public blockchain is a permissionless blockchain where all records are visible to the public and anyone can participate in the system, e.g., Bitcoin, Ethereum. A consortium blockchain is a partially decentralized system, as it is managed by several organizations. A private blockchain is considered a centralized network because one organization has full control over the system. Our system can be realized based on the smart contract, so it can be deployed in any type of blockchain. In this paper, we deploy the smart contracts to a private Ethereum [12].

2.2   Proxy Re-Encryption

Proxy re-encryption is a cryptographic technique to securely convert ciphertexts for data sharing. The ciphertext with the public key of the owner can be converted to another ciphertext with the public key of the requester, and the corresponding plaintext remains the same, and the converted ciphertext can be decrypted by the private key of the requester.

The general processes of proxy re-encryption are described as follows [3].

1. $(sk_i, pk_i, sk_j, pk_j) \leftarrow KeyGen(i, j)$: Given a security parameter λ and two users (i, j), two pairs of private and public keys (sk_i, pk_i) and (sk_j, pk_j) are generated.
2. $C_i \leftarrow Enc(pk_i, M)$: The ciphertext C_i of message M is generated by public key pk_i, and the ciphertext C_i can be decrypted by sk_i.
3. $rencKey_{ij} \leftarrow ReKeyGen(sk_i, C_i, pk_j)$: Given another public key pk_j, a re-encryption key $rencKey_{ij}$ is generated to convert C_i to C_j.
4. $C_j \leftarrow ReEnc(rencKey_{ij}, C_i)$: Given the ciphertext C_i and the re-encryption key $rencKey_{ij}$, a new ciphertext C_j is generated which can be decrypted by private key sk_j.
5. $M \leftarrow Dec(C_j, sk_j)$: The ciphertext C_j is decrypted by sk_j, and the plaintext M is output.

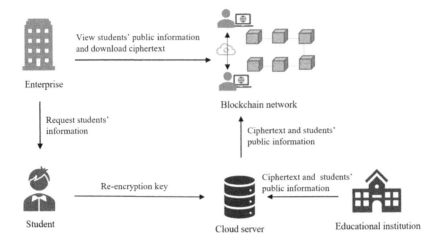

Fig. 1. System overview.

3   System Model

The section illustrates our system overview and the description and implementation of the workflow.

3.1   System Overview

We present a new architecture based on blockchain and proxy re-encryption mechanisms for securely storing and sharing students' educational credentials. We consider five entities in the system, including student, enterprise, educational institution, cloud server, and blockchain. Each educational institution, student, cloud server, and enterprise is represented by a pair of public-private keys (pk, sk) in the blockchain. The description of each entity is illustrated as follows.

– **Student** is the data owner and educational credentials from the educational institution. The student defines the sensitive information M_1 (e.g., personal information, academic certificate, course grade, etc.) and the non-sensitive information M_2 (e.g., major, degree, course information, etc.). The student authorizes the education institution to upload the ciphertext of M_1 and the plaintext of M_2 to the cloud service and blockchain. When an enterprise requests information, the student sends a re-encrypted key by the enterprise's public key to the cloud service if the student is willing to work at the enterprise.
– **Educational institution** provides student's educational credentials. The authorized educational institution is able to encrypt students' sensitive information M_1 to ciphertext C_i by students' public key pk_i to C_i, and then uploads C_i and students' public information M_2 with the signature σ by educational institution private key sk_{edu} to the cloud service and blockchain.

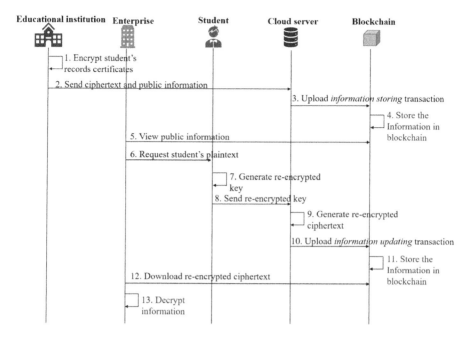

Fig. 2. Workflow of student's educational credential.

- **Enterprise** matches students' background based on students' public information M_2 in the blockchain and requests access to the students' private information M_1 if it finds a suitable student. Once the re-encrypted ciphertext C_j is uploaded to the blockchain, the enterprise downloads the ciphertext C_j, and decrypts the C_j to plaintext M_1.
- **Cloud server** is honest but curious. It is responsible for storing the encrypted educational credentials C_i provided by the educational institution. It also sends *information storing* transaction and *information updating* transaction to the blockchain. In addition, it is responsible for re-encrypting the ciphertext C_i to C_j using a re-encryption key.
- **Blockchain** stores the students' educational credentials including raw information M_2 and the hash index of ciphertext C_i and C_j. The smart contract of blockchain defines the rules of the system in Algorithm 1. Miners are responsible for maintaining the security of the blockchain.

3.2 Workflow

The workflow for student's educational credential sharing is illustrated in Fig. 2. The main steps are described as follows.

Encrypt Information. The educational institution encrypts student's sensitive information M_1 to generate the ciphertext C_i by using the student public

---

Algorithm 1. Smart Contract

Input: a legal transaction
1: **if** $msg.sender = server$ & *information storing* transaction **then**
2:     $studentMap[studentAddr] \leftarrow (M_2, H(C_i))$;
3:     store and publish *transaction*;
4: **else if** $msg.sender = server$ & *information updating* transaction **then**
5:     $enterpriseMap[enterprisAddr] \leftarrow (M_2, H(C_j))$;
6:     store and publish *transaction*;
7: **else**
8:     return error
9: **end if**

---

key pk_i.

$$C_i = Enc(M_1, pk_i) \tag{1}$$

Send Information. The educational institution sends the ciphertext C_i and the student's public information M_2 to the cloud service.

Upload Transaction. The cloud service uploads the hash index of ciphertext $H(C_i)$ and the plaintext of M_2 as a *information storing* transaction to the blockchain.

Verify Transaction. The miners validate the receiving transaction and pack the information into the block.

View Transaction. The enterprise views the students' public information M_2 and matches the suitable students.

Request Information. The enterprise requests access to the student's encrypted information and sends the public key pk_j to the student.

Generate Re-Encryption Key. Upon receiving the enterprise's request, the student calculates a re-encrypted key $rencKey$ and sends it to the cloud server.

$$rencKey = ReKeyGen(sk_i, pk_j) \tag{2}$$

Re-Encrypt Information. The cloud server re-encrypts the information from C_i to C_j using the re-encrypted key $rencKey$.

$$C_j = ReEnc(rencKey, C_i) \tag{3}$$

Upload Transaction. The cloud server uploads the hash index of re-encrypted ciphertext $H(C_j)$ and the plaintext of M_2 as a *information updating* transaction to update the state of smart contract in the blockchain.

Verify Transaction. The miners validate the receiving transaction and pack the information into the block.

Download Information. Once the state of smart contract is updated in the blockchain, the enterprise downloads the ciphertext C_j from the cloud server according to the hash index $H(C_j)$ in the blockchain.

Decrypt Information. The enterprise uses its private key sk_j to decrypt the ciphertext C_j to M_1. Additionally, the enterprise validates the signature σ by the public key of educational institution pk_{edu} by Eq. (5).

$$M = Dec(C_j, sk_j) \tag{4}$$

$$assert(\sigma == sign(M, pk_{edu})) \tag{5}$$

3.3 Detailed Implementation

We apply a proxy re-encryption scheme [4], which consists of six polynomial-time algorithms: setup, key generation, encryption, re-key generation, re-encryption, and decryption. We explain each phase in more detail as follows.

Setup (*params ← Setup(l).* Given secure parameter l, this algorithm generates q order ECC group G, and a corresponding generator is g. Hash functions are selected and denoted as H. The public parameters are now $params = \{G, q, g, H\}$.

User key generation (*$(sk_i, pk_i, sk_j, pk_j) ← KeyGen(params,i,j)$*) This algorithm randomly generate sk_i and compute pk_i as student's private key and public key, and sk_j and pk_j as enterprise's private key and public key.

$$sk_i \in Z_q^*, pk_i = g^{sk_i} \tag{6}$$

$$sk_j \in Z_q^*, pk_j = g^{sk_j} \tag{7}$$

Encryption (*$C_i ← Enc(pk_{i,M})$*). Given student's public key pk_i and plaintext M, an encrypted key $encKey$ is generated by Eq. (9) as a private key of symmetric encryption, and M is encrypted to C_{sym} by Eq. (10). The encryption information $C_i = (C_1, C_2, C_{sym})$ is stored in the cloud server, and the hash index $H(C_i)$ is uploaded to the blockchain.

$$c_1, c_2 \in Z_q^*, C_1 = g^{c_1}, C_2 = g^{c_2} \tag{8}$$

$$encKey = H_1(pk_i^{c_1+c_2}) \tag{9}$$

$$C_{sym} = Enc(M, encKey) \tag{10}$$

$$C_i = (C_1, C_2, C_{sym}) \tag{11}$$

Re-Encryption Key Generation ($rencKey_{ij}$ ← $ReKeyGen(sk_i,$ $C_i, pk_j)$). Given enterprise's public key pk_j, a re-encryption key $rencKey_{ij}$ is generated by Eq (13) and Eq. (14), and then re-encryption key information $(C_3, rencKey_{ij})$ is sent to the cloud server.

$$.c_3 \in Z_q^*, C_3 = g^{c_3} \tag{12}$$

$$d = H_2(C_3||pk_j||pk_j^{c_3}) \tag{13}$$

$$rencKey_{ij} = sk_i \times d^{-1} \tag{14}$$

Re-encryption (C_j ← $ReEnc(rencKey_{ij}, C_i)$). Given the ciphertext C_i and the re-encryption key $rencKey_{ij}$, a re-encrypted information $C_j = (C_1', C_2', C_{sym}, C_3)$ is generated by Eq. (16). The C_j is stored in the cloud server and the hash index $H(C_j)$ is uploaded to the blockchain.

$$C_1' = C_1^{rencKey}, C_2' = C_2^{rencKey} \tag{15}$$

$$C_j = (C_1', C_2', C_{sym}, C_3) \tag{16}$$

Decryption (M ← $Dec(C_j, sk_j)$). Enterprise downloads the re-encrypted information C_j from the cloud server. A decryption key $decKey$ is generated by Eq. (18), and the symmetric cryptographic algorithm is decrypted and outputs the plaintext M by Eq. (19).

$$d = H_3(C_3||pk_j||C_3^{sk_j}) \tag{17}$$

$$decKey = H_4((C_1' \times C_2')^d) \tag{18}$$

$$M = Dec(C_{sym}, decKey) \tag{19}$$

Table 1. Experiment environment

Hardware	Parameter
CPU	3.10 GHz i5-11300H
Memory	16 GB
Storage	256 GB

4   Experiment

The feasibility of the system is shown through a prototype implementation. The proxy re-encryption algorithm[1] and Ethereum Geth[2] are employed to realize this system. The experiment platform is shown in Table 1.

---

[1] https://github.com/SherLzp/goRecrypt.

[2] https://github.com/ethereum/go-ethereum.

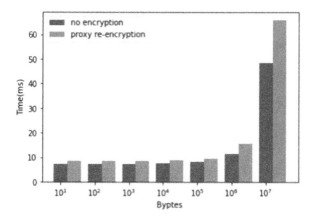

Fig. 3. Time cost of encryption with increasing information size.

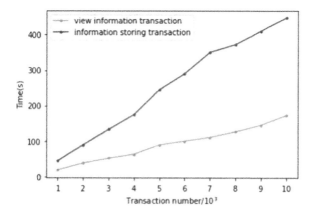

Fig. 4. Time cost of transaction with the increasing transaction number.

4.1 Cost of Proxy Re-Encryption

In the first experiment, we measure the impact of proxy re-encryption on the proposed system. The time cost of proxy re-encryption is analyzed and compared with no encryption method. There is no encryption method that just includes the key generation of blockchain and the signature algorithm of an educational institution. Proxy re-encryption adds encryption, re-encrypted key generation, re-encryption, and decryption.

Figure 3 shows the time cost with different sizes of sensitive information from 10^1 to 10^7 Bytes. It can find that no encryption method consumes more time cost with the increase of sensitive information, as the signature algorithm is more time-consuming. The proxy re-encryption method has a similar tendency, but it consumes more time cost than no encryption. Moreover, the cost gap increases

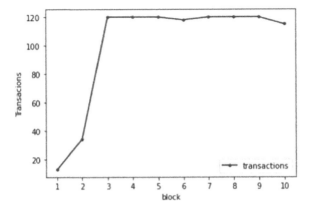

Fig. 5. Transaction number in each block (transactions $= 10^3$).

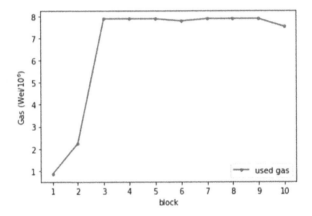

Fig. 6. Gas consumption in each block (transactions $= 10^3$).

with information size increases because symmetric encryption and decryption consume more time cost in the larger data.

4.2   Performance of Blockchain

In the second experiment, we evaluate the performance of blockchain. A private Ethereum blockchain with the gas limitation of 8×10^6 is employed in the blockchain. Figure 4 shows the latency of two types of transactions gradually increases due to the increase in transactions number from 10^3 to 10^4. Figure 5 and Fig. 6 show the transaction number and used gas in each block, respectively, when transaction number is 10^3. It can find the block stores at most 120 *information storing* transactions if the gas limitation is 8×10^6.

5   Conclusion

In this paper, a privacy-preserving educational credentials sharing scheme based on blockchain and proxy re-encryption for addressing the problems of centralized storage and encryption sharing. Students' private information is stored and encrypted in the cloud server. Enterprises can match students' public information in the blockchain and request private educational credentials by proxy re-encryption. The prototype is realized and deployed in a private Ethereum. Moreover, our experiments conduct that the time cost of proxy re-encryption is acceptable compared with no encryption method. In the future, we plan to extend the system by consortium blockchain to improve its security and scalability. Further, We look forward to developing an incentive mechanism to attract more students and enterprises to use our educational sharing platform.

References

1. Arenas, R., Fernandez, P.: Credenceledger: a permissioned blockchain for verifiable academic credentials. In: 2018 IEEE International Conference on Engineering, Technology and Innovation (ICE/ITMC), pp. 1–6. IEEE (2018)
2. Arndt, T., Guercio, A.: Blockchain-based transcripts for mobile higher-education. Int. J. Inform. Educ. Technol. **10**(2), 84–89 (2020)
3. Ateniese, G., Fu, K., Green, M., Hohenberger, S.: Improved proxy re-encryption schemes with applications to secure distributed storage. ACM Trans. Inf. Syst. Secur. **9**(1), 1–30 (feb 2006). https://doi.org/10.1145/1127345.1127346
4. Blaze, M., Bleumer, G., Strauss, M.: Divertible protocols and atomic proxy cryptography. In: Nyberg, K. (ed.) EUROCRYPT 1998. LNCS, vol. 1403, pp. 127–144. Springer, Heidelberg (1998). https://doi.org/10.1007/BFb0054122
5. Børresen, L.J., Meier, E., Skjerven, S.A.: Detecting fake university degrees in a digital world. In: Corruption in Higher Education, pp. 102–107. Brill (2020)
6. Daraghmi, E.Y., Daraghmi, Y.A., Yuan, S.M.: Unichain: A design of blockchain-based system for electronic academic records access and permissions management. Appl. Sci. **9**(22) (2019). https://doi.org/10.3390/app9224966
7. Han, M., Li, Z., He, J., Wu, D., Xie, Y., Baba, A.: A novel blockchain-based education records verification solution. In: Proceedings of the 19th Annual SIG Conference on Information Technology Education, pp. 178–183 (2018)
8. Li, Z., Ma, Z.: A blockchain-based credible and secure education experience data management scheme supporting for searchable encryption. China Commun. **18**(6), 172–183 (2021). https://doi.org/10.23919/JCC.2021.06.014
9. Mishra, R.A., Kalla, A., Braeken, A., Liyanage, M.: Privacy Protected Blockchain Based Architecture and Implementation for Sharing of Students Credentials. Inform. Process. Manage. **58**(3), 102512 (2021). https://doi.org/10.1016/j.ipm. 2021.102512
10. Srivastava, A., Bhattacharya, P., Singh, A., Mathur, A., Prakash, O., Pradhan, R.: A distributed credit transfer educational framework based on blockchain. In: 2018 Second International Conference on Advances in Computing, Control and Communication Technology (IAC3T), pp. 54–59. IEEE (2018)

11. Turkanović, M., Hölbl, M., Košič, K., Heričko, M., Kamišalić, A.: Eductx: a blockchain-based higher education credit platform. IEEE access **6**, 5112–5127 (2018)
12. Wood, G., et al.: Ethereum: a secure decentralised generalised transaction ledger. Ethereum project yellow paper **151**(2014), 1–32 (2014)
13. Young, A., Verhulst, S.: Creating immutable, stackable credentials through blockchain at mit (2018)

A Method of Students' Online Learning Status Analysis Based on Facial Expression

Mengya Wang, Chunling Jing, Zhiyi Huang, and Xiaohui Tan[✉]

Capital Normal University, Beijing, China
xiaohuitan@cnu.edu.cn

Abstract. In order to monitor students' emotional status during online learning, we propose a method to analyze students' online learning status by sentiment monitoring based on facial expressions. We provide visual feedback to teachers and students to improve online learning effectiveness. Firstly, the learning videos are used as input to recognize face AUs (action units) through convolutional neural networks, we get the discrete facial expression based on the recognized AUs. Secondly, the emotion index is calculated by building an emotion correlation matrix of emotions and AUs. Finally, we map the emotion index to the students' learning status. Various visual results are given for teachers to improve online teaching. Experiments show that our method can effectively reflect the status of students' online learning. By comparing our method with the student's self-report, the accuracy of our method reached 82.5%. Three types of visualizations presented in this paper (individual real-time feedback, feedback on the learning status of the class, and analysis feedback charts) provide students and instructors with privacy-preserving feedback on learning status.

Keywords: Face Recognition · Online Learning · Learning Status · Learning Feedback · Action Unit

1 Introduction

With the rapid development of online education and the spread of learner-centered independent learning, online learning is popular and widespread. Traditional teaching has become even more difficult under the impact of the new crown epidemic after 2019. Many primary and secondary schools, colleges, and universities actively conduct online teaching at home and abroad to ensure students' academic progress [1].

Many studies have shown a specific correlation between classroom emotion and students' learning effects [2]. Chao Yang's research proves that course interactivity is an essential factor affecting the effectiveness of lectures by studying the interactivity of online teaching. Therefore, in order to adopt reasonable and effective online classroom teaching strategies, teachers must understand and analyze the emotional state of students in the online classroom and adopt a practical learning condition monitoring approach [3], which is an essential guarantee for enhancing learners' listening efficiency. Currently, the commonly used emotion recognition methods in the teaching system mainly

© The Author(s), under exclusive license to Springer Nature Singapore Pte Ltd. 2023
W. Hong and Y. Weng (Eds.): ICCSE 2022, CCIS 1811, pp. 131–142, 2023.
https://doi.org/10.1007/978-981-99-2443-1_11

include the following three types: classroom state research method based on physiological parameters [4], classroom state research method based on learning behavior [5], and classroom state research method based on video images.

The first method mainly focuses on the relationship between the change in students' classroom state and physiological parameters [6]. The physiological parameters usually concerned are brain waves, eye movement changes, heartbeat, and other parameters. This method is based on physiological parameters to study the classroom state, which can get more accurate results, but it is not suitable for practical application scenarios. On the one hand, the cost of spreading the sensors across every student is relatively high, which is not conducive to widespread use. On the other hand, external devices will also cause interference for students themselves and affect the learning effect.

The second is the classroom state research method based on learning behavior [7]. This method is to judge the classroom status of learners by studying the video browsing progress, clicking times, discussion, question and answer, and other interactive behaviors of students during online learning. This method is greatly influenced by personal habits, behaviors, and emotions, resulting in lower reliability.

The third research method is the class state research method based on video images, which collects the images or videos of students during learning and concludes the classroom state of students by extracting the characteristics of essential parts, such as eyes, mouth, and eyebrows. Han Li's research [8] judges students' status by analyzing their facial expression changes through learning images of students. It is easy to capture images and videos in online teaching and obtain real-time and accurate results. Therefore, this method is most suitable for the problem of online classroom status analysis. This paper collects the videos or images of students and identifies the corresponding AUs with face recognition technology, carrying out relevant calculation processing.

In addition, the two commonly used learning status monitoring models show limitations. The first is the classroom status monitoring model based on learning behaviors. Personal habits and other factors predominantly influence the results of this method, resulting in lower credibility. The second is the text-based status monitoring model, which cannot follow up on learners' emotional states in real time and cannot capture the emotional state of learners who do not leave comment data on the platform. In contrast, the facial expression recognition-based method is wholly based on the actual state, follows up in real time, and solves the lack of intuitive and effective classroom status feedback.

Based on the analysis of the above problems, this paper proposes a method for online learning status assessment from various aspects such as learner's face detection, recognition, and feature extraction. The main contributions of this paper are as follows.

- Calculating the emotion index is adopted to improve the study of learners' emotion analysis. This emotion index can represent the accumulation of 19 emotion contributions.
- Through the real-time feedback of learners' emotional states to teachers, the effectiveness of the online classroom has improved significantly. We monitor the six emotions of learners: happy, sad, absorbed, bored, surprise, and puzzled by tracking their emotional feedback in real-time during the learning process.

- A variety of visual analysis results are generated by analyzing the data obtained from students' facial expressions. On the one hand, the individual emotion index change curve is presented to learners to help learners adjust their status. On the other hand, the classroom situation is feedback to the teacher through various visual charts to help the teacher adjust teaching strategies based on the sentiment analysis results.

The design and practice of this paper provide a novel way to evaluate students' online classroom status and classroom content and provide a scheme for assisting teachers in supervising students' online learning process and improving the online teaching effect.

2 Method

The main work of this research is to use student facial expression recognition based on AUs for classroom online learning status feedback. Based on Darknet-53's facial recognition algorithm, we classify and recognize the facial AUs and emotions in the video and get six emotions: happy, sad, absorbed, bored, surprise, and puzzled. Subsequently, we calculate the corresponding emotion indices based on our emotion index algorithm. After that, we monitor the online classroom learning status based on individual and group to provide the visual analysis results in real-time or summary form to students and teachers.

2.1 Online Expression Monitoring

In this research, the facial expression recognition algorithm is to identify the facial AUs and emotion indices of the students in the video. Twelve action units are involved in this method: AU1, AU2, AU4, AU5, AU6, AU9, AU12, AU15, AU17, AU20, AU25, and AU26. [9] Based on facial expression recognition of AUs, we correspond facial activity characteristics to happy, sad, absorbed, bored, surprise, and puzzled emotions. The correspondence between each emotion and facial features is shown in Table 1.

Table 1. The correspondence between emotions and AUs

Emotion	AU
Happy	AU6 + AU12 + AU25 + AU26
Sad	AU1 + AU4 + AU6 + AU9 + AU15 + AU17
Absorbed	AU5 + AU20 + AU25
Bored	AU9 + AU15 + AU17 + AU20 + AU25
Surprise	AU1 + AU2 + AU5 + AU25 + AU26
Puzzled	AU4 + AU17 + AU20

Different facial emotions correspond to different facial features. As shown in Table 2, the student's facial emotions [10] and the corresponding image features [11] are happy, sad, absorbed, bored, surprise, and puzzled from top to bottom.

Table 2. Facial emotional features

Emotion	Facial Features	Facial emotion images
Happy	Raise the corners of the mouth. Expose the teeth. Lift the cheeks.	
Sad	Raise the inner eyebrows and nose. Pull the mouth downward. Squeeze the lower lip upward. Lift the cheeks.	
Absorbed	Raise the upper eyelids. Pull the lips backward. Expose the teeth.	
Bored	Contract the nose. Pull the mouth downward. Squeeze the lower lip upward and pull it backward. Expose the teeth.	
Surprise	Raise the inner eyebrows. Raise the outer eyebrows. Raise the upper eyelids. Expose the teeth.	
Puzzled	Lower the eyebrows overall. Squeeze the lower lip upward to the top. Pull the lips backward.	

2.2 Emotional Index Calculation

We get the emotion index by building an emotion correlation matrix of emotions and AUs. The column vectors of the matrix represent the 12 AUs, and the row vectors represent the 19 emotions, which are happy, happy and surprised, surprised, happy and puzzled, surprised and puzzled, puzzled, neutral, surprised and absorbed, puzzled and absorbed, absorbed, surprised and bored, puzzled and bored, absorbed and bored, bored, surprised and sad, puzzled and sad, absorbed and sad, bored and sad, and sad. To establish the relationship between them, we construct the following emotional correlation vector.

$$r_i = \sum_{j-1}^{12} W_{ij} \times A_{j1} \times A_{j2} \tag{1}$$

W represents the sentiment correlation matrix, and A represents the AUs identification matrix. To represent the influence of different emotions on the emotion index, we introduce the emotion weight vector $C_{1 \times 19}$. After several adjustments, we get the most suitable sentiment weight vector [12].

$$C = \begin{bmatrix} 1, 0.5, 0.3, 0.6, 0.2, 0.1, 0, \\ -0.1, -0.2, -0.3, -0.35, -0.45, \\ -0.55, -0.6, -0.65, \\ -0.7, -0.8, -0.9, -1 \end{bmatrix} \tag{2}$$

Based on the Sigmoid function, we obtain the final sentiment index, which ensures that the value of the positive sentiment is greater than 0, while the value of the negative sentiment is less than 0, and the value of the neutral expression is in the middle. The formula for the emotion index is defined as the followings:

$$h = \frac{2}{1+e^{-\lambda \sum_{i-1}^{i-19} c_{1i} \times r_{i1}}} - 1 \tag{3}$$

$c_{1i} \times r_{i1}$ represents the value of the feature vector, which ensures that the value of the emotion index can fall in the range of $[-1,1]$. λ affects the sensitivity of the algorithm.

3   The Workflow of the Method

As shown in Fig. 1, videos of students' expressions are used as input to recognize AUs and their intensity in the video frame images and calculate the emotion index for each frame based on the Darknet-53 network model. A total of six expressions - happy, sad, absorbed, bored, surprise, and puzzled - are distinguished through facial expression recognition. The method generates various visual charts: individual real-time emotion index chart, group real-time emotion ratio distribution chart, and three stages of student emotion distribution chart, for teachers to understand students' online learning emotion.

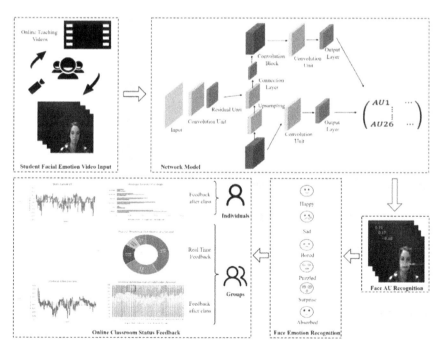

Fig. 1. Flow chart of the experiment system

3.1   Experiments

We select 14 subjects aged 16–30 years old for this experiment. The online teaching platform is the Superstar Learning Pass app, which includes three teaching videos for college Chinese, advanced mathematics, and college English. The content of the videos matches the cognition of the experimental subjects. The experimental subjects need to study the online videos on the platform, and we record their facial videos. Finally, we collect 42 facial video samples.

There are three questionnaires in this experiment: the questionnaire about the real-time emotions in watching instructional videos, the questionnaire about the feelings of videos after watching one instructional video, and the questionnaire about the whole experiment. Finally, we collect 140 experimental questionnaires.

To ensure the accuracy of the experiment, the experimental subjects should keep a proper distance from the camera when recording the facial video, whose faces need to appear entirely in the video throughout, avoiding situations such as facial obscuration. After collecting the videos of the facial expressions, we process the videos to analyze each subject's emotions during the three stages of watching the teaching videos and their feedback on the difficulty associated with the teaching videos.

3.2   Individual Feedback

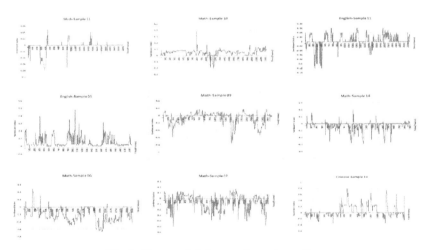

Fig. 2.   Exponential change of mood over time

In the experiment, based on data collected from students in the classroom, the individual student data from the online classes are plotted as an exponential change in mood over time. As shown in Fig. 2, the figures show the change in students' mood index at different moments in the classroom. When the emotion index is positive, the student's learning state is reasonable; when the emotion index is negative, it means that the student's state needs adjustment in time, and the figures can give feedback to the students and teachers. 42 experimental samples are divided into three categories, from top to bottom: emotionally stable learners throughout the lesson, those whose emotions are subjectively biased, and those whose emotions change drastically.

For the first group of learners, the mood is stable throughout the lesson, with little change in the learners' facial expressions. For the second group of learners, the overall mood is evident positive or negative, considering that this may be due to subjective factors of the learner, such as frequent smiles and depressed expressions. For the third group of learners, overall mood changes are more intense, considering that this may be due to the learner's mood being prone to events in the classroom that affect the learner's mood.

For all three types of learners, students and teachers can discover the turning point of emotional change by following the extreme points in the experimental results. Early detection of problems can serve as a warning reminder to students and help them adjust their moods in class promptly. According to the result, there are three minimum points in the students' emotions. The first and second lowest points occur in the middle part of the class, which means that students encounter more difficult knowledge or do not master it at this stage. Feedback of the results to students and teachers can help students improve learning efficiency and help teachers develop better teaching solutions. The third lowest point occurs in the second half of the class, which means that student's study for too long at the stage to become distracted or encounter a problematic point of knowledge. The results are fed back to students and teachers so that students can adjust their status in time, and teachers can consolidate the teaching effect of this stage.

3.3   The Overall Feedback

Real-Time Feedback.   As shown in Fig. 3, it is the proportion of students' emotions in three stages, with one second representing each stage. The figure contains six emotions: happy, sad, absorbed, bored, surprise, and puzzled. It can be seen from the figure that happy mood accounted for the most significant proportion, which is the dominant position in the three stages, accounting for about 42.86% to 50%, indicating that students have positive emotions in the whole class. With the progress of teaching, the proportion of puzzled emotions shows a downward trend, from the initial 21.43% to 8.33%, indicating that teachers play a role in answering doubts; After the problem is solved, the proportion of bored emotions begins to rise, from 21.43% initially to 25%.

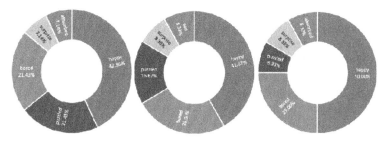

Fig. 3. Circle of emotion quantity distribution

Teachers can master the learning conditions of all students in the whole class through the proportion of the number of emotions. The overall emotional state of the students in the classroom is happy. In contrast, the puzzled emotion shows a linear downward trend, indicating that the teacher's arrangement of the lesson's difficulty and the arrangement of the teaching content is reasonable. The overall teaching effectiveness of the classroom is quite good.

Summative Feedback. According to the final experimental results, all sample data of a particular course are drawn into the exponential change of mood over time, as shown in Fig. 4. It shows that students' mood index changes at different moments in class. When the mood index is positive, it indicates that the student's overall state is good. When the mood index is negative, it means that the overall state of students needs to be adjusted. Teachers can find out the location of the mood change according to the trend of the overall line in the experimental results, grasp the change in students' mood in the classroom in time and make the corresponding adjustment to improve the quality of the classroom.

Fig. 4. Line chart of exponential changes in mood over time

The emotion index gradually decreases in the first half of the class with a range of [-0.04,0.07], from which we can infer that the interest of the students in learning has decreased and that probably because more difficult knowledge points appear or distractions. In the middle of the class, the mood index gradually rises and declines in [-0.08,0.02]. Students have mastered the knowledge points at this stage, but they encounter troubles with more profound knowledge. Teachers can review and practice students on this knowledge point in the follow-up course. In the latter part of the class, the mood index changes from an upward trend to a downward trend in [-0.06,0.03], which means students are distracted. Teachers can formulate more effective teaching plans for this stage.

After enlarging the rectangular box in Fig. 5, we get the trend chart of puzzled mood, in Fig. 6. To eliminate the inaccurate results caused by extreme emotions of students in a particular frame, we take 30 frames as one second to analyze the mood changes

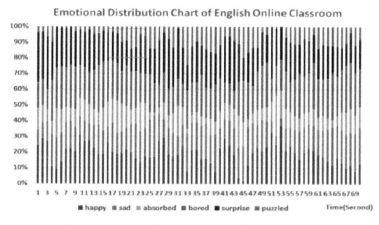

Fig. 5. Emotional distribution map of the whole class

in the whole class. On the one hand, students absorbed and puzzling emotions are less, mainly concentrated in the middle part of the course, and their emotional variation is not apparent. Therefore, we can assume that all students have an average learning effect throughout the lesson. On the other hand, positions 17s, 28s, and 42s show a trend of increasing confusion and subsequently decreasing confusion. It indicates that some students are puzzled at this content stage, but they resolve the questions as the class progresses. It shows that the students' learning effect has improved.

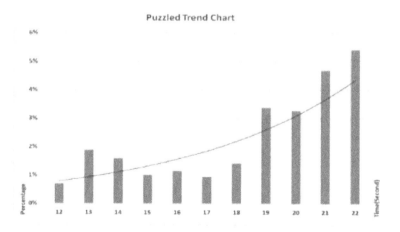

Fig. 6. Puzzled trend chart

4   Verification of Experimental Results

To prove the accuracy of the results, we verify from four aspects: expression monitoring accuracy, overall feedback accuracy, rational analysis, and robustness analysis.

4.1 Expression Monitoring Accuracy

Firstly, we conduct facial expression recognition processing on the collected face videos and obtain the expression data of the six emotions about 14 students. The experiment processes the video data at 30 frames per second, divides the teaching video into three stages, and obtains the frame number of each stage. Finally, the monitored emotional distribution is shown in Fig. 7.

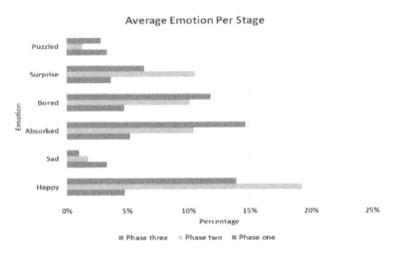

Fig. 7. Average emotion per stage

Secondly, we compare the facial expressions captured by the video with the real emotions of the subjects in the questionnaire and then analyze the accuracy of the experiment. In this experiment, the input video is divided into three stages. The most apparent facial expression detected in each stage is taken as the learning state of the subject in this stage and then compared with the actual learning state of the subject in the questionnaire filled in this stage. Finally, 126 pieces of accurate and monitoring data are collected, and 104 pieces of data are measured according to the learning state. Therefore, it can be concluded that the accuracy rate of facial expression detection in this experiment is 82.5%.

4.2 Overall Feedback Accuracy

After the experiment, we ask each experimenter to fill in their opinion about the difficulty level of the class, which is difficult, moderate, and accessible. We consider sad and puzzling emotions as difficult, happy, surprised, absorbed emotions as moderate, and bored emotions as easy. We compare the real emotion with the monitored emotion and obtain Fig. 8 based on the above criteria.

As shown in Fig. 8, the part of genuine emotion and monitored emotion overlap is accurate, while the non-overlap is inaccurate. The overall feedback accuracy is obtained as 78.57%, so the monitored value is considered accurate.

Number	Truth	Experiment	Result	Number	Truth	Experiment	Result	Number	Truth	Experiment	Result
1	Moderate	Moderate	Accuracy	15	Hard	Hard	Accuracy	29	Hard	Hard	Accuracy
2	Moderate	Moderate	Accuracy	16	Moderate	Moderate	Accuracy	30	Moderate	Moderate	Accuracy
3	Moderate	Moderate	Accuracy	17	Moderate	Moderate	Accuracy	31	Moderate	Moderate	Accuracy
4	Hard	Hard	Accuracy	18	Hard	Hard	Accuracy	32	Hard	Hard	Accuracy
5	Moderate	Moderate	Accuracy	19	Hard	Moderate		33	Hard	Easy	
6	Easy	Moderate		20	Moderate	Moderate	Accuracy	34	Hard	Hard	Accuracy
7	Moderate	Moderate	Accuracy	21	Moderate	Easy		35	Hard	Easy	
8	Easy	Easy	Accuracy	22	Easy	Easy	Accuracy	36	Easy	Easy	Accuracy
9	Hard	Hard	Accuracy	23	Hard	Easy		37	Moderate	Moderate	Accuracy
10	Easy	Moderate		24	Moderate	Moderate	Accuracy	38	Moderate	Moderate	Accuracy
11	Moderate	Moderate	Accuracy	25	Hard	Moderate		39	Moderate	Moderate	Accuracy
12	Hard	Hard	Accuracy	26	Moderate	Moderate	Accuracy	40	Moderate	Moderate	Accuracy
13	Moderate	Easy		27	Easy	Easy	Accuracy	41	Moderate	Moderate	Accuracy
14	Hard	Hard	Accuracy	28	Hard	Hard	Accuracy	42	Moderate	Moderate	Accuracy
Precision Rate					78.6%						

Fig. 8. Accuracy between real emotions and monitoring emotions

4.3 Robustness Analysis

To demonstrate the robustness of the experimental system, we add data with almost zero mood index to the overall data to study the effect on the experimental system before and after adding this kind of data. The interference data used in the experimental system are the student data obtained from real monitoring during the experiment.

As shown in Fig. 9, the comparison graph before and after the addition of the disturbance factor can be seen that its effect on the results is almost negligible. It demonstrates that the present experimental method can effectively avoid the influence of actual disturbing factors and verifies the robustness of the current experimental system.

Fig. 9. Comparison of emotion index before and after adding interference

5 Conclusion

This paper proposes a method to analyze and evaluate students' online learning status based on facial expressions. With facial action unit recognition by the convolutional neural network, this paper gets the emotion index of each frame and calculates the proportion of six emotions: happy, sad, absorbed, bored, surprise, and puzzled. Teachers and students get visual classroom feedback to improve teaching efficiency. A comparative analysis of the user's real emotions and the experimental results show that the method obtains an accuracy rate of 82.5% for emotion monitoring. At the same time, the experimental results remain almost consistent with the addition of distracting factors.

The experimental results show that the method proposed in this paper provides a solution to help teachers adjust their teaching strategies, assist them in supervising students' online learning status, and improve the effectiveness of online teaching. In the future, we will deploy the system in more online teaching platforms to further study classroom feedback with privacy protection.

Acknowledgment. This work was supported by the Beijing Municipal Natural Science Foundation [grant number 4222023]; The general characterization facilities are provided by International Science and Technology Cooperation Base of Electronic System Reliability and Mathematical Interdisciplinary at Capital Normal University.

References

1. Yang, Y.L.: Research on the hybrid online teaching mode based on Super Star platform under the epidemic situation: an example of "military theory" course. J. High. Educ. Res. **42**, 53–60 (2021)
2. Yang, C., Cheng, B.D., Heng, Y.: Differences in knowledge transmission effects between live and online lectures and the influence mechanism. China High. Educ. Res. **42**, 23–29 (2021)
3. Wang, X., Zhang, L., et al.: How online learning resources influence academic emotions and learning outcomes: a meta-analysis based on control-value theory. Mod. Dist. Educ. Res. **35**, 201 (2021)
4. Li, X., Zhang, Y., Tiwari, P., et al.: EEG based Emotion Recognition: A Tutorial and Review. ACM Comput. Surv. (CSUR) **55**, 1–36 (2022)
5. Han, Y.: Building a new teaching support system for higher education with information technology-an analysis based on online teaching practices during the epidemic resistance. High. Educ. Res. **41**, 80–86 (2020)
6. Wang, Z., Zhang, X.L., Liu, Y.Q., Zhou, J.Y., Shan, D.S.: Research on facial action recognition based on EEG sensors. Comput. Eng. Appl. **56**, 182–186 (2020)
7. Zhuang, J., Huang, W.: Design and implementation of intelligent teaching attendance system based on image recognition. In: Proceedings of the 2021 5th International Conference on Electronic Information Technology and Computer Engineering, pp. 516–520 (2021)
8. Han, L., Li, Y., Zhou, Z.J., et al.: Analysis of teaching effectiveness based on facial expressions in the classroom environment. Mod. Dist. Educ. Res. **31**, 103–112 (2017)
9. Zhuang, M.Q., Tan, X.H., et al.: 3D animation expression generation and emotional supervision based on convolutional neural network. J. Chongqing Univ. Technol. **36**, 151–157 (2022)
10. Zhou, Y.Y.: VGG-based face emotion recognition and classification
11. Luo, W.Y., Gong, K., et al.: Analysis of students' listening emotions in video streaming based on facial expression recognition. Mod. Comput. 117–121 (2021)
12. Pan, X.Z., Chen, J., Ma, R.L.: A classroom teaching feedback system based on facial expression recognition. Comput. Syst. Appli. 102–108 (2021)

Short Text Dynamic Clustering Approach for Semantic-Enhanced Knowledge

Mingyou Liu, Yingxue Zhu[(⊠)], and Li Li

School of Biology and Engineering, Guizhou Medical University, Gui'an New District, Guizhou, China
zyx@gmc.edu.cn

Abstract. Traditional text clustering algorithms largely rely on word co-occurrence information in text data to infer the hidden topics. However, due to the limited content length of the short text, the word co-occurrence information in the short text is very scarce, which we call the short text feature sparse problem. In order to solve the feature sparse problem in the dynamic clustering of short texts, and more better capture the dynamic evolution of topics in the dynamic short text data over time, this paper proposed a semantic-enhanced dynamic Dirichlet multinomial Mixture (SDDMM) model with enhanced semantics, which uses the additional semantic knowledge provided by word embedding to assist in improving the effect of short texts' dynamic clustering, at the same time, because the generation of topics in the dynamic clustering process is affected by inherited historical topics, the introduction of semantic knowledge can automatically adjust the strength of topic inheritance, making the dynamic evolution of the number of clusters more in line with the actual data. Experiments on synthetic data and real data show that the SDDMM model effectively improves the short texts' dynamic clustering effect.

Keywords: dynamic clustering · topic model · semantic-enhanced · word embedding · short texts

1 Introduction

With the rise of new media technologies on the Internet, online social media platforms have freed people from the shackles of lack of information, and have become an important platform for disseminating, acquiring and exchanging information. The text data published by social media has some characteristics: large quantity, variety, rapid growth, short length, and strong timeliness. It is called short text dynamic data [1]. It can be captured by mining and analyzing short text dynamic data that include popular news events, academic research hotspots, and topic evolution trends within a certain period of time.

Funded: Provincial Health Commission Science and Technology Foundation of Guizhou (No. gzwkj2023-590), Guizhou Medical University National Natural Science Foundation Cultivation Project (No. 21NSFCP40), National Natural Science Foundation of China (No. 32160668), 2021 Guizhou Medical University "Ideological and political course" Construction Project: (No. 1: SZ2021045, No. 2: SZ2021046), Guizhou Medical University Undergraduate Teaching Content and Curriculum System Reform Project: (No. 3: JG2022029).

2 Model Foundations

2.1 Problem Definition

As documents arrived in different time periods, the number of clusters, cluster labels, etc. will show a dynamic evolution over time. Generally, the dynamic clustering algorithm is essentially a function that satisfies the following conditions f:

$$\mathbf{D}_t = \{..., \mathbf{d}_{t-2}, \mathbf{d}_{t-1}, \mathbf{d}_t\} \xrightarrow{f} \mathbf{C}_t = \{c_1, c_2, ..., c_{K'}\} \tag{1}$$

Among them: $\mathbf{D}_t$ represents the short text dynamic data that arrived before time t (the length of the short text does not exceed 140 words), $\mathbf{d}_t$ is the short text data collection that arrived at the most recent time t, each document in the collection $d = \{w_1, w_2, ..., w_n\}$ is composed of words in the vocabulary $V = \{w_1, w_2, ..., w_V\}$, The length of the document can be different; $\mathbf{C}_t$ is the clustering result of the short text data arriving at time t, c_k which represents the kth cluster, K' which is the total number of clusters, and the actual number of clusters K' in each time period may be not equal.

2.2 GSDMM Model

The GSDMM model is a probabilistic topic model. The model assumes that each document in the data set is generated by a single topic, that is, all words in a document are generated from the same topic distribution. This assumption restricts the short text generation process and effectively improves the short text clustering effect. The generation process of the GSDMM model is as follows:

a) Sample topic distribution $\theta \sim Dirichlet(\alpha)$
b) For each topic $k \in \{1, 2, ..., K\}$

Sample topic-word distribution $\phi_k \sim Dirichlet(\beta)$.

c) For a document $d \in \{1, 2, ..., D\}$

A sample topic $z_d \sim Multinomial(\theta)$, For each word in the document $w \in \{w_{d,1}, w_{d,2}, ..., w_{d,N_d}\}$, Sample word $w \sim Multinomial(\phi_{z_d})$, Using Gibbs sampling algorithm to estimate the hidden parameters $z_d, \theta_z, \phi_{z,w}$ in the model, the results are as follows:

$$p(z_d = k | \mathbf{z}_{\neg d}, \mathbf{d}) \propto \frac{m_{k,\neg d} + \alpha}{D - 1 + K\alpha} \times \frac{\prod_{w \in d} \prod_{j=1}^{N_d^w} (n_{k,\neg d}^w + \beta + j - 1)}{\prod_{i=1}^{N_d} (n_{k,\neg d} + V\beta + i - 1)} \tag{2}$$

$$\theta_z = \frac{m_{k,d} + \alpha}{D - 1 + K\alpha} \tag{3}$$

$$\phi_{z,w} = \frac{n_k^w + \beta}{\sum_w^V n_k^w + V\beta} \tag{4}$$

2.3 Word Embedding to Obtain Semantically Similar Words

Word embedding (word embedding) can provide semantic lexical feature expression, its purpose is to preserve the context information of words in the global corpus, so word embedding can reflect semantic related information, that is to say, words that are semantically similar are mapping to the word vector space regrets more similarity. At the same time, due to the limited number of short text words, it is impossible for words with high semantic similarity to appear together frequently. Therefore, short text features can be expanded through additional global word embedding information, thereby it solves the short text feature sparse problem.

Literature illustrates that words obtained by word embedding can show strong similarities with example words in the literature. The examples in the literature also illustrate that semantically similar words may not appear frequently in short text sets. Therefore, through the auxiliary word embedding learned in a large corpus can effectively improve the effect of short text clustering to obtain semantically similar words.

3 SDDMM Model

The SDDMM model is a dynamic clustering algorithm that extends the GSDMM model to multiple time periods, and introduces a global background semantic knowledge through the GPU model, thereby it improving the probability of a word's semantically similar words appearing under a related topic. This section introduces the model generation process from two aspects: dynamic model construction and GPU model to enhance semantics. Table 1 shows the main symbols and meanings involved in the model generation process.

3.1 Dynamic Model Construction

Based on GSDMM, the SDDMM model assumes that if no new documents arrive in the time period t, and then all the distributions (document-topic distribution, topic-word distribution) remain unchanged from the previous time period t-1. Once there is a new document when the time period t arrives, the Dirichlet prior parameters of the document-topic distribution $\Theta_t = \{\theta_{t,z}\}_{z=1}^{K}$ of the current time period t in the above generation process will be composed of the previous time period distribution Θ_{t-1} and hyper parameters $\alpha_t = \{\alpha_{t,z}\}_{z=1}^{K}$. Similarly, the Dirichlet prior parameters of the topic-word distribution $\Phi_t = \{\phi_{t,z}\}_{z=1}^{K}$ will be composed of the previous the distribution Φ_{t-1} of a time period and the composition of hyper parameters $\beta_t = \{\beta_{t,z}\}_{z=1}^{K}$. Among them: $\theta_{t,z} > 0$ and $\sum_{z=1}^{K} \theta_{t,z} = 1$, K is the number of clusters in the current time period; $\phi_{t,z} = \{\phi_{t,z,w}\}_{w=1}^{V}$ is the word distribution corresponding to the topic z in the t time period, $\phi_{t,z,w} > 0$ and $\sum_{w=1}^{V} \phi_{t,z,w} = 1$, V is the size of the vocabulary in the current time period; among them $\beta_{t,z} = \{\beta_{t,z,w}\}_{w=1}^{V}$.

Table 1. Main notation Used

symbol	Paraphrase
d, z, w	Document, subject, word
t	time
K	Number of initial clusters
$K*$	Actual estimated number of clusters
V	Dictionary size
d_t	Document set in time slice t
N_d	Number of words in document d
$N_{d,w}$	Number of word w occurrences in document d
Θ_t, Φ_t	word distribution in time slice t
α_t, β_t	Dirichlet prior hyper parameters
M_w	The semantic similarity matrix of word w
$A_{w,w'}$	Semantic enhancement matrix of word w
μ	Enhanced weight

In the SDDMM model, the dynamic clustering model is constructed by assuming that the document-topic distribution and topic-word distribution in the current time period t depend on the distribution in the previous time period. Therefore, given the Dirichlet prior parameters $\alpha_t \Theta_{t-1}$, the obtained Θ_t conditional distribution is as follows:

$$P(\Theta_t|\Theta_{t-1}, \alpha_t) \propto \prod_{z=1}^{K} \theta_{t,z}^{(a_{t,z}\theta_{t-1,z})-1} \qquad (5)$$

Similarly, given the Dirichlet prior parameters $\beta_t \Phi_{t-1}$, the word distribution corresponding $\phi_{t,z}$ to each topic is as follows:

$$P(\phi_{t,z}|\phi_{t-1,z}, \beta_{t,z}) \propto \prod_{w=1}^{V} \phi_{t,z,w}^{(\beta_{t,z,w}\phi_{t-1,z,w})-1} \qquad (6)$$

3.2 GPU Model Enhanced Semantics

SDDMM enhances the semantically similar words of the text to a certain topic through the GPU model. The GPU model has been verified to have a good performance in improving the effect of Gibbs sampling, and is widely used in the semantic enhancement of the topic model use the GPU model for the SDDMM model to enhance semantics is mainly reflected as follows:

First, given a pre-trained word embedding (word vector), the cosine similarity between the word embedding of two words w and w' is used as a semantic similarity score. The score can be expressed as $sim(w, w')$, and then all construct a semantic similar word vector M_w with the words whose score of the current sampled word w is greater than the set threshold ε, that is $M_w = \{\langle w, w_z \rangle | sim(w, w_z) > \varepsilon\}$, the enhancement weight of the semantic similar words of each word is set through the enhancement matrix A, and the expression of the enhancement matrix is as shown in formula (7):

$$A_{w,w'} = \begin{cases} 1, & w = w' \\ \mu, & w' \in M_w \text{ and } w \neq w' \\ 0, & \text{other} \end{cases} \tag{7}$$

The above formula means: the number of co-occurrences of each word in the semantically similar word vector M_w will increase by μ ($0 < \mu < 1$) times; when the sampled word itself is enhanced, the number of co-occurrences will increase by 1; in other cases, no change occurs.

Secondly, since the SDDMM model assumes that all words appearing in a text belong to the same topic, but in fact, some words in the text are not related to the topic, and this type of words semantic enhancement will affect the aggregation of the model. Therefore, in the Gibbs sampling process of time period t, for each word w in the document $d \in \mathbf{d}_t$, an indicator variable $S_{d,w}$ is constructed according to the distribution probability of w under the current topic z_d to determine whether the word should be semantically enhanced. The enhancement strategy is shown as in formula (8):

$$S_{d,w} \sim Bernoulli(\lambda_{w,z_d}) \tag{8}$$

The calculation of the parameter sin formula (8) λ_{w,z_d} is shown in formula (9):

$$\lambda_{w,z_d} = \frac{p(z_d|w)}{p_{\max}(z'_d|w)} \tag{9}$$

It can be seen from Eqs. (8) and (9) that when the probability of word w being assigned to the topic z_d is greater, and the topic of document d is determined to be z_d, then the GPU model is more likely to be used to enhance the semantics of word w.

Finally, for the word w (when $S_{d,w} = 1$) that needs to be enhanced in the text d in the current period t, the semantic similar word matrix M_w of w is used to enhance the count $\tilde{n}_{t,z} \leftarrow \tilde{n}_{t,z,\neg d} + N_d \cdot A_{w,w'}$ under topic z, and the semantic similar words $w' \in M_w$ are assigned to the count $\tilde{n}_{t,z,w'} \leftarrow \tilde{n}_{t,z,w',\neg d} + N_{d,w} \cdot A_{w,w'}$ under topic z. Among them: $\tilde{n}_{t,z}$ represents the total number of words corresponding to the topic z in the current time period t, $\tilde{n}_{t,z,w'}$ represents the total number of words w with the topic z in the current time period t and the total number of semantically similar words in the word w, N_d represents the number of words in the document d, and $N_{d,w}$ represents the word w the number of occurrences in document d.

3.3 Model Derivation

The SDDMM model proposed in this paper is based on the GSDMM model in a single time period t. The semantic similar words of the document words are introduced through the GPU model to enhance the semantic knowledge. At the same time, the model parameters in the current time period are also compared with the previous time period. The

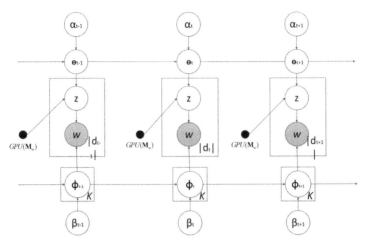

Fig. 1. Graphical representation of SDDMM model

parameters are deduced, and the model in a single time period is extended to multiple time periods, thereby realizing the dynamic construction of the model. The probability generation diagram of the model is shown in Fig. 1.

A split Gibbs sampling algorithm is used to derive the SDDMM model parameters. It is assumed that the document-topic distribution Θ_{t-1} and topic-word distribution Φ_{t-1} in the previous time period $t-1$ are known, and the initialization $t = 0$, the two parameters are set as: $\theta_{0,z} = 1 / K, \phi_{0,z,w} = 1 / V$. According to the generation process of SDDMM model deduced:

1) The generation probability of the topic z assignment of word w in the current time period t changes from Eq. (10) to:

$$p(z_d = k | \mathbf{z}_{t,\neg d}, \mathbf{d}_t, \Phi_{t-1}, \Theta_{t-1}, \alpha_t, \beta_t) \propto$$

$$\frac{m_{t,z} + \alpha_{t,z}\theta_{t-1,z} - 1}{\sum_{z=1}^{K} (m_{t,z} + \alpha_{t,z}\theta_{t-1,z}) - 1} \times \frac{\prod_{w \in d} \prod_{j=1}^{N_{d,w}} (\tilde{n}_{t,z,w,\neg d} + \beta_{t,z,w}\phi_{t-1,z,w} + j - 1)}{\prod_{i=1}^{N_d} (\tilde{n}_{t,z,\neg d} + i - 1 + \sum_{w=1}^{V} \beta_{t,z,w}\phi_{t-1,z,w})} \tag{10}$$

2) The document-topic distribution $\Theta_t = \{\theta_{t,z}\}_{z=1}^{K}$ in the current time period t is Eq. (11):

$$\theta_{t,z} = \frac{m_{t,z} + \alpha_{t,z}\theta_{t-1,z}}{\sum_{z=1}^{K} m_{t,z} + \alpha_{t,z}\theta_{t-1,z}} \tag{11}$$

3) Topic-word distribution in the current time period t is Eq. (12):

$$\phi_{t,z,w} = \frac{\tilde{n}_{t,z,w} + \beta_{t,z,w}\phi_{t-1,z,w}}{\tilde{n}_{t,z} + \sum_{w=1}^{V} \beta_{t,z,w}\phi_{t-1,z,w}} \tag{12}$$

In formula (10): if the indicator variable $S_{d,w} = 1$ is used to enhance semantically similar words using the GPU model, after the text d arrives, the total number of words corresponding to the current time period t subject z is updated as: $\tilde{n}_{t,z} \leftarrow \tilde{n}_{t,z,\neg d} + N_d \cdot A_{w,w'}$, and the current time period t subject is w of word z, its semantically similar words is: $\tilde{n}_{t,z,w} \leftarrow \tilde{n}_{t,z,w,\neg d} + N_{d,w} \cdot A_{w,w'}$, $\neg d$ means that all counts in document d are excluded from the total count in the current time period t; otherwise, the GPU model is not used to enhance the semantics. See algorithm 2 for the detailed process. $m_{t,z}$ represent the number of documents $\mathbf{d}_t$ with subject z in the document set. Algorithm 1 gives the detailed process of Gibbs sampling algorithm of SDDMM model in time period t.

Algorithm 1: Gibbs Sampling for SDDMM

Input: "document-topic" distribution Θ_{t-1} of the previous time slice; "topic-word" distribution Φ_{t-1} of the previous time slice; semantically similar word vector M_w; short text set and d_t in time window t; initialized α_t, β_t, μ, ε; Algorithm iteration number I.

Output: document and its category label; current document topic distribution Θ_t; current topic word distribution Φ_t.

1). Initialize the d_t parameters m_{t,z_d}, n_{t,z_d}, $n_{t,z_d,w}$ to 0

2). for each document $d \in \mathbf{d}_t$ do $L=\text{Multinominal}(1/K)$

3). $z_d \leftarrow L$

4). $m_{t,z_d} \leftarrow m_{t,z_d} + 1$

5). $n_{t,z_d} \leftarrow n_{t,z_d} + N_d$

6).   for each word $w \in d$ do

7). $n_{t,z_d,w} \leftarrow n_{t,z_d,w} + N_{d,w}$

8). $S_{d,w} \leftarrow 0$

9). for iteration=1 to I   do

10).   for each document $d \in \mathbf{d}_t$ do

11).   Record the category label $z = z_d$

12). $m_{t,z_d} \leftarrow m_{t,z_d} - 1$

13). $n_{t,z_d} \leftarrow n_{t,z_d} - N_d$

14).   for each word $w \in d$ do

15).   Update ($S_{d,w}$, A, d, w, False)

16).   Sampling from equation (10) to get zd

17). $m_{t,z_d} \leftarrow m_{t,z_d} + 1$

18).   for each word $w \in d$ do

19). $S_{d,w} \leftarrow S_{d,w} - \text{Bernoulli}(\lambda_{w,z_d})$

20).   Update ($S_{d,w}$, A, d, w, True)

21). Calculation parameters Θ_t and Φ_t

Algorithm 2: Update ($S_{d,w}$, A, d, w, Flag)

1). if Flag == true then

2).   if $S_{d,w} == 1$ then

3).   for each semantically similar word $w' \in \mathbf{M}_w$ do

4). $\tilde{n}_{t,z} \leftarrow \tilde{n}_{t,z,-d} + N_d \cdot \mathbf{A}_{w,w'}$

5). $\tilde{n}_{t,z,w} \leftarrow \tilde{n}_{t,z,w,-d} + N_{d,w} \cdot \mathbf{A}_{w,w'}$

6).   else

7). $\tilde{n}_{t,z} \leftarrow \tilde{n}_{t,z,-d} + 1$

8). $\tilde{n}_{t,z,w} \leftarrow \tilde{n}_{t,z,w,-d} + 1$

9). else

10). if $S_{d,w} == 1$ then

11).   for each semantically similar word $w' \in \mathbf{M}_w$ do

12). $\tilde{n}_{t,z} \leftarrow \tilde{n}_{t,z,-d} - N_d \cdot \mathbf{A}_{w,w'}$

13). $\tilde{n}_{t,z,w} \leftarrow \tilde{n}_{t,z,w,-d} - N_{d,w} \cdot \mathbf{A}_{w,w'}$

14). else

15). $\tilde{n}_{t,z} \leftarrow \tilde{n}_{t,z,-d} - 1$

16). $\tilde{n}_{t,z,w} \leftarrow \tilde{n}_{t,z,w,-d} - 1$

4 Experiments and Results

4.1 Evaluation Index

Normalized mutual information (NMI) and clustering purity (Purity) are used as the evaluation indicators of clustering effect.

NMI is an external clustering metric that can effectively evaluate the amount of statistical information shared by variables randomly assigned, it come from model clustering and actual categories marked by users. The calculation of NMI is as follows:

$$NMI(X, Y) = \frac{I(X, Y)}{[H(X)+H(Y)]/2} = 2 \frac{\sum_i \sum_j \frac{|x_i \cap y_j|}{N} \log \frac{N|x_i \cap y_j|}{|x_i||y_j|}}{-\left(\sum_i \frac{|x_i|}{N} \log \frac{|x_i|}{N} + \sum_j \frac{|x_j|}{N} \log \frac{|x_j|}{N}\right)} \quad (13)$$

In the formula, N is the total amount of data in a given data set, the category result of the training output is $X = \{x_1, x_2, \cdots, x_N\}$, and the standard actual category label is $Y = \{y_1, \cdots, y_N\}$. The value of NMI is between 0 and 1. The higher of the value, the more consistent of the output clustering and actual category, and the better of the clustering effect.

Purity is a simple and easy to implement cluster evaluation standard. In order to calculate the Purity value, the category with the largest sample size in each cluster is taken as the category represented by the cluster, then the number of correctly allocated categories is calculated, and then it divided by the total number of samples. The calculation expression is as follows:

$$purity(\Omega, C) = \frac{1}{N} \sum_k \max_j |w_k \cap c_j| \quad (14)$$

In the formula, N is the total number of samples, K is the number of clusters, $\Omega = \{w_1, \cdots, w_K\}$ is the clustering result set, and $C = \{c_1, \cdots c_j\}$ is the actual clustering set. The Purity value is between 0 and 1. The closer to 1, the better the clustering results.

4.2 Data Set

This paper will test our proposed method on one simulated data set and two real data sets.

Simulation data set TSet-T: The simulation data set used here comes from the TSet data set. Since the original data cannot express the chronological relationship between the documents, the data set is manually reconstructed, some of the data is intercepted and it is mapped to three time periods, and the data is mainly composed of 3000 (1000 documents/time period) documents in twenty-three categories (category labels 1–23).

Real data set: Twitter is one of the most widely used social media in the world. Its content is usually in the form of short texts, and the content changes over time, so use the twitter data set (https://archive.org/details/twitterstream) to verify Model validity.

4.3 Experimental Results and Analysis

Pre-training Word Vector. Each data set uses a 300-dimensional word vector (https://code.google.com/p/word2vec) pre-trained on the Google News corpus containing 100 billion words for semantic enhancement.

Compare Models and Parameter Settings. For each experimental data set, set the hyper parameters $\alpha_t = 0.5$, $\beta_t = 0.5$ in each time period; The maximum number of clusters K = 30; the number of iterations I = 1000; the semantic enhancement value $\mu = 0.1$ and the similarity threshold $\varepsilon = 0.5$, the setting of these two parameters is detailed in reference. In the experiment, the SDDMM model was compared with OSDMD model; DCT model, DMM model and DTM model to verify the effectiveness of the model. The SDDMM model is equivalent to the DCT model when the semantic enhancement value is $\mu = 0$.

Experimental Results. Performed twenty times independent experiments on the TSet-T data set to obtain the NMI value and Purity of SDDMM and each comparison model in each time slice, and averaged them to find that under the same parameter settings, the NMI of SDDMM value and Purity value are higher than other models, which means that the SDDMM model effectively improves the dynamic clustering effect of short texts by introducing semantic knowledge.

Experimental Results and Analysis of Real Data Sets. The same experimental settings as the simulation data set experiment were performed on the two sets of real data sets. The results obtained show that the NMI and Purity values of SDDMM are higher than those of other models. The clustering effect of the SDDMM model is better after the introduction of semantic knowledge. At the same time, the SDDMM model can obtain the number of clusters in each time period, and can effectively capture the dynamic changes of the number of clusters. As shown in Fig. 2, the SDDMM model is used for cluster analysis on the Twitter2016 data set at each time. The number of clusters estimated in each iteration of the segment.

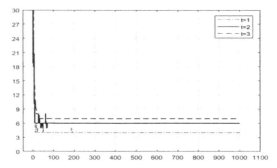

Fig. 2. Estimation of the number of clusters by SDDMM model with each iteration on Twitter2016 data set

The above experimental results show that the SDDMM model can effectively improve the dynamic clustering effect of short texts, and at the same time can capture the dynamic evolution of the number of clusters over time, so the model has a good dynamic clustering performance. As a result of the enhancement of semantics, the word cloud representation information shown in Fig. 3 shows that "coronaviru" and "covid" appear more frequently in the data set, and there is no information of this type of word in the pre-trained word vector, When the model performs semantic enhancement, it has no effect on this type of words, which leads to the insignificant improvement of the dynamic clustering effect. In summary, the dynamic clustering of short texts in a dynamic semantic environment will be considered in the subsequent work.

Fig. 3. Word cloud display of Twitter2020 data set

5 Summary

This research proposes a dynamic clustering method with enhanced semantics for short text dynamic data. Due to the limited number of short text words, it leads to the problem of feature sparseness, which makes the traditional dynamic clustering algorithm clustering poorly. The proposed method enhances the semantic similarity of words by introducing word embedding, and effectively solves this problem. At the same time, the model uses semantic information as background knowledge, which effectively improves the text clustering effect. The experimental results show that the short text dynamic clustering algorithm proposed in this paper has a better clustering performance.

Acknowledgments. We would like to thanks the Funded Project: Provincial Health Commission Science and Technology Foundation of Guizhou (No. Gzwkj2023–590), Guizhou Medical University National Natural Science Foundation Cultivation Project (No. 21NSFCP40), 2021 Guizhou Medical University "Ideological and political course" Construction Project: (Project Number 1: SZ2021045, Project Number 2: SZ2021046), and also thanks the members of the project team for their efforts in the development of the project.

References

1. Zhao, Y.: Research on Topic Model and its Application in Short Text Flow. Shandong University, Jinan (2017)
2. Huang, J., Li, P., Peng, M., et al.: Research on topic model based on deep learning. Chin. J. Comput. **43**(05), 827–855 (2020)
3. Zhou, X., Ouyang, J., Li, X.: Two time-efficient gibbs sampling inference algorithms for biterm topic model. Appl. Intell. **48**(3), 730–754 (2018)
4. Liang, S., Yilmaz, E., Kanoulas, E.: Dynamic clustering of streaming short documents. In: Proceedings of the 22nd ACM SIGKDD International Conference on Knowledge Discovery and Data Mining (KDD 2016), pp. 995–1004. ACM, New York (2016)
5. Liang, S., Ren, Z., Yilmaz, E., et al.: Collaborative user clustering for short text streams. In: Proceedings of the 31st AAAI Conference on Artificial Intelligence, pp. 3504–3510. ACM, New York (2017)
6. Peng, M., Yang, S., Zhu, J.: Topic modeling based on two-way LSTM semantic enhancement. J. Chin. Inf. Process. **32**(04), 40–49 (2018)
7. Gao, W., Peng, M., Wang, H., et al.: Incorporating word embeddings into topic modeling of short text. Knowl. Inf. Syst. **61**(2), 1123–1145 (2019)
8. Kumar, J., Shao, J., Uddin, S., et al.: An online semantic-enhanced Dirichlet model for short text stream clustering. In: Proceedings of the 58th Annual Meeting of the Association for Computational Linguistics, pp. 766–776. ACL, Stroudsburg (2020)

An Improved Perspective Transformation and Subtraction Operation for PCB Defect Detection

Guifang Shao[1]([⊠]) [iD], Qiao Sun[2], Fengqiang Gao[1] [iD], Tundong Liu[1], Jincai Luo[1], and Yubin Wei[1]

[1] Xiamen University, Xiamen 361005, FJ, China
gfshao@xmu.edu.cn
[2] University of Calgray, Calgary, AB T2N 1N4, Canada

Abstract. Defects appeared in the printed circuit board (PCB) will pose a serious damage on the following procedure. Image based inspection methods have been proposed to improve the efficiency and reliability of PCB defect detection compared to manual inspection. The machine learning and deep learning detection methods are popular one, however, they are complex, time consumption and require lots of labeled samples. Thus, we conduct the PCB defect detection and classification by using the template-based algorithm. To realize an accurate registration, the region of interest (ROI) among input image is first computed by utilizing the Grab Cut method. Furthermore, to ensure the complete overlap of feature points between the test image and template image, a perspective transformation based on four vertexes calculating is introduced. Once the different shape and posture images are transformed into a uniform imaging plane, a subtraction operation is used to extract the features of various defects. Experiments on a public data set prove the efficiency of our proposed method.

Keywords: PCB · Defect Detection · Perspective Transformation · Subtraction Operation · Image Registration

1 Introduction

Recently, various electronic products are widely used in daily life, such as air conditioner, cellphone and remote controller [1]. In all these applications, the printed circuit board (PCB) is an essential component. There is also a trend on PCB design with more complicated internal circuit and thinner appearance, which result in a higher quality demand on PCB production.

In fact, the manufacturing of PCB is too complex to ensure the quality of thousands of circuits and welding spots. Once the open circuit or short defects appeared in some circuit, the PCB may be out of use, even arouse severe defects, such as the components destroyed, welding point leakage welding and continuous welding [2]. The common defect in PCB is usually including welding points defect and circuit defect. Figure 1 shows the examples of different defects with various features. The first three rows illustrate the real defects in PCB images and the fourth row is the simulated diagram of some ideal defects. Obviously, there is a great challenge on PCB detect detection due to the same defect with various shapes and multiple defects occurred in one image. Thus, a useful method is needed to deal with different defects simultaneously.

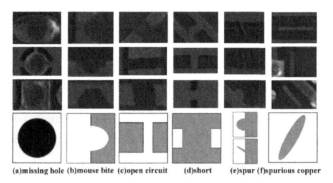

(a)missing hole (b)mouse bite (c)open circuit   (d)short   (e)spur (f)spurious copper

Fig. 1. Example of six types of defects.

In the past, the PCB defect detection is mainly depended on human visualization, and the detection precision will be affected by human experience, emotion and work efficiency. To improve the production efficiency of large-scale assembly line and avoid the hand touching problem, the automated optical inspection (AOI) system is developed [3], which consists of hardware system and image-based software system, as shown in Fig. 2.

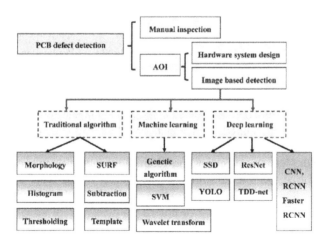

Fig. 2. The classification of PCB defect detection methods.

Once the PCB image is captured by the hardware system, three types of methods can be used to detect defects [4] and image captured from various sensors can also be used [5]. One is the traditional image processing method based on feature extraction or template operation. Here, PCB defects can be detected according to different image features, including gray histogram and geometric features [6], adaptive thresholding segmentation [7], SIFT [8] and SURF [9] features. As the PCB image is so complex that defect detection based on image processing without any reference is quite complicated and time consumption. Therefore, the template-based method is proposed, it is simple but requires a much higher registration accuracy [10]. Another method is based on machine learning algorithms, such as genetic algorithm [11], SVM [12] and wavelet transform [13]. This method doesn't require any reference information and extracts features automatically, as it usually depends on iterative computation, it is complex and large time consumption. The last one is deep learning-based method, including TDD-net [14], YOLO [15], ResNet [16, 17], SSD [18], and so on. These methods require a large amount of defect sample images and most need predefined label to train the network. As they can learn from standard information, there is a better performance of deep learning-based method. However, there exist a severe unbalance ratio between positive (normal) and negative (defective) samples in industrial applications, which will result in a great challenge on deep learning method. Therefore, some pioneering works have been done to build public PCB data sets, such as the DeepPCB [19] and the PKU-Market-PCB [20], the detail information of these two data sets are illustrated in Table 1.

Table 1. Information of public PCB data sets.

Data Set	Year	Image numbers	Resolution/Pixel	Defect Types
PKU-Market-PCB	2018	1386	4608 * 3456	Missing hole, mouse bite, open circuit, short, spur, spurious copper
DeepPCB	2019	1500	16000 * 16000	Pin-hole, mousebite, open, short, spur, copper

As there are a few PCB defect images can be captured in real application and a real-time defect detection is required, the template-based method is used in this paper. To improve the computation efficiency, the ROI is extracted based on Grab Cut method. To further improve the detection precision, the test image and template image are first registering by using the perspective transform, and the features are extracted with subtraction operation.

2   Methodology

To precisely detect the PCB image defects, there are two main operations involved in our proposed method. One is the image registration, which maps the captured PCB image into a uniform size and posture. Another is the defect detection based on subtraction operation and defect classification according to feature extraction.

2.1 Image Registration with Improved Perspective Transformation

During industrial application, there is a common problem aroused by camera capturing procedure, that is the image shift problem in imaging plane. This image coordinates changing phenomenon is attributed to the varied placing positions of PCB, which will result in the registration failure between the template image and the testing image. Therefore, we put forward an improved perspective transformation to transfer the captured varied PCB images into the fixed size and shape in image pixel coordinate system. As shown in Fig. 3, there are five operations in the proposed method. First of all, the input image is binarized by Otsu method to reduce the image data and improve the computation efficiency. Then, the Grab Cut method is introduced to overcome the large ROI extraction area problem. Furthermore, the contour and vertex are computed according to Canny edge detection algorithm. In addition, to reduce the position error between the template and the test ROI, a traversal algorithm on four vertexes in minimum external rectangle is utilized to extract the four feature points. Finally, the perspective transformation is used for transferring the PCB part into original image size.

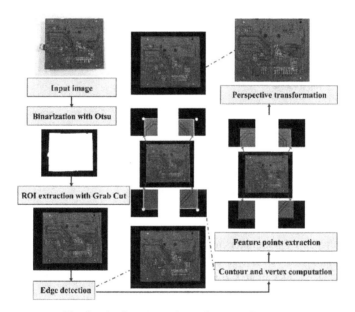

Fig. 3. The flowchart of PCB image registration.

Usually, the camera is put far away from the object and some useless background will be captured. To avoid the affection of these background on the computation and precision of feature points detection, ROI extraction is quite important. As there are some components in various sizes welt on the back of PCB, and some may be too big to extended to the outside of PCB, result in a large error on extracting the minimum external rectangle by using the Otsu thresholding. Thus, to meet the requirement of detection, Grab Cut method is utilized for the ROI extraction. The PCB undirected graph model is built, as shown in Fig. 4. Here, the texture and edge information of PCB image are utilized to extract a more accurate ROI. Grab Cut is an interactive image segmentation algorithm based on graph cut and the maximum flow technology, in which the minimum circumscribed rectangular box of PCB main part is only required as the prior knowledge for image segmentation.

In the undirected graph, imagine that there are virtual edges connecting two adjacent pixels in original PCB image, thus we can explore the minimum energy cut edge by the following energy formula,

$$E(p, k, \theta, z) = \sum_i D(p_i, k_i, \theta, z_i) + V(p, z) \tag{1}$$

In which, $D(p_i, k_i, \theta, z_i)$ denotes the probability negative logarithm that one pixel i can be classified into PCB main part or background, $V(p, z)$ represents the boundary energy term as the penalty term that can describe the discontinuity between two adjacent pixels m and n.

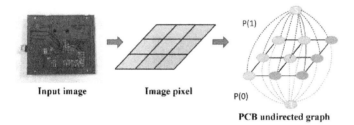

Input image   **Image pixel**   **PCB undirected graph**

Fig. 4. The PCB undirected graph.

According to the Gaussian probability density model, the PCB undirected graph model area term can be defined as

$$D(p_i, k_i, \theta, z_i) = -\log \pi (p_i, k_i) + \frac{1}{2} \log|\Sigma (p_i, k_i)| + \frac{1}{2} \left[z_i - \mu(p_i, k_i)\right]^T \Sigma(p_i, k_i)^{-1} \left[z_{i-}\mu(p_i, k_i)\right] \tag{2}$$

In which, there are 3 parameters in our built PCB main part Gaussian mixture model, one is the weights π for each Gaussian component, another is 3D mean vector μ and the other is the covariance matrix Σ of size 3×3.

$$\theta = \{\pi(p, k), \mu(p, k), \Sigma(p, k), p = 0, 1, k = 1, 2 \dots K\} \tag{3}$$

As the energy will be small when the information between two adjacent pixels varies greatly, Euclidean distance can be used to measure the similarity between two adjacent pixels, and the boundary energy term can be denoted as

$$V(p, z) = C \sum_{(m,n) \in N} \left[p_m \neq p_n\right] exp - \beta z_m - z_n^2 \tag{4}$$

In which, z_m and z_n are the pixel vector of two adjacent pixels, β is an adjust parameter to adapt to the image contrast variation, and a larger value is needed for lower contrast image to magnify its difference. C is a constant and its value is 50.

Furthermore, to reduce the affection of various postures on defect detection, the perspective transformation is utilized to map the extracted ROI into one a uniform pixel coordinate system. Meanwhile, four vertexes in PCB main part are chose as the feature points required by perspective transformation.

To simply the computation, we only extract the maximum edge contour by the following four operations. First is image binarization and filtering with mathematical morphological operation. Then, Canny edge detection is used to obtain the external contour of PCB main part. Subsequently, a minimum external rectangle is obtained. Finally, four vertexes of PCB main part are computed according to the theory that one PCB vertex is nearest to its minimum external rectangle vertex, as shown in Fig. 5. Find the point with the smallest distance from the four vertices of the image edge, which is the vertex of the PCB. The Euclidean distance in the image pixel coordinate system is used to evaluate the distance. Therefore, we can use these four vertexes of PCB main part as the feature points of perspective transformation.

$$d\left(E_i, C_{roi,j}\right) = \sqrt{\left(E_i(x) - C_{roi,j}(x)\right)^2 + \left(E_i(y) - C_{roi,j}(y)\right)^2} \tag{5}$$

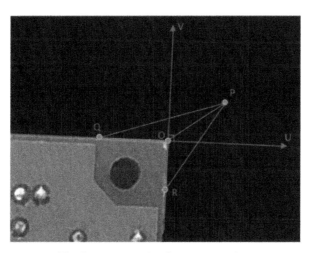

Fig. 5. The example of vertex extraction.

2.2 Defect Detection with Improved Subtraction Operation

To avoid the contrast variation in different PCB images, the histogram equalization is utilized to realize image contrast enhancement. Then the subtraction operation can be applied for the template image and test image, to extract the possible defective area. But this operation can only detect the growth type defects. Thus, a bool flag is introduced to describe the growth type and reduced type defects, respectively. What's more, the defect ROI is extracted to remove the redundant information interference. Here, a minimum external rectangle with rotation angle is used again to detect the defective area, as shown in Fig. 6. Here, it starts from the zero degree angle and does the counterclockwise rotation. And the angle that first touch the rectangle is defined as the rotate angle of the rectangle, at the same time, the first contacted edge is identified as a long edge, another edge is thus the short edge, as shown in Table 2.

Fig. 6. The examples of minimum external rectangle with rotation angle.

Table 2. The minimum external rectangle of defect with rotate angle.

Defect No.	Central coordinate of external rectangle (pix)	Rotate angle of external rectangle (°)	FLAG
1	[637.057,685.004]	47.976	reduced type 0
2	[721.374, 1593.070]	61.265	reduced type 0
3	[780.271,446.104]	43.569	growth type 1
4	[1197.160,1455.120]	45.053	growth type 1
5	[1370.980,441.519]	89.982	reduced type 0
6	[1507.940,1457.980]	88.663	growth type 1
7	[1613.020,1491.560]	0.208	growth type 1
8	[1637.470,1780.470]	0.013	reduced type 0
9	[1793.000,898.742]	12.308	reduced type 0
10	[1848.570,179.946]	24.060	growth type 1

To further determine the type of PCB defect and eliminate information interference outside the defect area, the image mask is used to extract the ROI of the detective part. Here, the minimum external rectangle with rotate angle is utilized to build the mask. What's more, to make use of the feature information around defects for determining defect types, the size of mask is set as the 1.5 times of the minimum external rectangle.

To classify the defect types, the circle similarity is defined as follows,

$$s = \frac{dist}{lS_{roi}}, \text{dist} = \sum_{i=0}^{n} distance\left(C_{ROI}^{i}, O_{ROI}\right) \qquad (5)$$

In which, C_{ROI} denotes the pixel set in external contour of defective area, and there are l pixels in this set. O_{ROI} is the centre of the minimum external circle that around the defective area, S_{roi} is the elementary area of input image.

Finally, various defect types can be classified according to the following rules and its flowchart as shown Fig. 7.

Rule 1: the missing hole defect is the only one welding points defect, it belongs to reduced type defect and its shape is similar to circle, and its gray value may be larger due to there are some solder around it.

Rule 2: the mouse bite defect is one circuit defect with semicircle shape, it also belongs to the reduced type defect.

Rule 3: the short defect is a common circuit defect and always in rectangle shape, it usually connects two adjacent circuits and belongs to the growth type defect.

Rule 4: the spurious copper defect is a growth type defect and normally appeared around the circuit.

Rule 5: the open circuit defect is also a popular circuit defect and among two circuits.

Rule 6: the spur defect is a special circuit defect with rectangle or semicircle shapes, it also belongs to the growth type defect.

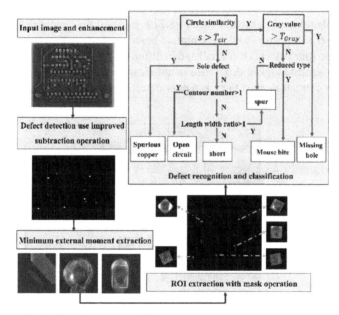

Fig. 7. The flowchart of PCB defect detection and classification.

3   Experiments and Discussion

3.1   Experiment Setting

To verify the efficiency of our proposed method, the data is drawn from a PKU-Market-PCB data set published by the Open Lab on Human Robot Interaction of Peking University. There are 1386 PCB images including 6 types of defects, here we randomly choose 534 PCB images [19]. All experiments are conducted on the Intel(R) Core(TM) i3–4160 CPU @ 3.60GHz with RAM 8.00 GB. Programs are built on Microsoft Visual Studio 2015 and opencv320. The precision and recall are utilized to evaluate the proposed method, here the recall is defined as the ratio between the defects number that are correctly detected and the total detects number, the precision is defined as the ratio of correctly detect defects number with all the defects number that are detected.

3.2   Experiment Results and Discussion

Figure 8 shows the defect detection result of our proposed method, and Table 2 shows the detail result of recall. As the PCB image is too complex and the defects are too small, even several defects appeared in one image, it is difficult to reach a 100% accuracy. From Fig. 8 we can see that there are some defects can't be detected correctly. However, no matter what defect it is, once there is a defect occurs, this PCB should be picked out and need a further consideration. Sometimes, although we can't detect all the defects in one PCB, each PCB containing defects or not can be confirmed. What's more, it can be seen from Table 3 that there is a highest recall 98.77% on spurious copper defect detection due to its bigger size feature and the template-based feature extraction in our method. However, as the spur defect is too small and in different shapes, such as circle shape and strip shape, its morphological difference is not clear result in it is prone to be ignored during contour extraction, thus there is a poor detection recall only 85.16%.

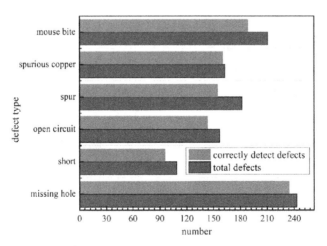

Fig. 8.   The PCB defect detection results.

Table 3. Defect Detection Results on Recall.

Defect Types	Total Defects Number	Correct Detect Defect Number	Recall
Missing hole	243	235	96.71%
Short	109	96	88.07%
Open circuit	157	144	91.72%
Spur	182	155	85.16%
Spurious copper	163	161	98.77%
Mouse bite	211	189	89.57%

To further prove the efficiency of our proposed method, the precision is computed as shown in Table 4. As the missing hole defect is detected according to the gray value of pixels surrounding it, so it is easy to judge and we can classify it fully success. However, the classification of open circuit defect is worst, its detection precision is about 89.44%. The reason is the feature of open circuit defect is similar to that of spurious copper defect, thus it is hard to classify them correctly when disturbed by surrounding circuits.

Table 4. Defect Detection Results on Precision.

Defect types	Total defect detect number	Correct detect defect number	Precision
Missing hole	235	235	100.00%
Short	97	96	98.97%
Open circuit	161	144	89.44%
Spur	173	155	89.60%
Spurious copper	168	161	95.83%
Mouse bite	203	189	90.14%

Figure 9 illustrates the examples of false detection and leak detection. It can be seen that two spurious copper defects are detected successfully by our method, as the pink rectangle of top two images in the middle column shown. As the spurious defect is similar to the circuit, there will be a false detection once affected by the surrounding circuits. For example, as shown inf Fig. 9c, the interval between these two spurious copper defects is taken as open circuit defect falsely. It is mainly attribute to the situation that it is too close between two spurious copper defects, which result in a similar feature between the open circuit defect and the interval part of two spurious copper defects. In addition, there will be a leak detection if the defect is too small to be detected.

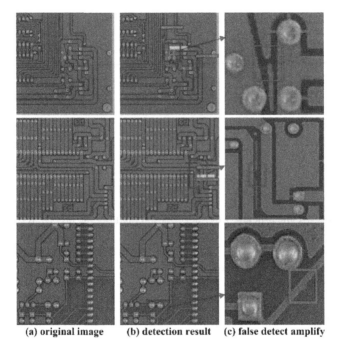

(a) original image   (b) detection result   (c) false detect amplify

Fig. 9. Examples of false detection and leak detection in our method. The detection result of open circuit is in green color and spurious cooper in pink color.

4   Conclusions

PCB is widely applied in various equipment and electronic devices. The defects detection of PCB plays an import role in industrial product quality control. To improve the precision and computation efficiency, here we make use of template-based method. First, the ROI is extracted by using Grab Cut and image registration based on perspective transformation is introduced. Then, the features of various defect are detected according to subtraction operation. Finally, different defects are classified based on feature matching according to six predefined rules. Experiments result on the public PCB dataset prove the efficiency of our proposed method. However, it is also need to be further improved owing to the false detection and leak detection.

Acknowledgements. This work was supported by the Natural Science Foundation of Xiamen under Grant 3502Z20227189.

References

1. Ling, Z.G., Zhang, A., Ma, D., Shi, Y.X., Wen, H.: Deep siamese semantic segmentation network for PCB welding defect detection. IEEE Trans. Instrum. Meas. **71**, 5006511 (2022)

2. Mamidi, J.S.S.V., Sameer, S., Bayana, J.: A light weight version of PCB defect detection system using YOLO V4 Tiny. In: 2022 International Mobile and Embedded Technology Conference (MECON), Noida, India, pp. 441–445 (2022)
3. Li, Z., Yang, Q.: System design for PCB defects detection based on AOI technology. In: 2011 4th International Congress on Image and Signal Processing, Shanghai, China, pp. 1988–1991 (2011)
4. Borthakur, M., Latne, A., Kulkarni, P.: A comparative study of automated pcb defect detection algorithms and to propose an optimal approach to improve the technique. Int. J. Comput. Appli. **114**(6), 27–33 (2015)
5. Li, M.K., Yao, N.F., Li, S.Q., Zhao, Y.Q., Kong, S.G.: Multisensor image fusion for automated detection of defects in printed circuit boards. IEEE Sens. J. **21**(20), 23390–23399 (2021)
6. Zhang, Z.Q., Wang, X.D., Liu, S., Sun, L., Chen, L.Y., Guo, Y.M.L: An automatic recognition method for PCB visual defects. In: 2018 International Conference on Sensing, Diagnostics, Prognostics, and Control (SDPC), Xi'an, China, pp138–142 (2018)
7. Luo, J.X., Chen X.C., Hu, Y.M.: A fast circle detection method based on threshold segmentation and validity check for FPC images. In: 2017 Chinese Automation Congress (CAC), Jinan, China, pp. 3214–3217 (2017)
8. Dai, L.H., Guan, Q., Liu, H.: Robust image registration of printed circuit boards using improved SIFT-PSO algorithm. J. Eng. **16**, 1793–1797 (2018)
9. Hassanin, A.-A., Abd El-Samie, F.E., El Banby, G.M.: A real-time approach for automatic defect detection from PCBs based on SURF features and morphological operations. Multimedia Tools Appli. **78**(24), 34437–34457 (2019). https://doi.org/10.1007/s11042-019-080 97-9
10. Putera, S.H.I., Ibrahim, Z.: Printed circuit board defect detection using mathematical morphology and MATLAB image processing tools. In: 2010 2nd International Conference on Education Technology and Computer, Shanghai, China (2010)
11. Srimani, P.K., Prathiba, V.: Adaptive data mining approach for PCB defect detection and classification. Indian J. Sci. Technol. **9**(44), 1–9 (2016)
12. Zhang, Z.Q., Wang, X.D., Liu, S., Sun, L., Chen, L.Y., Guo, Y.M.: An automatic recognition method for PCB visual defects. In: 2018 International Conference on Sensing, Diagnostics, Prognostics and Control (SDPC), Xi'an, China (2018)
13. Ibrahim, Z., Al-Attas, S.A.R., Aspar, Z., Mokji, M.M.: Performance evaluation of wavelet-based PCB defect detection and localization algorithm. In: 2002 IEEE International Conference on Industrial Technology, Bankok, Thailand (2002)
14. Ding, R.W., Dai, L.H., Li, G.P., Liu, H.: TDD-net: a tiny defect detection network for printed circuit boards. CAAI Trans. Intell. Technol. **4**(2), 110–116 (2019)
15. Adibhatla, V.A., Chih, H.C., Hsu, C.C., Cheng, J., Abbod, M.F., Shieh, J.S.: Defect detection in printed circuit boards using you-only-look-once convolutional neural networks. Electronics **9**(9), 1–16 (2020)
16. Zhang, H.A., Jiang, L.X., Li, C.Q.: Cs-resnet: cost-sensitive residual convolutional neural network for PCB cosmetic defect detection. Expert Syst. Appl. **185**, 115673 (2021)
17. Nguyen, V. T., Bui, H. A.: A real-time defect detection in printed circuit boards applying deep learning. EUREKA: Phys. Eng. **2**, 143–153 (2022)
18. Kim, J., Ko, J., Choi, H., Kim, H.: Printed circuit board defect detection using deep learning via a skip-connected convolutional autoencoder. Sensors 21(15), 4968 (2021)
19. Tang, S. N., He, F., Huang, X. L., Yang, J.: Online PCB defect detector on a new PCB defect dataset (February 2019)
20. Huang, W.B., Wei, P.: A PCB dataset for defects detection and classification. J. Latex Class Files **14**(8), 1–9 (2018)

An Overview of Smart Contract in Blockchian Technology: Security and Platforms

Wanting Hu[1], Qingfeng Wu[1], Zhiling Zhang[2], and Lu Cao[1(✉)]

[1] Xiamen University, Xiamen 361005, China
caolu2010@xmu.edu.cn
[2] Ningde Normal University, Ningde 352100, China

Abstract. With the continuous innovation of blockchain technology, smart contracts, as an important part of blockchain, are also receiving more and more attention. In this paper, we introduce smart contracts from three directions: basic technology, security, and development platform. The security of smart contracts is discussed from the perspective of the external environment and internal vulnerabilities of smart contracts, and a comparison of different development platforms for smart contracts is made. Finally, the problems faced by smart contracts and future application directions are summarized.

Keywords: blockchain · smart contract · security · platform

1 Introduction

The concept of smart contract was first introduced in 1995 by Nick Szabo: A smart contract is a computerized transaction protocol that executes the terms of a contract [1]. However, smart contracts have not been widely used due to the imperfect development of trusted environmental technology. In November 2008, a Satoshi Nakamoto scholar issued a research paper in which the concept of decentralized digital currency Bitcoin was first introduced [2]. As the focus on Bitcoin increases, the underlying blockchain technology is used has gradually been developed. Blockchain is a decentralized distributed ledger that combines blocks of data in a chronological manner in a chain to form a specific data structure, and cryptographically guarantees that the data is tamper-evident and unforgeable, enabling secure storage as well as simple verification of the data. Bitcoin combines cryptography, distributed technology, and economic incentives to usher in a new era of encrypted blocks. In 2014, Vitalik Buterin proposed the Ethereum blockchain platform, which uses a Turing-complete programming language to develop smart contracts known as Blockchain 2.0 [3].

Smart contracts utilize the decentralized consensus mechanism of blockchain to allow mutually untrusted users to complete data exchange without the intervention of third parties, providing a trusted execution environment, and smart contracts began to be widely applied to blockchain technology. Based on smart contracts, the ethereum platform has built a lot of dapps - similar to apps in the web2 world. Dapps are different from apps in that they are completely decentralized and run automatically through the ethereum network nodes without relying on any centralized servers. Dapps are divided into two parts, front-end and back-end, can write front-end code and user interfaces, and can be called back-end like traditional applications. By the end of 2021, the number of unique daily active wallets linked to dapps reached 2.7 million.

In contrast to traditional contracts, smart contracts run automatically without third-party arbitration. Also, contracts are written in code, are open and transparent, avoid semantic disagreements through computer language, and have little potential to cause disputes, so they can operate efficiently in certain application scenarios. But the security of smart contracts is still problematic: in the first quarter of 2022, the blockchain space attack-type security incidents caused losses of up to about $1.2 billion about 50% of the attacks were contract vulnerability exploits. There has been The DAO attack [4], and Parity wallet theft [5] are relatively high-impact security events.

As blockchain continues to grow in popularity and adoption, the literature related to the technology of smart contracts is also developing. [6] conducted a co-citation analysis using exploratory factor analysis to identify six different research directions involving technical, social, economic, and legal disciplines. [7] conducted an exploratory study was conducted to understand the problems and potential development directions developers face when developing smart contracts on the blockchain. [8] explored the applications that are currently important on smart contracts, as well as the inspiration from them. [9] presents the development trajectory of blockchain and smart contracts, exploring four aspects of cryptography, access management, social applications, and smart contracts structure. [10] outlines the challenges facing smart contracts, and platforms and gives a classification of smart contracts applications. [11] construct a smart contract-based access control framework built on top of a distributed ledger (blockchain) to ensure the sharing of electronic medical records among different entities involved in a smart healthcare system. In [12], some frequently occurring smart contract vulnerabilities are analyzed, and then the traditional mainstream smart contract vulnerability detection tools are described.

Although the aforementioned literature summarizes various aspects of smart contracts from different perspectives, smart contracts are evolving rapidly with a proliferation of programming languages, tools, and platforms. The construction of this article is divided into four parts: the first part is the background knowledge of smart contracts; the second part is the technical basics of smart contracts; the third part is the security of smart contracts; the fourth part is the popular platform of smart contracts and summarizes this paper.

2   Background Knowledge

2.1   Blockchain

In this section, blockchain as an innovation of several technology fusions, we introduce blockchain through Bitcoin and explain in detail three aspects: data structure, network propagation, and consensus protocol.

Data Structure
Hash pointer
A pointer is used to point to the location where the information is stored, while saving the hash value of the information being pointed to. The hash pointer is connected to a chain table, and each chain node is a block, which forms the most basic blockchain. Each block (except the Genesis block) holds the hash of the previous block. By the mechanism that this block's hash generation depends on the content of this block, and the content of this block contains the hash value of the previous block, the content of the block is guaranteed not to be tampered with.

Merkle tree
The Merkle tree operation generally involves grouping the data in the block body and inserting the resulting new hash into the Merkle tree, and so on recursively until only the last root hash remains and is recorded as the Merkle root of the block header. The advantage of this data structure is that only the Root Hash (root hash) needs to be remembered to detect modifications to any part of the tree.

Hashpointer and merkle tree are important data structures of the blockchain, a complete bitcoin block structure as Fig. 1.

Network Propagation. The network layer is a P2P network [13]. There are no priority nodes in the Bitcoin network, and each node is equal. When a new node wants to join the network, it first finds a seed node and informs itself about the nodes it knows through the seed node. The nodes communicate with each other using the TCP protocol, and when a node leaves, it simply exits itself, and other nodes delete it after a certain period without receiving a message from that node. Bitcoin network propagation does not guarantee a successful transmission. A transaction posted to the network may not be received by all nodes, nor may all nodes receive transactions in the same order.

Consensus Protocol. The PoW algorithm is a proof-of-work machine [14]. It requires the initiator to perform a certain amount of operations, which means that it consumes a certain amount of time and resources of the computer. By the time the operation produces a result that meets the requirements, it can be quickly verified by other nodes, specifically, the miner performs the hash operation, this process consumes arithmetic power and broadcasts it to the whole network, other miners or normal nodes synchronize the block and verify if it is correct. To motivate miners, miners are rewarded with blocks that can include a special transaction (mint transaction) in the block.

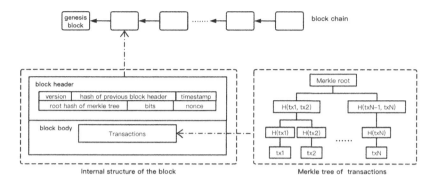

Fig. 1. A blockchain consists of a sequence of blocks, with a number of transactions stored within a block forming a merekle tree.

3 Smart Contract Technology

3.1 The Workflow of Smart Contracts

A smart contract is an executable code deployed on the blockchain that encodes a set of rules agreed upon by the users of the smart contract in a programming language. Once an event that satisfies these rules occurs, it will trigger a series of pre-defined operations in the smart contract. Similar to a self-service vending machine, as long as the user selects a product and pays enough, he or she can get the desired product. The workflow of a smart contract is shown in Fig. 2. The operational flow of a smart contract. The entire life cycle of a smart contract is divided into four parts.

1) Creation. First of all, the user must first register as a user of the blockchain platform. Users agree on a contract according to their needs, which contains the agreement to be reached; the contract is written in the form of a programming language, and then the compiler of the blockchain platform compiles the source code to obtain a bytecode and generates the application binary interface ABI.

2) Deployment. The smart contract is published to the blockchain network and stored in the blockchain. The contract is proliferated across the blockchain network in a peer-to-peer manner, and each node receives a copy. The validation node will take all the contacts saved in the recent period, pack them together into a collection and calculate the Hash value of this contract collection, and finally assemble the Hash value of this contract collection into a block structure that will be spread across the network. Smart contracts are modifiable or unmodifiable. In Ethereum, no modification of smart contracts is allowed after deployment.

3) Execution. When a condition is triggered, the corresponding statement will be executed automatically, so a transaction will be executed. The smart contract will push the transactions whose conditions are satisfied to the queue to be verified and wait for consensus; the transactions that do not satisfy the triggering conditions will continue to be stored on the blockchain. The transactions waiting for consensus verification will be spread to each verification node, and the transactions that pass the verification will enter the set of pending consensus, and after most verification nodes reach consensus, the transactions will be successfully executed and the users will be notified.

4) Completion. After the smart contract is executed, the new status of all participants will be updated. Therefore, the status of transactions and updates generated during the execution of smart contracts is stored in the blockchain. The blockchain marks the status of the contract as completed and then removes the contract from the latest block, and the smart contract completes its entire life cycle.

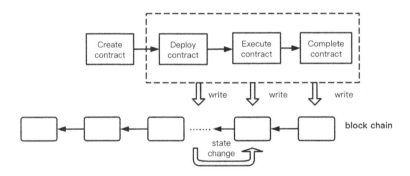

Fig. 2. The flow of smart contract operation.

3.2   Smart Contract Security

External Threats. The external threat to smart contracts comes mainly from the insecurity of external data. The blockchain is unable to actively obtain data from the real world outside the chain, for example, some other data such as weather, competition results, etc. But some of the needs of smart contracts are necessary to use these interactive data. But some of the needs of smart contracts are necessary to use these interactive data, and if the data from the outside world is false information, then it is also insecure for smart contracts.

Insider Threats to Smart Contracts. Due to programming flaws in programs running in the blockchain, smart contracts are prone to security vulnerabilities. [15] conducted a systematic study of 12 vulnerabilities in smart contracts, and [16] proposed a symbolic execution tool called Oyente for discovering four potential security vulnerabilities: transaction order dependency, timestamp dependency, reentrant attack, and exception handling. They found that 8,833 out of 19,366 Ethereum smart contracts had at least one of these security vulnerabilities. In 2020, [17] summarized 15 smart contract vulnerabilities in Ethereum and pointed out the high-impact security events and their vulnerabilities: re-entry attack, code injection, integer overflow, and denial-of-service attacks. The details of these four vulnerabilities are as follows.

1. Re-entry attacks. One of the features of Ethereum smart contracts is the ability to call the code of other external contracts. A re-entry vulnerability may occur when the contract processes a transfer by using a transfer first and then modifying the variable to reduce the amount. If the attacker uses fallback function recursive calls in the attack contract, thus not reducing the number of repeated transfers to the attacker's account.
2. Code injection. Solidity provides call(), delegatecall(), callcode() three functions to achieve direct contract calls and interactions. In the use of functions to directly call a contract or a method of the local contract, the delegatecall function after the call of the built-in variable msg value will not be modified for the caller, but the execution environment for the caller's operating environment, the attacker to take advantage of this point will occur injection vulnerability.
3. Integer overflow. An overflow occurs when an integer variable is above or below the range of an integer type. An attacker will use this overflow to bypass certain conditions and achieve the purpose of the attack, such as transferring the account amount. When writing solidity code, you can use the safemath library to do overflow judgment, which can effectively solve the integer overflow problem.
4. Denial of service attack. There are many ways to target DoS on the Internet, but they fall into three main categories: exploiting flaws in software implementation, exploiting vulnerabilities in protocols, and exploiting resource suppression [18]. Denial of service attacks can disrupt, abort, and freeze normal transaction operations performed by a contract, or worse, make the logic of the contract itself inoperable. DoS attacks belong to the means of exploiting protocol vulnerabilities, where the attacker locks data in the attacked contract by consuming contract resources and making the user exit the frozen contract. For developers, the contract needs to process the results of external function calls to enter a new state, so it is necessary to consider the case where the external call may always fail, such as adding a time judgment operation.

3.3   Smart Contract Defenses

Defensive Measures against the External Environment. So a concept like Oracle was born, where the prophecy machine acts like middleware between the blockchain and real-world data, collecting and verifying real-world data and submitting the information to the smart contract in an encrypted way. The operation principle of the oracle machine is that when a smart contract on the blockchain has a data interaction requirement, it will notify the oracle machine to collect real-world data outside the chain, and the oracle platform will verify and then feed the acquired data back to the smart contract on the chain [19]. The oracle has greater application scenarios and scalability in express tracking, data association, IoT, finance, etc., but still faces certain challenges that need to be improved. Oracle can be divided into centralized oracle and decentralized oracle. The current oracle platforms follow:

1) Provable proposed in 2015, it is the leading oracle smart contract and blockchain application service, relying on Amazon cloud host and Google software remote proof technology to provide data authenticity verification service, a provable and honest prophecy machine service, serving thousands of requests daily on platforms such as Ethereum, R3 Corda, and EOS. However, Provable as a single model prophecy machine network is difficult to integrate the resources of multiple prophets (Oracles) in terms of scalability as decentralized Oracles do.

2) Chainlink is the first decentralized prophecy machine, it went live in May 2019 and is currently the most popular oracle smart contract service provider. ChainLink's core functional goal is to connect two environments: on-chain and off-chain. The on-chain part completes the recording of all information within Chainlink, while the off-chain part is responsible for the specific execution of code and command lines and output data [20]. Meanwhile, Chainlink has a reputation evaluation system for nodes, where information demanders can select nodes with a specific reputation level, and the reputation score of nodes is updated after each information feedback. In both on-chain and off-chain versions, ChainLink is designed with modularity in mind. Each type of system is scalable, so those different components can be replaced as better technologies and competing implementations become available.

Defenses against Internal Vulnerabilities. A major feature of smart contracts is that they cannot be modified after deployment even if flaws and errors are found, and the only way to roll back transactions is by hard forking. The main approaches taken for automated vulnerability detection of smart contracts are fuzzy testing, symbolic execution, formal verification, taint analysis, machine learning-based vulnerability detection models, natural language processing-based approach to vulnerability detection, graph-based vulnerability detection, etc. Fourteen smart contract detection tools are summarized and compared in [17]. The new detection tools are: [21] proposed an integrated framework to enhance the security of smart contracts by improving the security of both recommendation and verification phases. This framework is used as an official development tool for the webank. [22] proposed a method to automatically learn smart contract features in Solidity, which can be used for clone detection, vulnerability detection, and contract validation of smart contracts. [23] combines deep learning to design an unsupervised graph embedding algorithm that encodes the graph into quantitatively comparable vectors that can improve the probability of identifying potentially vulnerable smart contracts. [24] propose a new Ethereum smart contract mutation testing tool is proposed. It is designed on the basis of the latest Solidity documentation and well-known mutation testing tools to implement a set of 44 mutation operators.

3.4   The Platform Comparison of Smart Contracts

Ethereum. Ethereum is one of the largest and most popular blockchain platforms. It is Turing-complete and supports multiple programming languages: solidity, vyper. Developers use the Ethereum platform to develop dapps in various fields, including finance, games, art, etc. Ethereum currently has some scalability issues that result in high cost per transaction and slow transaction processing speed. Ethereum initially used the pow algorithm, but due to scalability issues and wasted power resources of the pow algorithm, developers are moving to Ethereum 2.0, and the beacon chain is now live, which is a pos-based public chain, completely independent of the main Ethereum network, with plans to completely introduce pos to Ethereum in the next step by merging into the main Ethereum network. Switching from the proof-of-work pow algorithm to the proof-of-equity pos algorithm, Ethereum 2.0 can improve the speed, efficiency, and scalability of the Ethereum network, enabling it to handle more transactions. The upgrade timeline for Ethernet is shown in Fig. 3.

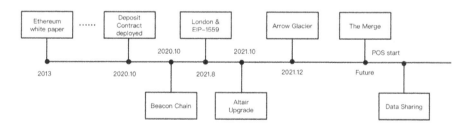

Fig. 3. Ethereum's upgrade timeline.

Hyperledger Fabric. Hyperledger (Hyperledger) is a global collaborative project hosted by the Linux Foundation and supports multiple programming languages: Go, Java. The main difference between fabric and Ethereum is the status of its nodes, which must be approved to join. Fabric is suitable for enterprise-level scenarios and allows for building blockchain applications for permission projects [25]. Like the public blockchain platform, the Hyperledger project has created a very useful set of tools to more efficiently allow developers to develop smart contracts at the application layer, including JavaScript-based tools and Hyperledger Composer.

Dfinity. One Internet Computer (IC for short) aims to be the next generation of Internet infrastructure, a third-generation blockchain that achieves infinite scalability, high performance, and neural network autonomy. IC supports multiple programming languages: Rust, Motoko. Developers can build programs and applications directly on this Internet ontology without the need for cloud services, databases, various types of interfaces, etc. And since there is no need to consider a lot of middleware, it also enables connection and building of applications. Ultimately, a scalable open cloud supported by a decentralized network of computers, capable of interfacing with AWS, Microsoft Azure, and Google Cloud Platform will be realized as one Internet computer. The permission model of IC is a hybrid model that gains the efficiency of licensed protocols while retaining the advantages of decentralized PoS protocols [26].

Table 1. Development platform comparison.

Blockchain system	Blockchain type	Consensus mechanism	Smart contract Turing completeness	Source support
Ethereum	Public	Pow/Pos	Turing complete	Solidity/Vyper
Fabric	Private	Pbft/Sbft	Turing complete	Go/Java
Dfinity	Public	Pos	Turing complete	Motoko/Rust
Cosmos	Public	Bft+Pos	Turing complete	Go

Cosmos. Cosmos sets itself up as a scalable and modular blockchain network. The goal is not to build its own blockchain, but to build an ecosystem of interoperable networks. Since the current throughput of the most mainstream blockchain platforms still falls short of what is needed, but the number of users of blockchain services is growing, it may be necessary for an entire public chain to serve the application separately if mainstream-level applications are to be developed. In 2021, the chain game Axie has chosen to develop its own sidechain, Ronin, to handle a large number of transactions. The development framework provided by Cosmos (Cosmos SDK) even allows developers to develop a chain in a very short time [27]. Besides, the cosmos communication protocol allows interconnection of blockchains, supports asset transfer between different blockchains, and enables interoperability of traffic between different chains.

Table 1 shows the consensus algorithms,blockchain types and supported programming languages for different platforms

4   Conclusion

This paper has provided an overview of smart contract technology regarding operational processes, security, and platforms. Smart contracts are still in the early stages of development, and there is still a lack of supporting tools, frameworks, and mature materials for developers compared to traditional development. In addition, the security of smart contracts and the tamper-evident nature of smart contracts require developers to maintain a relatively high level of coding, and detecting and fixing these bugs requires a lot of work from security personnel and data analysts. The combination of blockchain with other directions of knowledge is also an important aspect, for example, natural language processing, and graph algorithms can improve the security of intelligence. And in terms of applications, blockchain can be used in the Internet of Things, healthcare, gaming, finance [28–30], etc. More importantly, blockchain is the basis for digital assets from the physical world to the digital world, and with the development of blockchain technology and the change of transaction mode, the transaction mode of physical assets such as property rights and copyrights or equity assets may all gradually become the object of digital goods transaction and become digital assets [31].

References

1. Szabo, N.: Formalizing and securing relationships on public networks. First monday (1997)
2. Nakamoto, S.: Bitcoin: A Peer-to-Peer Electronic Cash System. Decentralized Business Review, p. 21260 (2008)
3. Buterin, V., et al.: A next-generation smart contract and decentralized application platform. White paper. vol. 3, no. 37 (2014)
4. Mehar, M.I., et al.: Understanding a revolutionary and flawed grand experiment in blockchain: the DAO attack. J. Cases Inf. Technol. (JCIT) 21(1), 19–32 (2019)
5. Palladino, S.: The parity wallet hack explained. OpenZeppelin blog. blog.openzeppelin.com/on-the-parity-wallet-multisig-hack-405a8c12e8f7 (2017)
6. Ante, L.: Smart contracts on the blockchain-a bibliometric analysis and review. Telematics Inform. 57, 101519 (2021)
7. Zou, W., et al.: Smart contract development: challenges and opportunities. IEEE Trans. Softw. Eng. 47(10), 2084–2106 (2019)
8. Hewa, T., Ylianttila, M., Liyanage, M.: Survey on blockchain based smart contracts: applications, opportunities and challenges. J. Netw. Comput. Appl. 177, 102857 (2021)
9. Kemmoe, V.Y., Stone, W., Kim, J., Kim, D., Son, J.: Recent advances in smart contracts: a technical overview and state of the art. IEEE Access 8, 117782–117801 (2020)
10. Zheng, Z., et al.: An overview on smart contracts: challenges, advances and platforms. Future Gener. Comput. Syst. 105, 475–491 (2020)
11. Saini, A., Zhu, Q., Singh, N., Xiang, Y., Gao, L., Zhang, Y.: A smart-contract-based access control framework for cloud smart healthcare system. IEEE Internet Things J. 8(7), 5914–5925 (2020)
12. Zhang, Y., Ma, J., Liu, Z., Liu, X., Zhou, R.: Overview of vulnerability detection methods for ethereum solidity smart contracts. Comput. Sci. 49(3), 52–61 (2022)
13. Yuan, Y., Wang, F.-Y.: Blockchain: the state of the art and future trends. Acta Automatica Sin. 42(4), 481–494 (2016)

14. Zheng, Z., Xie, S., Dai, H., Chen, X., Wang, H.: An overview of blockchain technology: architecture, consensus, and future trends. In: 2017 IEEE International Congress on Big Data (BigData congress), pp. 557–564, IEEE (2017)

15. Atzei, N., Bartoletti, M., Cimoli, T.: A survey of attacks on ethereum smart contracts (SoK). In: Maffei, M., Ryan, M. (eds.) POST 2017. LNCS, vol. 10204, pp. 164–186. Springer, Heidelberg (2017). https://doi.org/10.1007/978-3-662-54455-6_8

16. Luu, L., Chu, D.-H., Olickel, H., Saxena, P., Hobor, A.: Making smart contracts smarter. In: Proceedings of the 2016 ACM SIGSAC Conference on Computer and Communications Security, pp. 254–269 (2016)

17. Ni, Y., Zhang, C., Yin, T.: A survey of smart contract vulnerability research. J. Cyber Secur. 5(3), 78–99 (2020)

18. Bogdanoski, M., Suminoski, T., Risteski, A.: Analysis of the SYN flood dos attack. Int. J. Comput. Netw. Inf. Secur. (IJCNIS) 5(8), 1–11 (2013)

19. Beniiche, A.: A study of blockchain oracles. arXiv preprint arXiv:2004.07140 (2020)

20. Kaleem, M., Shi, W.: Demystifying pythia: a survey of ChainLink Oracles Usage on ethereum. In: Bernhard, M. (ed.) FC 2021. LNCS, vol. 12676, pp. 115–123. Springer, Heidelberg (2021). https://doi.org/10.1007/978-3-662-63958-0_10

21. Ren, M., et al.: SCStudio: a secure and efficient integrated development environment for smart contracts. In: Proceedings of the 30th ACM SIGSOFT International Symposium on Software Testing and Analysis, pp. 666–669 (2021)

22. Gao, Z., Jiang, L., Xia, X., Lo, D., Grundy, J.: Checking smart contracts with structural code embedding. IEEE Trans. Softw. Eng. 47(12), 2874–2891 (2020)

23. Huang, J., et al.: Hunting vulnerable smart contracts via graph embedding based bytecode matching. IEEE Trans. Inf. Forensics Secur. 16, 2144–2156 (2021)

24. Barboni, M., Morichetta, A., Polini, A.: SuMo: a mutation testing strategy for solidity smart contracts. In: 2021 IEEE/ACM International Conference on Automation of Software Test (AST), pp. 50–59, IEEE (2021)

25. Dhillon, V., Metcalf, D., Hooper, M.: The hyperledger project. In: Blockchain Enabled Applications, pp. 139–149. Apress, Berkeley, CA (2017). https://doi.org/10.1007/978-1-4842-3081-7_10

26. Team, D., et al.: The internet computer for geeks. Cryptology ePrint Archive (2022)

27. Alex, G.: Blockchain interoperability framework using cosmos SDK, CosmWasm, and polkadot substrate IBC implementation (2020)

28. Dai, H.-N., Zheng, Z., Zhang, Y.: Blockchain for Internet of Things: a survey. IEEE Internet Things J. 6(5), 8076–8094 (2019)

29. Azaria, A., Ekblaw, A., Vieira, T., Lippman, A.: MedRec: using blockchain for medical data access and permission management. In: 2016 2nd International Conference on Open and Big Data (OBD), pp. 25–30, IEEE (2016)

30. Treleaven, P., Brown, R.G., Yang, D.: Blockchain technology in finance. Computer 50(9), 14–17 (2017)

31. McConaghy, M., McMullen, G., Parry, G., McConaghy, T., Holtzman, D.: Visibility and digital art: blockchain as an ownership layer on the internet. Strateg. Change 26(5), 461–470 (2017)

Comparison Between Methods Based on LSTM and BLS for Stock Analysis and Prediction

Weizhen Jiang and Honghua Yu[✉]

School of Information Science and Technology, Jinan University, Guangzhou City, China
jiangwz@jnu.edu.cn, yuhonghua@163.com

Abstract. Broad Learning System (BLS) is a new model to expand the neural network from a horizontal perspective in recent years. Based on its outstanding performance in various aspects, this paper intends to apply it to the analysis and prediction of the stock market. Stock market data is a kind of time series data with strong correlation in time. After analyzing and summarizing the advantages and disadvantages of various existing time series prediction and analysis methods, this paper selects the LSTM (long - short term memory network) model, which is outstanding in time series prediction, to compare with the BLS model, and to examine the ability of these two methods in stock market data analysis and prediction. The experimental results show that the cyclic BLS system also has good performance in the prediction of time series data, especially in reducing the training time. The main reason is that the weight of each layer of LSTM is updated by gradient layer by layer, while the weight from hidden layer to output layer in BLS model is solved by pseudo-inverse calculation, which avoids the gradient update method and ensures the efficiency of network training. In addition, the BLS-based loop structure is adopted in this paper. The nodes in the feature layer or enhancement unit are connected circularly. The nodes can capture the dynamic characteristics of the time series, and well acquire and calculate the time-related information in the time series.

Keywords: Time Series · Broad Learning System · LSTM · Prediction

1 Introduction

Time series is composed of data arranged according to the sequence of time occurrence, and has strong correlation in time. Common time series data include such as stock price, temperature, grain output, rainfall and so on.

Time series data prediction method is to predict the long-term development trend of data by capturing the law between historical time series data. Typical time series data analysis, includes such as stock market trend, meteorological change, memory monitoring, etc. While financial time series data is a kind of time series data with nonlinear and unstable characteristics. It is often very difficult to predict such time series data. The change of data is affected by many uncontrollable factors such as national policies, so that, financial time series data prediction has always been a very challenging problem in the field of time series prediction.

2 Related Work

2.1 Time Series Prediction

After years of research, researchers have found that nonlinear prediction methods mainly include BP neural network [1], support vector machine [2], cyclic neural network [3], generative countermeasure network [4] and reinforcement learning [5], these methods can more comprehensively capture the nonlinear relationship between financial time series data and obtain relatively accurate prediction results than linear methods. As a result, nonlinear prediction methods are the research focus and trend in the field of financial time series data in the future.

Moreover, the research results of domestic and foreign scholars show that compared with the traditional machine learning algorithm, the deep learning algorithm can better extract features and improve the accuracy of stock price prediction. [6–8].

In 1997, Hochreiters et al. proposed a new structure–LSTM(long short term memory networks) [9], which is a neural network based on the recurrent neural network RNN. The network has the characteristics of long-term memory and has a good application in predicting long-term sequence data. In 2014, CHO et al. [10] proposed GRU (Gated Recurrent Unit) model, which is a recurrent neural network above on LSTM.

LSTM and GRU use their special gate structure to skillfully combine short-term memory and long-term memory, and solve the problem of gradient disappearance of RNN to a certain extent. Moreover, in the process of information transmission, the subsequent cell of LSTM can keep the previous information, which is suitable for processing and predicting important events with very long interval and delay in time series. Thus, LSTM and GRU, being deep learning methods, have a good performance in time series data analysis and prediction. [6–8].

2.2 About LSTM

The structure of unit of LSTM and time series data analysis and prediction process based on LSTM are shown in Fig. 1: at time t, the stock data x_t is put into the input layer; and then the output result of input layer, and the hidden layer state h_{t-1} at time t-1, and the cell unit information C_{t-1} at time t-1 are input into the LSTM unit. After the processing of each gate and cell unit, the output data is used as the input of the next hidden layer or output layer; Then the final prediction results are output through the neurons in the output layer. The model updates each weight through back propagation.

Since 2006, various research of deep learning have developed rapidly in various fields, new model structures based on it emerged quickly, and the number of layers gradually increase more and more. However, deep learning models often have a large number of parameters to be optimized, which usually takes a lot of time and machine resources to optimize, and can't be modified on demand or be modified according to the changes of input. For these reasons, in order to provide an alternative method for depth structure, Professor Chen proposed a broad learning system (BLS) [11] in 2018. The system is designed based on compressed sensing technology and pseudo-inverse theory, consists of feature nodes and enhancement nodes.

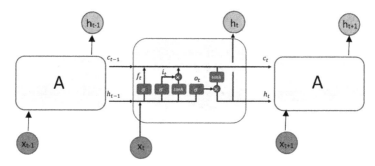

Fig. 1. The memory unit structure and prediction model based on LSTM.

3 Broad Learning System (BLS)

Compared with deep learning structure (such as deep neural network), BLS has the ability of fast incremental learning, and can reshape the system without cumbersome retraining process. BLS has a variety of variants. The structure of cascade mode also has the characteristics of long-term and short-term memory similar to LSTM and GRU models. Researchers have applied BLS in mainly in image classification [11], graph structure data classification [12] and numerical regression. It is also widely used in food safety, construction engineering [13], anomaly detection [14], pattern recognition [15] and other fields, and achieved good results. Peers have also applied cascade variants and cyclic variants of BLS in time series data analysis and prediction, and achieved good results [16]. However, at present, no one has applied BLS in stock market analysis and prediction. This paper intends to make a practice on this problem using BLS, and compare it with LSTM.

The general structure of the broad learning system is shown in Fig. 2: it consists of four parts: 1) input; 2) Feature node; 3) Enhanced nodes; 4) Output. Firstly, the input data is transformed into random features by feature mapping algorithm, and then the mapped features are randomly connected to the enhancement node. Finally, the feature node and enhancement node are connected to the output, and the weight of the output is trained by linear regression method [17]. The structure of BLS is very flexible. If the learning cannot achieve satisfactory accuracy, we can insert some enhancement nodes, feature nodes or input data through incremental learning [11]. The output of this system should be computed as Eq. (1):

$$Y = [Z_1, Z_2 \ldots, Z_n | H_1, H_2 \ldots, H_m] W_n^m = [Z^n | H^m] W_n^m \tag{1}$$

where Z is mapping feature node, H is enhance node, W is weight, Y is the given supervision output information. The objective function of BLS is shown in Eq. (2):

$$\min_{W_n^m} \|O - Y\|_2^2 + \lambda \|W_n^m\|_2^2 \tag{2}$$

In Eq. (2), the first item is empirical risk item, to reduce the error between the computing output of the model (O) and the given supervision information (Y), the 2nd item is structural risk term which is used to improve the generalization ability of the model and reduce the risk of over fitting, λ is the coefficient. Where W is weight same as in Eq. (1).

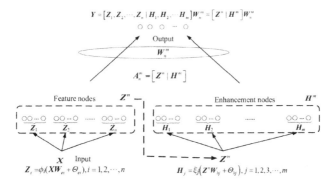

Fig. 2. The Structure of typical BLS

BLS system places the nodes horizontally, this mode not only has superior computing ability like deep net, but also avoids deep net's cumbersome training process.

As mentioned above, to achieve the good characteristics for long time memory, we decided to use BLS model with cyclic structure on the time series prediction in this paper.

The BLS based cyclic structure to be using in this paper, whose nodes in the BLS feature layer or enhancement unit are circularly connected in order to capture the dynamic characteristics of time series. Take the recurrent structure of enhancement nodes as an example, and its structure is shown in Fig. 3, in the figure we can see the nodes are connected with each other, constructs a cyclic structure.

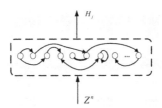

Fig. 3. The recurrent structure of the j_{th} group of enhancement nodes

In this paper, we call the BLS with the feature nodes recurrent structure "RFBLS", and call the BLS with the enhancement nodes recurrent structure "REBLS".

4   Experiment

4.1   Experimental Preparation

Datasets: using Shanghai stock index. This index can fully and accurately reflect the overall operation of China's A-share stock market, and is not easy to be manipulated.

The Shanghai stock index data selected in the dataset is the daily data of 25 years (from 1990 to 2015, there are almost 6100 data). 90% of the data in the dataset is used as the training set, and 10% of the dataset is used as the verification set to verify the effect of training.

Characteristic variables: We choose seven financial factors of the stock, including the highest price, lowest price, opening price, closing price, trading volume, MACD value, and stock prices change in a day. These factors have important value and significance in the price prediction of technical analysis and mean regression. We will take these financial factors as seven characteristics of stock data to predict the next day's closing price.

Predicting target label: we take the closing price of the next day as the target of prediction.

The performance of the evaluated prediction models is assessed by the root mean square error (RMSE), the mean square error(MSE), the mean absolute error(MAE), the goodness of fit(R^2), and the training time.

4.2   Experimental Parameter Setting of LSTM

Parameter setting: the neural network consists of 2 LSTM layers, the number of neurons in the LSTM (hidden) layer is 128. The LSTM layers use tanh function as the activation function, and the output layer uses sigmoid activation function. The batch size is set to 64 based on experience, and the initial learning rate is set to 0.001 based on experience, training epoch set to 20 times.

In order to avoid the over fitting problem, the dropout method is used, that is, the units are randomly discarded in the training process of neural network to prevent excessive adjustment of the connection weight of neurons. This is a more effective method than other regularization methods [18]. The dropout parameter is set to 0.2.

At the same time, in order to avoid the optimization algorithm consuming a lot of time and computing resources, the optimization algorithm of training neural network does not use gradient descent algorithm or random gradient descent algorithm, but uses Adam algorithm [19]. It uses the first-order estimation and second-order estimation of gradient to dynamically adjust the learning rate of each parameter, which has high computational efficiency and low memory requirements.

4.3   Experimental Parameter Setting of BLS

The main parameter settings: dataset standardized with zscore method; data is scaled to the $(-1,1)$ interval with the maximum normalization method; the number of feature points (N1) varies from 10 to 15, the number of feature groups (N2) varies from 10 to 30, and the number of enhancement points (N3) varies from 80 to 200. In order to obtain the weight of sparse mapping features in the training process, the regularization parameter is set to 2 ^ - 25, and the shrink coefficient of the enhancement node is set to 0.8. Based on experience, three model's parameters are set and listed in Table 1.

At the end, after predicting, use the average value and standard deviation value to restore normalized data.

Table 1. The parameters of BLS experiments.

Model	Number of feature points (N1)	Number of feature groups (N2)	Number of enhancement points (N3)
BLS	10	30	20
REBLS	10	20	160
RFBLS	15	10	80

4.4 Specific Experimental Steps:

Carry out the experiment according to the following steps:

1) Take the above dataset as the training sample dataset of this paper, which will be divided into training set and verification set in chronological order. The training set accounts for 90% (divided into several groups), and the verification set accounts for 10%.
2) Normalize and standardize the data, remove outliers data, and finish other data preprocessing job.
3) Each group of data is trained through the built model. After each group of training is completed, the weight value of the current group and the results of each group of training will be saved. During the data training of the next group, the weight value of the previous group will be used to continue the training until all data training is completed.
4) Test with the validation set according to the trained model, and analyze the results and efficiency.

4.5 Experimental Result

The Fig. 4 shows the prediction fitting effect of these four models on the Shanghai stock index. It can be seen from the Figs. 4 that the prediction fitting performance of the four models are all good and basically fit the development trend of stocks. The models' goodness of fit is very good, all be higher than 0.96.

Table 2. lists the test results of these models on the Shanghai Stock Index with set experimental parameters. It can be seen that, BLS is a little better than LSTM in performance, and the training time of BLS cyclic structure is much shorter than LSTM. In comparison between RFBLS and REBLS, it reveals that the performance index and goodness of fit of RFBLS is a little better.

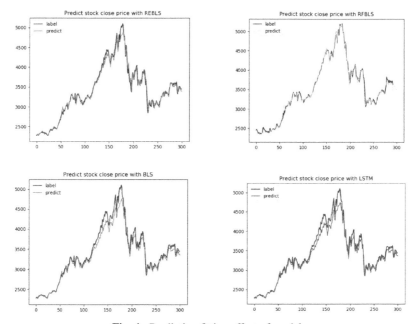

Fig. 4. Prediction fitting effect of models

Table 2. Experimental results of different models.

Model	Mae	Mse	Rmse	R^2	Traning time(s)
LSTM	86.23	15658.76	125.13	0.9601	155
BLS	79.42	15032.84	122.61	0.9701	20
REBLS	44.61	5527.64	74.34	0.9803	27
RFBLS	51.62	4950.06	70.35	0.9902	25

5   Conclusion and Prospect

The above experiments proves that the performance of BLS system is a little better than LSTM (mainly in the training time), and its cycle system can predict the time series well, which shows that it can capture the characteristics of time series well through the cycle structure.

The training time of BLS models is much shorter than LSTM, as is consistent with our prediction, BLS has no need to spend a lot of time in deep training. The underlying cause of this, is based on the below truth: in the deep neural network, the weight of every layer is updated by the gradient layer by layer. It is easy to encounter the problems of falling into local optimization, gradient disappearance or gradient explosion, and slow convergence speed. Although the LSTM in this paper adopts Adam optimization algorithm, this algorithm is still designed based on gradient descent. When the test accuracy of the model cannot meet the expected requirements, the whole network needs to be retrained, leads to serious time-consuming training. As for BLS, there are only three layers in the model: input layer, hidden layer and output layer. The weight of mapping feature node (W_e) and the enhanced node (W_h) in the hidden layer and the weight from hidden layer to output layer (W_m) need to be set or calculated. The initial values of We and W_h are randomly set, and then fine turned by sparse automatic encoder algorithm [11], they are set only once. While the weight from hidden layer to output layer (W_m) in BLS model is solved by pseudo-inverse computation, which avoids the gradient updating method, ensures the efficiency of network training, and greatly shortens the running time of the algorithm.

As for the better performance of RFBLS comparing with REBLS, we believe that, in principle, this is related to both the model structure and the data continuity of time series. Stock data are highly correlated, in RFBLS model, the data first input to the feature nodes, the feature nodes are cascaded, these feature nodes will acquire and compute the information well. While in REBLS mode, the information already has been processed and fused in previous mapping features layer, the continuity information will be changed, so the enhanced nodes get fewer continuity information to processing. Therefore, in the future, the next step should be to find the appropriate cascading model and stacking number through experiments. Furthermore, we can use incremental BLS model to improve the performance [20].

References

1. Wang, J., Wang, J., Zhang, Z.: Forecasting stock indices with back propagation neural network. Expert Syst. Appl. **38**(11), 14346–14355 (2011)
2. Tong-yuan, H., Fang-fang, C.: Application of kernel function of stock price forecasting based on SVM. J. Chongqing Univ. Technol. (Nat. Sci.) (2), 89–94 (2016)
3. Kim, T,. Kim, I.M.H.Y.: Forecasting stock prices with a feature fusion LSTM-CNN model using different representations of the same data. PLOS One **14**(2), 0212320 (2019)
4. Zhang, K., Zhong, G., Dong, J., Wang, S., Wang, Y.: Stock market prediction based on generative adversarial network. Proc. Comput. Sci. **147**, 400–406 (2019)
5. Lee, J., Kim, R., Koh, Y., Kang, J.: Global stock market prediction based on stock chart images using deep Q-network. IEEE Access **7**, 167260–167277 (2019)
6. Chen. K., Zhou, Y., Dai F.: A LSTM- based method for stock returns prediction: a case study of China stock market. In: IEEE International Conference on Big Data, pp. 2823–2824 (2015)
7. Jia, H.: Investigation into the effectiveness of long short-term memory networks for stock price prediction. https://arxiv.org/abs/1603.07893v1 (accessed 2016/8/28)
8. Nelson, D.M.Q., Pereira, A.C.M., de Oliveira, R.A.: Stock market's price movement prediction with LSTM neural networks. In: 2017 International Joint Conference on Neural Networks (IJCNN), pp. 1419–1426 (2017)
9. Hochreiter, S., Schmidhuber, J.: Long short-term memory. Neural Comput. **9**(8), 1735–1780 (1997)
10. Cho, K., Merrienboer, B.V., Gulceher, C., et al.: Learning phrase representations using RNN encoder-decoder for statistical machinetranslation. In: Proceedings of the Conference on Empirical Methods in Natural Language Processing, pp. 1724–1734 (2014)
11. Chen, C.L.P., Liu, Z.: Broad learning system: an effective and efficient incremental learning system without the need for deep architecture. IEEE Trans. Neural Netw. Learn. Syst. **29**(1), 10–24 (2018)

12. Guoqiang, L., Lizhuang, X.: Application of local receptive field based broad learning system. Comput. Eng. Appl. **56**(9), 162–167 (2019)
13. Meng, L., Zhongyu, R., Ming, L., Xinhui, Y., Liang, Z.: Identification of coal geographical origin using near infrared sensor based on broad learning, Appli. Sci. **9**(6), 1111 (2019)
14. Jiao, Y., Qiu, Y., Lichao, Z.: An anomaly detection approach on servers traffic in smart grid based on breadth learning algorithm. Comput. Modern. (9), 77–82,89 (2019)
15. Issa, S., Qinmu, P., Xinge, Y.: Emotion classification using EEG brain signals and the broad learning system. IEEE Trans. Syst. Man Cybern. Syst. **51**(12), 7382–7391 (2020)
16. Ye, H., Li, H., Chen, C.L.P.: Adaptive deep cascade broad learning system and its application in image denoising. IEEE Trans. Cybern. **51**(9), 4450–4463 (2021)
17. Meiling, X., Min, H., C.L. Philip, C., Qiu, T.: Recurrent broad learning systems for time series prediction. IEEE Trans. Cybern. **50**(4), 1405–1417 (2020)
18. Nitish, S., Geoffrey, H., Alex, K., Ilya, S., Ruslan, S.: Dropout: a simple way to prevent neural networks from overfitting. J. Mach. Learn. Res. **15**(56), 1929–1958 (2014)
19. Diederik, P., Kingma, J.L.B.: Adam: A method for stochastic optimization. In: The 3rd International Conference for Learning Representations, San Diego (2015)
20. Liang, Z., et al.: Analysis and variants of broad learning system. IEEE Trans. Syst. Man Cybern. Syst. **52**(1), 334–344 (2022)

The Application of Information Communication Technology in Design Education

Junjie Su, Siqing Che, Kunyu Chen, Hongzhe Wang, Yue Yin,
and Xinkai Wang[✉]

NingboTech University, No.1 South Qianhu Rd, Ningbo, China
xinkai.wang@nbt.edu.cn

Abstract. Information Communication Technology (ICT) revolution
has brought enormous changes to the world. The process of digitalization also impacted on the modern design education, including architecture and urban design. It has become an urgent problem for practitioners that how to conduct innovative practices by involving ICT. This
study is aimed at contributing to the literature of computer augmented
urban design education and its pedagogical meaning. A practical case of
extracurricular research project conducted by students in Ningbo Tech
University was analysed to introduce an entire process of design practice (including site investigation, data collection and analysis, and design
generation). Moreover, a research-led teaching practice was highlighted,
which improves students' ability to use ICT in urban design.

Keywords: Student education · Information Communication
Technology · Urban guidance system

1 Introduction

The rapid process of digitization brings both opportunities and challenges to
architecture education. A free and multi- channel communication platform,
impacted by the application of computer, has been established in Architecture
education. Architecture is discipline with both aesthetic and artistic features, but
also imagination and logical thinking in its nature. In fact, it integrates aesthetic
and engineering side of architec- ture design during an in-depth application of
diversified and pluralist technology, which facilitates an extensive requirement
of courses in the field of ICT in higher education [1].

Computer augmented design has been extensively discussed in architecture
and design arena. For instance, "Quan Zhu" Digital FUTURE Shanghai International Summer Work Shop was launched in 2018, which focus on the theme
of 'Cy- borg Futures Man-machine Symbiosis'. The improvement of modern
computer technology has strengthened the interaction and connection between
human beings and machines. New design patterns have been continuously formed
for the future design industry. The workshop provides students opportunities

W. Hong and Y. Weng (Eds.): ICCSE 2022, CCIS 1811, pp. 186–204, 2023.
https://doi.org/10.1007/978-981-99-2443-1_16

Identify applicable funding agency here. If none, delete this.to explore the cutting-edge ideas of digital design. Finally, participants provide a variety of exploration and contribution in digital design.

In China, education practitioners have dedicated to ped- agogic reform to cultivate diversified pattern of talent de- velopment for more than two decades. In terms of teaching methods, pioneers in colleges and universities started use advanced technology to enhance design education, especially enriching teaching content. Moreover, the application of new techniques raises the level of prac- tical ability and ethics, especially in the development thinking and innovative spirit. It also creates more opportunities for college students to join scientific research activities to promote the development of students' brains and intelli- gence. A comprehensive and extensive education reform has been launched in China, which is expected to be persisted by practitioners in the future.

In recent years, teaching with concept of ICT has gained prominence in higher education. Artificial intelligence, virtual reality, big data, blockchain, and other emerging ICTs have brought opportunities in the field of design education, but also a challenge for practitioners in adopting a new approach to achieve certain goal education modernization. In this study, an empirical evidence was provided to highlight the proprieties in adopting ICT in architecture and urban design.

2   Literature Review

The application of ICTs in site investigation has been extensively discussed, which promote the methods of site investigation as a comprehensive exploration by using modern technologies. The aim of site investigation is to understand the actual environment, including geographical and social-cultural information, spatial scale, surrounding conditions, etc. For instance, the adoption of automatic pilot bicycle could achieve a large-scale data collection in urban area where roads are not accessible for cars [2]. Also, the extensive use of mobile phone helps researchers and urban administrators to mange a largeset of data, e.g. the motion trail of individuals, traffic flow, spatial distribution of population, at the beginning stage of urban design [3].

ICTs have also increasingly adopted in the process of design analysis. Big data has gradually become a solid theoretical support for modern design and application. [4]Data mining plays an important role in facilities planning, road design, and urban management [5]. Long, Mengru Zhou, Hanbin Wei, Yafei Hu, analysed the street space based on the deep leaning based on more than 4 million images of street view. The widespread use of ICT is/will be a starting point of unfolding the in-depth and unrecognized side of data.

Design generation has also married with the concept of ICTs. In Harvard University, Stanislas Chaillou divided ar- chitectural design into four stages: modular design, computer- aided design, parametric design, and artificial intel- ligence de- sign. As suggested by Chaillou, these four stages are connected and permeated to each other, rather than four independent sections [6].

The artificial intelligence was firmly integrated into the four stages of design, which enables architects and urban designers to establish a knowledge map between the massive reality and its special characteristics. A large amount of empirical data was generated to guide and support the design conclusion. Moreover, the trained AI is also capable to evaluate the data which is continuously inputted during the process of design-making. It contributes to the goal of accurate, efficient, convenient in the actual design generation (Fig. 1).

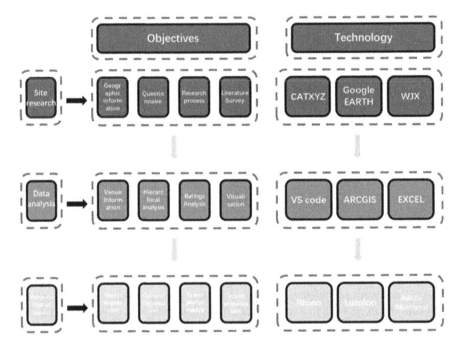

Fig. 1. Basic thinking diagram of the research process

As discussed above, existing literature lay emphasis on the application of ICT in each sections of design, instead of combining three major sections (investigation, analysis, generation) as a unit. This helps students to develop a mode of research-led thinking, but also enrich the outcome of design work. Furthermore, this provides a practical way for design education in the epidemic period.

3   Case Study: A Three-Step Design Process

3.1   Investigation: Cloud Investigation and On-Site Investigation

Students were blocked and unable to conduct on-site investi- gation at the initial stage of the project because of the epidemic control. A cloud investigation, thus, was launched by using Google Earth, Baidu Map street View, and other techniques (Fig. 2). A set of site data, such as site boundary, road grade, greening situation, and surrounding landmark buildings, was collected to support the pre-liminary analysis of research- led design. It also helps the participants to develop a research framework (Fig. 3), potential problems, data requirements, field trip routes, and other related issues before the field trip. Moreover, in this stage, literature in the field of road guidance system (Fig. 4) was also collected to help participants to fully prepared for the following steps of design.

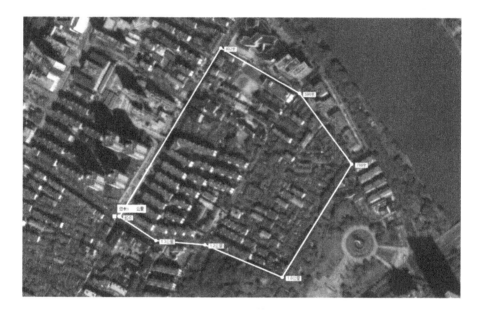

Fig. 2. Site Boundary map (Collected by using Google Earth)

On-site investigation was conducted by using app, e.g. 'Two Step Road' which could automatically record and generate a track image of the field trip. Also, images of built environment were recorded by using app, 'Mao Yan Xiang Xian' (Fig. 9) which also helps participants to made a continuous record of located site images. The trained AI, such semantic segmentation, was not currently capable in street view analysis of irregular street space, especially in the old commu-nity. Thus, built environment of guidance system, including surrounding green-ing, road conditions, and pedestrians, are recorded and manually highlighted by using Photoshop and Baidu Map (Fig. 6).It is noted that the street signs and its environment within research area remained at a limited condition (Fig. 5).

Generally, the issues of street signs could be concluded as follows:

– The street signs were not damaged to a large extent, but the size and location of signs were not designed and planned in order.
– The road condition remains limited because of subsidence. The built environ-ment constrains the attitude and experiences of pedestrian in using the road guidance system.

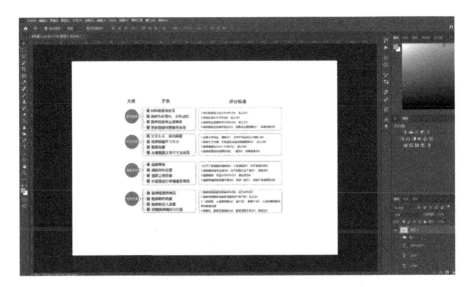

Fig. 3. Preliminary Research framework (Edited by using Photoshop)

Fig. 4. Bibliography (Edited by using Excel)

Fig. 5. Current situation of street signs in blocks (Edited by using Photoshop)

- Mobile navigation was not effective in old community. A certain of alleys and lanes were not included in the navigation.
- The greening on pedestrians were not regularly maintained. Road space is, to some extent, occupied by construction and facilities without permission (Fig. 7).

Fig. 6. Classification diagram of road signs

3.2   Investigation: Questionnaire

Data about the attitude of residents and visitors in using road guidance system was collected by questionnaires survey. The questionnaires were distributed online by using "Wenjuan Xing (Questionnaire Star)". Data were analysed and presented by Excel (Fig. 10).

3.3   On-Site Reinvestigation

An on-site reinvestigation and second-round data collection were conducted by team members to improve concept framework of the research. Panoramic images

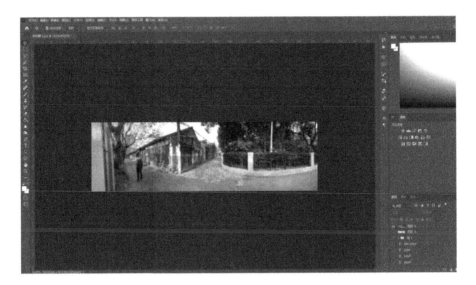

Fig. 7. View limit of block (Edited by using Photoshop)

Fig. 8. Schematic diagram of occlusion area (Edited by using Photoshop)

Fig. 9. Analysis of surrounding environment (Collected by using Mao Yan Xiang Xian)

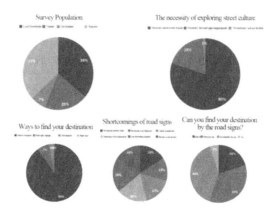

Fig. 10. Questionnaire (Questionnaire star +Excel)

of the site were further analysed to see the scaling relation between human activities, street, open public spaces, and facilities. Time-lapse photos were taken to examine the density of human activities. Intelligent behaviour recognition system was adopted in the image analysis to draw thermal map of human activities (Fig. 11).

Fig. 11. In-depth analysis of road sign visibility (edited by Photoshop)

3.4   Data Collection: Delphi Method

To evaluate the existing road guidance system, an evaluation framework (Fig. 12) was established by using Delphi. Thus, the importance and priorities of designing road signs were generated by collecting opinions with expertswho have architecture/urban design background. The Delphi was conducted by two rounds of written online questionnaires that allow all experts to share their opinions and achieve a common ground.

3.5   Data Analysis: The Fuzzy Evaluation Method

Fuzzy evaluation method is usually used to evaluate in the area of performance appraisal, for instance, product usability . Thus, in this study, the effectiveness of road signs is evaluated not only by subjective comments but also awarding fuzzy numbers. A set of factors, including single-factor fuzzy evaluation, first-level fuzzy comprehensive evaluation, and multi-level fuzzy comprehensive evaluation, were used and determined. Then, impact factors of road sign evaluation obtained from Delphi method were weighted (Table 1), which enhance the reliability of road sign design evaluation frameworkto a large extent.

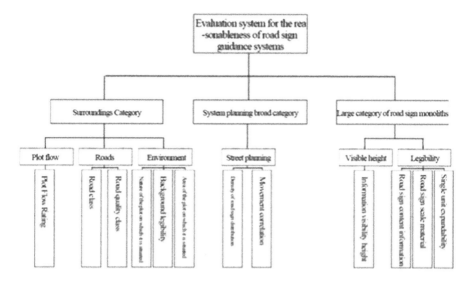

Fig. 12. Rationality evaluation index system of road sign guide System (questionnaire mini-program)

Table 1. Table captions should be placed above the tables.

Criterion Layer	B1			B2		B3
Weights	0.4151			0.3962		0.1887
Sub-criteria Layer	C1	C2	C3	C4	C5	C6
Weights	0.1905	0.3333	0.4762	0.3810	0.6190	1

3.6 Data Analysis: Human Activity Prediction Based on Deep Learning

The methodof deep learning was learned based on the study of Li et al. . It is suggested that the method could achieve a higher production accuracy and reliability on activity prediction. Based on matlab platform, the model is tested on time-lapse photographyduring the on-site investigation. Human activitiesin street or open public spacesare predicted and presented as an edited heat map (Fig. 13).

Fig. 13. Street Space vitality Map (MATLAB, Adobe Photoshop)

3.7 Data Analysis: Geographic Information System (GIS)

Points of interests (POI) data were collected based on Baidu API, and then analysed based on Arc GIS platform (Fig. 14). Spatial connection between road and POI data were made to comprehensively evaluate the conditions of areas (Fig. 15), in order to support the effectiveness evaluation of road guidance system.

3.8 Data Analysis: Visual Studio Code Editing

The Visual Studio Code editing platform is used to combine the road and facility data to visualize the data analysis, which reflect the rating of road signs evaluation (Fig. 16). The application of VSC helps a rapid formation of images of road sign evaluation.

3.9 Data Analysis: Revisit Research Area

To contribute to the reliability of results, the team revisit the four communities in Ningbo and Hangzhou to verify the performance of the framework in evaluating the road signs. The reliability assessment of the framework is about to compare with the scores generated base on framework and manual grading. Two images were put together to explore the differences of scores. It shows that there is limited differences between two images, which demonstrate the reliability of the framework (Fig. 17/18).

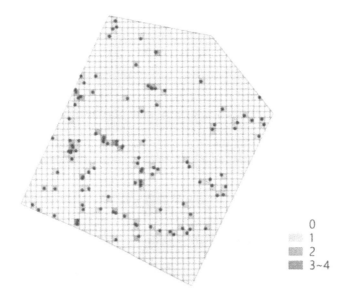

Fig. 14. POI data Analysis Diagram (Arc GIS)

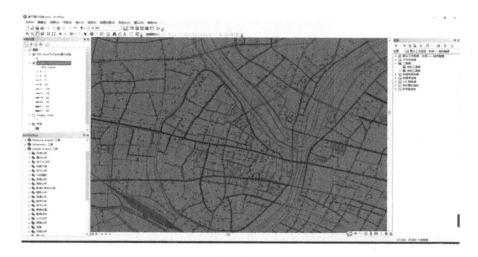

Fig. 15. Comprehensive analysis of Plot information (Arc GIS)

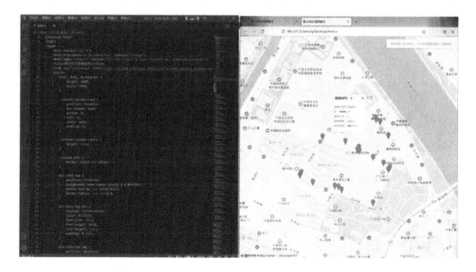

Fig. 16. Visual Road sign information (Visual Studio Code)

Fig. 17. Evaluation grade of Road signs in Hangzhou, Zhejiang Province (Adobe Photoshop)

Fig. 18. Evaluation grade of Road signs in Ningbo city, Zhejiang Province (Adobe Photoshop)

4   Design Generation: Computer Augmented Design

As third-year college students, a great passion has been established by adopting theoretical knowledge into practice. A set of ICTs are applied to contribute to the design generation to promote outcome of a research-led design. Based on the result of investigation and data analysis, the diversity of road sign design was improved as multi-scene and multi-product design. A more visualized design outcome, thus, presented by adopting ICTs, which consist of four sections, includes map generation, modelling, scenario design, and graphic design.

4.1   Map Generation

Map generation with ICTs is mainly conducted at the initial stage of design generation. A visualized map help designers to have an overview of the areas especially in architecture and urban design. The dataset of map was obtained by open map system, such as OpenStreetMap and Autonavi. Map with POI data could be made by using GIS system, such as Arc MAP and Arc GIS Pro (Fig. 19).

4.2 Modelling

Modelling with ICTs is mainly used in the middle stage of the design practice. Software, such as Rhino and SketchUp, could enhance the visual reorganization of design (Fig. 20/21), especially for the people without design background. It could also encourage designers to further polish the design, but also provide a solid ground in the following steps.

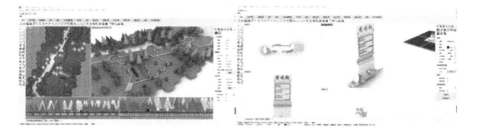

Fig. 19. Operation interface of customized map (Autonavi customized base map) and Traffic Flow map (GIS)

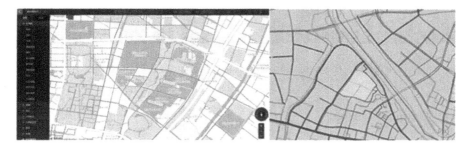

Fig. 20. Operation interface of modelling software (Rhino)

Fig. 21. Effect expression (Rhino, Photoshop)

4.3 Scenario Design

Based on the outcome of modelling, a couple of ICTs, such as Lumion and Vary were also applied in scenario design. This helps designers to promote the vitality of the scenario by predicting the human activities. Moreover, strategies of road sign design, especially in existing or old communities, could be developed to enhance the road sign designs in future (Fig. 22).

Fig. 22. 22 Scene representation (Lumion and Photoshop)

4.4 Graphic Design

Finally, graphic design is usually conducted to provide the most vivid product of design generation. Photoshop, Illustrator, and other graphic design software enhances the feasibility and diversity of design (Fig. 23–26). The semi-finished design products are completed and become reality to fully convey the concept of the design.

5 Discussion and Conclusion

This study elaborates a research-led design practice by implementing of ICTs. A case study was presented to enrich the empirical evidences in the field of computer augmented design. The concept of "investigation + analysis + design" was therefore highlighted by using a case of extracurricular research project conducted by undergraduate students. It shows that a whole process of ICT implementation in design enhance the self-learning climate, attitude of students, and diverse possibilities in architecture and urban design. Also, in this epidemic time, a teaching resilience could be achieved by gradually adopting ICT in design practice in higher education.

5.1   Establishment of Climate of Self-Learning

Through the whole process of project practice, the research-led design projects concluded as a problem-oriented process of design. By answering the questions raised in each section. the project participants shows a growing attitude of solving the problems by finding and learning ICTs. By learning different ICTs in a whole process of design, it articulates the different techniques in practice. we can realize the diversification of results, visualization of results expression and diversification of solutions.

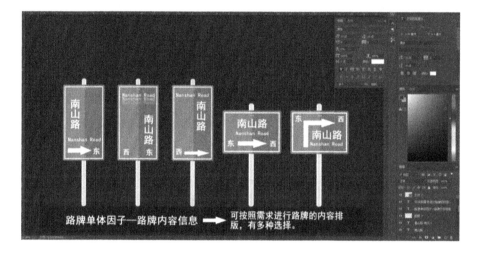

Fig. 23. Software Operation interface (Photoshop)

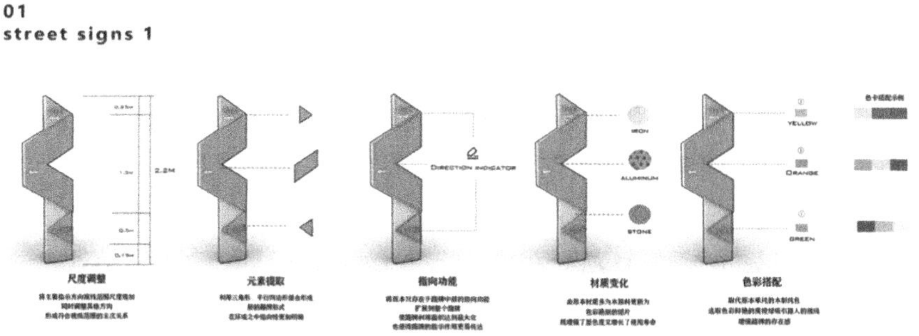

01
street signs 1

Fig. 24. Design Concept presentation (Photoshop)

Fig. 25. Visual expression of site data (Photoshop)

Fig. 26. Design Results display (Rhino, Photoshop)

5.2 Promotion of Studying Attitude

Compared with a traditional way of teaching in classroom, students directly conduct the process of studying rather than passively taking homework as the final goal. In traditional way, for instance observation, imitation, and other passive practices, students receive information driven mainly by taught classes. Under such conditions, the attitude of students remains limited. Thus, the breadth of knowledge remains in a low condition which subject to the learning interests of students.

By comparison, a research-led design project has its advantages in teaching, including team-work design, and an active and circulation process of learning (identifying problems, exploring measures, solving problems, identifying problems). Moreover, the muti-dimension project led to a diversity of ICT application. Project practitioners has a continues opportunity of getting familiar with the techniques, but also constantly absorb new knowledge and apply it in design.

6 Enrich Possibilities by Integrating ICT and Design

In this empirical study, project participants actively combine different ICT applications in order to achieve

- diversity of research directions
- multi-dimension of research methods
- diversity of design outcome

Taking the site investigation stage as an example, survey on built environment could be carried out through vertical maps, including Google Earth, which helps the data collection during following on-site investigation. Also, data of on-site survey was collected through"Two-step" and "Mao Yan Xiang Xian (Cat's Eye Quadrant)", but also on-line questionnaire data collected by "Questionnaire Star". Key site features of the research area were highlighted by using "X-Mind" mapping. All ICTs contribute to the in-depth research and design in this project. Furthermore, it has a profound enlightenment for students that a combination of different ICT applications and design can be continuously developed.

7 Improving Teaching Resilience Through ICT Application

In today's epidemic moment, teaching resilience is becoming a major issue which gained prominence from decision-makers and teachers. How to maintain the regular order of teaching is critical for both teachers and students. Especially for practical section of architecture and urban design, on-line education is being criticized for its teaching quality when compared with face-to-face teaching. The application of ICT in design education, to some extent, provides design teachers various path of teaching.

– Teaching timeliness:
Teaching through ICTs provides an alternative path of teaching when off-line class is not available. The application of on-line conference apps is easily accessible to ensure a communication between teachers and students but also the regular schedule of teaching.
– Teaching accuracy:
Students can access massive information resources from multiple datasets, which contribute to the accuracy of information convey and validation of design analysis even in this epidemic moment.
– Equity of teaching:
The extensive application of ICT in design education improved the equity of teaching. When students receive learning resources, they can have teaching resources without urban-rural vision. The MOOCs taught by advanced universities in the field of design also facilitate the education equity between different schools.

Acknowledgements. This research was funded by Zhejiang Soft Science Research Program (Key Project)grant number 2022C25070; Zhejiang Planning Program in Philosophy and Social Sciences (Youth Project) grant number 21NDQN2 96YB.

References

1. Jing, G., Huang Ming, F.: Research on informatization of architectural education-How to promote the informatization and lon g-distance construction education. Contemp. Educ. Pract. Teach. Res. **03**, 4 (2015). https://doi.org/10.16534/jcnk.i.cn13-9000/g.2015.0218
2. Weijian, L., long Ying, F.: Spatial agent: a fine governance scheme of urban public space driven by technology. Future Urban Des. Oper. **01**, 61–68 (2022)
3. Xinyi, N., Liang, D., Song Xiaodong, F., Identifying the urban spatial structure of Shanghai central city based on mobile phone data. J. Urban Plann. **06**, 61–67 (2014)
4. Tian Wangwang, F.: Research on the standard of information and communication technology in smart city. Digital Technol. Appl. **39**(01), 28–30 (2021). https://doi.org/10.19695/j.cnki.cn12-1369.2021.01.09
5. Wang Chengjin, F.: Problems and Countermeasures of the era of scientific data management. Suzhou University, Suzhou (2014)
6. Yang Liu, F.: Research on automatic generation of youth apartment Type based on deep learning. SCUT (2019). https://doi.org/10.27151/d.cnk.i.ghnlu.2019.003843
7. Zhou, R., Chan, A.H.S.: Using a fuzzy comprehensive evaluation method to determine product usability: a proposed theoretical framework. Work **56**(1), 9–19. https://doi.org/10.3233/WOR-162474
8. Li, J., Liu, H., Guo, W., Chen, X.: A spatial-temporal network for human activity prediction based on deep learning. Acta Geodaet. et Cartographica Sinia **50**(4), 522–531. https://doi.org/10.11947/j.AGCS.2021.20200230

Multi-targets Vital Signs Detection Using CW Radar

Chao Wang[1(✉)], Lin Shen[1], Ningxin Yu[2], and Yangjie Cao[1]

[1] School of Cyber Science and Engineering, Zhengzhou University, Zhengzhou, China
austin423@163.com, caoyj@zzu.edu.cn
[2] International College, Zhengzhou University, Zhengzhou, China

Abstract. This paper proposes a system to detect the vital signs of multiple targets. The radar system transmits a synthetic beam and this synthetic beam will scan the space. During the scanning process, the radar system will monitor the respirations of multiple targets. The respirations of the targets will be extracted from the changing phase difference between the reference and receiving signals. A phase comparator is used to obtain the phase difference and the phase comparator will output the voltage values according to the changing phase difference. The experiments using the proposed radar system with a 2 GHz signal verify that the radar system can monitor the respirations of two targets.

Keywords: CW radar · Phase difference · Multi-targets detecting · Vital-signs detecting

1 Introduction

Human vital signs detection has attracted more attention in recent years. Human vital signs detection consists of contact detection and non-contact detection. Since the COVID-19 has out broken, non-contact detection techniques have played a crucial role for detecting human vital signs. Microwave perception using radar systems is one kind of the most important and popular non-contact methods to detect human vital signs. According to the waveform, radar systems for vital signs detection can be classified to continuous-wave (CW) radar system and some ranging radar systems like FMCW radar system and so on. FMCW radar is introduced to detect several targets in distance range. The number and position of each target can be obtained concurrently. In contrast to CW radar, FMCW radar has no DC offset problem in data processing and it can recover range information [1]. However, compared to CW radar, FMCW radar needs a wide bandwidth to detect the vital signs. Thus, FMCW radar systems are generally provided with high cost and complicate system architecture. Stepped-frequency continuous-wave (SFCW), as a special case of FMCW, is employed in monitoring the human vital sign using the phase information. UWB radar system is also applied on human vital signs detection but the most UWB radar structures are complicate and have higher cost with a low SNR compared to CW radar.

CW radar has been widely employed on human vital signs detection since the radar systems were first introduced for vital signs detection in the 1970s s [2]. Up to now, many research groups [3] have used modified CW radar system to monitor human vital signs such as respiration rates (RRs) and heart rates (HRs). However, CW radar system still has some problems in detecting vital signs [4,5]. One of the major problems is that CW radar system lacks of the ability of detecting multiple targets simultaneously. In order to detect multi-targets vital signs, some research groups [6,7] have tried to use UWB radar systems to realize it. Groups in [8,9] obtained RRs or HRs by using FMCW radar systems. Also, the researcher in the [10] detected multi-targets vital signs via SFCW radar system. However, the groups above can only achieve monitoring the targets at the different distance and angles. Furthermore, they cannot detect multiple targets at the same distance with different angles. In 2018, Mehrdad Nosrati et al. in [11] firstly used a dual-beam phased array radar system with the CW signal to detect the RRs and HRs of two targets at two different angles but same distance apart from the system. However, more beams are needed in their work if the number of the targets increases, which will result in high cost. After that, more modified systems [12,13] have been proposed to detect RRs and HRs of multi-targets in an identical plane, but these systems using ranging radar techniques require complex system architectures and high cost compared to CW radar system.

In this paper, a phased array radar system with CW signal is proposed to simultaneously monitor the respirations of multiple targets located in the same distance but different angles. This system is equipped with MIMO technique and analogous beamforming technique with a scan method to detect multiple targets. Then the respiration information of the targets will be acquired according to the phase difference of the reference and receiving signals.

2   Multi-targets Vital Signs Detection System Design

The architecture of multi-targets vital signs detection radar system is shown in Fig. 1. The signal will be transmitted to the targets via the transmitting antennas in the transmitting module. The signal reflected by the targets will be received via the receiving module. Then a phase comparator will be used to obtain the phase difference between the transmitting and reflecting signal and output different voltage values. A data acquisition (DAC) will collect the voltage values output by the phase comparator. Then the vital signs of the targets can be extracted from the phase difference.

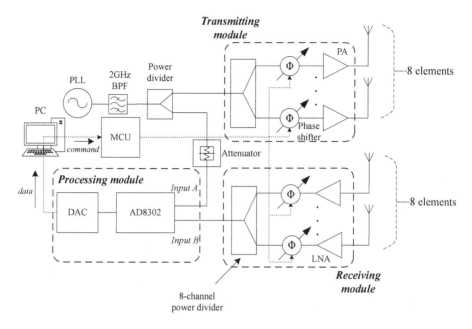

Fig. 1. System architecture. The radar system consists of transmitting module, receiving module and processing module.

In the transmitting module, the CW signal is generated by a phased locked loop (PLL). A filter is used to eliminate the harmonics generated by the PLL. Then, the signal will pass through a 2-channel power divider. One part of the signal will directly arrive at the processing module. After passing through the digital phase shifters (DPS) and the power amplifiers (PA), another part will be transmitted to the targets by the transmitting antennas.

In the receiving module, a 1×8 receiving antenna array receives the signals reflected by the targets. Some low noise amplifiers (LNAs) are used to amplify the reflecting signals. Then the signals will pass through the power combiner and become a synthetic signal. Finally, the synthetic signal will reach at the processing module and become another input of the phase comparator.

In the processing module, a phase comparator, AD8302 is used for comparing the phase difference between the reference and receiving signals. The chest of the target is vibrating because of the respiration. The vibration will result in the change of the phase difference between the reference and receiving signals. AD8302 will output voltage values according to the change of the phase difference. Then the voltage values output by AD8302 are collected by the DAC and analyzing by the PC.

3   Fundamental Theories of Detecting Multiple Targets

3.1   Transmitting Signal and Beamforming

A CW signal $S(t)$ used in the system generated by PPL is able to be expressed as:

$$S(t) = A_p \cos(2\pi ft - \phi) \tag{1}$$

where f is the frequency of the signal generated by the PLL and ϕ is the phase which is generated by the PLL. Then signal $S(t)$ will pass through the 2-channel power divider. The signal arriving the transmitting antennas is able to be expressed as $S'(t)$:

$$S'(t) = A'_p \cos(2\pi ft - \phi_0) \tag{2}$$

where ϕ_0 is the current phase. Considering that ϕ_0 is a constant so the ϕ_0 will be regarded as 0 in the following.

Assuming that a target is detected by the radar system. In order to enable the transmitting signals point at the target commonly, the digital phase shifters are employed to adjust the phase differences between each elements. As for the 1-D phased array, the phase difference between each antenna in the phased array is able to be expressed as:

$$\Delta\phi = \frac{2\pi l \sin(\theta)}{\lambda} \tag{3}$$

where l is the distance between each adjacent antenna, θ is the azimuth angle of the target position and λ is the wavelength. The phase difference within the array is identical because the spacing is same. In this work, the spacing within the array is $\frac{\lambda}{2}$. Thus, the phase difference is:

$$\Delta\phi = \pi \sin(\theta) \tag{4}$$

The DPS will adjust the phase difference in the antenna array. The signals will pass through the phase shifters. Then signals will be transmitted by the antennas and the synthetic signal reaching at the target can be expressed as:

$$S_T(t) = A \cos(2\pi ft - \Phi) \tag{5}$$

$$\Phi = i\Delta\phi + \frac{2\pi d_i}{\lambda} \tag{6}$$

where d_i is the distance of the target apart from the antenna i.

3.2   Receiving Signal and Phase Difference Analyzing

The signal $S_T(t)$ will be reflected by the target. Assuming that the target's chest does a displacement $x(t)$, the signal received by each of the antennas in the phased array radar can expressed as:

$$R_i(t) = B \cos(2\pi ft - \Phi - \frac{2\pi d_i}{\lambda} - \frac{4\pi x(t)}{\lambda}) \tag{7}$$

The signals will pass through the DPS and the phases will be adjusted, and then the signals are synthesized by a power combiner into signal $R(t)$:

$$R(t) = b\cos(2\pi ft - 2\Phi - \frac{4\pi x(t)}{\lambda}) \tag{8}$$

A phase comparator AD8302 is used to compare the phase difference between the reference and receiving signals. A part of signal from the transmitting module will be input to AD8302 as the reference signal $S_{ref}(t)$:

$$S_{ref} = A_{ref}\cos(2\pi ft) \tag{9}$$

AD8302 can extract the deformation information of the target's chest according to the phase difference. Thus, the vital signs are able to be obtained. AD8302 will output the corresponding DC voltage values according to the change of the phase difference between two signals. The phase difference between reference signal and reflecting signal is:

$$\Delta\Phi = 2\Phi + \frac{4\pi x(t)}{\lambda} \tag{10}$$

the change of the target chest vibration $x(t)$ results in different voltage values. Therefore, the vital signs of the target are able to be obtained by analyzing the voltage values changing.

Fig. 2. Radar system. The radar system is used to detect the respirations of two targets.

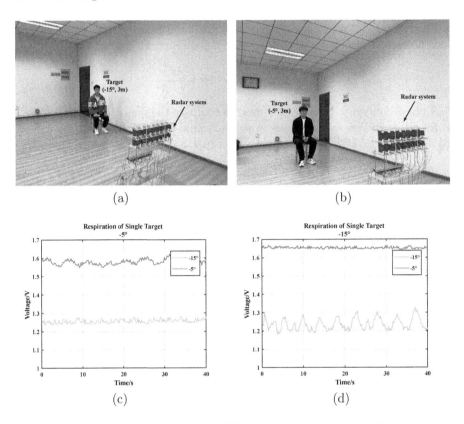

Fig. 3. Figure (a) shows the scenario of detecting the respiration of the target at position $-15°$. Figure (b) shows the scenario of detecting the respiration of the target at position $-5°$. Figure (c) shows the respiration wave of the target at position $-15°$. Figure (d) shows the respiration wave of the target at position $-5°$.

4   Experiment

The proposed vital sign detection radar system detects the respirations of two targets in this section. Figure 2 shows the vital sign detection radar system. A 2 GHz CW signal is employed to be transmitted at the targets.

It is vital to verify and ensure each target has no influence on other targets before using the radar system detects multiple targets. Thus, the radar system firstly detects single target located in $-15°$ and $-5°$, respectively. This experiment aims to verify that the adjacent targets have no influence on each other. Figure 3 show the detail testing scenarios. The target is located at position $-15°$ and $-5°$, respectively. In each angle, the synthetic beam scans the space from $-15°$ to $-5°$.

Figure 3 and Fig. 4 displays the respiration wave of the target located at $-15°$ and $5°$, respectively. In the figures, the respiration wave of the target at position $-15°$ can be detected but there are no respiration waves on position $-5°$. This experiment illustrates that the proposed system can distinguish the different targets' RR.

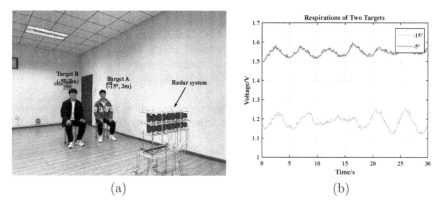

(a)   (b)

Fig. 4. Figure (a) shows the scenario of detecting the respirations of the two targets. Figure (b) shows the respiration wave of the two targets.

Then the two targets A and B are simultaneously detected by the radar system. The two targets A and B are located at the same distance but different angles. Figure 3 displays the experiment scene. Target A is in front of the radar system with angle $\beta_A = -15°$ while target B is at angle $\beta_B = -5°$. The distance between the targets and the system is 4 m. The chests of targets and the antenna elements in the phased array are at the identical horizontal height so that the system can perform a best capability of investigating the respirations of the targets. Figure 4 displays the change of voltage values and the change shows the targets' respirations. Curves in the figure show the respirations of targets at $\beta_A = -15°$ and $\beta_B = -5°$, respectively.

5   Conclusion

This work designs a multi-targets vital signs detection radar system to simultaneously detect the RRs of multiple targets. The system transmits a synthetic electromagnetic beam via beamforming technique. The synthetic electromagnetic beam scans the space to detect the targets located in different position. The respirations of different targets are obtained via analyzing the changing phase difference between the transmitting and reflecting signal. The experiments show that the proposed radar system successfully detects the respirations of two targets. Given time for further study, the proposed radar system and method can detect more targets respirations in the same azimuth and distance and the heart rates of the targets can also be extracted.

Acknowledgements. This work is financially supported by Collaborative Innovation Major Project of Zhengzhou (20XTZX06013).

References

1. Xiong, Y., Peng, Z., Xing, G., Zhang, W., Meng, G.: Accurate and robust displacement measurement for FMCW radar vibration monitoring. IEEE Sens. J. **18**(3), 1131–1139 (2018)
2. Gu, C.: Short-range noncontact sensors for healthcare and other emerging applications: a review. Sensors (Basel, Switzerland) **16**(8), 1169 (2016)
3. Gu, C., Peng, Z., Li, C.: High-precision motion detection using low-complexity doppler radar with digital post-distortion technique. IEEE Trans. Microw. Theory Tech. **64**(3), 961–971 (2016)
4. Li, C., et al.: A review on recent progress of portable short-range noncontact microwave radar systems. IEEE Trans. Microw. Theory Tech. **65**(5), 1692–1706 (2017)
5. Nosrati, M., Shahsavari, S., Tavassolian, N.: Multi-target vital-signs monitoring using a dual-beam hybrid doppler radar. In: IEEE International Microwave Biomedical Conference Imbioc, pp. 58–60 (2018)
6. Wu, S. et al.: Study on a novel UWB linear array human respiration model and detection method. IEEE J. Sel. Top. Appl. Earth Observ. Remote Sens. **9**(1), 125–140 (2016)
7. Rittiplang, A., Phasukkit, P.: UWB radar for multiple human detection through the wall based on doppler frequency and variance statistic. In: BMEiCON - Biomedical Engineering International Conference, pp. 1–5 (2019)
8. Mercuri, M., et al.: 2-D localization, angular separation and vital signs monitoring using a SISO FMCW radar for smart long-term health monitoring environments. IEEE Internet Things J. **8**(14), 11065–11077 (2021)
9. Fang, G.-W., Huang, C.-Y., Yang, C.-L.: Simultaneous detection of multi-target vital signs using EEMD algorithm based on FMCW radar. In: IEEE Mtt-S International Microwave Biomedical Conference (Imbioc), pp. 1–4 (2019)
10. Nahar, S., Phan, T., Quaiyum, F., Ren, L., Fathy, A.E., Kilic, O.: An electromagnetic model of human vital signs detection and its experimental validation. IEEE J. Emer. Select. Top. Circ. Syst. **8**(2), 338–349 (2018)
11. Nosrati, M., Shahsavari, S., Lee, S., Wang, H., Tavassolian, N.: A concurrent dual-beam phased-array doppler radar using MIMO beamforming techniques for short-range vital-signs monitoring. IEEE Trans. Antennas Propag. **67**(4), 2390–2404 (2019)
12. Su, W.-C., Juan, P.-H., Chian, D.-M., Horng, T.-S.J., Wen, C.-K., Wang, F.-K.: 2-D self-injection-locked doppler radar for locating multiple people and monitoring their vital signs. IEEE Trans. Microw. Theory Tech. **69**(1), 1016–1026 (2021)
13. Xiong, J., Hong, H., Zhang, H., Wang, N., Chu, H., Zhu, X.: Multitarget respiration detection with adaptive digital beamforming technique based on SIMO radar. IEEE Trans. Microw. Theory Tech. **68**(11), 4814–4824 (2020)

The Influence of English Learning Apps on College Students' English Learning

Liye Zhang, Haonan Mao, and Chen Ou[✉]

School of International Studies, NingboTech University, Ningbo, China
ocean79ou@163.com

Abstract. Under the mode of "dual-line" education, various English learning apps emerge. These apps have become a tool for students in colleges and universities to assist their English learning. This paper, based on the information collected from the undergraduate students in the NingboTech University, investigates the aim, habit, and preference of their using English learning apps. It also reveals the influence of English learning apps on those students, which leads to some proposals for the English teaching and learning as well as the design of the English learning apps.

Keywords: English Learning App · English Learning · Colleges and Universities · Students

1 Introduction

Since the beginning of the 21st century, the rapid development in the technological revolution of information and communication has brought about a comprehensive integration of the Internet into various social fields [1]. As a result, the integration of the Internet into the field of education thrives. Online teaching and learning have become increasingly popular nowadays and are developing at an even more rapid pace in the post-pandemic era [2, 3]. China has always been emphasizing the importance of online teaching and learning and are encouraging teachers and students to make full use of information technology to carry out in-class teaching and autonomous learning [4], which leads to the application of "dual-line" teaching mode in many colleges and universities [5]. In this mode, the use of learning applications (apps in brief) is indispensable, because these learning apps not only provide rich supplements for in-class teaching, but also offer bountiful resources for students' autonomous learning [6, 7]. It is widely acknowledged that the introduction of apps into the classroom is beneficial to both teachers and students.

This study aims to investigate how English learning apps are used by students in college and universities to aid their English learning and how these English learning apps have affected the students' English learning to put forward suggestions for facilitating the integration of learning apps into the "dual-line" teaching mode.

2 Methodology

2.1 Questionnaire

This study adopts questionnaire survey. The questionnaire, a total of 17 questions, mainly collects respondents' basic personal information such as gender, major and grade. It also asks about respondents' aim, habit, and preference of using English learning apps.

2.2 Data Collection

The questionnaire is compiled on the website (URL: https://www.wjx.cn/), in which a QR code is generated. Then the QR code is sent to the undergraduate students of NingboTech University. Once the QR code is scanned, the respondents will get a questionnaire to fill in. Altogether, 365 respondents complete the questionnaire, and all the questionnaires are valid.

2.3 The Composition of Respondents

Table 1 presents the composition of respondents. In terms of gender, 116 male respondents fill in the questionnaire, accounting for 31.78% of all the respondents, while 249 female respondents fill in the questionnaire, accounting for 68.22% of all the respondents. In terms of major, 176 English majors fill in the questionnaire, accounting for 48.22% of all the respondents, while 189 non-English majors fill in the questionnaire, accounting for 51.78% of all the respondents. In terms of grade, 92 freshmen fill in the questionnaire, accounting for 25.21% of all the respondents, while 162 sophomores fill in the questionnaire, accounting for 44.38% of all the respondents. Seventy-one juniors fill in the questionnaire, accounting for 19.45% of all the respondents, while forty seniors fill in the questionnaire, accounting for 10.96% of all the respondents.

Table 1. The Composition of Respondents

Item	Category	Number	Ratio
Gender	Male	116	31.78%
	Female	249	68.22%
Major	English Major	176	48.22%
	Non-English Major	189	51.78%
Grade	A freshman	92	25.21%
	A sophomore	162	44 38%
	A junior	71	19.45%
	A senior	40	10.96%

3 Results

3.1 The Number of English Apps Used

Table 2 reveals that 289 respondents usually (79.18% of all respondents) use one to two English learning apps, while 72 respondents (19.72% of all respondents) usually use three to four English learning apps. Only four respondents usually use five to six English learnings apps, while none of the respondents use more than seven English learning apps. This indicates that total number of English learning apps used by the respondents is quite limited. Most of them use fewer than four English learning apps in their normal study.

Table 2. The Number of English Learning Apps Frequently Used

Number of apps	Number of users	Ratio
1–2	289	79.18%
3–4	72	19.72%
5–6	4	1.10%
more than 7	0	0

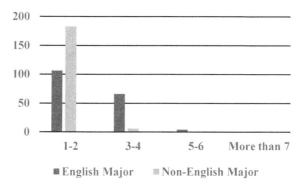

Fig. 1. The number of English majors/Non-English majors for English learning apps

Figure 1 shows that the majority of respondents who frequently use 3 to 4 English learning apps are English major students, and those who frequently use 5 to 6 English learning apps are all from English major. This indicates that major difference plays an important role in using English learning apps. English majors tend to use more English learning apps than non-English majors do. English majors are more enthusiastic about relying on English learning apps to assist their English learning. The reason why this occurs might due to the fact that English major students are required to learn more English courses than non-English major students. As their major, English major students study a wide range of English related courses, such as comprehensive English, extensive English, English listening, oral English, written English, English to Chinese translation,

Chinese to English translation, etc., and have to finish quite a lot of English related tasks. However, non-English major students only have to study one or two kinds of English related classes, and they do not have many English related tasks to complete. Therefore, English major students are more apt to use English learning apps.

3.2 The Selection of English Learning Apps

The study also asks respondents about the names of the English learning apps that they frequently use. The respondents are given a list of thirteen English learning apps that are commonly welcomed by ordinary students, and are quired to select three English learning apps that they like best out of the whole list. Figure 2 shows the proportion of English learning apps that popular among the respondents. "U-Dictionary" (23.93%), "The Words Cut" (17.72%) and "Memorizing Words" (11.81%) are the top three English learning apps that attract the respondents. All of them are apps that aim to assist users in memorizing words. This indicates that the difference in the function of English learning apps play an important role in respondents' selection of English learning apps. Respondents, regardless of their majors, tend to accept and love "words" apps more than other types of English learning apps. Their preference to "words" apps reflects that many students, English major or non-English major, tend to think that learning words is one of the most important things in English learning, and that they pay more attention to learning English words than other learning tasks.

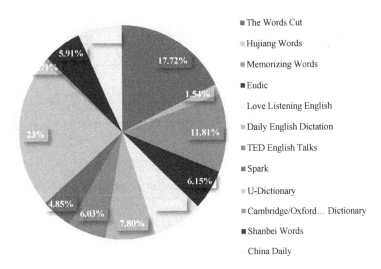

Fig. 2. The use of popular English learning apps

This phenomenon might be accounted by the hardships respondents might have encountered while they are learning English words. For many Chinese students, memorizing English words is not an easy task. Traditional way of mechanically memorizing

words which only focuses on spelling and meaning might be quite tedious and ineffective. The emergence of English word learning apps such as "U-Dictionary", "The Words
Cut" and "Memorizing Words" seems to shed light on memorizing English words. "The
Words Cut" app associates words with certain pictures. Once the learners have formed an
association between the words and their related pictures, they can easily get the meaning
of the words when they see the words. "Memorizing Words" app adopts special ways to
associate the meaning of stem and affix with the meaning of the entire word, which can
effectively facilitate learners to memorize words. In addition, "Shanbei Words" app finds
an interesting way to group words into different categories for the ease of memorizing
words, which can probably release learners from the heavy burden of memorizing words
[8]. Many of those word learning apps have audio or visual settings that can effectively
assist students in imitating or memorizing the words. Through the use of these word
learning apps, students' interest in learning words might be aroused and their learning
efficiency might be improved.

Figure 3 reveals the kinds of English learning apps that respondents find the most
helpful. It can be seen that 65.32% of all the respondents find English learning apps that
focus on language application the most useful. These apps probably give examples for
analysis, tell etymological stories, and present phrasal collocations. By using these apps,
students might find it easier to understand or memorize the English words or phrases.
The figure also shows that 18.91% of all the respondents find English learning apps that
aim to entertain the most useful. These apps probably offer videos and pictures that can
facilitate respondents to learn better. By using these apps, students might find it more
interesting to learn or practice English skills. The figure also shows that 13.62% of all
the respondents find English learning apps that functions as testing tools the most useful.
These apps probably offer tests for revision and reflection. By using these apps, students
might find it a convenient way to review what they have learned and get a satisfactory
mark in their exams.

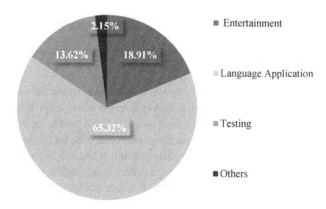

Fig. 3. The kinds of English learning apps that respondents find the most helpful

3.3 Time Spent on English Learning Apps

Table 3 reveal the time respondents spend on English learning apps per day. It shows that 211 respondents (57.81% of all respondents) spend less than an hour on English learning apps, while 123 respondents (33.70% of all respondents) spend one to two hours on English learning apps. Nineteen respondents spend two to three hours on English learning apps while twelve respondents spend more than three hours on English learning apps.

Table 3. Time Spent on English Learning Apps Per Day

Time	Number	Ratio
Less than 1 h	211	57.81%
1–2 h	123	33.70%
2–3 h	19	5.21%
More than 3 h	12	3.28%

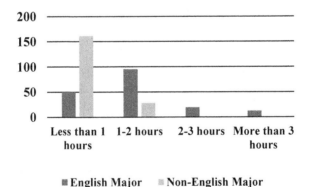

Fig. 4. Time spent on English learning apps per day (English major/Non-English Major)

Figure 4 shows that the majority of respondents who spend one to two hours on English learning apps are English major students, and it is not surprising to see that the respondents who spend more than two hours on English learning apps are all English majors. This indicates that major difference will affect the time learners spend on English learning apps. English majors tend to spend more time on English learning apps than non-English majors do. As it is mentioned in the previous part, English major students study more English related courses than non-English major students, and they are required to accomplish more English related assignments than non-English majors, so it is not surprising that English major students tend to depend more on English learning apps in their studies.

3.4   The Influence on the Improvement of English Skills

The percentage in Fig. 5 shows which English skill is mostly benefited if the respondents use English learning apps. Around 44% of all the respondents think that English learning apps contribute greatly to the improvement of their word learning. About 27% of all the respondents believe that their English listening comprehension has been enhance a great deal by using English learning apps. About 15% of all the respondents admit that their English reading comprehension has been improved greatly, while around 7% of all the respondents acknowledge the increase in their English writing or speaking skills. This indicates that the English learning apps tend to be more effective for learning words, practicing English listening comprehension, and improving English reading comprehension.

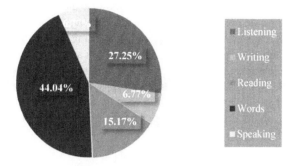

Fig. 5. The English skills benefited mostly from using English learning apps

4   Discussions

This section mainly presents a discussion on the impact of English learning apps based on the above data presentation.

The multi-function of the English learning apps can improve student's English learning. English learning apps feature audio and visual resources. They not only offer bountiful learning materials for students, but also arouse students' interest in learning. Once students become interested in learning, they will find it fun to learn. Figure 3 shows that 65.32% of all the respondents are fond of using English learning apps that focus on language application, 18.91% of all the respondents find English learning apps entertaining, and 13.62% of all the respondents even prefer to use English learning apps that functions as testing tools. It can be seen that the English learning apps cannot only improve students' autonomy and concentration, but also allow them to change passive way of learning into active way of learning. Students are really willing to conduct autonomous learning through a large number of app resources [9].

The diversity of the English learning apps can also benefit student's learning. It can be seen from Fig. 2 that the English learning apps that the respondents tend to use are diversified. Some English learning apps mainly focus on memorizing words, while others mainly deal with listening and speaking. The extensive resources offered by these apps will make the apps become the carriers of students' "third classes", assisting the students in English learning by helping them learn more comprehensively and effectively [9, 10].

The convenience in using English learning apps also facilitate students' autonomous learning. As far as the students are concerned, their autonomous learning are not always confined to a certain period of time. They may want to carry out study whenever they feel like to. Since English learning apps can be easily installed in mobile phones and are really handy, they can greatly cater for students' need for flexible learning. From the study, the respondents say that they will use English learning apps whenever they want to use. As far as the teachers are concerned, the English learning apps can pave the way for them to guide students to carry out autonomous learning. Teachers can take advantage of the apps to utilize the online resources, to assign extracurricular exercises, and to monitor students' learning process. In this way, the English learning apps can really play a certain role in students' autonomous learning [11].

From the study, it also can be seen that English learning apps really play an important role in assisting English majors' learning. Figure 1 indicates that English majors tend to use more English learning apps than non-English majors do, which proves that English majors are really keen on using English learning apps to facilitate their English learning. Figure 4 reveals that English majors tend to spend more time on English learning apps than non-English majors do, which also proves their enthusiasm in relying on English learning apps in the course of their studies.

Table 4. Respondents' Dissatisfaction of English Learning Apps

Reasons	Number	Ratio
It has limited functions	42	49.41%
The content is old and slow to update	14	16.47%
The software itself is full of bugs	7	8.24%
It costs to use apps	22	25.88%

However, the English learning apps are by no means perfect. Some respondents also express their dissatisfaction with the English learning apps in the survey. As is shown in Table 4, altogether 85 respondents are dissatisfied with the English learning apps. Among them, 42 respondents (49.41% of all respondents who have expressed dissatisfaction) complain that English learning apps have limited functions. Twenty-two respondents (25.88% of all respondents who have expressed dissatisfaction) complain that it costs much to use English learning apps. Fourteen respondents (16.47% of all respondents who have expressed dissatisfaction) complain that English learning apps are not updated in time. Seven respondents (8.24% of all respondents who have expressed dissatisfaction) complain that English learning apps are full of bugs which are really annoying. This indicates that some of the current English learning apps ought to be optimized in order to cater for students' needs.

5   Suggestions

Digitalization and intellectualization of English learning are the trend of future development [12]. Through data analysis, this study puts forward suggestions from three aspects: English app design, college students' English learning and college teachers' teaching.

5.1   Suggestions for the Design of English App

- The survey reveals that respondents are really interested in word learning apps and they pay much attention to edutainment and language applications. As a result, app designers could develop suitable English learning apps which are not only rich in content but also bear practical functions. More audio or visual resources that are closely related to English learning could be included in the apps, and advanced technology could be applied in the apps to create an authentic scene for communication. In this way, more and more students will be apt to use these English learning apps to assist their English learning.
- The study finds that the respondents think that the use of English learning apps have benefited their ability of learning words the most, and have contributed least to the improvement of their writing and speaking skills. Hence, the app designers could develop more apps that could effectively influence the users' writing or speaking skills.
- The survey shows that the respondents who are dissatisfied with the English learning apps think that the function of the apps is limited. In light of this, the app designers ought to take measure to figure out the needs of students with different tastes and to include more functions that will attract students to use.
- The survey also reveals that some respondents who are dissatisfied with the English learning apps complain about the bugs in some English learning apps. They also complain that some apps are not updated in time. Hence, it is important that the app designers optimize the English learning apps they develop to avoid annoying the users. Moreover, they ought to update their apps in time, which will surely generate a sound learning experience for the users.
- In this survey, some respondents also express their dissatisfaction with the English learning apps because they have to pay much to use the apps. It is highly demanded that the app designers release more free apps so that more and more students will be willing to use apps to assist their learning, which will finally improve the popularity of the English learning apps.
- Many of the current English learning apps used by students are designed by Chinese engineers rather than English natives. Therefore, the sentences they present might be labeled as "Chinglish", which will mislead students' learning. Therefore, people with language education background could be invited to offer suggestions for the development of apps so as to optimize the apps to better meet the learners' needs [13].

5.2   Suggestions for College Students' English Learning

- Students could develop good learning habits and enhance self-control in online learning. They could figure out a reasonable schedule of using English learning apps.

- Students ought to be aware of their own learning abilities and judge what kind of English learning apps suit them best. In this way, students could learn more efficiently and effectively.

5.3 Suggestions for College Teachers' Teaching

- Teachers could be more aware of the trend of the digitalization and intellectualization of English learning. They could update themselves with various English learning apps and judge whether the apps are suitable for the students or not before the apps are introduced to the students [2, 9].
- Teachers could strengthen their role in guiding their students to use apps effectively. After teachers select specific apps to assist teaching, they could tell their students the pros and cons of the English learning apps they have chosen, so that students can form a good habit of using apps [9, 14].

6   Conclusions

To sum up, under the "dual-line" education mode, college students' use of English learning apps helps them cultivate independent learning habits and improve their comprehensive English abilities. This study has conducted a survey of students in NingboTech University on their aim, habit, and preference of using English learning apps. The study also investigates the influence of English learning apps on those students, which leads to some proposals for the English teaching and learning as well as the design of the English learning apps.

This study finds that major difference really matters when it comes to the choice of English learning apps, and it will also affect the time respondents spend on English learning apps. The study also shows that most respondents find English learning apps that focus on language application the most useful. They prefer to use more "words" apps in comparison with other types of English learning apps. They believe that English learning apps contribute greatly to the improvement of their word learning. They also admit that using English learning apps is beneficial for the improvement of their listening comprehension and reading comprehension.

Acknowledgments. The authors gratefully acknowledge the research projects supported by the Zhejiang Provincial Planning Office of Philosophy and Social Science (Grant Number: 23NDJC347YB) and by the Major Humanities and Social Sciences Research Projects in Zhejiang higher education institutions (Grant Number: 2023QN052). This work was also supported by the Zhejiang Higher Education Teaching Reform Project for the 14th Five-Year Plan Period (Grant Number: jg20220689), the 2022 Key Project for Professional Comprehensive Reform at NingboTech University (Construction of International-Communication-Capacity-Oriented Experimental Teaching System and Cooperative Education Mechanism for New Liberal Arts) and the 2022 Project for Professional Comprehensive Reform at NingboTech University (Exploration and Practice of College English Teaching Model from the Perspective of New Engineering and New Liberal Arts Majors).

References

1. Wu, J.F., Fang, Y.: Research on digital compiling and publishing under the background of 'Internet Plus.' China Publ. J. **4**, 42–46 (2022). (in Chinese)
2. Yang, J.: Current situation analysis and countermeasure research of online teaching in colleges and universities. China J. Labor Relat. **2**, 19–24 (2022). (in Chinese)
3. Yuan, S.: Analysis on quality control strategy of online teaching in universities. Sci. Technol. Vision **28**, 48–50 (2021). (in Chinese)
4. Deng, Y., Long, J.: The influence of English learning apps on college students' self-learning. J. Jilin Radio TV Univ. **3**, 58–60 (2021). (in Chinese)
5. Tong, X.: Research on online and offline mixed English teaching mode in the post-epidemic Era. Mod. Bus. Ind. **4**, 157–159 (2022). (in Chinese)
6. Chen, Q.X.: Practice research on vocational college students' English learning assisted by mobile apps. Inf. Comput. **16**, 244–247 (2021). (in Chinese)
7. Zhang, Y.Q.: English Learning App Data Analysis and Application Research. Shanghai Normal University, Shanghai (2018). (in Chinese)
8. Zhang, X.S.: A study on English vocabulary memorization strategies of college students—a case study of The Word Cut, Momo, Shanbei Words and Memorizing Words. Engl. Squ. **155**, 119–121 (2021). (in Chinese)
9. Qi, J.: An empirical study on classroom participation of college students in the context of English apps pragmatics. J. Changchun Univ. **4**, 90–92+105 (2019). (in Chinese)
10. Zhou, X.C.: Thinking on college English courses from the perspective of core literacy in the era of "Internet +." Overs. Engl. **5**, 168–169 (2022). (in Chinese)
11. Yuan, X.W.: Research on the reform and development of college English teaching under the background of "Internet +" era. J. Hubei Open Vocat. Coll. **317**, 175–176 (2022). (in Chinese)
12. Xin, W.J., Lai, H.: Dissemination and application of educational apps in college students' foreign language learning. News Commun. **14**, 156–157 (2018). (in Chinese)
13. Lu, X.T.: Research on the Evaluation Index System of English APP for College Students. Henan University, Henan (2019). (in Chinese)
14. Huang, J.G.: Using mobile phone APP to cultivate higher vocational students' independent English learning ability exploration. J. Yangtze River Eng. Vocat. Tech. Coll. **3**, 72 (2016). (in Chinese)

Research Hotspots and Frontiers of Blockchain Technology Based on Citespace

Xueting Yang and Xia Zhao[✉]

School of Information Technology, Hebei University of Economics and Business,
Shijiazhuang 050000, China
2649805106@qq.com

Abstract. This paper uses Citespace bibliometric tool to visually analyze the core literature in the field of blockchain technology, and sort out the hot spots and frontiers of the research in the field of blockchain technology. 3522 core journal papers retrieved from CNKI database. Through author cooccurrence analysis, institution co-occurrence analysis, keyword clustering analysis and hotspot word emergence analysis of the above literature, it is concluded that the research hotspots of blockchain technology include consensus mechanism, smart contract and other technologies, as well as privacy protection, supply chain, copyright protection and other applications. The study found that future research should focus on the combination of blockchain with other fields or other hot technologies. The above research provides relevant reference for researchers in the field of blockchain.

Keywords: Citespace · The currency · Smart contracts · Consensus mechanism · Artificial intelligence

1 Introduction

In 2008, an article titled "Bitcoin: A Peer-to-Peer Electronic Cash System" was published under the pseudonym Satoshi Nakamoto. This paper proposes that blockchain is a data structure, the core technology of Bitcoin, used to record the accounting history of Bitcoin transactions.

Blockchain technology, known as distributed ledger technology, has the characteristics of securely storing data, and information cannot be forged and tampered with. It can automatically execute smart contracts without the need for review by any centralized organization, and can effectively solve the trust problem of all parties involved. It is widely used in finance, Internet of Things, medical care, transportation, education and other fields.

Blockchain technology has attracted much attention, and it is considered to be the next-generation disruptive core technology after steam engines, electricity, and the Internet. This paper uses Citespace5.8R3 software and adopts the visual bibliometric method

Supported by: The Scientific Research Program of Higher Education of Hebei Province (SD2021097).

to sort out the Chinese literature in the field of blockchain technology from 2014 to 2021, trying to outline the research hotspots and trends of blockchain technology in China, and for the future blockchain technology. Chain technology research hotspots are prospected.

2   Data Sources and Research Methods

As an excellent bibliometrics software, CiteSpace can visualize the relationship between documents in the form of a scientific knowledge map to display the research hotspots in related fields.

In this paper, CNKI database was used for literature retrieval. The data retrieval time was December 2021, and the time span was 2014–2021. Total number of documents: 3522; search conditions: (subject% = 'blockchain technology' or title% = 'blockchain technology' or title = xls('blockchain technology')) or v_subject = xls('blockchain technology') Technology')) AND ((Core Journal = 'Y') OR (CSSCI Journal = 'Y') OR (CSCD Journal = 'Y')); Scope: Journals.

This paper uses Citespace 5.8R3 to conduct author cooccurrence analysis, institutional co-occurrence analysis, keyword clustering analysis, and hot word emergence analysis on CNKI database to explore domestic research hotspots and research fronts in the field of blockchain technology.

3   Literature Statistical Analysis

3.1   Time Analysis

The annual number of published papers is an important indicator to measure the popularity and development trend of blockchain technology research. Through the statistical analysis of the number of documents related to blockchain technology in the time period selected in this paper, we can see the trend of changes in the number of documents related to blockchain technology as a whole. As can be seen from Fig. 1, the number of documents related to blockchain technology has gradually increased from 2014 to 2021, and there has been no downward trend. Slow growth in 20142016. 2019–2020 saw the fastest surge in publication volume. On the afternoon of October 24, 2019, the Political Bureau of the Central Committee of the Communist Party of China conducted the eighteenth collective study on the development status and trends of blockchain technology. Xi Jinping, general secretary of the Central Committee of the Communist Party of China, emphasized that the integrated application of blockchain technology plays an important role in new technological innovation and industrial transformation. We should take blockchain as an important breakthrough for independent innovation of core technologies, clarify the main direction of attack, increase investment, focus on conquering a number of key core technologies, and accelerate the development of blockchain technology and industrial innovation. In 2021, the number of published papers will be the largest, and the annual number of published papers will be 1,268, which is enough to show that the development of blockchain technology is hot. Because of the epidemic, people need more science and technology such as blockchain to solve problems in their lives. Therefore, the number of publications in 2020 and 2021 is higher.

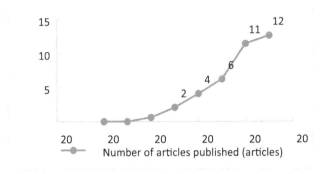

Fig. 1. Time distribution of the number of Chinese documents on.

3.2 Author Cooperation Network Analysis

In Citespace, set the Node type as Author, the time span is 2014–2021, the time slice is 1 year, and when CiteSpace is run, the number of nodes is 287, the number of connections is 212, and the density is 0.0052. Blockchain technology research Author co-occurrence knowledge graph. Each node represents an author, the size of the node represents the number of articles published by the author, the connection between the nodes indicates the existence of a cooperative relationship between the authors, and the thickness of the connection represents the closeness of the cooperative relationship between the authors. It can be seen from Fig. 2 that some authors have relationship lines, and many authors have no relationship lines and do not cooperate with other authors. There are more than 10 author cooperation networks. The centrality of the authors is all 0, the overall map is very loose, and there is no close cooperation network. The cooperative relationship presents a pattern of overall decentralization and partial concentration.

Table 1 shows the published papers of the top 11 core authors. Among them, Li Chao and Wang Feiyue published the most papers. Followed by Zhang Lihua. Li Chao posted the earliest and the most. Most of Li Chao wrote articles independently, and a few cooperated with Zhang Liang and others. Wang Feiyue co-authored many publications. Among the documents retrieved this time, Yuan Yong and Wang Feiyue's current situation and prospect of blockchain technology development are the most frequently cited. They proposed the basic architecture model of the blockchain system, expounded the basic principles, technologies, methods and application status of the blockchain and its related bitcoins, discussed the concept, application and significance of smart contracts, and introduced the concept, application and significance of smart contracts. The parallel social development trend of blockchain is committed to providing useful guidance and reference for future related research [6].

3.3 Co-occurrence Analysis of Institutional Cooperation

The research institutions are scattered and there is no obvious clustering. East China Jiaotong University publishes the most papers with 20 papers, followed by the School of Information and Computer of Taiyuan University of Technology. There is no cooperation

Table 1. Published papers of the top 11 core authors blockchain technology from 2014 to 2021.

author	Post volume	Year of the author's first publication
Li Chao	23	2014
Wang Feiyue	23	2016
Zhang Lihua	22	2014
Sun Chuanheng	20	2014
Zhu Yan	16	2014
Zhou Buxiang	16	2014
solemn	16	2014
Tang Yanjun	16	2020
Li Li	15	2014
Pang Xiaoqiong	15	2014
Xin Junchang	15	2014

between institutions. Table 2 shows the number of papers published by institutions with more than 10 papers and the time of their first publication.

Table 2. The number of papers issued by institutions with more than 10 papers.

mechanism	Post volume	Year of first publication
School of Software, East China Jiaotong University	20	2014
School of Information and Computer, Taiyuan University of Technology	1	2014
Southeast University School of Law	17	2014
School of Electrical Engineering, Sichuan University	17	2014
School of Information and Computer Engineering, Northeast Forestry University	16	2014
School of Information Management, Nanjing University	16	2018
School of Information, Central University of Finance and Economics	13	2017
School of Economics and Management, Jiangsu University of Science and Technology	13	2014
School of Management, University of Shanghai for Science and Technology	12	2019

(continued)

Table 2. (*continued*)

mechanism	Post volume	Year of first publication
Central University of Finance and Economics School of Law	12	2018
School of Computer Science and Technology, Wuhan University of Science and Technology	12	2014
School of Computer Science and Engineering, Northwest Normal University	11	2019
Northeastern University School of Business Administration	10	2014
School of Computer Science, Nanjing University of Posts and Telecommunications	10	2019
School of Information Engineering, Jiangxi University of Science and Technology	10	2018

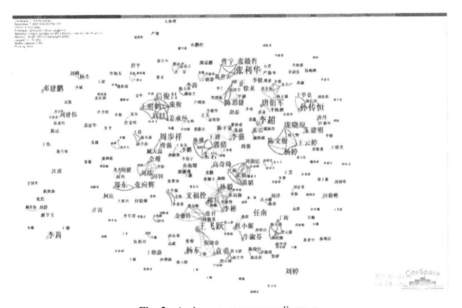

Fig. 2. Author co-occurrence diagram.

4 Keyword Clustering Analysis

4.1 Keyword Cluster Analysis

A keyword is a comprehensive, refined summary of the topic of an article. The keyword co-occurrence analysis was performed on the 3522 papers retrieved. In the CiteSpace operation, the Node types were set as the keyword Keyword, the time parameter was set as 2014–2021, and the time slice was set as 1 year. Table 3 is based on the key Top 10 information on word betweenness centrality. The frequency of keyword occurrence is not proportional to betweenness centrality. The higher the betweenness centrality of the keyword, the more important the keyword is, and it is the hub in the keyword. In addition to the "blockchain" itself, "smart contracts" have the highest centrality and frequency, and smart contracts are a hot spot in the blockchain field.

Table 3. Information on the top ten keywords.

keywords	frequency of occurrence	betweenness centrality	Year of first publication
blockchain	3365	1.20	2014
smart contract	634	0.16	2014
decentralization	199	0.08	2014
artificial intelligence	120	0.08	2014
digital currency	113	0.07	2016
Alliance chain	115	0.06	2014
consensus mechanism	213	0.05	2014
bitcoin	121	0.05	2014
Big Data	110	0.05	2016
Fintech	97	0.05	2016

Set the time span to "2014–2021", the time slice to 1, the nodetype to "Keyword" and the Selection Criteria to "k = 25". As shown in Fig. 4, the number of nodes is 560, the number of edges is 2169, and the network density is 0.0139. It can be seen that the Modularity Q value is 0.3837 > 0.3, which indicates that the network clustering structure is remarkable, and the Mean Silhouette value is 0.6812 > 0.5, which indicates that the network clustering has high internal homogeneity. Using LLR to extract keywords and automatically identify them, eight clusters are derived from this cluster. The cluster labels include blockchain, consensus mechanism, privacy protection, artificial intelligence, intelligent contract, digital currency, supply chain, copyright protection and differentiation, which indicates that blockchain technology is hot in the application of privacy protection, artificial intelligence, digital currency, supply chain and copyright protection of consensus mechanism, intelligent contract and other technologies (Fig. 3).

Blockchain is a consensus distributed network where all transactions are transparent and open. The public can see all transactions, but cannot see the link and identity information of the transaction, and the characteristics of the blockchain itself can protect privacy to a great extent [1]. The decentralization, non-tampering, and traceability features inherent in blockchain technology are complementary and compatible with the supply chain financial business model, transaction mechanism, and operation method [2]. The core legal problems facing copyright protection in the digital environment are lack of transparency of copyright ownership, repeated prohibitions on piracy, and difficulty

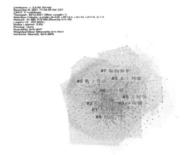

Fig. 3. Blockchain product clustering knowledge graph.

in obtaining fair compensation for authors. The core legal problems facing copyright protection in the digital environment are the lack of transparency of copyright ownership, repeated prohibitions on piracy, and difficulty in obtaining fair compensation for authors [3]. As the underlying technology of digital currency, the promotion and application of blockchain technology in the field of digital currency will help promote the in-depth development of digital currency, thereby promoting the rapid development of digital finance.

On the basis of outlining the definition, characteristics and current situation of digital currency, systematically combing and studying the technical characteristics and principles of blockchain, taking the application of blockchain technology in Bitcoin as the starting point, from the credit attributes of digital currency, payment and settlement Research on the value prospect and development trend of blockchain technology in the field of digital currency in terms of efficiency and transaction security [4]. Artificial intelligence is built on the basis of massive data and powerful computing power, and the characteristics of blockchain technology can be well integrated into artificial intelligence applications, thereby promoting the further development of artificial intelligence [5]. A smart contract is the core component (contract layer) of the blockchain. It is an event-driven, stateful computer program running on a replicable shared blockchain data ledger. It can process data actively or passively. Accept, store and send value, as well as control and manage various on-chain smart assets and other functions [6]. Blockchain technology is a universal underlying technology architecture. It generates and synchronizes data on distributed nodes through a consensus mechanism, and realizes the automatic execution of contract terms and data operations with the help of programmable scripts [7].

On the basis of the keyword clustering knowledge map, select "Summarization of Clusters" in the menu bar of "cluster" to get the keyword co-occurrence network clustering table (see Table 4).

Table 4. Co-occurrence network clustering table of blockchain technology keywords.

Cluster ID	cluster size	Markers (first five)
0	86	blockchain; sharing economy; electronic evidence; business model; credit bank
1	73	consensus mechanism; alliance chain; consensus algorithm; dpos; public chain
2	73	privacy protection; data sharing; decentralization; car networking; data security
3	69	artificial intelligence; fintech; big data; cloud computing; regtech
4	59	smart contract; ethereum; access control; ipfs; fairness
5	51	digital currency; bitcoin; cryptocurrency; virtual currency; blockchain technology
6	47	supply chain; traceability; agricultural products; safety; cross-border e-commerce
7	42	copyright protection; library; short video; digital publishing; digital copyright
8	25	differentiation; value consensus; archives management; technology; uncertainty

4.2 Keyword Timeline Map

Taking the vertical axis as the cluster name and the horizontal axis as the citation publication year, a timeline map of keyword clusters is generated. According to the timeline map, blockchain nodes have a purple outer circle, indicating that blockchain keywords have a strong centrality and play a pivotal role. In 2014, a number of prominent nodes appeared, indicating that keywords such as consensus mechanism, decentralization, artificial intelligence, and smart contracts were proposed in 2014, and the nodes became larger when they were constantly mentioned in the later period. In 2016, keywords such as credit, digital bills, cryptography, financial technology, database, and digital currency were proposed. Among them, financial technology, cryptography, and database nodes are relatively large, indicating that they are constantly mentioned in the later period, and the hot spots last for a long time. The latest keywords include chain code, knowledge graph, value chain, financing model, small and micro enterprises, digital archives, mechanism design, traceability system, copyright management, etc. The combination of blockchain technology and small and micro enterprises has gradually become a hot topic.

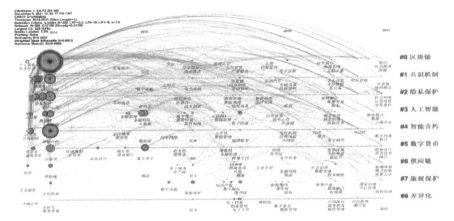

Fig. 4. Timeline graph knowledge graph.

5   Frontier Analysis of Blockchain Technology

Keyword prominence analysis can further observe the duration of keyword popularity, current research hotspots, and forecast the future research direction. Figure 5 shows the emergence of 25 key words. The "Year" in the figure indicates the year in which the keywords appeared. As the data time range is "2014–2021", the keywords all appeared continuously from 2014; "Strength" indicates the emergent strength of keywords; "Begin" means the initial time when the key words are highlighted, and the key words have become a research hotspot since that year; "End" means the time when the keyword fever ends. The blue part of the figure indicates the appearance and duration of keywords, and the red part indicates the duration of keywords becoming research hotspots. As can be seen from the figure, "Bitcoin" has the highest emergence intensity, reaching 10.59, which has become a research hotspot. "Distributed" lasts for the longest time, up to 4 years. "Electric Energy Trading" is the latest hot spot of trading, which started in 2019 and lasted until 2021. Attribute encryption, distribution and access control have been widely concerned since 2014, and their emergence intensity has reached more than 4, which has become a research hotspot. In the later stage, ico also had a high fever, and its emergent intensity reached more than 4. "Electric energy trading" is a new research hotspot.

Keywords	Year	Strength	Begin	End	2014 - 2021
attribute encryption	2014	5.21	**2014**	2016	
distributed	2014	4.92	**2014**	2018	
Access control	2014	4.52	**2014**	2016	
evolutionary game	2014	3.95	**2014**	2016	
privacy security	2014	2.96	**2014**	2017	
Differentiation	2014	2.76	**2014**	2017	
ipf	2014	2.57	**2014**	2016	
service quality	2014	2.56	**2014**	2017	
literature review	2014	2.56	**2014**	2017	
edge computing	2014	2.45	**2014**	2016	
reputation assessment	2014	2.36	**2014**	2017	
dpo	2014	2.36	**2014**	2017	
electricity trading	2014	2.25	**2014**	2017	
bitcoin	2014	10.59	**2016**	2018	
digital currency	2014	7.8	**2016**	2017	
Financial Supervision	2014	2.44	**2016**	2018	
commercial Bank	2014	2.29	**2016**	2017	
ico	2014	4.84	**2017**	2018	
digital assets	2014	3.38	**2017**	2018	
information security	2014	3.04	**2017**	2019	
RegTech	2014	2.88	**2017**	2019	
e-commerce	2014	2.28	**2017**	2018	
business model	2014	2.25	**2017**	2019	
Aggregate Signature	2014	2.34	**2018**	2019	
Electricity Trading	2014	2.46	**2019**	2021	

Fig. 5. Keyword Emergence Analysis.

6 Conclusion

Blockchain is a decentralized and distributed network, which is hot in recent years and has attracted the attention of many scholars. Blockchain technology has the characteristics of decentralization, time series data, collective maintenance, programmability, security and credibility, etc. It is especially suitable for building programmable monetary system, financial system and even macro social system. Blockchain technology can be used for sensitive information protection, supply chain, etc. Based on a total of 2,533 literatures from 2014 to 2021, this paper analyzes the authors, institutions, research hot keywords and keyword clustering of blockchain technology, and draws the following conclusions: (1) The popularity of blockchain technology continues to rise. Blockchain technology has been widely concerned by scholars, and the number of literatures has increased exponentially, and the achievements of authors in the field have been increasing. (2) The application and technology of blockchain are hot, including privacy protection, artificial intelligence, digital currency, supply chain, copyright protection, etc., while the technology includes smart contract and consensus mechanism. (3) There is basically no cooperation among institutions. There is no inter-agency cooperation. In the future development, blockchain technology will be widely used in the financial field. In the future, we should focus on privacy security, information security, and regulatory technology. It is hoped that the research results of this paper can provide intuitive and valuable reference information for the development direction of China's blockchain technology, and provide new ideas and methods for a fuller understanding of the research status of blockchain technology.

References

1. Han, Q., Wang, G.: Review of foreign research on blockchain technology. Sci. Technol. Prog. Countermeas. **35**(02), 154–160 (2018)
2. Liu, X.: Research on the supply chain financial model empowered by blockchain technology. Friends Account. **23**, 148–152 (2021)
3. Wang, J.: Copyright protection under blockchain technology: expectations, challenges and realistic paths. China Editor (11), 67–71 (2021)
4. Tong, M., Niu, Z., Chen, T.: Blockchain technology and its application in the field of digital currency. Finan. Account. Monthly (08), 137–142 (2018)
5. Pan, J., Huang, D.: The impact of blockchain technology on artificial intelligence. Comput. Sci. **45**(S2), 53–57+70 (2018)
6. Yuan, Y., Wang, F.: Current situation and prospect of blockchain technology development. J. Autom. **42**(04), 481–494 (2016)
7. Wang, Q., Li, F., Wang, Z., Liang, G., Xu, J.: Principles and key technologies of blockchain. Comput. Sci. Explor. **14**(10), 1621–1643 (2020)
8. Shao, Q., Jin, C., Zhang, Z., Qian, W., Zhou, A.: Blockchain technology: architecture and progress. J. Comput. **41**(425(05)), 969–988 (2018)

3D-LSTM Wireless Sensing Gesture Recognition —A Collaborative Bachelor and Master Project-Based Learning Case

Ming-Wei Wu$^{(\boxtimes)}$ ⓘ, Meng Zhang, Hao-Hui Zhuo ⓘ, and Yi-Chen Xu ⓘ

School of Information and Electronic Engineering, Zhejiang University of Science and Technology, Hangzhou 310023, China
wu_mingwei2004@aliyun.com

Abstract. When learning core theoretical courses in bachelor and professional master majors in electronic information engineering, such as communication engineering, electronic information engineering, artificial intelligence, etc., many students face difficulties in understanding abstract signals and deep learning knowledge taught using rigorous mathematical derivations. They are often at a loss applying the theoretical knowledge. We propose a collaborative bachelor and master student project-based learning (PBL) approach and present the Wi-Fi gesture recognition application case. The project not only provides undergraduates an intuitive understanding of signals, signal processing methods, and deep learning methods in real-life applications, but also improves their technical application skills and teamwork skills. The master student proposes a 3D-LSTM method in deep learning algorithm which improves the gesture recognition accuracy and significantly reduces the model complexity. The project not only improves the master student's research ability, but also improves his teaching and teamwork skills.

Keywords: project-based learning · bachelor and master collaboration · signal processing · deep learning · artificial intelligence · gesture recognition

1 Introduction

In undergraduate majors of electronic information engineering such as communication engineering, electronic information engineering and artificial intelligence, core theoretical courses such as digital signal processing, communication principles, wireless communication and deep learning are full of comprehensive knowledge, both theoretical and abstract. Core theoretical courses in new majors like

This work is supported by 2020 Zhejiang Provincial-level Top Undergraduate Courses (Zhejiang Provincial Department of Education General Office Notice (2021) No. 195), Classroom Teaching Reform Project at Zhejiang University of Science and Technology (No. 2018-ky3), Top Undergraduate Courses Development Project (Nos. 2020-k11, 2022-k4, 2020-k10).

artificial intelligence, such as machine learning and deep learning in particular, traditional teaching methods often rely on rigorous mathematical derivation, which poses a significant challenge to students in applied colleges and universities. Students usually lack an intuitive understanding of signals, signal processing methods, and deep learning methods, and are often at a loss when applying theoretical knowledge learnt through mathematical derivations. Due to a usually large student-teacher ratio in Chinese universities, the practical courses are often based on verification experiments, making it difficult to satisfy university goal to cultivate application-oriented talents as well as research-oriented talents [1].

In this paper, we design a project-based learning (PBL) case involving signal processing and deep learning for bachelor and master students majoring in electronic information engineering, using the application of wireless sensing gesture recognition as an example. The NIC wireless network card is used for signal collection, MATLAB is used for signal processing of Wi-Fi signals and Python is used for deep learning methods to realize the recognition of hand gestures. The program involves a few different courses, majors, workloads and students. In order to improve efficiency and focus on the respective learning goals of students at different levels, a bachelor and master collaboration scheme is adopted:

1. The supervisors is responsible for the topic and objectives of the project, guiding master students the direction of innovation, dividing sub-projects, setting up milestones, and forming interdisciplinary undergraduate teams based on expertise.
2. Master students are responsible for project technical solution design and experiment design, focusing on deep learning algorithm research while guiding undergraduate students to implement applications and conduct experiments.
3. Undergraduates in different majors learn related knowledge under the guidance of master students to realize technology application and reduce the burden of repetitive experiments for master students.

The system framework shown in Fig. 1 contains three parts: signal collection, signal processing and classification. First, engineering freshmen and sophomore undergraduates conduct experiments to collect gesture channel state information (CSI) [2] signal data through wireless network cards. Next, sophomore and junior students majoring in communication engineering and electronic information engineering remove interference and reduce noise using signal processing methods such as filtering and short-term Fourier transform (STFT) to obtain gesture-related features. Finally, master students choose and design suitable deep

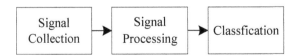

Fig. 1. System framework

learning models, and guide sophomore and junior students majoring in communication engineering and artificial intelligence to input feature data into the deep
learning model for training and testing to realize gesture recognition.

2   Signal Collection

Wi-Fi gesture signals are collected by one transmitter and three receivers in an
indoor environment. The experiment setup is shown in Fig. 2, where Tx represents a transmitter and Rx represents a receiver.

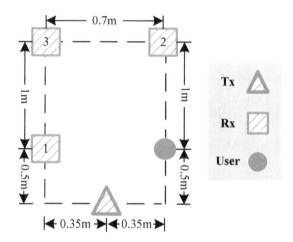

Fig. 2. Experiment setup

Data is transmitted at 1000 packet/s. The receiver is a laptop computer
running Linux system, with an Intel 5300 NIC wireless network card as shown
in Fig. 3. Gesture CSI signals are collected using the Linux open-source CSI Tool
based on the IEEE 802.11n protocol.

Figure 4 shows the instantaneous amplitudes of 30 sub-carriers of the collected CSI data, showing theoretical knowledge e.g. the orthogonal frequency
division multiplexing (OFDM) principle in the course Communication Principles
or Digital Communications and the frequency selectivity of multi-path fading in
the course Wireless Communications.

Figure 5 shows time variation of sub-carrier CSI amplitudes, i.e., the time-
varying characteristics of the multi-path fading channel in the course Wireless
Communications.

Four gestures are designed, i.e. wave, draw a circle, draw a zigzag, and push
& pull, as shown in Fig. 6. A total of 14 undergraduate students participated in
the gesture signal collection. They varied in genders, heights and weights, and
the distribution of their information is shown in Fig. 7. Each student collected

Fig. 3. Intel 5300 NIC

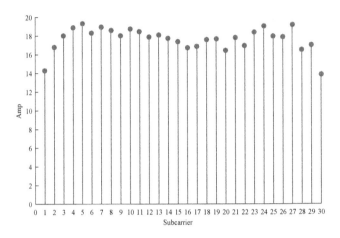

Fig. 4. Instantaneous amplitudes of 30 sub-carriers

20 gesture samples for each gesture. A total of $4 \times 20 \times 14 = 1120$ gesture signal data were collected.

In the practice of signal collection, undergraduate students from engineering majors practise Linux and basic computer skills. Students majoring in communication engineering and electronic information engineering gain intuitive understanding of signals, bandwidth, OFDM and multi-path fading in Communication Principles and Wireless Communications, and improve their hands-on ability and teamwork skills.

3   Signal Processing

CSI is a signal that contains physical layer information based on OFDM. The paths of the received signal consist of the static and dynamic paths due to the multi-path effect and movement. The CSI of the received signal with frequency

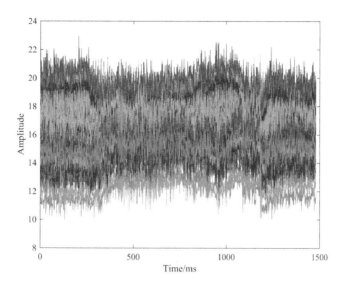

Fig. 5. Time variation of sub-carrier CSI amplitudes

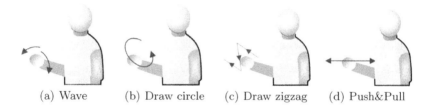

(a) Wave   (b) Draw circle   (c) Draw zigzag   (d) Push&Pull

Fig. 6. Gestures

f at moment t can be expressed as the sum of the static signal and the dynamic signal [3]:

$$H(f,t) = [H_s(f,t) + H_d(f,t)]\, e^{j\kappa(f,t)} \tag{1}$$

where $H_s(f,t)$ and $H_d(f,t)$ denote the static and dynamic components, respectively, and $\kappa(f,t)$ denotes the random phase shift. The static component describes the signal reflected by a static object, e.g. a wall, and the dynamic component describes changes in the signal

$$H(f,t) = [H_s(f,t) + H_d(f,t)]\, e^{j\kappa(f,t)} \tag{2}$$

containing the Doppler frequency shift (DFS) caused by the gesture. Therefore, gesture recognition can be performed by analyzing the dynamic component of CSI.

Figure 8 shows the schematic diagram of the whole signal processing process, which mainly contains the steps of conjugate phase multiplication [4], principal component analysis (PCA) [5], short-term Fourier transform (STFT), and body-coordinate velocity profile (BVP) [6] estimation. MATLAB is used to write the

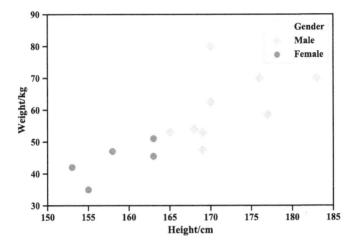

Fig. 7. Statistics of participants

relevant programs, and the open-source MATLAB-based CSI toolbox provides a large number of signal processing functions. Also, we add visual displays in the signal processing process, which allows students to understand the various methods of signal processing in a more intuitive way through visualization, as shown in Fig. 9.

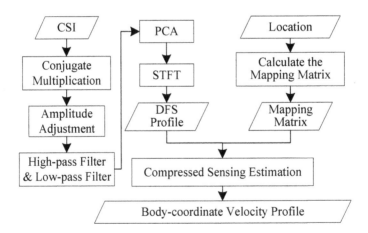

Fig. 8. Signal processing flow

Figure 9(a) shows the change in signal amplitude after conjugate multiplication, high-pass filtering and low-pass filtering, visualizing the process of high-pass filtering and low-pass filtering in the course Digital Signal Processing. Figure 9(b) shows the effect of PCA in the course Multivariate Statistical Analysis and

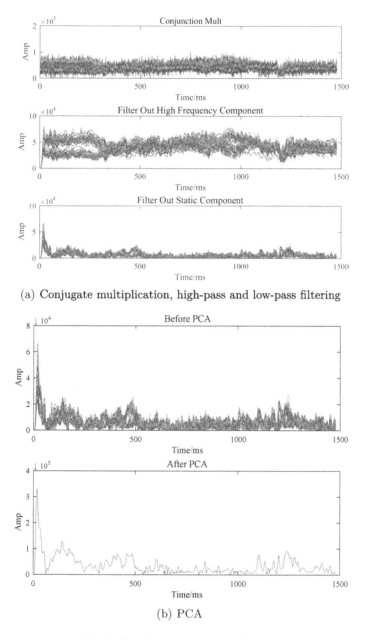

(a) Conjugate multiplication, high-pass and low-pass filtering

(b) PCA

Fig. 9. Signal processing visualization

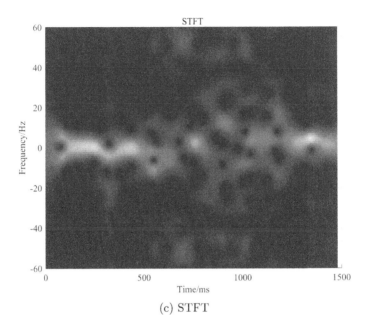

(c) STFT

Fig. 9. (*continued*)

Fig. 9(c) shows the effect of STFT in the course Digital Signal Processing. The visualization of the intermediate steps of signal processing gives communication engineering and electronic information engineering students a more intuitive understanding of Digital Signal Processing course knowledge, increases their further understanding of knowledge points, and improves their MATLAB programming skills.

4 Classification

BVP is similar to continuous video image frames, and each BVP data records the variation of velocity power distribution of each gesture, but the BVP features extracted from the same gesture are still affected by different human bodies, different motion amplitudes, speeds and directions, which increases the difficulty of recognition. In order to extract the accurate spatial-temporal features of BVP as much as possible, we combine 3D convolutional [7] neural network and long short-term memory (LSTM) [8] recurrent neural network model in the field of artificial intelligence to construct a 3D-LSTM network.

The reason for choosing 3D convolution is that it can better extract the information of features in the time dimension than 2D convolution, and the resulting features are more temporally correlated. In fact, 2D convolution is a special case of 3D convolution, which simplifies to 2D convolution when the depth of the convolution kernel is the same as the depth of the input tensor. The LSTM is chosen because the BVP mainly responds to the change of velocity distribution over time, and the LSTM can retain more temporal details than the Gated Recurrent Unit, which is also a recurrent neural network, which fits nicely the needs of this project.

As shown in Fig. 10, the model first uses two layers of 3D convolution to extract the effective features of the BVP data. The first 3D convolution layer contains 16 6×6×3 3D convolution kernels with a step size of 1, without zero padding, and uses ReLU as the activation function. The second 3D convolution layer contains 8 $3 \times 3 \times 3$ 3D convolution kernels, and all other parameters are the same as the first 3D convolution layer. Next, the data are dimensionalized by a maximum pooling layer of size $2 \times 2 \times 1$ to reduce the redundancy of features. The features processed by the pooling layer are expanded into a set of vectors and fed into an LSTM network with 32 cells to further extract the features in the temporal dimension. Finally, the features extracted by the LSTM are fed into a gesture classifier consisting of a fully connected layer containing four neurons corresponding to different gestures, which are mapped to each gesture using SoftMax as the activation function. A dropout layer with a coefficient of 0.3 is used between the LSTM layer and the dense layer to avoid overfitting.

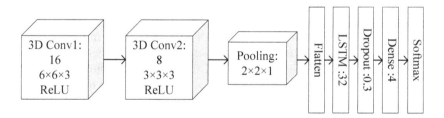

Fig. 10. Structure of 3D-LSTM

Python is used to program the deep learning model, calling numpy, keras, sk-learn and other libraries. Due to differences in the physical characteristics of the participating students at the time of signal acquisition, same-distribution sampling was used in dividing the training and test data sets and five-fold cross-validation was used to ensure the consistency of data distribution during model training. Table 1 shows the final gesture recognition accuracy of the proposed model and the number of parameters, compared with C-RNN [6], 3D-CNN [9] and LSTM [10].

Table 1. Accuracy and parameter comparison

Model	Accuracy/%	Parameter/k
LSTM	89.91	713
3D-CNN	90.72	835
C-RNN	91.52	106
3D-LSTM	**92.86**	**26**

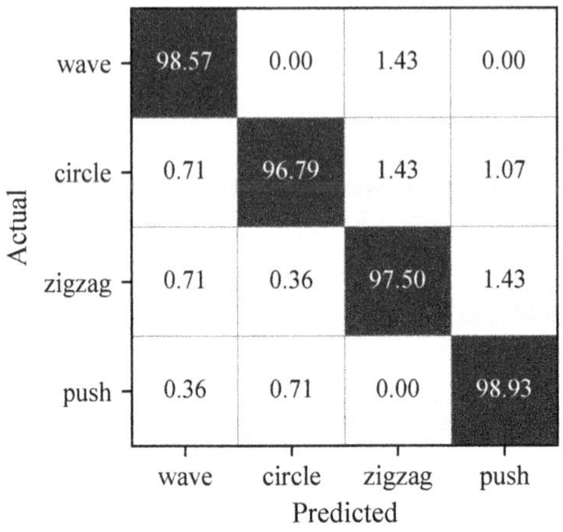

Fig. 11. Confusion Matrix

The proposed 3D-LSTM model improves by 1.34%-2.95% in the final recognition accuracy, and the number of parameters is only 26k, which is an order of magnitude less than the parameters of other models. Figure 11 shows the recognition confusion matrix of 3D-LSTM on four gestures, where the recognition accuracies of wave, draw circle, draw zigzag and push & pull are 94.64%, 92.50%, 91.79% and 92.50%, respectively. Since there are similar parts in the two gestures of wave and draw circle, the mutual mis-recognition rate of these two gestures is high, and similarly for draw zigzag and push & pull.

The classification module practice extended the knowledge of students majoring in artificial intelligence from Machine Learning and Deep Learning courses, and improves their Python programming skills and result analysis ability.

5   Conclusions

The practical teaching program in this paper involves a wide range of knowledge, and students from each major need to use their professional knowledge to cooperate with students from other majors during the project-based learning practice. Figure 12 shows the pyramidal structure of the majors of the students involved in the practical process of each module and related technical courses.

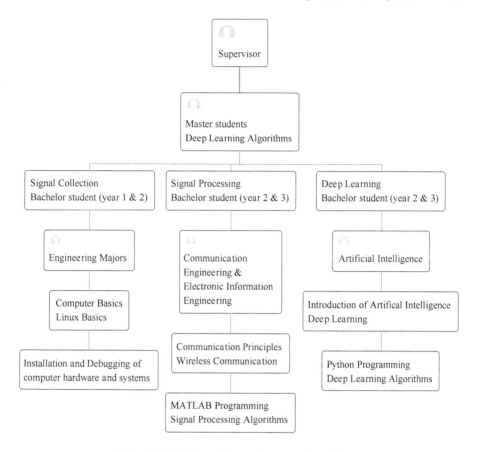

Fig. 12. Collaborative and practical teaching

Students from different majors and grades of Computer Science and Electronic Information participated in the project by dividing the work and cooperating with each other. Through specific application practice cases and visualization, students' understanding of knowledge points and their own hands-on ability were improved, and their team cooperation ability and interdisciplinary integration ability were also enhanced, laying a good foundation for the cultivation of talents in communication engineering, electronic information engineering and artificial intelligence. Based on this project and further applications of related technologies, the team of students majoring in communication engineering won a first prize and a third prize in Zhejiang Physics Science and Technology Innovation Competition, two innovation training projects granted at Zhejiang University of Science and Technology, a second prize in the "Internet+" College Innovation and Entrepreneurship Competition, and a third prize in the Challenge Cup extracurricular academic works. The master student proposed a 3D-LSTM model, which improves the accuracy of gesture recognition while significantly increasing the lightness of the model. A research paper was accepted by a core journal, and two invention patents were filed.

References

1. Long, T., Yang, D.: Research on the reform of practical teaching system of communication class under engineering practice mode. Indust. Sci. Tribune **20**(18), 160–161 (2021)
2. Zheng, Y., Zimu, Z., Liu, Y.: From RSSI to CSI: Indoor Localization via Channel Response. ACM Comput. Surv. **46**(2), (November 2013), 25:1–25:32 (2013)
3. Guo, L., et al.: Wiar: a public dataset for Wifi-based activity recognition. IEEE Access **7**, 154935–154945 (2019). https://doi.org/10.1109/access.2019.2947024
4. Li, X., et al.: Indotrack: Device-free indoor human tracking with commodity Wi-Fi. In: Proceedings of the ACM on Interactive, Mobile, Wearable and Ubiquitous Technologies **1**(3), 1–22 (2017). https://doi.org/10.1145/3130940
5. Inferring Motion Direction using Commodity Wi-Fi for Interactive Exergames. https://dl.acm.org/doi/10.1145/3025453.3025678
6. Zheng, Y., et al.: Zero-effort cross-domain gesture recognition with Wi-Fi. In: Proceedings of the 17th Annual International Conference on Mobile Systems, Applications, and Services, p. 313–325. ACM, Seoul, Republic of Korea (2019)
7. Tran, D., Bourdev, L., Fergus, R., Torresani, L., Paluri, M.: Learning spatiotemporal features with 3D convolutional networks. In: Proceedings of the IEEE International Conference on Computer Vision, (pp. 4489–4497)
8. Chung, J., Gülçehre, Ç., Cho, K., Bengio, Y.: Empirical Evaluation ofGated Recurrent Neural Networks on Sequence Modeling. CoRR abs/1412.3555 (2014)
9. Wang, Z., Chang, J.: CSI cross domain gesture recognition method based on 3d convolutional neural network. Comput. Sci. **48**(08), 322–327 (2021)
10. Liu, J., Wang, Y., Lei, Y.: CSI gesture recognition method based on LSTM. Comput. Sci. **46**(11), 283–288 (2019)

Research on Chinese Language Learning Behaviors of Students in Indonesia Primary School

Ling Shen[1], Yuanbin Fang[2], Wenyi Gao[3], and Huanhai Fang[4(✉)]

[1] School of the Humanities, Xuzhou Institution of Techonology, Xuzhou, China
gwhenling@163.com
[2] College of Business and Economics, Australia National University, Canberra, Australia
u5818784@anu.edu.au
[3] College of Asia and Pacific, National University, Canberra, Australia
u5833330@anu.edu.au
[4] School of Foreign Studies, Suqian University, Suqian, China
fanghuanhai@xmu.edu.cn

Abstract. In Chinese language teaching, even though students are in an identical learning environment, significant differences in learning efficiency still exist between individuals. The presence of these variations can have a considerable impact on students' Chinese language improvement. This study will investigate the formations and consequences of these differences in the learning behavior's four dimensions. This study employs SPSS statistical analysis software for data processing and analysis and concludes the following observations: 1) Chinese language achievement is positively related to students' learning behaviors in four dimensions; 2) The extent of Chinese language learning has a negative correlation with learning behavior; 3) Gender distinction resides in students' learning behaviors; 4) There is a significant relationship between the language used at home and the learning behavior. This study interprets the specific effects of the length of Chinese language learning, gender diversity, and the language used at home on the students' Chinese language learning patterns. Furthermore, this study proposes recommendations to teachers for improvement in Chinese language teaching in accordance with the present status of Chinese language teaching and students' learning behaviors.

Keywords: Chinese language teaching · learning behavior · computer aided education · Introduction

1 Introduction

Learning behaviors are basic behaviors determined by individuals themselves, which are also known as Basic Learning Behaviors or Stylistic Learning Behaviors. In recent years, Chinese and oversea scholars have gradually begun to emphasize student-centered instructional research, especially in the field of learners' learning behaviors. For instance, the statistical evidence detected by Durbrow et al. (2000) demonstrated that related learning behaviors are better predictors of academic performance than cognitive abilities.

McDermott et al. (1996) developed the Learning Behaviors Scale (LBS), which consists of 29 items. The comprehensive items capture the following four dimensions of learning behavior: learning motivation, learning attitude, learning attention, and learning strategy. Therefore, LBS is applicable to, examine the individual's learning behavior of different ages, genders, and ethnic groups. Schaefer (1996) and Hamlet (1999) both adopted the general American LBS to investigate and analyse learners' in-class learning behavior, and illustrated a significant positive correlation between learning behavior and academic performance. Durbrow et al. (2001) also contended that, in addition to cognitive ability, in- class attention and anxiety levels significantly contribute to an individual's academic performance.

Riding et al. (2003) explored the factors that influence middle school students' learning behaviors and performances with respect to their working memory, cognitive style, and gender. The findings emphasizes that learners with verbal cognition and analysis cognitive style had better learning behavior than those with other cognitive styles. It also indicated that no significant association was found between gender and learning behavior. MOS and Csizer (2008) remarked that the primary elements that affect second language learning are language learning attitudes and the Ideal L2 self, which provided empirical support for the self-system theory of second language motivation.

Throughout the academic literature on Chinese language education, studies on the relationship between learning behaviors and language teaching currently concentrate on learning motivation. The studies have not considered all four dimensions of learning behavior, and there are only two investigations of primary school students' Chinese learning behavior. Consequently, there is no dependable quantitative conclusion and valid interpretation of learning behavior variables. Accordingly, this paper selects an Indonesian primary school as a case study to investigate the Chinese teaching environment and analyse the students' Chinese learning behavior.

2 Hypothesis, Survey Respondents and Questionnaire Development

2.1 Hypothesis

This paper proposes the theoretical hypothesis of the survey on the basis of the previous research results, examines the respondents and obtains the required information through scientific methods, and eventually reaches a diagnosis and conclusion on the proposed hypothesis. This survey encompasses three theoretical hypothesizes,

Hypothesis 1: The language learning length causes differences in language learning behavior.
Hypothesis 2: gender differences exist in language learning behavior.
Hypothesis 3: There is a correlation between language learning behavior and home used language.

2.2 Survey Respondents

Tzu Chi Primary School in North Jakarta, Indonesia, was officially opened in July 2011. It is a trilingual international school with over 1,200 students. Chinese is one of the main courses at the school, accounting for 40% of the total language program. The students are all required to pass the new Chinese Proficiency Test (HSK) Level 3 before they graduate from primary school. The survey involved 522 Chinese language learners in grades one through six at Tzu Chi Primary School. Four classes were randomly selected from each grade (the only two classes in grade six were included). A total of 522 questionnaires were sent out and 522 valid questionnaires were received, with an effective response rate of 100%.

This study utilizes SPSS 23.0 to conduct the sample reliability scores for each grade level on four-dimensional variables, which are: motivation, attitude, strategy, and attention. The result reveals that grade one and grade two's Cronbach's alpha for each variable is less than 0.7, implying that the data for these two grades are unreliable. The explanation could be the learners' lack of self-awareness and self-evaluation in the lower grades. Therefore, this study only consists of 337 participants from grades three to grade six in the following analysis.

2.3 Questionnaire Development

The questionnaire is derived from the Learning Behavior Scale (LBS) developed by McDermott et al. (1996). The generic American LBS consists of 29 components and incorporates four dimensions: motivation, attitude, attention, and strategy. Hence it is applicable to measure students' learning behavior across diverse ages, genders, and ethnic groups. McDermott conducted a factor analysis test on the four dimensions of adaptive learning behavior in LBS and concluded that each dimension had high internal consistency and test-retest reliability. Since LBS is only specific to in-class learning behaviors, the study also referenced the questionnaire compiled by Politzer and McGroarty (1985). The questionnaire whilst is modified according to the specific situation of Tzu Chi primary school students and their Chinese learning environment. Ultimately, a questionnaire is developed that was tailored to investigate the Chinese learning behavior of Tzu Chi primary school students.

3   Analysis on Four Dimensions of Chinese Learning Behavior

The study adopts Confirmatory Factor Analysis (CFA) to conduct the validity of questionnaires. The MSA values for each question in the questionnaire were more prominent than 0.5, indicating excellent validity of the scale utilized in this study. The statistical results of the survey were presented in the following tables.

Table 1 presents the description of the four dimensions for each grade level, revealing that the third grade has the highest mean values in motivation, attitude attention and strategy, with the values 47.53, 65.11, 37.78, and 80.79, respectively. The fourth grade ranks second among the four grades, the fifth grade takes third place, and the sixth grade has the lowest numerical scores. The analysis of the statistics in Table 1 demonstrates that the higher the learner's grade level, the more inactive their learning behavior. One of the patterns observed in Table 1 is that there are significant differences in learning behaviors among different grade students while higher grade levels result in lower behavior scores. In a nutshell, primary school students' length of language learning time and learning behavior is negatively correlated.

Table 1. Learning behavior scores of students in different grades

		Quantity	Mean	Standard Deviation	Standard Error	95% Confidence interval		Min	Max
						Lower Bound	Upper Bound		
Motivation	Grade 3	98	47.53	7.795	0.787	45.97	49.09	30	65
	Grade 4	96	43.26	8.452	0.863	41.55	44.97	22	59
	Grade 5	95	42.77	6.717	0.689	41.40	44.14	22	55
	Grade 6	48	38.02	6.702	0.967	36.07	39.97	23	51
	Total	337	43.62	8.113	0.442	42.75	44.49	22	65
Attitude	Grade 3	98	65.11	9.947	1.005	63.12	67.11	39	85
	Grade 4	96	59.45	10.233	1.044	57.37	61.52	33	81
	Grade 5	95	58.65	9.616	0.987	56.69	60.61	34	78
	Grade 6	48	55.85	8.205	1.184	53.47	58.24	40	76
	Total	337	60.36	10.198	0.556	59.27	61.45	33	85
Attention	Grade 3	98	37.78	5.961	0.602	36.58	38.97	23	49
	Grade 4	96	34.07	6.048	0.617	32.85	35.30	16	48
	Grade 5	95	33.36	5.452	0.559	32.25	34.47	17	43
	Grade 6	48	31.94	5.632	0.813	30.30	33.57	20	46
	Total	337	34.64	6.150	0.335	33.98	35.30	16	49
Strategy	Grade 3	98	80.79	10.523	1.063	78.68	82.90	61	112
	Grade 4	96	76.60	11.704	1.195	74.23	78.98	50	106
	Grade 5	95	74.42	11.439	1.174	72.09	76.75	31	99
	Grade 6	48	73.08	10.353	1.494	70.08	76.09	44	100
	Total	337	76.70	11.424	0.622	75.48	77.93	31	112

Table 2 illustrates that female students have higher mean values versus male students on all four dimensions (motivation 45.10, attitude 62.23, attention 36.02, and strategy 78.51). Out of the 337 respondents, 170 (50.45%) were male students and 167 (49.55%) were female students. Comparing the statistical discrepancies in learning behaviors between the two genders, the mean differences between female and male students were motivation 2.94, attitude 3.71, attention 2.73, and strategy 3.58.

Table 2. Learning behavior scores of students in different gender

	Gender	Quantity	Mean	Standard Deviation	Standard Error
Motivation	Male	170	42.16	7.869	0.604
	Female	167	45.10	8.114	0.628
Attitude	Male	170	58.52	10.374	0.796
	Female	167	62.23	9.695	0.750
Attention	Male	170	33.29	6.028	0.462
	Female	167	36.02	5.980	0.463
Strategy	Male	170	74.93	11.103	0.852
	Female	167	78.51	11.495	0.889

The significance tests were conducted in SPSS for each of the four dimensions for both genders in Table 3. In the results of the independent sample T test, if the significance in Levene's homogeneity variance test is greater than 0.05, it indicates that the variances of the two groups of data are equal. The significance must then be tested by mean homogeneity t-test with equal variance assumed. On the contrary, if the significance in Levene's homogeneity variance test is less than 0.05, it denotes heterogeneity of variance between the two groups. Significance is required to be examined by mean homogeneity t-test with equal variance not assumed. If the significance value in the mean homogeneity t-test is less than 0.05, it means that there is a significant difference between the two groups; while if it is greater than 0.05, thus the difference is not significant. The significance values of four dimensions are less than 0.05, which indicates that there are significant differences in language learning behaviors between the male and female students.

Table 3. Significant test of genders differences in language learning behavior

	Equal Variance	Levene's homogeneity variances test		Mean homogeneity t-test						
		F-value	Significance	t-value	DF	Significance (Double tails)	Mean Difference	SE difference	95% confidence interval	
									Lower Bound	Upper Bound
Motivation	Assumed	0.298	0.585	−3.366	335	0.001	−2.931	0.871	−4.644	−1.218
	Not Assumed			−3.366	334	0.001	−2.931	0.871	−4.644	−1.218
Attitude	Assumed	0.747	0.388	−3.385	335	0.001	−3.704	1.094	−5.856	−1.552
	Not Assumed			−3.387	334	0.001	−3.704	1.094	−5.855	-1.553
Attention	Assumed	0.018	0.895	−4.182	335	0.000	−2.736	0.654	−4.023	−1.449
	Not Assumed			−4.182	335	0.000	−2.736	0.654	−4.022	−1.449
Strategy	Assumed	0.540	0.463	−2.908	335	0.004	−3.580	1.231	−6.001	−1.158
	Not Assumed			−2.907	334	0.004	−3.580	1.231	−6.002	−1.157

Durbrow et al. (2001) indicated that female students performed better academic performance in school and teachers also determined that female students were more disciplined than male students. In consist to previous studies, our study highlights that gender difference leads to variability in language learning and female students show more positive learning behaviors than male students. One explanation is that differences in brain architectures cause the disparities exhibited by genders. Compared to female students, male students are generally overactive and sensitive to any situation. Their behaviors are more visible in the classroom and these behaviors tend to cause disruptions.

Table 4 indicates that students whose home language is Chinese have the highest mean values in all four dimensions, with motivation 46.98, attitude 63.57, attention 36.66 and strategy of 80.80. While students with Indonesian as their home language have the lowest mean values in all four dimensions, with 41.76, 58.74, 33.93 and 74.23, respectively. With regard to learning attitudes, the most significant difference is found between students from Chinese language families and Indonesian language families, with a mean of 4.83. The discrepancy between students from English language families and

Table 4. Learning behavior scores for students with different home used languages

	Home speak language	Quantity	Mean	Standard Deviation	Standard Error	95% Confidence Interval		Min	Max
						Lower Bound	Upper Bound		
Motivation	English	89	44.30	7.727	0.819	42.68	45.93	27	65
	Chinese	56	46.98	7.129	0.953	45.07	48.89	33	64
	Indonesian	168	41.76	8.329	0.643	40.49	43.02	22	61
	Other	24	46.25	6.784	1.385	43.39	49.11	35	57
	Total	337	43.62	8.113	0.442	42.75	44.49	22	65
Attitude	English	89	61.40	10.710	1.135	59.15	63.66	39	85
	Chinese	56	63.57	8.483	1.134	61.30	65.84	47	81
	Indonesian	168	58.74	10.315	0.796	57.17	60.32	33	83
	Other	24	60.29	9.355	1.910	56.34	64.24	34	72
	Total	337	60.36	10.198	0.556	59.27	61.45	33	85
Attention	English	89	34.80	5.800	0.615	33.58	36.02	23	49
	Chinese	56	36.66	6.082	0.813	35.03	38.29	17	48
	Indonesian	168	33.93	6.124	0.472	33.00	34.86	16	49
	Other	24	34.38	7.014	1.432	31.41	37.34	20	46
	Total	337	34.64	6.150	0.335	33.98	35.30	16	49
Strategy	English	89	78.22	11.622	1.232	75.78	80.67	46	112
	Chinese	56	80.80	10.088	1.348	78.10	83.51	58	104
	Indonesian	168	74.23	11.446	0.883	72.48	75.97	31	100
	Other	24	78.83	9.783	1.997	74.70	82.96	54	96
	Total	337	76.70	11.424	0.622	75.48	77.93	31	112

other language families is not significant in any of the four dimensions. The maximum values of all four dimensions were found among students whose home language is English, and the minimum values were found among students in Indonesian language families.

According to Table 4, students from Chinese-speaking families have the highest mean values on the four dimensions compared to other languages. This result implies that students from Chinese-speaking families generally have better learning behaviors in Chinese language studies. SPSS significance test suggests significant differences in the motivation, attitude, and strategy among students from different language families. The causes of these discrepancies are the cultural backgrounds and language habits of the different families.

4 Conclusion

Several research have also demonstrated that students' learning progress is determined by their own learning behaviors and have emphasized the significance of students' developing good learning behaviors. This study analyses the current situation of behaviors in the process of Chinese language learning. The outcomes of this study's analysis will be utilized as reference suggestions for Chinese language teaching, thereby enhancing the efficiency of Chinese language teaching and learning. Chinese language teaching and discusses students' learning As an international trilingual school, As an international trilingual school, Tzu Chi Primary School adopted an immersion model, offered spoken Chinese classes, and even established a teaching team led by Chines teachers in order to create a suitable environment for the Chinese language. The regression analysis on learning behaviors could be proposed in future research as a suggestion for teachers to predict and measure students' learning behaviors. The teachers could speculate on students' learning behaviors according to their grade, gender, family and other influencing factors in order to develop customized teaching strategies.

Based on the research of Indonesian primary school students' Chinese learning behaviors, the study proposes several recommendations: 1) Teachers have to stimulate students' motivation in learning the Chinese language and develop students' good learning behaviors; 2) Teachers should create a language environment for non-native Chinese speakers. 3) Teachers should be aware of gender differences in teaching and discard gender discrimination, and provide feedback based on students' learning behaviors in class; 4) Teachers should design classroom instruction according to students' language learning behaviors, including the adoption of enriched and innovative materials, the application of flexible teaching methods, the utilization of a model-based practice model, and the examination of learning effects through classroom quizzes.

Acknowledgements. This work is supported by the Foundation of Center for Language Education and Cooperation (21YH019CX2). We are grateful to the workmates for their comments.

References

Abdullah, M.Y., Bakar, N.R.A., Mahbob, M.H.: Student's participation in classroom: what motivates them to speak up? Procedia. Soc. Behav. Sci. **51**, 516–522 (2012)

Barriga, A.Q., Doran, J.W., Newell, S.B., Morrison, E.M., Barbetti, V., Robbins, B.D.: Relationships between problem behaviors and academic achievement in adolescents: the unique role of attention problems. J. Emot. Behav. Disord. **10**, 233–240 (2002)

Beaman, R., Wheldall, K., Kemp, C.: Differential teacher attention to boys and girls in the classroom. Educ. Rev. **58**(3), 339–366 (2007)

Chen, M.L.: Age differences in the use of language learning strategies. Engl. Lang. Teach. **7**(2), 144–151 (2014)

Durbrow, E.H., Schaefer, B.A., Jimerson, S.R.: Learning-related behaviors versus cognitive ability in the academic performance of Vincentian children. Br. J. Educ. Psychol. **71**, 471–483 (2001)

Kormos, J., Csizér, K.: Age-related differences in the motivation of learning English as a foreign language: attitudes, selves, and motivated learning behavior. Lang. Learn. **58**(2), 327–355 (2008)

Lee, K.R., Oxford, R.: Understanding EFL learners' strategy use and strategy awareness. Asian EFL J. **10**(1), 7–32 (2008)

Magogwe, J.M., Oliver, R.: The relationship between language learning strategies, proficiency, age and self-efficacy beliefs: a study of language learners in Botswana. System **35**, 338–352 (2007)

McDermott, P.A.: National scales of differential learning behaviors among American children and adolescents. Sch. Psychol. Rev. **28**(2), 280–291 (1999)

McDermott, P.A., Leigh, J.L., Glutting, J.J.: Informing stylistic learning behavior, disposition, and achievement through ability subtests—or more illusions of meaning. School Psychol. Rev. **26**, 163–175 (1997)

McDermott, P.A., Leigh, N.M., Perry, M.A.: Development and validation of the preschool learning behaviors scale. Psychol. Sch. **39**(4), 353–365 (2002)

Politzer, R.L., Mcgroarty, M.: An exploratory study of learning behaviors and their relationship to gains in linguistic and communicative competence. TESOL Q. **19**(1), 103–123 (1985)

Riding, R.J., Grimley, M., Dahraei, H., Banner, G.: Cognitive style, working memory and learning behavior and attainment in school subjects. Br. J. Educ. Psychol. **73**, 149–169 (2003)

Schaefer, B.A., McDermott, P.A.: Learning behavior and intelligence as explanations for children's scholastic achievement. J. Sch. Psychol. **37**(3), 299–313 (1999)

Worrell, F.C., Vandiver, B.J., Watkins, M.: Construct validity of the learning behavior scale with an independent sample of students. Psychol. Sch. **38**(3), 207–215 (2001)

Hamlet, H.S.: Construct Validation of the Learning Behaviors Scale by Independent Measures of Student Performance. University of Pennsylvania, Philadelphia (1999)

Mooney, L.I.C.: The Assessment of Differential Student Learning Behaviors in Trinidad and Tobago: A Cross-cultural Construct Validity Study of the Learning Behaviors Scale. University of Pennsylvania, Philadelphia (2006)

Schaefer, B.A.: Relationship Between Learning Behaviors and Academic Achievement Among School-Aged American Children and Adolescents. University of Pennsylvania, Philadelphia (1996)

Santos, R.M., Ostrosky, M.M.: Understanding the impact of language differences on classroom behavior. Center on the Social and Emotional Foundations for Early Learning (2022)

Hetherington, M.E., Parke, R.D.: Gender roles and gender differences. http://highered.mheduc ation.com/sites/0072820144/student_view0/chapter15/index.html. Accessed 11 May 2016

Decoster, J.: Scale construction notes. http://www.stat-help.com/notes.html. Accessed 04 Oct 2016

Visualization Analysis on the Research Status and Trend of Recommendation System

Yi Zhang[1]([✉]) [iD], Nan Wan[2] [iD], and Chao Kong[1] [iD]

[1] Anhui Polytechnic University, Wuhu, China
zhangyi@ahpu.edu.cn
[2] Wannan Medical College, Wuhu, China

Abstract. In order to fully recognize the research status and development trend of the recommendation system, by using the software CiteSpace, taking reference to the literature in the recommendation system from 2012 to 2021 collected by the database Web of Science, this paper is to analyze the overall distribution characteristics on the years, journals, countries/regions, institutions/authors, important documents, research hotspots/research frontiers via the literature statistics and the visualization. As the result, there is going to be a knowledge map to be drawn to provide references for the researchers of the recommendation system.

Keywords: recommendation system · visualization · knowledge map · citespace

1 Introduction

With the rapid development of cloud computing, big data, Internet of Things and other technologies, the problem of 'information overload' is growing more and more serious. How to find out valuable information from a large quantity of data has become a key problem to be solved. To obtain valuable content, information retrieval by a search engine is one of the commonly used methods, such as Baidu and other retrieval systems. Another widely used and potential method is the recommendation system, which is based on the user's needs and interests to make personalized recommendation, as in the field of e-commerce and short videos. The system will be based on the user's past browsing records to recommend relevant products to users.

Academic circles are paying more and more attention to the research of recommendation system and have got some meaningful results. At present, there are four main types of recommendation system: (1) content-based recommendation, according to the user's past choice, it is to determine the user's choice preferences, select items to the user's interests in the recommended objects for the user; (2) collaborative filtering recommendation, assuming similar users with similar preferences, it is to find the potential preferences of users for the project; (3) hybrid recommendation, which is to combining different recommendation algorithms; (4) the recommendation system based on deep learning. This model can combine the explicit with the implicit feedback information, and fuse multi-source heterogeneous data into the recommendation system, so

W. Hong and Y. Weng (Eds.): ICCSE 2022, CCIS 1811, pp. 255–266, 2023.
https://doi.org/10.1007/978-981-99-2443-1_23

as to effectively alleviate the cold start and data sparsity problems faced by traditional recommendation, and effectively improve the recommendation effect.

By using the 5.8.R3 software of Cite Space to visually analyze the relevant literature in the field of recommendation system included in the core set of Web of Science, the author aims to quantitatively examine the representative research institutions, journals, literatures, research hotspots and frontiers in the field of recommendation system, and to draw a visualized knowledge map, so that the majority of researchers can more directly understand the recent developments in the field of recommendation system, to promote more researches on recommendation system [1].

2 Data Sources and Research Methods

The data in this paper comes from the core database of Web of Science. The following formula is used to retrieve: TI = 'recommendation system' OR TI = 'recommendationer system' OR TI = 'personalized recommendation' OR TI = 'personalized recommendation', and the time range is set for 2012–2021. The literature type was Article OR Proceedings Paper, with a total of 2791 records retrieved on March 17, 2022. This paper employed the visualization software Cite Space developed by Professor Chen Chaomei. Being a scientific metrology method widely used in the industry to visualize and analyze the collected data, Cite Space was to visualize the distribution of literature, journals, national and regional distribution, institutional distribution, author distribution, citation analysis, research hotspots and frontier analysis, to show the current situation of recommendation system research in the past decade [2].

3 Result Analysis

3.1 Literature Quantity Analysis

The annual number of published papers on related research topics in a period of time can help to understand the research level and development trend of in the field to a certain extent. Figure 1 shows the ten-year distribution of literature quantity in the research field of recommendation system. From the graph, it can be found that since 2012, the number of publications in the field of recommendation system research has been steadily increasing, especially during 2017–2021, at a high growth rate. It can be seen that recommendation system is the current hot research, with more and more researchers paying attention to it[3].

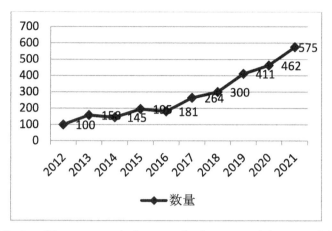

Fig. 1. Distribution of literature quantity in personalized recommendation research in the past ten years

3.2 Journal Distribution

By analyzing the highly cited and highly core journals in the field of recommendation system, the distribution of core journals in this field can be determined, which is of great help to retrieving and discovering high-quality literature in the field. By setting NodeTypes as Cited Journal in CiteSpace5.8.R3, running the software, we can get the journal co-occurrence map in the research field in recommendation system, as shown in Fig. 2. Table 1 shows highly cited journals in the field of recommended research. Intermediary centrality is an index to measure the importance of nodes in the network. According to the statistical results, the periods of centrality greater than 0.1 in Top10 are: IEEE T KNOWL DATA EN (0.15), KNOWL BASED SYST (0.14), EXPERT SYST APPL (0.12), ACM T INFORM SYST (0.11). This shows that these journals occupy an important position in the field of recommendation system research, and they are the core communication platform of recommendation system research. The published literature has high quality and reference value [4].

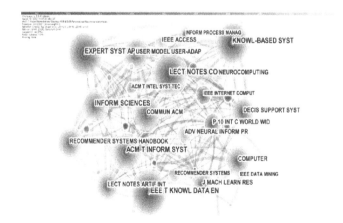

Fig. 2. Co-occurrence Map of Journals in Recommendation System Research

Table 1. 10 top Highly cited journals in personalized recommendation research

Ranking	Citation frequency	Journal title
1	1069	EXPERT SYST APPL
2	997	IEEE T KNOWL DATA EN
3	986	LECT NOTES COMPUT SC
4	917	KNOWL BASED SYST
5	743	ACM T INFORM SYST
6	693	INFORM SCIENCES COMMUN ACM
7	642	RECOMMENDER SYSTEMS HANDBOOK
8	615	COMMUN ACM
9	580	USER MODEL USER ADAP
10	520	LECT NOTES ARTIF INT

3.3 Distribution of Countries and Regions

Studying the distribution of countries allows us to know about the countries (regions) that have invested more in the field of recommendation systems and their research strength, facilitating exchanges and cooperation between countries. In CiteSpace5.8.R3, Node-Types was set as Country, by running software, we drew the nation (region) distribution map in the field of recommendation system research, as shown in Fig. 3. The nodes in the graph represent the country (region), and the size of the nodes represents the number of publications. The nodes with purple optical circles have higher centrality. In terms of the number of published papers, China comes first with 887 papers in the field of recommendation system, followed by the United States with 447 papers, Spain comes third with 215 and India the fourth with 203. Table 2 shows the top 10 countries (regions) that have made more achievements in the field of recommendation systems. Table 3 lists countries (regions) with centrality above 0.1. From the perspective of centrality, the primary countries include Germany (0.21), France (0.16), the United Kingdom (0.13) and the United States (0.12). The connections between nodes indicate cooperative relationship between different countries (regions). It can be seen from Fig. 3 that countries (regions) with closer cooperation are mainly Germany, France, the United Kingdom, the United States. The number of published papers from China ranks first, superior to Germany. But China's centrality is equivalent to that of Switzerland, indicating that there is still much work to be done about the cooperation in China.

Table 2. 10 top Number of PUBLICATION by countries (regions) in the recommended system field

Ranking	Number of articles	Countries and Regions
1	887	PEOPLES R CHINA
2	447	USA
3	215	SPAIN
4	203	INDIA
5	156	AUSTRALIA
6	153	SOUTH KOREA
7	126	TAIWAN(CHINA)
8	124	ENGLAND
9	104	ITALY
10	103	GERMANY

Table 3. 5 top Nation (region) centrality in recommendation system area

Ranking	centrality	Nation (region)
1	0.21	GERMANY
2	0.16	FRANCE
3	0.13	PEOPLES R CHINA
4	0.12	USA
5	0.11	NETHERLANDS

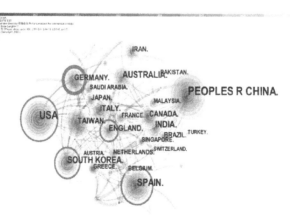

Fig. 3. Nation (region) distribution map of recommendation system research

3.4 Distribution of Institutions and Authors

In CiteSpace5.8. R3, NodeTypes is set as the Institution, and the appropriate threshold is certain. The software is run to obtain the distribution map of institutions engaged in the research of recommendation system (see Fig. 4). Node size is positively correlated with the number of papers published by the institutions, and the connections between the nodes represent a cooperative relationship between them. Table 4 lists the 10 top research institutions of recommendation system. Of them, seven are from China: the University of Chinese Academy of Sciences (47), the University of Electronic Science and Technology (31), Tsinghua University (27), Chongqing University (26), Wuhan University (24), Huazhong University of Science and Technology (23), and the University of Electronic Science and Technology (22). The number and centrality (0.20) of the papers published by the University of Chinese Academy of Sciences are at the top of the research institutions. It can be seen that the Chinese Academy of Sciences is in an absolute core position in the field of recommendation system research and has strong scientific research strength.

Table 4. 10 top Publication in Recommendation System Research by Institutions

Ranking	Number of articles	Institution
1	47	Chinese Acad Sci
2	31	Beijing Univ Posts & Telecommun
3	29	Univ Technol Sydney
4	27	Tsinghua Univ
5	26	Chongqing Univ
6	26	Univ Politecn Madrid
7	26	Islamic Azad Univ
8	24	Wuhan Univ
9	23	Huazhong Univ Sci&Technol
10	22	Univ Elect Sci&Technol China

In CiteSpace 5.8.R3, NodeTypes is set as Author, and the appropriate threshold is given. The software is run to obtain the distribution map of authors engaged in the research of recommendation system (see Fig. 5). The nodes in the figure represent the author, and the size of the node is positively correlated with the number of published papers. The connections between nodes represent that the authors have a certain cooperative relationship in the research of recommendation system. Based on the statistical analysis of the retrieved authors, it can be found that Professor JIE LU of Sydney University of Science and Technology (15 papers) and FERNANDO ORTEGA of Madrid University (15 papers) have the highest number of publications. Table 5 lists the 10 top authors in the field of recommendation system research.

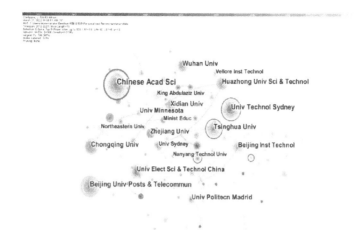

Fig. 4. Distribution Map of Institutions for Recommendation System Research

Table 5. 10 Top Authors in Recommendation System Research

Ranking	Number of articles	Author
1	15	JIE LU
2	15	FERNANDO ORTEGA
3	14	JASON J JUNG
4	14	JESUS BOBADILLA
5	12	XIN LUO
6	12	GUANGQUAN ZHANG
7	12	MIN GAO
8	12	MINGSHENG SHANG
9	11	FUZHI ZHANG
10	11	GIOVANNI SEMERARO

3.5   Citation Analysis

The citation frequency and its centrality can reflect the influence and value of literature. Generally, the higher the citation frequency of a single document, the greater the academic influence of the document in the research field. The centrality of node literature also reflects the importance of literature in the discipline. In CiteSpace5.8.R3, Node Types is set as Reference, and the appropriate threshold is given. The software is run to obtain the co-citation map of the research literature in the recommendation system, as shown in Fig. 6. Highly cited papers in recommendation system research are shown in Table 6.

In the 10 top papers cited, there were 3 papers with centrality above 0.1, BOBADILLA J, 2013 (0.15); Wang H, 2015 (0.18); Lu J, 2015 (0.11). By reading

Fig. 5. Distribution Map of Authors in Recommendation System Research

the three papers, we can have a comprehensive understanding about the recommendation system research. The recommendation system technology mentioned in the paper by Lu J (2015) mainly include: Content-based recommendation techniques, Collaborative filtering-based recommendation technique, Knowledge-based recommendation techniques, Hybrid recommendation technique, Computational intelligence-based recommendation techniques, Social network-based recommendation techniques, Context awareness-based recommendation techniques and Group recommendation techniques. The application scenarios of the recommendation system are: E-government recommender systems, E-business recommender systems, E-commerce/e-shopping recommender systems, E-library recommender systems, E-learning recommender systems, E-tourism recommender systems, E-resource service recommender systems and E-group activity recommender systems [5]. BOBADILLA J.(2013) mentioned that the effect of recommendation system recommendation is to be evaluated mainly from the following aspects: Quality of the predictions: mean absolute error, accuracy and coverage, Quality of the set of recommendations: precision, recall and F1, Quality of the predictions: mean absolute error, accuracy and coverage, Novelty and diversity, Stability and Reliability [6]. Wang H(2015) proposed a hierarchical Bayesian model called Cooperative Deep Learning (CDL), which jointly performs deep representation learning for the content information and collaborative filtering for the ratings (feedback) matrix, Extensive experiments on three real-world datasets from different domains show that CDL can significantly advance the state of the art [7]. The highly cited papers also include: Harper FM, (2016) [8], He XN, (2017) [9].

3.6 Research Hotspots and Frontier Analysis

Co-word (feature words or keywords) map is more conducive to the analysis of hotspots and hotspot evolution, especially with the use of burst term function. In CiteSpace5.8.

Table 6. A 10 Top Highly Cited Papers in Recommendation System Research

Ranking	Citation frequency	Cited Literature
1	136	BOBADILLA J,2013 Recommender systems survey
2	117	Harper FM,2016 The Movie Lens Datasets: History and Context
3	115	He XN,2017 BiRank: Towards Ranking on Bipartite Graphs
4	114	Lu J,2015 Recommender system application developments: A survey
5	77	Zhang SA,2019 Deep Learning Based Recommender System: A Survey and New Perspectives
6	70	Ricci F,2011 Introduction to recommender systems handbook
7	61	Wang H,2015 Collaborative deep learning for recommender systems
8	49	Wei J,2017 Collaborative Filtering and Deep Learning Based Recommendation System For Cold Start Items
9	48	Wu Y,2016 Collaborative Denoising Auto-Encoders for Top-N Recommender Systems,
10	44	Lu LY,2012 Recommender systems

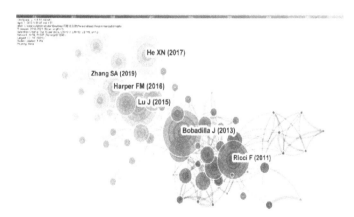

Fig. 6. Co-citation Map of Recommendation System Research Literature

R3, NodeTypes is set as Reference, and the appropriate threshold is certain. The software is run to obtain the research hotspot map of the recommendation system field, as shown in Fig. 7. Each node in the map represents a corresponding keyword. The larger the node, the greater the frequency of keywords. The research hotspots in the field of recommendation system reflected by the high-frequency keywords mainly include Model, Matrix Factorization, Deep Learning, Social Network, Trust, Accuracy and Machine Learning. The keywords with word frequency of 20 tops are listed in Table 7. Statistical analysis of hot keywords shows that the research on recommendation system mainly focuses on theoretical and technical methods, as well as application research. Key words involved include Collaborative Filtering, Matrix Factorization, Deep Learning, Social Network, Machine Learning, Neural Network, etc. The research progress of Machine Learning and Deep Learning provides new ideas to and technical support for the construction of recommendation system.

Table 7. A 20 Top High Frequency Keywords in Personalized Recommendation Research

Count	Keywords	Count	Keywords
883	Recommender System	43	Neural Network
389	Collaborative Filtering	29	Similarity
214	Model	29	Optimization
146	Matrix Factorization	27	Prediction
80	Deep Learning	20	Feature Extraction
78	Social Network	19	Genetic Algorithm
76	Trust	18	Knowledge
60	Accuracy	18	Internet of Thing
60	Machine Learning	14	Decision Making
52	Classification	14	Content-based Filtering

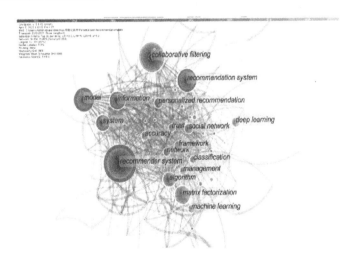

Fig. 7. Hot spots in recommendation system research

Tracking the frontier of disciplines is conducive for the academic community to better grasp the trend of discipline development and the direction of future research. Based on the expansion word exploration technology provided by CiteSpace5.8.R3, the expansion word list is obtained. Semantic Web is the keyword that occurred more frequently in the field of recommendation system in 2013. Deep Learning is a theory that has been widely applied in the field of recommendation system research in recent years.

4 Conclusion

Taking the literature in the field of recommendation system included in the Web of Science database as the source, this paper makes a visual analysis of the research status and trend in the field of recommendation system from 2012 to 2021 through the visualization software Cite Space. The conclusions are as follows:

(1) In terms of time distribution, the research on recommendation system in this period is divided into two stages.

The first stage from 2012 to 2016 is a period of stable development. The second stage, after 2017, shows a steady upward trend where the number of published papers increases year by year.

(2) In terms of periodical distribution, IEEE T KNOWL DATA EN, KNOWL BASED SYST, EXPERT SYST APPLPERT SYST APPL and ACM T INFORM SYST are highly cited and highly central.

(3) In terms of the research power, high-yield countries in this field include China, the United States and Spain, etc. From the perspective of centrality, countries(regions) with close cooperation mainly include Germany, France, the United Kingdom, the United States. The number of published papers in China ranks first, exceeding Germany. But the centrality is near to that of Switzerland, indicating that there is still much work to do about the cooperation. Universities and research institutes are the priamry force in this field, and the University of the Chinese Academy of Sciences takes lead in both publication volume and centrality.

(4) By citation analysis, it can be found that BOBADILLA J, 2013 (0.15), Wang H, 2015 (0.18), and Lu J, 2015 (0.11) are the 3 tops, in high citation, centrality and influence in the field of recommendation systems.

(5) The research about recommendation system mainly focuses on theoretical research, technical methods and application research. The keywords are Collaborative Filtering, Matrix Factorization, Deep Learning, Social Network, Machine Learning, Neural Network and so on.

(6) Through the analysis of research hotspots and frontiers, it can be found that Deep Learning and Machine Learning are widely used in recommendation system research in recent years. The research progress of Deep Learning and Machine Learning provides new ideas to and technical support for the construction of recommendation system.

Acknowledgment. This work was supported by the National Natural Science Foundation of China Youth Fund under Grant No.61902001 and the Open Project of Shanghai Big Data Management System Engineering Research Center under Grant No.40500–21203-542500/021. All opinions, findings, conclusions and recommendations in this paper are those of the authors and do not necessarily reflect the views of the funding agencies.

References

1. Chen, Y., Chen, C., Liu, Z., Hu, Z., Wang, X.: The methodology function of CiteSpace mapping knowledge domains. Stud. Sci. Sci. **33**(02), 242–253 (2015)
2. Li, J.: CiteSpace Chinese Guide. http://blog.sciencenet.cn/blog-554179-1066981.html
3. Qiu, J., Zhai, L.: Visualization analysis on the research of international knowledge engineering. J. Mod. Inf. **37**(06), 148–154+177 (2017)
4. Li, C., Zhao, J.: Information visualization analysis of tourism management research based on web of science. Tour. Tribune **29**(04), 104–113 (2014)
5. Lu, J., Wu, D., Mao, M., et al.: Recommender system application developments: a survey. Decis. Supp. Syst. **74**(Jun.), 12–32 (2015)
6. Bobadilla, J., Ortega, F., Hernando, A.: Recommender systems survey. Knowl.-Based Syst. **46**, 109–132 (2013)
7. Wang, H., Wang, N., Yeung, D.Y.: Collaborative deep learning for recommender systems. In: KDD, pp. 1235–1244 (2015)
8. Harper, F.M., Konstan, J.A.: The MovieLens datasets: history and context. ACM Trans. Interact. Intell. Syst. **5**(4), 19 (2015). https://doi.org/10.1145/2827872
9. He, X., Gao, M., Kan, M.-Y., Wang, D.: BiRank: towards ranking on bipartite graphs. IEEE Trans. Knowl. Data Eng. **29**(1), 57–71 (2017)

Research on Library Intelligent Service Based on Blockchain Technology

Xueqing Yuan[1(✉)] and Sicen Zhou[2]

[1] Wuhan University of Technology, Wuhan, China
vvf1@qq.com
[2] Peking Universtiy, Beijing, China

Abstract. Computer technologies such as big data, cloud computing, and artificial intelligence are changing the present and future of the library. More and more technologies are applied to the library field, making the library more modern, intelligent and intellectual. Blockchain technology is one of the database technologies that has emerged in recent years, which consists of a series of cryptographically generated and timestamped data blocks (namely blocks composition). It uses a peer-to-peer distributed database system construction method to establish an open account book.. Applying this technology to the library will bring about a series of changes in the functions and services of the library. This article attempts to start from the blockchain technology, connect the blockchain with the library development technology, and explore the application of blockchain technology in the library's intelligent service.

Keywords: Blockchain · Technology · library · intelligent

1 Introduction

The development of intellectual resources, preservation of cultural heritage, and social education are the important functions of today's libraries. However, with the in-depth development of intelligent technology, new technologies have changed the way that users obtain information and improved the library's organizational knowledge platform model. Never the less, some of the complex business problems in the library are gradually coming out, such as the accumulation of virtual and real collection resources, the construction of intelligent resource retrieval windows, and the improvement of traditional library service models. All these need to be supported by advanced technologies from multi-dimensional cognitive computing. Therefore, a new mutual trust mechanism which can realize the shaping and exploration of the management process of library resources, space, services and other business formats is required. As an emerging information technology, blockchain has built-in time stamp and smart contracts which empower library data credit. Besides, the smart services such as fragmented service superposition and scenario-based service reset that blockchain contains create a chain structure, providing conditions for in-depth communication between library services and users as well as the effective configuration of contextualized services.

At present, blockchain has been applied in many fields of life, which has brought great changes to people's live. Especially in the application of the library, the use of information technology to break the information barrier and to innovate the service model of the library truly providing intelligent services for readers. Under such a model, the sharing of knowledge, the efficiency of services and the convenience of use are the pursuit of library users. Blockchain technology can play a prominent role in library resource construction, copyright protection, book management and service content, contributing to provide users with intelligent library services.

2   The Concept and Features of Blockchain

2.1   The Concept of Blockchain

Blockchain technology originated from the development of Bitcoin. It is one of the underlying supporting technologies of Bitcoin which was first described in the paper "Bitcoin: A peer-to-peer" published by Satoshi Nakamoto on the Bitcoin Forum in 2008. From the perspective of comprehensive research and development, blockchain technology is a database technology that combines blocks in a chain. Blockchain technology is a distributed accounting technology, and the electronic account book it builds is decentralized and non-tampering. At the same time, blockchain technology is also an Internet application protocol, which can establish mutual trust without third-party supervision. Therefore, blockchain is a technical solution, which is a technology set integrated by multiple technologies, and is an innovative technology model in the Internet+ era.

Blockchain technology was first used in virtual currencies, such as Bitcoin and Ethereum. It exposes the complete record of transactions on each node and makes it immutable, while generating a large amount of related data. The application which is based on peer-to-peer for open source protocols and decentralized electronic device currency system is the 1.0 stage of blockchain development. This technology is widely used due to its simple encryption, low transaction costs, no personnel management, and high security performance. Subsequently, the blockchain concept attracted the attention of government departments, the financial industry, and technology companies. The British government established a working team specializing in blockchain research and released the "2016 Blockchain Research Report". The United States, the United Kingdom, and Japan established a blockchain development alliance; NASDAQ built Linq Securities Trading platform based on blockchain technology; Germany Siemens established a power grid platform based on blockchain technology. Dehler and Ernst & Young established a research and development team to design a blockchain-based customer audit service platform. Citibank, HSBC and other more than 40 global financial giants Signed a blockchain cooperation project with blockchain startup R3CEV. So far, blockchain technology has ushered in the 2.0 stage characterized by programmable financial systems. Blockchain technology is the prototype of the next generation of cloud computing. It is expected to completely reshape the form of human social activities like the Internet, and realize the transformation from the current information Internet to the value Internet. With the development of blockchain technology, the blockchain 3.0 stage characterized by a programmable society has arrived. Experts and scholars from educational institutions have begun to explore the application of blockchain technology in education, humanities and social sciences, such as using blockchain technology to establish credible learning systems, credit certification systems, degree acquisition systems, and digital publishing systems. As a decentralized, fast, low-cost, low-error, and high-security technology, blockchain technology is compatible with the large number, high speed, and complex nature of library user behavior big data mining. The combination of the two is based on the blockchain technology as the underlying supporting technology, the blockchain concept as a breakthrough in the data mining dilemma, and the application advantages of blockchain to provide impetus for the development of library intelligent services.

2.2 Features of Blockchain

The core technology of blockchain mainly includes consensus mechanism, distributed storage technology, P2P network technology, asymmetric encryption algorithm and so on. Due to the special data structure and operation mechanism adopted in the design of blockchain, the blockchain technology presents the following technical characteristics:

1) Decentralization: The blockchain removes the central control restrictions, and distributes the authority of recording and storage to all nodes in the system. Each node realizes self-verification, transmission and management of data information through a peer-to-peer mesh structure. The status of each node is equal, every node maintains the functions of the system together. If any node is damaged or abnormal, it will not affect the normal operation of the system, thus ensuring the security and reliability of the blockchain system.

2) Consensus mechanism: Blockchain technology confirms the consensus mechanism in the form of smart contracts, and uses technical rules to improve the reliability of credit. The way to achieve trust is no longer based on the endorsement of a third party but on the recognition and support of the consensus mechanism by all participating individuals. Under the consensus mechanism, transactions can only occur when more than 51% of the node members reach a consensus, which greatly reduces the possibility of dishonest behavior and counterfeit transactions in transactions.

3) Immutable: The blockchain is stored on a distributed network system composed of multiple nodes, encrypting the newly generated data block containing the transaction data of the whole network. The newly added information needs to be verified by all nodes before it can be added to the zone in chronological order on the blockchain and then permanently stored. Each node stores a copy of the entire blockchain, and records the historical transactions of the entire network with the "timestamp". The historical transaction records of the entire network can be tracked and queried in a short time. Therefore, the data stability and reliability of the blockchain are very high.

4) Openness: The blockchain system is an open system. Except for account information and private information of transaction parties, the data in the system is open to everyone, and the data content can be queried through the public interface. This is a highly transparent information storage method. The blockchain technology itself also has the characteristics of open source and transparency. The system participants can know the operating rules and data content of the system, and the data exchange

between any nodes is verified by digital signature technology, which not only ensures the security of the data, but also increases the transparency of data.

3 Integration Analysis of Blockchain and Library Intelligent Services

3.1 Promote the Co-construction and Sharing of Resources

Blockchain has the characteristics of decentralization (distributed ledger technology) non-tampering (high reliability) security (asymmetric encryption algorithm) traceability (time stamp technology, chain structure) smart contracts (consensus mechanism, credibility, reliability) openness (open source, transparency). Blockchain technology has great application potential in the field of information science, which can provide low-cost, better privacy, lower-risk, more transparent and fair processes, and more efficient processes, showing an unstoppable force for change. In November 2017, the U.S. government allocated $100,000 to the American Institute of Museum and Library Services to explore the application of blockchain technology in library digital management. The project brought together more than 20 experts in library, blockchain technology and urban planning. Its research focuses on the use of blockchain technology to advance library services so that it can achieve city or community goals. Digital copyright, information security, concepts, technical level, management mechanism, facilities and equipment, physical space distance and so on are the main factors that plague the promotion of cultural co-construction and sharing. The application of blockchain technology to public culture has the characteristics of distributed and open access to digital resources, distributed digital resource storage, peer-to-peer mutual transmission, protection of the rights and interests of various providers, and sharing of digital resource construction results. Under the concept of decentralization of blockchain technology, all cultural institutions are equal nodes on the chain, collectively maintaining and cooperating with each other under the highly trusted consensus mechanism, which promotes the real openness of resource sharing and breaks the imbalance of resources caused by geographical, economic and capital investment. Last but not least, this will reduce the burden of the country's repeated construction. The ownership and copyright protection of public cultural resources are also key issues in co-construction and sharing. Blockchain technology can realize the intelligent confirmation of public cultural resources, and ensure that resource builders, providers, and users have traces to follow. The use of resources can be traced back, and each institution is still the owner of the data resource, only authorized people can access it, which protects the legitimate rights and interests of the main body of each institution, being able to solve the problems of unclear ownership of public cultural resources and difficulty in tracing the source.

Through the incomparable security-level infrastructure and frictionless authentication process provided by the blockchain consensus mechanism, various cultural institutions can directly carry out point-to-point resource transmission, which reduces the trouble of resource collection and centralized storage, and is more flexible to deal with the addition, deletion and modification of resources. It avoids the cumbersome coordination and cooperation of multiple agencies and joint implementation as well. Under the existing mode, for privacy protection and information security considerations, institutions may not co-construct and share important user information and characteristic resources. Blockchain technology uses cryptography to ensure the security of data transmission and access. It avoids the risk of data leakage and can achieve complete open sharing. The traceability of the blockchain can also make the rights and responsibilities of various institutions clear, and perform performance evaluation of institutions through user behavior and feedback, so that institutions can pay more attention to the content and quality of resource construction, effectively improve service levels. It also helps to avoid face-saving projects, inefficient investment, useless construction and so on. Therefore, the decentralization and smart contracts of blockchain technology can perfectly solve the bottleneck encountered in the co-construction and sharing of cultural resources.

3.2   Copyright Protection and Efficient Preservation

The blockchain is composed of blocks, each block corresponds to the Hash value. If any block is modified, all the blocks behind it must be modified at the same time, and each block is connected through the principles of Cryptography. Which increases the difficulty of malicious tampering. This immutability can be applied in the fields of library big data collection, learning certification, and copyright dispute resolution. Smart contract technology is an embedded programmed contract, which is jointly formulated by all parties involved in the contract and to form a transparent script code that is deployed on the blockchain. After the operation, all parties to the contract cannot intervene, control, renege and tamper, which ensures the credibility of data operation and program operation. This technology can be applied to the library's business process optimization, library intelligent robot development and other fields. Because the blockchain adopts timestamp technology, any transaction and data processing will be recorded with timestamps. Since timestamps are unique and unforgeable, this ensures the traceability of all historical data. This feature can ensure the integrity of library big data acquisition and prevent malicious tampering and deletion.

The application of blockchain technology provides a peer-to-peer communication channel for the transmission of library network information. The blockchain network completes the distributed storage of data by itself, and saves the data efficiently, which can promote the effective integration of data between different systems and different regions. Blockchain technology can be used to process the information transaction network between devices and users, giving independent identities such as intelligent robots, borrowing and returning machines, and wearable devices in libraries without the need for interaction through cloud servers, setting up level management controls for library-related facilities. Thus, the application of blockchain technology can greatly reduce the virtual storage space of the library and improve the operation efficiency of the overall network.

Set up a mechanism for protecting intellectual property rights. Blockchain itself has the characteristics of being tamperproof, decentralized, and traceable, which can be described as a "magic weapon" for protecting information. Its existence effectively reduces the emergence of counterfeit products and establishes an indestructible "shield" for the security of resources in libraries. However, when using blockchain technology on the Internet, one has to face the problem that people can access various information resources at extremely low cost. The existence of such problems will increase the difficulty of library copyright protection. In response, libraries can use a digital identity authentication mechanism to verify the true identity of blockchain participants, and use timestamp technology to record the time when participants' works were posted, ensuring that their copyright is not stolen. In addition, smart contract technology can automatically record the operation process of transactions, and the entire transaction process is completely transparent. The advantage of blockchain is not only that, but also to further ensure the effectiveness of user access, promote the dissemination of works, and improve the interests of creators. For the modification of original works and other links, the blockchain can also add a timestamp to ensure its traceability, and in the property rights link, digital fingerprints can also be used to ensure originality.

3.3 More Intelligent Book Lending Management

When the library is lending books to readers, it may encounter the situation that the books cannot be correctly put back in right place after reading, or the borrowed books are overdue. The application of blockchain technology can effectively reduce the occurrence of such situations. Through the supervision of blockchain technology, readers are urged to return books in time and to place books in their proper places. If they fail to return the books in time, they will be affected when they want to borrow books from the library again. Because of the particularity of the blockchain, all nodes will be automatically supervised, which can help to achieve standardized management for the boooks. In the final borrowing process, through blockchain technology, the borrower and related books are automatically matched, making the process of borrowing books more efficient.

3.4 Optimize Processes and Increase Efficiency

In the era of intelligent Internet, the integration and transformation of library service is an important driving force for realizing the transformation from knowledge service to smart service. Although both knowledge service and smart service focus on information services, they have different emphases. Knowledge service tends to build users' personalized knowledge and service finished products, while smart service tends to meet the general needs of users, giving "life" to library literature resource data and user behavior data, and focus on data extraction and resources description. Although the library is in a stage of lack of deep mining blockchain applications, its fertile application soil coincides with the blockchain. Use a radical method based on copyright printing to ensure the correspondence between the works of professors and scholars in the fields of music and art in colleges and the copyright, and to realize the inseparability of the two. With the help of blockchain contract currency, the uniqueness of users' intellectual property rights can be effectively guaranteed and genuine intellectual property rights protected. In addition, the blockchain's unique traceability and anti-counterfeiting, unique identification, digital identity verification, data management and other industrial chains can be used in the fields of copyright tracking, identity recognition, smart learning certification, knowledge base crowdfunding and other smart services, which can better serve users.

3.5 Alleviate the Pressure on Library Funds

The decentralized characteristics of blockchain can save a lot of input costs in the construction of open access to digital resources in libraries and relieve the financial pressure of libraries. The library's open-access digital resources need to be purchased from third parties and then freely available to users. At present, the ownership of digital resources is not in the hands of authors, but in the hands of publishers and database providers. Resource authors cannot get corresponding remuneration, but resource users have to bear high costs, which brings great financial pressure to library resource construction. However, through the decentralized nature of the blockchain, the third-party platform is omitted, the direct connection between document authors and libraries is realized through peer-to-peer technology, which can greatly save the subscription fees from database providers that have risen year by year. If the library's open access digital resources are self-built, the library owns it, and it is freely available to users. The blockchain peer-to-peer technology can realize the direct connection between resource authors and the library, and realize the dissemination and sharing of information. The library does not need to build an intermediary platform, and naturally does not require maintenance. The corresponding construction and maintenance costs can be saved as well. If the library's open-access digital resources come from the co-construction and sharing between libraries, the co-construction and sharing of library digital resources is affected by factors such as system platform differences, spatial distance barriers and so on, which affect its sustainable development. Centralization can break the barriers of cross-platform resource sharing between libraries, promote the blockchainization of resource sharing, and reduce unnecessary costs caused by repetitive construction of resources.

3.6 Collaborative Development and Smart Service

The decentralized method adopted by the blockchain enables any node in the system to have an equal right to speak, and any node can obtain a complete record of transactions and data, which enhances the right of each node to speak. The decision-making and rule-making in the block are established through a consensus mechanism, which can enhance the trust between nodes, and control the security of transactions and data transmission through technical means. This can reduce the complexity of data processing and solve the problem of information asymmetry in negotiation in the library field.

Whether the information exchange is balanced and the information flow is equal is an important criterion for judging whether a smart service system is centralized or not. This system is an open and flat service system. The focus of the deep integration of blockchain and library is not service intelligence. Instead, it focuses more on dynamic modeling of the content of users' active needs, judging user behavior preferences, feedback on the status quo of user needs. With the assistance of big data analysis technology, the deep integration of blockchain and library activates library information and enhances users' dependence on the library, efficiently uses the blockchain to reshape the library service content, service tools, service methods and service system, so that the majority of users can feel the sense of belonging and satisfaction brought by the "blockchain + library" smart service platform. The essence of blockchain requires overall collaboration to be realized. Its function must not be limited to individual levels of library services. Intelligent joint products should be built from the perspectives of service intensification, high degree of cooperation, co-construction and coordination, integration and dispersion, and innovate new formats of library services.

4 Application of Library Intelligent Service Under Blockchain Technonlogy

The core driving force of library smart services is to improve service capabilities and meet users' needs for high-quality services. Blockchain will play an effective role in the pursuit of smart services. In October 2019, general secretary of the Central Committee of the Communist Party of China (CPC)Xi Jinping emphasized in his study that the blockchain should be taken as an important breakthrough for independent innovation of core technologies, clarify the direction of tackling, and accelerate the promotion of new breakthroughs in blockchain and industrial layout. As a hot topic in academic research in recent years, blockchain participates in multiple computing nodes to jointly perform digital calculation and processing through the network environment. The cooperation mode and supervision and incentive mechanism between different subjects will lead to an all-round reform of the library service distribution system and resource recommendation methods.

Under the practice of blockchain, library smart service is the organization and reconstruction of processes such as circulation affairs, learning space services, educational exploration, and file storage. Such management innovations help to adjust the direction of library services.

4.1 Research and Development of Intelligent Equipment Used in Library

On January 1, 2018, the first robot librarian in Shanghai Library officially took office. The era of library intelligence is coming, more and more intelligent devices will gradually enter the library to provide service for users. The application of blockchain technology to the research and development of library intelligent equipment will definitely become a development trend in the future. The distributed accounting technology, asymmetric encryption algorithm and smart contract technology of blockchain will provide effective technical support for the research and development of library robots, which integrates smart devices with readers' behaviors, exchanges data information at any time without restrictions on terminals, and realizes effective storage and analysis, providing big data support for robot learning.

4.2 Demand Response Applied to Intelligent Services

With more and more opportunities for big data to respond to forecasting services, blockchain can help forecasts to be implemented. The "test-response" model can be used to further reduce the compatibility between big data and blockchain and achieve the unity of data collection results in form and semantic mining, infer which smart brand services meet the current user situation needs, and realize mutual reference between blockchain and big data. Improving the library service industry through blockchain technology can further improve service efficiency and quickly respond to changes in user needs.

4.3 Learning Authentication Technology Applied to User Education

The blockchain can provide users with non-tamperable distributed data records, which can record the learning trajectory of learners in the application software at any time, and store the learning behavior and academic performance of learners. Therefore, the library can establish a public service platform of blockchain based on the cloud server to record the learning behavior of learners. These learning behaviors may not be limited to one library, but can be shared among libraries within the library alliance or even across the country and even the world. When evaluating the user's information ability, the library can also obtain the user's learning record from the cloud server, and issue a certificate based on the evaluation result.

4.4 Applied to Library Data Security

Big data technology is one of the most popular emerging technologies in recent years. The use of big data technology can realize the collection, arrangement, analysis and utilization of massive data. However, in reality, the collection and acquisition of big data is in dilemma. Considering multiple factors such as security, data ownership, and value density, there are many practical difficulties in the collection and processing of big data in many fields, including libraries. Blockchain technology is a high-speed, low-cost, high-security, low-error, non-tamperable, and decentralized system. Combining it with big data can break through the practical dilemma of big data collection. In this way, a consensus mechanism is established to ensure the security of data acquisition and the ownership of rights and interests, so as to solve the problem of library big data acquisition.

4.5 Applied to the Construction of Library Service Chain System

Nowadays, the library has become an intelligent service organization that provides knowledge services. In the construction of the service system, the concept of blockchain can also be used to build the library's service chain system and make various services into different blocks, and then connect them to form a closed service chain, establish good communication and communication channels with each other. The system will automatically record the content of the service and the footprint of the user. In this way, on the one hand, it can enhance the value of library services. On the other hand, it can also combine big data analysis technology to dig deeper into user needs and create more refined services.

4.6 Applied to the Construction of Library Resource Sharing

Both university libraries and public libraries are committed to building a perfect resource co-construction and sharing system. Today, when we talk about the sharing economy, the co-construction and sharing of library information resources can better reflect the economy and importance of sharing. Using the distributed ledger technology of blockchain, different information resources can be distributed and stored in different blocks. These blocks can be composed of a single library, each library is a node, through point-to-point transmission. In this way, all nodes will directly share information resources by agreement through a consensus smart contract, which can greatly improve the efficiency of sharing, and also solve the problems caused by information islands.

4.7 Applied to the Construction of Library Knowledge Base

Many libraries have developed institutional knowledge bases, building the scientific research results of the institution itself and its members in the knowledge base. Using blockchain technology, a more flexible and free knowledge base platform can be built and connected with other knowledge bases. Together, tthey can form a global open knowledge base system. Blockchain technology breaks the traditional mode of open resources using centralized management for authority verification, content storage and service. Instead, it uses a decentralized verification method and distributed storage method to share knowledge, so that knowledge users of the library can obtain access to the knowledge base at any time without the need for upper-level approval and authorization.

5 Conclusion

At present, the blockchain has moved from theory to practice in terms of digital currency, payment and settlement, and securities management. The technological innovation lead by blockchain is subverting the inertial thinking of many traditional service industries. The replacement of library technology and the recognition of the service market are a gradual process. During this period, in order to adapt to various application scenarios, library smart services require librarians, technical experts, and architecture makers to participate in mastering blockchain technology. The application development in the library's intelligent service allows the different transaction subjects involved in the service to maximize the benefits of cross-border transactions.

The construction of smart libraries is an inevitable trend in the development of libraries in the digital era. The construction of smart libraries can improve the service level and resource utilization efficiency of libraries, and achieve document resource sharing. However, in the construction of smart libraries, digital technology and related management measures need to be adopted to address copyright issues from multiple aspects. Only in this way can we achieve the legitimate use and sharing of digital resources and better serve readers.

In the future, the construction of smart libraries will continue to face various challenges, such as how to better maintain the copyright of digital resources, how to improve the utilization efficiency of digital resources, and other issues. Therefore, it is necessary to adopt more flexible and efficient management measures and technical means to solve it. In short, the construction of smart libraries is an inevitable trend in the development of libraries in the digital era. The construction of smart libraries requires full consideration of copyright issues, and corresponding management and technical measures to ensure the legitimate use and sharing of digital resources, better provide services to readers, and promote the development of the library industry.

Based on the concept of blockchain technology, the article embodies an accurate, transparent, open and efficient smart network, and realizes the substantive application and interactive exploration of library smart services in the "blockchain" technology concept, providing reference for the construction of smart library in the new era.

References

1. Satoshi, N.: Bitcoin: a peer-to-peer electronic cash system. Consulted, 1–30 (2008)
2. Chen, X.: Research on big data mining of library mobile user behavior based on blockchain concept. Libr. Work Res. (12), 63–68 (2018)
3. Fan, X., Li, T., Sun, Y.: Research on the research hotspots and development trends of blockchain in the subject of image and information files. Inf. Sci. **38**(06), 163–169 (2020)
4. Li, Q., Zhang, X.: Blockchain: promoting the openness and credibility of education with technology. Dist. Educ. J. (1), 36–44 (2017)
5. Tang S, Liu J.: Research on the new ecology of library smart reading services in the "5G+" era. Libr. Work Res. (06), 17–23 (2021)
6. Wang, F., Zhao, H., Ma, J., Li, X., Zhang, X.: Research and practice progress of data traceability from the perspective of data science. Chin. Libr. J. **45**(05), 79–100 (2019)
7. Yu, X., Zhao, Y., Ling, Y.: Research on smart library services driven by blockchain technology. Library (10), 47–52 (2020)
8. Yuan, Y., Wang, F.: Current situation and prospects of blockchain technology development. J. Autom. (4), 481–494 (2016)
9. Zhang, X., Liang, R.: Discussion on the application of blockchain technology in libraries in the scene era. Libr. Work Res. (07), 85–90 (2020)
10. Zhang, Z., Wang, L.: Analysis of application scenarios of blockchain technology in libraries. Books Inf. (06), 110–112 (2018)
11. Zhao, C., Nie, L.: An analysis of the application prospect of library technology under the concept of blockchain. Libr. Sci. Res. (21), 7–9+54 (2018)
12. Zhao, L., Xu, S.: Research on the accurate information service path of university libraries under blockchain technology. Libr. Inf. Work **65**(10), 31–37 (2021)
13. Zhi, Y.: Research on the application of 5G+ blockchain technology in library smart services. Libr. Work Res. (10), 12–17 (2020)
14. Zhi, Y.: An analysis of the promotion strategies for the co-construction and sharing of public cultural services in the new era. Library (02), 8–14 (2021)
15. He, B.: Research on constructing intelligent knowledge service system based on blockchain technology. Library (09), 41–45+65 (2020)
16. Ma A, Pan X, Wu L, et al.: Review of blockchain technology foundation and application research. Inf. Secur. Res. (11), 968–980 (2017)
17. Ai, Q., Liu, C., You, L.: Privacy protection and countermeasures for scientific research users to access foreign academic databases. Libr. Inf. Work **63**(10), 12–20 (2019)
18. Yang, X., Li, X., Wu, H., Zhao, K.: The application model and practical challenges of blockchain technology in the field of education. Mod. Dist. Educ. Res. (2), 34–45 (2017)

Towards Intelligent Serious Games: Deep Knowledge Tracing with Hybrid Prediction Models

Baha Thabet$^{(\boxtimes)}$ ⓘ and Francesco Zanichelli ⓘ

Department of Engineering and Architecture, Università di Parma, Parma, Italy
{baha.thabet,francesco.zanichelli}@unipr.it

Abstract. Combining Deep Knowledge Tracing (DKT) with serious games can establish an intelligent model for modeling the knowledge state of players. This model can help players to look one or more steps ahead and predict the performance of the next missions in gameplay. This helps also to provide players with proactive recommendations to be able to complete the next mission successfully. In this research, we introduce a novel Intelligent Serious Games model (ISG) based on the state-of-the-art DKT method combined with other components to improve players' programming skills. We propose novel hybrid prediction models for DKT and a Missing Sequence Padding (MSP) recursive method. Our findings revealed the effectiveness of integrating the Deep Knowledge Tracing (DKT) method with serious games. The proposed hybrid prediction models with a multi-layer learning approach for DKT achieved the best prediction performance among the other models. Whereas the results revealed the effectiveness of the MSP in predicting more steps ahead with missing values in the sequences. Also, the new approach in evaluating the DKT method based on each sequence within a fixed length enabled us to trace and investigate each knowledge state. Whereas concepts' dependency with order from basic to advance have positively influenced the performance.

Keywords: intelligent serious games · deep knowledge tracing · hybrid prediction · missing sequence padding · RNN · CNN

1 Introduction

Deep Knowledge Tracing (DKT) [1] based on recurrent neural networks has demonstrated excellent results for capturing hidden and long dependencies. DKT aims at modeling the knowledge state of learners during practice to predict the future learning performance. Traditionally, Intelligent Tutoring Systems (ITS) have been spread as adaptive learner-oriented environment. An ITS utilizes artificial intelligence [2] to improve learning performance. The intelligent model in the ITS is an adaptive environment represented by knowledge tracing [1, 3] and offering customized recommendations to comply with learners' knowledge level. Similarly, the intelligent model of the ITS can be integrated into Serious Games to focus more on the player model [4]. The adaptive model requires continuous estimation for the proficiency level of players during the gameplay. DKT in

W. Hong and Y. Weng (Eds.): ICCSE 2022, CCIS 1811, pp. 278–292, 2023.
https://doi.org/10.1007/978-981-99-2443-1_25

a serious game can help players to look one or more steps ahead to predict the result of the next missions in gameplay. Accordingly, a recommender can offer proactive recommendations for players to complete the next mission successfully. Our approach is aligned with the findings of a recent systematic literature review [5]. As future directions for serious games research, the authors suggest focusing more on the players with establishing an adaptive gaming experience and feedback. Also, they suggest applying neural networks to analyze data, with adopting a standard data format for the gameplay interaction.

In this research, we introduce an Intelligent Serious Games model (ISG) based on combining the DKT method [1] with other components for learning programming skills.

In this study we have the following contributions: (1) we introduced a novel Intelligent Serious Games model based on DKT method to look for one or more steps ahead during the gameplay and predict the result of the next missions; (2) we proposed and tested novel DKT-based hybrid prediction models for a multi-layer learning approach. We also investigated the influence of combining the RNN variants for sequential dependencies with CNNs for hidden features extraction; (3) we introduced and tested a novel recursive method called MSP to predict more steps ahead with possible of missing values in the sequences; (4) we assessed a new approach in evaluating the DKT method based on each sequence within a fixed-length sequences of submissions to trace each knowledge state; (5) we introduced a new questions/answers dataset C++CCH for programming skills, and we investigated the influence of the dataset size on the prediction performance. In addition to the impact of real sequence dependency and ordered concepts from basic to advance on the prediction performance.

2   Related Work

Modeling learners' knowledge state while practicing is a crucial task to improve learning achievements. Traditionally, the common approach for modeling the knowledge state is based on the probabilistic methods. Corbett and Anderson [3] introduced the Bayesian Knowledge Tracing (BKT) method based on the Bayesian probability and the Hidden Markov Model (HMM). According to [1, 6] the BKT and its successor extensions are suffering from the difficulty of capturing the hidden dependencies between the sequence of concepts. However, Piech et al. [1] have introduced a recent approach called Deep Knowledge Tracing (DKT) based on Recurrent Neural Networks (RNNs). The new approach aims at modeling learners' knowledge state over time to predict the future learning performance for learners. The DKT method has been applied in several studies such as [1, 6, 7] and outperformed previous PKT methods.

Despite the success of the DKT method, there are some limitations in terms of using inputs with non- fixed, unordered sequence lengths (timesteps) and the adopted neural network models [8]. Most of the previous studies used a non-fixed sequence length of students' submissions with undetermined sequence submission order. For this reason, they measured an overall prediction performance without assessing the impact of the non-fixed sequence length sizes on the performance of their models and without assessing the performance on each sequence length. This is unrealistic in real learning situation when we need to trace and predict each knowledge state of learners or players.

Also unordered submissions with non-fixed sequence length could negatively influence the performance as the new knowledge is dependent on previous knowledge. Another limitation is due to the absence of evaluating the method on different neural network models other than the RNNs and its variants. However, other authors have focused partially on these limitations. Wang et al. in [9] have evaluated the DKT method on one exercise question to predict the next one. While in 2022, Hooshyar et al. [8] have assessed the DKT method on the Convolutional Neural Network (CNN), but they evaluated the model on only three sequence lengths out of 20 fixed sequence lengths. To the best of our knowledge no prior studies having assessed the DKT method using hybrid neural models and on each sequence length within a fixed and ordered series of submissions, which is crucial to apply the model in real situation and trace each knowledge state.

3   The Intelligent Serious Games (ISG)

We introduce in this study a novel Intelligent Serious Games (ISG) model (see Fig. 1) as adaptive knowledge tracing and recommendation environment. The proposed model combines a novel conceptual serious games framework with an intelligent model of deep knowledge tracing and a Transformer-based recommender. The main goal of the new ISG, is to adapt and adjust learning trajectories of players according to their level of proficiency in gameplay. In particular, the model looks one or more steps ahead during the gameplay and predict the result of the next missions (success/fail) before they are happening in order to provide players with proactive recommendations to complete the missions successfully.

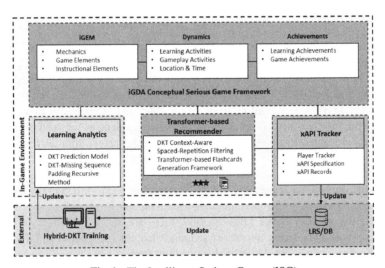

Fig. 1. The Intelligent Serious Games (ISG)

The ISG consists of four components as follows:

- iGDA Conceptual Serious Game Framework: a novel re-usable serious game framework, aiming at clearly identifying all game and learning components to be integrated at the early stage of design. In fact, the iGDA is aligned with the learning-based outcomes approach, to allow modeling the knowledge state of players with measurable achievements and easy integrate the DKT and a recommendation mechanism.
- Learning Analytics: located in two separated environments: in game environment which is a generic component can hold any analytics approach. In our study it consists of the DKT prediction model with the DKT missing sequence padding method integrated; externally, connected on-demand with the Hybrid-DKT training host which is responsible to update the DKT prediction model when needed.
- Transformer-based Recommender: the Transformer-based Recommender (TR) enables personalized guide for players. The recommendation and filtering techniques are context-aware with the DKT prediction results and the player's knowledge state. The TR provides recommendations based on fine-tuned transformer models [10] to auto generate flashcards in the form of questions, answers and supporting paragraphs. However, we will leave this part for the future work.
- XAPI Tracker: based on xAPIs1 data and communication standard. The main goal of this component is to provide a standard data format with communication protocol for tracking, capturing, storing, and sharing players' interactions with DKT and externally with other databases.

3.1 Each Sequence Length Approach

Our approach in the DKT based on each sequence length is to track the players interactions in real-time and predict the result of each knowledge state. Given an ordered player's game submission with interactions $x_1, x_2,..., x_s,... x_m$ the task is to predict the result of each next game challenge x_{s+1} (sequence) whether it will be completed successfully or not, where s from 1 to $m-1$. To feed the neural network, each submission should be transformed into vectors for each input and output. $m-1$ vectors with length 2 m to represent the inputs x_s as $\{Q_s, A_s\}^{2m}$, and $m-1$ vectors with length m to represent the outputs y_{s+1} as $\{A_{s+1}\}^m$ for each entry x_s and y_{s+1}, where $s = 1$ to $m-1$.

3.2 Hybrid-Deep Knowledge Tracing (RNN-CNN)

RNNs and CNNs are the most popular adopted for the time series and image recognition problems. Several prior studies have combined the LSTM and CNN together in other research areas [11–13] with excellent performance results.

In this study, we propose hybrid prediction models for the Deep Knowledge Tracing (Hybrid-DKT) based on combining the advantages of the RNNs variants and the CNN neural networks. The proposed hybrid network combines two key learning characteristics together: sequence dependencies learning and feature/pattern extraction. Unlike prior studies, we seek to improve the performance for each single sequence. Therefore, we expect from the hybrid combination to improve the performance along all the sequences in qualitative way by level-up the prediction performance ranges.

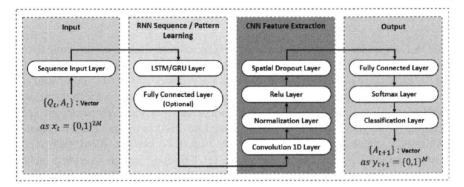

Fig. 2. Hybrid-based Deep Knowledge Tracing Models

The Hybrid-DKT model in Fig. 2 consists of four layers: input layer, RNN layer followed by CNN layer and output layer. This architecture enables a multi-level learning and feature extraction. Initially the input layer feeds the LSTM/GRU layer to capture the long-term and sequential dependencies from the input vectors. Accordingly, the LSTM/GRU passes its output to a fully connected layer to adjust weights and bias (as optional), then it feeds the 1D convolutional layer to discover the hidden patterns and low-level features and make more tunning for the network output. A normalization layer usually is used after learnable layers to normalize a mini batch of data across all channels, to speed up training and reduce the sensitivity to network initialization. The Rectified Linear Unit (ReLU) is an activation function for each input sequence, where any value less than zero is set to zero. ReLU usually used to overcome the vanishing gradient problem, allowing models to learn faster and perform better. The dropout layer offers a method to prevent neural networks from overfitting during training. The output layer is the last phase of training by passing the outputs from the CNN layer to a fully connected layer and applying the SoftMax function then the classification layer to infer the number of classes from the output size which 0 or 1 in our case.

3.3 DKT-Missing Sequence Padding Method

In a flexible gaming or learning scenario, there are two different strategies ahead for learners or players. Moving sequentially or randomly (jump-moving) to learn the difficult concepts first, and implicitly acquire the simple concepts. In reality, moving randomly raises an issue of missing previous sequences in the DKT prediction model as shown in Fig. 3.

	x_0	x_1	x_2	x_3	x_4	x_5	x_6	x_7	$P(x_8)$
Ideal DKT Prediction	1	0	1	1	0	0	1	1	?
Missing Sequence Values Problem	1	0	1	1		0			?

Fig. 3. Missing Sequence Values Prediction Problem

Generally, the DKT method needs a threshold of at least one value available within a series to predict the second one. For a given sequence set from 0 to s our goal is to predict the value of the sequence s + 1 as shown in the algorithm in Fig. 4.

1. Initially, at line 2 assign the threshold index $>= 0$ at which the model is able to predict the next value, for instance threshold $= 1$ which means that the model is capable to predict after the sequence x_1.
2. Assign the index i at line 3 which is the first missing value in the series and obviously it should be greater than the threshold.
3. The MSP algorithm initiates at line 5.
4. At line 11 the MSP algorithm starts predicting $Xs + 1$ recursively by decrementing the index and looking back to temporarily predict and fill the missing values only at lines 12 and 13.
5. When the decremented index reaches the first missing value (line 7), predict the missing value at line 8 and terminate the recursive calling at line 9 and exit the program.

	Output: DKT_Predict (x_{s+1})
1	Sequences: $[\ x_0, x_1, ..x_i, ...x_s]$
2	threshold $= 1$ // $x_s >$ A threshold should be $>= 0$
3	first_missing_Sequence $\leftarrow i$
4	If first_missing_Sequence $>$ threshold
5	Recursive_MSP (Sequences, $s + 1$)
6	end

Recursive_MSP (*vector, index)

7	If index $==$ first_missing_Sequence
8	DKT_Predict (vector, index)
9	return
10	end
11	Recursive_MSP (vector, index $- 1$)
12	If vector[index] $==$ missing_Sequence
13	DKT_Predict (vector, index)
14	end

Fig. 4. DKT-Missing Sequence Padding (MSP) Algorithm

4   Experiments and Results

4.1   C++Code Challenge Serious Game

We developed a serious game called C++Code Challenge based on the iGDA framework as a board-adventure game using UNITY 2D and simulates the campus environment to teach the basic skills of computer programming in C++. The game consists of challenges, quick timed-skills, library, badges, concept flashcards and an evidence-based achievement progress bar to track players' success. Moving on to the player role, the overall goal for players is to walk through 26 code challenges to acquire the programming skills in the form of learning achievements. Initially, players have to answer 4 code challenges before they can enter the board. Then, the player role is to roll the dice and choose one of the next possible places in the board with some criteria to move sequentially or randomly and try to overcome the rest of 22 code challenges.

4.2   Dataset 1: C++Code Challenge

To train the DKT prediction model of the game, we transformed the 26 code challenges into online quiz with extra 10 questions as multiple choices and sort statements questions using Microsoft Forms. For most of the questions, the associated source code produces two outputs, thus there are 22 possible answers. A total of 5394 exercise responses were collected from 174 students, but we selected only 4524 responses that belongs to 26 code challenges of the game.

4.3   Dataset 2: Simulated-5 (Standard)

Most of the previous studies have evaluated only the overall performance of their DKT models, unlike our own work. They mostly used some public datasets such as ASSISTments' skill builder, Algebra 0506 and Statics2011. In fact, those datasets have some limitations due to each student has a different length of responses; some questions have multiple associated scaffolding questions, therefore there are multiple sequence of responses with sub-sequences; undetermined submission order and repeated responses for each student where a student can keep trying until a mastery threshold is reached. However, Piech et al. [1] have simulated 5 concepts to cover a fixed-length and ordered sequence of 50 questions and answered by 4000 virtual students, and this dataset was used also to evaluate DKT method in [1, 14]. We randomly selected only 174 unique virtual student submissions from Simulated-5 dataset with total of 4524 exercise answers for 26 sequences like our dataset1. The purpose of this selection is to compare both datasets with the same size and investigate the impact of using a small dataset with fixed-length responses and ordered questions from basic to advance concepts on the prediction performance.

4.4   Experiments Design

In our experiments, we applied and evaluated the LSTM, biLSTM, GRU, CNN and the hybrid models across our dataset C++CCH and Simulated-5 dataset using MATLAB. The same network topologies and settings on all models and datasets were applied.

Initially, the proposed Hybrid-DKT topology (see Fig. 2) was used. For the CNN model we used the same Hybrid-DKT, but we removed the RNN layer and reconnected the input layer directly with the CNN layer. For the LSTM, biLSTM, GRU we removed the CNN layer from the Hybrid-DKT model as well and reconnected the RNN layer with the output layer. Moreover, we adjusted the hidden layers to 98, batch size to 25 for the RNN single models, and 70 for the CNN and the Hybrid models. We performed 30 training epochs with Adam algorithm [15]. For the CNN layer we adjusted the number of filters to 64, filter size to 5, dropout factor to 0.01 and padding value set to "same".

We trained the model to predict the next code challenge for each sequence length from 5 to 26. Whereas the first 4 challenges as we indicated before the players have to answer them when starting the game.

4.5 Results

We evaluated the prediction performance by four metrics: we constructed the confusion matrix and plotted the ROC curve to measure the area under the curve (AUC) for each sequence length. We also calculated the prediction accuracy ACC to compare it with the AUC results. Moreover, to simplify the comparison along 22 sequence lengths and 7 prediction models, we calculated the ACC/AUC average of all sequence lengths for each model to make a general comparison indicator between models and datasets. Finally, we considered to compare the AUC prediction performance categorized into four ranges over the percentage of all sequence lengths.

Table 1. Prediction Performance (Average for all Sequence Lengths)

Model	Simulated-5		C++CCH	
	ACC	*AUC*	*ACC*	*AUC*
LSTM	0.752	0.700	0.789	0.786
biLSTM	0.725	0.666	0.786	0.788
GRU	0.743	0.685	0.795	0.794
CNN	0.757	0.703	0.790	0.791
Hybrid (LSTM-CNN)	0.741	0.712	0.786	0.802
Hybrid (biLSTM-CNN)	0.709	0.712	0.784	0.804
Hybrid (GRU-CNN)	0.759	0.716	0.798	0.814

The results in Table 1 show that the Hybrid models on both datasets achieved better performance than the other baseline single models biLSTM, LSTM, GRU and CNN (for more details see Table 2). Among the hybrid models, the GRU-CNN model on C++CCH dataset achieved the best prediction performance with average AUC score of 0.814, higher than the biLSTM-CNN with a 0.804 AUC score and the LSTM-CNN with an AUC score of 0.802, which is confirming the fact of GRU model performs better on small datasets.

For the single models, the GRU model achieved also the best average AUC prediction performance with 0.794, followed by CNN and biLSTM with 0.791 and 0.788

respectively, the LSTM model was the last in the list with 0.786 AUC score. The results revealed that the CNN single model obtained similar performance to the RNNs variants and can be used in the DKT problem.

To compare the performance on the datasets level, the C++CCH dataset outperformed the Simulated-5 dataset on all models. This result is expected as the C++CCH dataset contains real submissions and sequence dependency ordered in ascending order from simple concepts to difficult. The best prediction performance for the Simulated-5 dataset was on the Hybrid GRU-CNN with AUC 0.716. Also, the Simulated-5 dataset showed significant differences between ACC and AUC scores on the single models.

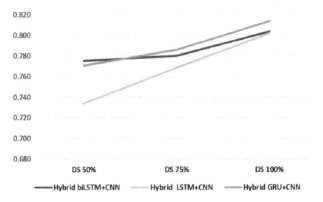

Fig. 5. Avg. Prediction performance AUC with dataset size

To investigate the influence of the dataset size over the prediction performance, the results in Fig. 5 confirmed that the Hybrid models achieves some performance improvements when increasing the dataset size. For instance, the average AUC score of the GRU-CNN model achieved around 5% of improvement when increasing the dataset size from 50% to 100% whereas the LSTM-CNN obtained around 9% of improvement.

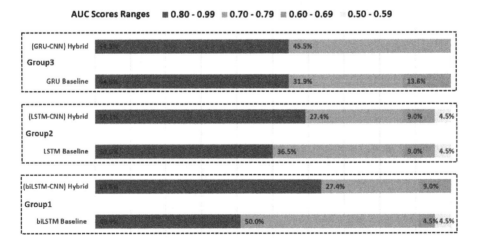

Fig. 6. Percentage of all 22 exercises AUC scores distributed in 4 score Ranges (Baseline V.S. Hybrid)

Figure 6 shows that along all the 22 sequence lengths, the hybrid models achieved the best prediction performance ranges.

The combination of the RNNs variants and the CNN network influenced the performance positively with an interesting behavior. Obviously, it leveled-up the overall prediction quality toward increasing the sequence lengths in the AUC interval 0.80–0.99 and decreasing those with AUC scores less than 0.70.

Group1 shows that 63.6% of the sequence lengths achieved AUC scores between 0.80 and 0.99 in the Hybrid biLSTM-CNN, while the biLSTM baseline percentage was 41%, with significant increase of 23% to the benefit of the Hybrid biLSTM-CNN. Also all the sequence lengths with score less than 0.60 improved and shifted up to the range 0.60–0.69.

Group2 shows that around 9% of the sequence lengths shifted up from the AUC range 0.70–0.79 to 0.80–0.99 in the Hybrid LSTM-CNN, while the rest ranges below 0.70 remained unchanged.

Group3 shows stability in the range 0.80–0.99 with 54.5% for both Hybrid GRU-CNN and GRU baseline, but 13.6% of the sequence lengths shifted from the score range 0.60–0.69 to 0.70–0.79, so that there are no sequence lengths with AUC performance under the score 0.70 as Fig. 7 shows the leveling-up trend for GRU baseline and Hybrid GRU-CNN.

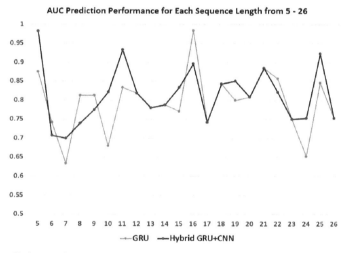

Fig. 7. Prediction performance trend for all sequence Lengths for GRU – Hybrid GRU-CNN

Table 2 demonstrates the AUC prediction performance trend at each sequence length from 5 to 26 on all models. The results show the impact of the multi-level learning and feature extraction in the proposed Hybrid-DKT model. For example, as shown in Fig. 8 the Hybrid GRU-CNN achieved the best prediction performance with top five AUC scores 0.982, 0.933, 0.833, 0.85 and 0.923 on the sequence lengths 5, 11, 15, 19 and 25 respectively, while the baseline results on the GRU model before applying the hybrid multi-level training were 0.875, 0.833, 0.771, 0.8 and 0.846. Similarly, on the Hybrid

Table 2. AUC Prediction's Performance on Each Sequence Length for C++CCH Dataset

Seq. Len.	biLSTM	LSTM	GRU	CNN	Hybrid biLSTM-CNN	Hybrid LSTM-CNN	Hybrid GRU-CNN
5	0.781	0.875	0.875	0.960	0.938	0.875	0.982
6	0.742	0.742	0.742	0.753	0.717	0.682	0.707
7	0.667	0.633	0.633	0.767	0.733	0.667	0.700
8	0.729	0.750	0.813	0.646	0.667	0.771	0.739
9	0.786	0.775	0.813	0.742	0.852	0.775	0.775
10	0.595	0.500	0.679	0.595	0.821	0.821	0.821
11	0.933	0.933	0.833	0.967	0.933	0.900	0.933
12	0.864	0.808	0.818	0.864	0.808	0.864	0.818
13	0.742	0.703	0.780	0.742	0.709	0.780	0.780
14	0.843	0.843	0.788	0.788	0.843	0.843	0.788
15	0.792	0.792	0.771	0.833	0.833	0.833	0.833
16	0.854	0.958	0.984	0.938	0.896	0.958	0.896
17	0.742	0.742	0.742	0.687	0.742	0.742	0.742
18	0.798	0.843	0.843	0.788	0.843	0.843	0.843
19	0.850	0.850	0.800	0.750	0.800	0.800	0.850
20	0.808	0.808	0.808	0.808	0.808	0.808	0.808
21	0.885	0.923	0.885	0.852	0.885	0.885	0.885
22	0.857	0.821	0.857	0.821	0.821	0.821	0.821
23	0.708	0.750	0.750	0.750	0.750	0.750	0.750
24	0.753	0.697	0.652	0.753	0.697	0.753	0.753
25	0.846	0.846	0.846	0.846	0.775	0.885	0.923
26	0.753	0.707	0.753	0.753	0.808	0.586	0.753

biLSTM-CNN, as shown in Fig. 9 the top five improvement ratios are 20%, 38%, 12%, 11% and 15% on the sequence lengths 5, 10, 11, 13 and 24.

For assessing the DKT Missing Sequence Padding (MSP) method across the three hybrid trained models, we recursively predicted the result of the 11th sequence given the results of all available sequences from 1 to 5 and missing results from element 6 to 10. The results in Table 3 revealed the effectiveness of the method with 5 missing values. The Hybrid GRU-CNN achieved the best AUC scores on sequences 7 and 11, while the other sequences are still in acceptable score ranges.

In summary, we tested three hybrid models, three single RNNs variants, and the CNN single model on two datasets. The Hybrid-DKT models obtained better prediction performance over the state-of-the-art DKT method with RNNs single variants LSTM, biLSTM and GRU on both datasets. The GRU-CNN hybrid model obtained the best prediction performance with slightly advantage over the biLSTM-CNN, while the LSTM-CNN

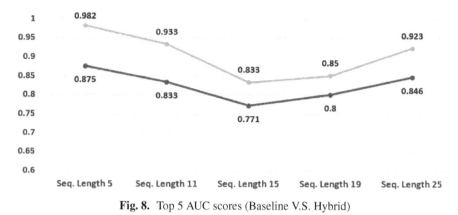

Fig. 8. Top 5 AUC scores (Baseline V.S. Hybrid)

Fig. 9. Top 5 Improvement Percentages (Hybrid)

Table 3. Seq. 11 Prediction with 5 Missing Sequences.

Sequence Length	Hybrid (biLSTM-CNN)	Hybrid (LSTM-CNN)	Hybrid (GRU-CNN)
	AUC	*AUC*	*AUC*
6 (missing)	0.673	0.632	0.668
7 (missing)	0.750	0.719	0.813
8 (missing)	0.749	0.792	0.764
9 (missing)	0.786	0.643	0.750
10 (missing)	0.750	0.679	0.786
11 (Predict)	0.752	0.719	0.813

was the third on the C++CCH dataset. For the single baseline models on the C++CCH dataset, the GRU obtained the best AUC score followed by the CNN, biLSTM and LSTM.

Along all the 22 sequence lengths, the hybrid biLSTM-CNN obtained the top five improvement ratio over the baseline biLSTM model, while the GRU-CNN model achieved the highest prediction performance AUC scores over five sequence lengths. Also, the results revealed that the hybrid models have positive impact to level-up the prediction quality toward increasing the sequence lengths in the AUC interval 0.80–0.99 by 23%, and decreasing those with AUC score less than AUC 0.70 to 0%.

The results demonstrated the impact of both increasing the dataset size and using submissions with real sequence dependency in improving the prediction performance.

Also, the results revealed the effectiveness of the DKT Missing Sequence Padding method and the ability to recursively predict far sequences with AUC score 0.813 on 5 missing values.

5   Conclusions and Future Work

In this work, we presented a novel Intelligent Serious Games model. This study revealed the effectiveness of integrating the Deep Knowledge Tracing (DKT) method with serious games in particular and with games in general. The study also, revealed that the DKT model can look one or more steps ahead during the gameplay to predict the result of the next missions. Accordingly, the game will be able to make a proactive action such as recommendations so that the player can successfully complete the next mission with high confidence.

Also, we introduced in this work, a new approach in evaluating the DKT method based on each sequence length within a fixed and ordered series of submissions. This approach is crucial to apply the model on real situation to trace the knowledge state of players/students at each sequence/mission.

Furthermore, we proposed and tested a novel DKT-based a hybrid prediction model, and we investigated the influence of combining the LSTM, biLSTM and GRU with CNNs as a multi-layer learning approach. The results revealed the effectiveness of this approach, the models LSTM, biLSTM and GRU are efficient for long-term and sequential dependencies, but this might not necessarily be useful for all sequence lengths, for this reason the CNN model as a second layer can enhance the performance with another technique as it is an efficient model to discover hidden patterns and features. Also, the study uncovered the fact of the CNN as a single model can be used in the DKT problem or in the time-series problem in general as it achieved performance close to the RNNs baseline variants.

Also, we introduced and tested a novel method for DKT-Missing Sequence Padding with recursive algorithm. The results revealed the effectiveness of this method to predict far sequences on series with missing values. Therefore, the model is able to look more steps ahead during the gameplay.

In this study, we introduced a new dataset called C++CCH for programming skills. Our investigation uncovered that the prediction performance can be improved by increasing the dataset size; and using real sequence dependency in the submissions as the concepts are ordered from basic to advanced.

Overall, this work can be replicated and extended in different disciplines and can be integrated with any online learning environment. Future prospective to extend this work by applying the concept of the DKT method on the entertainment games, which could positively impact the gaming industry. Another future opportunity also to expand the dataset to include more advanced programming skills, and to address the influence and the effectiveness of the complete ISG model on the players' attainments by implementing an ISG-based game and testing on real players. Furthermore, our efforts now dedicated to introducing A novel Transformer-based Recommender system by fine-tuning Transformer [10] based models such as GPT-2, BART and T5 to generate recommendation flashcards for players in programming skills.

References

1. Piech, C., et al.: Deep knowledge tracing. Adv. Neural Inf. Process. Syst. **28** (2015). https://proceedings.neurips.cc/paper/2015/file/bac9162b47c56fc8a4d2a519803d51b3-Paper.pdf
2. Hasanov, A., Laine, T.H., Chung, T.-S.: A survey of adaptive context-aware learning environments. J. Ambient Intell. Smart Environ. **11**(5), 403–428 (2019). https://doi.org/10.3233/AIS-190534
3. Corbett, A.T., Anderson, J.R.: Knowledge tracing: Modeling the acquisition of procedural knowledge. User Model. User-Adapt. Interact. **4**(4), 253–278 (1995). https://doi.org/10.1007/BF01099821
4. Zanichelli, F., Encheva, M., Thabet, B., Tammaro, A.M., Conti, G.: Serious games for information literacy: assessing learning in the NAVIGATE Project. In: IRCDL: Proceedings of the 17th Italian Research Conference on Digital Libraries, Padova, Italy (2021). http://ceur-ws.org/Vol-2816/paper7.pdf
5. Alonso-Fernández, C., Calvo-Morata, A., Freire, M., Martínez-Ortiz, I., Fernández-Manjón, B.: Applications of data science to game learning analytics data: a systematic literature review. Comput. Educ. **141**, 103612 (2019). https://doi.org/10.1016/j.compedu.2019.103612
6. Mao, Y., Lin, C., Chi, M.: Deep learning vs. bayesian knowledge tracing: student models for interventions (2018). https://doi.org/10.5281/ZENODO.3554691
7. Wang, Z., Feng, X., Tang, J., Huang, G.Y., Liu, Z.: Deep knowledge tracing with side information. In: Isotani, S., Millán, E., Ogan, A., Hastings, P., McLaren, B., Luckin, R. (eds.) AIED 2019. LNCS (LNAI), vol. 11626, pp. 303–308. Springer, Cham (2019). https://doi.org/10.1007/978-3-030-23207-8_56
8. Hooshyar, D., Huang, Y.-M., Yang, Y.: GameDKT: deep knowledge tracing in educational games. Expert Syst. Appl. **196**, 116670 (2022). https://doi.org/10.1016/j.eswa.2022.116670
9. Wang, L., Sy, A., Liu, L., Piech, C.: Deep knowledge tracing on programming exercises. In: Proceedings of the Fourth (2017) ACM Conference on Learning @ Scale, Cambridge Massachusetts USA, pp. 201–204 (2017). https://doi.org/10.1145/3051457.3053985
10. Vaswani, A., et al.: Attention is all you need. Adv. Neural Inf. Process. Syst. **30** (2017). https://proceedings.neurips.cc/paper/2017/file/3f5ee243547dee91fbd053c1c4a845aa-Paper.pdf
11. Zhang, J., Li, Y., Tian, J., Li, T.: LSTM-CNN hybrid model for text classification. In: 2018 IEEE 3rd Advanced Information Technology, Electronic and Automation Control Conference (IAEAC), Chongqing, pp. 1675–1680 (2018). https://doi.org/10.1109/IAEAC.2018.8577620
12. Alhussein, M., Aurangzeb, K., Haider, S.I.: Hybrid CNN-LSTM model for short-term individual household load forecasting. IEEE Access **8**, 180544–180557 (2020). https://doi.org/10.1109/ACCESS.2020.3028281

13. Agga, A., Abbou, A., Labbadi, M., Houm, Y.E., Ali, I.H.O.: CNN-LSTM: an efficient hybrid deep learning architecture for predicting short-term photovoltaic power production. Electr. Power Syst. Res. **208**, 10790 (2022). https://doi.org/10.1016/j.epsr.2022.107908

14. Yeung, C.-K., Yeung, D.-Y.: Addressing two problems in deep knowledge tracing via prediction-consistent regularization. In: Proceedings of the Fifth Annual ACM Conference on Learning at Scale, London United Kingdom, pp. 1–10 (2018). https://doi.org/10.1145/323 1644.3231647

15. Kingma, P., Ba, J.: Adam: a method for stochastic optimization. ArXiv14126980 Cs (2017). Accessed 29 Jan 2022. http://arxiv.org/abs/1412.6980

MOOCs Based Blending Teaching Reform for Integrated College Computer Course

Yue Yu[1(✉)], Ying Fu[1], Yufeng Chen[1], and Minzhi Li[2]

[1] Beijing Institute of Technology, Beijing, China
yuyue@bit.edu.cn
[2] Lanzhou Jiaotong University, Lanzhou, China

Abstract. As the development of new engineering, the integration of the computer technology with other disciplines brings the challenge to the basic college computer course. However, the limited class hours in the university makes it much more difficult to realize the computational thinking ability cultivation. So it is important to design the highly integrated and connotative college computer courses based on the limited class hours, meeting the requirements of the computer technology and the information quantity for the new engineering. This paper introduces the blending teaching method for integrated college computer course based on MOOCs. With the help of multiple high-quality MOOC resources, SPOC is constructed to deeply explore the mode of online and offline mixed teaching practice and the teaching method of flipped classroom, which is useful for the talent cultivation of new engineering. At last, a blended teaching reform and practice based on MOOCs is carried out in the course "Computer Science and Programming (C)" and some evaluation statistical analysis are conducted.

Keywords: Blending Teaching · Computational Thinking · MOOC · SPOC

1 Introduction

The development of the new era has put forward new goals for the education, which needs to cultivate the students with the innovative ability and the international vision. To realize this goal, it is necessary to propose the new teaching methods. In 2017, the Ministry of Education of China launched the research on the development of "new engineering". The new engineering emphasizes the practicability, intersection and comprehensiveness of the disciplines, especially the close combination of new technologies such as information communication, electronic control and software design with traditional industrial technology. The new engineering needs the new educational concepts and shows the new characteristics, such as the interdisciplinary, the cooperation and collaborative education between the university and the industry. The important task of the new engineering is to cultivate the innovative talents with the sustainable competitiveness.

MOOC (Massive Open Online Course) first emerged in the United States in 2012, and the MOOC learning platforms were built successively in 2014 in China, which had a great impact on the higher education [1]. The Internet+ education technology brings

W. Hong and Y. Weng (Eds.): ICCSE 2022, CCIS 1811, pp. 293–304, 2023.
https://doi.org/10.1007/978-981-99-2443-1_26

great changes to the modern education and teaching reform. First, the personalized features of the large-scale online teaching make personalized learning possible for the students; second, the teachers requires the full use of a large number of the digital teaching resources; third, a lot of objective, concrete, and real-time big data analysis can support the sustainable development of the curriculum.

Computation is considered the third pillar of the scientific method, along with theory and experimentation [2]. With the development of computer, big data, artificial intelligence, virtual reality and other technologies, the concept of computing has penetrated into the various domains such as society and nature, making the various disciplines develop in the direction of computing, virtualization and intelligence. Computer technology has been widely used in all fields of work and life. Therefore, it is necessary for the students to obtain the comprehensive computer technology to adapt to the social development.

In the context of the new engineering and MOOC, the basic college computer courses for all the freshman in the university face the opportunities and challenges. The opportunities are mainly in that the new engineering education needs the basic computer courses can realize the cross-fertilization of computing technology and other disciplines. The basic college computer courses should be prepared for the students cultivation with sustainable competitiveness. The challenges include that many MOOC resources cannot be fully utilized; it is difficult in building the courses for deep integration of the computing technology and various disciplines; it is not easy to carry out practical flipped classroom teaching.

The following parts of this paper are organized as follows. Section 2 presents the design of integrated college computer course. Section 3 shows MOOCs based blending teaching design. The practice process and effect evaluation are illustrated in Sect. 4. Section 5 concludes the paper finally.

2   Design of Integrated College Computer Course

Computational thinking emphasizes that the essence of computer education is for the students to master the computing technology and use the computing science to solve the problems. The United States began to popularize the computational thinking in 2005, Jeanette Wing published an article where she described the computational thinking as "a fundamental skill for everyone, not just for computer scientists in 2006 [3]. The Ministry of Education of China started to bring the computational thinking into the basic college computer courses in 2010. The content of the basic college computer courses has been replaced by "tool software" with "problem solving, system design and human behavior understanding" as the core content. Some definition of the computational thinking appropriate for elementary level instruction is proposed [4]. The basic college computer courses need to be guided by computational thinking, deepen the reform of teaching content, improve the curriculum system, support the interdisciplinary integration, and cultivate innovative and entrepreneurial talents with computational thinking skills.

At present, the main basic college computer courses mainly include two courses: college computer foundation and computer programming. Under the background of the new engineering and the class hour compression, how to design an integrated course to cultivate the ability of computational thinking under the limited class hours is of great significance. The integrated college computer course is designed for this purpose, integrating the basic principles of computer, the computer-based problem solving method and the programming technology, realizing the combination with the majors. The curriculum design of integrated college computer course is shown in Fig. 1. The whole course content is divided into four layers: the basic layer, the abstract layer, the practice layer and the application layer. The basic layer introduces the working principle of computer, including the digital processing of computer information, the basic working principle of computer hardware and software. The abstract layer cultivates the students' computational thinking ability. It focuses on the abstract representation of the problems on the basis of the computer principles, including the computer-based problem solving and the algorithm design and expression. The practical layer introduces the specific programming language, trains the students to realize the method of solving problems based on computer with specific programming language, and deeply understands the computational thinking ability. The application layer introduces different computer practical applications, such as the computer network, the multimedia data processing and the database, etc. Different contents can be selected for different majors, which is conducive to the in-depth integration of the course and the major, so as to realize the in-depth integration of computational thinking and the major.

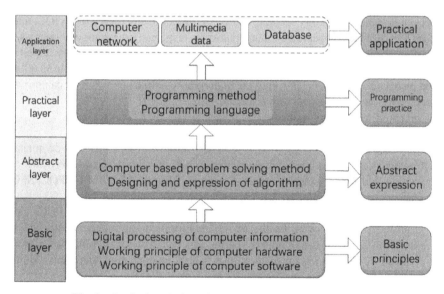

Fig. 1. Curriculum design of integrated college computer course

3 MOOCs Based Blending Teaching Design

3.1 MOOC and SPOC

The emergence of MOOC has brought the changes in teaching mode. MOOC refers to large-scale online open courses, which are generally open to all students in the society. "Large-scale" means supporting students to communicate across domains, "online" means supporting real-time guidance from experts, and "open" means supporting resource sharing. This is a new type of curriculum model, which should also have the same complete curriculum structure as traditional teaching. MOOC has many advantages, such as high-quality teaching resources, which can promote education fairness. However, MOOC also has its shortcomings. In terms of ability development, emotional interaction with students, and systematic knowledge, MOOC is not as good as traditional classrooms. The obvious advantage of MOOC is the knowledge transmission. MOOC is better than previous traditional online courses. The complete learning process in MOOC is recorded and the learning process can be evaluated.

SPOC (small private online course) refers to small-scale private online courses, which are open to some schools or some specific students. MOOCs + SPOC refers to an online open course with its own characteristics established based on the MOOC. It is an implementation mode of course collaborative construction based on MOOCs. MOOCs + SPOC avoids the repeated construction of resources and is also conducive to the promotion of high-quality teaching resources. Since the emergence of MOOC, many similar MOOCs have appeared on many platforms, especially the computer courses. In face of so many MOOCs, the selection of a proper MOOC has become very important for the teaching reform based on MOOCs + SPOC. When carrying out teaching reform based on MOOCs + SPOC, choosing the high-quality online open courses can provide guarantee for the development of teaching reform.

Compared with MOOC courses, the advantages of SPOC courses are:

(1) Easy access to high-quality MOOC teaching resources. SPOC teachers do not have to spend a lot of time, energy, and cost like MOOC teachers to record short videos of lectures and design a large number of exercise. Through MOOCs + SPOC, SPOC teachers can obtain all teaching resources in MOOC and reuse them.

(2) SPOC can realize the private management of their own students. The SPOC course is an independent course on the MOOC platform. It can independently use the platform's learning data statistics, performance statistics, and other functions to facilitate teachers to manage their own school students and view their MOOC learning results.

(3) Simply coordinate MOOC public resources and SPOC private teaching resources. The SPOC divides teaching resources, assignments/tests, and discussion areas into two parts: the MOOC area and the SPOC area, which are organically unified and provided to students for use. The SPOC teachers can maintain the unique content of the proprietary SPOC in private, while the content of the MOOC area are shared in the same course.

(4) Real-time sharing of online teachers and teaching assistant teams. MOOC courses have their own teachers and teaching assistants. Therefore, even if SPOC teachers

do not have time, there will still be MOOC teachers or other SPOC teachers and teaching assistants to answer questions for students, realizing the sharing of online teachers and teaching assistants. At the same time, due to the fact that assignments on MOOC are regularly released and closed by a dedicated person, and the system automatically scores and counts them, it saves time for SPOC teachers to assign assignments in class and correct assignments after class.

For a typical SPOC course, first of all, you need to publish your own course SPOC homepage, which specifies the content that SPOC students should learn and how to obtain their grades. Teachers tell students about course links, course selection passwords, and identity authentication information during class. For more complex SPOC, based on the differences in student groups, teaching content is restructured on the basis of MOOC, teaching videos are supplemented, characteristic test and homework, exams, and different achievement acquisition policies are set. Flipped classes can be carried out.

Although MOOC/SPOC has many advantages, its biggest disadvantage is that its learning process mainly relies on students' learning self-consciousness, and due to the limited self-control ability of students, there are also shortcomings in their learning self-consciousness. It is important to design the proper strategies to encourage students to participate in the activities in MOOC/SPOC effectively.

3.2 Blending Teaching Methods

SPOC is a mode of the integration between MOOC and the traditional classroom. It aims to combine the high-quality resources of MOOCs and the new classroom structure of the flipped classroom. It can not only play role of the structural advantages of flipped classroom focusing on discussion and interaction, but also make up for the lack of content systematisms of simple MOOC course [5, 6]. The blending teaching based on MOOCs + SPOC can be divided into the online and offline mixed teaching mode and the flipped classroom teaching mode. The online and offline mixed teaching mode based on MOOCs + SPOC is a mixed teaching mode to realize the complementarity of in class and out of teaching. The MOOC teaching content introduced into the traditional teaching can be carried out by means of the MOOC video supplementary for teaching content, the MOOC exercises supplementary for homework exercises, the MOOC online discussion assisting in Q&A. This mode is a traditional teaching method with MOOC supplementary learning mode, which is simple to implement and easy to popularize. It is especially easy to be popularized and applied in large class teaching. Generally, schools adopting this teaching method will consider MOOC learning as into the part of their evaluation methods. The flipped teaching mode based on MOOCs + SPOC is a discussion teaching mode that emphasizes students' autonomous learning. Students learn in advance through MOOCs and other methods according to teachers' requirements before class, and deeply understand the teaching content through the tests, the core and difficult knowledge analysis, the discussion and report in class. This method is conducive to the students' in-depth learning, but the students pay a high cost of learning time. It is not suitable for the large class teaching. For the practice of flipped teaching, a practical investigation is conducted on the time and the content of flipped classroom teaching. The investigation includes the following aspects:

(1) All teaching contents flipped.
(2) First traditional classroom teaching (30%), then flipped teaching(70%).
(3) First traditional classroom teaching (50%), then flipped teaching(50%).
(4) First traditional classroom teaching (70%), then flipped teaching(30%).
(5) No flipped teaching contents.
(6) First flipped teaching, then traditional classroom teaching.

The conclusion is shown in Fig. 2. It can be seen that students are not interested in the way that all teaching contents are flipped. It is a more suitable scheme to carry out traditional classroom teaching first and then flipped classroom teaching, and the proper flipped teaching content is less than 50%.

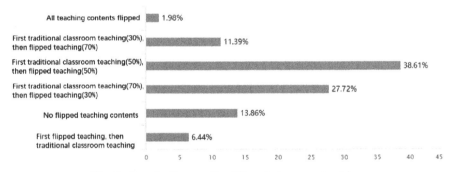

Fig. 2. Investigation results of flipped classroom teaching

It is important to adopt the online and offline mixed teaching mode based on MOOC. The fragmentation of MOOC knowledge points is conducive to students' further learning after class, especially for knowledge points that they do not understand in class, making up for the lack of the classroom teaching. In particular, the knowledge points in the basic college computer courses are numerous and complex, and MOOC resources can provide strong supplement and support for classroom teaching. The fragmentation of MOOC knowledge points is not conducive to the formation of a complete knowledge system for students, while classroom teaching is a systematic guide to students' whole knowledge, making students learn more comprehensively. In addition to the videos, MOOC also has a wealth of automated test assignments such as discussion questions, quizzes, unit tests, and assignments, providing students with more opportunities to practice and improving their awareness of learning. Unit tests and other assignments allow students to submit their work multiple times. This is designed to take advantage of students' high scoring psychology. If students find themselves doing something wrong, they can submit them repeatedly until they are satisfied. This process is conducive to students' continuous consolidation and reinforcement of knowledge.

It is significant to adopt the flipped classroom teaching mode based on MOOC. Learning MOOC videos in advance before class allows students to listen to the teacher with questions and key points in classroom, making learning process more efficient and targeted. The teacher's classroom becomes richer, using MOOC resource to realize micro flip based on local content and designing discussion topics that guide students' thinking, which is conducive to the explanation of the key and difficult knowledge. With the foundation of MOOC learning, teachers can shift from explaining knowledge and skills to cultivating computational thinking abilities within limited classroom teaching time. Through case studies and discussions, students can acquire the application ideas of computers in different disciplines based on the teaching of problem abstraction, solution ideas and methods, thereby improving their computational thinking abilities.

MOOCs + SPOC approach is an effective means to realize the implementation of MOOC. But there are still some problems. MOOCs + SPOC approach dependents on the existing MOOC resources; however, the existing MOOC resources are limited, and it is difficult to meet the learning needs of different discipline courses in colleges. The SPOC resource development is still led by the teacher, ignoring the main position and role of the learners. The SPOC resource application lacks dynamism and sticks to the predetermined teaching objectives, ignoring the process of dynamic development of teaching, the openness of learning resource application, and the personalization of the learners [7]. Therefore, in the implementation of the MOOCs + SPOC based process, the integration of multiple MOOCs and the dynamic teaching process approach should be adopted to achieve the purpose of effective students' cultivation.

4　Practice Process and Effect Evaluation

We have carried out a blended teaching reform and practice based on MOOCs in the course "Computer Science and Programming (C)". The course "Computer Science and Programming (C)" is an integrated college computer course that integrates the knowledge of computer, the computer technology, and the computer application by linking the two courses "College Computer" and "C Programming". Students can obtain the information quality through this course, that is, they can use computers for information acquisition, information analysis, and information processing, and provide computer-related knowledge and auxiliary skills for the study of other courses.

4.1　Course Content

Three MOOCs courses used in the process of teaching the MOOCs + SPOC based "Computer Science and Programming (C)" course are the excellent MOOCs named "College Computer" by Professor Fengxia Li of Beijing Institute of Technology and "C Programming (Part 1)" and "C Programming (Part 2)" by Professor Fengxia Li on China University MOOC platform. In the implementation process, the MOOC "College Computer" does not count as the evaluation grade and the MOOCs "C Programming (Part 1)" and "C Programming (Part 2)" count as the evaluation grade. The whole course content includes the following components:

(1)　Computer-based problem solving;
(2)　The digital foundation of computer information;

(3) Computer hardware platform;
(4) Computer software platform;
(5) Computer network platform;
(6) Data processing and database;
(7) Computing science;
(8) Algorithms and programming;
(9) Data types and operation rules in C programming language;
(10) Sequence structure programming in C programming language;
(11) Selection structure programming in C programming language;
(12) Loop structure programming in C programming language;
(13) Array in C programming language;
(14) Function in C programming language;
(15) Pointer in C programming language;
(16) Structure in C programming language.

4.2 Teaching Method Evaluation

The following teaching methods are adopted in the process of teaching the course "Computer Science and Programming (C)" based on MOOCs + SPOC:

(1) Traditional classroom - lectures;
(2) Flipped classroom - preview before class, feedback questions, teacher explains important points and problems in class;
(3) Flipped classroom - preview before class, questions in class, group discussion;
(4) Flipped classroom - preview before class, few lectures on knowledge points in class, more lectures on homework problems;
(5) Flipped classroom - preview before class, teacher asks questions in class, students answer them, and teacher explains in response to students' answers.

A study is conducted on the effectiveness of MOOCs + SPOC based flipped class-room teaching, as shown in Fig. 3. Most students think that the flipped classroom app-roach will increase the students' learning time, but at the same time, more students think that the flipped classroom approach will lead to a deeper understanding of the course content.

For specific course content, which content do students think is suitable for flipped classroom teaching? A investigation is conducted, and each student could choose up to 5 contents, and the results are shown in Fig. 4. It can be seen that the flipped classroom teaching method is more suitable for some more difficult teaching contents.

Statistical analysis is conducted for the different teaching methods expected for different teaching contents, and the results are shown in Fig. 5. Traditional classroom teaching still accounts for a large proportion of students' subjective willingness, but this willingness will gradually decrease as the teaching process proceeds, while the will-ingness of flipped classroom teaching will increase, so it is more appropriate to adopt traditional classroom teaching first and then flipped classroom teaching as a solution. Among different forms of flipped classroom, flipped classroom forms with weak student

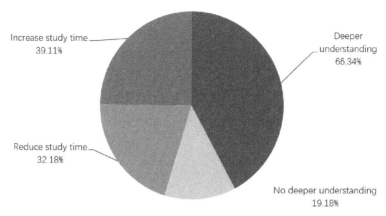

Fig. 3. Effectiveness of flipped classroom based on MOOCs + SPOC

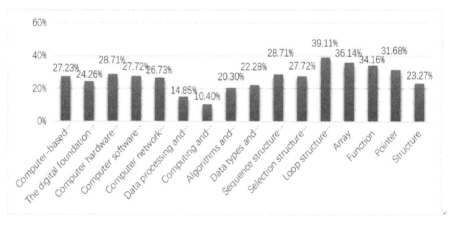

Fig. 4. Investigation results of teaching course content suitable for flipped classroom teaching

participation (e.g., analysis of important and difficult knowledge, explanation of exercises) are more popular among students than flipped classroom forms with strong student participation (e.g., questions and discussions), so how to motivate students' subjective initiative in flipped classroom is still a key issue to be considered in the teaching design.

Through the survey of students, the results of MOOCs' assistance in studying the course are shown in Fig. 6. The study resource in MOOCs includes video, discussion subject, quiz and assignment, online discussion and Q&A, and exercise.

Video: The teaching content is divided into several knowledge points, with each knowledge point recording a video.

Discussion subject: Set some discussion topics based on the video content to inspire students to think after watching the video.

Quiz and assignment: Assign homework based on the teaching content, so that students can achieve the required degree of the course and test their understanding of video knowledge.

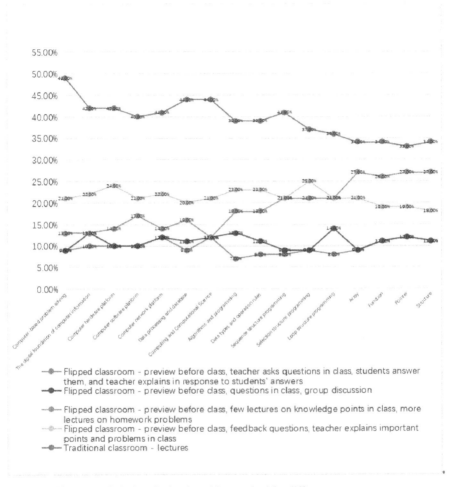

Fig. 5. Statistical analysis of teaching method for different course content

Online discussion and Q&A: The online discussion areas in MOOC can support discussions between students, Q&A between teachers and students, and Q&A among students.

Exercise: Set some exercise among different videos to enhance students' interactive learning in MOOC and deepen their understanding of video knowledge points, supporting the learning process.

It can be seen that very few students believe that the content in MOOC is not helpful for learning. In addition, as can be seen from Fig. 6, among the several learning process of MOOC, the relatively helpful parts for students are video, quiz and assignment. Therefore, it can be seen that using online video resources to assist teaching, and allowing students to complete assignments on MOOC are greatly helpful for students to learn the course, improving the teaching quality of basic college computer courses.

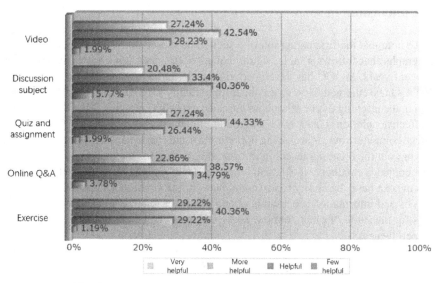

Fig. 6. Results of MOOCs' assistance in studying the course

The online and offline mixed teaching mode based on MOOCs, combining MOOC/SPOC online video resources are useful for the students to carry out self-learning and knowledge expansion. Participating in online discussions and completing online assignments can enhance the generalization and diversity of courses. The flipped classroom teaching mode based on MOOCs increases the depth of the course, including class questions, group discussion, in-depth explanation for the student answers, which is conducive to active learning and in-depth learning.

Although MOOC has many advantages, its biggest disadvantage is that its learning process mainly relies on students' learning self-consciousness, and due to the limited self-control ability of students, there are also shortcomings in their learning self-consciousness,

Finally, we analyze the role of three MOOCs in the blending teaching of "Computer Science and Programming (C)". In fact, MOOC content mainly includes three aspects: video teaching resources, MOOC homework and discussion. The help of these three parts to students' learning is shown in Fig. 7. MOOC video helps students preview in advance and consolidate after class. MOOC homework helps students strengthen training.

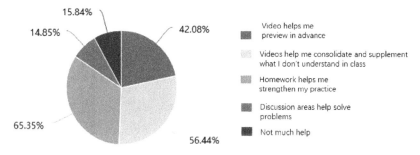

Fig. 7. Statistical analysis of MOOC resources

5 Conclusion

Please note that the first paragraph of a section or subsection is not indented. The first paragraphs that follows a table, figure, equation etc. does not have an indent, either. In recent years, MOOC has developed vigorously and a large number of high-quality MOOCs have emerged. How to use these high-quality MOOC resources and implement them in the teaching of our school has attracted extensive attention. MOOCs + SPOC is an effective solution. Under the background of new engineering and MOOC, the basic college computer courses are facing opportunities and challenges. Based on the MOOCs, carrying out the blending teaching reform and practice for the integrated college computer course is conducive to students' more in-depth access to information quality. The students can have the ability to use computers for information acquisition, information analysis and information processing, obtain computer related knowledge and auxiliary skills for the study of other courses. So the students can be cultivated with sustainable competitiveness.

Acknowledgment. This work was supported by National Natural Science Foundation of China (61807002).

References

1. Zhou, M.: Chinese university students' acceptance of MOOCs: a selfdetermination perspective. Comput. Educ. **92–93**, 194–203 (2016)
2. Grover, S., Fisler, K., Lee, I., Yadav, A.: Integrating computing and computational thinking into K-12 STEM learning. In: SIGCSE 2020, Portland, OR, USA (2020)
3. Wing, J.M.: Computational thinking. Commun. ACM **49**(3), 33–35 (2006)
4. Pietros, J., Sweetman, S., Shim, M.: How is computational thinking defined in elementary science. In: SIGCSE 2022, Providence, RI, USA (2022)
5. Xu, B., Li, T., Shi, X.: The analysis and educational revelation of learning motivation in MOOC, flipping classroom and SPOC. Dist. Educ. Online Learn. **368**, 47–52, 61 (2017)
6. Liu, C., Fu, G.: Research on the application path of SPOC flipped classroom in basic education in poor areas. E-Educ. Res. **6**, 107–113 (2018)
7. Zhong, L., Hu, Q., Hu, X.: Research on develop and application of generative learning resources for SPOC. China Educ. Technol. **5**, 118–123 (2018)

Sentiment Classification of Chinese Commodity-Comment Based on EMCCNN Model

Xiaoyan Ren[✉], Yunxia Fu, and Xiaoyan Yang

College of Computer and Information Technology, China Three Gorges University, Yichang, Hubei, China
450706780@qq.com

Abstract. Targeting at the great commercial and social values of sentiment analysis of online product reviews, this paper puts forward an emotion-semantics enhanced multi-channel convolutional neural network (EMCCNN) approach to dig automatically out the emotional position of the reviewer. This EMCCNN model is featured firstly with a completed construction of emotional symbols datasets which are composed of Chinese emotion words, degree adverbs, negative words, common Internet slang and emoticons, secondly with three input channels containing a relatively independent text sequence and emotional symbol sequence in each, thirdly with weighted pooling which summarizes different channel's convolution result with various weight, then joins with max pooling to form the final emotion vectors, which are subsequently classified with softmax function. The experiment result shows that, after the adjustment of super parameters, the F1 value of EMCCNN has been improved by 3.2% compared with the traditional CNN one.

Keywords: Sentiment Classification · Convolutional Neural Network · Natural Language Processing · Deep Learning

1 Introduction

With the rapid development of Web 2.0, a lot of User Generated Contents (UGCs), which show clearly writers' various emotions and positional tendencies, have been produced on the Internet. For example, more and more buyers have published massive commodity reviews in the form of short text on E-commerce platform platforms. These reviews often contain the user's buying experience and emotional perspective on the products, which are characterized by short length, clear themes, and strong emotions. With the rapid expansion of commodity comments, it is difficult to cope with the collection and processing of massive amounts of information by manual methods alone. Therefore, an efficient emotional information processing system is urgently needed to quickly obtain and sort out these related review information and dig out the true emotional tendencies, which have reference value for merchants, sellers, buyers. Compared with ordinary semi-structured texts, these commodity review texts are short and not strictly standardized.

© The Author(s), under exclusive license to Springer Nature Singapore Pte Ltd. 2023
W. Hong and Y. Weng (Eds.): ICCSE 2022, CCIS 1811, pp. 305–314, 2023.
https://doi.org/10.1007/978-981-99-2443-1_27

Accordingly, sentiment analysis of commodity review texts is more challenging and difficult to analyze than ordinary text analysis.

Sentiment analysis is a computational study of people's opinions and emotions on entities and events or their attributes [1]. Sentiment analysis can be divided into two categories in terms of granularity: one is for a coarse-grained emotion classification of positive (praise), neutral and negative (derogatory) sentiment polarity of a text; the other is subdivided fine-grained sentiment analysis such as "joy", "anger", "angry", and "sadness". The research scope of this article belongs to the former: coarse-grained sentiment analysis. At present, the mainstream methods in the field of sentiment analysis are mainly divided into four categories: the first category is the traditional feature-based statistical method; the second category is the calculation method based on the semantic dictionary [2–4]; the third category is based on the Support Vector Machine and Naïve Bayesian Model and other traditional machine learning methods; the fourth category is based on deep neural network methods. Compared with the first three types of methods, the deep network learning method avoids the limitations and huge costs of manual design features, and has better portability. Because of the successful application of deep learning models in the field of Natural Language Processing, more and more scholars have applied deep learning techniques such as CNN [5], LSTM [6], and BiGRU to research on sentiment classification and other related tasks, and have achieved good experimental results.

The main contributions of this article are:

- Chinese emotional words and emoticons are exploited to improve the emotional classification effect of commodity review text.
- Based on the uneven distribution of emotional intensity of product review text (the initial sentence and the last sentence usually have strong emotional tendenies),an emotional semantic enhancement multi-input channel convolutional neural network (EMCCCN) is proposed to adapt to this research problem.

2   Related Works

2.1   Construction of Emotional Symbols Dictionary

More recent approaches used deep learning model for UGC Chinese sentiment analysis research work, but most of the researchers did not consider the weight of the influence of different feature words on the overall position information of the sentence. Product review texts, such as Taobao's and JD's comments, have the characteristic of congenital sparse information. The length of these comments, which contain emoticons, sentimental words, links, pictures, stop words, and other information, is generally between 10 and 100 words. The analysis and induction of sample product review cases show that the key emotional characteristic words and emoticons in product reviews can roughly reflect the opinion tendency of reviewers. For example, the stop words "的de", "了le", "吧ba", "着zhe", have no practical effect on the emotional position analysis of the review text. On the contrary, emotional words and emoticons, such as "bad review", "like", "satisfied", "disappointed", ☺, and, can well reflect the emotional tendency of commentators. For product-review texts are sparse, colloquial, and non-standard, in addition, different words and emoticons have different contribution weights to emotional stance, to extract the commentators' stance efficiently and accurately from these unstructured texts we built an emotional symbols dictionary, which includes the following two modules:

- 8703 Chinese emotional words are selected based on the "HowNet" sentiment analysis vocabulary set (beta version) and Dalian University of Technology's "Chinese Sentiment Vocabulary Ontology Database". These emotion words are composed of positive evaluation words, positive emotion words, negative evaluation words, negative emotion words, degree adverbs, negative words, rhetorical words and double negative words.
- 75 web emoticons. According to the statistics of the Taobao's review data set, buyers use a large number of emoticons in the review text to express the purchase experience. Through the analysis and sorting of the Taobao's comment sampling data set, 129 emoticons are collected (as shown in the Table 1). We arrange emoticons in descending order of appearance frequency, and two researchers separately labeled the top 100 emoticons list. One tagging task is to determine the emotional expression tendency of emoticons, and another task is to determine the emotional expression tendency of the text where the emoticons are located. According to the order of emoticons, we calculated the Kapper values of the two taggings, and get the result shown in Fig. 1 below (where Top-n represents the first n emoticons in the sort list).

Table 1. Emoticons library

Emoticons	Emotional polarity	Amount
⊖ 🖐 ⊕ ……	positive	45
👀 👀 👀 ……	neutral	37
🏠 💢 👀 ……	negative	47

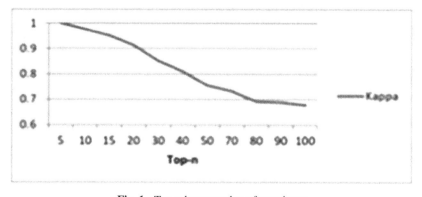

Fig. 1. Top-n kapper value of emoticons

As shown in the figure above, the top-ranked emoticons have a strong ability to express emotions, and the lower-ranked emoticons have a low contribution rate to the emotional tendency of the comments, but they cannot be completely ignored. After repeated testing and optimization, TOP-75 emoticons with a higher usage rate are collected as emotional symbol sets for the experiment of this article.

2.2 Emotional Semantic Enhancement Multi-input Channel Convolutional Neural Network Model

Aiming at the problem of Chinese short text sentiment classification of Taobao's product reviews, this article proposes an Emotional semantic enhancement Multi-input Channel Convolutional Neural Network model (EMCCNN), which is mainly composed of text multi-channel input word embedding layer, multi-convolution size and multi-convolution Kernel convolution layer, weighted pooling layer, fully connected layer and softmax classification layer (Fig. 2).

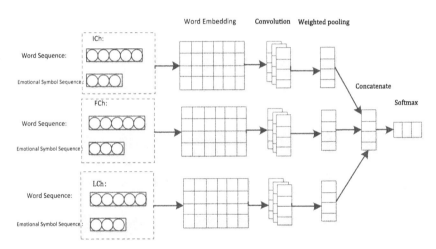

Fig. 2. EMCCNN Model Architecture

• Word embedding layer

After doing a lot of research and analysis on product review texts, we found that most of the first and last sentences of the reviews are far more emotional than the middle texts. For example: "Great! Saved my sensitive red skin in time. I like the faint fragrance of essential oil very much. Yes, I bought it. Absolutely empty bottle repurchase! Real love!" Both the first sentence and the last sentence of the comment express positive and affirmative intentions. Another example: "I feel not worth the price. It is very thin, the pattern is uncomfortable to the touch, and the color difference is also quite strong. Moreover, the neckline is already loose after washing it once… I am sorry for the quality at this price." The emotional inclination of the first and last sentence of this comment is extremely negative. For the above characteristics, we adopt three input channels to overcome traditional text classification's limitation. The three channels are: First-Channel (FCh), Integrated-Channel (ICh) and Last-Channel (LCh). FCh refers to the first sentence of the comment; LCh refers to the last sentence of the comment; ICh is the complete comment text. The word sequence input layer of each channel mainly includes two parts: the word sequence text, which is composed of filtered and segmented review text, and the emotional symbol sequence, which is extracted from the review text and is a subset of the self-built Chinese emotional symbol dictionary detailed in 2.1.

We convert the input layer data to word vector matrix by Tencent AI Lab's Chinese word vector, which transforms each Chinese word into a 200-dimensional vector by Tencent self-developed Directional Skip-Gram algorithm. The acquisition of the word sequence text vector matrix RT and the emotional symbol sequence vector matrix RE can be regarded as a process of looking up a dictionary. Assuming that the number of elements in the dictionary is N and the dimension of a single word vector is d, $W_e \in R_{NXd}$ represents the matrix of the entire word vector dictionary. For a text sequence $T = \{w_1, w_2,\ldots,w_n\}$ that are composed of dictionary elements, the word vector representation matrix of the entire text sequence is obtained by concatenating the word vectors of the dictionary elements at the corresponding positions in the text sequence:

$$R_T = v_1 \oplus v_2 \oplus \ldots \ldots \oplus v_n \tag{1}$$

where $\oplus$ represents the vector concatenation operation, $v_i \in R_{NXd}$ represents that the word wi corresponds to the word vector in the dictionary. The generation of the emotion symbol sequence vector matrix R_E is also searched in the emotion dictionary vector library, that is self-built according to the model and algorithm of Tencent's word vector library. In order to simplify the network model structure, we form each input module to a feature matrix by simple concatenation operation; that is to say $X = R_T \oplus R_E$. At the same time, a maximum length maxlen is set for the input of each channel. If the channel's length is less than maxlen, use a vector of all 0s to complete the feature matrix.

- Multi-channel Convolutional Layer

CNN has excellent feature self-extraction ability, which has obvious efficiency advantages compared with manual feature selection. In this work, we obtain local features of different channel inputs by convolution operation of multiple windows and multiple convolution kernels,and form a feature information map. Among them, the calculation method of feature extraction is:

$$S_i = f(C_{w*d} \cdot X_{i:i+w-1} + b) \tag{2}$$

where C (w * d) represents the convolution kernel, and w is the window size of the convolution kernel, and d is the word vector dimension. The $X_{i:\ i+w-1}$ represents the eigenvector matrix from the i-th input sequence to the (i + w-1)-th input sequence in the input channel, and b represents a bias term, and f represents the neuron activation function. By formula (2), we obtain S_i: the i-th eigenvalue after convolution. To overcome the loss of neuron information and gradient disappearance during the training process, the LeakyReLU is used as the activation function in the design:

$$f(x) = \max(0,x) + \gamma\min(0,x) \tag{3}$$

After the convolution kernel feature extraction, each input channel can get a feature map:

$$S = \left[S_1, S_2, \ldots\ldots, S_{maxlen-w+1}\right] \tag{4}$$

In this model, the convolution matrices after convolution sampling of the three channels correspond to S_{FCh}, S_{ICh}, S_{LCh} in turn.

- Weighted Pooling Layer

After the feature extraction is performed by the convolutional layer, since the dimensionality of the feature map is still very high, the feature map needs to be passed to the pooling layer to perform feature selection and information filtering through the pooling function. For the network of this experimental model has multiple input channels, in order to make full use of the feature information in each channel, we weight the convolution results under different input channels:

$$S_W = S_{FCh} \times W_f + S_{ICh} \times W_i + S_{LCh} \times W_l \tag{5}$$

Here W_f, W_i, W_l are the weights of S_{FCh}, S_{ICh}, S_{LCh} respectively. Then the result of a single point in the feature map is replaced by the feature map statistics of its neighboring area through the pooling function. In our experiment, the feature matrix weighted by the MaxPooling function is used to retain the maximum value while discarding other feature values.

- Fully Connected Layer and Softmax Classification

The fully connected layer itself does not have the ability to extract features. It is mainly used to integrate the distinguishing feature information in the pooling layer. In our experiment, the LeakyReLU function is used to adapt to complex text emotion classification tasks. In addition, the Dropout algorithm is added to the fully connected layer to prevent training produces overfitted. Finally, the Multiclass Cross Entropy function is used as the loss function and the normalized exponential function (Softmax) is used as the activation function to output feature classification labels to complete the text classification task.

3　Experimental Results and Analysis

3.1　Experimental Environment Configuration

See Table 2.

Table 2. Environment configuration

Experimental tools	Model or version
CPU	Intel Core™ I5-4200U
GPU	NVIDIA GeForce GT 740M
RAM	16G
Operating System	Linux
Programming language	Python 3.6
Deep learning framework	Tensorflow 1.7
Chinese word segmentation	PyNLPIR

3.2 Experimental Data Det

In view of the current lack of public datasets for Chinese product review text sentiment analysis tasks and the difficulty in obtaining methods, we use a topic-specific crawler to crawl review data from Taobao.com. Then we manually mark the emotional polarity of the crawled texts, and build a balanced distribution corpus, which is composed of 9000 comments.

3.3 Experimental Parameter and Evaluation Index

- Experimental parameter

Because the corpus is relatively small, we use 10-fold cross-validation in the experiment. This experiment is mainly based on Google's deep learning framework tensorflow to build a CNN model. The related experimental parameters are set as follows (Table 3):

Table 3. Parameter settings

Parameter name	Parameter value	meaning
Embedding_dim	200	Word vector dimension
Activation function	LeakyReLU	Unsaturated activation function
optimizer	Adam	Adaptive moment estimation
epochs	20	Number of training iterations
Batch_size	64	The number of samples selected for each iteration of training
Dropout_keep_prob	0.5	The Retention ratio of Dropout

- Evaluation index

The experiment uses a confusion matrix (as shown in Table 4) to record the test results.

Table 4. Confusion matrix

	Test Positive	Test Neutral	Test Negative
Gold standard Positive	*TPP*	*FPO*	*FPN*
Gold standard Neutral	*FOP*	*TOO*	*FON*
Gold standard Negative	*FNP*	*FNO*	*TNN*

In order to verify whether the proposed EMCCNN has the better capability to automatically implement the comment text classification, we compare the accuracy rate, the recall rate and F1-score of our method with the previous methods that realize text sentiment classification. Taking positive evaluation as an example, the calculation method of related evaluation indicators is as follows:

$$precesion = \frac{TPP}{FOP + FNP + TPP} \tag{6}$$

$$recall = \frac{TPP}{TPP + FPO + FPN} \tag{7}$$

$$F1 = \frac{2 * precision * recall}{precision + recall} \tag{8}$$

3.4 Experimental Comparison Model

In order to verify the effectiveness and robustness of the model in this paper, we compare the EMCCNN's evaluation index with the indexes of the following models:

- MNB model (Multinomial Naïve Bayes): As a representative of traditional machine learning, the MNB model has obtained relatively good text analysis results in short text analysis.
- CNN model: Based on the CNN model proposed by Kim, it is the most basic convolutional neural network.
- LSTM model (Long Short Term Memory Network): Use the simplest LSTM model to compare with CNN in classification performance and training time.

3.5 Analysis of Experimental Results

We use 4 models to conduct experiments on the pre-defined corpus detailed in 3.2 to analyze the sentiment polarity of the text. The following table shows the comparison results of the 4 groups of models in the balanced corpus (Table 5).

Table 5. Sentiment classification results of different models

Model	index	positive	neutral	negative
MNB	P	0.716	0.753	0.782
	R	0.765	0.709	0.730
	F1	0.740	0.730	0.755
CNN	P	0.711	0.750	0.861
	R	0.849	0.772	0.695
	F1	0.774	0.761	0.769
LSTM	P	0.735	0.770	0.868
	R	0.877	0.801	0.722
	F1	0.799	0.785	0.788
EMCCNN	P	0.758	0.869	0.811
	R	0.880	0.733	0.793
	F1	0.814	0.795	0.802

As can be seen from the above table, the EMCCNN model has achieved the better sentiment classification accuracy on this corpus. Compared with traditional CNN, EMCCNN has a 3.2% higher experimental data, which verifies the effectiveness of the emotional symbol library and multi-channel input proposed in this paper. Compared with LSTM, EMCCNN has a 1.3% higher experimental data too.

4 Conclusion

Identifying the orientation of UGCs has become one of the important topics of natural language processing in recent years. Different from the traditional machine learning that needs to construct a complex feature set reflecting the characteristics of the task, and it is also different from the traditional short text sentiment analysis method of treating different vocabulary equally, this paper proposes a multi-channel and enhanced sentiment CNN position detection method based on existing work. The experimental results on the Taobao official website data review set show that this method can effectively analyze the sentiment orientation of the product review text and achieve good performance.

This article also has certain limitations, that is the experimental data set of this article is not sufficient, the data scale is not large, and the corpus is not rich enough. In the next step, we will expand the corpus to improve the classification performance of the model.

References

1. Ravi, K., Ravi, V.: A survey on opinion mining and sentiment analysis: tasks, approaches and applications. Knowl.-Based Syst. **89**, 14–46 (2015)
2. Hu, M., Liu, B.: Mining and summarizing customer reviews. In: Proceedings of the 10th ACM SIGKDD International Conference on Knowledge Discovery and Data Mining, pp. 168–177. ACM, New York (2004)
3. Ding, X., Liu, B., Yu, P.S.: A holistic lexicon-based approach to opinion mining. In: Proceedings of International Conference on Web Search and Web Data Mining, pp. 231–240. ACM, New York (2008)
4. Turney, P.D.: Thumbs up or thumbs down?: Semantic orientation applied to unsupervised classification of reviews. In: Proceedings of the 40th Annual Meeting of the Association for Computational Linguistics, pp. 417–424. MIT Press, Cambridge (2002)
5. Kim, Y.: Convolutional neural network for sentence classification (2014). arXiv preprint. arXiv:1408.5882
6. Zhu, X., Sobihani, G.H.: Long short-term memory over recursive structure. IN: Proceedings of International Conference on Machine Learning, pp. 1604–1612. ACM, New York (2015)

Research on an Evaluation System of Individual Digitalization Capability

Binyue Cui[1(✉)] and Wenxing Hong[2]

[1] Hebei University of Economics and Business, Shijiazhuang 050061, China
binyuec@Heuet.edu.cn
[2] Xiamen University, Xiamen 361005, China

Abstract. The surge of digital economy will break the traditional business models, the way companies interact, and the way people obtain services, information and commodities, thereby changing the way people live. With the rapid development of new generation of information technology, international organizations and countries have attached great importance to the digital literacy of citizens, and improving the digital literacy of citizens has become an indispensable and important part in the development of digital economy. Based on literacy review of the origin of the digital literacy concept, the existed digital citizen's capability framework and our practices of digital talent training, this research proposed a 7-level digital literacy and skill framework for improving local citizens' individual digitalization capabilities (IDC) in China; based on this framework, the exam syllabus, curriculums and digitalization capability level certification are perform in local areas, all these practices constitute an evaluation system of citizens' IDC.

Keywords: Digital Economy · Digital Literacy · Individual Digitalization Capability (IDC) · Evaluation System

1 Introduction

Digital technologies are transforming the way people live, work, consume as well as the way of production, the way of providing services [1].

The rapid development of digital technologies, especially artificial intelligence, big data, block chain and other new-generation information technologies, accelerated the digitalization transformation in organizations, such as government departments, enterprises, education institutes etc. It's well known, digital transformation is a systematic project and involved many new production factors. Suitable and obtainable digital technologies may improve the business process and even change the business model of an organization, and then build a new ecosystem for the organization. Digital transformation prompts organizations to leverage technology to become more agile in the face of changes from both outsides and insides, thus the digital talents become one of the most important strategic resources in an organization. In recent years, the demands for digital talents continuously increased, and many countries paid attention to enhance citizens information literacy, digital literacy so that reduce the influences which occurred because of the digital divide, which refers to the gap between demographics and regions that have access to ICT, and those that don't or have restricted access [2]. In G20 2019 Osaka Summit [3], the participating countries reached consensus on the lack of digital literacy in public education will have influence on the sustainable development. In July 20, 2022 [4], the Third Digital Economy Working Group (DEWG) Meeting of Indonesia's G20 Presidency discussed on the second priority issue of DEWG, namely Digital Skills and Digital Literacy as well as the third priority issue etc.

2   Evolution of the Concept-Digital Literacy

The evolution of digital literacy is shown in Fig. 1 below. FR Leavis and his student Denys Thompson addressed the concept of Media literacy in 1933 to avoid the young people going astray under the situation that movies and televisions are very popular. Technology literacy was proposed by American technical education scholar Towers, E. R., Lux, D. G., and Ray, W. E. in *a rationale and structure for industrial-arts subject matter* in 1966 [5]. Technology literacy indicated that citizens with technology and skills should understand the significance of technology. With the development of information industry, Paul Chekowski, president of United States Information Industry Associate addressed Information literacy firstly in 1974 [6]. The objective is to enable citizens to utilize information technology and tools to solve problems. American Library Association (ALA) built Presidential Committee on Information Literacy in 1987. With the Internet era, the internet users are dramatically increased and make it very important for people to perform critical innovation, solve problems by information technologies. At the same time, the appearance of digital natives evoked the digital technology's application, thus Israeli scholar Yoram Eshet-Alkalai put forward the concept of digital literacy in 1994.

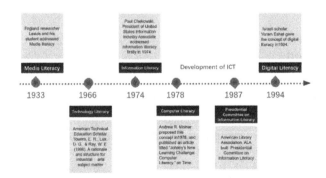

Fig. 1. The evolution of digital literacy concept

Digital literacy requires people have the skills in locating and using information with critical thinking. It also involves knowing digital tools and using them in communicative, collaborative ways through social engagement. ALA's Digital Literacy Task Force defines digital literacy as "the ability to use information and communication technologies to find, evaluate, create, and communicate information, requiring both cognitive and technical skills" [7].

Individual digitalization capability (IDC) is the basic competence for individuals, with IDC, individuals master the necessary digital technology knowledge and skill and utilize them suitably, reasonably in the way consistent with ethics in lives and works.

3   Digital Literacy Frameworks for Citizens

In digital economy era, besides excellent professional skills, digital literacy will be the key competence for people to work and live. The citizen digital literacy frameworks describe what knowledge and skills construct individuals digital literacy.

3.1   Digital Literacy Framework

Yoram Eshet-Alkalai proposed a comprehensive digital literacy framework in 2004 based on his experiences, literature review and pilot experiment. He added the sixth sill in 2012 [8]. This framework composed of six digital skills (Fig. 2):

Fig. 2. Yoram Eshet-Alkalai digital literacy framework

1) Photo-visual Digital Skills

    Take graphic user interfaces [9, 10] and children computer games [11] for example, helps users to intuitively understand instructions and messages presented in a visual-graphical form.

2) Reproduction Digital Skills

    This skill defined as the ability to create new meanings or new interpretations by combining preexisting, independent shreds of information in digital media (text, graphic, or sound) [12].

3) Branching Digital Skills

This skill is a good spatial-multidimensional sense of orientation, namely the ability to stay oriented and avoid getting lost in the hyperspace while navigating through complex knowledge domains, despite they dependent on some the navigation.

4) Information Digital Skills

The ability to identify false, irrelevant, or biased information, and critically think while getting information [13].

5) Socio-emotional Digital Skills

This requires users with critical and analytical thinking, very mature, and have a good command of information, branching, and photo-visual digital thinking skills.

6) Real-time Digital Skills

This demands the ability to process "simultaneous large fluxes of information" with high-speed real time.

3.2 DigComp of European Union

The European Union (EU) did great efforts to find the abilities that citizens with digital literacy should have science 2006 on the basis of studying the experiences of many European countries, and proposed Key Competences for lifelong learning: European Reference Framework [14], in which digital literacy is one of the eight competences that citizen should have. The EU released DigComp frameworks in 2013, described the details of digital literacy, and addressed that digital literacy includes five parts abilities: Information, Communication, Content creation, Safety as well as Problem solving. The EU launched DigComp2.1 and DigComp2.2 subsequently in 2017 and 2022. DigComp 2.2 composed of five main parts:

1) Information and data literacy, describe the ability to obtain, evaluate and manage the information.
2) Communication and collaboration emphasize the ability to leverage digital technologies in order to communicate with others online with proper, legal and safe ways.
3) Digital contents creation, namely develop, integrate digital contents by complying with the copyright and license.
4) Safety, means protect device, personal date and privacy, health and environment while taking advantage of digital technologies.
5) Problem solving, the highest demand in this framework, that indicates the citizen can utilize digital technologies fluently in identifying needs and problems, to resolve conceptual problems and problem situations in digital environments. The citizens are also able to use digital tools to innovate processes and products, and keep up-to-date with the evolution of digital technologies (Fig. 3).

In this framework, there are A, B, C three levels in each digital skill dimension. A is the basic level, B is the middle level, and C is the highest level. The hierarchical division of skills make citizens learn and assess their ability of digital skill more accurately.

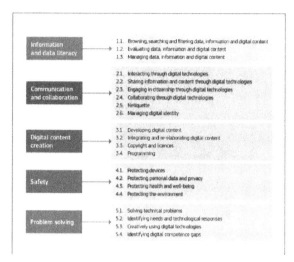

Fig. 3. Digital competence framework for citizens (DigComp) 2.2. (from official website of European Commission)

3.3 GFRDLSI of United Nation

In Jun., 2018, the United Nation (UN), Educational, Scientific and Cultural Organization proposed a Global Framework of Reference on Digital Literacy Skills for Indicator 4.4.2 (GFRDLSI) [15], in which there are 7 ability dimensions. Compared with DigComp 2.0, two dimensions are added in this framework. The first is No. 0 "Devices and software", to identify and use hardware tools and technologies. The second is No. 6 "Career-related competences", to understand, analyze and evaluate digital contents in special fields within a digital environment [16]. GFRDLSI put basic ability of both software and hardware, and digital ability in career into consideration, constructed a more comprehensive framework for digital literacy of citizens in digital era.

3.4 DL-S Framework of DCLC

In China, many efforts have been done to cater to the digital talent demands of digital economy. In Sept., 2018, National Development and Reform Commission issued the "Guiding Opinions on Developing Digital Economy to Stabilize and Expand Employment" (Develop & Reform Employment [2018] No. 1363), in this document, the objective of cultivating digital talent is the digital literacy of Chinese citizens will be no less than that of the average level in developed countries by 2025. The Central Cyber Security and Informatization Committee issued the Action Plan for Improving the Digital Literacy and Skills of all the People, Nov., 2021. In this document, the digital literacy and skills (DL-S) are described as a collection of a series of qualities and abilities of digital acquisition, production, utility, evaluation, interaction, sharing, innovation, security, ethics and morality that digital society citizens should have in their study, work and lives.

Dimensions	Description	Localization
Obtain, manage and evaluate digital contents	• Browse, Filter, evaluate digital contents. • Categorize, Save, callout and manage digital contents.	---
Develop and use digital contents	• Build, create and edit digital contents	• Digital contents includes: Text, picture, video and sound
Communication and collaboration	• Interact, communicate and collaborate via digital technologies while being aware of cultural and generational diversity • Be aware of the regulation of Copyright and License. • To participate in society through public and private digital services and participatory citizenship. • Manage one's digital presence, identity and reputation.	---
Digital skill and knowledge	• identify needs and problems and resolve conceptual problems and problem situations in digital environments • Innovate processes and products by digital tools. • keep up-to-date with the digital evolution • Master the basic digital technology knowledge (Big data, AI, Block chain, IoT etc).	• Master the basic digital technology knowledge (Big data, AI, Block chain, IoT etc).
Security	• Security of Networks, computer systems and inteligent mobile device systems. • Security of networks application. • Security of health and well-beings.	• Anti-fraud. • Health of both body and soul.
Ethics	• Digital ethics. • Networks ethics. • Science and technology ethics. • Digital community of destiny.	• Digital community of destiny.
Laws and Regulations	Policies and regulations about DL-S.	The main policies and regulations about DL-S inside China.

Fig. 4. DL-S framework of DCLC

Based on the concept of digital literacy and skill in Action Plan for Improving the Digital Literacy and Skills of all the People and the digital literacy frameworks aforementioned above, we proposed a DL-S framework of Digitalization Capability Level Certification (DCLC). After consulting experts of data science and computer science, we received many suggestions via online seminars, and revised the framework several times. And then, we performed three times suggestion collection with Delphi method, finally decided the 7-dimension framework shown in Fig. 4.

In DL-S framework of DCLC, there are 7 basic DL-S abilities of citizens. Integrated with China's national conditions, we added some localization contents to make it convenient for local organizations to take advantage of it. This framework is a guidance for individuals or organizations to training talents with up-dated DL-S, so that enhance their IDC. DL-S framework of DCLC is divided into three level. The first level is basic level of DL-S, all the citizens should reach the first level. The second level is medium level, this level is for the university students or employees who have to master some necessary digital skill and knowledge besides professional abilities. The third level is advanced level, all the employees that engaged in IT, or data science fields should master. Different level in the DL-S framework of DCLC will help different groups to learn and evaluate their IDC.

In this framework, we fully considered the literacy of citizens while they are using digital technologies. Thus, we put anti-fraud, healthy way to use digital technologies and so on into consideration.

4 Evaluation System of Individual Digitalization Capability

DL-S framework of DCLC is the foundation of evaluation system of individual digitalization capability (ES-IDC) in our research. This system is built for citizens including university students, Enterprise employees, teenagers and seniors, to learn and evaluate DL-S.

In this system, based on DL-S framework of DCLC, a project of group standards titled digital literacy and skill certificate hosted by Prof. W.X. Hong, and started in Mar.,

2022. Till Jun., 2022, over 14 universities and organizations took part in drafting team. The draffs for comments of this group standards is available, and will be promulgated in Oct., this year.

On the basis of the group standards of DL-S certificate draffs, the Exam syllabus is developed. Digital literacy supporting learning resources, ppt documents and relevant teaching videos, are also made at the same time. All this teaching and learning resource come from the digitalization capability (DC) curriculum that divided into general and industrial curriculum. The details about DC curriculum are introduced in our previous research [17]. We won't descript it here anymore.

All the learning resources are uploaded to the platform for industrial digitalization ability innovation, individual users or organization users are able to access to them on this platform (Fig. 5).

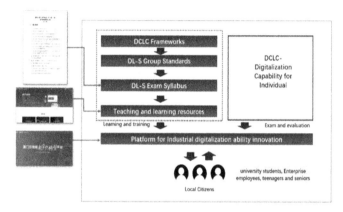

Fig. 5. Architecture of Evaluation System of Individual Digitalization Capability (ESIDC)

In addition, the DCLC is hosted by Computer Education Research Association of Chinese Universities (CRC-CE), a professional association in computer education fields all over the country, and DCLC official website is available online in Jun., 2022. Some learning resources can be visited on the DCLC official website as well, please refer to Fig. 6 below.

From Jul., 2020 to now, over 670 people of local state-owned commercial bank, manufacturing enterprise or public-sector organization have attended DL-S evaluation certification online via ES-IDC. In Jun., 2022, the DCLC-IDC had been held in two universities: Xiamen Huaxia University and Xiamen University of Technology. 197 freshmen had signed up and participated DCLC-IDC Digital Literacy Certification-level one online, the exam duration is one hour, test takers that passed the certification exam online received the first batch of DCLC-IDC certificates from the CRC-CE.

In the online examination of DCLC-IDC, we added a questionnaire about the importance of DL-S and the difficulty of the exam. We got 198 valid feedbacks, the statistics data showed that 36.04% test takers thought it's very important to learn and master DL-S, and 33.50% thought it's necessary to master DL-S for individuals nowadays. 40.61% respondents felt the difficulty of the questions in this exam is moderate.

Fig. 6. DCLC official website (Left) and learning resources of DL-S (Right)

5   Summary

Digital literacy now is a necessary living method for individuals live in digital economy era. To let citizens learn and master DL-S become one of the most essential country strategies in China. However, there are still no efforts have been made to find a way for the public to train and evaluate digital literacy systematically, although, there are some kinds of digital technology trainings for the technical talents to iteratively upgrade their knowledge system. Therefore, in this research, we addressed an evaluation System of Individual Digitalization Capability based on the literacy review about digital literacy concept and mainstream frameworks of digital literacy integrated with our training experiences in enterprises and universities in China.

We build a DL-S training and evaluation system for the individuals to enhance personal DL-S. Local people are able to take part in DCLC-IDC Digital Literacy certification hosted by CRC-CE, by which to test their ability of DL-S, so that find what to do next in order to keep up with the rapid development of digital technologies. The DCLC-IDC pilot works indicated that our ES-IDC achieved very good results. These practices provided a significant reference for cultivating and evaluating local citizens' IDC.

The next, we are going to improve the Hierarchy of DCLC-IDC, build Exam syllabus, text book, digital learning resources, DCLC certificate system according to the ability demands of each level, accumulate more practices and experiments for enhancing DL-S of Chinese local citizens.

Acknowledgment. This research is supported by Fujian science and technology plan project-innovation strategy research project-Platform for Industrial digitalization ability innovation-A preliminary exploration of the technical service system that empower the digital transformation of local enterprises, project No. 2021R0173.

Thanks for Xiamen DigiTwin Information Science and Technology Co., Ltd. Providing the data of DCLC-IDC pilot works.

References

1. The Digital Economy, Bank of Canada Review. Spring (2017). https://www.bankofcanada.ca/wp-content/uploads/2017/05/boc-review-spring17-dsouza.pdf. Accessed 5 2022

2. Cullen, R.: Addressing the digital divide. Online Inf. Rev. (2001)
3. G20 2019 Osaka. http://www.g20.utoronto.ca/2019/2019-g20-osaka-leaders-declaration. html. Accessed 5 2022
4. G20 2022 Indonesia. https://g20.org/g20-presidency-of-indonesia/. Accessed 5 2022
5. Towers, E.R., Lux, D.G., Ray, W.E.: A Rationale and Structure for Industrial Arts Subject Matter. The Ohio State University, Columbus (1966)
6. Badke, W.: Foundations of information literacy: learning from Paul Zurkowski. **34**(1), 48–50 (2010)
7. "Digital Literacy". Welcome to ALA's Literacy Clearinghouse, 19 January 2017. Accessed 5 2022
8. Eshet-Alkalai, Y.: Thinking in the digital era: a revised model for digital literacy. Issues Inf. Sci. Inf. Technol. **9**, 267–276 (2012). https://doi.org/10.28945/1621
9. Opperman, R.: User interface design. In: Adelsberger, H.H., Collis, B., Pawlowski, J.M. (eds.) Handbook on Information Technologies for Education and Training, pp. 233–248. Springer-Verlag, Berlin (2002)
10. Shneiderman, B.: Designing the user interface. Addison-Wesley, Reading (1998)
11. Carlsson, U. (ed.): Regulation, awareness, empowerment: young people and harmful media content in the digital age. In: The International Clearinghouse on Children, Youth and Media. University Press, Nordcom/Goteborg (2006)
12. Gilster, P.: Digital Literacy. Wiley Computer Publishing, New York (1997)
13. Paul, R., Elder, L.: A guide for educators to critical thinking competency standards: standards, principles, performance. Foundation for Critical Thinking, Dillon Beach (2005)
14. The Digital Competence Framework, European commission official website. https://joint-res earch-centre.ec.europa.eu/digcomp/digital-competence-framework_en. Accessed 5 2022
15. Vuorikari, R., Kluzer, S., Punie, Y.: DigComp 2.2: the digital competence framework for citizens - with new examples of knowledge, skills and attitudes. EUR 31006 EN, Publications Office of the European Union, Luxembourg (2022). ISBN 978-92-76-48883-5. https://doi. org/10.2760/490274. JRC128415
16. A Global Framework of Reference on Digital Literacy Skills for Indicator 4.4.2, Information Paper No. 51, UNESCO Institute for Statistics (2018)
17. Cui, B.Y., Hong, W.X., Zhu, J.C., Chen, X.L.: Digitalization capability evaluation system and practice. In: Proceedings of ICCSE 2021 (2021)

A Secure Privacy Preserving Authentication Schema for Remote Server Using Biometric

Shreeya Swagatika Sahoo[1]([✉]) [iD], Sujata Mohanty[2], and Dibyasundar Das[1] [iD]

[1] Siksha 'O' Anusandhan University, Bhubaneswar, Odisha, India
shreeya.swagatika@gmail.com, dibyasundar@ieee.org
[2] NIT Rourkela, Odisha, India

Abstract. Modern networking needs fast and secure-authentication to perform in an optimal state. Researchers have used smartcards and biometrics to provide security over a wide range of applications in recent decades. However, the current protocols are computationally intensive and have higher latency. Hence, this article proposes a biometric-based authentication scheme (SBAS) that requires less computational resources to provide adequate security. The SBAS uses only hash functions instead of the non-homogenous combination of functions to reduce the computational cost compared to the existing schemes. Moreover, the proposed protocol includes password protection to increase the efficiency of security. Protecting against security threats is one of the essential requirements of the security protocol. Hence, the proposed system is studied in-depth and found to satisfy desirable security features. The SBAS is impervious to online and offline password guessing attacks, insider attacks, and SC loss attacks. The low computational footprint of the protocol makes it suitable for low-power devices.

Keywords: Authentication · AVISPA · Biometric · BAN Logic · Cryptography

1 Introduction

The password-based security protocols are the primary choice of security researchers due to their intuitiveness and the ability to provide a secure environment for user authentication. Similarly, user-friendly smart cards provide authentication in many applications that need secure transmission over the open channel. Each session requires authentication to maintain integrity in two-party client-server communication over an insecure channel. Hence, the proposed model uses both password and smart-card-based security models to establish communication between two parties, namely the server and client. The very first password-based protocol was proposed by Lamport in 1981 [11]. This protocol uses the server stored one-way hash function to authenticate the user password. The limitations of storing one-way hash function in sever influenced many

W. Hong and Y. Weng (Eds.): ICCSE 2022, CCIS 1811, pp. 324–336, 2023.
https://doi.org/10.1007/978-981-99-2443-1_29

researchers [2,7,12,20] to develop new versions of the security model. Later Yang and Shieh used a combination of smartcard and password to propose a more secure authentication scheme. Their protocol uses timestamp and nonce (an arbitrary number that is used only once) to establish a secure connection [20]. The need for a password table makes many of the protocols susceptible to external attack. Hence, in the year 2000, Hwang et al. [8] suggested a security scheme using ElGamal's public-key cryptosystem. Their proposed model can resist message replaying attack. Chen and Zhang [4] have proposed a privacy-aware smart-card-based scheme that can withstand impersonation attack and provides user anonymity. It is observed from the literature that password-based mutual authentication schemes are popular and more secure. However, the suggested strategies are computationally inefficient as well as incur larger communication overhead [19]. The limitations of previous models influenced the development of a lightweight password-based authentication scheme that provides several security features and is secured against online/offline password guessing attack, lost SC attack, insider attack, forgery attack, and replay attack. The scheme has been simulated along with other existing schemes. It is noted that the proposed scheme has lower computational as well as communicational overhead, which makes it suitable for real-time applications.

The rest of the paper is organized as follows: The following section provides a brief description of the preliminaries. The proposed scheme and its various phases are demonstrated in Sect. 3. The formal and informal security analysis of the scheme is discussed in Sect. 4 and Sect. 5. The simulation and performance analysis of the protocol are described in Sect. 6 and Sect. 7, respectively. Finally, the chapter is summarized in Sect. 8.

2   Preliminaries

2.1   Adversary Model

The proposed protocol considers the Dolev-Yao (DY) model to determine the protocol's performance under different compromised conditions.

- We have used the Dolev-Yao threat model, in which both parties can communicate over an insecure channel [6]. Thus, the adversary $(\mathcal{A}_v)$ has control over the communication channel and can eavesdrop, modify, or delete the message. However, he could not get the information from the secure channel [6].
- A malicious attacker can extract saved information from the stolen smart card by using power analysis attacks. Moreover, the relation among the stored key can be reverse-engineered to exploit the protocol to grant unauthorized access [10].
- An $\mathcal{A}_v$ may be a privileged insider or an outsider.
- An adversary may compromise any particular entity to obtain his long-term private key to compromise the session key.

2.2   Hash Function

A one-way hash function $h : \{0,1\}^* \rightarrow \{0,1\}^k$ generates fixed length of output string y of variable length k input. It is considered as a deterministic algorithm which has the following properties:

1. For a given hash value y, it is difficult to find any input k such that $y = h(k)$.
2. It is computationally infeasible to find any k_2 for a given k_1, such that $k_1 \neq k_2$, where $h(k_1) = h(k_2)$.
3. It is difficult to find two different message (k_1, k_2) such that $h(k_1) = h(k_2)$.

2.3   Fuzzy Extractor

A fuzzy extractor can extract an almost random string σ from the biometric input w in an error-tolerant way [5]. The important thing about a fuzzy extractor is when an input changes but the input remains close to w, then it extracts the same output σ. To recover σ from new biometric input w, a uniformly random string θ will be generated by using two procedures

- Generation procedure (Gen) receives input $w\varepsilon\psi$ and generates the output of a random string $\sigma\varepsilon 0, 1^l$ and a auxiliary string θ, $\text{Gen}(w) = (\sigma, \theta)$.
- Deterministic reproduction procedure (Rep) procedure allows to receives input w' close to input w and corresponding random auxiliary string θ to recover σ, $\text{Rep}(w', \theta) = \sigma$.

3   The Proposed System

This article proposes a biometric-based authentication scheme using a fuzzy extractor. This scheme is divided into four phases, namely, registration phase, login phase, authentication phase, and password change phase. Each phase plays a significant role in providing security with user convenience. The protocols establish a secure connection by interacting between a server S_n, a user (U_i), and a smartcard (SC).

Before initializing the registration phase, the server S_k establishes and shares the public key. The public key q is randomly selected. Then, the server selects a secret key $x \in Z_p$, where Z_p is the set of residues. The proposed security model uses the hash function only. Hence, the server chooses an adequate hash function $h(): \{0,1\}^* \longrightarrow Z_m^*$ where Z_m^* is the multiplicative group of Z_p. Finally, the server shares the hash function $h()$ with terminals and smart cards.

3.1   Registration Phase

Initially, the users register with the server and follow the delineated steps:

   Step 1: The U_i chooses his identity (ID_i) and password (PW_i) of his own choice. And also selects a number b randomly.

   Step 2 : U_i computes new password PW_{i1} as $PW_{i1} = h(ID_i || PW_i)$

Step 3: After calculating new password PW_{i1}, the user sends the message $\{ID_i, PW_{i1}\}$ to the (S_n) through a secure channel.

Step 4: After obtaining the registration message, S computes the steps given in Table 2.

Table 1. Registration phase of the SBAS

User(U_i)	Server(S)
Selects a random number b.	
Choose ID_i and PW_i.	
$Gen(BM_i) = (\sigma_i, \theta_i)$	
$G_i = b \oplus h\ (ID_i \parallel PW_i \parallel \sigma_i)$	
Computes $PW_{i1} = h(\text{PW}_i \parallel b)$	
$\xrightarrow[\ (Secure channel)\ ]{\{ID_i, PW_{i1}\}}$	
	$A_i = h(ID_i \parallel PW_{i1}) \bmod (p)$
	$B_i = (h(h(PW_{i1} \parallel ID_i)) \oplus (A_i)) \bmod (p)$
	$C_i = (h(PW_{i1} \parallel x) \oplus h(A_i)) \bmod (p)$
	$L_i = h(A_i) \oplus PW_{i1} \bmod (p)$
$\xleftarrow[\ (Secure channel)\ ]{\{B_i, C_i, h(.)\}}$	
Stores G_i into SC	

3.2 Login and Authentication Phase

U_i puts his/her SC to the card reader and enters ID_i and (PW_i).

Step 1: The SC will first verify the authenticity of user by validating $B_i \stackrel{?}{=} B_i^*$.

Step 2: After verification, now the smart card computes the $\{M_1, R_1\}$ and sends to the server.

Step 3: now, the server will verify the user and if successful, then both will communicate.

The details are given in Tables 2 and Table 3. After successful login to the server, both U_α and S_β are mutually authenticated for further communication.

3.3 Password Change Phase

The valid user can only change the password on his own. An adversary cannot change the password as it needs to know the user identity, password, and biometrics of a legal user. However, it is infeasible work for an A_v to know all three credentials simultaneously.

Table 2. Login and Authentication phase of the SBAS

User(U_i)	Server(S)
Enters ID_i, PW_i, BM_i	
Smart Card computes	
$\sigma_i^* = Rep(BM_i, \theta_i)$	
$b^* = G_i \oplus h(ID_i \parallel PW_i \parallel \sigma_i^*)$	
$PW_{i1}^* = h(PW_i \parallel b^*)$	
$A_i = (B_i \oplus h(ID_i \parallel PW_{i1})) mod(p)$	
$B_i^* = (A_i \oplus h(h(ID_i \parallel PW_{i1})))mod(p)$	
Computes $L_i^* = (h\,(A_i) \oplus PW_{i1} \bmod)\,(p)$	
Checks $B_i \overset{?}{=} B_i^*$	
Then computes	
$M_1 = (h\,(L_i^* \parallel C_i) \oplus N_1) \bmod (p)$	
$Z_1 = h(ID_i \parallel L_i^* \parallel M_1)$	
$R_1 = h(M_1 \parallel Z_1 \parallel N_1)$	
$\dfrac{\{M_1, R_1\}}{(Public channel)} \longrightarrow$	
	Computes $N_1^* = M_i \oplus h(L_i \parallel C_i)$
	$Z_1 = h(ID_i \parallel L_i \parallel M_1)$
	$R_2 = h(Z_1 \parallel M_1 \parallel N_1^*)$
	Checks $R_1 \overset{?}{=} R_2$
	$N_3 = N_1^* \oplus N_2$
	$SK_{us} = h(ID_i \parallel R_2 \parallel N_2)$
	$M_2 = SK_{us} \oplus Z_1$
	$M_3 = h(SK_{us} \parallel N_2 \parallel Z_1)$
	$SK_{us} = M_2 \oplus Z_1$
$\overset{\{M_2, M_3, N_3\}}{\underset{(Public channel)}{\longleftarrow}}$	
Computes $SK_{us} = M_2 \oplus Z_1$	
Then, computes $N_2^* = N_1 \oplus N_3$	
Checks $N_2 \overset{?}{=} N_2^*$	
If they are equal, then goes to further steps	
Verifies $M_3 \overset{?}{=} h(SK_{us}^* \parallel N_2^* \parallel Z_1)$	
$M_4 = h(SK_{us} \parallel Z_1 \parallel M_3)$	
$\dfrac{\{M_4\}}{(Public channel)} \longrightarrow$	
	$M_4 \overset{?}{=} h(SK_{us} \parallel Z_1 \parallel M_3)$
$SK_f = h(SK_{us} \parallel Z_1 \parallel N_1^* \parallel N_2)$	
$\longleftarrow$	
	Stores the session key SK_f
Stores the session key SK_f	

4 Security Analysis of the Scheme

In this section, we use BAN logic [1] to prove the security of the session key between the server and user. One of the most common and widely used logic for assessing authentication schemes is BAN logic. It represents both the user's and the server's beliefs in a conversation. The suggested scheme's security features are then shown.

4.1 Authentication Proof Based on BAN Logic

In this section, by using BAN logic we have proof the authentication between the user and server [1,14]. Let symbol $\pounds$ and φ are principals, γ and α range over statements and K ranges over cryptographic key. We have taken some notations of the BAN logic as follows:

Table 3. BAN Logic Symbol

Notation	Description
$\pounds \mid\equiv \gamma$	$\pounds$ believes that γ is true
$\#(\gamma)$	γ is new, it has never existed before
$\pounds \Rightarrow \gamma$	$\pounds$ has perfect control over γ, and $\pounds$ believes γ to be true
$\pounds \lhd \gamma$	Someone sends message containing γ to $\pounds$
$\pounds \mid\sim \gamma$	$\pounds$ sends a message containing γ at some point in the past (or present)
$\{\gamma\}_\alpha$	The secret formula is combined γ and Y
$(\gamma)_h$	The key K is used to hash the formula γ
$(\gamma)_K$	K is used to encrypt the formula γ
$\pounds \overset{K}{\leftrightarrow} \varphi$	K is used as a secret key between $\pounds$ and φ
	Only $\pounds$ and Q are aware of the K; others are uninformed
SK	The user and server share a session key, which is used for secure transmission
The message meaning rule	
$\dfrac{\pounds\mid\equiv\pounds\overset{K}{\leftrightarrow}\varphi,\pounds\lhd(\gamma)_K}{\pounds\mid\equiv\varphi\mid\sim\gamma}$	$\pounds$ believes that $\pounds$ and φ shared the private key K and that $\pounds$ is the one who receives the K-encrypted message. $\pounds$ believes that φ sends messages with γ every once in a while
The nonce verification rule	
$\dfrac{\pounds\mid\equiv\gamma(\gamma),\pounds\mid\equiv\varphi\mid\sim\gamma}{\pounds\mid\equiv\varphi\mid\equiv\gamma}$	If $\pounds$ thinks γ is new and φ sends the message containing γ only once, then $\pounds$ thinks that Q considers γ
The jurisdiction rule	
$\dfrac{\pounds\mid\equiv\varphi\Rightarrow\gamma,\pounds\mid\equiv\varphi\mid\equiv\gamma}{\pounds\mid\equiv\gamma}$	$\pounds$ thinks that φ has entire authority on γ and that φ believes γ
	$\pounds$ thinks γ is correct
The freshness rule	
$\dfrac{\pounds\mid\equiv\#\gamma}{\pounds\mid\equiv\#(\gamma,\alpha)}$	If $\pounds$ feels that γ is new, then (γ,α) must also be new
The belief rule	
$\dfrac{\pounds\mid\equiv\varphi\mid\equiv(\gamma,\alpha)}{\pounds\mid\equiv\varphi\mid\equiv(\gamma)}$	If $\pounds$ believes that the φ believes message γ and α, then $\pounds$ believes φ believes the message γ

The objectives and the message are as follows.

Goal 1: $U_\alpha \mid\equiv U_\alpha \overset{SK_{us}}{\leftrightarrow} S_\beta$

Goal 2: $U_\alpha \mid\equiv S_\beta \mid\equiv U_\alpha \overset{SK_{us}}{\leftrightarrow} S_\beta$

Goal 3: $S_\beta \mid\equiv U_\alpha \overset{SK_{us}}{\leftrightarrow} S_\beta$

Goal 4: $S_\beta \mid\equiv U_\alpha \mid\equiv U_\alpha \overset{SK_{us}}{\leftrightarrow} S_\beta$

M1: $U_\alpha \rightarrow S_\beta : \{M_1, R_1, N_1\}_{U_\alpha \overset{Z_1}{\leftrightarrow} S_\beta}$

M2: $S_\beta \rightarrow U_\alpha : \{M_2, M_3, N_3\}_{U_\alpha \overset{SK_{us}}{\leftrightarrow} S_\beta}$

M3: $U_\alpha \rightarrow S_\beta : \{M_3\}_{U_\alpha \overset{SK_{us}}{\leftrightarrow} S_\beta}$

The assumptions are as follows:

$A_1 : U_\alpha \models \#N_1$

$A_2 : S_\beta \models \#N_2$

$A_3 : U_\alpha \models (U_\alpha \overset{Z_1}{\leftrightarrow} S_\beta)$

$A_4 : S_\beta \models (U_\alpha \overset{Z_1}{\leftrightarrow} S_\beta)$

$A_5 : U_\alpha \models S_\beta \models \Rightarrow (U_\alpha \overset{SK_{us}}{\leftrightarrow} S_\beta)$

$A_6 : S_\beta \models U_\alpha \models \Rightarrow (U_\alpha \overset{SK_{us}}{\leftrightarrow} S_\beta)$

The message is sent to the S_β by the U_α.

S1: $S_\beta \triangleleft (M_1, R_1, N_1)_{U_\alpha \overset{Z_1}{\leftrightarrow} S_\beta}$

From S1 and assumption A_3, by applying message meaning rule follows Step 2

S2: $S_\beta \models U_\alpha \mid\sim (U_\alpha \overset{Z_1}{\leftrightarrow} S_\beta, N_1)$

According to S2 and A_1, and freshness rule, S3 can be applied

S3: $S_\beta \models \#(U_\alpha \overset{Z_1}{\leftrightarrow} S_\beta, N_1)$

S4 is carried out in accordance with S2 and S3 by employing the nonce-verification rule.

S4: $S_\beta \models U_\alpha \models (U_\alpha \overset{Z_1}{\leftrightarrow} S_\beta, N_1)$

As a result of S4 and the belief rule, S5 produced the following results:

S5: $S_\beta \models U_\alpha \models (U_\alpha \overset{Z_1}{\leftrightarrow} S_\beta)$

The jurisdiction rule has been applied to get S6 based on S5 and A_4.

S6: $S_\beta \models (U_\alpha \overset{Z_1}{\leftrightarrow} S_\beta)$

S7 is as follows, according to M2.

S7: $U_\alpha \triangleleft (M_2, M_3, N_3, U_\alpha \overset{Z_1}{\leftrightarrow} S_\beta)_{(U_\alpha \overset{SK_{us}}{\leftrightarrow} S_\beta)}$

S8 can be applied based on S7 and A_5 by using the message meaning rule.

S8: $U_\alpha \models S_\beta \mid\sim (M_2, M_3, N_2, U_\alpha \overset{Z_1}{\leftrightarrow} S_\beta)_{(U_\alpha \overset{SK_{us}}{\leftrightarrow} S_\beta)}$

Applying the freshness rule to S8 and A_2, we obtain

S9: $U_\alpha \models S_\beta \#(M_2, M_3, N_2, U_\alpha \overset{Z_1}{\leftrightarrow} S_\beta)_{(U_\alpha \overset{SK_{us}}{\leftrightarrow} S_\beta)}$

Applying the nonce verification rule to continue over S10 by S8 and S9.

S10: $U_\alpha \models S_\beta \models (M_2, M_3, N_2, U_\alpha \overset{Z_1}{\leftrightarrow} S_\beta)_{(U_\alpha \overset{SK_{us}}{\leftrightarrow} S_\beta)}$

Based on S10 and the belief rule, we obtain

S11: $U_\alpha \models S_\beta \models (U_\alpha \overset{SK_{us}}{\leftrightarrow} S_\beta)$ (Goal-2)

Based on S11 and the jurisdiction rule, we have

S12: $U_\alpha \models (S_\beta \overset{SK_{us}}{\leftrightarrow} S_\beta)$(Goal-1)

Based on M3 and S13, we get

S13: $S_\beta \triangleleft (M_3, N_2, U_\alpha \overset{Z_1}{\leftrightarrow} S_\beta)_{(U_\alpha \overset{SK_{us}}{\leftrightarrow} S_\beta)}$

The message meaning rule has been applied according to S13 and $A3$.

S14: $S_\beta \mid\equiv U_\alpha \mid\sim (M_3, N_2, U_\alpha \overset{Z_1}{\leftrightarrow} S_\beta)_{(U_\alpha \overset{SK_{us}}{\leftrightarrow} S_\beta)}$

The freshness rule is applied from S14 and $A2$.

S15: $S_\beta \mid\equiv \#(M_3, N_2, U_\alpha \overset{Z_1}{\leftrightarrow} S_\beta)_{(U_\alpha \overset{SK_{us}}{\leftrightarrow} S_\beta)}$

Based on S15, by applying the belief rule

S16: $S_\beta \mid\equiv U_\alpha \mid\equiv (U_\alpha \overset{SK_{us}}{\leftrightarrow} S_\beta)$ (Goal-4)

The jurisdiction rule has been used to get S17 based on S16 and assumption $A4$.

S17: $S_\beta \mid\equiv (U_\alpha \overset{SK_{us}}{\leftrightarrow} S_\beta)$ (Goal-3)

Based on the Steps 11, 12, 16, 17, We demonstrated that the proposed strategy achieves all of the goals. The secure session key SKf is believed to be shared by both the server and the user.

5   Informal Security Analysis

We have proven in this part that the suggested scheme can withstand a variety of known attacks. Mutual authentication, session key security, and user anonymity are also possible with this technique.

1. **Session Key Security:** In SBAS, the server calculate the session keys SK. The secret session will be established between user and server for further communication. The session key is generated by using four parameters $\{SK_{us} \parallel Z_1 \parallel N_1^* \parallel N_2\}$. Out of these, two parameters (N_1, N_2^*) vary for each session key generation as they are generated randomly. M_1 and L_1 is needed to compute Z_1. Where L_1 is protected by one way hash function and M_1 is used random number N_1 and another parameter C_i for calculation. The compromising of secret key x will not disclose the session key.

2. **User Anonymity:** User anonymity ensures that only the user and the server are aware of the user's identity. No third party can not experience the user ID_i. The privacy of user identity is maintained throughout the communication. User ID_i has not been send in plain text in login message and authentication message. To get ID_i, intruder try to retrieve M_2 and M_3 where both the parameters are associated with Z_1. A one-way hash function is used to secure the parameter $Z1$. As a result, achieving user IDm is not a possible task. As a result, the suggested technique ensures user anonymity.

3. **Online password guessing Attack:** An adversary tries to guess the password by producing a genuine login message in an online password guessing attack. He retrieves the transmitted valid login message and stored information of the smart-card of a valid user. A password may be retrieved by an adversary from a valid login message. To create an actual message, an adversary may utilize the retrieved smart card information $\{B_i, C_i\}$. But this proposed scheme has overcome that weakness as follows:

For instance, the password PW_{i*} is guessed by the adversary. An adversary must construct a valid login message Bi, Ci, where $Ci = h(PWi1 \parallel x) \oplus h(Ai)$ to validate the PW_{i1}^*. Let adversary guess the secret key x' and tries to calculate PW_{i1}^*. Further to calculate PW_{i1}^* the adversary needs to know the random number b as $PW_{i1} = h(PW_i \parallel b)$. Again b is computed by the equation $b = G_i \oplus h(ID_i \parallel PW_i)$. To get random number b adversary needs to guess both ID_i^* and PW_{i1}^* simultaneously which is infeasible work for adversary. So the adversary can not compute the login message.

4. **Offline Password Guessing Attacks:** Assume the SC has been stolen and the data, $\{B_i, C_i\}$ has been retrieved from the SC. In addition A_v may listen to a valid message $\{M_1, R_1\}$ transmitted between U_i and server S without the knowledge of a real user. The adversary tries to retrieve the password PW_{i1} from C_i, which is computed by using one way hash function. He cannot retrieve the password from B_i because of unavailability of user id and password.

5. **Lost SC Attack:** Let user U_i's SC is stolen by the adversary or it has been lost. By using the smart card information he tries to login the system. To login into system, the adversary requires to know L_i and ID_i. But it is not possible as $L_i = h(A_i) \oplus PW_{i1}$. To compute L_i, the password PW_i is needed which is concatenated with random number b and it is protected by the one-way hash function. Again to calculate A_i both user ID_i and password PW_i is needed. So, this scheme can withstand smart card stolen attack.

6. **Insider Attack:** In this scheme, a real user submits PW_i to the server S rather than original password PW_i, where $PW_{i1} = h(PW_i \parallel b)$. The PW_i can not achieved by an insider because the random number b submitted to the server by hashing with password PW_i.

7. **Forgery Attack:** In order to carry out a forgery attack, the intruder must first create a login message $\{M_1, R_1\}$ and assure the mutual authentication between U_i and S_n. Without knowing N_1, L_i, x, b, PW_i, and ID_i, it is impossible to construct a message. Though the intruder can get B_i and C_i, but cannot compute PW_{i1} as it is hashing with user ID and using random number b. Hence, the SBAS resist forgery attack.

8. **Replay Attack:** Replay attacks are prevented under the proposed method. An intruder tries to listen in on a valid login message $\{M_1, R_1\}$ between the user and the server in a replay attack. After that, the attacker sends it back to the server's service. The nonce is utilised in this approach to keep such attacks in check. Because of the nonce N_1, the login message will be different each time.

Suppose the adversary sends the eavesdropped login message $\{M_1, R_1\}$ to the server. Then he will receive a message $\{M_2, M_3, N_3\}$ from the server for authentication. For completion of mutual authentication and set up a session key, the intruder has to calculate the parameter M_4. To compute M_4 he needs to know the session key and random number which is generated by the server. Moreover if the attacker tries to generate its own random number, then due to the difference of random number the authentication is not completed. The SBAS can resist replay attack.

9. **Mutual authentication:** The user verifies the legitimacy of the server by calculating the equation, $M_3 = h(SK_{us}^* \parallel Z_1 \parallel N_2)$. If this condition satisfies, then the server is valid. Otherwise the user will terminate the session. Then the server can verifies the user by computing the parameter $M_4 = h(SK_{us} \parallel Z_1 \parallel M_3)$. Likewise the server verifies the authenticity of the valid user. If the condition holds, the user is legal user and the server accepted the request. Otherwise server reject the request and terminates the session. Therefore, SBAS achieves proper mutual authentication.

10. **Secured Password Update:** A user can choose their own password and change it whenever they like. The password can only be changed if the former password is known. The attacker cannot change the password without knowing the correct login message and the old password.

6   Formal Security Verification Using AVISPA Tool

We simulated the proposed algorithm under both, OFMC and AtSe back-ends. The simulation results are shown in Fig. 1a and Fig. 1b respectively. The output demonstrates that proposed protocol is secure.

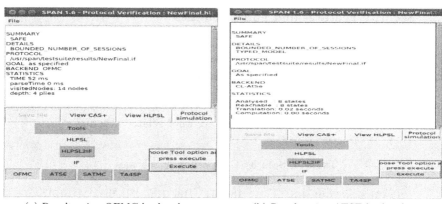

(a) Result using OFMC backend   (b) Result using ATSE backend

Fig. 1. Simulation result using AVISPA tool

7   Performance Analysis of the SBAS

This section demonstrates a comparison of computational cost, communication cost and security features between the proposed scheme and another related scheme in Table 4.

7.1   Computational and Communicational Cost:

This section compares the computational and communicational cost of the proposed SBAS with other existing schemes. The notations T_{HS}, T_{EN}, T_{MUL} are used as hash function, encryption/decryption function, and multiplictive function, respectively. Table 4 demonstrates both computational and communicational cost of the proposed schema with other related schema. From the table , it can observer that the computational cost is very less compared to others as only hash function is used.

Table 4. Computational and Communicational Cost Analysis of Scheme

Scheme	Registration phase	Log in Phase	Authentication Phase	Communication Cost
Xu et al. [18]	$1T_{EXP}+2T_{HS}$	$2T_{EXP}+3T_{HS}$	$2T_{EXP}+6T_{HS}$	2
Sood et al. [17]	$2T_{EXP}+2T_{HS}$	$3T_{EXP}+4T_{HS}+2T_{MUL}$	$2T_{EXP}+2T_{HS}+1T_{MUL}$	1
Song et al. [16]	$1T_{EXP}+2T_{HS}$	$3T_{HS}+1T_{EN}$	$1T_{EXP}+3T_{HS}+1T_{EN}$	2
Chen et al. [3]	$1T_{EXP}+1T_{HS}$	$2T_{EXP}+3T_{HS}+2T_{MUL}$	$1T_{EXP}+6T_{HS}+1T_{MUL}$	1
Ramasamy et al. [15]	$2T_{EXP}+3T_{MUL}$	$2T_{EXP}+3T_{MUL}$	$3T_{EXP}+2T_{MUL}$	2
jiang et al. [9]	$1T_{EXP}+1T_{HS}$	$3T_{EXP}+2T_{HS}+1T_{MUL}$	$2T_{EXP}+6T_{HS}$	2
Mishra et al. [13]	$3T_{HS}$	$3T_{HS}+T_{EXP}$	$6T_{HS}+3T_{EXP}$	2
SBAS	$7T_{HS}$	$7T_{HS}$	$6T_{HS}$	2

7.2 Security Features and Functionalities

Table 5 shows the security and functionality feature comparison of the proposed scheme with other related schemes. From this table, it is observed that the schemes in [16,18] could not resist insider attack, smart card loss attack, and online password guessing attack. In addition, the scheme in [3,15,17], and [9] are unable to achieve user anonymity. Hence, SBAS can resist various attack and provide many security features compared to other related schemes.

Table 5. Security Comparison of Schemes

ATTACKS ON SCHEMES	[18]	[17]	[16]	[15]	[3]	[9]	[13]	SBAS
User Anonymity	N	N	N	N	N	N	Y	Y
Session Key Security	Y	Y	Y	N	Y	Y	Y	Y
Offline password based attack	N	N	N	N	N	N	Y	Y
Online password based attack	N	N	N	N	N	N	Y	Y
Smart card loss attack	N	Y	N	Y	Y	Y	Y	Y
Insider attack	N	N	N	N	N	N	Y	Y
Forgery Attack	N	Y	Y	N	Y	Y	N	Y
Replay Attack	Y	Y	Y	N	Y	Y	Y	Y
Mutual authentication	Y	N	Y	N	N	Y	Y	Y

8   Conclusion

This article presents a cost-effective approach for remote user authentication using biometrics. The cost-effectiveness arises because the proposed approach uses only hash functions. Although some work had been reported by using the hash function only, however, they lack proper security features. It is found to be resistant to online and offline password guessing attack, smart-card attack. The security analysis of the scheme has been rigorously evaluated and proved to achieve user anonymity along with mutual authentication. Moreover, this scheme is resistant to attacks such as insider attack, replay attack, and forgery attack. In the future, we plan to improve this scheme in a real-time environment.

References

1. Burrows, M., Abadi, M., Needham, R.M.: A logic of authentication. In: Proceedings of the Royal Society of London A: Mathematical, Physical and Engineering Sciences. vol. 426, pp. 233–271. The Royal Society (1989)
2. Chang, C.C., Wu, T.C.: Remote password authentication with smart cards. IEE Proc. E-Comput. Digital Techniques **138**(3), 165–168 (1991)
3. Chen, B.L., Kuo, W.C., Wuu, L.C.: Robust smart-card-based remote user password authentication scheme. Int. J. Commun Syst **27**(2), 377–389 (2014)
4. Chen, L., Zhang, K.: Privacy-aware smart card based biometric authentication scheme for e-health. Peer-to-Peer Network. Appl. **14**(3), 1353–1365 (2021)
5. Dodis, Y., Reyzin, L., Smith, A.: Fuzzy extractors: how to generate strong keys from biometrics and other noisy data. In: Cachin, C., Camenisch, J.L. (eds.) EUROCRYPT 2004. LNCS, vol. 3027, pp. 523–540. Springer, Heidelberg (2004). https://doi.org/10.1007/978-3-540-24676-3_31
6. Dolev, D., Yao, A.: On the security of public key protocols. IEEE Trans. Inf. Theor. **29**(2), 198–208 (1983)
7. Fan, L., Li, J.H., Zhu, H.W.: An enhancement of timestamp-based password authentication scheme. Comput. Secur. **21**(7), 665–667 (2002)
8. Hwang, M.S., Li, L.H.: A new remote user authentication scheme using smart cards. IEEE Trans. Consum. Electron. **46**(1), 28–30 (2000). https://doi.org/10.1109/30.826377
9. Jiang, Q., Ma, J., Li, G., Li, X.: Improvement of robust smart-card-based password authentication scheme. Int. J. Commun. Syst. **28**(2), 383–393 (2015)
10. Kocher, Paul, Jaffe, Joshua, Jun, Benjamin: Differential power analysis. In: Wiener, Michael (ed.) CRYPTO 1999. LNCS, vol. 1666, pp. 388–397. Springer, Heidelberg (1999). https://doi.org/10.1007/3-540-48405-1_25
11. Lamport, L.: Password authentication with insecure communication. Commun. ACM **24**(11), 770–772 (1981)
12. Lin, C.W., Tsai, C.S., Hwang, M.S.: A new strong-password authentication scheme using one-way hash functions. J. Comput. Syst. Sci. Int. **45**(4), 623–626 (2006)
13. Mishra, D., Das, A.K., Chaturvedi, A., Mukhopadhyay, S.: A secure password-based authentication and key agreement scheme using smart cards. J. Inform. Secur. Appl. **23**, 28–43 (2015)
14. Odelu, V., Das, A.K., Goswami, A.: An effective and robust secure remote user authenticated key agreement scheme using smart cards in wireless communication systems. Wireless Pers. Commun. **84**(4), 2571–2598 (2015)

15. Ramasamy, R., Muniyandi, A.P.: An efficient password authentication scheme for smart card. IJ Netw. Secur. **14**(3), 180–186 (2012)
16. Song, R.: Advanced smart card based password authentication protocol. Comput. Stand. Interfaces **32**(5), 321–325 (2010)
17. Sood, S.K., Sarje, A.K., Singh, K.: An improvement of wang et al'.s authentication scheme using smart cards. In: Communications (NCC), 2010 National Conference, pp. 1–5. IEEE (2010)
18. Xu, J., Zhu, W.T., Feng, D.G.: An improved smart card based password authentication scheme with provable security. Comput. Standards Interfaces **31**(4), 723–728 (2009)
19. Yang, T., Zhai, F., Xu, H., Li, W.: Design of a secure and efficient authentication protocol for real-time accesses of multiple users in piot-oriented multi-gateway wsns. Energy Reports 8, pp. 1200–1211 (2022). https://doi.org/10.1016/j.egyr. 2022.02.061,www.sciencedirect.com/science/article/pii/S2352484722003080, 2021 International Conference on New Energy and Power Engineering
20. Yang, W.H., Shieh, S.P.: Password authentication schemes with smart cards. Comput. Secur. **18**(8), 727–733 (1999)

A Fast Dynamic Adaptive Sampling Algorithm for Large-Scale Online Social Networks

Jing Jin, Gang Lu[(⊠)] [iD], and Weiwei Gu

UrbanNet Lab, College of Information Science and Technology, Beijing University of Chemical Technology, Beijing 100029, China
lugang@mail.buct.edu.cn

Abstract. Sampling a representative subnetwork from a large-scale network is crucial for the research of online social net-works. Uniform sampling (UNI) is often used to evaluate the unbiasedness of sampling results, but the sampling efficiency and the representativeness of the sampled network are weak. In this paper, a dynamic adaptive UNI sampling method (DaptUNI) is proposed in order to overcome the disadvantages of UNI by dividing the user ID space into small equal intervals, and then sampling in the intervals according to the density of valid user IDs. Dynamical programming is applied during the sampling process so that the intervals can be merged or split adaptively. In addition, another method called DaptUNI + N is proposed, in which the neighbors of the sampled nodes are sampled, too. That further improves the sampling efficiency. Finally, our methods outperform other classical methods in terms of sampling efficiency and the sampled network is better when it comes to representativeness.

Keywords: Complex Networks · Large-scale Online Social Net-works · UNI · Adaptive Sampling · Dynamic Programming

1 Introduction

Online social networks (OSNs) as a type of the complex networks [1] play an important role in society, which promotes information exchange and adoption of healthier behaviors [2, 3] that can lead to effective interventions on epidemic spreading [4–7]. Social networks are also the mainstay of our communities [8], and essential for our livelihoods and urban economies [9–11]. The rapid growth of OSNs and the unprecedented large volume of data have made social network analysis increasingly challenging. Facebook, in particular, was the first OSN that exceeds 1 billion registrations and now has more than 2.91 billion monthly active users (MAUs)[1]. Twitter has reached 174 million average profitable daily active users (monetizable DAUs, mDAUs) in Q3 2021, compared to 152 million in the same period of last year[2]. And Sina Weibo is the most popular OSN in

---

[1] https://investor.fb.com/investor-events/event-details/2022/Meta-Q4-2021-Earnings/default.aspx.

[2] https://s22.q4cdn.com/826641620/files/doc_financials/2021/q3/Final-Q3'21-Shareholder-letter.pdf.

W. Hong and Y. Weng (Eds.): ICCSE 2022, CCIS 1811, pp. 337–349, 2023.
https://doi.org/10.1007/978-981-99-2443-1_30

China. According to its financial results disclosed in Q3 2021, it had approximately 573 million MAUs[3].

A crucial challenge in the study of OSNs is to produce a sampled network that maintains the properties of the original network [12]. At present, there are several network sampling methods to deal with the problem of OSN sampling [13–15]. Network sampling algorithms can be classified into three groups: graph traversal sampling, random walk sampling, and random selection sampling [16–18]. The graph traversal sampling methods mainly include BFS [19], DFS [20], FF [21], SBS [22], etc.; random walk sampling methods include RW [23], MHRW, RWRW [24], etc.; random selection sampling methods include RN, RE, etc. All of these methods have numerous improvements [14, 25, 26]. Gjoka proposed a sampling method, the Uniform Sampling (UNI) method, in a study of Facebook [17]. The UNI method, which is based on the acceptance-rejection method, is a uniform sampling method where the probabilities of being sampled for the nodes are the same, which are independent of the topology of the original network. In this way, it can be assumed that the sampling process is unbiased with respect to the characteristics of the nodes concerned. As a result, UNI can be used as a benchmark for the evaluation of other sampling methods [17]. However, UNI is very inefficient if the valid user IDs sparsely distribute in the userID space (generally $[0, 2^{32} - 1]$ or $[0, 2^{64} - 1]$, depending on the system). To solve this problem, Cai et al. [12] proposed adpUNI, which used the feature of nonuniform distribution of valid user IDs in OSN and the property that the target rate of the UNI sampling method is related to the density of valid user IDs. In adpUNI, the user ID space is divided into intervals evenly with their sampling probabilities being adjusted dynamically to improve the sampling efficiency.

On this basis, we propose a new method to improve the sampling efficiency further by dynamically adjusting the intervals. It is called as Dynamic adaptive UNI (DaptUNI) sampling. Moreover, DaptUNI is further improved by DaptUNI + N, in which neighbors of the sampled nodes are also sampled. By comparing DaptUNI and DaptUNI + N with other network sampling methods in the datasets of Sina Weibo and Twitter, the sampling efficiency and effectiveness of each method are analyzed.

2   Methods

In [12], it has been shown that the distribution of user IDs is not uniform. That means if the whole user IDs space is divided into intervals, sampling can be processed among the intervals according to the density of valid user IDs in them. That is the basic idea of adpUNI. Basing on adpUNI, a dynamic adaptive UNI sampling method (DaptUNI) is proposed, in which the intervals of user IDs space are dynamically merged or split. Given the range of user IDs L, which is divided into N small intervals with same size, each interval i has an initial length $l_i = L/N$. However, in DaptUNI, the intervals are dynamically merged or split as the sampling process goes on, so their length $l_i(t)$ will be changed along with time t. As a result, being similar to [12], the following definitions

---

[3] http://ir.weibo.com/news-releases/news-release-details/weibo-reports-third-quarter-2021-una udited-financial-results/

are given: For each interval i, the sampling rate at time t is defined as

$$SP_i(t) = \frac{S_i(t)}{l_i(t)}, \tag{1}$$

where $l_i(t)$ denotes the length of the interval i at time t and $S_i(t)$ denotes the sampling times at time t. If a valid user ID is sampled, it is called *targeted*. Then by following the definitions of adpUNI in [12], $T_i(t)$ is the cumulative number of targeted user IDs in the interval i at time t, while the target rate $TP_i(t)$ and the sampling probability of interval i as $P_i(t)$ are defined respectively as follows:

$$TP_i(t) = \frac{T_i(t)}{S_i(t)}, \tag{2}$$

$$P_i(t) = TP_i(t-1) \times [1 - SP_i(t-1)], \tag{3}$$

where $P_i(t)$ decides the probability of sampling in interval i at time t. The definition of $P_i(t)$ makes DadpUNI to avoid local optima traps. Also, a minimum sampling threshold for each interval at $\alpha = 1/N$ is followed from [12] to solve the cold start problem. In addition, to dynamically shape the intervals, two more thresholds are defined, which are the interval adjustment probability *prob* and the minimum interval length l_{min}. The detailed process of DaptUNI is shown as Algorithm 1.

The first half of Algorithm 1 is similar to adpUNI. In the second half, a process of dynamic programming for the intervals begins. For each interval i, if $TP_i(t) \leq prob$, this interval is considered as relatively sparse. Moreover, if $l_i(t) \geq l_{min}$, this interval should be evenly split into two small intervals. If $TP_i(t) > prob$ and $TP_{i+1}(t) > prob$, it means that both interval i and $i+1$ are dense intervals with high relative target rates. As a result, the two intervals are merged into a bigger one. If we initially divide the entire user space S into N intervals and the size of samples to be collected is M, the average time complexity will be $O(N) + O(S)O(\max(S/l_{min}, N))$, where $\max(S/l_{min}, N)$ represents the maximum number of intervals in the sampling process.

By the process of dynamic programming, the adjacent dense intervals can be combined into one interval in order to avoid local optima traps more effectively; also, a relative sparse interval can be divided into two intervals with the purpose of trying not to ignore the valid IDs in it.

The adpUNI + N method has been advanced in [12] to further improve the adpUNI method. Similarly, in order to further improve the sampling efficiency and sampling performance of DaptUNI, DaptUNI + N is proposed. In the sampling process, when a valid user ID is sampled, all neighbors of that node will also be added to the sample set. The process of adding each neighbor is considered as one sampling, with updating the attribute values of corresponding intervals. Adding neighboring nodes helps to sample more quickly.

```
Algorithm 1 DaptUNI(L,I,DSS,prob,lmin)

Input:
1) L(User IDs space),
2) N(Number of intervals),
3) DSS(Desired sample size),
4) prob(Interval adjustment probability),
5) lmin (Minimum interval length)
Output: A set of targeted IDs
1:  α = 1/N; l = L/N; intervalDict = {}
2:  #divide the user ID space L into N intervals
3:  for i in range(N) do
4:      It = Interval()#create an instance of Interval class
5:      It.S = 0; It.T = 0; It.SP = 0; It.TP = 0
6:      It.P = α # sampling probability
7:      It.low,It.up = i * l,(i + 1) * l - 1
8:      It.key = str("It.low_It.up")
9:      intervalDict[It.key] = It
10:end for
11:testID = set(); # save all tested IDs
12:targetID = set(); # save all targeted IDs
13:while len(targetID) <= DSS do
14:   for It in intervalDict do
15:      RP = random(0, 1)
16:      if It.P >= RP then
17:          id = randint(It.low,It.up)
18:          while id in testID do
19:              id = randint(It.low,It.up)
20:          end while
21:          testID .add(id)
22:          It.S+ = 1; It.SP = It.S/(It.up - It.low)
23:          if id exists in the OSN then
24:              It.T+ = 1; It.TP = It.T/It.S
25:              targetID .add(id)
26:          end if
27:          b = It.TP * (1 - It.SP)
28:          It.P = b if b < α else α
29:      end if
30:   end for
31:   # dynamic programming
32:   for It in intervalDict do
33:      if It.TP <= prob then
34:          if It.up - It.low >= 2 * lmin  then
35:              divide It into two intervals
36:          end if
37:      else
38:          find next interval as NIt
39:          if NIt.TP > prob then
40:              merge intervals It and NIt
41:          end if
42:      end if
43:   end for
44:end while
```

3   Experiments

Two datasets are taken as the original networks to simulate the real OSNs, which are a connected subnetwork of the Sina Weibo network crawled in 2014, and the social network from Twitter used in [17]. The details of these two datasets are shown in Table 1. The userIDs in both datasets are numeric which range in $[0, 2^{32} - 1]$. In the experiments, the datasets are stored in a MySQL database, so that the validity of a random ID can be verified by accessing the database during the sampling process. Additionally, network statistics including degree distribution, clustering coefficient distribution, and k-core distribution are used to evaluate the sampling results by calculating their KS distance from the original whole networks.

Table 1. Basic information of the datasets.

Dataset	Nodes	Edges	Expected TP
Sina Weibo	10,314,647	25,139,163	0.24%
Twitter	41,652,230	1,468,365,182	0.97%

3.1   *prob* and l_{min}

Since *prob* and l_{min} need to be set in advance, in this section, we investigate their effects on the sampling performance of DaptUNI and DaptUNI + N.

Sampling Efficiency: We show the variation of the number of target nodes for our method (DaptUNI, DaptUNI + N) and other rejection sampling methods (UNI, adpUNI, adpUNI + N) on Sina Weibo (see Fig. 1) and Twitter (see Fig. 2) as the number of samples increases. Meanwhile, Table 2 shows the number of sampling attempts required by DaptUNI and DaptUNI + N with different *prob* and l_{min} for a sample size of 5 $\times$ 10^5 from Sina Weibo and 1 $\times$ 10^6 from Twitter, with a comparison with adpUNI, adpUNI + N and UNI. From Table 2, we can observe that the proposed methods require fewer attempts than adpUNI, adpUNI + N and UNI when sampling Sina Weibo, while DaptUNI has better robustness when sampling Twitter. Both DaptUNI and DaptUNI + N have much better sampling efficiency than the UNI method. Furthermore, the sampling efficiency on Twitter dataset is significantly higher than that on Sina Weibo because Twitter has more densely distributing nodes with a greater opportunity for a random ID to be a valid user ID. However, the sampling efficiency of DaptUNI and DaptUNI + N is greatly improved on Sina Weibo, a network with sparse node distribution, indicating that these two methods are more suitable for the OSNs with the relatively lower expected *TP* and uneven user ID distribution. From Fig. 1 and Fig. 2, it can be seen that several curves representing different results by different values of *prob*. They almost overlap under the same minimum interval length l_{min}. This illustrates that the effect of the interval adjustment probability *prob* on sampling efficiency is not obviously significant in the sampling process, regardless of the data set network.

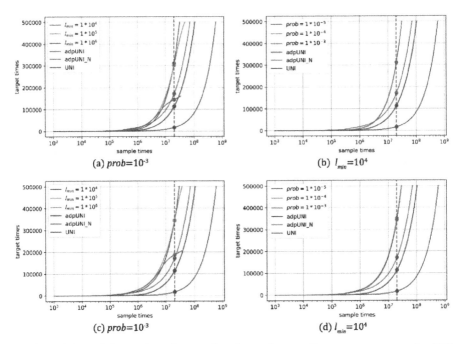

Fig. 1. Variation of the number of targeted nodes as the sampling process goes on for UNI, adpUNI, adpUNI + N, and DaptUNI (a, b), DaptUNI + N (c, d) on Sina Weibo dataset, with different *prob* (a, c) and different *lmin* (b, d).

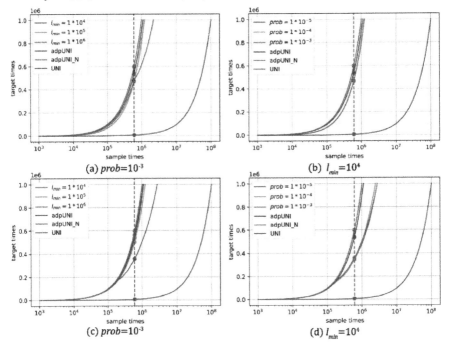

Fig. 2. Variation of the number of targeted nodes as the sampling process goes on for UNI, adpUNI, adpUNI + N, and DaptUNI (a, b), DaptUNI + N (c, d) on Twitter, with different *prob* (a, c) and different l_{min} (b, d).

In addition, Fig. 3 shows the overall target rate variation for DaptUNI (a, b) and DaptUNI + N (c, d) comparing with adpUNI, adpUNI + N, UNI and MHRW during the sampling process on Sina Weibo (a, c) and on Twitter (b, d). Obviously, our methods outperform UNI and MHRW in terms of Overall Target Rate (OTR) and is much higher than the expected values listed in Table 1. It is worth to mention that MHRW has a poor performance in terms of sampling efficiency. Since the sampling scale and the original network are huge, MHRW is easily trapped in one node, so it takes a very long time to collect tens of thousands of nodes, thus only the OTR of the collected nodes of MHRW will be compared with other methods. When sampling Sina Weibo (see Fig. 3(a, c)), the OTR of DaptUNI and DaptUNI + N is higher than UNI, MHRW, adpUNI and adpUNI + N in the sampling process. When sampling Twitter (see Fig. 3(b, d)), the OTR of DaptUNI and DaptUNI + N still has a distance with adpUNI and adpUNI + N. This is probably because the Twitter dataset has relatively higher expected TP as Table 1 lists. Furthermore, for different *prob*, the curves are relatively similar. For different l_{min}, the curves have a peak and a very significant decrease.

Table 2. The number of sampling attempts required when the sample size is 1×10^5 for Sina Weibo and 1×10^6 for Twitter (in a unit of 10^6)

	DaptUNI					DaptUNI + N					adpUNI	adpUNI + N	UNI
prob	10^{-5}	10^{-4}	10^{-3}	10^{-3}	10^{-3}	10^{-5}	10^{-4}	10^{-3}	10^{-3}	10^{-3}			
l_{min}	10^4	10^4	10^4	10^5	10^6	10^4	10^4	10^4	10^5	10^6			
Sina Weibo	**31.42**	31.58	31.53	48.52	-	**29.39**	29.48	29.47	36.88	-	106.82	72.42	599.12
Twitter	1.25	**1.24**	1.26	**1.24**	2.25	2.81	2.50	2.78	1.26	**1.08**	1.12	**1.00**	101.81

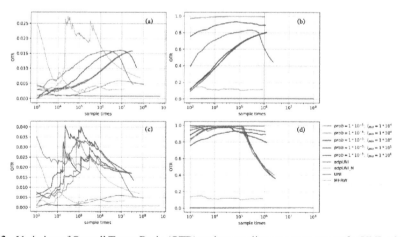

Fig. 3. Variation of Overall Target Ratio (OTR) as the sampling process goes on for UNI, adpUNI, adpUNI + N, MHRW and DaptUNI(a, b), DaptUNI + N(c, d) on Sina Weibo(a, c) and on Twitter(b, d).

Performance Analysis: Figure 4 and Fig. 6 show the KS distance between the sampled

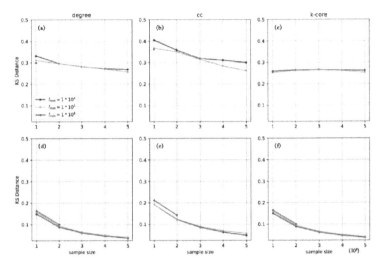

Fig. 4. Effects of DaptUNI (a–c), DaptUNI + N(d–f) on Sina Weibo sampling representativeness under different values of *lmin*.

networks and the original network in terms of the corresponding statistics as the sampling progress goes on, for DaptUNI (a-c) and DaptUNI + N(d-f), by $prob = 1 \times 10^{-3}$ and l_{min} as different values, for the two datasets, respectively. Similarly, Fig. 5 and Fig. 7 show the results by $l_{min} = 1 \times 10^4$ and *prob* as different values.

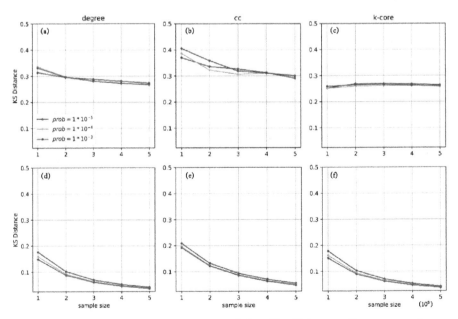

Fig. 5. Effects of DaptUNI (a–c), DaptUNI + N (d–f) on Sina Weibo sampling representativeness under different values of *prob*.

From these figures, it can be observed that the curves are quite similar. So that it can be concluded that *prob* and l_{min} have a small effect on the sampling effect. It is also observed that, in general, the sample size affects more on the sampling performance.

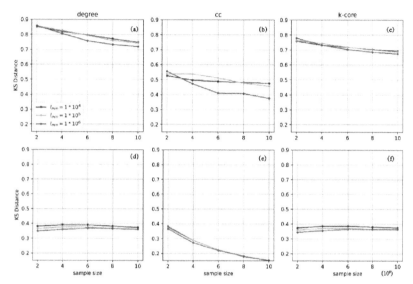

Fig. 6. Effects of DaptUNI (a–c), DaptUNI + N (d–f) on Twitter sampling representativeness under different values of l_{min}.

3.2   Representativeness Analysis

In this section, the sampling results of DaptUNI, DaptUNI + N are compared with those of UNI, adpUNI, adpUNI + N and other classical network sampling methods, including RN, BFS and RW, on the aspect of sampling representativeness. The cumulative degree distributions, clustering coefficients and k-core of the original network and the sampled networks by each method for Sina Weibo are illustrated in Fig. 8, while those for Twitter in Fig. 9, respectively. The KS distance between the sampled network and the original network correspondingly, see Table 3 for Weibo and Table 4 for Twitter.

From Fig. 8, we can see that for the k-core distribution and the clustering coefficient distribution, the curve of DaptUNI + N is the closest to the curve of the original network. In contrast, the curve of DaptUNI is farther away from the original network. For the degree distribution, it can be seen in Fig. 8(a) that there are more nodes with small degree values and fewer nodes with large degree values in the subnets sampled by DaptUNI + N, with a certain distance between their curves. However, as shown in Table 3, DaptUNI + N has the smallest KS distance from the original network in every statistic, which proves that DaptUNI + N is able to obtain a more representative sampled network from the dataset which has relatively lower expected target rate.

Table 3. The KS distance between the sampled networks and original network in terms of the degree distribution (degree), k-core distribution (k-core), and clustering coefficient distribution (cc) for each method on Sina Weibo dataset

Sampling Method	degree	k-core	cc
UNI	0.0649	0.0658	0.1428
DaptUNI	0.2683	0.2622	0.2791
DaptUNI + N	**0.0360**	**0.0374**	**0.0493**
adpUNI	0.0734	0.0742	0.1714
adpUNI + N	0.2050	0.2049	0.1387
RN	0.0612	0.0616	0.1324
BFS	0.4995	0.4995	0.2592
RW	0.3277	0.3277	0.1998

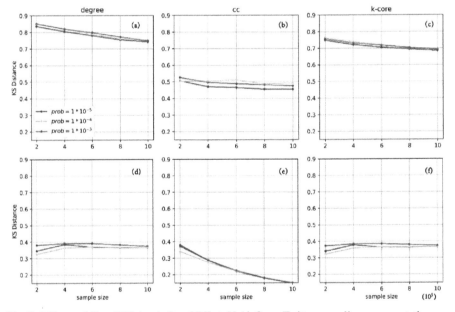

Fig. 7. Effects of DaptUNI (a–c), DaptUNI + N (d–f) on Twitter sampling representativeness under different values of *prob*.

From Fig. 9 and Table 4, it can be found that when sampling Twitter, the curves of each method have a certain distance from the curve of the original network, which can be due to the sampling size is only 2.4% of the original network. However, the KS distances between adpUNI + N and DaptUNI + N and the original network are smaller in terms of the distribution of clustering coefficients, as can be observed from the table. This indicates that these two methods can preserve the local characteristics

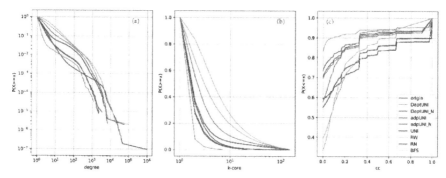

Fig. 8. Degree distribution (a), k-core distribution (b), and clustering coefficient distribution (c) by different sampling methods on Sina Weibo dataset.

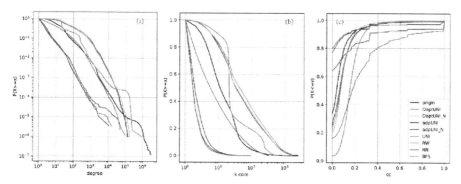

Fig. 9. Degree distribution (a), k-core distribution (b) and clustering coefficient distribution (c) by different sampling methods on Twitter dataset.

Table 4. The KS distance between the sampled networks and original networks in terms of the degree distribution (degree), k-core distribution (k-core), and clustering coefficient distribution (cc) for each method on Twitter dataset

Sampling Method	degree	k-core	cc
UNI	0.7358	0.6700	0.5586
DaptUNI	0.6738	0.7203	0.3755
DaptUNI + N	0.3649	0.3638	0.1469
adpUNI	0.7834	0.7675	0.7348
adpUNI + N	**0.3241**	0.3312	**0.1172**
RN	0.3500	0.3368	0.5630
BFS	0.4317	0.4117	0.5605
RW	0.3340	**0.3290**	0.1916

of the original network quite well. It can also be observed from the figure that the distributions of the curves of DaptUNI, adpUNI and UNI methods are relatively similar, while the distributions of the curves of DaptUNI + N, adpUNI + N and RW methods are relatively similar. That means when the neighbors of the sampled nodes are also sampled, DaptUNI and adpUNI act like RW; while if not, they act like UNI. That also proves on the aspect of network representation that since the Twitter network has relatively higher expected target rate, the method based on the uneven distribution of user IDs does not improve much.

4 Conclusion and Discussion

In this paper, DaptUNI and DaptUNI + N are proposed for sampling large-scale OSNs. The efficiency and subnetwork representativeness of these two methods are demonstrated in the process of experiments. DaptUNI is based on the UNI algorithm with the addition of interval division and dynamic programming of intervals. The main process of DaptUNI is to divide the user ID space uniformly, and gradually adjust their sampling probabilities. At the same time, the intervals are merged or split dynamically according to their target rates-merging two neighboring intervals with relatively high target rates and splitting the intervals with relatively low target rates. DaptUNI improves the sampling efficiency of UNI according to the user ID distribution, as well as avoids reducing the representativeness of the sampled networks. By adding neighboring, DaptUNI + N can significantly improve sampling efficiency and obtain more representative subnets. In summary, DaptUNI and DaptUNI + N are much better than UNI sampling in terms of sampling efficiency and sampling effect. DaptUNI + N can collect a subnet with more similar distribution and more representative of the original network, especially in the OSNs with sparse node distribution.

Future research will focus on the following topics. First, the datasets used in this paper are all 32-bit integers, but in practice, the user ID space in OSNs is not limited to this. Therefore, we want to study how to make our methods applicable to the OSNs with a larger arbitrary user ID space. Moreover, the experiments in this paper are conducted on crawled datasets to simulate a sampling process on real OSNs.

We would like to apply our methods to a real sampling process on real OSNs in the future.

Acknowledgments. This research was conducted on the High Performance Computing Service Platform of the College of Information Science and Technology, Beijing University of Chemical Technology.

References

1. Mordeson, J.N., Mathew, S., Malik, D.S.: Networks. In: Fuzzy Graph Theory with Applications to Human Trafficking. SFSC, vol. 365, pp. 139–155. Springer, Cham (2018). https://doi.org/10.1007/978-3-319-76454-2_4
2. Centola, D.: The spread of behavior in an online social network experiment. Science **329**(5996), 1194–1197 (2010)

3. Centola, D.: An experimental study of homophily in the adoption of health behavior. Science **334**(6060), 1269–1272 (2011)
4. Liu, X., Yan, M., Deng, L., Li, G., Ye, X., Fan, D.: Sampling methods for efficient training of graph convolutional networks: a survey. IEEE/CAA J. Automatica Sinica **9**(2), 205–234 (2022)
5. Li, R., Tang, M., Hui, P.-M.: Epidemic spreading on multi-relational networks. Acta Physica Sinica **62**(16), 168903 (2013)
6. Li, R., Wang, W., Di, Z.: Effects of human dynamics on epidemic spreading in Cote d'Ivoire. Physica A **467**, 30–40 (2017)
7. Li, R., Richmond, P., Roehner, B.M.: Effect of population density on epidemics. Physica A **510**, 713–724 (2018)
8. Heidemann, J., Klier, M., Probst, F.: Online social networks: a survey of a global phenomenon. Comput. Netw. **56**(18), 3866–3878 (2012)
9. Dong, L., Li, R., Zhang, J., Di, Z.: Population-weighted efficiency in transportation networks. Sci. Rep. **6**(1), 1–10 (2016)
10. Li, R.: Simple spatial scaling rules behind complex cities. Nat. Commun. **8**(1), 1–7 (2017)
11. Li, R., et al.: Assessing the attraction of cities on venture capital from a scaling law perspective. IEEE Access **9**, 48052–48063 (2021)
12. Cai, G., Gang, L., Guo, J., Ling, C., Li, R.: Fast representative sampling in large-scale online social networks. IEEE Access **8**, 77106–77119 (2020)
13. Gjoka, M., Butts, C.T., Kurant, M., Markopoulou, A.: Multigraph sampling of online social networks. IEEE J. Sel. Areas Commun. **29**(9), 1893–1905 (2011)
14. Wang, D., Li, Z., Tyson, G., Li, Z., Xie, G.: Unbiased sampling of social media networks for well-connected subgraphs. In: Proceedings of the 2017 IEEE/ACM International Conference on Advances in Social Networks Analysis and Mining, pp. 212–215 (2017)
15. Lohr, S.L.: Sampling: Design and Analysis. Chapman and Hall/CRC (2021)
16. Leskovec, J., Faloutsos, C.: Sampling from large graphs. In: Proceedings of the 12th ACM SIGKDD International Conference on Knowledge Discovery and Data Mining, pp. 631–636 (2006)
17. Gjoka, M., Kurant, M., Butts, C.T., Markopoulou, A.: Walking in facebook: a case study of unbiased sampling of OSNs. In: 2010 Proceedings IEEE Infocom, pp. 1–9 (2010)
18. Cui, Y., Li, X., Li, J., Wang, H., Chen, X.: A survey of sampling method for social media embeddedness relationship. ACM Comput. Surv. **55**(4), 74:1–74:39 (2023)
19. Yoon, S., Lee, S., Yook, S.-H., Kim, Y.: Statistical properties of sampled networks by random walks. Phys. Rev. E **75**(4), 046114 (2007)
20. Even, S.: Graph Algorithms. Cambridge University Press (2011)
21. Kurant, M., Markopoulou, A., Thiran, P.: On the bias of BFS (Breadth First Search). In: Proceedings of IEEE 22nd International Teletraffic Congress, pp. 1–8 (2010)
22. Frank, O.: Survey Sampling in Networks. In: The Sage Handbook of Social Network Analysis, pp. 389–403. Sage (2011)
23. Gkantsidis, C., Mihail, M., Saberi, A.: Random walks in peer-to-peer networks. In: Proceedings of IEEE INFOCOM 2004, vol. 1 (2004)
24. Rasti, A.H., Torkjazi, M., Rejaie, R., Duffield, N., Willinger, W., Stutzbach, D.: Respondent-driven sampling for characterizing unstructured overlays. In: Proceedings of IEEE INFOCOM 2009, pp. 2701–2705 (2009)
25. Zhao, J., Wang, P., Lui, J.C.S., Towsley, D., Guan, X.: Sampling online social networks by random walk with indirect jumps. Data Min. Knowl. Disc. **33**(1), 24–57 (2018). https://doi.org/10.1007/s10618-018-0587-5
26. Li, Y.: Walking with perception: efficient random walk sampling via common neighbor awareness. In: Proceedings of IEEE 35th International Conference on Data Engineering, pp. 962–973 (2019)

A Preliminary Research on Online Learning Engagement of International Students Staying at Home Country: Take CFL Course as an Example

Menglu Chen, Yiyang Li, Chenxintong Cheng, Yujie Huang, and Huan Wang(✉)

NingboTech University, Ningbo, China
eletahuan@163.com

Abstract. Discouraged by COVID-19 pandemic restrictions, many international students resort to studying online in their home countries despite their enrollment in universities outside of their own countries. In order to ensure academic achievement and prevent dropping out, it is necessary to investigate the influences on online learning engagement of international students who are still staying in their home country. With an explanatory sequential mixed method, this study first delivered a questionnaire to the class of international students who were learning Chinese as a foreign language (CFL) online away from China, by which the researchers collect preliminary data about their learning engagement as online learners, and identified participants who would consent to attend further qualitative research. In the second phase of the study, qualitative data from learning profiles and further interviews were collected, explaining the general data that emerged in the previous quantitative research phase. It is found that online CFL learners may suffer from many negative factors, including internet problems, lack of online learning strategies, cultural differences, low Chinese proficiency, and pessimistic personality. Meanwhile, some other factors, including strong motivation to learn and language identity as CFL learners, as well as multilingual aptitude may stimulate them to overcome these difficulties and engage in Chinese learning positively. In addition, three components of engagements display an interdependent relationship with non-linear interaction. This complex relationship may result in at least three categories of emotional and cognitive engagements: nervous CFL learners, anticipating CFL learners, and confident CFL learners. Some implications are concluded for the improvement of learning engagement in online Chinese courses for international students away from China.

Keywords: online learning engagement · international students staying at home country · CFL course

1 Introduction

In the background of COVID-19, many international students are prohibited to enter host countries but resort to attending online classes remaining at home. To ensure the

W. Hong and Y. Weng (Eds.): ICCSE 2022, CCIS 1811, pp. 350–362, 2023.
https://doi.org/10.1007/978-981-99-2443-1_31

teaching quality of online Chinese as a foreign language (CFL) education, many efforts are supposed to make in terms of online learning infrastructure and online learning materials [1]. Despite the convenience of online education to both teachers and students, many new problems have been emerging constantly, including reduced synchronizing interaction in class, poor performance in exercises after class, and students' emotional fluctuations [2–4].

These problems may influence students' learning engagement, which has been demonstrated to significantly relate to students' academic achievement or dropout [5–7]. According to Fredricks, Blumenfeld and Paris, (2004), learning engagement has been considered a multidimensional construct of three components: behavioral engagement (how they do), emotional engagement (how they feel), and cognitive engagement (how they think) [5]. Some other researches refer to emotional engagement with the terms of affective engagement and extract academic engagement independently from behavioral engagement [6, 7]. Despite the terminological difference, all these above studies agree that these components of engagement are interdependent, but a nonlinear interaction exists between components of learning engagement [5–7]. It has been demonstrated that changes in the education context may influence students' learning engagement [5, 6, 8].

This study investigates international students' learning engagement in an online CEL learning context with the following contributing questions: 1) What are the influences on students' online engagement? 2) How do components of learning engagement interact with each other?

2 Methodology

Considering the fact that international students confined in their home countries by the pandemic is still a relatively new research topic, and that diverse influence factors were aimed to explore, this research adopted Creswell's explanatory sequential mixed method with two phases [9]. In the first phase, the researchers collected quantitative data through a questionnaire on a class of international students, and analyzed the results; based on these results, the researchers identified 13 participants who granted consent to participate in further qualitative research in the second phase. Finally, the results found in the second phase were related to the results in the first phase.

2.1 Participants and Setting

Participants involved in this research were from a class of international graduate students majoring in Industrial Designing. They had been admitted to a university in East China but were not allowed to enter China owing to the COVID-19 pandemic restrictions. So, they had to stay in their home countries and attended classes online while some of their classmates were having classes offline in China. They were arranged to take Chinese as a compulsive course, and the first four researchers functioned as teacher assistants (TA) to help them, including giving feedback on homework, answering questions, introducing Chinese culture, and accelerating these instruction recordings in students' learning profiles.

These 13 participants, who consented to attend the second phase, formed a relatively small but typical group sampling the variety of online international students in those less developed countries. As displayed in Table 1, they were from 12 countries, 5 in Asia and 7 in Africa. Their Chinese proficiency varies from beginning learners with no Chinese learning experience to fluent learners with HSK level 4/5 certificates. In addition, their foreign language learning experience also differs from each other, some took Chinese as their first or second foreign language, while others had learned 3 or 4 other foreign languages beforehand.

Table 1. Information about participants.

Participants	Gender	Nationality	Chinese is my ...	HSK[a] level
M1	Female	Lesotho	2nd foreign language	None
M2	Female	Bangladesh	2nd foreign language	None
H1	Male	Afghanistan	2nd foreign language	None
H2	Male	Rwanda	3rd foreign language	None
H3	Male	Tanzania	3rd foreign language	None
X1	Male	Cambodia	2nd foreign language	None
X2	Female	Malaysia	1st foreign language	Level 5
X3	Male	Nigeria	/	None
X4	Male	Ethiopia	/	/
Y1	Male	Nepal	2nd foreign language	Level 5
Y2	Male	Morocco	4th foreign language	None
Y3	Male	Zambia	2nd foreign language	Level 4
Y4	Female	Lesotho	5th foreign language	None

[a]HSK (*Hànyǔ Shuǐpíng Kǎoshì*) stands for an international Chinese proficiency test for CFL learners

2.2 Data Collection

Three sorts of data were collected in this explanatory mixed research. Firstly, a questionnaire was conducted on the whole class at the end of the semester, ending up with 13 participants granting consent to attend the second phase. Then these 13 participants' learning profiles collected during the semester were identified. Finally, semi-structured interviews were conducted by the first four researchers afterward.

Questionnaire. A questionnaire (see Appendix 1) was carried out at the end of the semester to collect international students' reflections on their Chinese learning experience in this course. Nine multiple-choice questions and one semi-open question were included. Question 1, 2, and 4 were designed to examine their emotional engagement, focusing on how they feel about learning Chinese, and distance learning, as well as factors that hinder their communication between teachers and students in class. The exploration of foreign students' behavioral engagement was based on Question 3 and 5, collecting data concerning the amount of time they spent in Chinese learning after class, as well as their communication with teachers in class. Question 6 to 10 were related to the benefit they reaped from TAs and their feelings and suggestion on TAs' feedback.

Learning Profile. Data from learning profiles stands for participants' behavioral engagement, including their class attendance, frequency of handed-in homework, and their communication frequency with teacher assistants. The assessment rule for their learning profile was set as follows: 1' for "seldom", 2' for "occasionally" and 3' for "usually".

Semi-structured Interview. Additionally, semi-structured interviews were conducted for further information on their online learning engagement. Interview questions (see Appendix 2) include the factors that influenced their online learning, their comments on Chinese learning experience in this distance learning context, and their comments on their contact with teachers and TAs. Each of the first four researchers interviewed 2–4 participants, whom they had assisted this semester. The relatively close rapport between the interviewer and interviewee was believed to ensure the smoothness of the interview. Due to some issues like time difference, these interviews were conducted flexibly in two modes via DingTalk: asynchronous text messages and synchronous voice chat. Then all the text messages and interview transcripts were gathered into one file for further analysis.

2.3 Data Analysis

Accordingly, a mixed data analysis method was adopted to investigate these online learners' behavioral engagement, emotional engagement, and cognitive engagement. Firstly, a quantitative analysis was conducted by descriptive statistics on data from the questionnaire and learning profile, focusing on participants' comments on the factors that influence their learning engagement.

Then, a qualitative analysis was performed on the interview transcripts focusing on three questions: 1) what factors influence their online learning? 2) what emotion have they experienced about their online learning? 3) what are their comments on their online learning? For the sake of research credibility and reliability, the researcher who had interviewed a specific participant would not be involved in the data analysis of that interview data. Three rounds of analysis had been taken in sequence: in the first round, two researchers code the transcripts sentence by sentence separately, then these coding themes were relayed to another researcher in the second round for check, and finally, in the third round all these coding themes were rechecked by the last researcher [10]. Researchers discussed together whenever any disagreement emerged.

Finally, these categories were employed to re-analyze the learning engagement and influence factors that had been suggested in the quantitative data from the questionnaire.

3 Results

3.1 Behavioral Engagement

Data from learning profiles (Table 2) shows that these participants vary in their behavioral engagements: While M2, H1, and H3 indicated high behavioral engagement (with a score of 3), X3, X4, M1, Y2, and H2 indicated moderate behavioral engagement (with a score of 2.3), and Y1, Y3, Y4 indicated relatively low behavioral engagement (with the score below 2). In addition, X2's score for behavioral engagement was 2.6, which was close to 3.

Table 2. Score of behavioral engagement from learning profile.

Participant	Attendance	Homework	Communication with TA	Behavioral engagement
X1	3	2	2	2.3
X2	3	3	2	2.6
X3	1	3	3	2.3
X4	3	2	2	2.3
M1	2	2	3	2.3
M2	3	3	3	3
Y1	1	1	1	1
Y2	2	3	2	2.3
Y3	1	2	1	1.3
Y4	2	2	1	1.7
H1	3	3	3	3
H2	3	2	2	2.3
H3	3	3	3	3

3.2 Influence on Learning Engagement

Both questionnaire data and interview data suggest some factors that might influence participants' distance learning engagement on participants' behavioral engagement, some overlapping and some complementary. Table 3 displays the influence factors based on the data from the questionnaire. It was suggested that "Internet problem" and "Lack of live practice" consisted of major factors (with the same ratio of 76.9%), and "Psychological introversion" was the least chosen (with the same ratio of 23.1%). What's more, "Low Chinese proficiency", "Negative emotions" and "Teacher's neglect" were three moderate factors with the same ratio of 30.8%.

Table 3. Influence factors suggested in questionnaires response.

Influence factors	Number	Percentage
Internet Problem	10	76.9%
Psychological Introversion	3	23.1%
Low Chinese Proficiency	4	30.8%
Negative Emotions	4	30.8%
Teacher's Neglect	4	30.8%
Lack of Live Practice	10	76.9%

Analysis of interview data (see Table 4) partly overlaps the factors found in questionnaires and displays some other factors. Some of the added factors are negative, including the problems caused uniquely by distant learning modes (e.g., time difference, lack of online learning strategies, and lack of learning material). Some other additional factors are relatively positive, including their strong motivation to learn Chinese and their multilingual learning experience.

Table 4. Influence factors in interview response.

Categories	Coding themes	Participants
Negative Factors	Lack of Live Practice	M1, H1, H3, X2, Y3
	Time Difference	H1, H3, Y1, Y2
	Lack of Online Learning Strategy	H1, H3, X2, Y3, Y2, Y1
	Teacher's Neglect	H2, M2, M1, Y4
	Internet Problems	H1, H2, H3, Y2
	Lack of Study Resources	Y2
	Low Chinese Proficiency	M2, Y1, Y2, Y3
	Psychological Introversion	Y1
Positive Factors	Strong Motivation to Learn	X2, Y3, Y2
	Language Identity as CFL learner	Y2
	Interest in Chinese Culture	H3, Y1, Y2, Y4
	Multilingual Aptitude	Y1

3.3 Emotional and Cognitive Engagement

Analyses of the questionnaire suggest that all participants expressed strong desires to have a good knowledge of Chinese and many of them noted that they were interested in learning a new language. Combined analysis of the questionnaire data and interview texts results in at least three categories of CFL distance learners: Nervous Learner, Anticipating Learner, and Confident Learner.

M2, H1, and H3 were Characterized as Nervous CFL Learners. These three participants are all Chinese learning beginners who had difficulty in following teachers in class. They confessed that they "always feel nervous in distance learning" (in the questionnaire). They also complained about various problems in distance learning, such as poor Internet, lack of online learning strategy, low Chinese proficiency, and psychological introversion (as shown in Table 4). These negative factors contribute to their low emotional engagement at the beginning of the semester. For instance, H1 mentioned that he was "very worried" when he found that the network was not good during the class. In their interviews, these three Nervous CFL Learners stated their strong desire to study in China. They all complained about the pandemic limitation and felt sad for not participating in classroom discussions personally.

However, these three participants all expressed their appreciation for the support from TAs. H1 mentioned in the interview that he "can release [his] negative emotions" with the help of TA. Besides, he said that TA "gives [him] confidence in learning Chinese" in the process of asking them relative questions, which indicates the improvement in H1's cognitive engagement. That indicates that support from TA may help those participants turn from low emotional engagement to high emotional engagement, which also contributes to their improvement of both cognitive and behavioral engagement. With support from TAs, participants overcame language learning difficulties and enhanced their emotional engagement and cognitive engagement.

The Group of Y1, Y3, and Y4 Displayed the Characteristics of Anticipating Learners. These students are facilitated with their Chinese proficiency or language learning aptitude. To them, Chinese learning is not very difficult. Their high self-efficacy in Chinese learning might relate to their Chinese proficiency. For example, Y1 remarked that "it does no matter whether [he] can study in China or not" since he is fluent in Chinese. Y3 also mentioned in the interview that "Chinese learning is okay because [he] could use the textbook to follow and learn more after class." It might also be related to their multilingual learning experience in Y2's case, who said in the interview that "I am a linguist so I love learning a different language all the time."

These participants expressed their strong anticipation to communicate with the teacher in class. The teacher in the class was faced with students both offline and online at the same time. In such a blended learning context, "the teacher used to focus more on those in class so online students got left out in so many times" (Y4's interview). In fact, they are more intended to communicate with the classroom teacher and hope their own voice to be heard by the teachers and classmates (e.g., Y4). The contradiction between their behavioral and cognitive engagement might be associated with their failure to catch enough attention from the teacher in distance learning. Y3 also mentioned that the "only difficulty [he] had was practicing communication skills".

However, their behavioral engagement is relatively lower than other students as suggested in the learning profile and questionnaire. They seldom talked with professors or TAs as well as occasionally failed to finish and submit their homework on time. They showed high cognitive engagement in the interview.

As an Exception, X2 is Categorized as a Confident CFL Learner. As she had passed HSK level 5, she demonstrates high confidence in her Chinese learning. In her interview, she stated that "except for Chinese pronunciation, the other section is quite easy for her to understand."

Different from those anticipating learners, her behavioral engagement is relatively high. As is displayed in Table 2, X2 attended all the online classes, finished all homework carefully, and submitted them on time, but with occasional communication with TA. In addition, X2 said in the interview that "I usually read Chinese novels and listen to Chinese music and Chinese drama."

At the same time, X2 indicated both high emotional and cognitive engagement. For instance, she responded that "I believe even though it is easy, I might also learn something new, and that right now I have learned a lot about the pinyin." Moreover, X2 also has an interest in Chinese, "more importantly is must have keen and interest to learn." Additionally, X2's self-concept and self-efficacy are high. X2 can clearly know her disadvantage and advantage, "however, I had also face difficulty in the pronunciation, but the other section is quite for me to understand.".

4   Discussions, Conclusions and Limitation

This research discusses the engagement of CFL Learners who are staying in their home countries. In accordance with previous studies on distance Chinese teaching [2–4], it is found that many factors may hinder these online learners' engagement in Chinese learning, ranging from lack of online learning strategies, cultural differences, low Chinese proficiency, as well as a pessimistic personality like shyness. However, some other positive factors are also found in this study, including strong motivation to learn, multilingual aptitude, and language identity as CFL learners may stimulate them to overcome these difficulties and engage in Chinese learning positively.

This study also discusses the non-linear interaction between the components between behavioral engagement, emotional engagement, and cognitive engagement. It is found that the inconvenience of distance learning is likely to cause anxiety in Chinese learners, both those beginning learners and those learners with high anticipation in distance courses.

These results about anticipating learners indicate that behavioral engagement may be influenced by cognitive and affective engagement. If problems with cognitive or affective engagement went unnoticed, it may cause some observable issues with behavior engagement [7]. To those anticipating CFL learners, non-participation in school-related activities will lead to emotional withdrawal and lack of identification with the school [6]. Under such estranged feelings and an isolated Chinese learning environment that contributes to the dropout problem [5], they may have a lower level of emotional engagement [11].

To those nervous CFL learners, TAs play a vital role in improving their behavioral and emotional engagement. With support from TAs, these beginning learners tried to overcome difficulties in Chinese learning and enhanced their emotional engagement. At the same time, it is found their cognitive engagement and behavioral engagement improved. Finn and Zimmer (2012) demonstrated that engagement can be manipulated to enhance educational performance and brought about significant payoffs for students at risk of school failure, which works in concert with this study [6]. These findings also support the result of Reschly, Pohl and Christenson, that while negative emotions may narrow learners' attention and behavior, positive emotions are argued to broaden attention and behavior [7].

The case of X2 appears to be an exceptional category in her learning engagement. As a confident CFL Learner who has high self-efficacy and proficiency in Chinese learning, she also exhibits relatively high behavioral engagement. Similar to the finding of Choi (2005), those "who have a high degree of self-perceptions tend to attain higher academic achievement" (p. 204) [12]. Despite her high proficiency in Chinese, X2 still recognized the field that she was not very good at (for example, knowledge about *Pinyin*), and knew the strategy to improve her Chinese in her own spare time (e.g., reading novels and news articles). It is her confidence in Chinese learning that contributes to her high behavioral engagement in return.

Although much effort has been made to increase the trustworthiness of mixed research with features of both quantitative and qualitative research, some limitations are unavoidable in this preliminary education research. First, as a multi-case education study of 13 participants, the population is relatively small, and the quantitative result can reflect only partially the learning engagement features of distance international students, especially those in some less developed countries in Asia and Africa. So, qualitative data like learning profiles and semi-structured interviews were collected for the effect of compensation. Besides, this study only takes the CFL courses as the research object, therefore, it's uncertain whether these results will be applicable to other online courses. Thus, more future researches are necessary to be conducted on distance international students with larger sample size, in others regions of the world, and/or in other online courses.

5   Research Significance and Implications

Although this study is driven by the teaching practice under the influence of the Covid-19 pandemic, research on students' engagement in online courses is still of high importance. With the ever-changing development of technology, online learning has become an indispensable part of future education, especially the international distance courses that are designed in one country and taken by international students in other countries. In order to improve students' learning engagement in terms of behavior, emotion, and cognition, this study provides certain implications for international online course design:

First of all, enough consideration should be allocated to various gaps between the countries of the course designer and course addressee, including digital gaps and time differences. Thus, online learning strategies for that specific course are supposed to be highlighted either in the course orientation or throughout the course. Then, alternative forms of learning materials and exercises should be designed to match the variety of students' cognitive and behavioral features. In addition, both synchronized and asynchronized discussions should be supplied to facilitate communication between teachers and students in different time zones.

Secondly, the accessibility of one-on-one tutoring is important to smooth students' learning anxiety, and thus boost their learning engagement. Given the non-linear interaction between the components between behavioral engagement, emotional engagement, and cognitive engagement, an abnormal fluctuation in behavioral engagement might indicate a possible fluctuation in students' emotional or cognitive engagement. With the help of teachers or teacher assistants, an adjustment in students' emotional engagement may also contribute to the improvement in behavioral and cognitive engagement.

Acknowledgment. The authors gratefully acknowledge the research project supported by the 15th Batch of "National Training Program for College Students' Innovation and Entrepreneurship" Project (CXCYGJ20210098), and Project of Zhejiang Association of International Education (FHKT2022018).

Appendix 1: Questionnaire on Online Learning Engagement

Dear friends:

Thanks for taking the time to complete this questionnaire. This research seeks to understand factors that may influence your engagement in distance learning and your opinions and suggestions for your teaching assistant (TA). The whole questionnaire may take you five to ten minutes. Your information will be greatly valued. When it comes to personal information, we promise not to let it out.

Name in Passport:

Student number:

Choice Question (If the question is marked with "*", you can choose more choices):

Q1: How much do you like Chinese? ()
    A. very simple B. simple C. average D. difficult E. very difficult.

*Q2: Which part is difficult in your Chinese learning this semester? ().
    A. Pinyin rules B. Reading C. Speaking D. Translation E. Writing.

Q3: How much time per week do you spend in learning Chinese after class? ()
    A. more than 5 h B. about 3–5 h.
    C. about 1–2 h D. less than 1 h.

*Q4: What do you think of Chinese learning in form of distance education? ().
    A. I always feel nervous about distance learning.
    B. I find it a useful method as we are not able to have face-to-face classroom education at present.
    C. I think it reduces the communication between my classmates.
    D. It influences my efficiency in learning Chinese.

Q5: Do you often communicate with teachers in Class? ()
   A. Yes B. No.

Further question:

*If yes, why or how can you benefit from communicating with teachers in class? ( )
   A. I can follow teachers' lectures better.
   B. I can get more information from teachers.
   C. I can get teachers' feedback quickly.
   D. I can release my negative emotions

*If not, what hinders your communication in class? ( )
   A. Internet problem
   B. I am not accustomed to answering teachers' questions in class learning habit
   C. I am not accustomed to interrupting teachers' lectures in class
   D. I am too shy to communicate in class
   E. I have difficulty keeping up with class

Q6: Do you often contact the teacher or your TA? ()
   A. Yes B. No.

Further questions:

*If yes, how can you benefit from the contact with the teacher or your TA? ( )
   A. It improves my level of learning Chinese.
   B. It helps me ease my anxiety, tension, worry, fatigue, or something else.
   C. It makes me feel closer to my teacher and TA.
   D. It gives me confidence in learning Chinese.

*If not, what hinders your contact with the teacher or TA? ( )
   A. the degree of interest in Chinese
   B. time difference between China and my home country
   C. shortage of electronic equipment
   D. less available time

Q7: Have the questions you asked been answered and resolved? ()
   A. All of them B. Most of themC. Part of them D. None of them.

Q8: How long does it usually take to get feedback from TAs? ()
   A. 1–3 Days B. 3–7 Days C.7–15 Days D. more than 15 Days.

Q9: Can you understand the TA'S homework feedback? ()
   A. All of them B. Most of themC. Part of themD. None of them.

Q10: Do you like the form of TAs' feedback? ()
   A. Yes B. No.

Further questions (short-answer questions):

*If yes, how have you benefited from TAs?

*If not, what is your suggestion to improve TAs' work?

Thank you very much for your support and cooperation!

Appendix 2: Semi-structure Interview Questions

Factors that influence online learning

- What factors influenced your interest in online Chinese learning this semester?
- Did you have any difficulty learning Chinese online?
- How many hours did you invest in Chinese learning after class? What factor influenced the amount of time?
- How about your class attendance? Would you please explain the causes provided you missed any classes?

Comments on Chinese learning experience in the distance learning context

- Which one do you prefer, online Chinese teaching under the guidance of teaching assistants or face-to-face teaching?
- What do you think are the shortcomings of Chinese teaching in the distance learning context? How to improve it?
- Do you think learning Chinese online this semester is effective? Why or why not?

Comments on contact with the teachers and TAs

- Did you often ask your teaching assistant for help when it comes to questions? Why or why not?
- Do you feel that we, as teaching assistants, have been helpful to you? In what ways have we truly helped you?
- Do you have any expectations for this way of online Chinese learning with the help of teaching assistants?

References

1. Wen, Q., Yang, J.: Analysis of strategic values of online Chinese language education through comparative study of online language education by international institutes under the epidemic COVID-19. Lang. Teach. Res. (period 6), 1–8 (2020)
2. Song, F., Zhang, M.: Application of online virtual reality technology in Chinese teaching. Int. Chin. Educ. **6**, 91–100 (2021)
3. Qiu, J., Bei, Y.: Research on the online course construction for advanced comprehensive Chinese courses under the background of normalization. Int. Chin. Educ. **6**, 3–11 (2021)
4. Jing, W.: Innovation and development of international Chinese online education and online teaching resources construction. Int. Chin. Lang. Educ. **6**, 3–6 (2021)
5. Fredricks, J.A., Blumenfeld, P.C., Paris, A.H.: School engagement: potential of the concept, state of the evidence. Rev. Educ. Res. **74**, 59–109 (2004)
6. Finn, J.D., Zimmer, K.S.: Student engagement: What is it? Why does it matter?. In: Christenson, S.L., et al. (eds.) Handbook of Research on Student Engagement, pp. 97–131. Springer, Boston (2012). https://doi.org/10.1007/978-1-4614-2018-7_5

7. Reschly, A.L., Pohl, A.J., Christenson, S.L. (eds.): Springer, Cham (2020). https://doi.org/10.1007/978-3-030-37285-9

8. Yang, X., Zhou, X., Hu, J.: Students' preferences for seating arrangements and their engagement in cooperative learning activities in college English blended learning classrooms in higher education. High. Educ. Res. Dev. (2021). https://doi.org/10.1080/07294360.2021.1901667

9. Creswell, J.W.: Research Design: Qualitative, Quantitative and Mixed Methods Approaches, 4th edn. SAGE, Los Angeles (2014)

10. Yu, J., Zhou, X., Yang, X., Hu, J.: Mobile-assisted or paper-based? The influence of the reading medium on the reading comprehension of English as a foreign language. Comput. Assist. Lang. Learn. **35**, 1–2, 217–245 (2022)

11. Salta, K., Paschalidou, K., Tsetseri, M., Koulougliotis, D.: Shift from a traditional to a distance learning environment during the COVID-19 pandemic. Sci. Educ. **31**, 93–122 (2021)

12. Choi, N.: Self-efficacy and self-concept as predictors of college students' academic performance. Psychol. Sch. **42**, 197–205 (2005)

Bibliometric Analysis for Intelligent Assessment of Data Visualization

Jimei Li[(✉)], Lai Chulin, Xinyu Li, and Qian He

School of Information Science, Beijing Language and Culture University, Beijing, China
ljm@blcu.edu.cn

Abstract. In the era of digital economy, high-quality visualization of data can better support decision making to show the value of data. In this paper, data visualization journal papers and conference proceedings papers were obtained through CNKI, and the annual number of published papers, literature sources, literature authors and hot keywords were counted. We have analyzed the statistical results from the whole to the specific order to get the current development status of data visualization and given the future development trend, especially for intelligent assessment of data visualization works, which can improve the popularization rate of data visualization, promote the development of data visualization technology, and give full play to the deep value of big data.

Keywords: Big Data · Data Visualization · Digital Economy · Intelligent Assessment · Bibliometrics

1 Introduction

After 2011, the amount of data began to rise exponentially with the development of information sciences and technology. The big data has played an irreplaceable role in many fields [1]. As the saying goes "A picture is worth ten thousand words" [2]. People are usually more willing to obtain information in the form of images [3]. The required technology is data visualization.

Data visualization is a scientific and technical study on the visual representation of data [4, 5]. It displays the results of data processing through visualization. Data visualization has made many outstanding research achievements in big data processing on how to better deal with diverse data types and improve real-time data transmission [6]. As data has become indispensable in people's daily life and almost every field involved data, it is an important research topic of how to improve the popularity rate of data visualization and enable more talents in other fields to quickly master data visualization technology in order to give full play to the infinite value behind big data [7].

In addition, the tremendous value of real-time data can be creatively found through effective visualization. Therefore, more and more people have begun to engage in the research of data visualization and integrate various fields with data visualization [8, 9].

This paper used bibliometric methods to find journal papers and conference papers related to data visualization. Through the analysis of the annual number of papers,

W. Hong and Y. Weng (Eds.): ICCSE 2022, CCIS 1811, pp. 363–373, 2023.
https://doi.org/10.1007/978-981-99-2443-1_32

authors and keywords, this paper drew some current development trends and future development possibilities in the field, and gave some ideas for promoting the popularity and development of data visualization technology.

2   Data Acquisition

In order to ensure the accuracy of the search data, we determined that the scope of the search was CNKI's Chinese Journals Full-text Database as well as the Chinese and International Conference Papers Full-text Database. The "data visualization" and the synonym "information visualization" were used as the subject words for accurate search. The time range of literature release was set from *January 1, 2012* to *December 31, 2021*, and the search date was *March 27, 2022*. A total of 9,574 academic journals and 469 Chinese and international conference records were obtained, including 420 Chinese conference papers and 49 international conference papers. The obtained journal papers as well as Chinese and international conference papers were used as analysis data to carry out relevant specific statistical analysis, and we conducted statistics and analysis of the annual number of documents, literature sources, authors, and related hot keywords [10, 11].

3   Literature Analysis Method

Bibliometric analysis method makes use of the law of publication of research papers, based on quantitative research methods such as mathematical statistics, and uses visual analysis method to directly explain the internal relationship between different research categories. Especially for the visualization of key words, core author groups and all kinds of co-occurrence, it can scientifically and effectively predict the development trend and trend of scientific research [12, 13].

This paper made a statistical analysis of the obtained literature from three dimensions, analyzed the overall development trend from the total number of documents published, and then analyzed the source and author of the literature to understand the research groups in the field of data visualization. Finally, it detailed the hot keywords and analyzed the hot research direction of data visualization.

A complete analysis of the literature related to data visualization was carried out from whole to refinement as following.

1) The development status of data visualization field from 2012 to 2021 was analyzed from the annual number of documents published, in order to analyze the development trend in the future.
2) The data visualization research community and the current development status of the field was analyzed through statistical literature sources and authors.
3) We performed statistical analysis of keywords in the literature to understand research hotspots and research trends in the field of data visualization.

4 Statistical Analysis Results of the Literature

4.1 Volume Analysis

In this paper, 9,574 journal papers and 469 conference papers obtained were counted in the unit of year, and a bar chart of publication volume from 2012 to 2021 was drawn to observe the development stage of data visualization in the past 10 years and inferred the future development trend [14, 15]. The data showed that the number of articles was increasing at a relatively stable rate, and the research on data visualization was developing gradually.

1) Preliminary development stage: In 2012, there were only 582 articles, which was still a small literature volume stage. In comparison, from 2012 to 2014, the growth rate of articles was relatively slow, the number of articles was increasing by about 50 every year, indicating that the development of data visualization was still in the preliminary stage, there were not so many industries to combine with data visualization, and there were relatively few studies on data visualization.
2) Rapid development stage: From 2015 to 2021, the number of articles published increased at a fast speed, with the annual increase of more than 100 articles and even 152 articles from 2014 to 2015. In addition, in 2017, the annual number of articles exceeded 1,000, reaching 1,076. In 2021, the number of annual papers has reached 1,414, accounting for 14.1% of the total number of papers. Data visualization was developing rapidly at this time, and the academic research on data visualization has entered the upsurge stage.

In general, the number of research papers on data visualization has been on a steady rise, with the growth rate fluctuating only in a small range. The annual number of papers published in 2021 was basically 2.4 times that of 2012. More and more papers were related to data visualization, and the number of papers was likely to continue to grow steadily after that. With the development of science and technology and the increasing amount of data, more and more attention has been paid to the research of data visualization in the academic circle, and the amount of literatures has also increased, as is shown in Fig. 1.

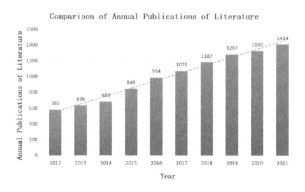

Fig. 1. Comparison of Annual Publications of "Data Visualization" Literature

4.2 Literature Source Analysis

Journal Source Analysis

In this paper, the number of articles published in the source journals was calculated according to 5,400 journals that provided complete source journals.

Table 1. Statistics of journals with an article volume greater than or equal to 10

Serial Number	Periodical	Volume of Posts
1	Software Guide	11
1	Computer Science	11
1	Computer Measurement and Control	11
1	Computer Engineering and Applications	11
1	Journal of System Simulation	11
6	Software	10
6	Devise	10
6	Journal of Computer-Aided Design and Graphics	10
6	Computer System Applications	10
6	Computer Science and Exploration	10
6	Computer	10
6	Computer Engineering	10
6	Computer and Digital Engineering	10
6	Automation & Instrumentation	10
6	Technology Horizons	10
6	Technology Dissemination	10
6	Fujian Computer	10
6	Computer Programming Skills and Maintenance	10
6	Computer Knowledge and Technology	10
6	Electronic Design Engineering	10
6	Surveying and Mapping Bulletin	10
6	Surveying and Mapping Science	10
6	Mapping Geographic Information	10
6	Mapping and Spatial Geographic Information	10
6	Digital Technologies and Applications	10
6	Intelligence Science	10
6	Intelligence Theory and Practice	10
6	Intelligence Exploration	10
6	Geospatial Information	10

(*continued*)

Table 1. (*continued*)

Serial Number	Periodical	Volume of Posts
6	Geographic Information World	10
6	Journal of Graphics	10
6	Packaging Engineering	10
6	Chinese Numeral Medicine	10
6	China Media Technology	10
6	Chinese Journal of Medical Library and Information	10

Table 1 shows journals with publications of 10 or more. Among them, "Software Guide", "Computer Science", "Computer Measurement and Control", "Computer Engineering and Application" and "Journal of System Simulation" had the most publications. This was followed by 30 journals with 10 articles. From the statistical journal names, data visualization papers were mostly in the key words of "computer", "software", "computer", "mapping" and "information" journals.

However, the journals with the largest number of publications accounted for only 0.2% of the total number of publications, indicating that the literatures on data visualization were published in scattered journals, and there were almost no journals specialized in data visualization.

Analysis of Conference Proceedings
We made conference source statistics for 376 conference papers with complete conference sources, and there were 16 conferences with more than 4 papers in total.

Table 2 shows the names of conferences with four or more publications. The Annual Conference of Chinese Urban Planning and The Annual Conference of Chinese Meteorological Society had the largest number of articles, which was 8. The second one was The Annual Conference of Information Technology in Electric Power Industry, and the number of articles published was 7. The next one had 6 articles, including China Command and Control Conference, China Earth Science Association Annual Conference and Annual Meeting of the Hydraulic Society.

Through the statistics of the conference categories, it was found that the categories were basically different, and were almost other areas of the conference. We could conclude that data visualization has been applied in many other fields [16], and organically combined with other fields such as "urban planning", "meteorology", "electricity" and so on [17].

However, the number of papers published in China Urban Planning Annual Conference and China Meteorological Society Annual Conference with the largest number of papers accounted for only 2.1% of the general conference, indicating that the academic community basically did not set up special conferences related to data visualization.

Literature Author Analysis
The maturity of authors in this field can be understood by analyzing the amount of authors' publications [18, 19]. Table 3 lists the authors with more than 13 papers and their affiliated institutions. It shows that among 10,043 journal and conference papers,

Table 2. Statistics of meetings with an issue of articles greater than or equal to 4

Serial Number	Meeting	Number of Posts Posted
1	The Annual Conference of Chinese Urban Planning	8
1	The Annual Conference of Chinese Meteorological Society	8
3	The Annual Conference of Information Technology in Electric Power Industry	7
4	China Command and Control Conference	6
4	China Earth Science Association Annual Conference	6
4	Annual Meeting of the Hydraulic Society	6
7	National Conference on Psychology	5
7	China Intelligent Transportation Annual Conference	5
9	Academic Exchange Meeting of Surveying and Mapping Societies in Six Provinces and One City in East China	4
9	National BIM Academic Conference	4
9	China Management School Year's Meeting	4
9	National Conference on Signal and Intelligent Information Processing and Application	4
9	National Seminar on Teaching and Research of Digital Technology in Architecture	4
9	Smart Grid Conference	4
9	Industrial Design Research	4
9	China Federation of Journalists and Technicians	4

Chen Yi has the largest number of papers (27), followed by Hou Jianhua, Chen Wei, Zhao Ying. Price's law states that only half of all papers in a research field are written by key authors in that field. According to Price's law,

$$N = 0.749 * (Nmax)^{1/2}$$

(N represents the lowest number of papers published by core authors, and Nmax represents the number of papers published by the most productive authors).

$$N \approx 0.749 * (27)^{1/2} \approx 4$$

N was calculated by analyzing the author data of 10043 papers and conference proceedings on "data visualization". A total of 529 authors with at least 4 papers were obtained, accounting for 2.59% of the total number of authors. The number of papers published was 2,863, accounting for 28.5% of the total number of papers, less than half

Table 3. Authors and Affiliates with a Volume Greater Than or Equal to 13

Serial Number	Author	Number of Posts Posted	Affiliation
1	Chen Yi	27	Beijing Technology and Business University
2	Hou Jianhua	21	Dalian University
3	Chen Wei	19	State Key Laboratory of CAD&CG, Zhejiang University
4	Zhao Ying	16	School of Information Science and Engineering, Central South University
5	Chen Hongqian	15	Beijing Technology and Business University
5	Qiu Junping	15	Wuhan University
7	Wu Yadong	13	Southwest University of Science and Technology
7	Zhao Rongying	13	Wuhan University

of all papers. It could be concluded that the high-yield author group has not yet formed [20].

Literature Keyword Analysis

Keywords are the author's refinement of academic papers. Keywords that appear frequently in a field are often regarded as research hot issues. High-frequency keywords to some extent reflect the basic trend of research in a certain field [21].

In this paper, VOSviewer was used to study the keywords in the literature [22]. It was found that there were 1,392 keywords that appeared more than or equal to five times in the literature, which were divided into 21 groups, as is shown in Fig. 2.

Table 4 shows hot keywords with frequencies greater than or equal to 80. Among them, "Visualization" appeared most frequently, with a total frequency of 4,371 in Both Chinese and English. "Data visualization" followed with 2,042 occurrences in Both Chinese and English, followed by "Information visualization," "Big Data", "Visual analytics", "Data journalism". "Citespace", "Python", "Echarts" and "Data Mining" were tools for visualizing big data [23, 24].

Through in-depth research on visualization tools, we could better get the information hidden behind the data [25], so that big data could play its role more fully. "Data journalism", "Knowledge graph", "Bibliometrics" and "Geographic information system" applied big data to news generation, knowledge graph construction, bibliometrics and other fields and solved practical problems in them [26].

This shows that the cross research and mutual combination of big data and other fields were getting good development.

Among the literature, there were only a few articles related to big data visualization teaching [17, 18], and there was no keyword of "Intelligent assessment" found in the literature. It could be seen that the research on data visualization teaching has not been widely concerned.

Fig. 2. Relationship between Keywords in the "Data Visualization" Literature

Table 4. Word Frequency Statistics of Keywords in the "Data Visualization" Literature

Serial Number	Keyword	Frequency
1	Visualization	4,371
2	Data visualization	2,042
3	Big data	1,482
4	Information visualization	1,251
5	Visual analytics	740
6	3D visualization	635
7	Data mining	547
8	Data journalism	494
9	Data analysis	430
10	Knowledge Graph	375
11	Citespace	259

(continued)

Table 4. (*continued*)

Serial Number	Keyword	Frequency
12	Gis	197
13	Visualization technology	180
14	Bim	148
15	Research hotspots	141
16	Python	118
17	Visual analysis	110
18	Data acquisition	108
19	Big data visualization	106
20	Bibliometrics	103
20	Geographic information system	103
22	Visualization analysis	97
23	Bibliometrics	94
24	The era of big data	93
25	Data processing	90
26	Echarts	84
26	Visual management	84
28	Information technology	80

5 Conclusion

In the data-driven environment of big data era, data visualization is indispensable. In this paper, we used bibliometrics software to statistically analyze the current hot spots and development trends of data visualization. It can be concluded that data visualization is in the stage of rapid development, and there have been many research papers organically combined with other research fields. It was also found that the academic community has not formed a corresponding organization or group of authors to do special long-term research on data visualization [27].

In addition, through our investigation and literature search, we found that data visualization has not been extensively studied in teaching, and almost no literature and words related to intelligent assessment have appeared [28, 29]. In the major automatic evaluation software, there was almost no automatic evaluation function for data visualization without code. In the face of the increasing number of learners of data visualization, the demand for data visualization problems to achieve automatic evaluation results also increased. If visual works can be added into the automatic evaluation function, it may improve the efficiency of learners' visual learning. When we no longer need a large number of manual participation in the evaluation of visualization works, we can meet the needs of people to learn data visualization skills by themselves, so as to solve the teaching pressure caused by the increasing demand for a certain amount of contemporary visualization skills [30, 31].

In this paper, we propose that further research on data visualization teaching can be strengthened in the future. In the teaching of data visualization without code, manual correction of learners' works can be optimized for automatic evaluation of works, so that stand-alone training and manual evaluation can be transformed into online intelligent assessment. By replacing manual correction of visual results of learners, it will be convenient for people to teach without code data visualization, improve teaching efficiency and reduce the waste of human resources [32]. At the same time, it can also reduce the learning cost of data visualization, and facilitate more people who are interested in code zero basis to start the learning road of data visualization. When more and more people are exposed to data visualization, it will greatly promote the development of data visualization. We will also continue to make efforts for the future development and innovation of data visualization, so that big data can be better used to provide greater value realization, and contribute to social development and better life [33, 34].

Acknowledgment. This work was partly supported by Research on International Chinese Language Education of the Center for Language Education and Cooperation "Research on identification and influence of teaching methods of International Chinese Education based on classroom video" (No. 21YH11C), by New Liberal Arts Program of Ministry of Education (No. 2021180006), by New Engineering Program of Ministry of Education (No. E-SXWLHXLX 20202604), by the Cooperative Education Program of the Ministry of Education (NO. 202101110002), and by the Science Foundation of Beijing Language and Cultural University (supported by "the Fundamental Research Funds for the Central Universities") (No. 22YJ080004).

References

1. Cheng, X., Jin, X., Wang, Y., Guo, J., Zhang, T., Li, G.: Big data system and analysis technology review. J. Softw. **25**(9), 1889–1908 (2014). https://doi.org/10.13328/j.cnkijos.004674
2. Ren, L., Du, Y., Ma, S., Zhang, X., Dai, G.: Big data visual analysis review. J. Softw. **25**(9), 1909–1936 (2014). https://doi.org/10.13328/j.cnkijos.004645
3. Zeng, Y.: Research on the Concept of Data visualization in the Context of Big Data Era. Zhejiang University (2014)
4. Zuo, Y., Wang, Y., Jiang, S., et al.: A review of data visualization analysis. Sci. Technol. Innov. **11**, 82–83 (2019)
5. Tu, C.: Big data era under the background of data visualization application study. J. Electron. (5), 118 (2013). https://doi.org/10.16589/j.cn11-3571/tn.2013.05.069
6. Wei, C.: Visualization and visual analysis of big data. Electron. Finan. **11**, 62–65 (2015)
7. Liu, Z., Zhang, Q.: Big data technology research review. J. Zhejiang Univ. (Eng. Sci.) **6**(13), 957–972 (2014)
8. Di, C., Guo, X., Wei, C.: The latest progress in the challenge of data visualization. J. Comput. Appl. **5**(7), 2044–2049 + 2056 (2017)
9. Wei, W.: Structural characteristics and hot spots in the field of big data and social governance in China: bibliometric and visual analysis based on CNKI. J. Leshan Normal Univ. **33**(01), 102–109+119 (2018). https://doi.org/10.16069/j.cnki.51-1610/g4.2018.01.016

10. Chen, J., Xie, W., Chen, Y., Li, Z.: A comparative study of academic papers on big data visualization at home and abroad: based on bibliometric and SNA methods. Sci. Technol. Manag. Res. **37**(08), 44–53 (2017)

11. Raparelli, E., Lolletti, D.: Research, innovation and development on Corylus avellana through the bibliometric approach. Int. J. Fruit Sci., 1–17 (2020)

12. Li, H., Yuan, C., Li, Y.: Big data based on bibliometrics research review. J. Intell. Sci. **32**(6), 148–155 (2014). https://doi.org/10.13833/j.cnkiis.2014.06.026

13. Qiu, J., Su, J., Xiong, Z.: Based on bibliometrics, information resource management research at home and abroad comparative analysis. J. Chin. Libr. (05), 37–45 (2008)

14. Yang, R.: Big data research literature measurement analysis. J. Intell. Sci. (8), 152–156 (2015). https://doi.org/10.13833/j.carolcarrollnkiis.2015.08.028

15. Li, Y., Qi, X.: CiteSpace-based government WeChat research literature measurement and research trend analysis. Procedia Comput. Sci. **199**, 665–673 (2022)

16. He, Q.: Development and application of visualization technology. West China Sci. Technol. **04**, 4–7 (2008)

17. Gao, Z., Niu, K., Liu, J.: For big data analysis technology. J. Beijing Univ. Posts Telecommun. **20**(3), 1–12 (2015). https://doi.org/10.13190/j.jbupt.2015.03.001

18. Ren, H., Zhang, Z.: Scientific knowledge map based on bibliometrics development research. J. Intell. **28**(12), 86–90 (2009)

19. Wang, F.: Visual analysis of big data research based on knowledge graph. J. North China Univ. Sci. Technol. (Soc. Sci. Ed.) **17**(01), 56–62 (2017)

20. Huang, Y.: Bibliometric analysis of digital research on teaching Chinese as a foreign language. In: Proceedings of the 11th International Symposium on the Modernization of Chinese Teaching, pp. 313–321 (2018)

21. Kai, G.: Application research of document metrology analysis software VOSviewer. Sci. Technol. Inf. Dev. Econ. **25**(12), 95–98 (2015)

22. Tang, G., Feng, Z., Li, D., Ai, X.: Review and prospect of industrial internet: based on bibliometric analysis. Comput. Integr. Manuf. Syst., 1-21 (2021)

23. Pei, D.: Realization of data visualization based on ECharts. Beijing University of Posts and Telecommunications (2018)

24. Xiao, H.: Research review of Python technology in data visualization. Electron. Test (13), 87–89 (2021). https://doi.org/10.16520/j.cnki.1000-8519.2021.13.029

25. Yong, G.E.: Feasibility analysis of production data visualization based on Python. Hongshui River **40**(4), 138–141 (2021)

26. Chen, J., Yu, Z., Zhu, Y.: Infrared and laser engineering (05), 339–342 (2001)

27. Liu, K., Zhou, X., Zhou, D.: Research and development of data visualization. Comput. Eng. (08), 1–2+63 (2002)

28. Yang, Y., Liu, B., Qi, M.: Information visualization research review. J. Hebei Univ. Sci. Technol. **35**(01), 91–102 (2014)

29. Yang, B., Lu, G., Cao, S., Goh, T.-T.: Research on data visualization evaluation standard of online learning system. Educ. China (12), 54–61 + 80 (2017). https://doi.org/10.13541/j.cnki chinade.20171222.010

30. Liu, W., Qi, Z., Wang, M.: Automatic subjective topic assessment study. J. Beijing Univ. Posts Telecommun. (Soc. Sci. Ed.) **17**(4), 108–116 (2016)

31. Liu, B., et al.: Review of data visualization research. J. Hebei Univ. Sci. Technol. **42**(06), 643–654 (2021)

32. Wang, Y.: Literature review of big data and information visualization. Ind. Des. **04**, 121–122 (2018)

33. Chu, Z.: The application research of automatic evaluation assisted teaching platform. J. Liaoning Univ. Technol. (Soc. Sci. Ed.) **19**(05), 133–135 (2017)

34. Jing, P.: Research on visualization of information evaluation. Libr. Inf. Serv. **03**, 74–76 (2008)

A Study to Evaluate Training Systems for Reducing Sensory Conflict Using Virtual Reality

Zhehang Jin[1], Keisuke Tsukamoto[1], Hironari Sugai[1], Yuuya Usami[1], Masaru Miyao[2], Tomoki Shiozawa[3], Masumi Takada[4], Kikuo Ito[5], and Hiroki Takada[1(✉)]

[1] Graduate School of Engineering, University of Fukui, Fukui 910-8507, Japan
takada@u-fukui.ac.jp
[2] Nagoya Industrial Science Research Institute, Nagoya 456-0058, Japan
[3] School of Business, Aoyama Gakuin University, Tokyo 150-8366, Japan
[4] Department of Nursing, Chubu Gakuin University, Gifu 504-0837, Japan
[5] Neuro Sky Co. Ltd., Tokyo 103-0014, Japan

Abstract. Walking is an aerobic exercise that can help prevent lifestyle-related diseases. Indoor training using a treadmill or ergometer can be used as a substitute for outdoor walking. However, during such indoor training, sensory conflicts between the vestibular and visual systems may occur, potentially inducing motion sickness. Notably, virtual reality (VR) can be used to create a realistic sensation of outdoor walking. Therefore, the purpose of this study was to develop a VR system for reducing sensory conflicts and evaluating patients' biological conditions. As a result, we gained a deeper understanding of the types of VR images able to reduce sensory conflicts.

Keywords: 3D images · Virtual reality (VR) · VR sickness · Visually induced motion sickness (VIMS) · Stabilometry

1 Introduction

Walking is an aerobic exercise, and it is well-known that walking can help prevent lifestyle-related diseases [1]. Virtual reality (VR) can be used to create a sense of realism when training indoors on a treadmill or ergometer as a substitute for outdoor walking. Previous research [2] has shown that a treatment combining VR, e.g., viewing 3D images using a head-mounted display (HMD) and treadmill exercise, can alter brain activity and dramatically reduce fall accidents in patients with Parkinson's disease and other neurodegenerative disorders. Training using treadmills and ergometers as a substitute for outdoor walking has also gained popularity in view of the coronavirus disaster, and there are apps being used overseas for training in VR [3].

However, VR uses 3D images. As such, certain corresponding health concerns remain unresolved, such as those concerning 3D image viewing causing eye fatigue, motion sickness, and other unpleasant symptoms [4].

© The Author(s), under exclusive license to Springer Nature Singapore Pte Ltd. 2023
W. Hong and Y. Weng (Eds.): ICCSE 2022, CCIS 1811, pp. 374–384, 2023.
https://doi.org/10.1007/978-981-99-2443-1_33

Video-induced motion sickness (VIMS) is affected by auditory [5], visual [6, 7], olfactory [8], and deep sensory [9] factors. In early studies, the mechanism of the onset of motion sickness was explained using overstimulation theory. According to this theory, the acceleration of the vehicle in which the affected individual is riding overstimulates the internal and vestibular organs and excites the hypothalamus, inducing vestibular-autonomic reflexes and causing various symptoms of motion sickness to occur. However, as motion sickness was discovered even in microgravity environments in the latter half of the 20th century, the overstimulation theory was rejected, and it became necessary to further elucidate the mechanism(s) of motion sickness.

According to the sensory conflict theory [10, 11], actual sensory information such as visual, vestibular, and somatosensory information is compared with information from past experiences in the central nervous system. Only when the combination of sensory information differs from what would be expected from memory is motion sickness induced [12]. Vestibular stimuli are transmitted via the vestibular-autonomic nervous system to the area postrema (vomiting center) in the medulla oblongata. The vestibular and autonomic nervous systems are closely linked anatomically and electrophysiologically, strongly suggesting that the relationship between them is involved in the unpleasant symptoms of motion sickness [13]. When rats are subjected to a rotational load for inducing motion sickness, the histamine levels in the brainstem and hypothalamus increase; this has been found to be related to vomiting at the onset of motion sickness [14].

The severity of motion sickness can be quantitatively assessed by analyzing the body sway, which is considered as an output of the equilibrium system. In general, visual information helps subjects to maintain an upright posture. Thus, in the test with eyes open, it is difficult to obtain significant differences regarding the sway values estimated from the stabilometry, such as area of sway, total locus length, and total locus length per unit area [15]. Recently, numerical analyses of mathematical models for the body sway have shown the possibility of obtaining significant differences in the test with eyes open [16]. In addition, studies have considered autonomic neurodynamics when tracking the severity of motion sickness [17, 18]. The initial symptoms are seen to be associated with increased parasympathetic activity [18]. In addition, although the exact mechanism is unknown, theories of "discrepancy between convergence and lens body segment" and "effect of excessive disparity" have been proposed as causes of the fatigue caused by stereopsis, in addition to differences in individual visual functions. The former theory states that a discrepancy between the convergence distance and lens accommodation distance causes visual fatigue and increases the adjustment load. We have shown that this theory, despite being common, does not explain stereoscopic VIMS [15]. The latter theory states that the stereoscopic disparity increases to emphasize the stereoscopic effect.

The effects of binocular stereoscopic display systems on our bodies can be explained by the discrepancy between the convergence and lens body segment. During stereopsis, we only focus on the surface of the display and simultaneously adjust our convergence to the three-dimensional objects popping out from it, resulting in a discrepancy between the convergence and lens accommodation [19–21]. Many researchers believe that there is a discrepancy between the convergence distance and adjustment distance during stereopsis, but it has also been reported that the lens body segment is not necessarily fixed to the surface of the display during stereopsis [22]. The mechanism of VR viewing and sickness may vary depending on the type of VR viewing device. In particular, there are very limited research examples of VR viewing using HMDs, which have been rapidly increasing in recent years.

Table 1. Characteristics by Viewing Method

	Panoramic Exposure	Synchronization of Vertical Movement	Projection of 3D Images
Screen	± (weak)	+	Liquid Crystal Shutter
Liquid-Crystal Display	-	+	Circular Polarization, etc.
Augmented Reality (AR)	±	±	HMD
Virtual Reality (VR)	+	-	HMD

The effectiveness of an exercise method combining VR and a treadmill is summarized in Table 1. When VR is not used, there are limitations on the surfaces that images can be projected on, and significant distortions owing to the construction of the laboratory. In contrast, in VR viewing, goggles are worn and information from the outside world is completely blocked. Therefore, the information does not move up and down when walking, which is different from what someone would naturally see when walking. In general, there have been relatively few studies on the relationship between VR viewing discomfort symptoms and indoor simulation training systems (treadmills and ergometers). However, for the development of the industry in this field and the widespread use of these therapies, it is necessary to study their relationships with VR viewing, and to develop VR systems that can diminish the sensory conflict.

Therefore, in this study, experiments combining VR and an indoor simulation training system were conducted to investigate the effects of sensory conflicts between the vestibular and visual systems on an organism.

This paper was written based on the papers cited [23].

2   Material and Method

In this study, the subjects wore an HMD and walked on a treadmill while viewing an image (Fig. 1). In the experiment, the subject walked on the treadmill for 300 s, at a speed of 5 km/h while viewing the image from the first-person viewpoint with the HMD. An omni-directional portable action camera L-FL360 (LET'S) was used to capture the images of running at a constant speed of.

(1)   0 km/h (static image),
(2)   3 km/h,
(3)   5 km/h,

(4)   8 km/h (4.5 mph).

The various image sequences (Fig. 2) were presented to subjects in an arbitrary order, and not necessarily in the order given above.

In this study, to investigate the biological effects of VR viewing during walking, the test items were the stabilometry, motion capture using a web camera, electroencephalogram /electrocardiogram, and subjective evaluation (i.e., the Simulator Sickness Questionnaire (SSQ)). The experimental protocol is shown in Fig. 3. In addition to the measurement of the stabilometry and motion capture before and after walking, the amount of change in the SSQ subscore was also tracked. The data obtained from motion capture was evaluated using PoseNet to estimate the subject's body inclination, stride length, and walking speed. The vision model was based on a skeletonization of the body (Fig. 4).

Fig. 1. Experimental scene

Fig. 2. Typical example of driving video

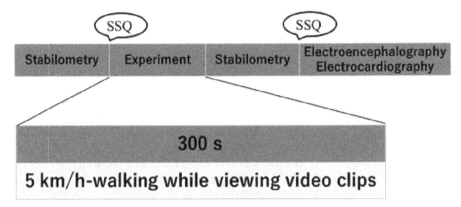

Fig. 3. Experimental protocol

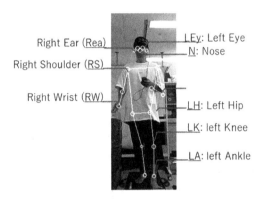

Fig. 4. Skeletonization of the body

We considered the stabilometry and SSQ among the above-mentioned test methods for the purpose of weighing degrees of intoxication. The Wii Balance Board (Nintendo) was used for the stabilometry. The sampling frequency was 100 Hz, and was resampled at 20 Hz. The experimental posture was the standing Lomberg posture, and the eyes were opened and closed before and after walking for 60 s each.

This study was approved by the Research Ethics Committee for Human Subjects, Department of Intelligent Systems Engineering, Graduate School of Engineering, University of Fukui (H2021002).

3   Results

The experiments were conducted with healthy young subjects (aged 21–24). Before and after walking with each VR image viewing, we performed the stabilometry and subjective evaluation with the SSQ.

The total locus length, area of sway, total locus length per unit area [24], and sparse density [25] were calculated based on the stabilograms obtained from the stabilometry.

Compared to these sway values in the test with eyes open, those in the test with eyes closed, except for the total locus length per unit area, tends to increase, and the standing posture becomes unstable. This is because visual information is used to maintain the upright posture. In addition, from comparing the change in the sway values before and after walking, the sway values except for the total locus length per unit area increases after walking, and the standing posture tends to become unstable. Of these sway values, there is a significant difference in the total locus length of the test with eyes open ($p <$ 0.05) in which subjects viewed the static image (1). However, no significant difference is observed in the test with eyes closed (Fig. 5).

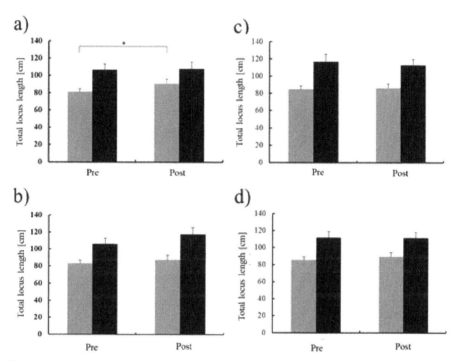

Fig. 5. Change in total locus length. a) before and after viewing the static image (1), b) before and after viewing the virtual reality (VR) image of running at a constant speed of 3 km/h (2), c) before and after viewing the VR image of running at a constant speed of 5 km/h (3), d) before and after viewing the VR image of running at a constant speed of 8 km/h (4).

Next, we compared the amount of change in the SSQ subscore to weigh the degree of motion sickness (Fig. 6). In this study, the Wilcoxon signed rank test was used for the statistical comparison, and the Holm method was used to conduct for multiple comparisons. The SSQ subscores show high values except for those during the 8 km/h visual image exposure (4). This indicates that the subjective evaluation values increase compared to the control owing to the effects associated with VR video viewing, including static images. In particular, statistically significant differences ($p < 0.05$) are found for

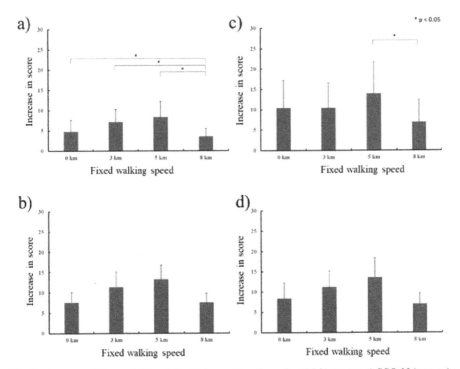

Fig. 6. Amount of change in Simulator Sickness Questionnaire (SSQ) scores. a) SSQ-N (nausea), b) SSQ-OD (eye fatigue), c) SSQ-D (non-disorientation), d) SSQ-TS (total)

SSQ-N (nausea) and SSQ-D (disorientation), and the increase in subjective evaluation values described above is suppressed by the exposure to the 8 km/h video clip (4).

4 Discussion

Sensory conflicts between the vestibular and visual systems are observed during indoor training using treadmills and ergometers. In the present study, we investigated the following hypothesis:

"There is increased parasympathetic activity associated with sensory conflicts between the vestibular and visual systems in subjects walking using an indoor simulation training system." [18].

We produced VR images for diminishing the sensory conflict by examining the possibility that subjects may develop motion sickness symptoms immediately after walking under the VR image (3); this image was produced according to the subject's running speed on the simulator. For comparison, we produced VR images (2) and (4) which were slower and faster than the subject's running speed on the simulator, respectively, in addition to the static image (1).

The subjects walked on the treadmill while viewing VR images (1)–(4) in any order for 5 min. The biological evaluation was conducted before and after the images were viewed. We compared the results of the stabilometry before and after walking to identify and weigh any motion sickness. The results show that the total locus length during the open-eye test increases significantly ($p < 0.05$) after walking with exposure to the static image (1). This confirms that the above hypothesis is valid. However, no significant difference is observed during the closed-eye test (Fig. 5), suggesting that the degree of motion sickness is not excessive.

The VR images (2)–(4) produced in this study are effective in diminishing the sensory conflict between the vestibular and visual systems of the subjects, as there is no significant increase with the viewing of the other images. Notably, the change in the sway values accompanying the viewing of VR image (4) is the smallest (Fig. 5.d), and not VR image (3), which was shot at the same speed as the subject's walking speed. The reasons for this include that there is no vertical movement of the visual information associated with walking owing to the visual recognition through VR, and that the altitude of the video recording is not necessarily the same as the height of the subject's eyes. However, the feedforward type of motor-sensory control may be predominant when applied to faster speeds than the actual walking speed. As for the subjective evaluation, it supports the above results (Fig. 6).

There are various theories concerning the mechanisms of stereoscopic motion sickness. One theory considers the range in which objects appear to be in focus both in front of and behind the exact plane of focus of the crystalline lens at a particular adjustment. This "range of focus" is known as the depth of field (DOF), and is approximately ±0.2–0.3 diopters (D) in humans [26, 27]. If a three-dimensional object is presented within the DOF, there will be no discrepancy between the convergence the lens accommodation [28]. This will also eliminate the problem of discrepancy during stereopsis, and suppress the discomfort observed in some studies [29, 30]. However, another study showed that fatigue occurred when there was a temporary change in the binocular disparity, even though the change was within the DOF [31, 32]. Another theory speculates that simultaneous changes in convergence and lens accommodation in the opposite directions cause instability in visual functions, and that the effort to fuse the images produced by the two eyes causes fatigue [33–35]. Here, preliminary experiments were also conducted on the illuminance of the experimental environment to interpret the previous experimental data. When the illuminance of the environment changed, the pupil diameter was affected. In general, as the illuminance decreases, the pupil diameter increases and the DOF becomes shallower. We believe that the misalignment between the lens accommodation and surface of the display, which was not included in the DOF range, induced the motion sickness [15, 36]. For the illumination environment of the VR system developed in this study, it is considered that the sensory conflict between the vestibular and visual systems can be diminished without inducing VR motion sickness.

Notably, differences have been reported in the energy expenditure between indoor level walking and treadmill walking. There is also a report on comparing outdoor walking with treadmill walking by conducting an expiratory gas analysis under the condition that both walking speeds are kept constant, suggesting that outdoor walking is suitable as an aerobic exercise because it shows lower values than treadmill walking in regards to the subjective exercise intensity and respiratory quotient [37]. However, the cause of this is seen as a psychological influence, leading toother limitations.

This discrepancy can be reduced by viewing under conditions of greater DOF as bright screen, large viewing distance, etc. [21]. The VR system developed in this study is not only novel, but is also valuable as a research material for 3D VIMS.

In the report "Development of Infrastructure for a Data-driven Society in Japan" [38], it was pointed out that it is necessary to elucidate the causes of discomfort symptoms for the development of the industry in this field, and that this is an urgent issue for the deployment of viewing services to an unspecified large number of people using 5G. In the future, it will be possible to construct a system for estimating the running speed on a simulator based on data measured by a web camera of the subject's movement, and for changing the playback speed of the 2D images according to the estimated running speed. For the estimation of the walking speed, we have focused on machine learning, and have used the posture estimation deep learning model PoseNet. The research using the artificial intelligence in question has already begun to be applied to the rehabilitation field [39]. We have built mathematical models, algorithms, and artificial intelligence (competitive neural networks) for biological signal processing; these can also be applied to the biological evaluation in this study [40]. In addition, although conducting measurements during walking outdoors is challenging, we can develop and carry out this research with the further developed preamplifier technology of NeuroSky Inc., with whom we are collaborating.

5   Conclusion

Sensory discrepancies between the vestibular and visual systems are observed during indoor training using treadmills and ergometers. In the present study, we examined the possibility that subjects may develop motion sickness symptoms immediately after walking, and produced VR images to diminish the sensory discrepancies. In particular, we compared the relationship between the walking speed and running speed when producing first-person VR images, and obtained significant findings.

Augmented reality (AR) viewing is being used in various areas owing to its convenience. In particular, following the coronavirus pandemic, AR viewing opportunities are increasing, and indoor training using treadmills and ergometers is becoming more popular. In addition, indoor training is necessary for physical and mental health in the current situation, where teleworking and other forms of exercise are increasing and people are becoming less physically active. Therefore, it is important to provide basic data on safety standards for VR/AR viewing and to ensure safety and security during training through this research, which will not only be important in future society, but will also help the development of this technology.

We would like to express our sincere gratitude to the Descente and Ishimoto Memorial Foundation for their support of this research [23]. Also, this work was supported in part by the Japan Society for the Promotion of Science, Grant-in-Aid for Scientific Research (C) Number 20K12528 and 20K11925.

References

1. Takei, M.: Health promotion by exercise: easy walking, good health today. Juntendo Igaku **48**(3), 330–334 (2002)

2. Mirelman, A., et al.: Addition of a non-immersive virtual reality component to treadmill training to reduce fall risk in older adults (V-TIME): a randomised controlled trial. Lancet **388**(10050), 1170–1182 (2016). https://doi.org/10.1016/S0140-6736(16)31325-3
3. Ministry of Internal Affairs and Communications: White paper on information and communications in Japan, pp. 6–16. MIC, Tokyo (2018). http://www.soumu.go.jp/johotsusintokei/whitepaper/index.html. Accessed 3 Mar 2023
4. Ujiie, H.: Report of ISO international workshop on biological safety of images. VISION **17**(2), 143–145 (2005). https://doi.org/10.24636/vision.17.2_143
5. Takane, S., Suzuki, Y., Sone, T., Kim, H.Y.: A study on control of distance perception by simulation of HRTF. In: Proceedings of the Virtual Reality Society of Japan Annual Conference, vol. 1, pp. 55–58. IAP, Tokyo (1996)
6. Inoue, T.: Eye movement and accommodation when viewing 2D and 3D images. J. Ins. Telev. Eng. Japan **50**(4), 423–428 (1996)
7. Kennedy, R.S., Berbaum, K.S., Dunlap, W.P., Hettinger, L.J.: Developing automated methods to quantify the visual stimulus for cybersickness. Hum. Fac. Ergo. Soc. Ann. Meet. **40**(2), 1126–1130 (1996)
8. Ohsuga, M., Tatsuno, T., Shimono, F., Hirasawa, K., Oyama, H., Okamura, H.: Bedside wellness, development of a virtual forest rehabilitation system. Stu. Health Tech. Inform. **50**, 168–174 (1998)
9. Kolasinski, E.M.: Simulator sickness in virtual environments (ARI Technical Report 1027), U.S. Army Research Institute for the Behavioral and Social Sciences, Alexandria (1995)
10. Reason, J.T., Brand, J.J.: Motion Sickness. Academic Press Inc., London (1975)
11. Balaban, C.D., Porter, J.D.: Neuroanatomic substrates for vestibulo-autonomic interactions. J Vesti. Res. **8**, 7–16 (1998)
12. Hirayanagi, K.: A present state and perspective of studies on motion sickness. Jap. J. Ergo. **42**(3), 200–211 (2006)
13. Barmack, N.H.: Central vestibular system: vestibular nuclei and posterior cerebellum. Brain Res. Bull. **60**, 511–541 (2003)
14. Takeda, N., et al.: Histaminergic mechanism of motion sickness neurochemical and neuropharmacological studies in rats. Acta Otolar. **101**, 416–421 (1986)
15. Matsuura, Y., Takada, H.: Evaluation studies of motion sickness visually induced by stereoscopic films. Adv. Sci. Tech. Eng. Syst. J. **6**(4), 241–251 (2021)
16. Kinoshita, F., Takada, H.: Numerical analysis of SDEs as a model for body sway while viewing 3D video clips. Mech. Syst. Cont. **47**(2), 98–105 (2019)
17. Nishike, S., Watanabe, H., Matsuoka, K., Oyama, H., Akizuki, H., Takeda, N.: Autonomic responses to virtual reality. J. Aeros. Env. Med. **42**(4), 22 (2005)
18. Nakagawa, C.: A study on evaluation of sway sickness using physiological reaction. Ph.D. thesis, Department of Fundamental Science and Engineering, Graduate School of Science and Technology, Keio University, p. 63 (2007). http://iroha.scitech.lib.keio.ac.jp:8080/sigma/handle/10721/2269. Accessed 3 Mar 2023
19. Toates, F.M.: Vergence eye movements. Doc. Ophthalmol. **37**(1), 153–214 (1974). https://doi.org/10.1007/BF00149678
20. Emoto, M., Niida, T., OkanoF.: Repeated vergence adaptation causes the decline of visual functions in watching stereoscopic television. J. Display Tech. **1**, 328 (2005)
21. Ito, T., Arai, J.: Three-dimensional image technology. Jap. J. Appl. Phys. **82**(1), 20–26 (2013)
22. Miyao, M., Ishihara, S., Saito, S., Kondo, T., Sakakibara, H., Toyoshima, H.: Visual accommodation and subject performance during a stereographic object task using liquid crystal shutters. Ergo. **39**(11), 1294–1309 (1996). https://doi.org/10.1080/00140139608964549
23. Takada, H., Miyao, M., Shiozawa, T., Takada, M., Ito, K.: Development and evaluation of a training system to reduce sensory conflict using augmented reality. Descente Sports Sci. **43**, 62–70 (2022). https://doi.org/10.57488/descente.43.0_62(InJapanese)

24. Suzuki, J., Matsunaga, T., Tokumatsu, K., Taguchi, K., Watanabe, Y.: Handbook and Q&A of the stabilogram 1995. Equil. Res. **55**(1), 64–77 (1996)
25. Takada, H., Kitaoka, Y., Ichikawa, M., Miyao, M.: Physical meaning of geometrical index for stabilometry. Equil. Res. **62**(3), 168–180 (2003)
26. Cambell, F.W.: The depth of field of the human eye. J. Mod. Opt. **29**, 157–164 (1957)
27. Charman, W.N., Whitefoot, H.: Pupil diameter and depth-of-field of the human eye as measured by laser speckle. Opt. Acta **24**, 1211–1216 (1977)
28. Kawai, T., Morikawa, H., Ohta, K., Abe, N.: Basic Principles and Production Technology of Stereoscopic Images. Ohmsha, Tokyo (2010)
29. Hiruma, N., Fukuda, T.: Viewing conditions for binocular stereoscopic images base on accommodation response. IEICE Trans. Info. Syst. **73**(12)D-2, 2047–2054 (1990)
30. Nojiri, Y., Yamanoue, H., Hanazato, A., Okano, F.: Measurement of parallax distribution and its applacation to the analysis of visual comfort for stereoscopic HDTV. Proc. SPIE **5006**, 195–205 (1993)
31. Yano, A., Emoto, M., Mitsuhashi, T.: Two factors in visual fatigue caused by stereoscopic HDTV images. Displays **25**, 141–150 (2004)
32. Speranza, F., Tam, W.J., Renaud, R., Hur, N.: Effect of disparity and motion on visual comfort of stereoscopic images. Proc. SPIE **6055**, 94–103 (2006)
33. Emoto, M., Masaoka, K., Yamanoue, Y., Sugawara, M., Nojiri, Y.: Horizontal binocular disparities and visual fatigue while viewing stereoscopic displays. Vision **17**(2), 101–112 (2005)
34. Ukai, K., Howarth, P.A.: Visual fatigue caused by viewing stereoscopic motion images, background, theories and observations. Displays **29**, 106–116 (2008)
35. Lambooji, M., Ijsselstejin, W., Fortuin, M., Heynderickx, I.: Visual discomfort and visual fatigue of stereoscopic displays: a review. J. Imaging Sci. Tech. Tech. **53**(3), 1–14 (2009)
36. Takada, H., Miyao, M., Fateh, S. (eds.): CTEHPM, Springer, Singapore (2019). https://doi.org/10.1007/978-981-13-1601-2
37. Takahara, T., Miyamae, A., Kobayashi, J., Akahoshi, K., Nagata, M.: Comparison of physiological responses in outdoor walking and treadmill walking. Physiotherapy **36**(S2), A3P1085 (2009). https://doi.org/10.14900/cjpt.2008.0.A3P1085.0
38. VR/AR Study Committee: Development of Infrastructure for a Data-driven Society in Japan: Report of research study on infrastructure and environment development for content creation to discover new social needs, Commerce and Information Policy Bureau, Ministry of Economy, Trade and Industry, Digital Content Association of Japan, Tokyo (2017)
39. Usami, Y., Takada, H., Hirata, T.: AI image processing analysis for rise testing. In: Proceedings 2021 Annual Conference of the IEEE Industrial Electronics Society. IEEJ, pp. 869–871 (2021)
40. Nakane, K., Ono, R., Takada, H.: Numerical analysis for feature extraction and evaluation of 3D sickness. Adv. Sci. Tech. Eng. Syst. J. **6**(2), 949–955 (2021)

A Divisive Approach for All Pairs Shortest Path on Large-Scale Graphs with Limited Resources

Yanwei Liu, Gang Lu$^{(\boxtimes)}$![ORCID], and Weiwei Gu

UrbanNet Lab, College of Information Science and Technolgy, Beijing University of Chemical Technology, Beijing 100029, China
lugang@mail.buct.edu.cn

Abstract. Solving the all pairs shortest path (APSP) problem is crucial for graph theory and various practical applications, but remains challenging for large graphs with an enormous number of nodes and edges when the computing resources is limited. In this work, based on an effective graph partition method, we further propose a divisive approach to obtain the APSP for large graphs. A large graph is firstly divided into smaller subgraphs that may not be of an equal size, and then getting the APSP of each subgraph separately. By concatenating the APSPs of the subgraphs, the APSP of the whole graph can be obtained. Experimental results confirm the effectiveness and correctness of our approach for obtaining APSP on large graphs with limited computing resources.

Keywords: all pairs shortest path · limited resources · large-scale graphs · dvide-and-conquer

1 Introduction

All pairs shortest path (APSP) problem aims to find shortest paths between each pair of vertices in a graph. It is the basis of calculating average shortest path length [1] and betweenness centrality measure of vertices or edges in complex networks [2], which are important for better understanding the topology of graphs, crucial for epidemic spreading dynamics [3–7], and other practical applications, including traffic engineering [8–10]. However, for large- scale graphs with an enormous number of vertices and edges, the calculation of APSP would consume more and more computer resources such as memory and CPU time.

In order to cope with the challenge of large graph data, some distributed graph computing systems are designed, which are able to be horizontally expanded to process distributed graph computing on a distributed cluster. Being different from general big data processing systems such as MapReduce [11], Spark [12], etc., these dedicated graph computing systems are designed and optimized for the data structure of graph, as well as keeping scalability of the system. Nevertheless, distributed clusters are not always available to users with limited budget, and calculating APSP of large graphs directly on a single machine is usually impossible due to excessive resource consumption. Therefore, it would be meaningful to find an effective way to solve the problem.

In this work, an approach based on a divide-and-conquer strategy for calculating APSP of large graphs on a single machine with limited resources is proposed. In this approach, firstly an effective graph partitioning algorithm is implemented, to divide the whole graph into several smaller subgraphs with relatively a few vertices overlapping. Then APSP in each subgraph is calculated. After that, the APSPs of the subgraphs are concatenated to obtain the APSP for the whole graph. We test the approach on real-world large graphs and find that it performs well.

2   Related Work

Researchers have proposed dozens of graph computing systems for large graphs computing issues, including shortest paths of the large graphs.

With the advent of the era of big data, the scale of graph data is growing rapidly. There have been many new technologies and new methods proposed to build graph processing system for large graphs. They can be classified into different types according to the number of main machines and whether external memory is used.

Today, the capacity of a single computer has advanced much. Multi-core architecture and large memory make it possible for a single computer to process graph data with over a hundred of billions of edges. Ligra [13], Galois [14], GraphMat [15], Polymer [16] are all excellent stand-alone memory graph processing systems, which can complete graph computations in single-machine memory.

GraphChi [17], X-Stream [18], GridGraph [19], and other stand-alone systems [20, 21] bypass the memory capacity limitations by storing graph data on external memory.

An obvious way to solve the memory limitation of single computer is to develop a distributed graph computing system with more computers. Being different from mainstream big data platforms such as Hadoop [22] or Spark [12], some dedicated graph computing systems are designed and optimized for the data structure of graphs, and maintaining the scalability of the system. Pregel [23], GraphLab [24], PowerGraph [25], Giraph [26], GraphX [27], Gemini [28] and other distributed graph computing systems [29, 30] have been proposed in the past few years.

Chaos [31] extended the X-Stream system to multiple machines and became the first graph system to achieve efficient processing of graph data in a distributed external memory environment.

The shortest path related problems are important and classical in graph computing, which have been researched for decades. Dijkstra [32], Bellman-Ford [33], Floyd-Warshall [34], A* [35], SPFA [36], Johnson [37] algorithms are several classical algorithms for calculating single source shortest paths.

In addition to this, many shortest path algorithms have been proposed. [38] gives detailed introduction to the related algorithms, while the author of [39] uses a variety of combined acceleration methods to optimize the algorithm. Among them, the dijktra algorithm optimized with binary heap reduces the complexity of the algorithm to $O(N\log(N + E))$, and is widely used in solving the shortest path problem.

Most of the above system traverses the single source shortest path based on BFS to obtain the result of APSP. When calculating the APSP of a large graph, the single-machine system faces huge challenges such as high complexity and increased resource consumption, while the cost of the distributed system is too high. So this paper uses a new idea and heap-optimized Dijkstra algorithm to calculate APSP for large-scale graphs.

3 Algorithm

This paper proposes a divide-and-conquer solution to solve the problem of APSP for large graphs. Firstly, by defining the expected number of subgraphs in advance, a large graph is divided into several smaller subgraphs. Secondly, the APSP of each subgraph is calculated. Finally, the APSP of the whole graph is obtained by concatenating the APSPs of the subgraphs.

3.1 Basic Definitions

Basing on the graph theory, some definitions which are used in our work are given as follows.

Definition 3.1: Graph. $G = (V, E)$ is an undirected and unweighted graph, with $|V|=N$, $|E| = M$, where V is the set of vertices and E is the set of edges. N represents the number of vertices, and M represents the number of edges.

Definition 3.2: Shortest Paths and Distances. Among all the paths from u to v, the path with the shortest distance is called the shortest path. $Dist(u,v)$ is uesd to represent the shortest path length between u and v, which is called the distance between two vertices.

Definition 3.3: Graph Partitioning. An undirected unweighted graph $G = (V, E)$ is divided into n subgraphs, which are denoted as $G_1 = (V_1, E_1)$, $G_2 = (V_1, E_1)$,..., $G_n = (V_n, E_n)$, where $V = V_1 \cup V_2 \cup... \cup V_n$ and $E = E_1 \cup E_2 \cup... \cup E_n$. With this definition, there are following discussions.

Graph partitioning algorithms can be classified into two categories, which are edge-based partitioning and vertex-based partitioning. By edge-based partitioning method, the split edges and corresponding vertices are copied between corresponding subgraphs, with $E_1 \cap E_2 \cap... \cap E_n \neq \varnothing$. By vertex-based partitioning algorithm, the graph is split on vertices. The split vertices will be copied to corresponding subgraphs, with $E_1 \cap E_2 \cap... \cap E_n =\varnothing$. Figure 1 and Fig. 2 illustrate examples of the two types of algorithms.

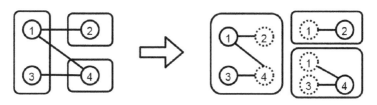

Fig. 1. An edge-based partitioning algorithm example.

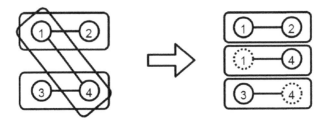

Fig. 2. An vertex-based partitioning algorithm example.

From the examples in Fig. 1 and Fig. 2, it can be seen that by edge-based partitioning, adds four vertex copies and three edge copies are added; while vertex-based partitioning only adds two vertex copies are added by vertex-based partitioning. For the division of large-scale graphs, the vertex-based partitioning algorithm is more advantageous in the aspect of data redundancy.

Definition 3.4: Boundary Vertices. For the subgraphs G_x and G_y divided by the vertex-based partitioning algorithm, if $B(G_x, G_y) = V_x \cap V_y \neq \varnothing$, then the vertices in $B(G_x, G_y)$ are called *boundary vertices*.

Definition 3.5: Path Matrix. For an undirected unweighted graph G, an $N \times N$ matrix M is used to store the shortest path lengths between all pairs of vertices, which is called the *path matrix*. The element m_{ij} in M represents the shortest distance $dist(i,j)$ between i and j. All the elements are initialized as 0.

By sorting the vertex of G by their IDs, it is stipulated that each subset has K vertices, and V is divided the vertices of G into $P = \lceil \frac{N}{K} \rceil$ vertex sets. If $N \bmod K \neq 0$, the number of vertices in the last set is $N \bmod K$. Basing on this statement, the following definition is given.

Definition 3.6: Grid. The path matrix of graph G is divided into $P \times P$ sub-matrices. Each sub-matrix is called a *grid*.

Given two vertex i and j, the grid in which $dist(i, j)$ is can be calculate as follows, with the sequence number starts from 0: The row number of the grid is $\frac{i}{K}$, while the column number of it is $\frac{j}{K}$. Then, the index of the grid is $index = f(i, j, K, P) = P \times \frac{i}{K} + \lceil \frac{j}{K} \rceil$.

3.2 OVSA Algorithm for Graph Partitioning

Given an undirected unweighted graph G, by dividing it into two subgraphs $G_1 = (V_1, E_1)$, $G_2 = (V_2, E_2)$, we get $|V_1| = N_1, |V_2| = N_2$, and $|B(G_1, G_2)| = n$. By calling Dijkstra algorithm for each vertex, the APSP of G_1 and G_2 can be solved separately, which are called as $APSP_1$ and $APSP_2$, with the time complexity of $O(N^3)$. The APSP of G can be obtained by concatenating the paths of $APSP_1$ and $APSP_2$ through n boundary vertices. The number of paths to be concatenated is $N_1 \times n \times N_2$, and the time complexity is also $O(N^3)$. So the total time complexity is $O(N^3)$. At the same time, considering $N_1 + N_2 - n = N$, there is.

$$N_1 \times n \times N_2 = n \times N_1 \times (N + n - N_1) = n \times N_2 \times (N + n - N_2) \tag{1}$$

Then when n is determined, we can get

$$\begin{cases} max(N_1 \times n \times N_2) = \frac{n \times (N+n)^2}{4}, N_1 = N_2 \\ min(N_1 \times n \times N_2) = n \times (N + n - 1), N_1 = 1 \, or \, N_2 = 1 \end{cases} \tag{2}$$

That means, the more evenly the graph is partitioned, the more paths need to be concatenated.

In the 2017 DataCastle Masters Competition, Professor Ren Tao from Northeastern University put forward an idea for partitioning graphs by deleting vertices, which fits vertex-based graph partitioning. We call his idea as Optimal Vertex Sorting Algorithm (OVSA), which can quickly and unevenly partition a graph with fewer boundary vertices. The idea of OVSA is to find a vertices sequence by which deleting vertices makes the graph break into pieces as quickly as possible. The steps of OVSA are as follows:

Step 1, define an empty sequence S to record the order in which vertices are deleted, and sort all the vertices of the graph in ascending order of degree. The degree sequence is denoted by D.

Step 2, move vertex of $D[0]$ with the smallest degree into S.

Step 3, find the next vertex with the smallest degree and the least connections to S in D, and then move it into S.

Step 4, Step 3 is repeated until all the vertices in D have been moved into S.

Step 5, S is reversed to get the final vertex-deleting sequence for partitioning the graph.

3.3   APSP Solution Based on CPA Algorithm

In the process of concatenating path, the most important problem is how to ensure that the connected path between two vertices is the shortest path in the whole graph for them. Being similar to traditional algorithms, the path length between two vertices will be updated at any time once a path between them with shorter length is found. At the same time, the distance value in corresponding grid will be updated, too. Subgraphs are concatenated one by one by their boundary vertices. When a new subgraph is joining the previously concatenated ones, the path lengths between the vertices of previously concatenated subgraphs will be updated by the paths in the new one. Finally, APSP of the whole graph can be get when all the subgraphs are concatenated.

Based on above idea, Concatenating Path Algorithm (CPA) is proposed. By this algorithm, the path lengths related to boundary vertices in the new incoming subgraph are used to update the path lengths in previously concatenated subgraphs. The steps of CPA are as follows:

Step 1, APSP of the first subgraph is calculated by running Dijkstra algorithm for every vertex. The path lengths are saved to the corresponding grid according to the vertex numbers at both ends.

Step 2, for another subgraph, if it shares the boundary vertices with the previous subgraphs, then the paths across them can be obtained by concatenating the paths in each subgraph through the boundary vertices. At the same time, APSPs in previous subgraphs are updated by APSP of this new subgraph.

Step 3, continue to update the path for the remaining subgraphs as described above.

There are two processing strategies for Step 2. The straightforward one, called as Sequential Solution, is calculating APSP for every subgraph in advance, and then concatenating them together. The other one is to concatenating the paths and updating the previous path lengths as soon as a path length related to some boundary vertices in the new subgraph is gotten. This is called as Simultaneous Solution. By the latter once, only one paths traversing is needed, which may enhance the performance of the algorithm.

3.4 Grid Management Strategy Based on LRU

LRU (Least Recently Used) algorithm is a page replacement algorithm widely used by most operating systems to maximize page hit ratio for memory management. The idea of the algorithm is to replace the page that has not been used for the longest time when the page missing interruption occurs hence a new page will be loaded into the memory.

In the case of insufficient memory space, a limited number of grids are kept in memory, and the others are placed on disk. For those grids in memory, the time of accessing them is maintained and updated in real time. When calculating APSP of each subgraph, the index numbers of corresponding grids can be calculated according to the ending vertex numbers of each path. If a grid needed is not in the memory, it will be loaded from the disk. However, if the number of in-memory grids has reached the limit, the grid with the oldest accessing time will be swapped out to the disk. The principle is that if a grid has been accessed recently, it has a high probability of being accessed in the future. Keeping frequently accessed grids in memory as long as possible by LRU lowers the frequency of disk I/O so that enhances performance.

3.5 Time Complexity Analysis

When calculating the APSP of subgraphs, in order to reduce the cost of selecting vertex with the shortest distance from the source vertex, a priority queue is maintained to record candidate vertices using the data structure of heap, and the performance of Dijkstra algorithm is greatly improved. We call it Heap Optimized Dijkstra algorithm (HOD). The main step of the HOD is to find vertices to be sorted and then sort them with a heap. After heap sorting, the vertices are stored in a complete binary tree being adjusted to a small top heap. Since the vertices to be sorted are the neighbors of all the labeled vertices, the running time of this step mainly depends on the number of neighbors of the labeled vertices, so the maximum searching times is $O(E)$. During the sorting process, the time complexity of each adjustment cannot exceed the height of the full binary tree, which is $\log N$. The two processes need to be executed iteratively for N times, so the time complexity of the whole algorithm is $O(N(\log N + E))$. As a result, the time complexity of solving the APSP on the subgraph using the improved Dijkstra algorithm is $O(N^2(\log N + E))$.

For CPA, assuming that graph $G(N, E)$ is evenly partitioned into m subgraphs, with n border vertices between every pair of subgraphs. The border vertices are used to concatenate the shortest paths across two subgraphs. In this case, the number of paths needed to be concatenated is $O(\frac{m \times (m-1)}{2} \times (\frac{N-mn}{m})^2 \times n$, which is $O(N^3)$ in fact.

4 Experiments

4.1 Experimental Environment

The experimental environment is a server with two 12-core Intel Xeon Gold 5118 @2.3GHz CPUs and 64GB memory, on which Centos7 operating system is installed. Part of the data for the experiment comes from open datasets by SNAP group of Stanford University[1]. Table 1 shows the specific information of the used datasets, including the number of vertices, the number of edges, the number of boundary vertices, the number of subgraphs to be divided, and the number of vertices K in the grid. In addition, Table 1 also shows the correlation coefficient of each dataset. Email-Eu-core and P2P-Gnutella08 in Table 1 are regarded as undirected graphs, and the isolated vertices in Email-Eu-core are removed.

Table 1. Basic statistics of networks.

Graph	Email-Eu-core	Facebook	P2P-Gnutella08
Vertex	986	4,039	6,301
Edge	16,376	88,234	20,777
Boundary vertices	2	1	7
Subgraphs	3	12	6
K	600	2,000	3,000
Average clustering coefficient	0.3994	0.6055	0.0109
Number of triangles	105,461	1,612,010	2,383
Fraction of closed triangles	0.1085	0.2647	0.006983
Diameter	7	8	9
90-percentile effective diameter	2.9	4.7	5.5
Average degree	33.848	43.691	6.595

4.2 Performance of the Algorithms

Analysis of CPA: There are two ideas in CPA mentioned in Sect. 3.3, which are Simultaneous Solution and Sequential Solution. Their performance is compared in terms of their execution time as follows.

It can be seen from Table 2 that the Simultaneous Solution on Email-Eu-core and Facebook is more efficient, and the execution time of the Sequential Solution on P2P-Gnutella08 is shorter. From Fig. 3 it can be seen that the degree distributions of Email-Eu-core and Facebook are relatively uneven. Uneven degree distribution usually means less border vertices between subgraphs, because OVSA preferentially selects vertices

---

[1] Http://snap.stanford.edu/data/.

with larger degrees for segmentation, thus becoming boundary vertices. On one hand, Sequential Solution increases the time to traverse all paths again. On the other hand, Simultaneous Solution need to check whether the end vertex of a path is a border vertex. That checking will slow down CPA if there are too many border vertices resulting from the more uniform degree distribution.

Table 2. Comparison on execution time for two concatenating path strategies in seconds.

Graph	Simultaneous	Sequential
Email-Eu-core	17.63	20.98
Facebook	1,147	16,642.9
P2P-Gnutella08	421.37	244.61

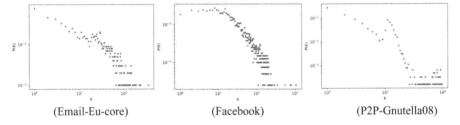

| (Email-Eu-core) | (Facebook) | (P2P-Gnutella08) |

Fig. 3. Degree distribution of networks.

Applying HOD Algorithm: In Table 3, the execution time for the three networks by Dijkstra, HOD, Dijkstra + CPA, and HOD + CPA are compared. In addition, Fig. 4 also showed the memory space occupied by the algorithm in the execution process in the space dimension.

Table 3. Execution time of different algorithms in seconds

Graph	Dijkstra	HOD	CPA + Dijkstra	CPA + HOD
Email-Eu-core	12.26	10.93	18.18	17.63
Facebook	282.65	212	1,246.76	1,147
P2P-Gnutella08	58.81	39.74	538.5	421.37

It can be seen that HOD has the least execution time and less memory usage than the normal Dijkstra algorithm. The larger the network size is, the more obviously the optimization affects. The execution time and memory usage of the algorithms with CPA are higher than others. However, the algorithms with CPA are for large graphs which cannot be loaded into memory at a whole. For those large graph, traditional algorithms without CPA will not work.

Table 4. Comparison of LRU strategy with different number sub-path matrix.

LRU	0	2	4
excution time (s)	3,103.88	1,233.56	4.99
file access frequency	2,110,193	1,160,390	12

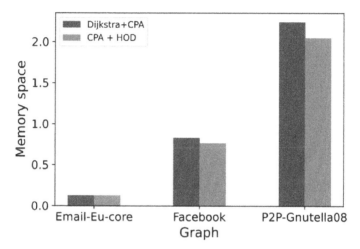

Fig. 4. Comparison of memory space occupied by different algorithm in three networks.

Effect of LRU Strategy: In the above experiments using HOD and CPA, LRU strategy is applied at the same time. Next, the results of the algorithms without LRU strategy on the Email-Eu-core will be compared. At the beginning, all grids are stored on disk as files, with the execution time and file access times recorded. After that, the number of grid kept in memory under LRU strategy is changed, and the changes in execution time and file access times are observed.

As can be seen from Table 4, when the memory is sufficient, using LRU strategy can greatly improve the execution efficiency compared to placing all grids on the disk. The more grids are kept in memory, the faster the computation and the fewer access times to the file. If the memory is insufficient when calculating APSP, the number of grids kept in memory can be different, which may lead to different results from those in Table 4. Future experiments will be conducted on large-scale graphs in this regard and their results will be analyzed.

Comparison of Different Numbers of Subgraphs: In order to explore the effect of different numbers of subgraphs on the execution time of the algorithm, we firstly select the number of subgraphs that each graph could easily be divided into, and then increase the number of subgraphs in turn. The effects of different numbers of subgraphs on the three datasets by executing HOD and CPA algorithms by Simultaneous Solution are analyzed.

By analyzing the topological structure and degree distribution of the three networks, we think that for large-scale graphs, the number of subgraphs has different effects on the execution efficiency due to the particularity of the topology structures of the networks. From Fig. 5, Fig. 6 and Fig. 7, it can be seen the general trend is that the number of subgraphs has little effect on the execution time of the algorithm until it reaches a certain number. At that time, the execution time will increase rapidly. Different graphs have different thresholds for the number of subgraphs.

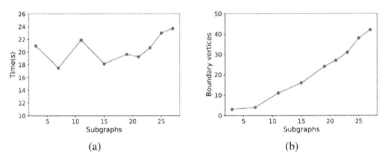

(a)   (b)

Fig. 5. Execution time and the number of boundary vertices for the Email-Eu-core network with different numbers of partitioned subgraphs.

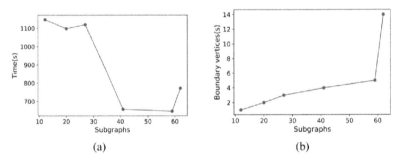

(a)   (b)

Fig. 6. Execution time and the number of boundary vertices for the Facebook network with different numbers of partitioned subgraphs.

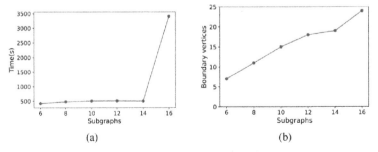

(a)   (b)

Fig. 7. Execution time and the number of boundary vertices for the P2P-Gnutella08 network with different numbers of partitioned subgraphs.

5   Conclusion

By the proposed approach for APSP of large graphs in this paper, the average shortest path length of large graphs can be correctly calculated with limited memory space. The approach is based on the divide and conquer idea. Firstly, the OVSA algorithm included in the approach is used to effectively and quickly divide a large graph into several subgraphs. After that, on the subgraphs, APSPs of them is solved separately. Finally, the APSPs of the subgraphs are concatenated to obtain the APSP of the whole graph. In this progress, some optimization strategies are used, such as heap sorting in Dijkstra algorithm, and LRU strategy.

In general, because the approach is based on the divide-and-conquer idea, it is possible to be parallelized on modern multi-core CPU architectures, as well as on a distributed environment in the future to improve the execution efficiency. In addition, more researches on larger datasets would be interesting, too.

References

1. Evans, T.S., Chen, B.: Linking the network centrality measures closeness and degree. arXiv preprint arXiv:2108.01149 (2021)
2. Newman, M.: Networks. Oxford university press, Oxford (2018)
3. Li, R., Richmond, P., Roehner, B.M.: Effect of population density on epidemics. Phys. A **510**, 713–724 (2018)
4. Li, R., Wang, W., Di, Z.: Effects of human dynamics on epidemic spreading in Cote d'Ivoire. Phys. A **467**, 30–40 (2017)
5. Li, R., Tang, M., Hui, P.M.: Epidemic spreading on multi-relational networks. Acta Phys. Sin. **62**(16), 168903 (2013)
6. Li, R., Wang, W., Shu, P., Shu, P., Yang, H., Tang, M.: Review of threshold theoretical analysis about epidemic spreading dynamics on complex networks. Complex Syst. Complex. Sci. **13**(1), 1–39 (2016)
7. Pastor-Satorras, R., Castellano, C., Van Mieghem, P., Vespignani, A.: Epidemic processes in complex networks. Rev. Mod. Phys. **87**(3), 925 (2015)
8. Dong, L., Li, R., Zhang, J., Di, Z.: Population-weighted efficiency in transportation networks. Sci. Rep. **6**, 26377 (2016)
9. Li, R., Dong, L., Zhang, J., Wang, X., Wang, W., Di, Z., et al.: Simple spatial scaling rules behind complex cities. Nat. Commun. **8**, 1841 (2017)
10. Li, R., Gao, S., Luo, A., Yao, Q., Stanley, H.E.: Gravity model in dockless bike-sharing systems within cities. Phys. Rev. E **103**(1), 012312 (2021)
11. Dean, J., Ghemawat, S.: MapReduce: simplified data processing on large clusters. In: Proceedings of the 6th Conference on Symposium on Opearting Systems Design & Implementation. vol. 6. USENIX Association (2004)
12. Zaharia, M., Chowdhury, M., Franklin, M.J., Shenker, S., Stoica, I.: Spark: cluster computing with working sets. In: 2nd USENIX Workshop on Hot Topics in Cloud Computing (2010)
13. Shun, J., Blelloch, G.E.: Ligra: a lightweight graph processing framework for shared memory. In: Proceedings of the 18th ACM SIGPLAN Symposium on Principles and Practice of Parallel Programming, pp. 135–146 (2013)
14. Nguyen, D., Lenharth, A., Pingali, K.: A lightweight infrastructure for graph analytics. In: Proceedings of the Twenty-Fourth ACM Symposium on Operating Systems Principles, pp. 456–471 (2013)

15. Sundaram, N., Satish, N.R., Patwary, M.M.A., Dulloor, S.: GraphMat: high performance graph analytics made productive. arXiv preprint arXiv:1503.07241 (2015)

16. Zhang, K., Chen, R., Chen, H.: NUMA-aware graph-structured analytics. In: Proceedings of the 20th ACM SIGPLAN Symposium on Principles and Practice of Parallel Programming, pp. 183–193 (2015)

17. Kyrola, A., Blelloch, G., Guestrin, C.: GraphChi: large-scale graph computation on just a PC. In: 10th USENIX Symposium on Operating Systems Design and Implementation, pp. 31–46 (2012)

18. Roy, A., Mihailovic, I., Zwaenepoel, W.: X-stream: edge-centric graph processing using streaming partitions. In: Proceedings of the Twenty-Fourth ACM Symposium on Operating Systems Principles, pp. 472–488 (2013)

19. Zhu, X., Han, W., Chen, W.: GridGraph: large-scale graph processing on a single machine using 2-level hierarchical partitioning. In: 2015 USENIX Annual Technical Conference, pp. 375–386 (2015)

20. Han, W.S., Lee, S., Park, K., Lee, J.H., Yu, H.: TurboGraph: a fast parallel graph engine handling billion-scale graphs in a single PC. In: Proceedings of the 19th ACM SIGKDD International Conference on Knowledge Discovery and Data Mining, pp. 77–85 (2013)

21. Zheng, D., Mhembere, D., Burns, R., Vogelstein, J., Szalay, A.S.: FlashGraph: processing billion-node graphs on an array of commodity SSDs. In: 13th USENIX Conference on File and Storage Technologies, pp. 45–58 (2015)

22. Turkington, G.: Hadoop beginner's guide. Packt Publishing, Packt Publishing (2013)

23. Malewicz, G., Austern, M.H., Bik, A.J.C., Dehnert, J.C., Czajkowski, G.: Pregel: a system for large-scale graph processing. In: Proceedings of the 2010 ACM SIGMOD International Conference on Management of data, pp. 135–146 (2010)

24. Low, Y., Gonzalez, J., Kyrola, A., Bickson, D., Guestrin, C.: Distributed GraphLab: a framework for machine learning in the cloud. arXiv preprint arXiv:1204.6078 (2012)

25. Gonzalez, J.E., Low, Y., Gu, H., Bickson, D., Guestrin, C.: PowerGraph: distributed graph-parallel computation on natural graphs. In: 10th USENIX Symposium on Operating Systems Design and Implementation, pp. 17–30 (2012)

26. Avery, C.: Giraph: large-scale graph processing infrastructure on hadoop. In: Proceedings of the Hadoop Summit. vol. 11(3), Santa Clara, pp. 5–9 (2011)

27. Xin, R.S., Gonzalez, J.E., Franklin, M.J., Stoica, L.: Graphx: a resilient distributed graph system on spark. In: First International Workshop on Graph Data Management Experiences and Systems, pp. 1–6 (2013)

28. Zhu, X., Chen, W., Zheng, W., Ma, X.: Gemini: a computation-centric distributed graph processing system. In: 12th USENIX Symposium on Operating Systems Design and Implementation, pp. 301–316 (2016)

29. Chen, R., Shi, J., Chen, Y., Zang, B., Chen, H.: PowerLyra: differentiated graph computation and partitioning on skewed graphs. ACM Trans. Parallel Comput. 5(3), 1–39 (2019)

30. Shao, B., Wang, H., Li, Y.: Trinity: a distributed graph engine on a memory cloud. In: Proceedings of the 2013 ACM SIGMOD International Conference on Management of Data, pp. 505–516 (2013)

31. Roy, A., Bindschaedler, L., Malicevic, J., Zwaenepoel.: Chaos: scale-out graph processing from secondary storage. In: Proceedings of the 25th Symposium on Operating Systems Principles, pp. 410–424 (2015)

32. Dijkstra, E.W.: A note on two problems in connexion with graphs. Numer. Math. 1(1), 269–271 (1959)

33. Bang-Jensen, J., Gutin, G.: The Bellman-Ford-Moore algorithm. Digraphs: Theory, Algorithms and Applications, p. 56 (2008)

34. Kleene, S.C.: Representation of events in nerve nets and finite automata. Automata stud. 34, 3–41 (1956)

35. Hart, P.E., Nilsson, N.J., Raphael, B.: A formal basis for the heuristic determination of minimum cost paths. IEEE Trans. Syst. Sci. Cybern. **4**(2), 100–107 (1968)
36. Duan, F.: A faster algorithm for shortest-path—SPFA. J. Southwest Jiaotong Univ. **29**(2), 207–212 (1994)
37. Johnson, D.B.: Efficient algorithms for shortest paths in sparse networks. J. ACM **24**(1), 1–13 (1977)
38. Zhang, Z.: Study of shortest path problem on large-scale graph. University of Science and Technology of China (2014)
39. Wagner, D., Willhalm, T.: Speed-up techniques for shortest-path computations. In: Thomas, W., Weil, P. (eds.) STACS 2007. LNCS, vol. 4393, pp. 23–36. Springer, Heidelberg (2007). https://doi.org/10.1007/978-3-540-70918-3_3

Long Short-Term Conditional Probability Matrix Prediction in Energy Efficient Ethernet

Yujie Hu, Ying Wang, Jie Wang, Renfu Yao, Ping Zhong,
and Wanchun Jiang$^{(\boxtimes)}$

School of Computer Science and Engineering,
Central South University, Changsha, China
`jiangwc@csu.edu.cn`

Abstract. Recently, much research on Energy Efficient Ethernet(EEE) have been carried out. For example, the recently proposed Frame Coalescing with Dynamic Threshold(FC-DT) strategy takes account of users' target delay and can achieve good energy savings. This paper reveals the issue of large prediction error in FC-DT. To solve this problem, we propose FC-DT+ with improving the prediction algorithm. In addition, we enhance the FC-DT strategy by choosing the low power mode according to the actual data arrival rate when the target delay is within [2.75 µs, 4.44 µs]. Simulation results confirm that FC-DT+ has better prediction accuracy about 8% higher than that of FC-DT and accordingly has a better tail delay which is 1.5 µs lower than that of FC-DT on average. Moreover, FC-DT+ can reduce the energy consumption by 20–30% with the enhanced low power mode selection mechanism.

Keywords: Energy Efficient Ethernet · FC-DT · prediction · algorithm · delay

1 Introduction

The IEEE 802.3bj standard defines two low power idle(LPI) modes for 40/100 Gb/s Energy Efficient Ethernet(EEE) [1,2] interfaces. IEEE provides the new modes but does not provide useful strategies. Afterward, several different strategies have been proposed, there are Dual-Mode [3], Frames Coalescing(FC) [4], and Frames Coalescing with States Selection based on History Information (FC-SSHI) [5]. The primary goal of these strategies is to make the interfaces stay in the low power mode longer for better energy savings. Moreover, an efficient way to achieve this goal is to collect arriving frames in the low power state and transmit them in the Active state. In this way, the energy-saving effect can be greatly improved, but simultaneously the delay of coalescing frames will be increased.

The FC-DT strategy [6] further considers the issue of delay based on the previous strategies. It sets the users' target delay as a parameter, which determines

---

Y. Wang—Co-first author.

W. Hong and Y. Weng (Eds.): ICCSE 2022, CCIS 1811, pp. 398–411, 2023.
https://doi.org/10.1007/978-981-99-2443-1_35

the LPI mode that EEE interfaces will only enter, and it proposes a dynamic queue threshold set by the target delay and the real-time load. In this way, FC-DT can keep the average delay close to the users' expectations while reducing the consumption of state transitions between two LPI modes.

However, when calculating the queue threshold for the next cycle, there is an unreasonable prediction algorithm for the load in real time in FC-DT, which directly takes the arrival rate of the previous cycle as the arrival rate of the next cycle. Moreover, when the target delay is within [2.75 μs, 4.44 μs], FC-DT directly selects Fast-Wake mode and takes much energy consumption. Aiming at the above problems of FC-DT, in this paper, we propose an improved strategy FC-DT+. Firstly, a prediction algorithm with conditional probability matrix is proposed in FC-DT+ to obtain a more accurate prediction of arrival rate. With the predicted value, an enhanced LPI mode selection mechanism is also proposed as a supplement for FC-DT.

After that, some NS3 simulation experiments are conducted, the results confirm that in FC-DT+, the better prediction accuracy brings a lower tail delay and choosing LPI mode better achieves more efficient energy savings.

2   Background and Motivation

2.1   Background

To reduce the energy consumption of 40/100 Gb/s EEE interfaces and the additional delay caused by state transitions, the IEEE 802.3bj proposed two energy efficient low power modes [1], which are known as the Deep-Sleep mode and the Fast-Wake mode. The parameters of these two low power modes are shown in the Table I. T_s is the time that interfaces cost from the Active state to LPI mode, T_w is the time needed by the interfaces for transmitting to the Active state from the LPI mode, and φ_{off} is the proportion of energy consumed in the low power mode compared with that in the Active state [2].

Since IEEE only devotes to formulating the EEE standards which instruct the production of EEE physical interfaces, without designing the strategies applied in EEE interfaces. Thus, the performed excellently strategies for 40/100 Gb/s EEE are significantly essential, which means they can achieve small delay while reducing energy consumption. To reach this goal, these strategies not only need to determine when the interfaces enter and exit the LPI mode, but also choose the better LPI mode.

2.2   Related Work

The original scheme designed for 40/100 Gb/s EEE to reduce the energy consumption is the Dual-Mode strategy [3,4]. It proposes [3] that when there is no frame needs to be transmitted, the EEE interfaces will enter the Fast-Wake mode, and set a timer T_F at the same time. If there is no frame arriving until the timer expires, the interface will transmit to the Deep-Sleep mode. On the contrary, when there is any frame arrives, the interface would exit the LPI mode and

Table 1. Two Low Power Modes

LPI mode	Active to LPI	LPI to Active	Energy consumption
Deep Sleep	$T_s^d = 0.9\mu s$	$T_w^d = 5.5\mu s$	$\varphi_{off}^d = 0.1$
Fast Wake	$T_s^f = 0.18\mu s$	$T_w^f = 0.34\mu s$	$\varphi_{off}^f = 0.7$

enter the Active state to transmit data, and this state transition takes T_w^f time. Similarly, if a frame arrives in the Deep-Sleep mode or the transition period, the interface will wake up as well.

With this mechanism, the interface wakes up whenever there is a frame arrives, which brings much additional energy consumption. Therefore, based on the Dual-Mode strategy, the FC strategy adds two counters C_F and C_D to coalesce arriving frames in the Fast-Wake mode and the Deep-Sleep mode, for the sake of prolonging the duration of the interfaces in the low power mode. When the interface is in the Fast-Wake mode, it will wake up unless the timer expires and the number of coalescing frames is larger than C_F. While in the Deep-Sleep mode, only when the number of coalescing frames exceeds the C_D, it will exit LPI mode and wake up.

Without a timer in the Deep-Sleep mode, the average delay in FC strategy is terrible. Afterward, the FC-SSHI policy [5] sets two timers T_D and T_F in two LPI modes and a counter C_D as the threshold, then the interfaces choose one of the low power modes dynamically by comparing the total number of arriving frames in the previous cycle with the threshold, which can reduce the times of state transitions.

In the light of the parameters in the above strategies are static, when the network load changes, the delay and energy consumption cannot show good effects at the same time in these mechanisms. Thus, To adapt to the changes of network load, FC-DT proposes a target delay W^* and configures a dynamical queue threshold Q_w with W^* and arrival rate λ [6], where $Q_w = (2W^* - T_w)\lambda + 1$. On the one hand, FC-DT makes the interfaces choose LPI mode according to W^*. Combined with the characteristics of 40/100 Gb/s EEE, FC-DT calculates the target delay threshold $\tilde{W}$ under different bandwidth. When W^* is larger than $\tilde{W}$, FC-DT gives priority to the Deep-Sleep mode to get better energy savings. Otherwise, the interfaces will directly choose the Fast-Wake mode to ensure that they can meet the small target delay. On the other hand, FC-DT calculates Q_w with W^* and real-time load, it uses the packets arrival rate of the previous cycle to predict the real-time load. Under these circumstances, FC-DT is able to keep the average delay close to the target delay and reduce the energy consumption as much as possible.

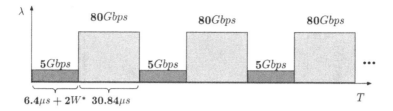

Fig. 1. The Synthesized traffic

In short, the performances of the above strategies depend on the config-urations of their timers or counters, but these parameters can not fully and accurately adapt to the network load in real time. Although FC-DT predicts the real-time network characteristics, it is obviously unreasonable to directly take the packets arrival rate of the previous cycle as the packets arrival rate of the next cycle in its prediction mechanism. A more accurate prediction algorithm is needed in the current EEE strategy research.

2.3 Motivation

Analyzing the mechanisms of existing strategies, the key to improving the per-formance of the strategy lies in controlling the time for the interfaces to enter and exit LPI mode and choosing which low power state to enter. If we can predict the arrival of data frames more accurately, this will make a significant contribution to this improvement work.

In the previous energy-saving strategies, only FC-DT considers the prediction of future traffic. Before the start of each cycle, FC-DT calculates the Queue Threshold Q_w in the low power mode with load prediction according to the users' target delay, for making the interfaces choose the proper time to exit the low power mode.

However, when FC-DT predicts the real-time load, it is unreasonable to directly take the arrival rate of the previous cycle as that of the next cycle. The arrival of packets in EEE is random, there is much difference between two contiguous periods. In addition, FC-DT uses arrival rate of packets for predic-tion, but the size of each packet is obviously not the same. For these reasons, the prediction mechanism of FC-DT will show poor accuracy, which will make the setting of Q_w inappropriate. If Q_w is large, it will increase the frame delay, and when Q_w is small, it will reduce the energy savings, thus the inaccurate predic-tion of packets arrival rate will worsen the overall performance of the strategy.

To verify that our opinion is correct, the Synthesized traffic was constructed to apply the FC-DT and compared with the FC-DT strategy applied in the Pareto traffic environment. Under the bandwidth of 100 Gb/s, there are two network nodes, one as the sending node and the other as the receiving and forwarding node. The Synthesized traffic is periodic, each cycle is divided into a low load part(5 Gb/s) and a high load part(80 Gb/s). The low load part lasts

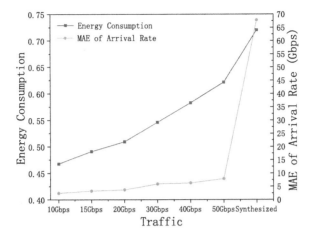

Fig. 2. Energy Consumption and Tail Delay When W*= 8 μs

$6.4\,\mu s + 2W^*$ (W^* is set by the users), while the high load part lasts $30.84\,\mu s$, the arrival rate of each part is constant, and the size of each packet is 1200 bytes. The average load of the traffic is about $48\,\text{Gb/s}$. The description of the traffic is shown in Fig. 1.

The experimental results are shown in Fig. 2. As shown in Fig. 2, when the traffic has extremely periodic changes, the mean average error of predicted data arrival rate will become very large, which shows the particularly poor prediction performance of FC-DT. Additionally, with inaccurate prediction, the energy-saving effect is quite terrible, which can be seen in Fig. 2.

Furthermore, we analyzed the $1\,\text{Gb/s}$ real traffic trace statistics, it's similar to the Synthesized traffic, the short-term(like $100\,\mu s$ or 1 ms) arrival rate is fluctuating violently in the real traffic environment. However, there is a significant finding that for a long term (10 ms and above), the fluctuation of the average data arrival rate is small. The total amount of arriving data in each long term of the same length fluctuates lightly. Therefore, in this paper, we proposed the improved prediction method of the FC-DT strategy with long-term average arrival rate, to achieve a more accurate prediction of the arrival rate. By the way, we abandon the practice of using arrival rate of packets to calculate the buffer threshold in FC-DT, and set bytes volume of the frame as the standard for caching. This will reduce the impact of the default packet size of 1500 bytes in FC-DT and improve the accuracy of arrival rate prediction.

In addition, to meet the users' target delay W^* and bring lower energy consumption, FC-DT calculates the delay threshold $\tilde{W}$ and the corresponding arrival rate threshold $\tilde{\lambda}$. Then it proposes [6] that when the W^* is larger than $4.44\,\mu s$, the interfaces choose to enter the Deep-Sleep mode under any load conditions, and when W^* is smaller than $2.75\,\mu s$, the interfaces can only enter the Fast-Wake mode, otherwise, it will not meet the target delay. However, when W^* is in $[2.75\,\mu s, 4.44\,\mu s]$, the selection of LPI mode is related to the load condi-

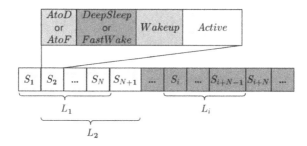

Fig. 3. Large cycle and small cycle

tions, but according to FC-DT, in most cases within this range, the traffic load is higher than $\tilde{\lambda}$. As a consequence, FC-DT proposes to choose the Fast-Wake mode in this interval. This is contrary to the principle of minimizing energy consumption under the constraint of W^*. Under the conditions of low load, the interfaces should be also allowed to enter the Deep-Sleep mode. Thus, we also enhanced the LPI mode selection mechanism with the load prediction.

3   Design of FC-DT+

In the previous section, we have got that the long-term average arrival rate is relatively stable so that we can predict it easily, simultaneously it has a strong correlation with the short-term arrival rate. Thus, we propose that use the prediction of the long-term average data arrival rate as a condition, then combine this condition with the data of the latest short term to make a more accurate prediction for the real-time load. At the same time, when the target delay is in the interval of $[2.75\,\mu s,\ 4.44\,\mu s]$, we consider comparing the predicted data arrival rate with $\tilde{\lambda}$ to choose the LPI mode to get better energy-saving effect.

3.1   Long-term Average Arrival Rate

Due to the stability of the change of the total amount of arriving data for a long time in the real network traffic, this longer term can be regarded as a large cycle. During this period, the real-time load will fluctuate around the average data arrival rate of the large cycle. Therefore, it can be involved in prediction of real-time load to obtain a more accurate prediction value.

FC-DT+ keeps using the cycle in FC-DT as the basic unit, which is later called cycle or small cycle, which is represented by S. And we call the long term as large cycle, which is represented by L, and each large cycle includes N small cycles. These two types cycles are shown in Fig. 3.

Firstly, we predict the average data arrival rate λ_{L_i} of the large cycle. In addition, the longer the distance from current small cycle, the more unreliable the historical information is, so that we give priority to the latest cycle. For this

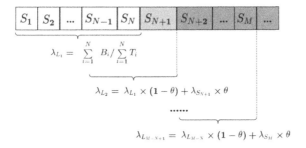

Fig. 4. Calculation of Li

reason, the exponential weighting method is adopted for the calculation of λ_{L_i} here. The calculation method is as follows.

In the first large cycle L_1, the algorithm will run the original FC-DT algorithm and calculate the first long-term average data arrival rate λ_{L_1}, which is given by the formula

$$\lambda_{L_1} = \frac{\sum\limits_{i=1}^{N} B_i}{\sum\limits_{i=1}^{N} T_i}, \tag{1}$$

where B_i is the total number of bytes arrived in the ith small cycle S_i and T_i is length of S_i.

At the end of subsequent small cycles, the average predicted value of large cycle is calculated as

$$\lambda_{L_i} = \lambda_{L_{i-1}} \times (1 - \frac{1}{N}) + \lambda_{S_{i+N-1}} \times \frac{1}{N}, \tag{2}$$

The calculation of λ_{L_i} is shown in Fig 4.

3.2   Prediction Algorithm

In FC-DT+, we get the average value of the data arrival rate λ_{L_i} of ith large cycle, and we take it as the first condition. We think that the data arrival rates of small cycles in the large cycle fluctuate around the value of large cycle, so we use λ_{L_i} as the first parameter to provide the benchmark. On this premise, we predict the data arrival rate λ_{S_k} of kth small cycle, where $k = i + N$. At the same time, We give more trust to the recent cycle, so we use the situation of the historical small cycle close to the current small cycle as an additional condition for prediction.

We propose a random variable R_k to represent the level of data arrival rate of S_k. After a large cycle pasted, the maximum λ_{max} and minimum λ_{min} of the short-term data arrival rate in this long term can be obtained, we take these two values as the two endpoints of the data arrival rate level interval, then the interval is divided into h levels. Here we can get the load quantization step v

$$v = \frac{\lambda_{max} - \lambda_{min}}{h}, \tag{3}$$

and the whole interval $[0, +\infty)$ of the load level can be divided into h levels by v. We give related formulas as follows

$$R_k = 1 \iff \lambda_{S_k} \in (0, \lambda_{min} + v),$$
$$R_k = 2 \iff \lambda_{S_k} \in [\lambda_{min} + v, \lambda_{min} + 2v),$$
$$\vdots \tag{4}$$
$$R_k = h \iff \lambda_{S_k} \in [\lambda_{min} + v(h-1), \infty).$$

Based on the above assumptions, a conditional probability matrix P is constructed to store the similarity between each small cycle and its previous cycle, which indicates the conditional probabilities of load level of S_{k+1} is r', given that the load level of S_k is r. The elements of the matrix are defined as

$$P(r, r') = \mathbb{P}[R_{k+1} = r' | R_k = r], r, r' \in \{1, \ldots, h\}. \tag{5}$$

According to the conditional probability matrix, we can predict the data arrival rate of the current small cycle with the condition of the average arrival rate of the large cycle and the previous small cycle. Here, we defined E represents the similarity between the current small cycle and the historical small cycle,

$$E = \mathbb{P}(R_k \in [r - 1, r + 1] \mid R_{k-1} = r). \tag{6}$$

When $E \geq \theta$, it is considered that the similarity between the current small cycle and the recent historical small cycle is high, then we let $\lambda_{S_k} = \lambda_{S_{k-1}}$. Otherwise, we think that the similarity is not high enough, and the value of historical small cycle should be revised by the average value of the large cycle. Here, we take the weighted value as α, which indicates the contribution of S_{k-1} to the prediction of the fluctuation amplitude of the arrival rate of current small cycle relative to the average value of large cycle

$$\lambda_{S_k} = \lambda_{S_{k-1}} * \alpha + \lambda_{L_i} * (1 - \alpha). \tag{7}$$

In this algorithm, the conditional probability matrix is used to monitor the change of traffic, and the arrival rate of long-term data is used to revise the predicted value when the short-term traffic fluctuates sharply. In this way, the prediction performance can be noticeably improved.

3.3   Low Power Mode Selection

Compared with the original prediction method, we have obtained a predicted value of real-time load which is more accurate and less affected by burst traffic. Except for setting the dynamic frame queue threshold, this predicted value can also be used to choose the low power mode when the users' target delay is in the [2.75 μs, 4.44 μs] range.

The relationship between the data arrival rate threshold $\tilde{\lambda}$ and the target delay has been obtained from FC-DT [6]. Then, after the users set the target delay parameters, $\tilde{\lambda}$ can be calculated by this formula [6]

$$\tilde{\lambda} = (T_w^d - 2W^* + \frac{2a}{\sqrt{b^2 - 4a(1-c)} - b})^{-1}, \tag{8}$$

where a = $cT_s^d T_w^f - T_s^f T_w^d = -0.072$, b = $T_w^d - T_s^f + c(T_s^d - T_w^f) = 7$ and c = $(1 - \varphi_{off}^d)/(1 - \varphi_{off}^f) = 3$ [6].

When the buffer is empty, the conditional probability matrix is used to calculate the predicted value of data arrival rate λ_{S_k} before entering the low power mode, and then $\tilde{\lambda}$ of the target delay is compared with λ_{S_k} to choose the LPI mode. If the predicted value λ_{S_k} is larger than the $\tilde{\lambda}$, the PHYs will choose to enter the Fast-Wake state, if λ_{S_k} is smaller than the $\tilde{\lambda}$, the PHYs will enter the Deep-Sleep state. The selection process is shown here,

$$\begin{aligned} \lambda_{S_k} > \tilde{\lambda} &\Longrightarrow Fast - Wake, \\ \lambda_{S_k} <= \tilde{\lambda} &\Longrightarrow Deep - Sleep. \end{aligned} \tag{9}$$

4   Evaluation

To evaluate the performance of the FC-DT+, the following traffic and parameters are used for experiments with the 100 Gb/s channel bandwidth.

Firstly, we designed some experiments for the LPI mode selection strategy with target delay W* between 2.75 μs and 4.44 μs, which are carried out mainly under low loads of Pareto traffic. Furthermore, Pareto traffic is also used to compare the original FC-DT algorithm with FC-DT+, then we set the target delays as 4.5 μs and 8 μs, and the traffic loads vary from 1 to 90 Gb/s. Additionally, the constructed traffic and real traffic are also used to conduct the comparative experiments. We recorded and compared the energy consumption, mean absolute error(MAE) of data arrival rate, tail delay and average delay of each experiment.

4.1   LPI Mode Selection

To evaluate the effect of the improvement for LPI mode selection with small target delay threshold, we conducted following experiments to validate the better energy-saving effect of our strategy.

We set the target delay as 4.3 μs, while the traffic loads vary from 1 to 10 Gb/s. As shown in Fig. 5, the MAE of arrival rate which indicates the actual

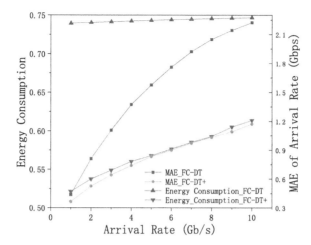

Fig. 5. Energy Consumption and MAE of Arrival Rate When W*=4.3 μs

arrival rate differs from the predicted value in our strategy is better than FC-DT, so that in these cases FC-DT+ has more accurate prediction of real-time load. What's more, we can see in Fig. 5 that our strategy has better energy-saving effect than FC-DT. This is because we add the option of the Deep-Sleep mode while keeping the delay close to the target value, and above experiments prove that our judgment is correct.

4.2 Prediction Error with Pareto Traffic

When W* is larger than 4.44 μs, FC-DT strategy directly chooses the Deep-Sleep mode, in this way, the energy-saving effect is excellent. As we adjust the queue threshold more accurately with the more accurate prediction of arrival rate, not only do we have the efficient energy savings, but also get the lower tail delay which better meets the needs of users.

Figure 6 shows the MAE of predicted arrival rate with applying FC-DT+ and FC-DT, it can be seen that the prediction accuracy of FC-DT+ is higher than that of FC-DT under all load conditions. With this improvement of prediction accuracy, Fig. 7 shows that we have obtained the better tail delay. Meanwhile, Fig. 8 shows that FC-DT+ can keep the energy consumption not more than FC-DT and the average frame delay of FC-DT+ is less than that of FC-DT. These experimental results validate the more efficient performance of FC-DT+ than that of FD-DT.

4.3 Prediction Error with Constructed Traffic

In part *II*, we proved the poor prediction performance of FC-DT with the Synthesized traffic we constructed, then we applied FC-DT in this traffic environment and got some experimental results. Here we applied FC-DT+ and FC-DT

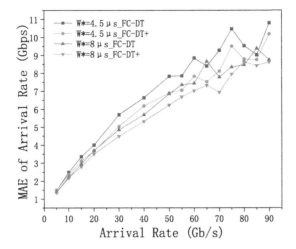

Fig. 6. MAE of Arrival Rate When W*=4.5 μs and 8 μs

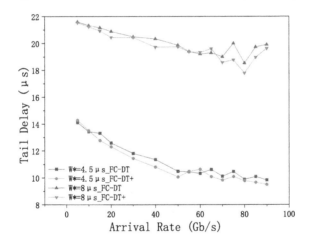

Fig. 7. Tail Delay When W*=4.5 μs and 8 μs

in this Synthesized traffic under different target delays and compared their performances. We set W* from 4.5 μs to 16 μs, as shown in Fig. 9, we have much higher accuracy of arrival rate than FC-DT, meanwhile, we also have better energy-saving effect which can be seen in Fig. 9. The comparisons in this traffic condition also validate the excellent accuracy of our prediction algorithm and the great performance it brings to the energy savings.

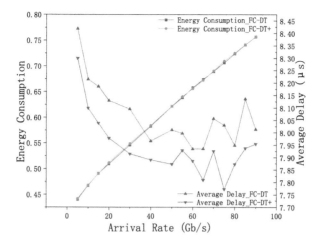

Fig. 8. Energy Consumption and Average Delay When W*=8 μs

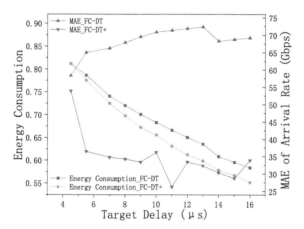

Fig. 9. MAE of Arrival Rate and Tail Delay with Constructed Traffic

4.4   Prediction Error with Real Traffic

We also evaluated FC-DT+ with real traffic which is available in MAWI Working Group Traffic Archive [7]. We used the daily traces at the transit link of WIDE to the upstream ISP which were collected during 2020 on a 1 Gb/s IX link. We assumed that the PHYs in these traces had the same behaviors as the EEE interfaces and then we adjusted the arrival rate to 100 Gb/s. Here we got some results.

Firstly, Fig. 10 shows that in the scenario of real traffic, FC-DT+ greatly improves the prediction performance of FC-DT, which reduces the prediction error of arrival rate notably. In addition, Fig. 11 shows that for tail delay and energy consumption, FC-DT+ also shows better performance than FC-DT.

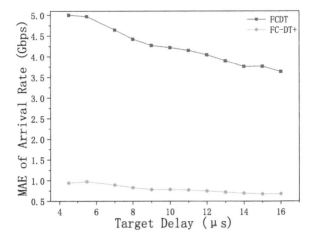

Fig. 10. MAE of Arrival Rate with Real Traffic

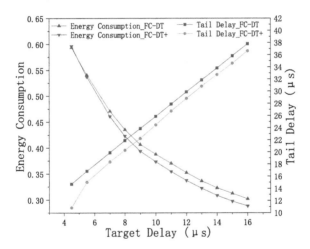

Fig. 11. Energy Consumption and Tail Delay with Real Traffic

5   Conclusions

This paper proposes FC-DT+, which combines the long-term average arrival rate with the conditional probability matrix to predict short-term arrival rate accurately. Thus, with the better prediction, more effective queue threshold can be got to bring the more efficient energy savings. This prediction method can be used not only in FC-DT, but also in other strategies with prediction mechanism.

What's more, a strategy about choosing the LPI mode according to the actual traffic load with the small target delay threshold is described in this paper. After the predicted value of arrival rate is obtained, we compare it with the arrival rate threshold to indicate which LPI mode is better. Finally, we conduct some experiments under different conditions which have verified that FC-DT+ has better tail delay effect and excellent energy savings.

Acknowledgment. The authors sincerely thank the reviewers for their helpful comments on this paper. This work is partially supported by the key research and development project of Hunan province under grant No. 2022SK2107 and the academic research project on education of central south university. In addition, This work was also carried out in part using computing resources at the High Performance Computing Center of Central South University.

References

1. Amendment 2: Physical Layer Specifications and Management Para-meters for 100 Gb/s Operation Over Backplanes and Copper Cables, IEEE Standard 802.3bj-2014, Sep. 2014. https://doi.org/10.1109/IEEESTD.2014.6891095
2. Barrass, H.: Options for EEE in 100G. IEEE 802.3bj Meeting, Jan. 2012. http://www.ieee802.org/3/bj/public/jan12/barrass_01a_0112.pdf
3. Mostowfi, M.: Packet coalescing for dual-mode energy efficient Ethernet: A simulation study. In: Proceedings of the 8th EAI International Conference Simulation Tools Techn. (SIMUTools), pp. 335–342 (2015)
4. Mostowfi, M.: A simulation study of energy-efficient Ethernet with two modes of low-power operation. IEEE Commun. Lett. **19**(10), 1702–1705 (2015)
5. Mostowfi, M., Shafieb, K.: Dual-mode energy efficient ethernet with packet coalescing: analysis and simulation. Sustain. Comput. Inform. Syst. **18**, 149–162 (2018)
6. Herrería-Alonso, S., Rodríguez-Pérez, M., Fernández-Veiga, M., López-García, C.: Optimizing dual-mode EEE interfaces: deep-sleep is healthy. IEEE Trans. Commun. **65**, 3374–3385 (2017)
7. Packet traces from MAWI Working Group Traffic Archive. Used: 20201025, Accessd May 2022. http://mawi.wide.ad.jp/mawi/

An Experiment Aiding System Driven by Eye Movement in Mixed Reality

Zhigeng Pan[1,3], Jiaxin Liu[1], Qingshu Yuan[2(✉)] ⓘ, Kailiang Shou[2], Yuxin Zeng[2], Zihan Wang[1], and Luxiao Zhu[2]

[1] Alibaba Business School, Hangzhou Normal University, Hangzhou, China
[2] School of Information Science and Technology, Hangzhou Normal University, Hangzhou, China
yuanqs@hznu.edu.cn
[3] School of Artificialrtificial Intelligence, Nanjing University of Information Science and Technology, Nanjing, China

Abstract. Experimental learning is crucial in secondary school. During experimental learning, students generally use laboratory manuals. However, it is inconvenient and unintuitive to read. Current experiment aids require users to interact by their hands to acquire guidance, affecting hands-on experiments. In order to facilitate students exploring experiments in an intuitive and non-affecting operations way, an experiment aiding system driven by eye movement in mixed reality is proposed. It identifies actual experiment scenarios and presents the virtual aid information in real-time. Reminders and warnings about experiments can be obtained by implicit eye-movement interaction. It takes the experiment "Oxygen production with potassium permanganate" as an example. Three modules including apparatus identification, experiment aiding and specification test are designed. Questionnaires demonstrate that students can get a better experience and are more satisfied with this system.

Keywords: Mixed Reality · Eye-movement Interaction · Experiment-aiding System

1 Introduction

Chemistry is an experiment-based science that studies substances and their changes. Chemical experiments are the physical manifestation of chemical concepts. Students reinforce the memory of theoretical knowledge by observing experiment phenomena. And the hands-on experiments also improve students' practical ability [1]. Modern teaching pays more attention to the comprehensive quality of students, so experimental learning becomes an important part of secondary education.

Students conduct experiments by following laboratory manuals in secondary school chemistry class. However, the laboratory manuals are brief, and the reminders of details are not obvious. Students frequently overlook necessary operation steps, resulting in failed experiments or even laboratory safety incidents. Furthermore, reading the manual while doing experiments also affects the operations and distracts their attention [2]. How to intuitively present guidance and cautions during operating is a key issue in experimental learning.

Several studies have attempted to use modern information technologies to help students do experiments. Students browse related learning resources (such as diagrams, videos) during experiments via apps, e-teaching resources and other media [3–5], helping them understand experimental operations clearly. But the assistance does not correspond exactly with the real experiment, incurring additional cognitive load during students match them [6].

Some studies have also used Augment Reality (AR) technology to solve the problems, presenting the virtual aid information in experiment scenarios. Current studies mainly focused on projective and handheld AR applications [7, 8]. Handheld AR applications require users to hold and interact with a mobile device to acquire guidance, which is inconvenient for hands-on experiments. Projective AR applications can separate the display device from the user, but digital information is not interactive and alterable, lacking flexibility and usability during experiments.

Using implicit eye-movement interaction mode in Mixed Reality (MR) technology implements the connection between digital information and actual environments without affecting current activity, assisting users learning in a natural and immersive way.

Main contribution of this study is the design and implementation of an experiment aiding system driven by eye movement in mixed reality. It is based on HoloLens2 MR device and combines object detection, eye-movement interaction, spatial anchors and other technologies. It identifies actual experiment scenes and presents the virtual aid information based on implicit eye-movement instructions, assisting students in exploring experiments without affecting hand-on operations. This preliminary study hopes to fill the gaps in existing research and provide a reference for designing similar systems.

The organization of the rest of this paper is as follows. Section 2 introduced related works. Section 3 designed the interactive instructions of eye movement during experiments. Section 4 focuses on the implementation of MR experiment aiding system. Next, user study is presented in Sect. 5. Finally, conclusion and future work are shown in Sect. 6.

2 Related Work

2.1 Experimental Learning Aids

To help students better understand experimental operations, Lo et al. developed a multimedia online learning system for organic chemistry courses, combining multimedia videos (experiment explanations and demonstrations) and interactive components [3]. Mao et al. designed the "Computer Simulation Experiment Organic Chemistry Experiment", utilizing multimedia technology to introduce organic chemistry experiments. It is designed three sections: basic knowledge, operation demonstration and comprehensive experiments, including many illustrations, texts, animations and other materials about multiple experiments [5].

Compared with the conventional laboratory manuals, multimedia experimental learning aids help students intuitively understand the experiment procedures, reducing operational errors. However, the experiment settings in the multimedia resource are not exactly consistent with the real scenario, resulting in extra cognitive load during students consulting for reference [6]. In addition, students have to pause their current operations to get guidance by interacting with the devices. This disruption will impact experiment continuity and immersion.

AR technology can connect the real experiment scenario with virtual aiding information. Ge et al. designed a projective AR learning-aiding system for chemical experiments, presenting reminders of the experiment by projection [7]. Nevertheless, the computer, camera, projector, and other devices are required to build this AR setting, and the projection is non-interactive and unalterable, which is inconvenient to use in chemistry experiments. Woźniak et al. designed the "ARchemist system", utilizing a tablet computer to identify the experimental apparatus and display the experimental works' relevant solutions. It was discovered that this system has significant potential to assist students in experimenting [8]. However, a tablet computer is required holding to acquire assistance during the experiment, limiting experimental operations.

2.2 Mixed Reality Aids

MR technology augments the real world by presenting digital information in the tangible environment and interacting virtual objects with physical objects in real-time, bringing a novel interaction and visual effect to assist users to complete tasks effectively. For example, Su et al. proposed a maintenance guiding system based on MR, assisting workers in checking equipment and implementing maintenance operations [9]. Molero et al. developed an MR system to assist piano learning, presenting the highlighted keys and standard gestures in real-time [10]. Strzys et al. proposed an MR experimental scene named Holo. Lab. It augmented displays the thermal state of objects in gradient color to help students understand the abstract concept of thermodynamics in an intuitive way [11].

2.3 Implicit Interaction and Eye-Movement Interaction

Schmidt defined implicit human-computer interaction (IHCI) as "an action performed by a user whose primary purpose is not to interact with the computer system, but the system interprets it as an interactive input" [12]. During IHCI, sensors form and perform interactive instructions by capturing data of user's state changes (gaze, expression, posture, etc.) and environment information (position, temperature, humidity, etc.). However, users are unconscious of these processes [13]. It reduces users' cognitive costs and attention demands, decreasing unnecessary energy consumption, thus improving the efficiency of tasks.

Humans acquire external information mainly through their eyes and form motion instructions through cognitive processors to guide interactive behavior [14]. Eye movement can reflect user's focus and interests during their activity. Therefore, many researchers use vision as an interactive input channel, analyzing intentions by eye movement and realizing implicit interaction.

For example, Starker and Bolt proposed a system using eye-movement interaction to facilitate users browsing product information. It analyzes user's eye movements and gaze patterns in real-time to infer the most attractive item, zooming in on it to help the user view closer [15]. Orlosky et al. designed a modular AR system. It integrates eye-tracking to control visual augmentation (e.g., optical zoom or vision expansion), improving digital graphics' flexibility and presentation effect [16]. Guo et al. proposed a reading-aiding method based on eye-movement interaction [17]. It translates and summarizes the regions of interest judged by the user's gaze pattern during reading, improving the reading efficiency and subjective experience.

Implicit interaction based on eye movement implements the interactive functions during user focus on their tasks, benefiting experimental learning that requires concentration and immersion. Therefore, eye-movement instruction for aiding experiments has been proposed to provide users with a better experience.

3   Design of Eye-Movement Instructions

Users obtain assisted information additionally will interrupt experimental operations and distract their attention. How to acquire prompt information naturally and smoothly is the key problem during experiments. An implicit interactive instruction is designed based on eye-movement technology. Assistance is incorporated into user's operation and can be presented unaffectedly when users need it.

Gaze duration is used to analyze whether the user needs prompt and gaze point's position control where aiding information presented. The detailed function of eye-movement interaction is shown in Fig. 1.

- During the user inspects the experimental apparatus, their eyes linger on the apparatus for a while. It is regarded as an interactive input when the gaze point is detected to stay on an apparatus for a specified time. The detailed information about this apparatus will be obtained and displayed above it.
- As usual, the user conducts experiments following the experimental procedure is required to find the specified apparatus and operate it. It is regarded as interactive input when the gaze point is not detected to stay on the specified operative object within a period of time. A noticeable mark will be displayed above this object.
- After operating, the user is frequently required to observe the experimental phenomenon. It is regarded as interactive input when the gaze point is not detected to stay at the specified position. A reminder about the position that needs to be observed will be presented for user.

User's intent can be identified actively by implicit interaction based on eye-tracking, allowing users to control assisted information more naturally and conveniently during the experiments.

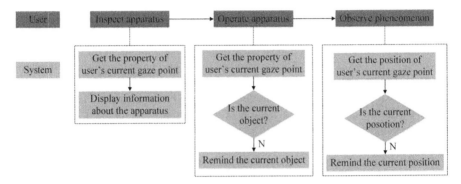

Fig. 1. The function of eye-movement interaction

4   Implementation

Basing on the design of eye-movement interactive function and referencing chemistry textbooks, an experiment aiding system driven by eye movement in mixed reality was proposed. The system concept diagram is shown in Fig. 2.

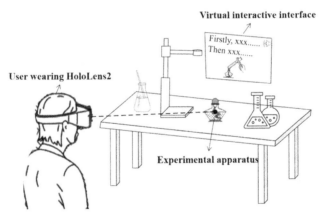

Fig. 2. The concept diagram of MR experiment aiding system. When the user gazes at an experimental apparatus, the related operative information will be augmented displayed above it.

4.1   Hardware

HoloLens2 MR headset from Microsoft is the core hardware of the system. It is equipped with a depth camera, infrared cameras, visible-light tracking cameras, RGB cameras and optical components, etc. [18]. HoloLens2 implements multiple functions such as spatial awareness, simultaneous localization and mapping, eye-movement tracking and hologram augmented display.

4.2 System Architecture

The system architecture is shown in Fig. 3. It mainly includes augmented display module, interaction module and data processing module.

Augmented display module mainly identifies experimental apparatus by the target database and transmits their detailed information to the data processing module. Meanwhile, it builds the corresponding virtual scene according to these data by 3D tracking registration. Finally, it augmented displays the digital information returned by the data processing module.

Interaction module is mainly responsible for the recognition and transmission of instructions. Firstly, it obtains and identifies user's gaze instructions using Application Programming Interface (API) and instruction database, then transfers interactive information to the data processing module.

Data processing module is the core of the whole system. It mainly receives and retrieves the gaze instruction data transmitted from outside, then manages and controls the assisted information according to the data logic of the script resource database. Finally, it transmits the data that needs to be presented to the augmented display module.

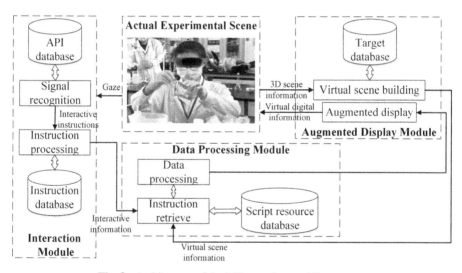

Fig. 3. Architecture of the MR experiment aiding system

4.3 Object Recognition and 3D Registration Algorithm

Object recognition and 3D registration are implemented with the Vuforia software development kit. Features from Accelerated Segment Test (FAST) algorithm is used to query the feature point data of the recognized target [19]. Error minimization method is used to estimate the projective transformation matrix of the target point set and detected point set, as in (1).

$$\begin{pmatrix} x'_1 \\ x'_2 \\ x'_3 \end{pmatrix} = \begin{bmatrix} h_{11} & h_{11} & h_{13} \\ h_{21} & h_{22} & h_{23} \\ h_{31} & h_{32} & h_{33} \end{bmatrix} \begin{pmatrix} x_1 \\ x_2 \\ x_3 \end{pmatrix} \tag{1}$$

where (x_1, x_2, x_3) is the point in the target coordinate system, $\left(x'_1, x'_2, x'_3\right)$ is the point in the camera coordinate system. According to the projective transformation matrix, the appropriate camera model is used to estimate the camera pose, and the virtual object is correctly placed on the position of the object.

4.4 Gaze Point Calculation

Gaze point tracking is implemented with the Mixed Reality Toolkit of HoloLens2. The principle of gaze ray collision detection is shown in Fig. 4.

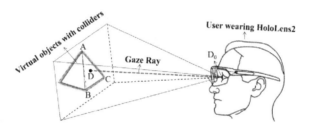

Fig. 4. Principle of calculating the gaze ray collision detection

Assuming that a ray is sent from $D_0(X_0, Y_0, Z_0)$ to the direction of eye gaze, it impacts the virtual object with collider at D. The coordinate of D on the ray can be expressed as:

$$D = D_0 + E \times M \tag{2}$$

where M is the module and E is the unit vector.

Assuming that there are three known reference points A $(X_A, Y_A, Z_A), B$ (X_B, Y_B, Z_B) and C (X_C, Y_C, Z_C) on the collider of the virtual model, any other point on the plane that constitutes by these three points can be represented by A, B, C and two other variables k, v. So D can also be expressed as:

$$D = A + k \times (B - A) + v \times (C - A) \tag{3}$$

$$(k > 0, v < 1, k + v < 1)$$

From (2) and (3) can get:

$$\begin{cases} X_0 + E \times M = (1 - k - v) \times X_A + k \times X_B + v \times X_C \\ Y_0 + E \times M = (1 - k - v) \times Y_A + k \times Y_B + v \times Y_C \\ Z_0 + E \times M = (1 - k - v) \times Z_A + k \times Z_B + v \times Z_C \end{cases} \quad (4)$$

The values of variable k, v and M can be obtained from (4), and the coordinate of D can be obtained by solving (3). This coordinate is the current gaze point of the user.

4.5 System Development

To help students be familiar with experimental apparatus and operations, three modules were designed for the MR experiment-aiding system, including experimental apparatus identification, experiments aiding and experimental operation specification test.

The process of the experimental apparatus identification module is shown in Fig. 5. Real apparatus will be identified first and the corresponding virtual object will be placed in the same position, then texture of the virtual object will be transparent. Meanwhile, the user's eyes will be tracked. When the gaze ray impacts a virtual object over 3 s, the corresponding aiding information (such as name, classification and cautions) will be displayed in the form of holographic (as shown in Fig. 6).

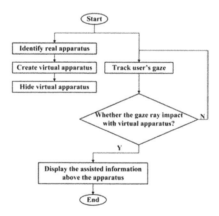

Fig. 5. Process of the experimental apparatus identification module.

The process of the experiments aiding module is shown in Fig. 7. Operation guidance is presented in the form of text and graphics step by step on the interactive interface, and the voice prompt is also played at the same time. After the voice prompt is finished, the collision detection event is triggered. When it is detected that the gaze ray does not impact the specified object within 5 s, the target's position is returned and a virtual red arrow is rendered above it (as shown in Fig. 8). When the system detects the collision between the gaze ray and the "Next" button lasts for 3 s, the operation guidance will be switched to the next one.

Fig. 6. The aiding information augmented display above the experimental apparatus.

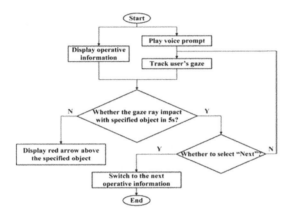

Fig. 7. Process of the experiment aiding module.

The process of the experimental operation specification test module is shown in Fig. 9. The system first collects spatial posture information and anchors the virtual test interface in the center of the user's vision, meanwhile tracking the user's eyes. The interaction event will be triggered when the gaze ray impacts the options button for 3 s. When the option selected by the user is detected to be the correct one for the current question, the question will be directly switched. Otherwise, the correct option will be marked as green, and the wrong one will be marked as red (as shown in Fig. 10). The question will be switched until the gaze ray is detected to impact with the "Next" button.

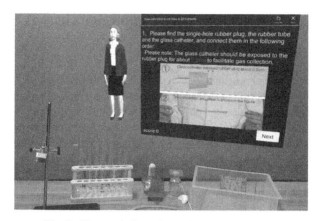

Fig. 8. The reminders of experimental operations.

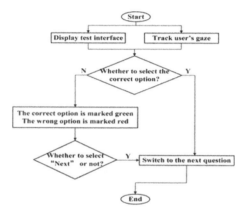

Fig. 9. Process of the experimental operative specification test module.

Fig. 10. The reminders of the experimental operative specification.

5   Comparative Experiment Design and Data Analysis

5.1   Comparative Experiment Design

A comparative experiment is designed to investigate the differences in students' attitudes toward using the MR experiment aiding system versus the laboratory manual. It was conducted in the chemistry laboratory of a public school in Hangzhou, Zhejiang Province. Twenty students who had experiment experience and could complete the chemistry experiment independently were invited to participate in this comparative experiment. All of the participants were informed and willing to participate in the experiment. They will be trained to use HoloLens2 before the formal experiment begins, ensuring that they can interact with it independently.

The overall flow of the comparative experiment was designed referring to the study of Alfalah [20]. Each participant will complete the tasks in the experimental and control group separately (as shown in Fig. 11). In the control group, participants follow the laboratory manual to perform the tasks in the experiment "Oxygen production with potassium permanganate". In the experimental group, participants need to wear HoloLens2 and finish the experiment with the help of MR experiment-aiding system. At the end of each task, participants were required to submit a subjective perception scale about the experiment aids.

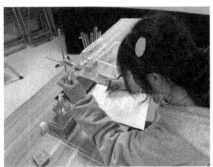

Fig. 11. Student does experiment following laboratory manual (left) and MR experiment aiding system (right), respectively.

5.2   Questionnaire Design

For measuring whether experiment aids improve students' experiment experience, a questionnaire about the satisfaction degree was designed. It is based on the scale proposed by Davis in 1989, which is used to predict user acceptance of computers [21], and referred to the subjective perception scale designed by other similar researchers [22] [23]. It is made up of 12 statements that cover the dimensions of learning content, user experience, learning motivation and usefulness. A 5-point Likert scale is used to score all of the questionnaire items [24]. Each statement has 5 answers: "strongly disagree",

"disagree", "neutral", "agree" and "strongly agree", which correspond to 1, 2, 3, 4, and 5 points, respectively. Students were asked to complete two identical scales based on their experience of doing experiments using the laboratory manual and the MR experiment-aiding system, measuring their satisfaction with different experiment aids.

5.3 Data Analysis

The data reliability of the two groups' questionnaires was analyzed using SPSS 26.0 statistical software. The results of the analysis are shown in Table 1. The Cronbach's α value of control group (using the laboratory manual) and experimental group (using the MR experiment aiding system) respectively were 0.880 and 0.958, indicating that both data sets are quite reliable.

Table 1. The result of questionnaires reliability analysis.

Comparison criteria	Cronbach's α
Control Group	0.880
Experimental Group	0.958

Two groups' scores of all questions in the satisfaction scale were averaged (as shown in Table 2). The results showed that students scored relatively high on the MR experiment-aiding system. The control group scored between 2.9 and 3.9 on average, indicating that students were dissatisfied with using the laboratory manual to aid experiment. The average score of the experimental group was between 4.0 and 4.6, which reflects the students' approval of the MR experiment-aiding system. Statements 9 and 11 demonstrate that the MR experiment-aiding system has obvious advantages over the laboratory manual in improving experiment experience while not interfering with the experiment operation. Students' overall satisfaction with the laboratory manual and the MR experiment-aiding system (as shown in Fig. 12) shows a clear preference for the latter, indicating that this type of experiment aid provides a more satisfactory interaction and better experiment learning experience.

Table 2. Questionnaire results comparing mean value for two groups.

Statements	Mean score of control group	Mean sore of experimental group
1. It helps me complete chemical experiments	3.30	4.40
2. It provides me with timely help and guidance in experimental operations	3.40	4.50

(continued)

Table 2. (*continued*)

Statements	Mean score of control group	Mean sore of experimental group
3. It deepens my understanding of experimental knowledge	3.25	4.40
4. It is easy and convenient to use	3.20	4.10
5. Using it can quickly get the information I want	3.05	4.60
6. I can use it independently	3.90	4.00
7. Using it gives me confidence in experimental learning	3.20	4.50
8. It is presented in a very interesting way	3.05	4.35
9. It improves my interest and efficiency in the experiment	3.05	4.60
10. It makes the experiment more convenient	2.95	4.45
11. It will not affect the experimental operation process	2.90	4.20
12. I would like to use it in more experiments	3.25	4.40

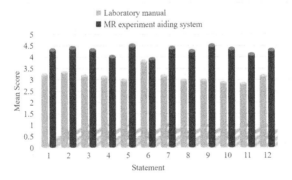

Fig. 12. Questionnaire results comparing each statement's mean values for the laboratory manual and the MR experiment aiding system.

6 Conclusion

An aiding system for chemistry experiments using MR and eye-movement interaction technologies is proposed in this paper. It realizes present virtual aiding information to the actual experimental scenario according to user's eye-movement instructions, and aid students in a convenient and natural way without affecting their experiment operation. An experimental study was conducted to compare it with conventional laboratory manual. The results of the satisfaction questionnaires clearly demonstrated that students were satisfied with the MR experiment aiding system, thus confirming its usefulness.

It was proved that MR and eye-movement interaction technology have great potential in experimental learning in this study. MR technology superimposes more information on the operative environment, whereas implicit eye-movement interaction minimizes the interactive burden in the operating process. This way of obtaining high-quality aid through low-cost interaction can bring a fantastic experience to users. Based on current achievements, we intend to explore more forms of aid information (such as operation animation) and functions in the future. In addition, we will further study whether and how the MR experiment-aiding system influences user's experimental learning efficiency.

References

1. Hofstein, A., Lunetta, V.N.: The role of the laboratory in science teaching: neglected aspects of research. Rev. Educ. Res. **52**(2), 201–217 (1982)
2. Baloian, N., Pino, J.A., Hoppe, H.U.: Dealing with the students' attention problem in computer supported face-to-face lecturing. J. Educ. Technol. Soc. **11**(2), 192–205 (2008)
3. Lo, C.M., Tang, K.Y.: Blended learning with multimedia e-learning in organic chemistry course. In: 2018 International Symposium on Educational Technology (ISET), pp. 23–25. IEEE, Japan (2018)
4. Seibert, J., Luxenburger-Becker, H., Marquardt, M., et al.: Multitouch experiment instruction for a better learning outcome in chemistry education. World J. Chem. Educ. **8**(1), 1–8 (2020)
5. Mao, Y., Huang, C.: Application of director in organic chemistry experiment. Chem. Eng. Trans. **62**, 175–180 (2017)
6. Kalyuga, S.: Cognitive load theory: how many types of load does it really need? Educ. Psychol. Rev. **23**, 1–19 (2011)
7. Ge, T., Wang, J.M., Zhu, Y.N., et al.: Research on interaction design of chemical inquiry virtual experiment based on augmented reality technology. In: 2021 IEEE 7th International Conference on Virtual Reality (ICVR), pp. 340–351. IEEE, China (2021)
8. Woźniak, M., Lewczuk, A., Adamkiewicz, K., et al.: ARchemist: towards in-situ experimental guidance using augmented reality technology. In: Proceedings of the 18th International Conference on Advances in Mobile Computing & Multimedia, pp: 58–63. ACM, USA (2020)
9. Su, X., Cheng, Z., Luo, B.: An auxiliary industrial equipment maintenance system using mixed reality. In: 2021 IEEE 8th International Conference on Industrial Engineering and Applications (ICIEA), pp: 503–508. IEEE, Japan (2021)
10. Molero, D., Schez-Sobrino, S., Vallejo, D., Glez-Morcillo, C., Albusac, J.: A novel approach to learning music and piano based on mixed reality and gamification. Multimedia Tools Appl. **80**(1), 165–186 (2020). https://doi.org/10.1007/s11042-020-09678-9
11. Strzys, M.P., Kapp, S., Thees, M., et al.: Physics holo. lab learning experience: using smartglasses for augmented reality labwork to foster the concepts of heat conduction. Eur. J. Phys. **39**(3), 035703 (2018)
12. Schmidt, A.: Implicit human computer interaction through context. Pers. Technol. **4**, 191–199 (2000)
13. Ju, W., Leifer, L.: The design of implicit interactions: Making interactive systems less obnoxious. Des. Issues **24**(3), 72–84 (2008)

14. Kang, Z., Bass, E.J.: Supporting the eye tracking analysis of multiple moving targets: Design concept and algorithm. In: 2014 IEEE International Conference on Systems, Man, and Cybernetics (SMC), pp. 3184–3189. IEEE, USA (2014)

15. Starker, I., Bolt, R.A.: A gaze-responsive self-disclosing display. In: Proceedings of the SIGCHI Conference on Human Factors in Computing Systems, pp. 3–10. ACM, USA (1990)

16. Orlosky, J., Toyama, T., Kiyokawa, K., et al.: Modular: eye-controlled vision augmentations for head mounted displays. IEEE Trans. Visual Comput. Graphics 21(11), 1259–1268 (2015)

17. Guo, W., Cheng, S.: An approach to reading assistance with eye tracking data and text features. In: Adjunct of the 2019 International Conference on Multimodal Interaction, pp. 1–7. ACM, USA (2019)

18. Furlan, R.: The future of augmented reality: hololens-microsoft's AR headset shines despite rough edges [Resources_Tools and Toys]. IEEE Spectr. 53(6), 21 (2016)

19. Drummond, T.: High speed matching and tracking. http://www.qualcomm.com/media/doc uments/high-speed-matching-andtracking-slides

20. Alfalah, S.F.M., Falah, J.F.M., Alfalah, T., Elfalah, M., Muhaidat, N., Falah, O.: A comparative study between a virtual reality heart anatomy system and traditional medical teaching modalities. Virtual Reality 23(3), 229–234 (2018). https://doi.org/10.1007/s10055-018-0359-y

21. Davis, F.D.: Perceived usefulness, perceived ease of use, and user acceptance of information technology. MIS Q. 13(3), 319–340 (1989)

22. Tsai, C.Y., Ho, Y.C., Nisar, H.: Design and validation of a virtual chemical laboratory—an example of natural science in elementary education. Appl. Sci. 11(21), 10070 (2021)

23. Tarng, W., Lin, Y.J., Ou, K.L.: A virtual experiment for learning the principle of daniell cell based on augmented reality. Appl. Sci. 11(2), 762 (2021)

24. Likert, R.: A technique for the measurement of attitudes. Arch. psychol. 22(140), 55 (1932)

Big Data Management and Analysis System for Field Scientific Observation and Research Stations

Junyi Tang and Shouliang Li[⊠]

School of Information Science and Engineering, Lanzhou University, Lanzhou, China
{tangjy20,lishoul}@lzu.edu.cn

Abstract. With the diversification of sensors and the refinement of observations, field scientific observation and research teams can collect a large amount of rich and accurate data. The traditional data analysis and storage methods face huge challenges for the big data. In order to promote the scientific and standardized management of field research data, this paper analyzes the needs and difficulties faced by the scientific observation and research, and proposes the design of the scientific research data management platform based on the Hadoop framework. A data management system of B/S architecture is implemented through the strategy of separating the front and back ends, which used the Vue.js and SpringBoot frameworks. Practice has proved that the system design meets the requirements of field observation and research.

Keywords: Big data · Web server · Hadoop platform · Data management

1 Introduction

Since the beginning of the 21st century, with the comprehensive development of informatization and intelligence in various fields, scientific data has gradually become the main driving force for scientific research activities [1]. With the help of new technologies, the field scientific observation and research team can collect richer and more accurate data on land resources, water resources, climate resources, biological resources and crop growth by various sensors and equipment when conducting observations and experiments in the field. These massive data have obvious diversity and heterogeneity, which not only has the problem of data normative management, but also faces many difficulties and challenges in its in-depth application. Field scientific observation and research needs to solve the problem of how to store, organize and utilize big data [2]. Based on this background, this paper researches the current situation of field scientific observation and research data management, and finds that the current experimental data management has the following problems: 1) The field scientific observation and research usually involves multi-disciplinary parallel research, and the number of experimental projects is large. The traditional manual data management method is under great pressure; 2) There is no unified standardized management of monitoring and experimental data, and the storage formats and locations are different. They make data difficult to find and use. Sometimes the stored data cannot be found in time, and the experiment has to be repeated. This will result in an increase in the cost of the experiment; 3) In the multidisciplinary collaborative research, the decentralized data management of each team is not conducive to data correlation analysis and interdisciplinary research; 4) The amount of data stored in system is increasing to GB and TB levels. It is difficult to process these massive data by traditional analysis methods; 5) When working in the field, data timely inputting the system and data sharing are generally inconvenient.

To solve these problems, this paper proposes a data management platform design based on B/S architecture, which enables sensors, PCs and mobile terminal devices to access the platform by the Internet anytime and anywhere, and facilitates the upload and download of field scientific data.[1] The distributed data management, parallel data analysis and sharing of large data sets are realized through the Hadoop cluster server, which is convenient for scientific research work to form the final research report.

The paper offers an effective solution to the big data management and analysis for field scientific observation and research. Section 2 of this paper introduces the related research. Section 3 and Sect. 4 describe the system overview and design. Section 5 shows the system implementation.

2   Background and Relate Work

Through research on more than 100 relevant scientific research data management platforms around the world and the measures taken by governments of various countries. It is found that scientific research data management platforms can be attributed to five elements and four functions. The five elements include platform-based management, multi-type data fusion, multi-condition retrieval data, online and offline multi-use communication, and user authority. The four functions refer to data upload, download, online analysis, and online query. According to different user needs and application scenarios, the design elements and functions of data management platform are personalized.

Scientific data management is not simply data standardization. It involves workflow and data management such as data collection, processing, storage, sharing, etc. The establishment of a standard system must not only meet the needs of basic management, but also form a well-structured system content. It covers technology, work, management and many other aspects. It also needs to focus on the effective connection between different data sets and promote the open sharing of data [3].

For multi-dimensional, multi-quality and massive marine data management, Zhang Minghua et al. proposed to build a marine data management platform that integrates storage, management, service and display. It adopts a layered architecture to realize data collection, data storage, data management, data export and import functions [4]. Hadoop is a widely used implementation framework for distributed data management. It can not only meet the distributed storage requirements of big data, but also solve many data related processing problems. For example, a clinical data integration and management system based is designed on Hadoop platform. The system has some significant features:

---

[1] The work was partially supported by Lanzhou University College Student Innovation and Entrepreneurship Action Plan (No.20210250077).

bulk-storage memory, standardized medical information sharing, fast retrieval and query, high performance parallel processing capabilities, reliable data management service [5]. For continuously improving the overall efficiency of scientific research comprehensive management, improving the scientific and technological support ability in an all-round way, the platform of scientific research project management is designed, which realizes the authority control through the web login, and can provide the functions of adding, deleting, modifying and querying according to the different authority on the login user [6].

Synthesizing the advantages of the above data management system, the management system designed in this paper covers two parts of field experiment project and experimental data management. In addition, the characteristics of field expedition data terminal mobility and unattended are considers, and the further expansion of system functions is easy.

3   System Overview

This paper provides a design scheme of data management platform, which focuses on the structure of the data management platform, operation authority management, data upload, data query, data analysis and sharing. A scientific research station data management platform is designed and implemented based on B/S architecture, so that users can connect to the platform without being limited by time and place. Data management becomes particularly convenient, especially for scientific research workstations that frequently carry out field experiments. The overall architecture of the platform is shown in Fig. 1, which includes Hadoop server, Web server, testing equipment/sensors and clients.

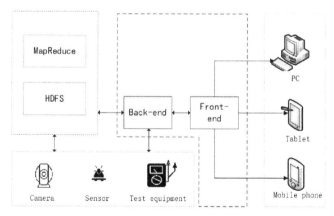

Fig. 1. Overall framework of data management platform for field scientific observation and research

The client is mainly to provide users with an operation terminal with good human-computer interaction, which can facilitate operators to view monitoring data, upload experimental data and issue control instructions to testing equipment in a timely manner.

The web server is implemented using a development method that separates front and back ends. The frontend includes two sub-interfaces, the experimental data management system and the personnel and equipment management system. The client can enter the two sub-interfaces from the main interface of the system. The backend is the logic implementation of various business function modules. Through the configuration of frontend routing, web pages can be loaded on demand to achieve local performance improvement. At the same time, it also achieves high cohesion and low coupling. So that the backend can better pursue high concurrency, high availability and high performance, and the frontend can better improve page performance and load more quickly [7]. In addition, there is no need to install and maintain application software for user. The system update and maintenance is simple and convenient, only need to change the front-end webpage files or back-end logic, then all users can be updated synchronously. Hadoop stores and analyzes massive data in a reliable, efficient and scalable manner in a distributed environment. The client can control to test equipment such as sensors and cameras through the web server, and the collected data can be automatically uploaded to the Hadoop for storage, and then transmitted to the client for display.

4   System Design and Function

4.1   Platform Feature

The platform is divided into experimental data management subsystem and personal and equipment management subsystem, and their system functions are shown in Fig. 2. The experimental data management system is used by experimenters, the personnel and equipment management subsystem is used by platform administrators and project managers.

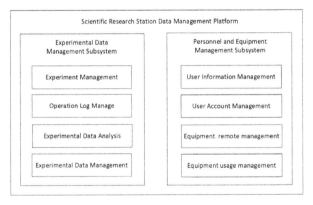

Fig. 2. System function module

The experimental management module is responsible for the management of the labor division and progress information of the experimental project. The experimental data management module includes functions such as uploading, downloading, modifying, counting and querying experimental data and files. The data analysis module can perform correlation analysis and data mining on experimental data to generate visual statistical charts. The log module records any operation of the user for trace back by viewing the log management. The equipment remote management module is responsible for remotely setting the parameters of the test equipment, checking the running status of the equipment, and adding job tasks for the equipment. The equipment usage management module is responsible for recording the usage status of the experimental equipment, such as whether the equipment is in use, and which team the equipment is used by.

4.2 Web Server

The subsystems of the platform are developed in a way that the front-end and back-end are separated, as shown in Fig. 3. The back-end adopts the current mainstream Java Web development framework SpringBoot, and the front-end uses the popular VUE + Element UI framework [9].

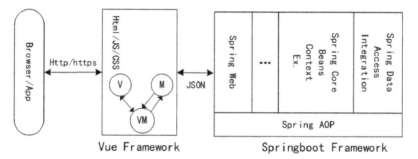

Fig. 3. Web server development architecture

Vue.js is a progressive framework for building user interfaces, and its basic working principle is based on MVVM (Model-View-ViewModel) [10]. Model is mainly responsible for encapsulating business data. View is DOM (Document Object Model) view, which is responsible for view processing. ViewModel is the data model that connects the view and data. It is the Vue instance object, which is responsible for monitoring the modification of the Model or View. It realizes the mutual decoupling of view and model. Since Vue is mainly written in JavaScript, it is also very easy to reintegrate with existing projects. On the other hand, when combined with modern toolchains and various supporting libraries, Vue is also fully capable of powering complex single-page applications. Its built-in methods and features make the code reusable. Spring is a mainstream Java web development framework, which is a highly cohesive and attractive lightweight application framework. Its functional elements generally include modules such as Core Container, Data Access/Integration, Web Development (Web), and AOP (Aspect Oriented Programming). Using basic JavaBeans to do what was previously only possible with EJBs (Enterprise Java Beans) replaces the inefficient development model of EJBs. Spring Boot is an extension of the Spring framework, it removes the complex and routine configuration required to set up a Spring application. At the same time, Spring Boot integrates a large number of commonly used third-party libraries for development, such as JSON library Jackson, non-relational database Redis [11], mail sending service Mail, etc.

4.3 Hadoop Platform

The types of data obtained by the field scientific observation and research team can be divided into structured data, picture files, and video files. Data storage and analysis are implemented through the Hadoop framework. Hadoop enables users to develop distributed applications without knowing the underlying details of the distribution. The core of Hadoop is HDFS (Hadoop Distributed File System) and MapReduce [12]. HDFS is used to store massive data, and MapReduce is used for distributed computing and processing of massive data. As shown in Fig. 4.

HDFS is a file system used for storing large datasets in a default block of size 64 MB (or 128 MB) in distributed manner on Hadoop cluster. Input files are stored in HDFS and computed using MapReduce defined program and the result is stored back in HDFS output folder [13]. HDFS has master-slave architecture, in which NameNode is the master node which controls DataNodes and it contains metadata. DataNode is responsible for serving read and write request for the client. For each MapReduce there is one JobTracker node which is responsible for distributing of mapper and reducer functions to available TaksTrackers and monitoring the results. Map Reduce is the heart of Hadoop for processing of large data sets in parallel by dividing it into multiple subtasks across distributed commodity of Hadoop cluster [14].

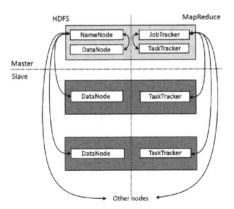

Fig. 4. Hadoop architecture [8]

5   System Implementation

Users can log in to the scientific research data management platform through any browser. The system on the PC side is shown in Figs. 5 and 6, and the user can implement the preceding operations on the browser.

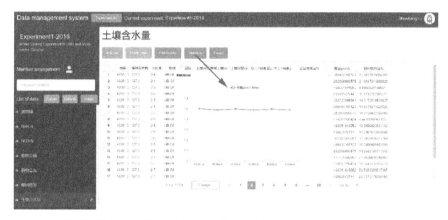

Fig. 5. Main interface of the experimental data management subsystem

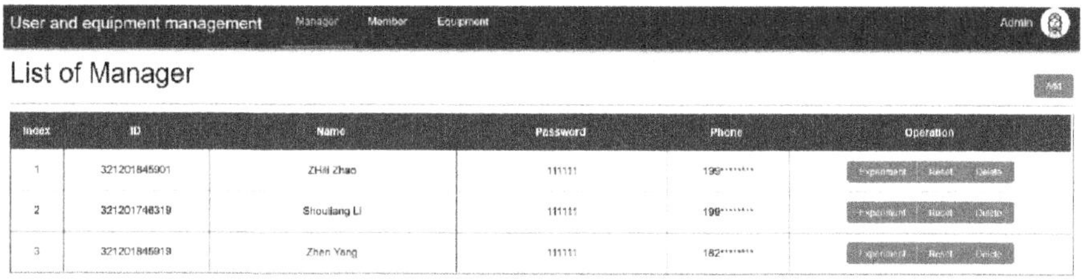

Fig. 6. Main interface of the personal and equipment management subsystem

When entering the experiment data management subsystem shown as Fig. 5, the experiment data can be created via the "Create" button or imported via click the "Import" button. The "Statistics" button can realize the analysis of the data. First select the data for x-axis and y-axis, and then selecting the appropriate statistical method and the required visual chart form. The statistical chart shown in the Fig. 5 will be automatically generated.

Figure 6 is the interface of the personnel and equipment management subsystem. The system administrators can set user information and rights in this interface, and experiment managers can set the permissions of experiment members. The setting and running status of the equipment parameters, and the usage of the equipment can be viewed in "Equipment".

6 Conclusion and Future Work

This paper focuses on the basic functions of the data management platform of the field scientific observation and research station. A system architecture is provided and implemented that integrates distributed data management, Web server and user interface. The big data analysis Hadoop clustering servers are adopted for the massive experimental test and monitoring data being comprehensively analyzed and managed in the system. The analysis results can be visualized with histogram, pie chart, curve, etc. Although the functional modules of the system are optimized, there is still room for further improvement in data security and data backup. In terms of data security, system optimization can be carried out based on encryption algorithms or the dividing databases of different security levels. In the data backup, it is necessary to further formulate reasonable backup strategy to reduce the risk and harm of server dropped and abnormal operation.

References

1. Huang, X., Jiang, R., Hu, X., Wang, L.: Thoughts on the ecological environment management innovation driven by big data. In: International Conference on Big Data, Artificial Intelligence and Internet of Things Engineering (ICBAIE). IEEE (2020)
2. Liao, X., Feng, Z., Gao, X., et al.: The development of field scientific observation and research stations (networks) and scientific data centers. In: ACTA GEOGRAPHICA SINICA. vol.75, no.12, pp. 2669–2683 (2020)
3. Chen, L., Wang, Q., Liu, J., et al.: Establishment of data management standard system for agricultural scientific research and experiment station. Trans. Chin. Soc. Agric. Eng. **36**(4), 193–201 (2020)
4. Zhang, M., et al.: Construction of a platform for management of multi-dimension heterogeneous and mass ocean data. In: International Conference on Electrical and Control Engineering. IEEE (2010)
5. Lyu, D.-M., et al.: Design and implementation of clinical data integration and management system based on Hadoop platform. In: The 7th International Conference on Information Technology in Medicine and Education (ITME). IEEE (2015)
6. Ying, Y., et al.: Design and research of scientific research integrated management platform. In: International Conference on Management Science and Software Engineering (ICMSSE). IEEE (2021)
7. Serge, B., et al.: Web infrastructure for data management, storage and computation. In: Medical Imaging 2021: Biomedical Applications in Molecular, Structural, and Functional Imaging. vol.11600. International Society for Optics and Photonics (2021)
8. Kalia, K., Gupta, N.: Analysis of Hadoop MapReduce scheduling in heterogeneous environment. Ain Shams Eng. J. **12**(1), 1101–1110 (2021)
9. Luo, H., Wen, Y., Zhang, X.: Research on intelligent pet management platform system based on big data environment. In: IEEE International Conference on Artificial Intelligence and Industrial Design. IEEE (2021)
10. Fang, Z., et al.: Design and implementation of energy management system based on spring boot framework. Information **12**(11), 1–13 (2021)
11. Wang, Z., Tang, F., Yu, Z.: Design and implementation of a health status reporting system based on spring boot. In: International Conference on Artificial Intelligence and Computer Engineering (ICAICE). IEEE (2020)
12. Akram, E., Larbi, H., Abderrahim, M.: New data placement strategy in the Hadoop framework. Int. J. Adv. Comput. Sci. Appl. **12**(7), 676–684 (2021)
13. Dubey, A.K., Jain, V., Mittal, A.P.: Stock market prediction using Hadoop Map-Reduce ecosystem. In: The 2nd International Conference on Computing for Sustainable Global Development (INDIACom). IEEE (2015)
14. William, V.-C., et al.: Analysis of the state of learning in university students with the use of a Hadoop framework. Future Internet **13**(6), 1–25 (2021)

A Novel Cooperative Package Pickup Mechanism for Door-to-Door Pickup Scenes

Pengfei Sun[1](✉) , Yu Shi[2], and Leixiao Li[1]

[1] Inner Mongolia University of Technology, Hohhot, China
{pfsun,lileixiao}@imut.edu.cn
[2] Inner Mongolia University, Hohhot, China
31909149@imu.edu.cn

Abstract. With the rapid development of express delivery industry, more and more focus has been shifted to express delivery mechanism design. For door-to-door pickup scenes of couriers, we present the cooperative package pickup system to reduce the users' express fee in form of sharing the express fee of users assigned the same express station. We formulate the *Cooperative Package Pickup (CPP)* problem to minimize all users' comprehensive cost, which is the sum of express fee and pickup cost of courier. The *Cooperative Package Pickup Mechanism (CPPM)* is proposed to solve *CPP* problem. First, *CPPM* transforms *CPP* into *Transformed Cooperative Package Pickup (TCPP)* problem according to the properties of the triangle inequality. Then, an approximate algorithm, *TCPPA*, is proposed to solve *TCPP* problem based on submodular function minimization. Furthermore, according to the package assignments of *TCPPA*, we present a polynomial time algorithm, *PPOA*, to optimize pickup path of couriers. Additionally, in order to incentivize users to deliver their packages by this system, we propose a cooperative cost allocation scheme to incentive the user to deliver the package. Through extensive simulations, we demonstrate that *CPPM* reduces the comprehensive cost by 8.84% on average compared to the door-to-door behavior in the non-cooperative mode.

Keywords: Express delivery · door-to-door pickup · cooperative package pickup · cooperation cost

1 Introduction

The explosive growth of e-commerce market has also driven the rapid development of express delivery industry in China for the past few years. The flourishing development of shopping online has accelerated the advancement of express delivery industry, which involves delivering goods to customers after online shopping. There are huge business opportunities in the express delivery industry. As shown in Fig. 1, China's express delivery business involved 108.3 billion pieces of goods delivered in 2021 and grown by 28.25% on average in the past five years according to statistics from the State Post Bureau [1]. The efficiency, punctuality and economy is increasingly an urgently problem in the field of express delivery service, which leads to some new and interesting research such as "last mile" delivery [2], crowdsourced parcel delivery [3], and transportation scheduling [4].

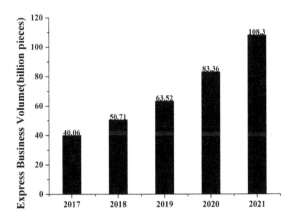

Fig. 1. Express business volume statistics from 2017 to 2021 in China

In the traditional express network, the user who requires delivering package initiates an order to the express platform online, the platform usually will assign the order to the courier closest to the user to pick up the package. Then the courier will pick up the packages one by one according to the assignment of express platform. Finally, user charges the express fee according to the packages billing rules of express companies. Generally speaking, the pickup cost of courier for each package is fixed. Therefore, if the packages assigned the same Express Station (ES) can be lumped into one big package, the users can share the express fee, which billed by large package. The billing rules of local packages for different express companies is shown in Table 1. Specifically, the users with small packages, whose weight is less than the first heavy, can share the first heavy price. In addition, the fact that the continued heavy price is far lower than the first heavy price for each express company also can ensure the users with big packages to benefit from the cooperation.

Table 1. Billing rules of different express companies.

Company	First Heavy (1 kg)	Continued Heavy (0.5 kg)
Deppon	CNY 10	CNY 1
EMS	CNY 12	CNY 1
SF-Express	CNY 12	CNY 1

Many existing studies focused on the design of cooperative models or mechanisms for logistics and express delivery [5,6] and large-scale express delivery problems model [7]. The cooperative strategy in express service also has been widely used, mainly in terms of efficiency improvement [12]. However, none of above researches considers the cooperative package assignment mechanism and the cooperative cost sharing.

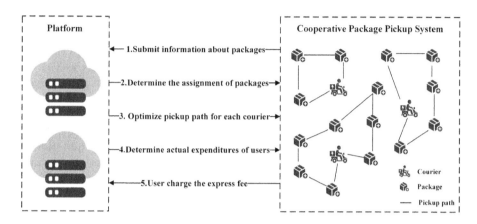

Fig. 2. Illustration of cooperative package pickup system

As shown in Fig. 2, the cooperative package pickup system is designed to determine an optimal assignment of packages for every ES. First, each user submits information about package to platform. Then, platform will determine the assignment of packages and optimal pickup path for every ES and each ES assigns the courier to pick up the packages. Afterwards, the user charges the express fee according to cooperative cost allocation scheme after the packages are lumped. Compared with the traditional express deliver scheme, where the couriers pick up the packages one by one and charge the express fee billed alone after ordering online, our system reduces the user's express fee by a way of cooperation. Therefore, such system can attract more users to deliver packages, which can improve the revenue of express companies potentially in the long run. Furthermore, such system will push the express companies to develop the more rational express billing rules from the perspective of social competition.

The main contributions of this paper are as follows:

- We present a cooperative package pickup system for door-to-door pickup scenes of couriers, and formulate it as the *Cooperative Package Pickup (CPP)* problem.
- Considering that *CPP* is a variant of the traveling salesman problem [8], which was proved NP-hard, we proposed the *Cooperative Ptextitackage Ptickup Mechanism (CPPM)* to solve *CPP* problem, including problem transformation, packages assignment by a $\frac{\ln n + 1}{1-\varepsilon}$-approximate algorithm, *TCPPA* based

on submodular function minimization [9], and a polynomial time algorithm, *PPOA*, to optimize pickup path of couriers.

- We propose a cooperative cost allocation scheme, which can incentive the user to deliver the package by the cooperative package pickup system.
- The extensive simulations verify that *CPPM* reduces its comprehensive cost by 8.84% on average compared to the non-cooperative mode.

2   System Model

We construct a cooperative package pickup system, which consists of a set $N = \{1, 2, \cdots, n\}$ of n users and a set $M = \{1, 2, \cdots, m\}$ of m ESs as well as an express cloud platform. We assume each user is only with one package to deliver. Therefore, the notation i is reused to represent the package delivered by user i. The notation N is reused to represent the package set delivered by all users. Besides we consider that all the couriers are from the same courier company and there is only one courier to pick up the package for each ES. The notation l^j represents the location of the ES $j \in M$. When there is a delivering demand, each user $i \in N$ need to submit the information $B_i = (l_i, w_i)$ to the cloud platform, where l_i is the location information in two-dimensional space and w_i is the actual weight of the package of user i, respectively.

2.1   Billing Rule

According to the billing rule of express company adopted in practice, we define ϕ_i as the express fee of any user i's package in any ES j as:

$$\phi_i = \begin{cases} p^f, & w_i \leq H^f \\ p^f + \left(w_i - H^f\right) p^c, & w_i > H^f \end{cases} \tag{1}$$

where H^f is the first heavy of ES. p^f is the first heavy price per kg of ES and p^c is the continued heavy price per kg. of any ES j, respectively. Generally speaking, the billing rule for all express companies should satisfy following:

$$p^f \geq p^c H^f \tag{2}$$

Then, the user i's comprehensive cost can be calculated as the sum of express fee and pickup cost of courier j:

$$c_i(j) = \phi_i + \chi \cdot 2d(l^j, l_i) \tag{3}$$

where χ and $d(l^j, l_i)$ are the unit pickup cost of courier and the distance between user i and ES j, respectively.

2.2   Cooperation Model

Once the users are assigned to the same ES, the increased cost should be considered in all aspects of express deliver such as lumping, separating and delivering packages to different terminal ESs. Therefore, in order to compensate the increased cost, we introduce the cooperation cost function $p(\cdot)$.

Meanwhile, the notation G_j represents the set of packages assigned to ES j and we assume the sum of the weight of packages in G_j is not lower than the first heavy of ES j. The total express fee $\phi(G_i)$ can be calculated as:

$$\phi(G_j) = \begin{cases} p^f + (\sum_{i \in G_j} w_i - H^f)p^c + p(G_j), & if \ G_j \neq \emptyset \\ 0, & otherwise \end{cases} \tag{4}$$

where $p(G_j)$ is the cooperation cost of G_j and we assume that $p(\cdot)$ is a nonnegative, monotone and submodular function. Specifically, $p(G_j) = 0$ if $|G_j| = 1$. Then, the comprehensive cost $c(G_j)$ is defined as the sum of pickup cost of courier j and total express fee of all users in G_j :

$$c(G_j) = \phi(G_j) + \chi \cdot TSP(G_j) \tag{5}$$

where $TSP(G_j)$ is the pickup distance function of courier j visiting all users in G_j and go back to l^j.

2.3   Problem Formulation

Our objective is to minimize the comprehensive cost of all users and we must ensure that each package is assigned to exactly one ES at the same time. So we refer to it as _Cooperative Package Pickup (CPP)_ problem, which can be formulated as follows:

$$(CPP) : \min \sum_{j \in M} c(G_j) \tag{6}$$

$$\textbf{Subject to:} \ \ N \subseteq \bigcup_{j \in M} G_j \tag{6-1}$$

$$G_j \cap G_{j'} = \emptyset, \forall j \neq j', j \in M, j' \in M \tag{6-2}$$

The constraint (6-1) ensures that packages of all users should be assigned out-and-out. The constraint (6-2) ensures that each package can be assigned to at most one ES. The two constraints ensure that each package is allocated to one ES exactly.

3   Cooperative Package Pickup Mechanism

In this section, we propose the _Cooperative Package Pickup Mechanism (CPPM)_ to deal with the _CPP_ problem.

3.1 Problem Transformation

It can be seen that the CPP aims to minimize $\sum_{j \in M} c(G_j)$, if $\phi(G_j)$ is a constant, obviously, $c(G_j)$ is a variant of the traveling salesman problem, which was proved NP-hard [9]. Additionally, we can get $\sum_{i \in G_j} 2d(l_i, l^j) \geq TSP(G_j)$ according to the properties of the triangle inequality. Then the transformed comprehensive cost $c^T(G_j)$ is the sum of the pickup cost of courier j and express fee of all users in G_j:

$$c^T(G_j) = \phi(G_j) + \chi \cdot \sum_{i \in G_j} 2d(l_i, l^j) \tag{7}$$

So we transform CPP into $\underline{T}$ransformed $\underline{C}$ooperative $\underline{P}$ackage $\underline{P}$ickup $(TCPP)$ problem:

$$(\boldsymbol{TCPP}) : \min \sum_{j \in M} c^T(G_j) \tag{8}$$

$$\textbf{Subject to:} \quad (6-1) \ and \ (6-2)$$

3.2 Packages Assignment

In this section, we contract the $\underline{T}$ransformed $\underline{C}$ooperative $\underline{P}$ackage $\underline{P}$ickup $\underline{A}$lgorithm $(TCPPA)$ to decide the assignment of the packages for the $TCPP$ problem.

Theorem 1. *The transformed cost function $c^T(\cdot)$ is a monotone, nonnegative and submodular function [10].*

Proof. The non-negativity and monotonicity of $c^T(\cdot)$ is obvious. We next show that $c^T(\cdot)$ is submodular. We consider two user set $A \subseteq B \subseteq N$. Let $e \in N\backslash B$. Due to $p(\cdot)$ is a monotone, nonnegative and submodular function, which can infer that $p(A \cup \{e\}) - p(A) \geq p(B \cup \{e\}) - p(B)$, so we have

$$
\begin{aligned}
&c^T(A \cup \{e\}) - c^T(A)\\
&= \phi(A \cup \{e\}) + \chi \cdot \sum_{i \in A \cup \{e\}} 2d(l_i, l^j) - \phi(A) - \chi \cdot \sum_{i \in A} 2d(l_i, l^j)\\
&= \phi(A \cup \{e\}) - \phi(A) + \chi \cdot \sum_{i \in A \cup \{e\}} 2d(l_i, l^j) - \chi \cdot \sum_{i \in A} 2d(l_i, l^j)\\
&= p^f + (\textstyle\sum_{i \in A} w_i - H^f)p^c + p(A \cup \{e\})\\
&\quad -(p^f + (\textstyle\sum_{i \in A \cup \{e\}} w_i - H^f)p^c) - p(A) + \chi \cdot 2d(l_e, l^j)\\
&= w_e p^c + \chi \cdot 2d(l_e, l^j) + p(A \cup \{e\}) - p(A)\\
&\geq w_e p^c + \chi \cdot 2d(l_e, l^j) + p(B \cup \{e\}) - p(B)\\
&= \phi(B \cup \{e\}) + \chi \cdot \sum_{i \in B \cup \{e\}} 2d(l_i, l^j) - \phi(B) - \chi \cdot \sum_{i \in B} 2d(l_i, l^j)\\
&= c^T(B \cup \{e\}) - c^T(B)
\end{aligned}
$$

Thus $c^T(\cdot)$ is a monotone, nonnegative and submodular function.

Next, we will analyze the complexity of the $TCPP$ problem.

Theorem 2. *The TCPP problem is NP-hard.*

Proof. First, given an instance of *TCPP*, we will determine that *TCPP* belongs to NP. We need to determine whether all packages are assigned and whether the total comprehensive cost is at most v. This process can be finished in polynomial time. Next, we will prove the *TCPP* is NP-hard by giving a polynomial time reduction from <u>W</u>eighted <u>S</u>et <u>C</u>over *(WSC)* problem [11], which has been proved NP-hard.

Instance of *WSC* (denoted by A): For an universe set $N = \{1, 2, \cdots, n\}$ of n elements, a positive real v and a family of sets $G = \{G_1, G_2, ..., G_k\}$, there is a weight value $c^T(G_j)$ for $j \in \{1, 2, ..., k\}$. The question is whether exists a set $G' \subseteq G$ with $\sum_{G_i \in G'} c^T(G_i) \leq v$ such that every element in N belongs to at least one member in G'?

Instance of *TCPP* (denoted by B): For a universe set $N = \{1, 2, \cdots, n\}$ of n packages and a family of package sets $G = \{G_1, G_2, ..., G_k\}$, each ES j is associated with a package set G_i and a cost $c^T(G_j)$. The question is whether exists a set $G' \subseteq G$ with $G' \subseteq G$ with $\sum_{G_i \in G'} c^T(G_i) \leq v$ such that every package in N is assigned to at least one ES in G'? Note that if the coverage G' exists, G' must be a partition of N, i.e., each package in N can be assigned exactly to one ES because the monotonicity of the cost function $c^T(\cdot)$.

The reduction from A to B can be ended up in polynomial time. We can simply see that q is a solution of A if and only if q is a solution of B.

As the following Theorem 2 shows, the *TCPP* is NP-hard. Thus, illustrated in Algorithm 1, we propose an approximate algorithm, *TCPPA*, to solve the *TCPP* problem based on greedy strategy.

Algorithm 1 : TCPPA

Require: $N, M, \forall i \in N, \forall j \in M, B_i, p^f, p^c, H^f$
 1: **for** $j \in M$ **do**
 2:    $G_j \leftarrow \emptyset$;
 3: **end for**
 4: $\mathbf{G} \leftarrow (G_1, G_2, ..., G_m)$;
 5: $N' \leftarrow N$;
 6: **while** $N' \neq \emptyset$ **do**
 7:    **for** $j \in M$ **do**
 8:        $S_j \leftarrow \mathbf{BS}(j, G_j, N')$;
 9:    **end for**
10:    $j \leftarrow \arg\min\limits_{j' \in M} \frac{c^T(G_{j'} \cup S_{j'}) - c^T(G_{j'})}{|S_{j'}|}$;
11:    $G_j \leftarrow G_j \cup S_j$; $N' \leftarrow N' \backslash S_j$;
12: **end while**
13: **return G**;

Let $\mathbf{G} = (G_1, G_2, ..., G_m)$ be the set of packages set of all ESs. By calling $\mathbf{BS}(\cdot)$, we can find a feasible unassigned package set S_j, which minimizes the marginal comprehensive cost effectiveness for all ES $j \in M$ in each iteration (Line 8). Then we find the ES j with minimum marginal comprehensive cost effectiveness (Line 10). The assigned package set S_j, is merged to ES j's current package set G_j (Line 11). The iteration will terminate until all packages are assigned exactly.

Algorithm 2 : BS($\cdot$)

Require: N', G_j, j

1: $low \leftarrow 0$;
2: $high \leftarrow \frac{c^T(G_j \cup N') - c^T(G_j)}{|N'|}$;
3: $mid \leftarrow \frac{low + high}{2}$;
4: **while** (1) **do**
5:      $S \leftarrow \arg \min\limits_{S' \subseteq N', S' \neq \emptyset} (c^T(G_j \cup S') - c^T(G_j) - mid|S'|)$;
6:      **if** $|\frac{c^T(G_j \cup S) - c^T(G_j)}{|S|} - mid| \leq \varepsilon$ **then**
7:          **return** S;
8:      **end if**
9:      **if** $c^T(G_j \cup S) - c^T(G_j) - mid|S| \geq 0$ **then**
10:         $low \leftarrow mid$;
11:     **else**
12:         $high \leftarrow mid$;
13:     **end if**
14:     $mid \leftarrow \frac{low + high}{2}$;
15: **end while**

BS($\cdot$) is illustrated in Algorithm 2. We first initialize low and $hign$ to be the indicator for left boundary and right boundary, respectively. Due to $S = N'$ is a feasible solution for minimizing $\frac{c^T(G_j \cup S) - c^T(G_j)}{|S|}$, we set $high = \frac{c^T(G_j \cup N') - c^T(G_j)}{|N'|}$ initially (Line 2). In each iteration, we compute the minimum of $(c^T(G_j \cup S) - c^T(G_j) - mid|S|)$ (Line 5) using submodular function minimization [9]. The binary search operation will terminate until the value of $(\frac{c^T(G_j \cup S) - c^T(G_j \cup S)}{|S|} - mid)$ satisfies the preset search precision $\varepsilon \in (0, 1)$ (Line 6).

Theorem 3. *TCPPA is a polynomial algorithm.*

Proof. Above all, we will analyze the time complexity of **BS($\cdot$)**. The binary search operation with search precision ε takes $O(\log \frac{n}{\varepsilon})$ time. Minimizing submodular function (Line 5) takes $O(n^7 \log n)$ time using the algorithm proposed in [9], which is a strongly polynomial algorithm. Thus, the running time of **BS($\cdot$)** is $O(n^7 \log n \log \frac{n}{\varepsilon})$.

TCPPA (Algorithm 1) is dominated by finding the unassigned package set S_j for each ES $j \in M$ (Line 8), which takes $O(mn^7 \log n \log \frac{n}{\varepsilon})$. The while loop operation (Lines 6–12) is executed at most n times because there are n packages that need to be allocated and it will assign at least one package for each iteration of the loop. Thereby the running time of $TCPPA$ is $O(mn^8 \log n \log \frac{n}{\varepsilon})$. Thus, $TCPPA$ is a polynomial algorithm.

Theorem 4. $TCPPA$ is a $\frac{\ln n + 1}{1 - \varepsilon}$-approximate algorithm for the $TCPP$ problem.

Proof. The $TCPP$ problem is equivalent to the WSC problem [11] on the basis of Theorem 2. So the $TCPPA$ is $\ln n + 1$-approximate if it can find the optimal solution to minimize the ratio of the marginal comprehensive cost of ES's package set to the number of newly joined packages. The binary search approximates the optimal solution within a factor of $1/(1 - \varepsilon)$, considering the search precision $\varepsilon \in (0, 1)$. Thus, $TCPPA$ is a $\frac{\ln n + 1}{1 - \varepsilon}$-approximate algorithm.

3.3   Couriers' Pickup Paths Optimization

In this section, we present the *P*ick-up *P*ath *O*ptimizing *A*lgorithm *(PPOA)* based on the greedy approach to optimize pickup paths for couriers according to the assignment of the packages by $TCPPA$.

Algorithm 3 : PPOA

Require: $M, N, B_i, l^j, \forall j \in M, \forall i \in G_j$
 1: **for** $j \in M$ **do**
 2:     $p_j \leftarrow \emptyset, G'_j \leftarrow G_j$;
 3: **end for**
 4: $\mathbf{P} \leftarrow (p_1, p_2, ..., p_m)$;
 5: **for** $j \in M$ **do**
 6:     $l^{temp} \leftarrow l^j$;
 7:     **while** $G'_j \neq \emptyset$ **do**
 8:         $i \leftarrow \arg \min_{i' \in G'_j} d(l_{i'}, l^{temp})$;
 9:         $p_j \leftarrow p_j \cup \{i\}$;
10:         $G'_j \leftarrow G'_j \backslash \{i\}$;
11:         $l^{temp} \leftarrow l_i$;
12:     **end while**
13: **end for**
14: **return** $\mathbf{P}$;

Specifically, the courier j takes the current location l^j as the starting point, selects the user i closest to l^j to join p_j, is the pickup path of the courier j. Then removes user i form G^j and update l^j with l_i. Return to the courier's pick-up path p_j until all users are selected. $\mathbf{P}$ is the couriers' optimal pickup paths set.

Theorem 5. $PPOA$ is a polynomial algorithm.

Proof. It is not difficult to see that contains at most G^j packages. $PPOA$ selects the user with the smallest distance from the user to the latest joining path each time. There are at most m assignments, so the running time of Algorithm 3 is $O(mn)$. So $PPOA$ is a polynomial time algorithm.

3.4   Cooperative Cost Allocation Scheme

In order to incentivize users to deliver their packages by this system, we propose the cooperative cost allocation scheme, which can calculate actual comprehensive cost for each user. The final comprehensive cost $c_i^T(G_j)$ of user i is proportional to the margin comprehensive cost of his package in ES j:

$$c_i^T(G_j) = c^T(G_j) \frac{c^T(G_j) - c^T(G_j\setminus\{i\})}{\sum\limits_{i'\in G_j} (c^T(G_j) - c^T(G_j\setminus\{i'\}))}, \forall i \in G_j \qquad (9)$$

4   Performance Evaluation

In this section, we will verify the performance of *CPPM* by experience simulations based on the real distribution of ESs and users in Gulou district of Nanjing. As shown in Fig. 3, We randomly choose 120 residential communities as users, indicated by red nodes. Furthermore, we randomly choose 12 ES in the area, indicated by blue nodes.

Fig. 3. Distribution of ESs and users in Gulou district of Nanjing

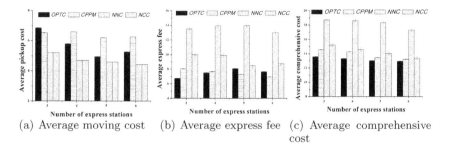

(a) Average moving cost   (b) Average express fee   (c) Average comprehensive
cost

Fig. 4. Impact of number of express stations (m)

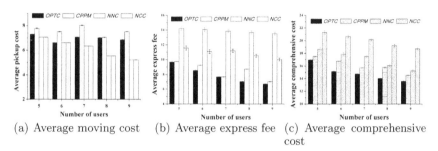

(a) Average moving cost   (b) Average express fee   (c) Average comprehensive
cost

Fig. 5. Impact of number of users (n)

4.1   Simulation Setup

We compare our algorithms *CPPM* with the following three benchmark algorithms:

- *NCC (Nearest Cooperation Collection)*: After the user applies for the platform to deliver the package, the courier closest to the user's location picks up
  the package and pays the express fee according to formula (9). In addition,
  the moving cost of courier j is calculated as $\chi \cdot 2d(l_i, l^j)$.
- *NNC (Nearest Noncooperation Collection)*: Different from *NCC*, user pays
  the express fee according to formula (3) independently.
- *OPTC*: Optimal solution of *CPP* problem. We enumerate all possible partitions of packages to find the optimal solution.

We assume that weights of packages are randomly distributed over [1 kg,
2 kg]. We use cooperation cost function $p(G_j) = 2\log(|G_j|)$ for any ES j. The
default unit moving cost is 0.06 and the search precision is 0.3, respectively. We
conduct the simulations on a Windows machine, which is with 16 GB memory
and Intel(R) Core (TM) i7-7560U CPU. There are averaged over 100 instances
for each measurement. The benchmark algorithms are implemented in Java platform.

4.2   Cost

We vary the number of ES from 3 to 6. As shown in Fig. 4, when more courier points are added, the pickup cost of all algorithms will be decreases because users can choose to send their packages from closer ESs. With the growth of the number of ESs, the average express fee of the *OPTC*, *NNC* and *NCC* algorithms increases slightly. The reason for this phenomenon is that some of added ESs may disperse the users to more ESs, which can reduce the pickup cost. In general, when the number of ES is increased, the comprehensive cost of all algorithms tends to decrease and the comprehensive cost gap between *CPPM* and *OPTC* is relatively small.

As shown in Fig. 5, when more users join, the express fee of *CPPM* gradually decreases. The reason for this phenomenon is that the average cooperative number of users increases for every ES, thereby reducing his express fee and increasing the cooperative surplus, which proves formula (9) is possible to reduce express fee. Due to the attraction of cooperative surplus, users in *CPPM* tend to join farther ES, resulting in a slight float but overall reducing in the pickup cost. *CPPM* is also effective in optimizing the pickup cost of the couriers. From the perspective of comprehensive cost, as the number of users increases, the comprehensive cost shows a decreasing trend.

Table 2. Running time of *OPTC*, *CPPM*, *NNC* and *NCC*

Users	OPTC (ms)	CPPM (ms)	NNC (ms)	NCC (ms)
5	664391.17	91.42	<10	<10
6	938742.6	1494.18	<10	<10
7	5603728.95	9759.19	<10	<10
8	72090372.77	33943.65	<10	<10
9	15063608.07	99650.38	<10	<10

The running time of *CPPM*, *NNC*, *NCC* and *OPTC* is shown in Table 2. With the increasing number of users, the running time of *OPTC* and *CPPM* grows rapidly. However, Compared with *OPTC*, *CPPM* greatly shortens the running time, which shows great scalability.

In general, compared with *NCC*, *CPPM* reduces the comprehensive cost by 8.84% on average. Meanwhile, the average comprehensive cost of *CPPM* is 6.5% higher than that of *OPTC*. The experimental results show that the performance of *CPPM* has been greatly improved, and it has good practicability.

5   Conclusion

This paper constructs a *CPP* problem for door-to-door pickup scenario. Considering the complexity of *CPP*, we propose *CPPM* to solve the *CPP* problem including problem transformation, packages assignment and couriers' pickup paths optimization. In problem transformation phase, we transform CPP into $TCPP$ problem according to the properties of the triangle inequality. Then, a $\frac{\ln n+1}{1-\varepsilon}$-approximate algorithm, $TCPPA$, is proposed to $TCPP$ problem to decide the assignment of the packages using submodular function minimization in packages assignment phase. Furthermore, $CPPM$ optimizes pickup paths of couriers by an $O(mn)$ polynomial time algorithm, $PPOA$. Additionally, in order to incentivize users to deliver their packages by this system, we propose a cooperative cost allocation scheme, which can calculate actual comprehensive cost of users in same assignment. Through extensive simulations, we verify that $CPPM$ reduces its comprehensive cost by 8.84% on average compared to the door-to-door behavior in the non-cooperative mode.

Acknowledgements. This work has been supported in part by the Inner Mongolia Autonomous Region Special Program for Engineering Application of Scientific and Technical Payoffs under Grant 2021CG0033 and 2020CG0073, in part by the scientific research project of Inner Mongolia University of Technology under Grant ZY202111.

References

1. Statistical Report of China Postal Industry (2017–2021). http://www.spb.gov.cn
2. Lee, H.L., Whang, S.: Winning the last mile of e-commerce. MIT Sloan Manag. Rev. **42**(4), 54–62 (2001)
3. Kang, Y., Lee, S., Chung, B.D.: Learning-based logistics planning and scheduling for crowdsourced parcel delivery. Comput. Ind. Eng. **132**(1), 271–279 (2019)
4. Zhou, H., Liu, B., Luan, T.H.: Chaincluster: engineering a cooperative content distribution framework for highway vehicular communications. IEEE Trans. Intell. Transp. Syst. **15**(6), 2644–2657 (2014)
5. Ferdinand, F.N., Chung, K.H.: Collaborative system design in express delivery services: formulation and solution heuristic. ICIC Exp. Lett. Part B, Appl. Int. J. Res. Surv. **5**(1), 1–8 (2014)
6. Yao, X., Cheng, Y., Song, M.: Assessment of collaboration in city logistics: from the aspects of profit and CO2 emissions. Int. J. Logist. Res. Appl. **1**(1), 1–16 (2019)
7. Jiang, L., Sun, P., Xu, J., et al.: Cooperative package assignment for heterogeneous express stations. IEEE Trans. Intell. Transp. Syst. (2021). https://doi.org/10.1109/TITS.2021.3082919
8. Shi, X.H., Liang, Y.C., Lee, H.P.: Particle swarm optimization-based algorithms for TSP and generalized TSP. Inf. Process. Lett. **103**(5), 169–176 (2007)
9. Iwata, S., Fleischer, L., Fujishige, S.: A combinatorial strongly polynomial algorithm for minimizing submodular functions. J. ACM **48**(4), 761–777 (2001)
10. Krause, A., Golovin, D.: Submodular function maximization. Tractability **3**(1), 71–104 (2014)
11. Golab, L., Korn, F., Li, F., et al.: Size-constrained weighted set cover. In: Proceedings of 2015 IEEE 31st International Conference on Data Engineering, pp. 879–890 (2015)
12. Dahl, S., Derigs, U.: Cooperative planning in express carrier networks-an empirical study on the effectiveness of a real-time decision support system. Decis. Supp. Syst. **51**(3), 620–626 (2011)

Adaptive Iterative Learning Control for Permanent Magnet Linear Synchronous Motor

Baobin Liu$^{(\boxtimes)}$ and Wei Zhou

Jiangsu Vocational Institute of Commerce, Nanjing 211100, People's Republic of China
jsliubaobin@163.com

Abstract. For the parameters uncertainties and nonlinear disturbances for permanent magnet linear synchronous motor (PMLSM), an adaptive iterative learning control (AILC) algorithm is designed to track iterative varying references. At the same time, learning law is utilized and update for parametric uncertainties. In the learning process, composite energy function (CEF) is used to prove the asymptotical stability of control system. To validate the proposed control method, simulation analysis is conducted by using MATLAB software.

Keywords: Adaptive Iterative Learning Control (AILC) · Non-Repetitive Reference Trajectory · Iteration-Varying Initial Condition · Permanent Magnet Linear Synchronous Motor (PMLSM)

1 Introduction

Permanent magnet linear synchronous motor (PMLSM) converts electric energy into kinetic energy and drives feed mechanism directly. Unlike other ordinary rotating motor, PMLSM is famous for improving transmission accuracy of servo system and ensuring advanced processing technology. Nevertheless, in controller design of PMLSM, special structure remains a large obstacle. It is well known that external disturbance and variation of parameters in the operation process of PMLSM have an influence on controlled system directly. Effective techniques are developed to overcome such limitations and improve the tracking performance [1–3]. In [4], an adaptive jerk control theory was considered for PMLSM with several uncertainties. To avoid the influence by dynamic error, the model-based feedforward control was developed. For PMLSM servo system, an adaptive backstepping control based direct thrust control algorithm was developed [5]. It solves the problems of degrading system performance caused by traditional direct thrust control. Furthermore, unknown estimators are update online. In the references mentioned above, they considered PMLSM system with known parameters and developed different control method to compensate for the susceptibility of uncertainties.

Iterative learning control (ILC) can be applied to repetitive systems. ILC approach facilitates system output to track desired trajectories within finite time [6–10]. ILC method has been utilized to highspeed train [10], PMLSM [11], electric dynamic load simulator [12], spacecrafts [13, 14], three-phase standalone inverters [15], etc. Recently, Zhou et al. [16] has developed a D-type ILC to solve synchronization track problem for neural networks under the iteration-independent commutation topology. Furthermore, the protocol was extended to the iteration-varying switching topology. A robust iterative learning control was developed for continuous-time PMLSM systems in [17] under the identical initial condition and repetitive reference trajectories. Although ILC method was presented originally for systems operate repetitively over finite time interval, repetitiveness becomes obstacle for ILC application since identical initial condition assumption is difficult to satisfy in practice.

Nonrepetitive conditions can be classified into two classes: uncertain iterative varying law and known iterative varying law. For uncertain varying law, [18] tracks iteration-varying reference trajectory and design adaptive iterative learning controller by incorporating a Recursive Least Squares (RLS) algorithm and achieve the pointwise convergence. In several kinds of varying laws, proportional varying [19] and high-order internal model (HOIM) [6] are typical laws in ILC study. In ILC design, scholars take nonrepetitive varying law as parametric uncertainties and incorporate varying law into control algorithm using different math method such as internal model theorem [6]. In this paper, time-iteration-independent initial condition is not necessary. Additionally, iteration-varying reference will be imported into the system.

In the past decades, many ILC methods for continuous-time systems are proposed [20, 21]. However, control approach for discrete-time plants needs more attentions since control system is always applied in discrete-time in practice. By considering the PMLSM system as parametric unknown discrete-time plants, an AILC approach is employed to track time-iteration-varying reference trajectories in this paper. Except for the time-iteration-varying tracking objective, the robustness to ripple force is also taken into account. Through matrix transformation, the inherent correlations of time-iteration-varying uncertainties is identified. A learning approach for unknown matrix similar with [22] is developed in the estimation. According to the composite energy function (CEF) methodology, we verify the convergence of the AILC algorithm rigorously.

The remainder of this paper is organized as follows. In Sect. 2, the system description of PMLSM and discretization are presented, as well as useful assumptions. In Sect. 3, the AILC algorithm for partial nonlinear system are constructed. Furthermore, the estimation updating law of uncertainty is designed. The iterative learning theorem and convergence certification are given in Sect. 4. In Sect. 5, a PMLSM simulation example is given to show the effectiveness of the proposed AILC protocol. Finally, the conclusions of the paper are presented in Sect. 6.

2 The Dynamic of PMLSM System

With the development of application technology and the improvement of material performance for permanent magnet, PMLSM has become representative motor of linear servo motor with its high thrust strength, low loss, fast response, and small electrical time constant. However, simplified mechanic structure of PMLSM also enhances difficulties in electrical control. End-effect, system parameter perturbations and load disturbances, etc. can affect controller without buffer. Without loss of generality, the theoretical analysis of multivariable PMLSM system is based on several assumptions.

Assumption 1. Assume that motor hysteresis, eddy current and flux distortion can be ignored.

Assumption 2. The magnetic field is sinusoidal spatial distribution.

Assumption 3. Assume that nonlinear friction can be ignored.

Assumption 4. Assume that mutual inductance coefficient of stator winding is 0.

Based on Assumptions 1–4, consider the following mechanical equation of PMLSM:

$$F_e = M\dot{v}(t) + Bv(t) + f_1 \tag{1}$$

where t denotes time. Meanwhile, F_e and $v(t)$ denote electromagnetic thrust and speed of mover, respectively; M is mass of load, B is viscous friction coefficient; f_1 is other uncertainties and disturbances.

On the premise of considering only the fundamental component of each variable, direct-quadrature decomposition is used to electromagnetic thrust equation. Hence, the electromagnetic thrust equation can be written as:

$$F_e = \frac{3\pi}{2\tau}\psi_f i_q(t) + \frac{3\pi}{2\tau}(L_d - L_q)i_d(t)i_q(t) \tag{2}$$

where τ is polar distance of permanent magnet; ψ_f is flux linkage; L_d and L_q denote inductance of direct axis and quadrature axis, respectively; $i_d(t)$ and $i_q(t)$ denote current of direct axis and quadrature axis, respectively.

In order to cope with coupling variables of stator current and rotor permanent magnetic flux, we reserve quadrature component in stator current only, namely, $i_d = 0$. Considering PMLSM is a dynamic system, this approach is feasible. Only permanent magnet torque component remains in motor torque which means that no reluctance torque left. By using those D-Q decomposition, stator current becomes smaller and more efficiency. Hence, decoupling stator current facilitate the modified electromagnetic thrust equation as:

$$F_e = \frac{3\pi}{2\tau}\psi_f i_q(t) \tag{3}$$

From electromagnetic thrust Eq. (3), we can see that current of d-axis i_d is equivalent to excitation current and q-axis current i_q is proportional to electromagnetic thrust, which means i_q is equivalent to armature current. Thus, the ideal position control of PMLSM can be implemented by controlling the q-axis current i_q.

After decoupling with $i_d = 0$, substituting (1) into (3), we have:

$$F_e = \frac{3\pi}{2\tau}\psi_f i_q(t) = M\dot{v}(t) + Bv(t) + f_1 \tag{4}$$

Considering the inherent structural characteristics of linear motor core breaking, we can see that inner and outer disturbances will affect the motor directly, especially nonlinear factor of thrust ripple. The thrust fluctuation will increase the positioning error. Moreover, among the various uncertainties, the thrust fluctuation caused by the end effect has a great influence on the PMLSM. Thus, periodic thrust ripple force f_{ri} is considered as:

$$f_{ri} = F_{r\max} \sin(2\pi x(t)/\tau) \tag{5}$$

where $F_{r\max}$ is the amplitude of thrust ripple, $x(t)$ denotes shift of moving part along the moving direction.

To carry the subsequent AILC approach forward, we make the following definitions. Denote $\pi \psi_f/\tau = K_1$ and $3K_1/2 = K_f$. K_f represents electromagnetic thrust coefficient. Equation (4) can be expressed as:

$$\dot{v}(t) = K_f i_q(t)/M - Bv(t)/M - f_{fr}/M - f_{ri}/M \tag{6}$$

Based on the first-order forward Euler difference, define:

$$\begin{cases} \dot{v}(t) = \dfrac{v(T+1) - v(T)}{T_0} \\ \dot{x}(t) = \dfrac{x(T+1) - x(T)}{T_0} \end{cases} \tag{7}$$

where T and T_0 are discrete-time variable and discrete-time interval, respectively. Substituting (7) into (6), we have

$$\begin{cases} v(T+1) = (1 - T_0B/M)v(T) + (T_0K_f/M)i_q(T) - T_0f_{fr}/M - T_0f_{ri}/M \\ x(T+1) = T_0v(T) + x(T) \end{cases} \tag{8}$$

3 AILC Algorithm Design

In this part, we will introduce AILC design with a novel estimation updating law for unknown terms of system (8). Resistance R, inductance L_q, etc. will be drifted in practical procedure. After that, shift parameters will cause control deviation. To avoid these problems, we will design AILC approach for partial nonlinear system as

$$x_k(t+1) = A(t)x_k(t) + B(t)u_{kq}(t) + D(x_k, t) \tag{9}$$

where k is the iteration number, t is the time index; $A(t) \in R^{2\times2}, B(t) \in R^{2\times1}, D(x_k, t) \in R^{2\times1}$ denote unknown system parameters, control input gain and disturbance varying in time and iteration domain, respectively; $x_k(t)$ consists of position and velocity of PMLSM; $u_{kq}(t)$ is the system input in the kth iteration which is q-axis current in practice.

With respect to actual operation of PMLSM, the following two assumptions are given before control design.

Assumption 5. $B(t)$ is uniformly bounded $0 < B_{\min} \leq \|B(t)\| \leq B_{\max}$, where $B_{\min}$ and $B_{\max}$ are bound of control gain respectively. Without generality, assume that the control gain is positive.

According to the analysis of the periodic thrust ripple caused by the end effect of PMLSM, f_{ri} increases linearly with motor position. Hence, thrust ripple satisfies the linear boundedness condition.

Remark 1. The control gain $B(t)$ should always be positive or negative in (9) practically. If the input gain is negative, the inverter can play a part. Furthermore, it's nonsense in practice if $B(t) = 0$ which means the system responds nothing to any input.

Assumption 6. f_{ri} is linear bounded $f_{ri} \leq C_1 + C_2 \|x_k(t)\|$, where C_1 and C_2 are positive constants.

For the initial state and tracking reference, due to the varying initial positions and tasks of PMLSM in practice, the initial position and reference trajectories of linear motor system changes, that is, iteration-varying. Hence, the initial state $x_k(0)$ and reference objective $x_k^d(t)$ vary in iteration domain.

Remark 2. The initial state and reference trajectory discussed in the paper can be defined as nonrepetitive circumstances in ILC which means that the AILC method designed can track reference target varying in iterations. Besides, the system plant worked iteratively in practice with different initial condition.

We target at designing appropriate input series $u_{kq}(t)$ to ensure that the system state tracks reference trajectory asymptotically in limit time with the iteration index tends to infinity.

The AILC law is designed as

$$u_{kq}(t) = \hat{\theta}_k(t)\xi_k(t) \tag{10}$$

where $\hat{\theta}_k(t)$ is the estimation of uncertainty $\theta(t)$ at kth iteration; $\xi_k(t)$ consists of state variables $x_k(t)$ and tracking reference $x_k^d(t+1)$. $\theta(t)$ and $\xi_k(t)$ are designed as

$$\begin{cases} \theta(t) = [F^{-1}(t)B^{\mathrm{T}}(t), -F^{-1}(t)B^{\mathrm{T}}(t)A(t), -F^{-1}(t)B^{\mathrm{T}}(t), -F^{-1}(t)B^{\mathrm{T}}(t)D_2(t)] \\ \xi_k(t) = [x_k^{d,\mathrm{T}}(t+1), x_k^{\mathrm{T}}(t), D_1(x_k(t)), 1]^{\mathrm{T}} \end{cases} \tag{11}$$

where $F(t) = B^{\mathrm{T}}(t)B(t)$; $D_1(x_k(t))$ is disturbance caused by thrust ripple; $D_2(t)$ is white noise in system position measurement.

The estimation updating law of unknown time-varying part in the kth iteration is

$$\hat{\theta}_k(t) = \hat{\theta}_{k-1}(t) + \frac{pB^{\mathrm{T}}(t)e_{k-1}(t+1)\xi_{k-1}^{\mathrm{T}}(t)}{q + \xi_{k-1}^{\mathrm{T}}(t)\xi_{k-1}(t)} \tag{12}$$

where p and q are learning gains which satisfy $q > 0$, $0 < p < 2/b_F$, b_F is defined as boundedness of matrix $F(t)$; $e_{k-1}(t+1)$ is the dynamics of the tracking error. The (k-1)th iteration of it can be given by $e_{k-1}(t+1) = x_{k-1}^d(t+1) - x_{k-1}(t+1)$.

It is worthwhile to point out that although the AILC algorithm presented in the paper is designed for a class of permanent magnet linear synchronous motor, the iterative learning control input (10) with estimation updating law of unknowns (12) can be extended to a class of partial nonlinear system (9) satisfies Assumptions 5 and 6.

Theorem. Suppose that partial nonlinear system (9) satisfies Assumptions 5 and 6. For given positive learning gains p and q satisfying $0 < p < 2/b_F$, the system state tracks iteration-varying reference objective along the iteration axis asymptotically under the AILC law (10) as well as the parameter updating law (12). Control input $u_{kq}(t)$ and system state $x_k(t)$ are both bounded.

It is worth noting that ILC control method was also proposed in [17] for PMLSM with iteration invariant initial condition. However, it is impossible to start at the same position every time in actual operation. Hence, in this paper, we purchase the AILC problem for PMLSM with iteration-varying initial states in every iteration. Moreover, the nonrepetitive circumstances of $x_k(0) \neq x_k^d(0)$ are also considered in the paper.

4 Design of AILC and Robust Convergence Result

We analyze the performance of the AILC law in this part. Firstly, we will simplify the expression. The correlation function $h(t)$ and matrix $L(t)$ are represented by the simplified expression h and L.

Define nonrepetitive estimation error in the kth iteration $\tilde{\theta}_k(t) = \theta(t) - \hat{\theta}_k(t)$. Subtract $\theta(t)$ from both sides of Eq. (12) we have

$$\tilde{\theta}_k(t) = \tilde{\theta}_{k-1}(t) - \frac{pB^T e_{k-1}(t+1)\xi_{k-1}^T}{q + \xi_{k-1}^T \xi_{k-1}} \tag{13}$$

The CEF of plant (9) is defined as $E_k(t) = \text{trace}(\tilde{\theta}_k^T(t)\tilde{\theta}_k(t))/p$. Then, the difference of CEF between two sequential iterations is

$$\Delta E_k(t) = E_k(t) - E_{k-1}(t) \tag{14}$$

Substituting (13) into (14), we get

$$\Delta E_k(t) = \text{trace}[-\tilde{\theta}_{k-1}^T \frac{B^T e_{k-1}(t+1)\xi_{k-1}^T}{q + \xi_{k-1}^T \xi_{k-1}} - \frac{[B^T e_{k-1}(t+1)\xi_{k-1}^T]^T}{q + \xi_{k-1}^T \xi_{k-1}}\tilde{\theta}_{k-1}]$$
$$+ \text{trace}[\frac{p[B^T e_{k-1}(t+1)\xi_{k-1}^T]^T[B^T e_{k-1}(t+1)\xi_{k-1}^T]}{(q + \xi_{k-1}^T \xi_{k-1})^2}] \tag{15}$$

Based on matrix transformation

$$\tilde{\theta}_{k-1}^T B^T e_{k-1}(t+1)\xi_{k-1}^T = [B^T e_{k-1}(t+1)\xi_{k-1}^T]^T \tilde{\theta}_{k-1}, \tag{16}$$

Equation (15) be expressed as

$$\Delta E_k(t) = \text{trace}[-2\tilde{\theta}_{k-1}^T \frac{B^T e_{k-1}(t+1)\xi_{k-1}^T}{q + \xi_{k-1}^T \xi_{k-1}}]$$

$$+\text{trace}[\frac{p[B^T e_{k-1}(t+1)\xi_{k-1}^T]^T[B^T e_{k-1}(t+1)\xi_{k-1}^T]}{(q + \xi_{k-1}^T \xi_{k-1})^2}] \tag{17}$$

$$= -2\frac{e_{k-1}^T(t+1)B\tilde{\theta}_{k-1}\xi_{k-1}}{q + \xi_{k-1}^T \xi_{k-1}} + \frac{p e_{k-1}^T(t+1)BB^T e_{k-1}(t+1)\xi_{k-1}^T \xi_{k-1}}{(q + \xi_{k-1}^T \xi_{k-1})^2}$$

Since $\frac{\xi_{k-1}^T \xi_{k-1}}{(q+\xi_{k-1}^T \xi_{k-1})^2} \le \frac{1}{q+\xi_{k-1}^T \xi_{k-1}}$, it can be obtained that

$$\Delta E_k(t) \le \frac{p e_{k-1}^T(t+1)BB^T e_{k-1}(t+1) - 2e_{k-1}^T(t+1)B\tilde{\theta}_{k-1}\xi_{k-1}}{q + \xi_{k-1}^T \xi_{k-1}} \tag{18}$$

Substituting system plant (9) into tracking error renders to

$$e_k(t+1) = x_k^d(t+1) - Ax_k - Bu_{kq} - D_k \tag{19}$$

Due to the definition of control gain matrix $B(t) \in R^{2 \times 1}$, we have

$$B^T e_k(t+1) = B^T B[\theta \xi_k - \hat{\theta}_k \xi_k] = B^T B\tilde{\theta}_k \xi_k \tag{20}$$

It follows that

$$\tilde{\theta}_k \xi_k = F^{-1} B^T e_k(t+1) \tag{21}$$

where $F(t) = B^T(t)B(t)$. Substituting (21) into (18), it can be obtained that

$$\Delta E_k(t) \le -\frac{e_{k-1}^T(t+1)B[-p + 2F^{-1}]B^T e_{k-1}(t+1)}{q + \xi_{k-1}^T \xi_{k-1}} \tag{22}$$

Noticing the range of learning gains p and q in Theorem, it can be concluded that $2F^{-1} - p > 0$. Furthermore, according to the Assumption 5, we have $\Delta E_k(t) < 0$ holds. Due to the definition of nonnegative function $E_k(t)$, we get the conclusion that estimation error of unknown parameters $\tilde{\theta}_k(t)$ is bounded.

Taking the sum of both sides in Eq. (22) from $k = 1$ to $k = i$ for each discrete time, it can be concluded that

$$E_i(t) \le E_0(t) - \sum_{k=1}^{i} \frac{e_{k-1}^T(t+1)B[-pB^T B + 2]e_{k-1}(t+1)}{q + \xi_{k-1}^T \xi_{k-1}} \tag{23}$$

Then we analyze inequality (23). Noticing that $E_0(t)$ is bounded and $E_i(t)$ is non-negative, we have the conclusion that $\lim_{k \to \infty} \|e_k(t+1)\| = 0, \forall k \in Z^+$. Namely, tracking position and velocity error of PMLSM converges to zero asymptotically in limited time. Similarly, we can also get the bounded conclusions of $u_k(t)$ and $x_k(t)$.

5 Simulation Example

In this section, we will give illustrative example using AILC law proposed in Section 3 for the PMLSM system with parameters as: $M = 10$kg, $B = 1.2$N $\cdot$ s/m, $K_f = 25$N/A, $f_{ri} = 30\sin(25x_k(t))$. The white noise varying in $[-0.01, 0.01]$ is produced in the process of position measurement. The sampling interval is $0.001s$.

The desired trajectory varies in time iteration domain as

$$\begin{cases} v_k^d(\tau) = (x_{0,k} - x_f)(60\tau_1^3 - 30\tau_1^4 - 30\tau_1^2) \\ x_k^d(\tau) = x_{0,k} + (x_{0,k} - x_f)(15\tau_1^4 - 6\tau_1^5 - 10\tau_1^3) \end{cases} \tag{24}$$

where $\tau_1 = t/(t_f - t_0)$, t_f and t_0 are terminal and start time of PMLSM, respectively; $x_f = 0.6$m is terminal position of PMLSM, $x_{0,k}$ denotes start position. The initial position $x_{0,k}$ is assumed to be generated by random in $(0, 0.1$m) as iteration number changes. As a result, desired reference trajectory and ripple force are non-repetitive in iteration domain.

The tracking error is defined as maximum absolute error max $|e_k|$ in every iteration. max $|e_k(1)|$ and max $|e_k(2)|$ are shown in Figs. 1 and 2 after the AILC control. Notice that for PMLSM with non-repetitive initial state, uncertainties and desired trajectories, the tracking can be achieved. From these two figures we can see that the maximum tracking error converges in a small bound asymptotically along the iteration axis with several non-repetitive problems in PMLSM. Furthermore, we can also get that the maximum absolute tracking error of velocity is about 0.017 m/s and that of position is about 0.19 m at the very beginning of learning control. When reference trajectories are iteration varying, tracking error converges rapidly in finite time interval in these two figures.

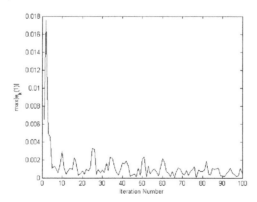

Fig. 1. The convergence of the maximum absolute tracking error of velocity in iteration domain

Non-repetitive initial position $x_k(2)$ in the 100 iterations is shown in Fig. 3. Desired trajectories of velocity at 5th and 28th iterations are shown in Fig. 4. Solid line means tracking trajectory at 5th iteration. Dotted line means reference at 28th iteration. From these two figures we can see the non-repetitiveness of initial states and desired trajectories.

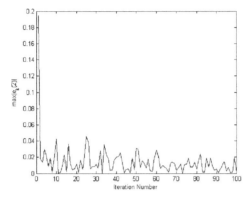

Fig. 2. The convergence of the maximum absolute tracking error of position in iteration domain

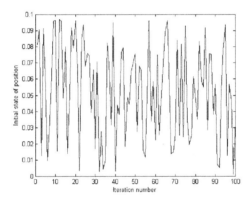

Fig. 3. System initial states of position along the iteration axis

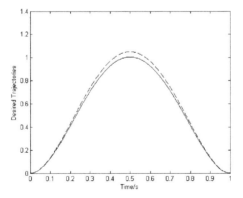

Fig. 4. Desired trajectories of velocity at 5th and 28th iterations

6   Conclusions

The AILC method for PMLSM system with time-iteration-varying uncertainties and non-repetitive initial position has been proposed in this paper. Furthermore, the tracking reference trajectories also vary nonrepetitively. Since the proposed method is designed for a class of partial nonlinear systems, the obtained results can also be extended. By using matrix transformation, the non-repetitive uncertainties are simplified into unknown problems varying in time domain. Hence, AILC algorithm and unknown estimation are designed. With the help of CEF, the learning performance has been verified strictly. The simulation result certificate the asymptotic convergence by exploring property profiles of PMLSM.

Acknowledgments. This research is supported by the Natural Science Foundation for the Universities of Jiangsu Province of China (18KJB510009), the Senior Visiting Scholar Project for the Higher Vocational School of Jiangsu Province (2021GRFX015) and the Major Project of Jiangsu Vocational Institute of Commerce (JSJM001).

References

1. Huang, W.T., Hua, W., Yin, F., Yu, F., Qi, J.: Model predictive thrust force control of a linear flux-switching permanent magnet machine with voltage vectors selection and synthesis. IEEE Trans. Ind. Electron. **66**(6), 4956–4967 (2019). https://doi.org/10.1109/TIE.2018.2835381
2. Chai, S., Wang, L.P., Rogers, E.: A cascade MPC control structure for a PMSM with speed ripple minimization. IEEE Trans. Ind. Electron. **60**(8), 2978–2987 (2013). https://doi.org/10.1109/TIE.2012.2201432
3. Liu, W., Xu, Y., Ding, R., Shu, F., Yang, X.: Time-iteration-domain integrated learning control for robust trajectory tracking and disturbance rejection: with application to a PMLSM. IET Control Theory Appl. (2021). https://doi.org/10.1049/cth2.12197
4. Yuan, H., Zhao, X.: Adaptive jerk control of permanent magnet linear synchronous motor servo system. Trans. China Electrotechnical Soc. **35**(16), 3406–3413 (2020). https://doi.org/10.19595/j.cnki.1000-6753.tces.190675 (in Chinese)
5. Tang, C., Duan, Z.: Direct thrust-controlled PMSLM servo system based on back-stepping control. IEEE Trans. Electr. Electron. Eng. **13**(5), 785–790 (2018). https://doi.org/10.1002/tee.22630
6. Zhou, W., Yu, M., Liu, B.B.: Iterative learning control design with high-order internal model for discrete-time nonlinear systems. Int. J. Robust Nonlinear Control **27**(16), 3158–3173 (2017). https://doi.org/10.1002/rnc.3732
7. He, T.F., Wu, Z.: Multirate iterative learning disturbance observer with measurement delay compensation for flexible spacecraft attitude stabilization subject to complex disturbances. J. Vib. Control (2020). https://doi.org/10.1177/1077546320977362
8. Zhang, H., Chi, R., Hou, Z., Huang, B.: Data-driven iterative learning control using a uniform quantizer with an encoding-decoding mechanism. Int. J. Robust Nonlinear Control (2022). https://doi.org/10.1002/rnc.6027
9. Chi, R., Wei, Y., Wang, R., Hou, Z.: Observer based switching ILC for consensus of nonlinear nonaffine multi-agent systems. J. Franklin Inst. (2021). https://doi.org/10.1016/j.jfranklin.2021.06.010

10. Li, Z., Yin, C., Ji, H., Hou, Z.: Constrained spatial adaptive iterative learning control for trajectory tracking of high speed train. IEEE Trans. Intell. Transp. (2021). https://doi.org/10.1109/TITS.2021.3106653

11. Lee, T.H., Tan, K.K., LIM, S.Y., Dou, H.F.: Iterative learning control of permanent magnet linear motor with relay automatic tuning. Mechatronics **10**(1–2), 169–190 (2000). https://doi.org/10.1016/S0957-4158(99)00074-4

12. Dai, M., Qi, R., Zhao, Y., Li, Y.: PD-type iterative learning control with adaptive learning gains for high-performance load torque tracking of electric dynamic load simulator. Electronics **10**(7), 811 (2021). https://doi.org/10.3390/electronics10070811

13. Buelta, A., Olivares, A., Staffetti, E., Aftab, W., Mihaylova, L.: A Gaussian process iterative learning control for aircraft trajectory tracking. IEEE Trans. Aerosp. Electron. Syst. (2021). https://doi.org/10.1109/TAES.2021.3098133

14. Zhu, X., Zhu, Z.H., Chen, J.: Dual quaternion-based adaptive iterative learning control for flexible spacecraft rendezvous. Acta Astronaut. **189**, 99–118 (2021). https://doi.org/10.1016/j.actaastro.2021.08.040

15. Basit, B.A., Rehman, A.U., Han, H.C., Jung, J.W.: A robust iterative learning control technique to efficiently mitigate disturbances for three-phase standalone inverters. IEEE Trans. Industr. Electron. (2022). https://doi.org/10.1109/TIE.2021.3071695

16. Zhou, X., Wang, H., Tian, Y., Dai, X.: Iterative learning control-based tracking synchronization for linearly coupled reaction-diffusion neural networks with time delay and iteration-varying switching topology. J. Franklin Inst. **358**, 3822–3846 (2021). https://doi.org/10.1016/j.jfranklin.2021.02.026

17. Zhang, H., Yu, F., Bu, X., Wang, F.: Robust iterative learning control for permanent magnet linear motor. Electric Mach. Control **16**(6), 81–86 (2012). https://doi.org/10.3969/j.issn.1007-449X.2012.06.014 (in Chinese)

18. Chi, R., Hou, Z., Xu, J.: Adaptive ILC for a class of discrete-time systems with iteration-varying trajectory and random initial condition. Automatica **44**, 2207–2213 (2008). https://doi.org/10.1016/j.automatica.2007.12.004

19. Xu, J.-X.: Direct learning of control efforts for trajectories with different magnitude scales. Automatica **33**(12), 2191–2195 (1997)

20. Huang, J., Wang, W., Su, X.: Adaptive iterative learning control of multiple autonomous vehicles with a time-varying reference under actuator faults. IEEE Trans. Neural Netw. Learn. Syst. (2021). https://doi.org/10.1109/TNNLS.2021.3069209

21. Liu, Q., Tian, S., Gu, P.: P-type iterative learning control algorithm for a class of linear singular impulsive systems. J. Franklin Inst. **355**(9), 3926–3937 (2018). https://doi.org/10.1016/j.jfranklin.2018.03.011

22. Chen, Y., Chu, B., Freeman, C.T.: Generalized iterative learning control using successive projection: Algorithm, convergence, and experimental verification. IEEE Trans. Control Syst. Technol. (2020). https://doi.org/10.1109/TCST.2019.2928505

Tracing Knowledge State with Individualized Ability and Question Difficulty

Bing Xiao[1,2(✉)], Hua Jiang[1], Junliang Ma[1,2], and Ruihuan Zhang[1]

[1] Shaanxi Normal University, Xian, Shaanxi, China
{bingxiao,junliangma}@snnu.edu.cn
[2] Key Laboratory of Modern Teaching Technology, Ministry of Education,
Xian, Shaanxi, China
https://www.snnu.edu.cn

Abstract. Knowledge tracing(KT) refers to the task of modeling students' evolving knowledge state according to their historical learning trajectories. Although many methods have been proposed to solve KT task, most of them ignore the difference of students and questions, i.e., the students' learning ability are different from each other. To this end, in this paper, a learning ability estimation module is proposed to extract students' learning ability according to their learning history and a novel method to obtain questions' representation is designed. Besides, a knowledge state estimation module is proposed to estimation students' knowledge state which takes both students' learning ability and their learning interaction into consideration when modeling. Extensive experiments demonstrate that the proposed model could improve thr results of knowledge tracing through modeling individualized students' learning ability and questions' difficulty in learning process.

Keywords: knowledge tracing · learning ability · question difficulty · temporal convolutional network

1 Introduction

With the advancement of online intelligent tutoring systems such as MOOCs, which aim to help students learn related knowledge and improve teachers' teaching efficiency [5]. knowledge tracing (KT) has attracted more and more researchers' interest. KT is a fundamental task for developing personalized learning systems, which aims at modeling students' knowledge state over time based on their historical activities.

Learning curve [15] found by Newell and Rosenbloom demonstrates that the error rate of students' performance will decrease as the amount of practice increase. However, it's simply gives the generalized relationship between the students' performance in the future and their historical learning activities. And many knowledge tracing models such as DKT [19] only takes students' learning history to predict students' future performance. However, students are different from each other, for example, to solve a same question some students will take many practices while some students will take few since the learning abilities of students are different.It means that the students' personalized learning abilities should not be neglected when modeling students' learning process.

Item response theory(IRT) [20] also known as latent trait theory, is usually used to measure students' latent variables such as ability, mastery level of knowledge concept, and attitude. Item response function shows that the probability of a correct answer is not only related to students' ability but also the questions' difficulty. It means that the questions' difficulty should be took into consideration when predict student future performance in knowledge tracing task.

Therefore, a novel Individualized Ability and Question difficulty Knowledge Tracing(IAQKT) model is proposed to model students' personalized learning ability and questions' individualized difficulty according to their learning activities. Contributions of this paper are given specifically: (1) A novel learning ability estimation nmodule is proposed to model students' learning ability which not only considers students' learning history students' current learning activities. (2) A novel question representation method is desighed, which could not only estimate individualized question difficulty but also could avoid over-parameterization compared with embedding every question directly. (3) Finally, students' learning abilities could impact their knowledge state , therefore, a knowledge state estimation module is proposed which takes students' learning ability and their learning interaction into consideration when modeling.

2   Related Work

The existing knowledge tracing methods could be classified into traditional machine learning-based methods and deep learning-based methods. Furthermore, Machine learning-based traditional methods could be grouped into probabilistic methods and logistic methods.

One representative model of probabilistic models is Bayesian Knowledge Tracing (BKT) [6] which could be viewed as a Hidden Markov Model(HMM) [2]. In BKT, student's knowledge state during the learning process is represented by a set of binary variables: mastered or not. In particular, BKT models each concept state separately. Based on logistic functions, logistic models take the factors which will affect students' knowledge state into consideration to estimate student knowledge state. The logistic models include Item Response Theory (IRT) [26], Additive Factor Model (AFM) [3], Performance Factor Analysis (PFA) [9], Knowledge Tracing Machine (KTM) [23]. In recent years, with the advancement of deep learning, a serious of deep learning-based KT models have been proposed. DKT [19] is the first deep learning-based model which models the students' knowledge state during students' process based on recurrent neural networks (RNNs) [25]. In order to model student's mastery level of every latent knowledge concept, Dynamic Key-Value Memory Network (DKVMN) [28] uses a static key matrix and a dynamic value matrix to model the latent concepts and their mastery respectively. A self-attention model for knowledge tracing (SAKT) [16] is a transformer-based model, which use a purely attention mechanism to model student learning process.

In addition to these generalized methods mentioned above, which ignore the difference of students and questions, there are several methods proposed to model the individualization of students and questions. To model students' personalized prior knowledge, Prior Per Student(PPS) model [17] personalized prior knowledge parameter of BKT [6] for every student. Similarly, based on BKT, KT-IDEM [18] individualized the guess and slip parameter to represent questions difficulty. These two methods all need to design a model for every skills separately. DKT-DSC [14] split students' learning sequence into several time intervals, and then the students will be assign into different group according to there learning performance in every interval. In particular, the K-means clustering algorithm is uesed in every interval to devide every student into different group. However, this method suffers from the problem of data leakage which may mix student's future answer information since it directly splits the student's whole answer sequence. Convolutional Knowledge Tracing(CKT) [21] proposed to utilize convolutional neural networks to capture students' personalized learning rates and prior knowledge. It's not accurately and comprehensively to estimate students' personalized learning ability simply according to their answer sequence in CKT.

Aiming at above problems, IAQKT is proposed, in which a student ability estimation module is designed to extract students' personalized dynamic ability according their historical learning process based on temporal convolutional networks(TCN) [1, 10]. Moreover, a novel question embedding method is designed to characterize question difficulty, which could avoid data sparsity and overparameterization problem. Learning ability is taken into consideration when modeling knowledge state since the learning ability could impact the knowledge state.

3   Problem Definition

In knowledge tracing, given a student's historical interactions sequence $X = \{(q_1, c_1, a_1) \ldots (q_t, c_t, a_t)\}$ from initial time step to time step t where the $q_i \in N^+$ is the question index, $c_i \in N^+$ is the concept index covered by the question, and $a_i \in \{0, 1\}$ is student's answer, the goal is to predict the student will answer q_{t+1} correctly at time step $t + 1$, $i.e. P(r_{t+1} = 1 \mid q_{t+1}, X)$.

4   The Proposed Method

The overview architecture of the proposed method is given in Fig. 1. The model could be divided into two components:learning ability estimation module, knowledge state estimation module.

4.1   Learning Ability Estimation Module

As Fig. 1 shows, based on TCN [1,10] architecture, a learning ability estimation module is proposed to model students' learning ability according to their learning history. AS [12] shows that the students' individualized abilities would

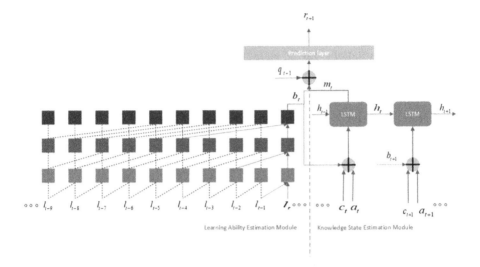

Fig. 1. The overview of proposed method

impact skilled performance. It means that the student learning ability could be extract from student historical learning performance sequence. In [14,21], they only consider a part of students' learning ability through computing the correct rate or counting number of different knowledge concepts the students answered. Therefore, we take a further step to model students' learning ability from two perspectives based on these two methods. On the one hand, we compute the students' average learning ability according to their learning history like [14,21]. On the other hand, we take students' current learning activities into consideration which reflect students' present learning state.

To measure students' average learning ability from their learning sequence, we count the number of different knowledge concepts n_t and compute the correct rate d_t that student answered from initial time step to time step t.

$$n_t = \sum_{i=1}^{t} \text{distinct}\,(c_i) \tag{1}$$

$$d_t = \frac{\sum_{i=1}^{t} a_i == 1}{t} \tag{2}$$

where c_i represents the student answered knowledge concept c at time step i, and the $distinct\,(c_i) = 0$ if the concept c_i has been answered before time step i otherwise $distinct\,(c_i) = 1$; $a_i == 1$ represents the student's answer is correct at time step t.

Actually, student's current learning activity reflect the his/her present learning ability. For example, for the same question, the students with higher learning ability could only takes less attempts to solve it while the lower takes more.

Therefore, we count the number of the attempts e_t and the number of hints f_t the student used at time step t.

Finally, we randomly initialize $\boldsymbol{n_t} \in R^d$, $\boldsymbol{d_t} \in R^d$, $\boldsymbol{e_t} \in R^d$, $\boldsymbol{f_t} \in R^d$ as the embedding of n_t, d_t, e_t, f_t respectively. And then the learning ability $\boldsymbol{b_t}$ at time step t is obtained as follows:

$$k_t = [\boldsymbol{n_t}, \boldsymbol{d_t}, \boldsymbol{e_t}, \boldsymbol{f_t}] \tag{3}$$

$$l_t = \boldsymbol{W} k_t + \boldsymbol{b} \tag{4}$$

$$b_t = \text{TCN}\,(L) \tag{5}$$

where $[,]$ is concatenation operation, the $\boldsymbol{W}$, $\boldsymbol{b}$ are parameters of feed forward layer, which are learned during training, l_t represents the learning ability feature and $L = (l_1, l_2, \ldots, l_i, \ldots, l_t)$ represents the student's learning ability feature sequence from initial time step to time step t.

4.2   Knowledge State Estimation Module

The knowledge state estimation module consists of a Long Short-Term Memory network(LSTM) [8], instead of simply using the student's answer sequence as input, we extra takes the student's ability into consideration to model student knowledge state . Similarly, we use a embedding matrix $\boldsymbol{C} \in R^{M \times d}$, where M is total count of different knowledge concepts of the dataset and d is the number of dimensions, to vectorize every knowledge concept, and it will be learned during training process. To distinguish the influences of right and wrong responses on student knowledge state, inspired by [11], the representation of learning interaction $\boldsymbol{x_t}$ is obtained as follows:

$$x_t = \begin{cases} [\boldsymbol{c_t}, \boldsymbol{a_t}], & \text{if } a_t = 1 \\ [\boldsymbol{a_t}, \boldsymbol{c_t}], & \text{if } a_t = 0 \end{cases} \tag{6}$$

where $\boldsymbol{a_t} = (0, 0, ..., 0)$ is a zero vector and its dimension is d.

Then take the estimated ability $\boldsymbol{b_t}$ and the interaction representation $\boldsymbol{x_t}$ as the input of knowledge state estimation module to model the student knowledge state at time step t. The knowledge state $\boldsymbol{m_t} \in R^d$ is computed as follows:

$$\begin{aligned}
s_t &= [\boldsymbol{b_t}, \boldsymbol{x_t}] \\
f_t &= \sigma\left(\boldsymbol{W_f} \cdot [h_{t-1}, s_t] + b_f\right) \\
i_t &= \sigma\left(\boldsymbol{W_i} \cdot [h_{t-1}, s_t] + b_i\right) \\
o_t &= \sigma\left(\boldsymbol{W_o}\,[h_{t-1}, s_t] + b_o\right) \\
g_t &= f_t \otimes g_{t-1} + i_t \otimes \tanh\left(\boldsymbol{W_c}\,[h_{t-1}, s_t] + b_c\right) \\
h_t &= o_t \otimes \tanh\left(g_t\right) \\
m_t &= h_t
\end{aligned} \tag{7}$$

where f_t, i_t, o_t, g_t, h_t are the activation vector of the forget gate, input gate, output gate, memory cell state and the hidden state of the LSTM cell separately, W_f,W_i,W_o,W_c are weight matrices, and b_f,b_i,b_o,b_c are bias vectors which need to be learned during training.$\otimes$ denotes element-wise product. The $\sigma()$ and $\tanh()$ denote the Sigmoid and Hyperbolic Tangent function seperately.

4.3   Question Embedding

It's obviously that the questions which cover same knowledge concepts are similar. However, there are still some difference among these questions since every question has its own characteristic such as the difficulty. But, in [22,24] , questions are used in place of concepts, which may lead a catastrophic failure because the interactions between students and questions are extremely sparse. According to [7], the questions are designed for the purposed of helping students mastery corresponding concepts. Therefore, in this paper, the question is characterized based on the question deviates and the concept embedding that question covers. It is represented as follow:

$$q_{t+1} = \mu_{q_{t+1}} \cdot c_{t+1} \tag{8}$$

where $\mu_{q_{t+1}}$ is a scalar coefficient which reflects the question's difficulty. It's learned during training process. c_{t+1} is the concept embedding that question covers.

4.4   Prediction and Training

Learning ability b_t, knowledge state m_t and the question q_{t+1} that student will answer in the next time step are all together input into prediction layer, the probability p_{t+1} of the student will answer correctly q_{t+1} is computed as follow:

$$p_{t+1} = \sigma\left(w_p\left[b_t, m_t, q_{t+1}\right] + b\right) \tag{9}$$

where w_p and b are trainable parameters.

Finally, the cross entropy log loss is choosed as the objective function of our model, which is computed between predicted probability of the model and the actual answer of the student:

$$\mathcal{L} = -\sum_t \left(a_t \log\left(p_t\right) + \left(1 - a_t\right) \log\left(1 - p_t\right)\right) \tag{10}$$

where the p_t denotes the predicted probability of student will answer correctly at time step t, and the a_t is the student's real answer at time step t.

5 Experimental Analysis

Five datasets: ASSISTment2009, ASSISTment2012, ASSISTmen2015[1], Ednet[2], Junyi Academy[3], are used to evaluate the performance of our model and several baseline knowledge tracing models on the task of predicting future learner responses. The ASSISTments datasets are collected from online tutoring system ASSISTments and widely used for KT tasks. Ednet is collected by [4] and collected over more than 2 years. As the result of the limitation of hardware, instead of using all students' logs of EdNet-KT1 dataset, we randomly sample 5000 students' records to experiment. For the Junyi Academy, which has more than 200000 students' interactions, and we remove the students who has less than three records. The detailed statistics of these datasets is shown in Table 1.

Table 1. Dataset statistics

	Students	Concepts	Questions	Records
ASSISTment2009	4,151	123	17,650	346,680
ASSISTment2012	46,674	265	179,999	6,123,270
ASSISTment2015	19,840	100		683,801
Ednet	5,000	188	13,169	222,141
Junyi Academy	247,606	41	722	25,925,922

To evaluate the effectiveness of our model, we compare it with several baseline knowledge tracing models, including DKT, DKT+ [27], DKVMN [28], and SAKT [16]. In addition to these non-individualized knowledge tracing models, two individualized models CKT [21] and DKT-DSC [14] are selected to validate our intuition. For the evaluation metric, we choose the area under the receiver operating characteristics curve (AUC), which is the most widely used indicator in KT.

5.1 Student Performance Prediction

Table 2 shows all KT methods' results on predicting learners responses across all datasets. We could see from the table that our model outperforms other KT methods including non-individualized methods and individualized methods on all datasets. This result suggests that students and the questions are different from each other and these differences should not be ignored when predict students' future performance. Particularly, on the ASSISTment datasets, our model achieve an AUC of 0.8337, 0.8724 and 0.7576 respectively, which denotes a significant gain of 2.59% on average compared with the closest baseline. And on the Ednet dataset, our model could improves the AUC by 1.24% over the closest baseline, although it dose not have students' current learning ability feature.

---

[1] https://sites.google.com/site/assistmentsdata/home.

[2] https://github.com/riiid/ednet.

[3] https://pslcdatashop.web.cmu.edu/DatasetInfo?datasetId=1198.

Table 2. results of comparison on students' performance

	DKT	DKT+	DKVMN	SAKT	DKT-DSC	CKT	**IAQKT**
ASSIST09	0.7356	0.7383	0.7394	0.7156	0.8104	0.8223	**0.8337**
ASSIST12	0.7013	0.7120	0.6752	0.7034	0.8310	0.8015	**0.8724**
ASSIST15	0.7310	0.7313	0.7012	0.7212	0.7053	0.7326	**0.7576**
Ednet	0.6616	0.6732	0.6711	0.6780	0.7062	0.7042	**0.7186**
Junyi	0.7421	0.7404	0.7014	0.7043	0.7506	0.8466	**0.8627**

5.2　Ablation Study

To validate the effectiveness of our proposed ability estimation module, we introduce the proposed ability estimation module to several non-individualized methods. Therefore, we re-implement several ability-supplement models based on their original models: DKT-AE, DKT+-AE, DKVMN-AE, SAKT-AE, which take the output of ability estimation module as supplementary feature of original models' input to predict students' future performance.

Table 3. The performance of introducing ability estimation module to non-individualized methods

	DKT	DKT-AE	DKT+	DKT+-AE	DKVMN	DKVMN-AE	SAKT	SAKT-AE
ASSIST09	0.7356	**0.7902**	0.7383	**0.8273**	0.7394	**0.7903**	0.7156	**0.8260**
ASSIST12	0.7013	**0.7758**	0.7120	**0.7804**	0.7225	**0.7659**	0.7034	**0.8066**
ASSIST15	0.7310	**0.7495**	0.7313	**0.7488**	0.7012	**0.7061**	0.7212	**0.7406**
Ednet	0.6616	**0.7041**	0.6732	**0.7082**	0.6711	**0.7012**	0.6780	**0.7050**
Junyi	0.7421	**0.7624**	0.7404	**0.7768**	0.7014	**0.7558**	0.7043	**0.7936**

Table 3 shows the results of introducing ability estimation module to non-individualized methods. We can observe that all ability-supplement models outperform their original non-individualized models on all datasets. In general, these results suggest that our ability estimation module is effective at extracting the students' learning ability according to their learning history and could improve the results of knowledge tracing.

To further investigate the impact of learning ability on knowledge state. We reimplement a model named IAQKT-A which removed the learning ability estimated by learning ability estimation module and simply takes students' learning interactions as knowledge state estimation module's input to estimation student knowledge state. From Table 4 we could observe that the model's performance decreases after removing students' learning ability feature when estimate students' knowledge state. It means that the learning ability should not be neglected when modeling students' learning process.

To further explore whether our proposed ability estimation module could extract the students' dynamic learning ability according to their learning history,

Table 4. The result of removing learning ability when estimate students' knowledge state

	ASSIST09	ASSIST12	ASSIST15	Ednet	Junyi
IAQKT	0.8337	0.8724	0.7576	0.7186	0.8627
IAQKT-A	0.8032	0.7965	0.7388	0.7073	0.8102

we randomly select 400 students' 20 consecutive answer sequences on dataset ASSISTment2009 to extract their learning ability through ability estimation module. We select students' estimated ability every 5 time steps and then we utilize t-SNE [13] to project the multi-dimensional ability vectors to the 2-D points. Figure 2(a,b,c,d) shows the clusters of students' 4 consecutive time intervals' learning ability and the students with similar learning ability are labeled with same color. From these 4 pictures we can observe that the students' abilities are different from each other, and students' learning ability change dynamically during the learning process since the number of students of a cluster and the number of different clusters change over time. Specifically, as Fig. 2(e,f) show, we select two students'(student A, student B) 20 consecutive answer sequences to investigate their learning ability difference. We can observe that in the first time interval these two students' abilities are similar since they have similar answer sequence and they are grouped in the same cluster. However, in the second interval student A has mastered knowledge concept 's34' and try to learn knowledge concept 's52', while student B still struggle for knowledge concept 's34'. Therefore, in the Fig. 2(b), the student A is far from student B after clustering. In the third interval, student B finally mastered knowledge concept 's34' and try concept 's52', while student A has mastered 's52' and try to concept 's68'. And in the Fig. 2(c) student A and student B are classified into different cluster. In the Fig. 2(d), we can observe that student A is close to student B since in the last interval, student B mastered concept 's52' fast and attempts to learn concept 's68', while student A still tries to master concept 's68'. In summary, the proposed ability estimation module is able to capture students' dynamic learning ability.

5.3   Question Embedding Analysis

Similarly, we select 10 knowledge concepts and compute the corresponding questions' embedding via learned deviation coefficient and knowledge concept embeddings. Then we utilize t-SNE [13] to project the multi-dimensional embedding vectors to the 2-D points and the questions labeled in the same color are related to same concept. As Fig. 3 shows, we can observe that question embeddings are well structured. The questions cover the same concept are close to each other, and questions that cover different concepts are well separated. Specifically, we can see that deviation coefficients control how far these questions deviate from the concepts they covered, the greater the absolute value of the coefficients, the farther away from the center of the cluster.

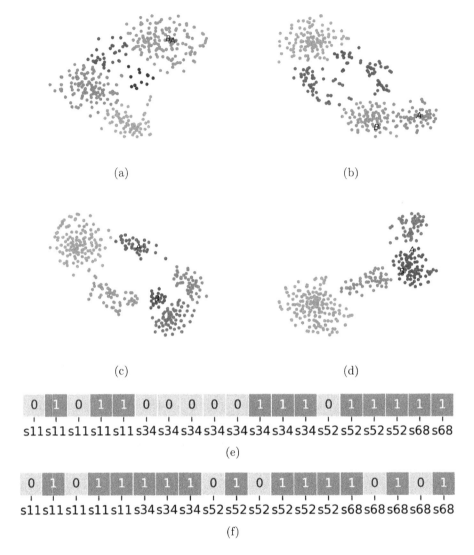

Fig. 2. The clusters of students' ability of four consecutive intervals on dataset ASSIST-ment2009, (a),(b),(c),(d) are four clusters, (e),(f) are two students'(student A and student B) 20 consecutive answer sequence.

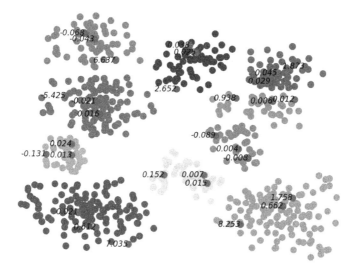

Fig. 3. Visualization of selected questions' embedding

6   Conclusion

In this paper, we proposed a novel method called IAQKT to model individualization of students and questions in KT task. Specifically, based on temporal convolutional network, we propose a learning ability estimation module to model students' learning ability according to their learning history. In addition, instead of simply taking students' learning interaction to model student knowledge state, we take students' learning ability as supplementary feature which will impact students' learning efficiency to estimate students' knowledge state more accurately. Finally, to individualize questions' difficulty, we design a novel method to obtain every question's representation instead of embedding every question directly which may lead overparameterization problem.

Acknowledgements. This research was funded in part by the National Natural Science Foundation of China (No. 62177032), Public Course Reform Project of Shaanxi Normal University (No. 21GGK-JG02) and the Fundamental Research Funds for the Central Universities (No. GK202205020).

References

1. Bai, S., Kolter, J.Z., Koltun, V.: An empirical evaluation of generic convolutional and recurrent networks for sequence modeling. arXiv preprint arXiv:1803.01271 (2018)
2. Baum, L.E., Petrie, T.: Statistical inference for probabilistic functions of finite state markov chains. Ann. Math. Stat. **37**, 1554–1563 (1966)

3. Cen, H., Koedinger, K., Junker, B.: Lncs 4053 - learning factors analysis - a general method for cognitive model evaluation and improvement (2006). http://www.carnegielearning.com

4. Choi, Y., et al.: EdNet: a large-scale hierarchical dataset in education. In: Bittencourt, I.I., Cukurova, M., Muldner, K., Luckin, R., Millán, E. (eds.) AIED 2020. LNCS (LNAI), vol. 12164, pp. 69–73. Springer, Cham (2020). https://doi.org/10.1007/978-3-030-52240-7_13

5. Cingi, C.C.: Computer aided education. Proc. - Social Behav. Sci. **103**, 220–229 (11 2013). https://doi.org/10.1016/j.sbspro.2013.10.329, https://linkinghub.elsevier.com/retrieve/pii/S1877042813037749

6. Corbett, A.T., Anderson, J.R.: Knowledge tracing: Modeling the acquisition of procedural knowledge. User Modeling User-Adapted Interact. **4**, 253–278 (12 1994). https://doi.org/10.1007/BF01099821

7. Freischlad, S.: Design of exercises and test items for internetworking based on a framework of exercise classes. In: Kendall, M., Samways, B. (eds.) Learning to Live in the Knowledge Society. ITIFIP, vol. 281, pp. 261–268. Springer, Boston, MA (2008). https://doi.org/10.1007/978-0-387-09729-9_40

8. Hochreiter, S., Schmidhuber, J.: Long short-term memory. Neural Comput. **9**, 1735–1780 (1997)

9. Jr, P.I.P., Cen, H., Koedinger, K.R.: Performance factors analysis-a new alternative to knowledge tracing. Online Submission (2009)

10. Lea, C., Flynn, M.D., Vidal, R., Reiter, A., Hager, G.D.: Temporal convolutional networks for action segmentation and detection, pp. 156–165 (2017)

11. Liu, Q., et al.: Ekt: Exercise-aware knowledge tracing for student performance prediction. IEEE Trans. Knowl. Data Eng. **33**, 100–115 (2019)

12. Lopes, A., Roodt, G., Mauer, R.: The predictive validity of the apil-b in a financial institution. SA J. Ind. Psychol. **27**, 61–69 (2001)

13. Maaten, L.V.D., Hinton, G.: Visualizing data using t-sne (2008)

14. Minn, S., Yu, Y., Desmarais, M.C., Zhu, F., Vie, J.J.: Deep knowledge tracing and dynamic student classification for knowledge tracing. IEEE (2018), https://ieeexplore.ieee.org/document/8594965/

15. Newell, A., Rosenbloom, P.S.: Mechanisms of skill acquisition and the law of practice. cognitive skills and their acquisition, jr anderson, editor (1981)

16. Pandey, S., Karypis, G.: A self-attentive model for knowledge tracing. arXiv preprint arXiv:1907.06837 (2019)

17. Pardos, Z.A., Heffernan, N.T.: Modeling individualization in a Bayesian networks implementation of knowledge tracing. In: De Bra, P., Kobsa, A., Chin, D. (eds.) UMAP 2010. LNCS, vol. 6075, pp. 255–266. Springer, Heidelberg (2010). https://doi.org/10.1007/978-3-642-13470-8_24

18. Pardos, Z.A., Heffernan, N.T.: KT-IDEM: introducing item difficulty to the knowledge tracing model. In: Konstan, J.A., Conejo, R., Marzo, J.L., Oliver, N. (eds.) UMAP 2011. LNCS, vol. 6787, pp. 243–254. Springer, Heidelberg (2011). https://doi.org/10.1007/978-3-642-22362-4_21

19. Piech, C., et al.: Deep knowledge tracing. In: Advances in Neural Information Processing Systems, vol. 28 (2015)

20. Rasch, G.: Probabilistic models for some intelligence and attainment tests. ERIC (1993)

21. Shen, S., et al.: Convolutional knowledge tracing: Modeling individualization in student learning process, pp. 1857–1860. Association for Computing Machinery, Inc (7 2020). https://doi.org/10.1145/3397271.3401288

22. Sonkar, S., Waters, A.E., Lan, A.S., Grimaldi, P.J., Baraniuk, R.G.: qdkt: Question-centric deep knowledge tracing. arXiv preprint arXiv:2005.12442 (2020)
23. Vie, J.J., Kashima, H.: Factorization machines for knowledge tracing. Knowl. Tracing Mach. **33**, 750–757 (2019)
24. Wang, T., Ma, F., Gao, J.: Deep hierarchical knowledge tracing (2019)
25. Williams, R.J., Zipser, D.: A learning algorithm for continually running fully recurrent neural networks. Neural Comput. **1**, 270–280 (6 1989). https://doi.org/10.1162/NECO.1989.1.2.270
26. Wilson, K.H., Karklin, Y., Han, B., Ekanadham, C.: Back to the basics: Bayesian extensions of irt outperform neural networks for proficiency estimation. arXiv preprint arXiv:1604.02336 (2016)
27. Yeung, C.K., Yeung, D.Y.: Addressing two problems in deep knowledge tracing via prediction-consistent regularization, pp. 1–10 (2018)
28. Zhang, J., Shi, X., King, I., Yeung, D.Y.: Dynamic key-value memory networks for knowledge tracing, pp. 765–774 (2017)

An NI-PSO-LightGBM Model Based on Adversarial Validation: Mortality Prediction in ICU Diabetic Patients

Xiaodong Liang[✉] and Minyi Ke

Hubei University of Technology, Wuhan, China
1492113422@hbut.edu.cn

Abstract. The number of diabetic patients and mortality rates are increasing year by year, imposing a heavy burden on health economies and families. ICU mortality prediction is crucial for patient care and allocating hospital resources. In the paper, a NI-PSO-LightGBM diabetic inpatient mortality prediction model based on adversarial validation is developed. The model was trained and tested using MIT's GOSSIS dataset provided from MIT, which gives various factors involved in hospitalization of diabetic patients. Based on these factors, patients are predicted to survive or not, and the dataset has 91,713 samples with 84 features. Adversarial validation was used to partition the dataset to ensure an even distribution of the training and test set samples and to avoid the model being much less effective on the test set than on the validation set. Feature extraction was performed on the samples using Null Importance to find the optimal subset of features containing the most information. The particle swarm optimization algorithm(PSO) was introduced to adjust the hyperparameters of the LightGBM model to obtain the final NI-PSO-LightGBM model and compare it with the Bayes-optimized LightGBM model (Bayes-LightGBM). The experimental results show that for the Bayes-LightGBM model, the average AUC = 88.66% for 5-fold cross-validation on the validation set, AUC = 88.88% and ACC = 92.84% on the test set. For the NI-PSO-LightGBM model, the validation set Average AUC = 89.52% for 5-fold cross-validation, AUC = 89.53% and ACC = 93.09% on the test set. The difference between the AUC values of the two models in the validation and test sets is extremely small, indicating that the adversarial validation prevents overfitting, and the NI-PSO-LightGBM proposed in the paper performs better than Bayes-LightGBM in both validation and test sets in terms of AUC and ACC, indicating that the NI-PSO-LightGBM model has better predictive ability.

Keywords: LightGBM · PSO · null importance · adversarial validation · death prediction

1 Introduction

According to the IDF (International Diabetes Federation) Global Diabetes Map 2021 [1], the number of adults with diabetes will reach 537 million, accounting for 10% of the world's adults. In 2021, approximately 6.7 million adults aged 20–79 will die from

© The Author(s), under exclusive license to Springer Nature Singapore Pte Ltd. 2023
W. Hong and Y. Weng (Eds.): ICCSE 2022, CCIS 1811, pp. 472–483, 2023.
https://doi.org/10.1007/978-981-99-2443-1_41

diabetes or its complications, and diabetes will account for 9% of global health care expenditures, or nearly $1 trillion. Quality of life, and is one of the most important resources for hospitals [2]. The estimated mortality of ICU patients plays a significant role in determining how hospitals should spend crucial resources [3]. With the rise of machine learning, more and more scholars are combining machine learning and medical prediction. Liu et al. proposed a cost-sensitive principal component (CSPCA) strategy for feature extraction, with the best performing model being SVM (AUC = 0.77) [4]. With the help of five models (elastic network penalized logistic regression, random forest, stochastic gradient boosting, neural network, and support vector machine), Kutyrev et al. successfully predicted mortality in patients with spinal epidural abscesses within 90 days [5]. In order to predict mortality, Naghmeh Khajehali et al. used KNN, decision trees, random forests, logistic regression, neural networks, and integrated learning [6]. The AdaBoost model produced the best results.

In the above context, this paper trains and tests the model using MIT's GOSSIS dataset, which is structured data [7] and contains a large number of missing values, and is well suited to solve the problem with tree models, because tree models can handle missing values automatically, which is a better performance than the manual way of filling in missing values. 2017, Ke et al. proposed the LightGBM algorithm (Light gradient boosting machine) [8]. The performance, effectiveness, and running speed of LightGBM have been demonstrated experimentally [9–12] to be superior to those of GBDT, XGBoost, and conventional machine learning algorithms. The value of the hyperparameters has a direct impact on the model's performance and generalizability. There are four common tuning methods: manual tuning, Grid Search, Random Search, and Bayesian Optimization, with the latter being the most effective [13]. Excellent global search algorithm [14] with promising parametric optimization [15–18] applications is the Particle Swarm Optimization (PSO) algorithm, which James Kennedy and Russell Eberhar proposed. Adversarial validation [19] can be used to verify whether the distributions of the test and training sets are consistent. If the distribution is inconsistent, the most similar samples from the training set and the test set are selected as the validation set, which can effectively avoid the model performing well on the validation set but poorly on the test set. Null Importance is a feature extraction method proposed by Kaggle GrandMaster Olivier [20], which uses XGboost/ LightGBM to train the model to get the importance of the features to judge the stability and goodness of the features.

The main contributions of this paper are as follows:

a. Use adversarial validation to partition the dataset and effectively prevent model overfitting.
b. Get the optimal feature subset by Null Importance, the number of features becomes about 65.47% of the original number of features.
c. Under the same conditions, the proposed NI-PSO-LightGBM model is superior to the Bayes-LightGBM model in terms of performance.

2 Adversarial Validation

Adversarial validation can be used to verify whether the distributions of the test and training sets are consistent. The details of some of the features used in our work are shown in Table 1.

Table 1. Features table

Features	Feature Description
patient_id	Unique identifier associated with a patient
age	The age of the patient on unit admission
bmi	The person's body mass index
d1_resprate_min	The patient's lowest respiratory rate
d1_resprate_max	The patient's highest respiratory rate
h1_heartrate_min	The patient's lowest heart rate during the first hour of their unit stay
apache_4a_icu_death_prob	The patient's in-ICU mortality is predicted probabilistically by APACHE IVa using the APACHE III score
d1_spo2_min	The patient's lowest peripheral oxygen saturation
d1_spo2_max	The patient's highest peripheral oxygen saturation
hospital_death	Whether the patient died during this hospitalization

In this dataset, there are various factors given, which are involved when a patient is hospitalized. Due to the large number of features only some of them are shown here.

2.1 The Idea of Adversarial Validation

First, train a binary classifier to determine whether it can correctly identify whether the samples are from the training set or the test set. If it can, it indicates that there is a significant difference between the training set and the test set sample distribution; otherwise, it indicates a minor difference.

2.2 Steps to Adversarial Validation

1. Set the label of the training set to 0 and the label of the test set to 1, and merge the training and test sets into a new data set.
2. Break up the new data set and re-partition it.
3. Build a binary classifier to train the model, in our work XGboost is used.
4. Use the trained model to predict the test set and get the AUC.
5. Check if the AUC value is close to 0.5.

a. If the AUC is close to 0.5, it means that the model cannot distinguish between the training and test sets, which means that the training and test sets are evenly distributed.
b. Only when AUC value exceeds 0.5, the samples that are most similar to the test set are chosen as the validation set because the model can distinguish between the training set and the test set, indicating that they are not equally distributed.

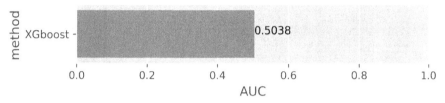

Fig. 1. AUC value of XGboost

As shown in Fig. 1, according to the steps of adversarial validation, the final AUC value of XGboost = 0.5038, which is very close to 0.5, indicating that the divided training set and test set samples are evenly distributed.

3 NI-PSO-LIGHTGBM Model

3.1 Null Importance

Really stable and important features will have good importance under the original labels, but once the labels are disrupted, the importance of these important features will become worse. Conversely, if certain features have ordinary importance under the original labels, but also increase in importance after the labels are disrupted, these features are obviously not good features.

The null importance steps are as follows:

1. The features and the original labels are sent to the LightGBM model for training, which gives the importance of each feature.
2. Break up the labels and send them to the model for training to get the importance of each feature, repeat n times, and take the average of the n times feature importance.
3. Compare the importance of each feature obtained under the original label in step 1 with the importance of each feature obtained by disrupting the labels n times in step 2.

The feature importance here refers to the "split" and "gain" of the LightGBM model. "split"- the frequency with which a feature is used to divide the data between all trees, "gain"-when applied to trees, the feature's average gain. After 80 times, split and gain scores were obtained. In this paper, split scores > 0 and gain scores > 0 were used as the criteria for selecting features, and finally 55 features were obtained from 84 features (Fig. 2).

Features' split and gain scores

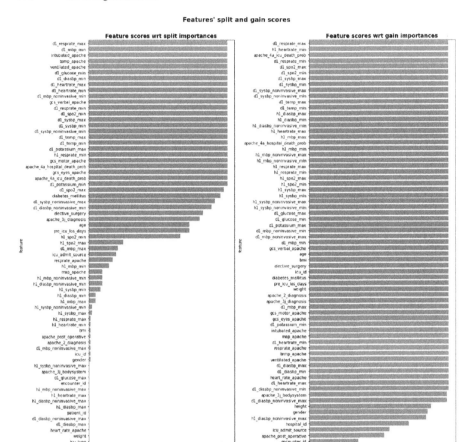

Fig. 2. Each feature split and gain score

3.2 PSO

The performance and generalizability of the LightGBM classification model are significantly influenced by the hyperparameters. Nowadays, among the four mainstream tuning methods (manual tuning, grid search, random search, and Bayesian optimization), Bayesian optimization has the best performance. The particle swarm optimization algorithm is an optimization algorithm that supports global stochastic parallel search with simple parameters, fast convergence, simple operation, and strong merit-seeking ability. Therefore, in this paper, the particle swarm algorithm is used to find the optimal hyperparameters to improve the performance and generalization ability of the model for predicting the risk of death of diabetic inpatients. The optimal hyperparameters of the LightGBM model are found in the 9-dimensional parameter space depicted in Table 2 using the particle swarm optimization algorithm and Bayesian optimization, respectively. The remaining hyperparameters are fixed to make it easier to compare the two optimization algorithms.

Table 2. LightGBM parameters to be optimized

Params	Params Description	Params Range
num_leaves	quantity of leaf nodes	[31, 500]
min_data_in_leaf	Minimum samples per leaf node	[20, 200]
bagging_fraction	Proportion of samples used in each iteration	[0.1, 0.9]
feature_fraction	What percentage of features are selected to build the tree during each iteration	[0.1, 0.9]
learning_rate	The smaller the value, the slower the training	[0.01, 0.3]
min_child_weight	Minimum value of the leaf node sample weights added together	[0.00001, 0.01]
reg_alpha	L1 regularization term on weights	[0, 1]
reg_lambda	L2 regularization term on weights	[0, 1]
max_depth	Maximum depth of the tree	[−1, 50]

The basic principle of the particle optimization algorithm is as follows.

There are N particles in a particle swarm in a D-dimensional target search space, with the ith particle represented by a D-dimensional vector:

$$X_i = (x_{i1}, x_{i2}, \cdots x_{iD}), i = 1, 2, \cdots, N \qquad (1)$$

The i-th particle's velocity is also a D-dimensional vector:

$$V_i = (v_{i1}, v_{i2}, \cdots v_{iD}), i = 1, 2, \cdots, N \qquad (2)$$

When the i-th particle of the t-th generation of particles iterates to the $t + 1$ generation, the velocity and displacement update formulas are as follows:

$$x_{ij}(t + 1) = x_{ij}(t) + v_{ij}(t + 1) \qquad (3)$$

$$v_{ij}(t + 1) = wv_{ij}(t) + c_1 r_1 \Big[pbest_{ij}(t) - x_{ij}(t) \Big] + c_2 r_2 \Big[gbest_j(t) - x_{ij}(t) \Big] \qquad (4)$$

t is the number of population iterations, $v_{ij}(t + 1)$ is the velocity of the ith particle in the jth dimension of generation $t + 1$, w is the inertia weight, $v_{ij}(t)$ is the velocity of the ith particle in the jth dimension of generation t, c_1 and c_2 are learning factors, r_1 and r_2 are random numbers between (0,1), $pbest_{ij}(t)$ is the single-particle historical optimum, $gbest_j(t)$ represents the population historical optimum, and $x_{ij}(t)$ is the position of the particle.

The number of particles N = 30, the number of iterations is set to 15, the fitness value is set to the AUC value obtained from the LightGBM model, and the obtained fitness iteration curve is shown in Fig. 3, and it is found that the optimal AUC value is obtained at the 8th iteration, and the position vector where the particles are located is the optimal hyperparameter of the LightGBM model at this time.

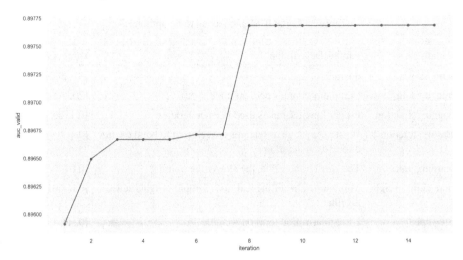

Fig. 3. Fitness value iteration curve

3.3 LightGBM

The Microsoft DMTK team's Gradient Boosting Decision Tree (GBDT) was the foundation for the open source algorithm known as LightGBM. Exclusive feature bundling (EFB) and gradient-based one-side sample (GOSS) are used instead of the conventional gradient boosting tree, which increases the model's speed and precision. It has been used to solve classification and regression issues thanks to its benefits of quick training speed, small memory footprint, high accuracy, support for parallelism, and capacity for large-scale data processing.

3.4 NI-PSO-LightGBM Prediction Process

The prediction flow of the NI-PSO-LightGBM model is shown in Fig. 4. First, the MIT GOSSIS dataset is a complete dataset and is not divided into a training set and a test set. Considering that the sample distributions of the test and training sets need to be consistent, adversarial validation is used to avoid the model running well on the training and validation sets, but not on the test set. Second, the dataset divided by adversarial validation was feature filtered using null importance to obtain the optimal subset of features to re-form the new training and test sets, which successfully filtered the original 84 features to 55, reducing the number of original features to about 65%. The LightGBM model was trained using the new training set. In the end, a particle swarm optimization algorithm was employed to identify the model's ideal hyperparameters.

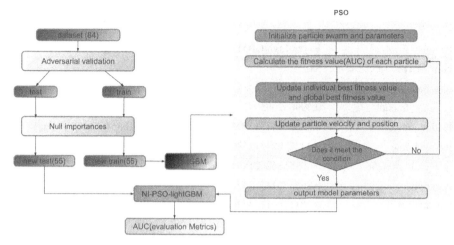

Fig. 4. NI-PSO-LightGBM model prediction process

The flow of the PSO algorithm is as follows:

1. Initialize particle swarm and parameterst.
2. Calculate each particle fitness value.
3. Update the historical best fitness value of the particle individual and the historical best fitness value of the group.
4. Update particle position and velocity.
5. Determine whether the termination condition is met, termination condition is the number of iterations.
6. If the conditions are not met, continue to execute from step 2.
7. If the condition are met, output the optimal hyperparameters of the model.

The model hyperparameters of NI-PSO-LightGBM are set to the optimal hyperparameters obtained by PSO, a 5-fold cross-validation is carried out on the training set, the prediction is carried out on the test set, and the AUC value is used as the evaluation metric. The forecasting process of the model is briefly described above.

3.5 Model Comparison

The optimal hyperparameters of the Bayes-LightGBM after Bayesian optimization and the NI-PSO-LightGBM after particle swarm optimization algorithm are shown in Table 3 and Table 4, respectively, in the 9-dimensional parameter space displayed in Table 2. Table 4 also displays the fixed parameters for both models.

Table 3. LightGBM adjustment parameters list

Params	Bayes-LightGBM	NI-PSO-LightGBM
num_leaves	58	60
min_data_in_leaf	48	58
bagging_fraction	0.39963209507789	0.358519604748816
feature_fraction	0.8605714451279329	0.27410864656673
learning_rate	0.22227824312530747	0.019685575152797
min_child_weight	0.001568626218019941	0.00112607614190026
reg_alpha	0.8661761457749352	0.221649602472921
reg_lambda	0.6011150117432088	0.701825304976611
max_depth	29	26

Table 4. LightGBM fixed parameter list

Params	Params Description	Bayes-LightGBM NI-PSO-LightGBM
metric	Evaluation Metrics	'auc'
objective	Set whether classification or regression	'binary'
boosting_type	Base learner model algorithm	'gbdt'
num_iterations	Controls the number of boosting rounds	20000
early_stopping_round	No improvement in accuracy on the validation set, stop training	200
save_binary	Speed up training next time	True

Due to the uneven proportion of positive and negative samples, the accuracy value (ACC) is not a good judge of the model, and many scholars use Area under the ROC curve value (AUC) as the evaluation metric in this case, which is because AUC is not sensitive to whether the sample categories are balanced or not, and the nearer to 1 the AUC value, the greater the classification impact of the model. In this paper, the AUC value is used as the main evaluation metric of the model.

Bayes-LightGBM and NI-PSO-LightGBM perform 5-fold cross-validation to obtain the ROC curve and AUC value of each fold as shown in Fig. 5 and Fig. 6.

Experiments show that NI-PSO-LightGBM has higher AUC values than Bayes-LightGBM in each fold of training, and the AUC value breaks through to 90.05% in the 3rd fold.

The performance of Bayes-LightGBM and NI-PSO-LightGBM on the test set is shown in Table 5. NI-PSO-LightGBM outperforms Bayes-LightGBM in both AUC values and ACC values, indicating that the NI-PSO-LightGBM proposed in this paper has better prediction.

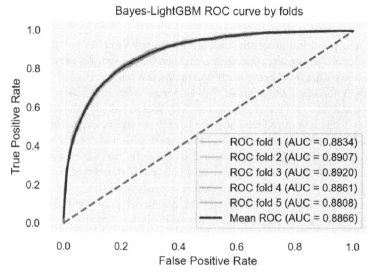

Fig. 5. Bayes-LightGBM ROC curve by folds

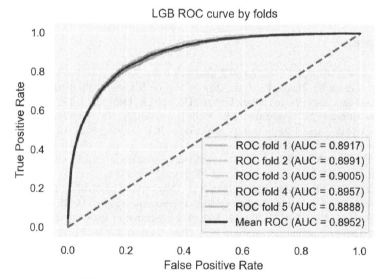

Fig. 6. NI-PSO-LightGBM ROC curve by folds

Table 5. Model performance on the test set

Model	AUC	ACC
Bayes-LightGBM	88.88%	92.84%
NI-PSO-LightGBM	89.53%	93.09%

4 Conclusion

In Sect. 2, this paper introduces the idea and implementation steps of adversarial validation, and successfully ensures that the training and test set samples are evenly distributed to prevent the model from being overfitted on the test set.

In Sect. 3, the ideas and steps of Null Importance filtering features are introduced, and the optimal subset of features is successfully found, reducing the number of features by about 34.52%. It is introduced how the particle swarm optimization algorithm finds the optimal hyperparameters of the NI-PSO-LightGBM model, and compared with the Bayesian optimization algorithm obtained in the same parameter search space of the Bayes -LightGBM model is compared, and finally it is found that NI-PSO-LightGBM achieves better AUC and ACC values than Bayes-LightGBM.

This indicates that NI-PSO-LightGBM has better prediction and generalization ability than Bayes-LightGBM and can be used in clinical practice.

Acknowledgment. I would like to express my sincere gratitude to my teacher, Minyi Ke, for his guiding comments and helpful suggestions on my thesis. Sincere thanks to MITISHA AGARWAL for providing the processed dataset.

References

1. International Diabetes Federation. IDF Diabetes Atlas, 10th edn, Brussels, Belgium (2021)
2. Xu, J., Zhang, Y., Zhang, P., et al.: Data mining on ICU mortality prediction using early temporal data: a survey. Int. J. Inf. Technol. Decis. Mak. **16**(01), 117–159 (2017)
3. Karimi Moridani, M., Setarehdan, S.K., Motie Nasrabadi, A., et al.: Non-linear feature extraction from HRV signal for mortality prediction of ICU cardiovascular patient. J. Med. Eng. Technol. **40**(3), 87–98 (2016)
4. Liu, J., Chen, X.X., Fang, L., et al.: Mortality prediction based on imbalanced high-dimensional ICU big data. Comput. Ind. **98**, 218–225 (2018)
5. Karhade, A.V., Shah, A.A., Bono, C.M., et al.: Development of machine learning algorithms for prediction of mortality in spinal epidural abscess. Spine J. **19**(12), 1950–1959 (2019)
6. Khajehali, N., Khajehali, Z., Tarokh, M.J.: The prediction of mortality influential variables in an intensive care unit: a case study. Pers. Ubiq. Comput. **27**, 1–17 (2021)
7. Eberendu, A.C.: Unstructured data: an overview of the data of big data. Int. J. Comput. Trends Technol. **38**(1), 46–50 (2016)
8. Ke, G., Meng, Q., Finley, T., et al.: Lightgbm: a highly efficient gradient boosting decision tree. Adv. Neural Inf. Process. Syst. **30**, 1–9 (2017)
9. Al, D.E.: Comparison between XGBoost, LightGBM and CatBoost using a home credit dataset. Int. J. Comput. Inf. Eng. **13**(1), 6–10 (2019)
10. Rufo, D.D., Debelee, T.G., Ibenthal, A., et al.: Diagnosis of diabetes mellitus using gradient boosting machine (LightGBM). Diagnostics **11**(9), 1714 (2021)
11. Wang, M., Yue, L., Yang, X., et al.: Fertility-lightgbm: a fertility-related protein prediction model by multi-information fusion and light gradient boosting machine. Biomed. Signal Process. Control **68**, 102630 (2021)
12. Sun, X., Liu, M., Sima, Z.: A novel cryptocurrency price trend forecasting model based on LightGBM. Financ. Res. Lett. **32**, 101084 (2020)
13. Hutter, F., Kotthoff, L., Vanschoren, J. (eds.): Springer, Cham (2019)

14. Kennedy, J., Eberhart, R.: Particle swarm optimization. In: Proceedings of ICNN 1995-International Conference on Neural Networks, vol. 4, pp. 1942–1948. IEEE (1995)
15. Liu, S., Liao, X., Shi, H.: A PSO-SVM for burst header packet flooding attacks detection in optical burst switching networks. In: Photonics, vol. 8, no. 12, p. 555. Multidisciplinary Digital Publishing Institute (2021)
16. Liang, Z., Di, X., Zhen Liu, X., Liu, X.Z., Zhi, Y.: Predicting students' academic performance based on improved PSO-Xgboost: a campus behavior perspective. In: Lai, Y., Wang, T., Jiang, M., Guangquan, X., Liang, W., Castiglione, A. (eds.) Algorithms and Architectures for Parallel Processing: 21st International Conference, ICA3PP 2021, Virtual Event, December 3–5, 2021, Proceedings, Part I, pp. 402–421. Springer International Publishing, Cham (2022). https://doi.org/10.1007/978-3-030-95384-3_26
17. Wu, S.: Simulation of classroom student behavior recognition based on PSO-kNN algorithm and emotional image processing. J. Intell. Fuzzy Syst. **40**(4), 7273–7283 (2021)
18. Ren, X., Liu, S., Yu, X., et al.: A method for state-of-charge estimation of lithium-ion batteries based on PSO-LSTM. Energy **234**, 121236 (2021)
19. Zygmunt, Z.: Adversarial validation, part one (2016). http://fastml.com/adversarial-validation-part-one/
20. Altmann, A., Toloşi, L., Sander, O., et al.: Permutation importance: a corrected feature importance measure. Bioinformatics **26**(10), 1340–1347 (2010)

IGFClust: Clustering Unbalanced and Complex Single-Cell Expression Data by Iteration and Integrating Gini Index and Fano Factor

Han Li[1] , Feng Zeng[1,2,3] , and Fan Yang[1,2,3]([⊠])

[1] Department of Automation, Xiamen University, Xiamen, China
`lihan20@stu.xmu.edu.cn`, `{zengfeng,yang}@xmu.edu.cn`
[2] National Institute for Data Science in Health and Medicine, Xiamen University, Xiamen, China
[3] Xiamen Key Laboratory of Big Data Intelligent Analysis and Decision, Xiamen, China

Abstract. With ScRNAseq, we are able to obtain genome-wide transcriptome data from single cells. However, it is very difficult to identify all cell subpopulations in single cell expression data, especially when these subpopulations are unbalanced and the number of subpopulations is unknown. In this paper, we propose a new clustering algorithm, IGFClust. We design an ensemble method to identify unbalanced subpopulations using Gini index and Fano factor. In addition, we design an iterative clustering framework to avoid the problem that only some subpopulations can be identified during the clustering process. We generated four sets of labeled simulation data and compared IGFClust with existing methods. Afterwards, we analyzed 576 glioblastoma primary tumor cells. We show that IGFClust performs accurately and robustly in identifying complex and unbalanced single-cell expression data.

Keywords: scRNA-seq · Clustering · Ensemble clustering · Unbalanced data

1 Introduction

ScRNAseq is able to provide researchers with genome-wide transcriptome data from single cells [2,3,10]. An important step in analyzing this data is dividing the raw data into cell subpopulations based on differences in gene expression, which is accomplished through unsupervised clustering. Proper clustering facilitates more efficient cell analysis and can even lead to the discovery of new cell types or functions, such as cancer cells, stem cells, and other rare but important cells [6,17]. However, like the complexity of organisms, the data obtained through scRNAseq is very complex [12,13], with two main aspects of complexity: 1) the number of subpopulations is unknown, and 2) the number of cells in different subpopulations can vary greatly. These challenges present significant obstacles to the design of clustering methods.

Several clustering algorithms have been proposed for scRNAseq [18,19]. These algorithms can be categorized based on the type of cells they are able to identify. The first category of algorithms can only detect common cells, such as Fano factor-based k-means, SC3 [14], and scAIDE [24]. Fano factor-based k-means identifies highly variable genes based on Fano factor [5] and then performs k-means clustering. SC3 integrates multiple clustering methods to detect common cells. ScAIDE generates a low-dimensional representation using autoencoder and then uses a random projection hashing based k-means algorithm for clustering. These methods do not consider rare cells in feature selection or in the selection of clustering algorithms, and rare cells are often overlooked in the clustering process. Therefore, these methods have limited ability to detect rare cells.

The second category of clustering algorithms is specifically designed to detect rare cells. Examples of such algorithms include GiniClust [11] and MCC [8]. GiniClust selects genes with high Gini index as features and performs clustering using DBSCAN [4]. MCC transforms the challenge of detecting rare cells into identifying highly expressed gene-cell subsets with constraints, which are then solved using a modified version of the CPGC algorithm. However, these methods have a limitation in that they focus on the detection of rare cells and may not be effective in identifying common cells.

The third categories of algorithms can detect both normal and rare cells, such as GiniClust2 [23], RaceID3 [9] etc. GiniClust2 identifies cells by integrating Fano factor-based k-means and GiniClust. It performs clustering using GiniClust and Fano factor-based k-means, respectively, and then assigns larger weights to rare cells in the result of GiniClust and larger weights to common cells in the result of Fano factor-based k-means. Finally GiniClust2 integrates these clustering results. RaceID3, on the other hand, first divides the data into large clusters by k-means, and then finds outliers among them, i.e. rare cells, by calculating the transcript count probability of each cell. These methods generally add detection methods for rare cells to traditional clustering algorithms to achieve the goal of detecting both common and rare clusters.

Regardless of how these methods are designed, they are assuming that the data are composed of rare cells and common cells. But such an assumption is too simple. Suppose there exists a data where the number of cells in each subpopulation is 1000, 500, 250, 100, 50, 10. It would be difficult to define which cells are common and which cells are rare. Therefore, it is difficult for the existing methods to detect all subpopulations in such data. However, it is worth noting that although we cannot determine all cell types, we know that the smallest subpopulation is rare and can detect it with the methods used to detect rare cells. Similarly, we can discover the largest subpopulation with the algorithm used to detect common cells. After that, we can iteratively perform the above steps to identify other subpopulations. In this way we can detect all subpopulations.

Here, we propose a new clustering algorithm, IGFClust, to address these challenges. First, we design an ensemble clustering method. Inspired by GiniClust2, we combine Fano factor-based k-means and GiniClust to achieve simultaneous detection of both common and rare cells. To adapt our proposed clustering algorithm to more complex data, we designed an iterative framework to re-cluster those subpopulations that we are not sure are accurate. We show that this iterative integrated clustering algorithm is able to accurately and robustly identify different subpopulations in complex data.

2   Preliminaries

First, we introduce the methods involved in the algorithm we designed.

2.1   Feature Selection

The dimensionality of single-cell gene expression data is high, therefore, appropriate feature selection is an important step [21]. There are two main feature selection metrics used in IGFClust, Fano factor and Gini index.

The Fano factor of a gene is defined as the ratio of the variance to the mean. It is used to measure the variation in the expression of a gene on different cells. Obviously, the greater the variation in expression on different cells, the greater the variance of that gene and the greater the Fano factor. However, the variance is calculated for the whole cells, which results in the variance of the gene marker for rare cells will not be large. Therefore the genes found by Fano factor do not help us to identify rare cells.

The Gini index is originally used in finance to measure the imbalance of people's income, and GiniClust finds that this index could be used to find gene markers for rare cells. The Gini index is defined as:

$$Gini_i = \sum_j (2j - n - 1)v_{ij}/(n^2 mean(v_i))$$ (1)

where v_i is the expression value of gene i, v_{ij} is the expression value of gene i on j-th cells, $mean(v_i)$ is the mean value of the vector v_i which has been sorted in ascending sort order, and n is the number of cells. In other words, the more a gene is expressed in only a few cells, the higher the Gini index of that gene. This is exactly in line with the characteristics of rare cell gene markers.

2.2   Clustering Algorithm

Two traditional clustering algorithms, kmeans and DBSCAN, are used in IGF-Clust.

Kmeans assumes that the data are approximately normally distributed, and its objective function is:

$$\min \sum_i \sum_j u_{ij}(x_i - c_j)^2$$ (2)

where x_i is i-th cell and c_j is the center of j-th cluster. $u_{ij} = 1$ if x_i belongs to c_j, otherwise $u_{ij} = 0$. K-means can be divided into two steps. In the first step, the cluster centers c_j are updated. In the initial state, samples x_i are randomly selected as cluster centers. In the non-initial state, the average of all samples belonging to the cluster is used as that cluster center. In the second step, the distance of each sample to the centers of all clusters is calculated and it is assigned to the nearest cluster. These two steps are iterated continuously until the termination condition is reached. K-means is efficient, but sensitive to data distribution. It has difficulty in identifying rare clusters in unbalanced data.

DBSCAN is a well-known data clustering algorithm for density-based clustering. It defines a neighborhood range. A sample with a number of samples in its neighborhood that exceeds a threshold is called a core point. A core point and the samples within its neighborhood are grouped into a cluster. If another core point exists within the neighborhood of that core point, then this core point and the samples within its domain are also grouped into that cluster. Since DBSCAN focuses on local information, it is able to cluster imbalanced data. However, because DBSCAN needs to calculate the distance between each sample, the computational complexity is high.

3 Method

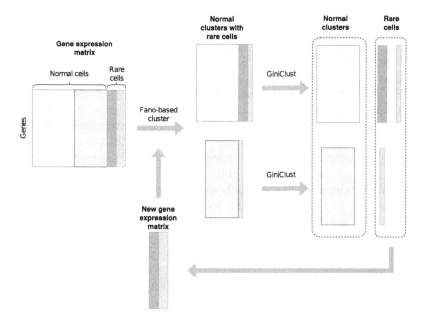

Fig. 1. Overview of IGFClust.

3.1   Framework

The framework of IGFClust is shown in Fig. 1 let us explain the overall idea of IGFClust. Consider a cell dataset $\{x_i\}_{i=1}^N$ with clustering labels $\{c_i\}_{i=1}^N$ for each cell. Instead of assigning clustering labels to all cells directly, IGFClust iteratively assigns labels to cells. Initially, each cell is labeled as $c_i = -1$, indicating that it has not been assigned any label. In each iteration, only the unlabeled cells participate in the clustering, and only normal cells are labeled in that iteration. This process continues until all cells have been assigned cluster labels. The specific method of label assignment can be divided into three steps: Fano factor-based k-means, GiniClust and reconstructing the dataset.

3.2   Fano Factor-Based K-means

First, we calculate the Fano factor for each gene. Based on the Fano factor, we selected the top 1000 genes for clustering. Then, we reduce dimensions of the data to 50 by PCA [1]. Finally, we use kmeans for clustering. The parameter k of k-means is unknown, and there are many methods to determine k [15]. We use the Gap Statistic to determine k [22]. This process is implemented using the clusGap function in R. The specific hyperparameters in this step follow GiniClust2.

3.3   GiniClust

After the first step, the data is divided into several clusters. These clusters are not the final result, because the rare cells in these clusters cannot be detected in the first step. The purpose of GiniClust is to detect these rare cells among the them, after which the non-rare clusters among them are the subpopulations we want. Assuming that the outcome of k-means clustering is represented as $\{C_j^t\}_{j=1}^k$, we will apply GiniClust to each cluster C_j^t during iteration t. Specifically, we first calculate the Gini index for each gene. Then the Gini index is normalized according to the steps of GiniClust, and genes whose normalized Gini index is significantly above zero are selected for clustering. Finally, the Jaccard distance matrix between each sample is calculated and DBSCAN is performed. The cluster with the largest number of cells obtained from GiniClust clustering in cluster C_j^t is selected, and new cluster labels are assigned to the cells in that cluster. Again, the specific parameters in this step follow GiniClust.

3.4   Reconstructing the Dataset

All rare clusters obtained in the second step are uncertain because these rare clusters may have been split into multiple parts in the first step. Therefore, in this step, we merge them back together to form a new dataset, and then repeat steps one and two until no new rare clusters appear in step two. What is important in the iterative process is that in order to accurately identify all subpopulations in the data, the features in the first and second steps need to be reselected based on the current data.

Algorithm 1. IGFClust

Input: Dataset $\{x_i\}_{i=1}^N$

  Initialize cluster labels $\{c_i = -1\}_{i=1}^N$, unlabeled dataset $X_u = \{x_i\}_{i=1}^N$

  while X_u is not empty **do**

    Obtain $\{C_j^t\}_{j=1}^k$ by performing Fano Factor-based K-means on X_u

    for $j = 1$ to k **do**

      Obtain clusters by perform GiniClust on C_j^t

      Assign new cluster labels to the cells in the cluster with the largest number of cells

    end for

    Update unlabeled dataset X_u

  end while

---

4 Result

In this section, we demonstrate that our proposed algorithm, IGFClust, is able to accurately detect both common and rare cells. We first test IGFClust on 4 simulation data with labels and compare it with existing algorithms. The purpose of this experiment is to demonstrate the accuracy and robustness of IGFClust in the task of identifying complex data. Afterwards, we apply IGFClust to a real dataset to evaluate its performance on real data.

4.1 Evaluation Metric

Since the number of clusters obtained by the algorithm is different from the actual number of clusters, here we use NMI [20] and Purity as evaluation metrics. NMI is defined as:

$$NMI = \frac{2I(X,Y)}{H(X) + H(Y)} \tag{3}$$

where $I(X,Y)$ is the mutual information between the clustering result and the true label, $H(X)$ is the information entropy of the clustering result and $H(Y)$ is the information entropy of the true label.

  Purity is defined as:

$$Purity = \sum_{j=1}^k \frac{m_j}{m} p_j \tag{4}$$

where m is the total number of samples, m_j is the number of samples in the jth cluster, k is the number of clusters, and p_j is the maximum proportion of each type of sample in the jth cluster.

  Since the data are unbalanced, to avoid that the evaluation metrics ignore the importance of identifying rare clusters, we assign a weight to each sample. A sample's weight is defined as the reciprocal of the number of samples in its class cluster. In this way, the correct identification of rare cells contributes equally to the evaluation metrics as the correct identification of common cells.

4.2   Simulation Data

We created four sets of simulation data using the same method as GiniClust, with highly imbalanced parameters shown in Table 1. The first simulation data contains a lower proportion of rare cells, while the last three simulations have more complex distributions. We evaluated the performance of IGFClust against RaceID3, SC3, GiniClust2, and scAIDE on these datasets, and the results are presented in Table 2.

Table 1. The cell numbers of each subpopulation in each simulation data.

Simulation data	Number of cells in each subpopulation
Simulation data 1	2000 1000 10 6 4 3
Simulation data 2	1000 1000 100 100 10 10
Simulation data 3	1500 1000 1000 100 100 10
Simulation data 4	1500 1000 500 250 100 50

Table 2. The result of simulation data experiment.

Dataset	Simulation data 1		Simulation data 2		Simulation data 3		Simulation data 4	
Metrics	NMI	Purity	NMI	Purity	NMI	Purity	NMI	Purity
GiniClust2	1	1	1	1	0.819	0.667	0.652	0.5
RaceID3	0.824	0.889	0.948	0.983	0.95	1	0.935	1
SC3	0.524	0.333	0.819	0.667	0.931	0.833	1	1
scAIDE	0.425	0.444	0.819	0.667	0.931	0.833	0.931	0.833
IGFClust	1	1	1	1	**0.969**	**0.983**	1	1

As we can see from the experimental results, no method can accurately identify all the clusters. Among these, GiniClust2 performs well on Simulation data 1 and Simulation data 2, while it performs the worst on Simulation data 4, with an NMI of only 0.652 and Purity of only 0.5, which indicates that GiniClust2 can effectively detect rare cells but performs poorly on data with complex distribution. This is most likely due to GiniClust2's overly simple assumptions on the data. In contrast to GiniClust2, SC3 and scAIDE perform well on Simulation data 4 but perform poorly on Simulation data 1. This is most likely due to the small percentage of rare cells in Simulation data 1. This indicates that SC3 and scAIDE have very limited ability to detect rare cells. RaceID3 performs better on all simulation data, but neither can accurately identify all clusters. Low NMI and high Purity indicate that the results of RaceID3 are over-clustered. IGF-Clust achieved 1 in both Purity and NMI on Simulation data 1, Simulation data 2 and Simulation data 4, and achieved the best results on Simulation data 3. The result shows IGFClust's good ability to identify unbalanced and complex data.

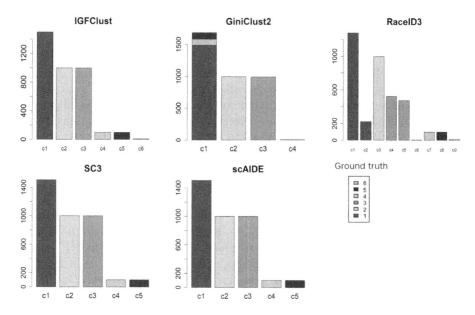

Fig. 2. The results of each clustering method on simulated data 3. The X-axis represents the cluster index and the Y-axis represents the cell number. Different colors in the same cluster represent the proportion of different cell types.

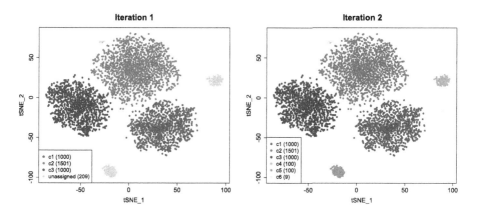

Fig. 3. The t-SNE plot of the clustering result of IGFClust on simulated data 3 for each iteration. IGFClust was iterated twice, with the left figure showing the results of the first iteration and the right figure showing the results of the second iteration.

To gain insights into how the algorithms recognize the data, we analyzed the results on Simulation data 3. Figure 2 displays the results of this experiment. As expected, GiniClust2 accurately identified rare and normal cells but misclassified cells in between. scAIDE and SC3 both misclassified rare cells and grouped them with the first cluster. RaceID3, while able to identify each class of cells, showed severe overclustering, dividing the data with only six subpopulations into nine clusters. IGFClust accurately identified all subpopulations. While IGFClust misclassified one cell from c6 to the c1 cluster in the final result, this misclassification does not affect researchers' analysis of cell subgroups. However, GiniClust2, SC3, and scAIDE can prevent researchers from discovering some cell subpopulations, while RaceID3's overclustering significantly increases the analysis cost for researchers.

We further investigated the clustering process of IGFClust. Figure 3 shows the result. We use visual graphs based on t-SNE to display the results of each iteration of IGFClust in assigning cell labels. It can be seen that, IGFClust identified three class clusters with the highest number of cells, while 209 cells were labeled as rare and remained unassigned in the first iteration. During the second iteration, these 209 cells were further clustered to obtain the remaining three clusters. This entire iterative process meets our expectations. The figure also reveals that the clustering error is caused by the omission of one rare cell in the first iteration, which is subject to further improvement in the future.

4.3 Real Data

Finally, we performed the experiment on glioblastoma primary tumor cells [16]. This scRNA-seq data includes 576 cells with 23233 genes. Our method divides it into a total of 8 subpopulations. There are two subpopulations with cell numbers above 100, namely c3 and c7. Their cell numbers are 136 and 248, respectively. There are six subpopulations with cell numbers below 100, namely c1, c2, c4, c5, c6 and c8. their cell numbers are 42, 7, 54, 35, 27, 27, respectively. The results of gene differential analysis of these clusters are shown in Fig. 4. The detailed gene marker for each cluster is shown in Table 3. It can be seen that the genes that are mainly expressed in each cluster are different. By relying on the information on PanglaoDB [7], we are able to gain an understanding of these cells. For example, the rare cluster c2 mainly expresses two genes, PLP1 and SLC5A11, indicating that it is likely to be Oligodendrocyte. In the original study, this subpopulations could only be detected by using prior knowledge. Of course, it is also detected in GiniClust, but GiniClust cannot detect other common clusters. The common cluster c3 expresses a series of fibroblast genes such as HHIPL1 and SEC61G. This experiment confirms the ability of IGFClust in detecting real data.

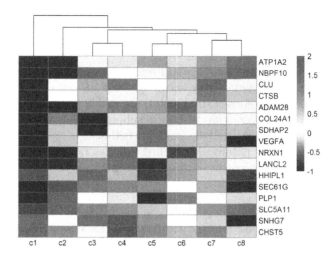

Fig. 4. A heatmap of differentially expressed genes for the clustering results of the glioblastoma primary tumor cells.

Table 3. The result of simulation data experiment.

Clusters	Gene markers
c1	CHST5, SNHG7, etc.
c2	PLP1, SLC5A11, SLC31A2, MAG, RNASE1, etc.
c3	HHIPL1, SEC61G, KIAA0895L, CHD5, SHF, etc.
c4	NRXN1, LANCL2, CD82, LHFPL3, DCX, etc.
c5	VEGFA, SDHAP2, NDRG1, ZNF395, C7orf68, etc.
c6	ADAM28, COL24A1, CLEC4A, RPL13AP17, etc.
c7	CLU, CTSB, ANXA2P2, ANXA2, MAP1B, etc.
c8	ATP1A2, NBPF10, FIGNL1, SEC14L1, TIMP4, etc

5   Discussion

ScRNA-seq provides us with high granularity data, allowing us to detect both common and rare cell types in complex tissues. Many clustering algorithms have been proposed, but it is still a challenge to robustly identify all cell subpopulations in scRNA-seq data with complex distribution. In this paper, we propose an iterative ensemble clustering algorithm, IGFClust. IGFClust identifies common cells by using Fano factor-based k-means, identifies rare cells by GiniClust, and then identifies cell subpopulations that cannot be identified by traditional methods. In simulated data experiments, IGFClust achieved the highest NMI and Purity, which means that compared with other algorithms, IGFClust has excellent ability to detect rare cells and complex data. After the simulation data experiment, we used IGFClust to detect glioblastoma primary tumor cells and divided them into 8 clusters. These clusters contain common and rare subpopulations, among which there are subpopulations that could only be detected based on a priori knowledge in the original study.

Of course, our proposed model is still relatively simple, and there are many places where we can achieve higher accuracy. First, in our idea, each iteration needs to find at least one correct subpopulations, and in IGFClust, this identified subpopulations are not very sure to be the subpopulations we want. Secondly, there is no method to accurately determine whether it is over-clustered or not. Finally, there exist many details in IGFClust that can be refined by using statistical methods. The improvement of these shortcomings is the focus of our future work.

Acknowledgements. This work is partially supported by the National Natural Science Foundation of China under Grant No. 62173282, the Natural Science Foundation of Guangdong Province under Grant No. 2021A1515011578, the Natural Science Foundation of Xiamen City under Grant No. 3502Z20227180 and the Shenzhen Fundamental Research Program under Grant No. JCYJ20190809161603551. The funders did not play any roles in the design of the study, in the collection, analysis, or interpretation of data, or in writing the manuscript.

References

1. Abdi, H., Williams, L.J.: Principal component analysis. Wiley Interdisc. Rev.: Comput. Stat. **2**(4), 433–459 (2010)
2. Aldridge, S., Teichmann, S.A.: Single cell transcriptomics comes of age. Nat. Commun. **11**(1), 4307 (2020)
3. Chen, G., Ning, B., Shi, T.: Single-cell rna-seq technologies and related computational data analysis. Front. Genet. **10**, 317 (2019)
4. Ester, M., Kriegel, H.P., Sander, J., Xu, X., et al.: A density-based algorithm for discovering clusters in large spatial databases with noise. In: kdd. vol. 96, pp. 226–231 (1996)
5. Fano, U.: Ionization yield of radiations. ii. the fluctuations of the number of ions. Phys. Rev. **72**(1), 26 (1947)
6. Feng, C., et al.: Dimension reduction and clustering models for single-cell rna sequencing data: a comparative study. Int. J. Mol. Sci. **21**(6), 2181 (2020)
7. Franzén, O., Gan, L.M., Björkegren, J.L.: Panglaodb: a web server for exploration of mouse and human single-cell rna sequencing data. Database 2019 (2019)
8. Gerniers, A., Bricard, O., Dupont, P.: Microcellclust: mining rare and highly specific subpopulations from single-cell expression data. Bioinformatics **37**(19), 3220–3227 (2021)
9. Grün, D. et al.: Single-cell messenger rna sequencing reveals rare intestinal cell types. Nature **525**(7568), 251–255 (2015)
10. Hedlund, E., Deng, Q.: Single-cell rna sequencing: technical advancements and biological applications. Mol. Aspects Med. **59**, 36–46 (2018)
11. Jiang, L., Chen, H., Pinello, L., Yuan, G.C.: Giniclust: detecting rare cell types from single-cell gene expression data with gini index. Genome Biol. **17**(1), 1–13 (2016)

12. Kharchenko, P.V.: The triumphs and limitations of computational methods for scrna-seq. Nat. Methods **18**(7), 723–732 (2021)
13. Kiselev, V.Y., Andrews, T.S., Hemberg, M.: Challenges in unsupervised clustering of single-cell rna-seq data. Nat. Rev. Genet. **20**(5), 273–282 (2019)
14. Kiselev, V.Y., et al.: Sc3: consensus clustering of single-cell rna-seq data. Nat. Methods **14**(5), 483–486 (2017)
15. Kodinariya, T.M., Makwana, P.R., et al.: Review on determining number of cluster in k-means clustering. Int. J. **1**(6), 90–95 (2013)
16. Patel, A.P., et al.: Single-cell rna-seq highlights intratumoral heterogeneity in primary glioblastoma. Science **344**(6190), 1396–1401 (2014)
17. Peng, L., et al.: Single-cell rna-seq clustering: datasets, models, and algorithms. RNA Biol. **17**(6), 765–783 (2020)
18. Petegrosso, R., Li, Z., Kuang, R.: Machine learning and statistical methods for clustering single-cell rna-sequencing data. Brief. Bioinform. **21**(4), 1209–1223 (2020)
19. Qi, R., Ma, A., Ma, Q., Zou, Q.: Clustering and classification methods for single-cell rna-sequencing data. Brief. Bioinform. **21**(4), 1196–1208 (2020)
20. Strehl, A., Ghosh, J.: Cluster ensembles–a knowledge reuse framework for combining multiple partitions. J. Mach. Learn. Res. **3**(Dec), 583–617 (2002)
21. Su, K., Yu, T., Wu, H.: Accurate feature selection improves single-cell rna-seq cell clustering. Briefings Bioinform. **22**(5), bbab034 (2021)
22. Tibshirani, R., Walther, G., Hastie, T.: Estimating the number of clusters in a data set via the gap statistic. J. Royal Stat. Soc: Series B (Statistical Methodology) **63**(2), 411–423 (2001)
23. Tsoucas, D., Yuan, G.C.: Giniclust2: a cluster-aware, weighted ensemble clustering method for cell-type detection. Genome Biol. **19**, 1–13 (2018)
24. Xie, K., Huang, Y., Zeng, F., Liu, Z., Chen, T.: scaide: clustering of large-scale single-cell rna-seq data reveals putative and rare cell types. NAR Genomics Bioinform. **2**(4), lqaa082 (2020)

A Bibliometric Review on Supplier Evaluation and Selection

Minhao Huang, Jia Huang(⊠), Mingshun Song, and Xinghua Fang

School of Economics and Management, China JiLiang University, Hangzhou 310018, Zhejiang, China
Jiahuangshu@foxmail.com

Abstract. Supplier selection and evaluation is an important part of supplier management. Identifying important authors, institutions and their cooperative network relationships, and revealing the theme evolution and research hotspots in this field can provide reference for relevant research in the future. This study based on the CNKI database, 662 relevant documents were obtained using the keywords of "supplier evaluation" and "supplier selection". Integrating CiteSpace and other software, a bibliometric review of supplier evaluation and selection was conducted with the help of descriptive statistics, cooperative network analysis, and timeline view. The results show that the research on supplier selection evaluation has attracted extensive attention of many scholars, with a wide variety of decision-making methods and diversified application fields. "Cold Chain Logistics", "Prefabricated Components" and "Sustainable" are the hot spots in recent years. It is worthy of paying more attentions to constructing new models for Supplier selection and evaluation, and some artificial intelligence technologies, such as neural network and machine learning are popular methods to advance the development of this filed.

Keywords: Supplier Evaluation · Supplier Selection · Bibliometric Method · CiteSpace

1 Introduction

Suppliers are the starting point for the entire supply chain, and any decision about suppliers will directly affect the overall profit and operation efficiency of the enterprises [1]. Therefore, how to evaluate and select suppliers is very important. So far, the methods used for supplier evaluation and selection can generally be divided into qualitative analysis, quantitative analysis and qualitative and quantitative comprehensive analysis [2]. Among them, qualitative analysis method includes bidding method and negotiation method. Qualitative analysis can evaluate indicators that are difficult to quantify, but it is too dependent on expert experience and lack of objectivity. Quantitative analysis methods include Activity Based Costing method, procurement cost method, etc. This method can objectively evaluate the indicators, but it can not fully express the subjective ideas of experts. Qualitative and quantitative comprehensive methods makes up for the

© The Author(s), under exclusive license to Springer Nature Singapore Pte Ltd. 2023
W. Hong and Y. Weng (Eds.): ICCSE 2022, CCIS 1811, pp. 496–507, 2023.
https://doi.org/10.1007/978-981-99-2443-1_43

shortcomings of the above methods and it has become the mainstream supplier evaluation and selection method in recent years, such as Fuzzy Comprehensive Evaluation Method and Analytic Hierarchy Process(AHP), etc.

In recent 20 years, many scholars have launched a comprehensive study on the field of supplier evaluation and selection. For example, Liu Xiao et al. [3] analyzed and summarized some main models and methods related to supplier selection from 1973 to 2002, and divided supplier selection methods into Cost Method, Linear Programming Method, Fuzzy Programming Method, Multi-objective Pro-gramming Method and various intelligent methods.In order to manage the supply chain better and achieve a "win-win" among enterprises, He Hongyan et al. [4] classified supplier selection methods from qualitative and quantitative perspectives, and analyzed their advantages and disadvantages. Han Kaijun and Li Jinhua [5] summarized a supplier selection method based on the integration of multiple methods, which is used to evaluate and select suppliers in the supply chain environment. Liang Ting and Yan Shi [6] sorted out the literature on logistics supplier selection methods from 2000 to 2015, and provided a reference for enterprises to choose logistics providers.

The above studies all adopt qualitative or descriptive analysis methods to review the selection of supplier evaluation, and these methods have poor verifiability and low accuracy [7]. Bibliometric analysis method can use data analysis tools to obtain invisible knowledge from a large amount of bibliographic data, and use statistical methods to analyze and summarize the fundamental nature and development direction of a discipline [8]. Thus, this study uses bibliometric analysis methods to review the field of supplier evaluation and selection, which can be divided into the following aspects: (1) statistical analysis of annual publication volume and journal distribution; (2) analysis of influential authors and institutions and their cooperative network atlas; (3) the use of keyword co-occurrence analysis, burst keyword analysis and keyword timeline view analysis of the theme.

2 Research Methodology

2.1 Research Methods

The bibliometric method is to use the characteristics of literature and quantitative data as the research object, so as to further analyze and explain its research law [9]. Bibliometric review is a review analysis of a certain field by using bibliometric method, which is an important part of review research [10]. Commonly used bibliometric analysis tools mainly include Histcite, CiteSpace, Vosviewer, Network Workbench tool, etc. Zhang Yun et al. [11] took the three journal citation subdatabases collected by the WoS core collection as the research object, and used Histcite and CiteSpace to explore current research hotspots. Xiang Xiaoqin et al. [12] sorted out the research literature on domestic public transport development through Citespace and Bibexcel, and summarized the main research fields, hotspots, and development trends in China. Yu Xiaohai et al. [13] used Bicomb and Vosviewer to conduct a comprehensive study of university think tanks in China, and proposed shortcomings and improvement measures in the field. Through the analysis, it is found that CiteSpace is a systematic modeling software based on bibliometric method, and it can obtain valuable core terms from the literature and overcome the subjective bias of traditional literature review through scientific mapping procedures [14]. To sum up, based on CNKI database, this study selects the core literature in the field of supplier evaluation and selection from 2001 to 2021, and uses CiteSpace and other software for bibliometric analysis, so as to reveal the research status and evolution trend of this field.

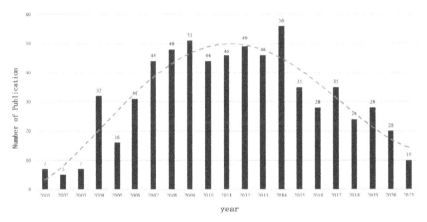

Fig. 1. Publication distribution according to years.

2.2 Data Collection

This article is based on the CNKI database, and the search criteria include: (1) the subject term is "supplier evaluation" or "supplier selection"; (2) time period is from 2001 to 2021; (3) the literature category is "Chinese Core Journal" or "CSSCI"; (3) only journal papers are retained, excluding books, conference papers, etc. Through the literature screening, 662 articles were finally obtained.

3 Results and Discussion

This section first uses Excel to conduct statistical analysis of the annual publication volume, journal distribution. Secondly, this study lists several important authors with the largest amount of publications in the field of supplier evaluation and selection. Then, this study uses CiteSpace to analyze the collaboration networks of the authors and organizations. Finally, keyword analysis is conducted on the selected literature to analyze the development process and research hotspots of this research direction through clustering and timeline mapping methods.

3.1 Annual Publication Analysis

The number of publication reflects the changes of scientific knowledge and the research progress in the field to a certain extent. It is an important index to measure the development of scientific research [15]. Figure 1 presents the publication distribution according to years and the quantity change trend.The following conclusions can be drawn from the figure:

In terms of the number of annual publication, the supplier selection evaluation mainly goes through three stages: exploration period (2001–2006), active period (2007–2014) and mature period (2015–2021). From 2000 to 2006, scholars' research on supplier selection and evaluation focused on the stage of current situation elaboration and theoretical exploration. Since 2007, the research on supplier selection evaluation has attracted the attention of many scholars, and lots of high-level papers have been published in this period. 2014 was the year with the highest number of high-level papers published of any year. The number of articles published this year reached 56. Since 2015, the field has entered a mature period, and high-level papers have tended to be stable.

3.2   Journal Analysis

There are 196 journals in total contributing to the selected publications on this topic. Figure 2 shows the journals with more than ten publications.As can be seen Statistics & Decision and Logistics Technology are the leading journals in this field with 38 articles, followed by Science and Technology Management Research with 29 articles. It is worth noting that the total number of articles published in these ten journals amounted to 217, and these represent about 1/3 of the total literature. The main topics covered by the literature in this area include management, mathematics, statistics, electronic information science and macroeconomic management and sustainable development.

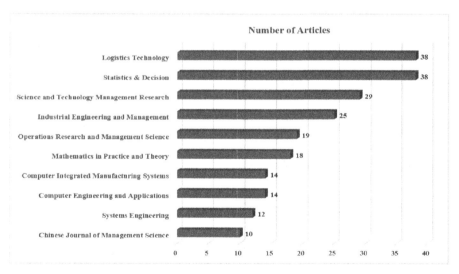

Fig. 2. Publication distribution according to journals.

3.3 Author Analysis

The publication quantity, the total number of citations and the average number of citations are three key indicators used to measure the author's contribution in this field [16]. Table 1 presents the relevant information of the 10 authors with the largest number of articles. It can be seen that most authors have published about five articles, and only Li Wu has more than 10 articles. In regards to the total citations and average ciation, Sun Linyan, Wang Daoping and Guan Zhimin rank the top three.

Table 1. The top 10 contributing authors.

No.	Author	Publication quantity	Author	Tocal citation	Author	Average citation
1	Li Wu	16	Sun Linyan	527	Sun Linyan	105
2	You Jianxin	5	Wang Daoping	258	Wang Daoping	52
3	Sun Linyan	5	Guan Zhimin	196	Guan Zhimin	49
4	Chen Zhengsong	5	Yao Jianming	183	Yao Jianming	37
5	Wang Daoping	5	Li Wu	154	You Jianxing	30
6	Wang Xu	5	You Jianxin	150	Liu Qiusheng	24
7	Yao Jianming	5	Liu Qiusheng	94	Geng Xiuli	22
8	Guan Zhimin	4	Geng Xiuli	89	Chen Zhengsong	17
9	Liu Qiusheng	4	Chen Zhensong	84	Wang Xu	16
10	Geng Xiuli	4	Wang Xu	78	Li Wu	10

On the other hand, the key collaborative networks among authors of the selected 662 articles are depicted in Fig. 3. The thicknesses of different lines stand for the frequency of two collaborated authors and the color denotes the year they were firstly co-authored. Figure 3 shows eight main cooperation teams. This study takes Group #1, Group #2 and Group #3 as examples:

Group #1 is the largest cooperative team in the current field with Li Wu as the core. The main members of the team include Hu Huanan, Chen Yan, Fu Yingzi and other 16 people. In this group, Li Wu has authored with Chen Yan for 3 times since 2009, with Fu Yingzi for 3 times since 2007, and with Hu Huanan for 2 times since 2010. The team focuses on supplier selection problems for ordinal preference and multi-attribute group decision making. For example, Li Wu et al. [17] considered the decision-making problem of the weight of decision-makers under each attribute, and proposed the concept of group ideal solutions under ordinal preferences to improve the supplier ranking result.

Li Wu et al. [18] established a multi-criteriand multi-level group decision model, and used linear weighted sum method and TOPSIS method to select library suppliers. In view of the existence of both cardinality evaluation information and ordinal preference, Hu Huanan et al. [19] established a hybrid group decision model for book suppliers, and used 0–1 programming and linear weighted sum method to calculate the final ranking and determine the best supplier.

Group #2 is composed of Wang Daoping, Wang Xu and Wang Yan. This group have published 5 relevant articles since 2007. Wang Daoping has authored with Wang Xu for 4 times since 2009, with Wang Yan for 3 times. This group focuses on the evaluation and selection of suppliers in the steel industry and green supply chain. Wang Daoping et al. [20] constructed a steel enterprise selection index system from cost-based and benefit-based, and this model improved the traditional Data Envelopment Analysis(DEA) and provided reference for steel enterprises to select suppliers. Wang Xu et al. [21] constructed a four-dimensional supplier selection index system from the supplier qualification, supplier ability, supplier culture and supplier environment, and identified the key elements of supplier selection by using factor analysis method. Wang Yan et al. [22] Optimized ranking results based on the combined model of DEA and TOPSIS, so as to select the green suppliers of steel enterprises.

Group #3 is a research team with You Jianxing and You Xiaoyue as its core. This team often uses fuzzy theory to solve supplier selection problems. For example, You Xiaoyue et al. [23] combined Two-Tuple Linguistic variables, AHP and VIKOR to evaluate supplier corporate social responsibility. You Jianxin and Wang Qinlan [24] ranked 26 supplier selection criteria according to their importance based on fuzzy mathematics and Quality Function Deployment(QFD), and proposed a systematic supplier selection criterion. You Xiaoyue and You Jianxin [25] used Two-Tuple Linguistic and VIKOR to select outsourcing suppliers and the method better takes into account subjective and objective weights and decision maker preferences.

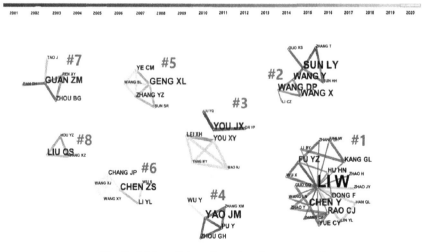

Fig. 3. Main collaborative networks among authors.

3.4 Institutional Analysis

Research institutions provide an efficient research platform for scholars, and especially those that produce a large number of high-quality articles, which act as a barometer and weathervane for other research institutions in the field [9]. Statistics show that a total of 252 institutions participated in the supplier selection and evaluation research, including 229 universities, 18 enterprises (electric power, medical, aero-space, etc.) and 5 research institutes. It can be seen that the main supporting platform for domestic supplier selection and evaluation research is the major high-level colleges.

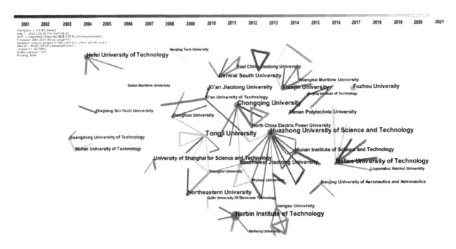

Fig. 4. Collaborative networks among organization

Figure 4 portrays the collaborative networks among organizations. We can see that Tongji University, Huazhong University of Science and Technology and Dalian University of Technology are prominently located on the map. Among them, Tongji University has the most cooperation with other institutions, and its number of publication has reached 19. In addition to cooperating with domestic universities and enterprises, Tongji University also cooperated with internationally renowned universities such as Cambridge University, Exeter University and Florida International University. In addition, from the perspective of the overall cooperation network, the average degree of the network is 1.93, and the average cooperation frequency of institutions is between [1, 2]. Most universities and enterprises cooperate independently or internally. In terms of cooperation intensity, the average cooperation network density of institutions in this field is only 0.0017, indicating that a typical fixed academic cooperation network has not been formed in the field of supplier selection and evaluation.

3.5 Keywords Analysis

Keywords are a high generalization of the theme of the article. Therefore, this study uses CiteSpace to analyze the keywords of the selected articles, including keyword co-occurrence analysis, keyword burst analysis and keyword timeline analysis. In this part, keyword co-occurrence analysis is used to identify keywords with high frequency in this field. Then, keyword burst analysis is used to reveal the research hotspots and research trends in a certain period of time. Finally, keyword timeline analysis uses cluster analysis to classify closely related words, which highlights the research focus according to the similarity between samples, and show the evolution trend of the research field in the form of time map [26].

Figure 5 shows the high-frequency keywords in the field of supplier selection evaluation. "Supply Chain", "Fuzzy Set", "TOPSIS", "AHP" and "Low Carbon" appear most frequently, so they occupy a prominent position in the figure. It can be seen from the figure that there are many kinds of decision-making technologies used in supplier selection and evaluation. It includes model driven methods represented by "TOPSIS", "AHP" and "DEA", knowledge driven methods represented by "Fuzzy Set", "Rough Set" and "Two-Tuple Linguistic", statistical probability driven methods represented by "Markov Chain", "Factor Analysis" and "Entropy Method", and data driven algorithms represented by "Genetic Algorithm" and "BP Neural Network". In addition, "Cold Chain Logistics", "Steel Enterprises" and "Auto Parts" are more applied in the research of supplier evaluation and selection. "Green Supply", "Sustainable" and "Carbon Emission" are the relevant contents of research in this field under the background of national development strategy in recent years.

Fig. 5. Co-occurrence keywords

Figure 6 presents ten keywords with the strongest citation bursts from the year 2001 to 2021. The strength value denotes the burst score of a keyword and the red line depicts its active years from the beginning to end. We can see from the figure that "Supply Chain" is the keyword with the highest strength. Scholars focused on the relationship between suppliers and the whole supply chain from 2003 to 2006. "Rough Set" and "Entropy Method" are common decision-making methods in the active period of the field, and "Prospect Theory" has been widely used in supplier selection and evaluation in recent years. With the diversification of decision-making methods, combined weighting and integrated decision-making have become the mainstream trend. In addition, with the rise of e-commerce platforms and online shopping, the selection of suppliers in the logistics

Keywords	Strength	Begin	End	2001 - 2021
Supply Chain	6.49	2003	2006	
Low Carbon	4.51	2014	2018	
Reverse Logistics	4.25	2012	2014	
Order Allocation	3.8	2016	2018	
Entropy Method	3.67	2010	2013	
Prospect Theory	3.6	2015	2021	
Combined Weighting	3.52	2013	2021	
Rough Set	3.52	2011	2014	
Logistics Service	3.27	2011	2012	
Prefabricated Component	3.21	2017	2021	

Fig. 6. The keywords with the strongest citation bursts

industry has attracted the attention of scholars from 2011 to 2014. Due to the reform of construction supply chain, scholars began to pay attention to the research on the supplier selection of prefabricated components in recent years.

Figure 7 depicts the time line visualization of co-occurrence keywords networks and associated clustering analysis result.According to this figure, and the development of supplier selection evaluation field is divided into exploration period (2001–2006), active period (2007–2014) and mature period (2015–2021). On the one hand, all keywords were divided into eight clusters, and the cluster "#0 supplier" gathers the most keywords. Then, a large number of supplier decision-making methods are gathered in clustering "#1 Entropy Method", clustering "#3 Rough Set" and clustering "#7 Fuzzy Sets", and clustering "#2 Carbon Emission", as an application background, is representative in the field of supplier selection and evaluation. On the other hand, from the time evolution of keywords, we can find that during the exploration period, the traditional competitive relationship is gradually replaced by partnership between suppliers and enterprises. Model driven decision-making methods occupy a dominant position in the field, and the evaluation index and decision-making methods have limitations. During the active period, decision-making methods have sprung up, including Rough Set, Entropy Method, BP Neural Network, Regression Support Vector Machine etc. The research on supplier selection and evaluation in the fields of steel, library and logistics has attracted more attention from scholars at this period. In the mature period, decision-making technology is mainly based on fusion application and improvement, and combined weighting has become the mainstream trend. Fuzzy Set, Prospect Theory and Two-Tuple Linguistic are the focus methodology. In the context of big data, machine learning and various intelligent algorithms have become a new generation of decision-making methods.

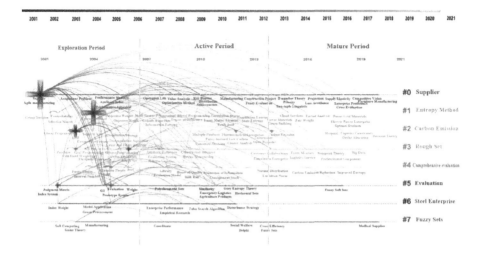

Fig. 7. Keyword time line analysis result

4 Conclusion

In this study, 662 literatures related to supplier selection and evaluation from 2001 to 2021 were bibliometrically analyzed, and it is an innovation of the summary research on supplier selection and evaluation. This article mainly draws the following conclusions:

On the one hand, the research on supplier selection evaluation has attracted the attention of many scholars. Many domestic high-level journals publish relevant papers on supplier selection and evaluation, including China Management Science, Operations Research And Management, Industrial Engineering And Management, etc. Li Wu is the author with the highest number of documents in the field of supplier selection evaluation, and Sun Linyan ranks first in the total number of citations and the average number of citations. The above two are important authors in the current field. Tongji University, Huazhong University of science and technology and Dalian University of technology are important institutions in the field, which play an important role in institutions cooperation. But the cooperation between industry-university-research institutions needs to be improved.

On the other hand, in the past 20 years, the supplier selection evaluation method has gradually become mature, and the trend of diversification in application fields is significant. The multi-attribute decision-making method represented by TOPSIS and AHP is the most widely used in supplier selection and evaluation. In addition, the data-driven approach fits well with the current big data background, which will be the mainstream decision-making method in the future. The supply network under the epidemic background, the introduction of deep learning decision-making technology and the constrained decision-making under the double carbon policy are several key points worth thinking about in the future supplier selection evaluation.

Therefore, this article attempts to briefly describe the potential development trends in this field from the perspective of key technology development and policy background:

(1) Firstly, the big data background has prompted data driven methods to become the mainstream research technology in the future. Machine learning algorithms such as decision trees and random forests have the advantages of high accuracy and training speed. Convolutional neural networks and cyclic neural networks have fast convergence speed and processing results for high-dimensional data. These methods are very suitable for large-scale supplier database optimization.

(2) Secondly, the COVID-19 has a important impact on agricultural products, cold chain logistics and other supply chains. There is a high degree of uncertainty in suppliers' supply capacity and transportation efficiency. Geographical location, supply elasticity and other factors have risen in the supplier evaluation index system. Therefore, the research on the construction of supplier evaluation and selection index system in the context of epidemic situation is the future research trend. In addition, social network analysis can identify the centrality and structural holes of suppliers in complex supply networks, which can be used to analyze the importance of suppliers in decision-making networks and provide effective reference for decision-making.

(3) With the promulgation of policies such as "dual carbon" and "zero carbon plan", green and low carbon has become a new factor in supplier decision-making in automotive, steel, and other industries. "Low carbon" or "zero carbon" as important constraints will be considered in supplier decision-making issues. In addition, there are significant differences between traditional vehicles and new energy vehicles in terms of energy, operation, and management. How to optimize the supplier evaluation index system in the new energy industry is a major research direction.

Acknowledgments. The authors are very grateful to the respected editor and the anonymous referees for their insightful and constructive comments, which helped to improve the overall quality of the paper. This work was supported by the National Natural Science Foundation of China (no.72001196), and the The Project Supported by Zhejiang Provincial Natural Science Foundation of China (no. LQ21G010004).

References

1. Wei, J.: Optimization Study on Supplier Management of Flextronics Group. Lanzhou University (2020)
2. Jia, J., Fan, L., Jia, l.: Neuro-fuzzy system-based research of supplier selectior. J. East China Univ. Sci. Technol. (Soc. Sci. Ed.) **28**(6), 38–44 (2013)
3. Liu, X., Li, H., Wang, C., Chu, C.: A survey of supplier selection models and approaches. Chin. J. Manag. Sci. **21**(1), 139–148 (2004)
4. He, H., Zhu, J., Xu, L., Wang, Y.: Discussion and investigation of supplier selection method. Hebei J. Ind. Sci. Technol. **22**(5), 308–311+2 (2005)
5. Han, K., Li, J.: Survey of supplier selection methods based on supply chain. Logistics Sci.-Tech. **32**(10), 133–134 (2009)
6. Liang, T., Yan, S.: Statistics and overviews of research literature on logistics supplier selection. Logistics Sci.-Tech. **39**(7), 24–26+46 (2016)
7. Zhang, E.: Reasearch on optimization of H warehousing equipment manufacturing company's purchasing management. Guangdong University of Technology (2020)

8. Qiu, J.: Bibliometrics. Science and Technology Literature Press (1988)
9. Mao, X.: The status quo and prospect of the research on the development of new urbanization in china——a bibliometric analysis of the publications with CSSCI journals in latest decade. J. Zhongzhou Univ. **37**(5), 32–37 (2020)
10. Li, W.: Overview and enlightenment of editorial aesthetics research in recent 30 years——from the perspective of bibliometric analysis from 1988 to 2017. Sichuan Drama **32**(9), 175–179 (2019)
11. Zhang, Y., Hua, W., Yuan, S.: Bibliometric measurement and analysis of the research on co-citation clustering from WoS. J. Intell. **35**(9), 152–157 (2016)
12. Xiang, X., Yang, C., Chen, J.: Bibliometric analysis of transit-oriented development research. Urban Rapid Rail Transit **33**(1), 15–21 (2020)
13. Yu, X., Wang, Q., Ling, Y.: A survey of Chinese university think tank research: based on bibliometric analysis. Inf. Sci. **38**(8), 164–169 (2020)
14. Li, Y., Zhang, Y., Zeng, K., Zhang, S.: Comparison of different literature information analysis tools. Chin. J. Med. Libr. Inf. Sci. **24**(11), 41–47 (2015)
15. Zhou, J., Liu, Y., Liu, J.: Exploration of intellectual structure and hot issues in sentiment analysis research. J. China Soc. Sci. Tech. Inf. **39**(1), 111–124 (2020)
16. Huang, J., You, J., Liu, H., Song, M.: Failure mode and effect analysis improvement: a systematic literature review and future research agenda. Reliab. Eng. Syst. Saf. **199**, 106885 (2020)
17. Li, W., Dong, F., Chen, Y.: Dynamic programming approach to multi-attribute group decision-making with ordinal preferences. J. Huazhong Univ. Sci. Technol. (Nat. Sci. Ed.) **37**(10), 48–51 (2009)
18. Li, W., Hu, H., Fu, Y.: Hybrid multi-person, multi-criteria and multi-level evaluation on books supplier. Libr. Inf. Serv. **54**(2), 92–95+54 (2010)
19. Hu, H., Dong, F., Li, W.: Hybrid multi-attribute group decision-making approach to books supplier selection. Comput. Eng. Appl. **46**(15), 208–210 (2010)
20. Wang, D., Wang, X., Wang, Y.: Hybrid multi-attribute group decision-making approach to books supplier selection. Comput. Eng. Appl. **46**(15), 208–210 (2010)
21. Wang, X., Wang, D., Wang, Y.: An empirical study on the green vendor selection index of china iron and steel industry based on factor analysis. Soft Sci. **23**(10), 46–49 (2009)
22. Wang, Y., Wang, X., Wang, D.: The study on the green vendor selection in the iron & steel enterprises based on the combination model of DEA and TOPSIS. Econ. Manag. **24**(4), 49–52 (2010)
23. You, X., Lei, X., Mao, R., Yang, M.: Evaluating supplier corporate social responsibility using an extended ITL-VIKOR method. Chin. J. Manag. **16**(12), 1830–1840 (2019)
24. You, J., Wang, C., Tala, M., Zhang, H.: Multinational supplier selection based on fuzzy quality. J. Tongji Univ. (Nat. Sci.) **47**(6), 878–887 (2019)
25. You, X., You, J.: Outsourcing supplier selection by interval 2-tuple linguistic VIKOR method. J. Tongji Univ. (Nat. Sci.) **45**(9), 1407–1414 (2017)
26. Lang, Z., Liu, H., Meng, N., Wang, H., Wang, H., Kong, F.: Mapping the knowledge domains of research on fire safety – an informetrics analysis. Tunnelling and Underground Space Technology (2020, prepublish)

Prediction of Vehicle Drag Coefficient Using Machine Learning

Zhuo Li, Feng Jiang, and Xingchen Liu$^{(\boxtimes)}$

Wuhan University of Technology Wuhan, Wuhan, China
lubenn@whut.edu.cn

Abstract. In view of the problem that numerical simulation of the vehicle was time-consuming, the support vector regression (SVR) model based on the simulation data was proposed to the prediction of the vehicle drag coefficient. The typical angles of the MIRA model were chosen as input dataset, and the results of simulation were chosen as output. The Multiple Linear Regression (LR), BP neural network (BP) and Support Vector Regression algorithm (SVR) were used to predict vehicle drag coefficient, respectively. The prediction effects under different machine learning algorithms were also compared. The penalty factor c and kernel function parameter g of the SVR algorithm were optimized by PSO algorithms. The simulation results show that the PSO-SVR model has high prediction accuracy and great generalization performance.

Keywords: support vector regression · machine learning · drag coefficient · aerodynamics

1 Instruction

At present, electric vehicles are still in the market promotion stage, and generally need to reduce costs to improve market acceptance. This makes electric vehicles rely more on styling optimization rather than adding aerodynamic accessories to reduce the drag of coefficient. In styling optimization, how to determine the value of typical angles is difficult, and it requires repeated fluid simulation, making it difficult to meet the demand when the task is urgent.

Machine learning is one of the fastest growing branches of artificial intelligence, which can mine the mathematical features of the original data, make predictions on new data, and solve various classification and regression problems. Numeral calculations is an important tool for aerodynamics research, which can provide high-precision analysis results, but there are generally problems such as time-consuming and high computing resource requirements. One of the main directions of combining machine learning and aerodynamics research is to use machine learning algorithms to obtain data information for CFD simulations, so that results of numeral calculations can be predicted [1].

In this paper, different supervised learning algorithms are applied to the prediction of drag coefficients of vehicles, and the data set is obtained by steady-state flow field simulation. Multiple Linear Regression, BP neural network and SVR were used to establish

W. Hong and Y. Weng (Eds.): ICCSE 2022, CCIS 1811, pp. 508–520, 2023.
https://doi.org/10.1007/978-981-99-2443-1_44

the prediction model. The results show that the standard SVR has the best prediction effect, and then the particle swarm optimization algorithm is used to find the best SVR hyperparameters. The PSO-SVR model can obtain drag coefficient prediction with high accuracy in short time and small samples, thus providing a new method to obtain drag coefficient of vehicles quickly.

2   Model Generation

2.1   Vehicle Model

In the development of CAS of the car, the selection of typical angles will have a large impact on the drag coefficient of the car, such as the inclination of front windshield angle, inclination of rear windshield angle, front inclination of hood angle, inclination of rear windshield angle and rear upturn angle [2].

This paper mainly discusses the prediction of drag coefficient based on the typical angles, but the common car model is complex, with many rounded corners and unnecessary surface, it is difficult to modify the modeling directly, so a simplified model of the car is selected as shown in Fig. 1, in which the front inclination of hood angle is 80°, the inclination of front windshield angle is 30°, and the inclination of rear windshield angle and tail upturn angle are 15°.

Fig. 1. simplified vehicle model

2.2   Numerical Simulation

The realizable K-ε turbulence model was used for the numerical simulation, and a constant density gas model was selected with a gas density of 1.15 kg/m^3, a static temperature of 25C, a reference pressure of 98400 Pa, and a turbulence intensity and viscosity ratio for the initial conditions. The specific boundary condition settings are shown in Table 1.

The width of the computational domain is 30 m, the height is 11.5 m, and the length is 63 m. The distance between the velocity inlet and the front end is more than three times the length of the vehicle, and the distance between the pressure outlet and the rear end is more than eight times the length of the vehicle, and the obstruction ratio is 0.69%.

Table 1. Boundary condition settings

Boundary condition	Setting
in	velocity 33.33 m/s
out	Pressure 0 Pa
ground	No slip
side and Top	Free slip
body surface	No slip

The surface mesh size of the simplified model of the body is 8 mm, and the boundary base mesh size of the calculation domain is 256 mm. 6 prismatic layers are generated on the surface of the model, and the extension rate of the prismatic layers is set to 1.2.

In order to ensure the calculation accuracy, the surface mesh of the body is controlled by surface encryption, and in addition, four layers of body encryption areas are set, as shown in Fig. 2. The location and dimensions of the encryption zones are shown in Table 2. The mesh size of C and D of the encryption area is set to 64 mm and 128 mm respectively.

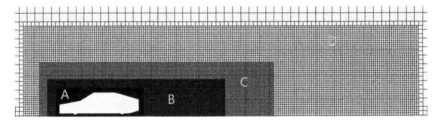

Fig. 2. encrypted domain

Table 2. Encrypted field location and size

Encrypted field	Location
A	Close to the body
B	0.5 m in front and side of the car, 5 m behind the car, 0.5 m high area
C	1 m in front and side of the car, 8 m behind the car, 1.5 m height area
D	2 m in front and side of the car, 12 m behind the car, 3.5 m height area

The body face encryption size and the grid size of the encryption area close to the body are crucial to the simulation results. Several grid size matching schemes are tried and simulated separately, and the results are shown in Table 3.

When the number of Volume mesh grid reaches 11.79 million, the drag coefficient error is within 0.43%, which has reached a high calculation accuracy, so project 3 is

Table 3. Grid-independence verification

num	Grid size of dense area (mm)			Cd
	Close to the body	*A*	*B*	
1	20	32	48	0.47
2	16	20	32	0.468
3	8	16	32	0.464
4	8	12	32	0.462
5	7	16	32	0.462

chosen to set the grid size. This setting method is used as the benchmark for prediction model dataset.

3 Drag Coefficient Prediction

3.1 Simulation Dataset

According to the simulation results flow chart using STAR CCM+ as a tool, it can be seen that the inclination of front windshield angle and front inclination of hood angle will both have an effect on the vortex above the hood, while the change of the inclination of rear windshield angle will change the distance from the tail vortex to the rear of the car, which will have a greater impact on the wind resistance of the whole car, so these three characteristic parameters are chosen as the prediction model input variables Fig. 3.

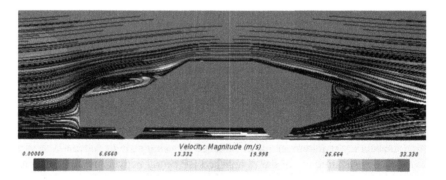

Fig. 3. velocity Streamline

The inclination of front windshield angle needs to meet the driver's vision requirements to ensure driving safety; the head height and inclination of hood angle need to meet the internal structure of the engine compartment requirements; the inclination of rear windshield angle is related to the man-machine arrangement, including the rear view

Table 4. Typical angles.

typical angles	Range of variation (unit/degree)				
hood Inclination	80	82.5	85	87.5	90
front windshield Inclination	25	30	35	40	45
rear windshield Inclination	10	15	20	25	/

and head wrap line. The final choice of the inclination of front windshield, inclination of hood and inclination of rear windshield range and gradient is shown in Table 4.

Under the condition that all simulation settings are the same as the baseline setting method, 100 sets of simplified models with the combination of the three characteristic parameters in the table are simulated and calculated to obtain the drag coefficients of all models. The three typical angles and the corresponding drag coefficients are input and output as data sets respectively. Among them, 20 sets of samples are randomly selected as the test set, and the remaining 80 sets of samples are used as the training set.

The data preprocessing maps the original data to the interval $[-1,1]$, thus ensuring that the difference in the input data range does not affect the training time and effect [3, 4].

3.2 Algorithm Selection

Multiple linear regression.Multiple linear regression is a type of linear model in which the model output is a linear combination of the sample characteristics and the parameters of the linear model itself, with two and more influences [5, 6]. The mathematical expressions are defined as follows, where x_1, x_2 and x_3 are the input variables, θ_0 are constant terms, θ_1, θ_2 and θ_3 are the weight values of the input variables, respectively.

$$y_\theta(x) = \theta_0 + \theta_1 x_1 + \theta_2 x_2 + \theta_3 x_3 \tag{1}$$

Multiple linear regression is modeled by fitting the data as a straight line and minimizing the loss function. In general, it is believed that the lower the front windshield lie-flat angle is, the smaller the drag coefficient is, so there is a possibility of linear correlation.

BP neural network. The number of input variables of the data set is 3, and the prediction accuracy requirement can be satisfied by using a single hidden layer neural network. The basic structure of the established BP neural network is shown in Fig. 4, which consists of an input layer, an implicit layer and an output layer, with the input layer consisting of three neurons and the output layer consisting of one neuron, and the weights and thresholds of the connections between different neurons are different [7].

Support vector regression The regression function $f(x) = \langle \omega, x \rangle + b$, whose accuracy is ε, then the distance from the sample data points to the function curve is

$$d_i = \frac{|\langle \omega, x \rangle + b - y_i|}{\sqrt{1 + \|\omega\|^2}} \tag{2}$$

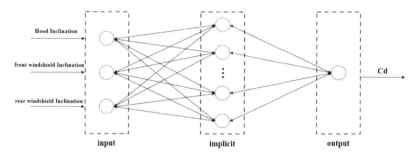

Fig. 4. the structure of BP neural network

The optimization objective is to maximize the upper bound of d_i, but since there may be linearly indivisible points in the sample set, it is necessary to introduce the slack variables ζ_i and ξ_i^*, the penalty factor C. The optimization problem is finally transformed into the problem of minimizing the structural risk.

$$\min R(\omega, \xi_i, \xi_i^*) = \frac{1}{2}\|\omega\|^2 + C\sum_{i=1}^{m}(\xi_i + \xi_i^*) \tag{3}$$

The LaGrange function is introduced, and the kernel function $K(x, y)$ is used to map the sample to a high-dimensional space regression, and the minimization problem is transformed into a dyadic form, which is solved to obtain the support vector regression expression.

$$f(x) = \sum_{i=1}^{l}(a_i - a_i^*)K(x_i, x) + b \tag{4}$$

The basic idea of support vector regression is to find the optimal classification surface so that all samples have the minimum error from that optimal classification surface, and when the sample set is linearly indistinguishable, the kernel function is used to map the sample set to a high-dimensional space for regression [8]. The Gaussian radial basis kernel function also has good support for small samples, and the parameter σ is chosen as the inverse of the eigenvalue, and the number of input variables is 3, $\sigma = 0.33$; the penalty factor C is chosen as the default value of 1; the loss function p is set to 0.01.

3.3 Algorithm Test Results and Discussion

In addition to MSE (mean squared error), MAPE (mean absolute percentage error) and (coefficient of determination) are commonly used to evaluate the prediction accuracy, and the expressions are shown below. The closer the MSE and MAPE are to 0, and the closer R^2 is to 1, the higher the prediction accuracy of the model. The comparison of the prediction results of each algorithm is shown in Table 5.

$$MSE = \frac{1}{n}\sum_{i=1}^{n}(y_i - y_i)^2 \tag{5}$$

$$MAPE = \frac{1}{n} \sum_{i=1}^{n} \left| \frac{y_i - y_i'}{y_i} \right| \tag{6}$$

$$R^2 = \frac{(n \sum_{i=1}^{n} (y_i y_i') - \sum_{i=1}^{n} y_i \sum_{i=1}^{n} y_i')^2}{[n \sum_{i=1}^{n} y_i^2 - (\sum_{i=1}^{n} y_i)^2][n \sum_{i=1}^{n} y_i'^2 - (\sum_{i=1}^{n} y_i')^2]} \tag{7}$$

Table 5. Comparison of prediction results

indicators(%)	SVR	BP	LR
MSE	0.256	0.572	6.05
MAPE	0.36	0.47	1.73
R^2	98.52	97.20	63.20

The test results of the three algorithms are shown in Fig. 5. The green solid line represents the multiple linear regression, which has the worst prediction effect, indicating that the relationship between the typical angles and the drag coefficient is not simply linear; the BP neural network has stronger prediction accuracy than the multiple linear regression, but the best number of neurons in the hidden layer is not easy to get, and the initial weights and thresholds are randomly determined again during each training, which results in large fluctuations and poor robustness. The solid red line represents the standard SVR model, which fits the true value best. The standard SVR prediction model has the highest accuracy, can avoid repeated testing to determine the model parameters, and has high robustness, so the standard SVR algorithm is finally chosen to build the base prediction model.

The standard SVR prediction model takes default parameters, there is still room for optimization to improve the performance of the prediction model. The values of SVR model hyperparameters, such as penalty factor C and kernel function parameter, can greatly affect the model performance, and the most appropriate parameter and penalty factor C need to be determined by the intelligent optimization algorithm.

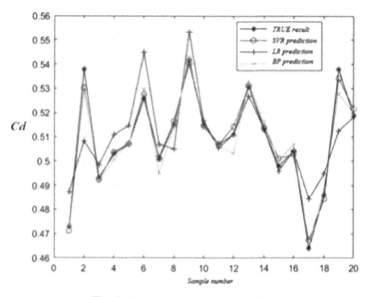

Fig. 5. Comparison of prediction effect

4 PSO-SVR Model

4.1 Particle Swarm Optimization Algorithm

The basic principle of PSO algorithm is to randomly generate some initial particles in two-dimensional space and randomly assign them initial velocity, calculate the individual fitness extremes and population fitness extremes of the initial particles, and the particles pursue the current individual extremes and population extremes to iteratively update and finally find the location with the most fitness [9].

The equations of particle update velocity and position are as follows.

$$v_i = \omega \cdot v_{i-1} + c_1 \cdot r_1 \cdot (p_i - x_i) + c_2 \cdot r_2 \cdot (p_g - x_i) \tag{8}$$

$$x_i = x_{i-1} + v_i \tag{9}$$

In the formula, v represents the velocity, including the velocity of generation i and generation i-1; x represents the position, including the position of generation i and generation i-1; p represents the extreme value, divided into group extreme value and individual extreme value; r_1 and r_2 are random numbers in the interval [0, 1]; c is the learning factor, and ω is the velocity weight.

4.2 Parameter Optimization of SVR by PSO

The initial population size of PSO is set to 100, the number of evolution is set to 200 generations, the particle velocity is restricted to the interval [-5,5], and the learning factor c1 = c2 = 1.5. The prediction error of support vector regression for the corresponding parameters at different particle positions is returned as the fitness function of the particle swarm optimization algorithm, which enables the use of the PSO algorithm to find the optimal hyperparameters of support vector regression [10, 11], The flow of the model is shown in Fig. 6.

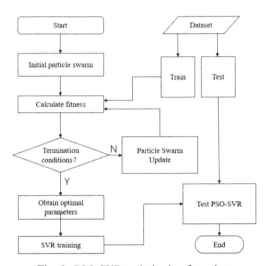

Fig. 6. PSO-SVR optimization flow chart

The detailed prediction results are shown in Table 6, and the prediction accuracy of the PSO-SVR model is significantly improved compared with the standard SVR. Figure 7 adaptation curve shows that the PSO algorithm converges quickly and the population reaches the individual optimal adaptation in only the 20th generation, and the PSO-SVM prediction error has reached a minimal value in less iteration time. Figure 8 shows that the PSO-SVR prediction results and simulation values have been basically consistent.

4.3 Analysis of Sample Size on Prediction Accuracy

PSO-SVR has been able to reveal the relationship between typical angle such as front wind inclination angle and drag coefficient, and all three evaluation indexes are at the appropriate level, which proves that it is feasible to predict drag coefficient by establishing PSO-SVR model, but the data set capacity is 100, which requires too many simulations to meet the engineering requirements. It is necessary to verify the prediction accuracy with different sample sizes to determine whether the accuracy requirement can be achieved with a smaller sample size. Random selection and orthogonal experiment selection, are used to design the data set with small sample size [12].

1) Random sample selection. Twenty samples were randomly selected as the test set, and the remaining 80 samples were trained with a gradient of 10, respectively, and the results are shown in Table 7.

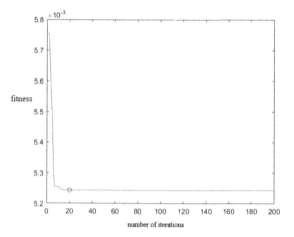

Fig. 7. Fitness

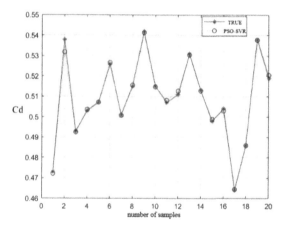

Fig. 8. Prediction result

Table 6. Comparison of prediction results

indicators(%)	SVR	PSO-SVR
MSE	0.256	0.099
MAPE	0.36	0.18
R^2	98.52	99.42

Table 7. The effect of sample size on prediction results

R^2	sample size							
	10	20	30	40	50	60	70	80
SVR	0.73	0.87	0.94	0.97	0.98	0.98	0.98	0.98
PSO-SVR	0.53	0.98	0.99	0.99	0.99	0.99	0.99	0.99

Table 8. The effect of sample size on training results

R^2	sample size				
	5	10	15	20	25
SVR	0.379	0.932	0.953	0.974	0.985
PSO-SVR	0.772	0.967	0.990	0.986	0.991

As seen in the figure, the standard SVR has poor generalization until the number of samples in the training set reaches 60. In contrast, the SVR model after optimization by particle swarm algorithm only needs to train 20 samples to achieve a high prediction accuracy.

2) Orthogonal experiment method to select samples

The orthogonal experiment method can select the representative samples in the original data set. The standard orthogonal table, which is widely used, $L_{25}(5^6)$ is selected as the benchmark, and the redundant three factors are removed by the combination method, and the standard orthogonal table is processed by the proposed level method to obtain the training sample set.

Using the selected 25 samples as the base, different numbers of samples were randomly selected as the training set, and 20 sets of data were randomly selected as the test set among the remaining 75 samples, and the test results are shown in the following Table 8.

The test results of the two previous schemes show that PSO-SVR not only improves the prediction accuracy based on the standard SVR, but also significantly improves the generalization ability of the model;

(1) when randomly selecting samples, the standard SVR requires 60 or even more training samples to obtain high prediction accuracy, while PSO-SVR only requires 20 training samples to ensure the prediction accuracy;

(2) Compared with random selection, the orthogonal experiment method can still effectively reduce the number of training samples while ensuring the prediction accuracy of the model. The standard SVR model requires only 25 training samples to obtain satisfactory prediction accuracy, and the number of samples is much smaller than 60 randomly selected data sets. The PSO-SVR model, on the other hand, has already

reached a great value of the coefficient of determination when the number of training samples is 15, and the subsequent increase in the number of samples has no significant effect on improving the prediction accuracy. It can be seen that the method of PSO-SVR is still feasible to predict the drag coefficient under the smaller sample size.

5   Summary

In this paper, the prediction of drag coefficient is realized by machine learning method.

(1) The simplified model is simulated and calculated for the external flow field and verified for grid irrelevance, and the grid size is determined as the simulation benchmark for the subsequent data set.
(2) Using the three typical angles of the simplified model and the corresponding drag coefficients as the input and output of the prediction model, the data set is established, and the multiple linear regression, BP neural network and SVR algorithms are used for prediction respectively, and the SVR is finally selected to build the base prediction model.
(3) The particle swarm optimization algorithm is used to optimize the SVR parameters, and the PSO-SVR prediction model is established to verify the prediction accuracy of the model under different numbers of data sets.
(4) The results show that the drag coefficient prediction model with smaller number of training samples still has high prediction accuracy, which proves that it is practical to use machine learning methods for drag coefficient prediction and it provides a new idea for fast and accurate prediction of vehicle drag coefficient.

Acknowledgment. This paper is partially funded by: Ministry of Education Industry-University Cooperation Collaborative Education Program (202102210002/202102292022). National Research Project on Computer Basic Education Teaching in Higher Education Institutions (2021-AFCEC-456).

References

1. Zhang, T., Qian, W., Zhou, Y.: Preliminary thinking on the combination of artificial intelligence and aerodynamics. Adv. Aeronaut. Eng. **10**(1), 1–11 (2019)
2. Wang, J., Yang, Z., Zhu, H.: Simulation analysis of the influence of typical angles on vehicle aerodynamic drag characteristics. Comput. Simul. **30**(10), 184–188 (2013)
3. Yuan, M.: Basic Principles, Algorithms and Practices of Machine Learning. Tsinghua University Press (2018)
4. Liu, M., Zhang, Q., Liu, Y., Wang, W.: Prediction of hot rolling force based on machine learning. Forging Technol. **46**(10), 233–241 (2021)
5. Leng, Y.: Introduction to Machine Learning to Practice. Tsinghua University Press (2019)
6. Jaffar, F., Farid, T., Sajid, M., Ayaz, Y., Khan, M.J.: Prediction of drag force on vehicles in a platoon configuration using machine learning. IEEE Access **8**, 201823–201834 (2020)

7. Huang, J., Su, H., Zhao, X.: Prediction of airfoil aerodynamic coefficient based on BP neural network. Adv. Aeronaut. Eng. **1**(01), 36–39 (2010)
8. Zhu, L., Zheng, S., Yuan, W.: Prediction of steady-state noise and sound quality in vehicle based on genetic-support vector regression. Noise Vibr. Control. **40**(3):170–174, 193 (2020)
9. Sun, H.: Prediction of vehicle exterior aerodynamic noise based on support vector regression. Wuhan University of Technology (2021)
10. Peng, D., Chen, Y., Qian, Y., Huang, C.: Transformer winding temperature soft measurement model based on particle swarm optimization-support vector regression. J. Electrotech. Technol. **33**(08), (2018)
11. Shen, Y., Guo, B., Gu, T.: Particle swarm optimization algorithm and its comparison with genetic algorithm. Univ. Electron. Sci. Technol. China **05**, 696–699 (2005)
12. Sun, H., Wang, Y., Zhang, C., et al.: Prediction method for aerodynamic noise of automotive rearview mirror based on machine learning. Chinese J. Autom. Eng. **11**(2), 142–148 (2021)

Research on Food Recommendation Method Based on Knowledge Graph

Yandi Guo, Yi Chen[✉], Wenqiang Wei, and Hanqiang Li

Beijing Key Laboratory of Big Data Technology for Food Safety, Beijing Technology and Business University, Beijing, China
chenyi@th.btbu.edu.cn

Abstract. Food recommendation is a crucial task in the field of food computing, which aims to match a user's preferences with appropriate food options by uncovering their latent preferences. However, traditional content-based and collaborative filtering methods may not effectively capture these preferences, as they overlook the rich information contained in food data. To address this issue, this paper explores the use of a Knowledge Graph-based approach to food recommendation. Specifically, we construct a food knowledge graph that contains abundant relational information and data on food products. We propose a novel recommendation model called the Knowledge-Aware Attention Graph Convolutional Network, which aggregates neighbor information using knowledge-aware attention and captures higher-order neighbor information by stacking multiple layers. We also employ different aggregation methods for user entities and internal entities of the knowledge graph. We conducted experiments on a large food recommendation dataset, and our results show that our proposed model significantly outperforms the benchmark approach.

Keywords: Food Recommendation · Food Knowledge Graph · Message Passing · Graph Convolutional Network

1 Introduction

Food plays an important role in daily life. In recent years, many online services related to food recommendation have emerged, such as Meituan, Koubei, Foodspotting, etc. Food recommendation is one of the tasks in the field of food computing [1]. The purpose of food recommendation is to find the right food for users and meet their individual needs. Food recommender systems can not only provide users with food products that match their preferences, but also influence their eating habits [2] and provide them with nutritional and health recommendations. Existing food recommendation methods mainly use machine learning methods to learn users' preferences from their interaction history with food and recommend foods that match their preferences and meet their personalized needs.

In recent years, Knowledge Graph-based recommender systems have gradually become the focus of research in the field of recommender systems. Knowledge Graph

W. Hong and Y. Weng (Eds.): ICCSE 2022, CCIS 1811, pp. 521–533, 2023.
https://doi.org/10.1007/978-981-99-2443-1_45

can provide rich auxiliary information for recommender systems, and knowledge Graph-based recommender systems can not only provide certain interpretability for recommendations by modeling higher-order user relationships, but also better construct user and item representations, better model user preferences, mine implicit association relationships, alleviate data sparsity problems and achieve high-quality recommendations.

In this paper, we address the food recommendation problem by providing a new exploration of food recommendation, i.e., using food knowledge graphs as auxiliary information for food recommendation. In summary, this work makes the following main contributions:

(1) We constructed a food knowledge graph for food recommendation, and combined the food knowledge graph and the user-recipe interaction bipartite graph to build a collaborative knowledge graph, which provides rich auxiliary information for the recommendation task, improves the performance of the recommendation while effectively alleviating the data sparsity problem.

(2) We develop a recommendation model based on a knowledge graph attention network, which performs knowledge graph attention-based message passing on a collaborative knowledge graph, and demonstrate the effectiveness of the model through extensive experiments.

2   Related Work

2.1   Food Recommendation

Food is a necessity for human life, and the field of food recommendation has received more and more attention in recent years. Most of the existing food recommendation methods are directly borrowed from recommendation methods in other fields, mainly CF-based methods [3] and CB-based methods [4]. Trattner et al. [5, 6] made a summary of the techniques in food recommendation systems and some of the challenges faced by food recommendation. They compared a series of CF-based and CB-based approaches and showed that CF-based approaches consistently outperformed CB-based approaches, but CB-based approaches were able to solve the cold start problem more effectively. However, the CF-based approach mainly focuses on mining user's preferences through the user-food interaction history, which is equivalent to directly borrowing recommendation methods from other domains, without considering the characteristics of the food recommendation domain itself, that is, ignoring the rich information contained in the food data itself, such as food composition, nutrition index, food taste, food image information, and so on. In order to enhance the performance of food recommendation, it is necessary to incorporate diverse auxiliary information. Gao et al. [7] introduced visual-aware to food recommendation and proposed a hierarchical attention-based approach that can learn user's preferences from visual images of food and treat food recommendation as a multimedia task. Gao et al. proposed a graph convolutional neural network-based method FGCN [8], adding rich association relations among foods to construct a heterogeneous graph containing food-related domain knowledge, which provides rich auxiliary information to the recommender system dataset, allowing the model to learn fine-grained representations and thus improve the performance of recommendations, which is better than the CF-based method and the CB-based. This method has better results than the CF-based method and CB-based method, indicating that adding some correlations to the food domain recommendation dataset can help the model to better model user's preferences and effectively improve the recommendation performance.

2.2 Food Knowledge Graph

The concept of a Knowledge Graph was first introduced by Google in 2012, and Knowledge Graph is a semantic network containing rich information describing concepts, entities, and connections among them in the objectively real world. Existing large knowledge graphs include Freebase, DBPedia, YAGO, and so on.

In recent research, Knowledge Graph technology has been gradually applied to the food domain [9]. A food knowledge graph can represent rich food data information into a unified and standardized structure, which can transform food information silos into a more reusable food net and be applied to various tasks in the food domain. The construction of a food knowledge graph can provide rich information for many tasks in food computing. Qin et al. [10] constructed a food safety knowledge graph and implemented a food safety knowledge graph-based question-and-answer system to help people with information about substandard foods. Haussmann et al. [11] constructed a dietary knowledge graph that provides relationships between foods, recipes, and nutrition, and implemented a food recommendation for a QA system was implemented to evaluate the usefulness of this knowledge graph.

3   Food Knowledge Graph Construction

In this research, the food recommendation system dataset used is foodRecSys-V1 [12], from the open source dataset site Kaggle.com, which collects 3794003 interaction histories from 1160627 users, 49698 recipes and the corresponding food composition, food images and nutritional metrics from Allrecipes.com. Allrecipes.com is a large food recipe website with more than 1.5 billion visits per year, and the data provided by the website is used in several studies related to food computing.

We selected 40128 recipes from the food recommendation dataset and established a food knowledge graph by linking the recipes to Freebase [13] and extracting relevant entities and relationships. The specific process of building the knowledge graph is divided into three steps, which are: entity extraction, entity linking, and entity refinement. In the first step, we extract food ingredient entities from the original dataset. Second match these entities to their corresponding KB entities in Freebase, and extract the entities and relationships linked to these KB entities in the knowledge base. Finally, refine the extracted entities and relationships.

3.1   Entity Extraction

In this step, we extracted available ingredient entities from the ingredient data that make up the recipes. Out of the 40,128 recipes that were selected, there were 34,156 ingredients, not all of which could be directly linked to entities in Freebase. Therefore, named entity recognition was performed on the ingredient data in order to obtain available ingredient entities. We utilized Spacy for named entity recognition on these ingredients. In the end, 31,389 ingredient entities were obtained.

3.2 Entity Linking

After extracting the ingredients entities through entity extraction, the next step was to extract these entities and their corresponding relations from a large knowledge base to construct a knowledge graph. We selected Freebase as our knowledge base for entity and relation extraction. Freebase is a large-scale knowledge base composed of nodes and edges, where each node represents an entity (such as a person, place, organization, etc.) and each edge represents a relationship between two entities. Freebase covers a wide range of domains, including art, history, food, and many others, and contains rich entities and relationships between them, making it a valuable knowledge base. In this step, we linked the extracted ingredients entities to their corresponding entities in Freebase and extracted the neighboring entities and relationships of the corresponding entities in Freebase. Through entity linking, we obtained 269,423 triples and 45 relationships from Freebase.

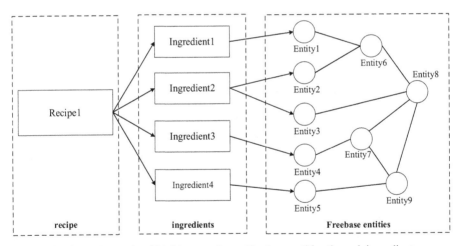

Fig. 1. An Example of Linking a recipe to Freebase entities through ingredients

Figure 1 shows an example of linking a recipe to entities in the Freebase knowledge base. Recipes are first broken down into the ingredients that make up the recipe, then these ingredients are linked to their corresponding entities in Freebase, and finally, the other entities linked by these entities and the relationships between them are extracted.

3.3 Entity Refinement

The triplets obtained by entity linkage contain a lot of noisy information, and the extracted triplets need to be refined. We keep the triplets with high quality and then add recipe-ingredients relationships to these triplets to form our final food knowledge graph.

The final food knowledge graph data contains 391156 triplets and 21 relationships. We combined the obtained knowledge graph with the user-item bipartite graph in the recommender system dataset to build the collaborative knowledge graph and implemented our recommendation model based on the collaborative knowledge graph.

3.4 Collaborative Knowledge Graph

In this recommendation task, we define the user as $U = \{u_1, u_2, ..., u_n\}$, the recipe as $I = \{i_1, i_2, ..., i_m\}$, and we define the user-recipe interaction bipartite graph as $S = \{(u, y_{ui}, i)|u \in U, i \in I\}$, $y_{ui} = 1$ means there is an interaction between user u and recipe i, and $y_{ui} = 0$ means vice versa.

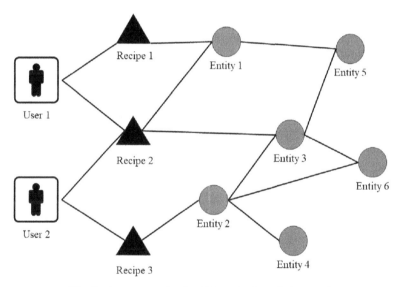

Fig. 2. A toy example of collaborative knowledge graph

The food knowledge graph we construct is denoted as *FKG*, which is composed of many triplets, denoted as $\{(h, r, t)|h \in H, r \in R, t \in T\}$, with h denoting the head entity, t denoting the tail entity, and r describing the relationship between them, e.g. (*dumpling, cuisine, Chinese cuisine*) such a triple describes the fact that dumpling belongs to the Chinese cuisine. A knowledge graph is a graph structure with rich semantic information consisting of many such facts. As shown in Fig. 2 we combine the food knowledge graph and the user-recipe interaction bipartite graph to construct a collaborative knowledge graph, and our collaborative knowledge graph is defined as *CKG*, which contains both user interaction information and knowledge graph information, and considers users as entities on the collaborative knowledge graph as well.

4 Method

Our model framework consists of three components: (1) embedding layer, which parameterizes each entity in *CKG* as a vector by knowledge embedding; (2) Knowledge-Aware attention Graph Convolutional Network layer, which performs Knowledge-Aware attention-based message passing on *CKG*, allowing each entity to recursively receive messages from its neighbors and update its own vector representation (3) prediction layer, which obtains all user entity representations and recipe entity representations from the Knowledge-Aware attention Graph Convolutional Network layer and outputs the predicted match scores between the two of them.

4.1 Embedding Layer

CKG is a heterogeneous graph network containing rich semantic information. To capture the structural information in *CKG*, we use TransR [14] as a knowledge graph embedding method to embed entities and relations in *CKG* into a continuous vector space, which preserves the structural information in *CKG* while facilitating computation, and the TransR method used in our model is described below.

TransR is a knowledge embedding method based on the translation principle. For a triplet (h, r, t) existing on the graph, it learns the embedding of entities and relations by optimizing $W_r e_h + e_r \approx W_r e_t$, TransR sets a transformation matrix $W_r \in R^{k \times d}$ for each relation r, through which the head entity h and tail entity t in the triplet are projected into the d-dimensional relation space represented by relation r. Herein, $e_h, e_t \in R^k$, $W_r e_h$ and $W_r e_t$ represent the embedding representation of the two entities h and t projected into the relation space r through the relation transformation matrix. The energy score for a triplet (h, r, t) is shown in Eq. (1).

$$g(h, r, t) = ||W_r e_h R^{k \times d} + e_r - W_r e_t R^{k \times d}||^2 \tag{1}$$

A lower $g(h, r, t)$ score indicates that this triple is more likely to be true and vice versa. The loss of TransR is the Bayesian personalized ranking loss, which aims to maximize the margin between positive and negative samples.

$$L_{kg} = \sum_{(h,r,t) \in \varepsilon^+} \sum_{(h,r,t') \in \varepsilon^-} - \ln \sigma \left(g\left(h, r, t'\right) - g(h, r, t) \right) \tag{2}$$

The loss function of TransR is shown in Eq. (2), where ε^+ represents the set of true triples in the knowledge graph, i.e., positive samples, and ε^- represents negative samples, which are constructed by randomly selecting a t' replacement of the true tail entity from the false tail entity, and σ is the sigmod function.

4.2 Knowledge-Aware Graph Convolutional Network Layer

In this layer, we perform the general paradigm of graph neural networks: message passing. Each entity on *CKG* goes iteratively to receive information from neighboring entities and combines the neighboring information to update its own representation, and by overlaying multiple layers of such operations, each entity is able to receive information from higher-order neighbors, thus capturing the higher-order similarity between entities. Specifically, the neighborhoods of user entities on *CKG*.

Message Passing. The knowledge graph attention network layer performs message passing on *CKG* to obtain the higher-order similarity between entities, inspired by KGAT [15], we add a knowledge-aware attention mechanism in, we add a knowledge-aware attention mechanism in the message passing process, which can better distinguish different relations on *CKG*. For an entity v on *CKG*, its neighborhood information passing is calculated as follows:

$$e_{N(v)} = \sum\nolimits_{(r,t)\in N(v)} \pi_r(v,t)e_t \tag{3}$$

where $N(v)$ denotes all neighbors of entity v, e_t is the representation of neighbor t, and $\pi_r(v,t)$ is the relational attention coefficient of v and t under relation r The relational attention coefficient is used to measure the importance of entity t to entity v under relation space r. When entity t is more closer to entity v under relation space r, then it will be given more weight and convey more information. The formula of the relational attention coefficient is as follows:

$$\pi_r(v,t) = (w_r e_t)^T tanh((w_r e_v + e_r)) \tag{4}$$

Using *tanh* as the nonlinear activation function, the attention coefficient depends on the distance between e_v and e_t under the relationship space r. The closer the distance, the larger the attention coefficient, and vice versa. The attention coefficients corresponding to all neighbors connected by entity v are normalized using the *softmax* function.

$$\pi_r(v,t) = \frac{exp\,(\pi_r(v,t))}{\sum_{(r',t')\in N(v)} exp\,(\pi_{r'}(v,t'))} \tag{5}$$

Message Aggregation. After obtaining all messages in the neighborhood of entity v, the next step is to perform message aggregation on it. In a traditional graph convolutional neural network, the usual way for message aggregation is as follows:

$$m_v = f(W(e_v + e_{N(v)})) \tag{6}$$

where m_v denotes the representation of the entity v after aggregating the neighborhood message, $f(\cdot)$ denotes the nonlinear activation function, and W is the feature transformation matrix. In LightGCN [16], it is demonstrated that nonlinear activation and feature transformation are not significant for performance improvement under collaborative filtering tasks, but increase the training difficulty of the model. We are inspired by Light-GCN to remove the redundant nonlinear activation function and feature transformation for the user-recipe interaction part, while retaining the nonlinear activation and feature transformations, we use bi-interaction for neighborhood information aggregation, and the specific aggregation formula is described below.

In the user-recipe interaction bipartite graph section, the aggregation function is as follows:

$$f_{u-i} = \left(e_u + e_{N(u)}\right) + \left(e_u \odot e_{N(u)}\right) \tag{7}$$

where e_u is the representation of user u, $e_{N(u)}$ is the neighborhood information of user u, and $\odot$ is the Hadamard product.

In the knowledge graph section, the aggregation function is as follows:

$$f_{kg} = LeakyReLU \left(W_1 \left(e_i + e_{N(i)}\right)\right) + LeakyReLU \left(W_2 \left(e_i \odot e_{N(i)}\right)\right) \tag{8}$$

where e_i is the representation of entity i, $e_{N(i)}$ is the neighborhood information of entity i, the activation function uses LeakyReLU, W_1 and W_2 are trainable parameter matrices, and the representation of the entity is updated after a layer of Knowledge-Aware attention Graph Convolutional Network is performed.

$$e_v^{(l)} = f \left(e_v^{(l-1)}, e_{N(v)}^{(l-1)}\right) \tag{9}$$

After performing one layer of such message passing, entities are able to acquire information from first-order neighbors. By stacking more Knowledge-Aware attention Graph Convolutional Network layers, the entities on *CKG* are able to capture information from higher-order neighborhoods and thus mine the potential preferences of users. Where $e_v^{(l)}$ denotes the representation of the entity on *CKG* at the l th layer, and the entity updates its own indication based on the aggregated neighborhood information.

4.3 Prediction Layer

After the message passing on the graph convolution layer, we obtain the final representation of the user e_u^* and the final representation of the recipe e_i^*, and we compute the inner product between them as the predicted matching score.

$$y_{ui} = e_u^* \cdot e_i^* \tag{10}$$

We use Bayesian personalized loss ranking to optimize the parameters of the model, Formally:

$$L_y = \sum_{(u,i)\in S^+,(u,j)\in S^-} -ln\,\sigma\,(y_{ui} - y_{uj}) \tag{11}$$

where S^+ is the positive sample set, i.e., the observed positive interaction between user u and recipe i, S^- is the negative sample set, where there is no interaction between user u and recipe j, and σ is the sigmod function.

4.4 Objective Function

Our objective function is optimized for the two loss functions L_{kg} and L_y mentioned in the previous section, and we combine the learning of the knowledge graph entity representation and the objective function of recommendation prediction, using an end-to-end approach for joint learning, i.e., the loss of the knowledge graph is also incorporated into the training of the final loss function, Formally:

$$L = L_{kg} + L_y + \lambda \|\Theta\|_2^2 \tag{12}$$

Table 1. Dataset Statics

	Item	Count
User-Recipe Interaction	#Users	53792
	#Recipes	40128
	#Interactions	1495445
Food Knowledge Graph	#Entities	59123
	#Relationships	21
	#Triplets	391156

5 Experiments

5.1 Dataset Description

The data statistics of the food recommendation dataset and the food knowledge graph used in this paper are presented in Table 1.

5.2 Settings

The parameters of our model training are set as follows: vector embedding dimension is set to 64, 3 layers of Graph Convolutional Network are used, batch_size is set to 1024, 200 epochs are trained, Adam is used to optimize the parameters of our model, learning rate is set to 0.0001, GPU is RTX3090. Some parameters are shown in the Table 2.

Table 2. Parameter Settings

Parameter	Value
Embedding Dimention	64
Layers	3
Batch_size	1024
Epoch	200
Parameter_update	Adam
Learning_rate	0.0001
Message_dropout	0.1
Node_dropout	0.1

5.3 Baselines

We compare our model with the following models:

CKE [17]: Collaborative Knowledge base Embedding, it fuses knowledge graphs with collaborative filtering for joint training to extract semantic features from structured knowledge.

CFKG [18]: Collaborative Filtering with Knowledge Graph, This model uses knowledge inference based on knowledge embedding on the knowledge graph for personalized recommendations.

LightGCN: LightGCN makes the model lightweight and efficient by simplifying the GCN in the neighborhood aggregation operation and using linear propagation to obtain the final user/item embedding representation.

NFM [19]: Neural Factorization Machines, it is an advanced decomposer model that introduces DNN on the basis of FM to learn more data information using nonlinear structure.

5.4 Evaluation Metrics

In this paper, we adopt two evaluation metrics that are widely used in recommender systems: Recall and NDCG.

Recall's formula is as follows:

$$Recall = \frac{\sum_{u \in U} |R(u) \cap T(u)|}{\sum_{u \in U} T(u)} \tag{13}$$

$R(u)$ are recipes recommended for the user, $T(u)$ is the set of recipes that the user has ever selected on the test set, recall reflects the proportion of recipes in the final recommendation list that the user may like to the overall user history interaction list, higher recall proves the higher relevance of our recommendation results. Recall@K represents the recall value of the top K items of the recommendation results.

NDCG, Normalized Discounted Cumulative Gain, formula is as follows:

$$NDCG = \frac{DCG}{IDCG} = \frac{\sum_{i=1}^{p} \frac{rel_i}{\log_2(i+1)}}{\sum_{i=1}^{rel} \frac{rel_i}{\log_2(i+1)}} \tag{14}$$

where DCG is the Discounted Cumulative Gain, IDCG is the result of normalizing DCG, and rel_i is used to describe the magnitude of similarity between the recipes selected by users and the recommended recipes. NDCG reflects the importance of the ranking order in the final recommendation list, the higher the real items are, the larger the NDCG value is. NDCG@K represents the NDCG value of the top K items of the recommendation results.

Table 3. Performance of compared models

Models	Recall@20	NDCG@20
CKE	0.12667	0.11260
CFKG	0.11871	0.10874
LightGCN	0.12298	0.11012
NFM	0.11811	0.10897
Our model	0.12929	0.11893

5.5 Performance Comparison

We first present a comparison between the proposed model and several baseline models in Recall@20 and NDCG@20 metrics, and Table 3 shows the performance comparison.

By analyzing the results of the performance comparison, our model performs the best in both metrics, and it can be found that the CKE model, which is also based on knowledge graph plus collaborative filtering for recommendation, achieves the second best result, which also proves that the use of knowledge graph as auxiliary information can significantly improve the performance of the model for better modeling of user preferences.

To investigate the performance of our model on sparse interactions, we set up a second set of comparison experiments. We divided the test set into five groups based on the sparsity of the number of user interactions, the number of interactions per user in each group is less than or equal to 19, 34, 62, 162, and 3886, respectively, and averaged the total number of interactions in each group as much as possible. Since the CKE model is most similar to our model in terms of performance, we compared the NDCG@20 of the CKE model and our model at different sparsity levels, and the comparison results are shown in Fig. 3.

The horizontal coordinates in the figure represent the sparsity of this group of user interactions, with smaller representing more sparse. We can observe that our model always outperforms CKE for all sparsity groups, and we can find that the advantage of our model is more obvious for the group with the highest sparsity, which proves that the knowledge graph can provide users with rich information for more intensive interactions, and thus can better capture users' preferences.

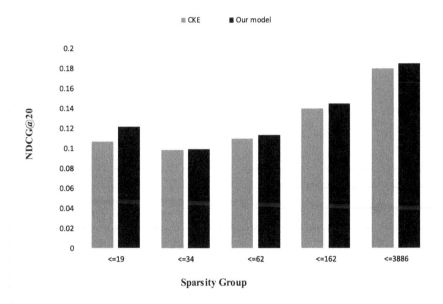

Fig. 3. Performance comparison on different sparsity groupings, the smaller the horizontal coordinate the sparser. NDCG@20 is used for the metrics.

6 Conclusion

In this paper, we propose to use a knowledge graph as auxiliary information to solve the food recommendation task. We construct a knowledge graph of recipes, give detailed construction steps, and design a knowledge graph attention network-based model for food recommendation based on this knowledge graph, which enhances the representation of entities on the graph by performing different message passing on the user-recipe interaction bipartite graph and the food knowledge graph, which can effectively tap the higher-order preferences of users and alleviate the problem of data sparsity. In our subsequent work, we will focus on the nutritional health aspects of food recommendations and incorporate nutritional health recommendations into food recommendations.

Acknowledgment. This work was supported by the National Natural Science Foundation of China (No. 61972010) and 2022 Postgraduate Research Capability Improvement Program Project.

References

1. Min, W., Jiang, S., Liu, L., Rui, Y., Jain, R.: A survey on food computing. ACM Comput. Surv **52**(5), 1–36 (2020). https://doi.org/10.1145/3329168
2. Chen, M., Jia, X., Gorbonos, E., Hoang, C.T., Yu, X., Liu, Y.: Eating healthier: exploring nutrition information for healthier recipe recommendation. Inf. Process. Manag. **57**(6), 102051 (2020). https://doi.org/10.1016/j.ipm.2019.05.012

3. Pecune, F., Callebert, L., Marsella, S.: A recommender system for healthy and personalized recipes recommendations. In: HealthRecSys@ RecSys, pp. 15–20 (2020)
4. Nilesh, N., Kumari, M., Hazarika, P., Raman, V.: Recommendation of Indian cuisine recipes based on ingredients. In: 2019 IEEE 35th International Conference on Data Engineering Workshops (ICDEW), pp. 96–99. IEEE (2019)
5. Trattner, C., Elsweiler, D.: An evaluation of recommendation algorithms for online recipe portals. In: CEUR Workshop Proceedings (2019)
6. Trattner, C., Rokicki, M., Herder, E.: On the relations between cooking interests, hobbies and nutritional values of online recipes: implications for health-aware recipe recommender systems. In: Adjunct publication of the 25th Conference on User Modeling, Adaptation and Personalization, pp. 59–64. Association for Computing Machinery, New York (2017). https://doi.org/10.1145/3099023.3099072
7. Gao, X., et al.: Hierarchical attention network for visually-aware food recommendation. IEEE Trans. Multimedia **22**(6), 1647–1659 (2019). https://doi.org/10.1109/TMM.2019.2945180
8. Gao, X., Feng, F., Huang, H., Mao, X.L., Lan, T., Chi, Z.: Food recommendation with graph convolutional network. Inf. Sci. **584**, 170–183 (2022). https://doi.org/10.1016/j.ins.2021.10.040
9. Min, W., Liu, C., Jiang, S.: Towards building a food knowledge graph for internet of food. ArXiv, abs/2107.05869 (2021)
10. Qin, L., Hao, Z., Zhao, L.: Food safety knowledge graph and question answering system. In: Proceedings of the 2019 7th International Conference on Information Technology: IoT and Smart City, pp. 559–564. Association for Computing Machinery, New York (2019). https://doi.org/10.1145/3377170.3377260
11. Haussmann, S., et al.: FoodKG: a semantics-driven knowledge graph for food recommendation. In: Ghidini, C., et al. (eds.) ISWC 2019. LNCS, vol. 11779, pp. 146–162. Springer, Cham (2019). https://doi.org/10.1007/978-3-030-30796-7_10
12. Kaggle (2018). foodRecSys-V1 (2020). https://www.kaggle.com/elisaxxygao/foodrecsysv1
13. Bollacker, K., Evans, C., Paritosh, P., Sturge, T., Taylor, J.: Freebase: a collaboratively created graph database for structuring human knowledge. In: Proceedings of the 2008 ACM SIGMOD International Conference on MANAGEMENT of data, pp. 1247–1250 (2008)
14. Lin, Y., Liu, Z., Sun, M., Liu, Y., Zhu, X.: Learning entity and relation embeddings for knowledge graph completion. In: Proceedings of the AAAI Conference on Artificial Intelligence, vol. 29, no. 1 (2015)
15. Wang, X., He, X., Cao, Y., Liu, M., Chua, T.S.: KGAT: Knowledge graph attention network for recommendation. In: Proceedings of the 25th ACM SIGKDD International Conference on Knowledge Discovery & Data Mining, pp. 950–958 (2019). https://doi.org/10.1145/3292500.3330989
16. He, X., et al.: LightGCN: simplifying and powering graph convolution network for recommendation. In: Proceedings of the 43rd International ACM SIGIR Conference on Research and Development in Information Retrieval, pp. 639–648 (2020). https://doi.org/10.1145/3397271.3401063
17. Zhang, F., et al.: Collaborative knowledge base embedding for recommender systems. In: Proceedings of the 22nd ACM SIGKDD International Conference on Knowledge Discovery and Data Mining, pp. 353–362. Association for Computing Machinery, New York (2016). https://doi.org/10.1145/2939672.2939673
18. Ai, Q., Azizi, V., Chen, X., Zhang, Y.: Learning heterogeneous knowledge base embeddings for explainable recommendation. Algorithms **11**(9), 137 (2018)
19. He, X., Chua, T.S.: Neural factorization machines for sparse predictive analytics. In: Proceedings of the 40th International ACM SIGIR Conference on Research and Development in Information Retrieval, pp. 355–364. Association for Computing Machinery, New York (2017). https://doi.org/10.1145/3077136.3080777

Visualization and Immersion: Fascination 3D

Carsten Lecon[✉]

Faculty of Computer Science, University of Applied Sciences, Aalen, Germany
carsten.lecon@hs-aalen.de

Abstract. Three-dimensional (3D) imaging has always been somewhat fascinating in its own right because it corresponds to natural spatial vision. With the increasing emergence of personal computers (PCSs), 3D applications first found their way into games and soon into "serious" applications, especially in training and education. Starting with a brief flashback, we'll look at some of the possibilities of 3D visualization per se and the uses of virtual reality in a 3D learning environment, as well as the current challenges associated with it.

Keywords: 3D visualization · 3D environment · virtual 3D room · immersion · training · education

1 Introduction

The three-dimensional representation of objects used to be reserved for art classes first, but since the 1980s, three-dimensional representations could be programmed and animated with simple computers (PCS). The display is usually on 2D screens. In order to achieve a better spatial effect, two images (for each eye) are generated from the 3D model using stereoscopy, so that a three-dimensional image results when using suitable 3D glasses. This technology is now mostly used in 3D cinema films, in which the spectators view the film with 3D glasses. Real immersion in a virtual reality (VR) application can be achieved using a 3D Head Mounted Display (HMD). This means that not only3D objects can be displayed more vividly, but one also is able to generate a spatial environment (e.g. as a learning environment).

In the following we first look at 3D Visualization (section II), then at virtual 3D environments (section III), whereby a 3D visualization can take place also in a virtual 3D environment (III.E). For both (3D visualization, virtual 3D environments) we present two examples in each case.

Furthermore, there exist some challenges in the context of using three-dimensional visualization and virtual 3D environments, some of these are depicted in section IV. The paper ends with a summary and a depicting of our next steps.

The main focus of this paper is not the detailed description of example applications, but rather the discussion of a few essential properties and the identification of the challenges in the design of 3D visualization and applications.

In this paper we only consider VR application and not general XR technologies, for example Augmented Reality (AR); some aspects considering XR learning settings in general can for example be found in [14].

© The Author(s), under exclusive license to Springer Nature Singapore Pte Ltd. 2023
W. Hong and Y. Weng (Eds.): ICCSE 2022, CCIS 1811, pp. 534–544, 2023.
https://doi.org/10.1007/978-981-99-2443-1_46

2   3D Visualization

2.1   Overview

3D visualization refers the spatial perception of human beings: The subject can be observed from all sides with adjustable size, one can look inside and can eventually interact with the 3D object. As an example, we look at the history in schools. Then this kind of presenting information already exists in the eighties of last century. Because the teaching object 'computer science' mostly was not part of the school curriculum, subject matters of the existing subjects were addressed, for example the 3D visualization of the effects of vector geometry by animated 3D figures on the screen of a personal computer (Apple IIe, …). Nowadays there exist 3D learning objects for nearly every teaching matter [3], beginning in elementary schools (application in the early childhood are in progress) [1, 12]. Up to now, 3D visualization is to find in education, training, visualization, etc. in nearly all areas.

The advantages of a computer-generated 3D visualization include:

- Any scalability
- Any level of detail
- (Color) marking of individual components of an object
- Animated exploded drawing
- Viewing from all sides, looking inside
- Display of items and even events that are no longer or not yet available
- Display of invisible thinks (wind flow, spreading viruses, electric field, etc.)
- Import of 3D data from CAD tools, geo databases, etc., since this data is also available electronically (although it may be reduced during the transfer)

Machines, objects, people (avatars), etc. available as 3D models can also be easily integrated into computer-generated virtual spaces (chapter III).

Regarding the visual presentation of the 3D subject, there exist a least three possibilities:

- *2D screen*: changing the viewpoint normally is done by mouse and keyboard. This is still the most widespread alternative and is mostly also used for computer games since no additional 3D hardware is required.
- *Head Mounted Display*: By this, a full immersion (visual and acoustic) is given. The control of the viewpoint is performed by controller, head movement, and eventually other input devices like steering wheel or pedal, etc. This alternative is more cost-intensive and require a more complex installation and calibration.
- *Augmented Reality* (AR): The 3D object is visualized by a hologram. This requires a AR glass (like *Hololens* or *Google Glass*) or an apparatus to split the 3D picture (stereoscopic) in combination with a mobile device (for example *Google Cardboard*). Because this apparatus is light weighted and cost-effective many companies can easily offer 3D presentations for their customers. Even without such an apparatus, holograms can be viewed on tablet computers and on the screen of a mobile device.

When using a 2D screen or an AR device, multiple persons can see the 3D objects inclusive the animations (at AR for the most part). The overall view to the scene is very limited, if a head mounted display is necessary. In this context, one should note, that the full immersion given by head mounted displays cannot be described, but have to be experienced oneself.

2.2 Example Applications

Of course, there exist a lot of applications. As an example, we show two rather actual approaches.

A classical and grateful subject is the archelogy: The history can be revived. As an example, in [28] the history of an UNESCO city is visualized by a virtual open-air museum (see Fig. 1).

Fig. 1. Virtual open-air museum

Another typical scope of application of virtual 3D visualization is manufacturing, for example training of workflows like in [2], see Fig. 2 (lean manufacturing training).

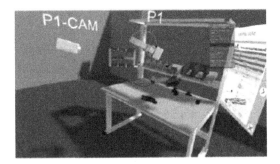

Fig. 2. Lean manufacturing training in VR

The individual work steps to be carried out can be displayed.

It is also possible to work on new, unavailable devices.

The number of training participants is not limited, since in principle an unlimited number of laboratory spaces is available.

3   Virtual 3D Environments

3.1   Overview

Even today in times of pandemics, video conference systems are a preferred communication medium. An alternative are virtual 3D environments.

Nowadays that are exist more and more providers (see subsection III.C). Virtual 3D environments are advantageous in many ways in contrast to 2D video conferences. Simple conversational situations are perceived as more natural than in 2D environments [9]. The virtual environment can be design comfortable and friendly, so that this environment can trigger relaxation, silence and pleasure at the user. The induced positive emotions can be a decisive factor for collaborative working and self-regulated learning [4, 25], which also is reinforced by the intensive flow and presence experience [29]. In general, for collaborative learning and working, the spatial and social immersion are central characteristic of these environments [11, 15] as well as the appropriate usability [20]. Spatial immersion means to feel being at another place as in reality. In addition to the proven way to use virtual environment in training scenarios [22], virtual 3D environments also allow to address a constructivism approach in teaching scenarios [5]. Because of the comparatively simple (also dynamic) adjustment of the settings, some implementations of virtual 3D environments allow an adaptive learning [26].

The technical backbone of a virtual 3D room is often a game engine. By the gameplay mechanism, acting in the virtual 3D room feels like playing a (serious) computer game, which leads (in the best case and given an appropriate didactic concept) to a 'game flow' [13]. This flow can be increased when using a head mounted display [27].

3.2   Features of Virtual 3D Environments

Some - partially distinct - properties of virtual 3D spaces are listed below.

Location-Independency: The use can participate from any place; in particular, this is interesting in times of pandemics. Since most of the available virtual 3D rooms do not place great demands on the technical equipment of the end devices (in order to serve a large, heterogeneous target group), access via mobile devices such as smartphones and tablets is usually also possible. Some systems react to a recognized overload by reducing the level of details temporarily.

Time Flexibility: Some sessions are scheduled (e.g. group discussions), otherwise the room can be used flexibly (e.g. according to the respective time zone for worldwide events).

There is a broad *spatial and social presence*. The virtual buildings, the furnishings and other (interactive) objects are adaptable to the special needs of the desired training or learning scenario. There is no distraction by for example ambient noises (road noise, projector blower, air condition system, etc.). The participants – represented as (configurable) avatars – are visible for all other participants; all see the same surrounding, for example when pointing. All persons can simultaneously interact with 3D object in the virtual world.

Anonymizing: The avatar (representation of a person) can serve like a protection shield. In this way, perhaps some people feel freer to talk and act. This presumption was confirmed in [17]: 'the relative lack of identity […] makes them less afraid to speak and more participatory'.

Recording and Replaying: Because the environment and the persons (avatars) are 'only' a piece of software, a complete session can be recorded and replayed – eventually from another point of view by adjusting the virtual camera. In addition, the recorded session can be reused as a multimedia-learning object.

The spatial presence, which can be configured as desired using virtual 3D rooms according to the desired scenario, plays a major role in training and learning and complements the didactic triangle [14], see Fig. 3.

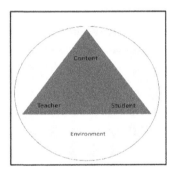

Fig. 3. Enriched didactic triangle (following [18])

3.3   Available Virtual 3D Environments

After virtual 3D learning and working spaces seemed somewhat suspicious to education providers up until the mid-1980s, there are now more and more commercial and non-commercial (sometimes also open-source) providers of virtual 3D environments. There are various business models, including:

- Temporary rental of virtual rooms (available via the Internet), possibly with (purchased) customization
- Client/Server: Local installation of a client that accesses the functionalities of the server; the available access time and the number of participants can be limited, a time extension as well as a possible adjustment of the room can be subject to a fee
- Purchase of the infrastructure with own adaptation (by programming)

There is no listing of specific providers at this point.

3.4   Example Applications

Besides of commercial training scenarios (flight simulator, operating a machine/system, rescue training, etc.,), 3D VR environments more and more are used as teaching/ learning setting in universities. One example is the transfer of teaching programming lectures from the conventional computer pool to a virtual environment [18] (Fig. 4), whereas a gamification approach lead to more motivated students. The group composition is heterogeneous in order to bring together students with different programming skills. This strategy supports as well individual learning as well learning by observation.

Fig. 4. Teaching programming in a virtual environment

In addition to many areas of application, there are now a number of 3D visualizations in the medical sector, especially for training purposes. But the training itself can also take place in 3D: In a virtual 3D environment and with 3D avatars representing the participants. A virtual 3D room is used in [17] for learning workshops (see Fig. 5). The workshops also took place with another group as a real life workshop. The comparison showed the advantages for the virtual 3D space.

Fig. 5. Medical workshop in a virtual environment

3.5 3D in 3D

Because of an easy integration of (animated) 3D objects into the virtual 3D environment, activity oriented training scenarios can be realized, where a benign interaction with these

3D objects takes place; this was early recognized [4, 19]. Also cyber-physical and even digital twins [6, 8] can be integrated in virtual 3D environments.

Up to date, the virtual 3D room mostly is visited without a head mounted display. In [16] an example is described to do and/ or record a lesson using a head mounted display. The movement of the teacher is tracked by a lightweight wireless motion capture system, the spatial learning setting as well as the teaching media (texts, images, videos, …) are integrated in der computer generated virtual 3D environment. The teacher itself sees the surrounding in which she/ he acts (see Fig. 6).

Fig. 6. Teaching in a virtual environment

4 Challenges

The use of 3D for the visualization of learning and training settings and for virtual 3D learning spaces is fascinating and more and more state of the art. However, there are some pitfalls – positively formulated: challenges – that has to be considered.

On the basis of many practical examples one can see, that these challenges are tradable in principle. And we think, that these challenge become less important in the near future.

4.1 Lack of Experience

As VR Learning is not yet widely used in training and at universities, there is currently little experience of how to design VR learning applications. Best practices or guidelines for the development of such learning applications presently rarely exist. In contrast to classical teaching methods, different aspects like motion sickness (also see section D), immersion or usability have to be considered when designing learning modules for VR (and AR). Moreover, the didactic concepts need to be adapted to the new opportunities opened up by the XR technology.

Even if a learning concept exists, further challenges follow: Which virtual 3D environment is suitable (and affordable; an in-house development is usually out of the question because of the immense effort involved) and how should the environment be adapted to the desired scenario if necessary (also depending on of the possibilities that the selected environment offers at all)? Meanwhile some providers offer appropriate editors, for example to choose the available rooms, the items (flipchart, media wall, rest room, etc.). But mostly, one has to outsource the realisation of the desired environment to the provider, or one has to implement the features – which require an open source software, software engineering professionals and a lot of time.

4.2 Interaction

The conventional user interface with foldable menu, keyboard input, mouse clicking, etc. doesn't work when wearing a head mounted display.

For this, VR techniques allow new interaction possibilities for selection and manipulation. Instead of using keyboard and mouse, in VR applications it is possible to use the full body to interact with the (virtual) worlds: Besides of using controllers, head movements and full body capture is possible. Also by eye tracking (integrated in a head mounted display), the orientation of the virtual environment can be influenced.

4.3 Head Mounted Displays

The currently available VR-Headsets are often still in the development phase and have some usability issues. Due to its size and weight, the hardware is uncomfortable to wear for a longer time and can causes headaches or neck pain. Moreover, the interaction with these devices is presently not intuitive or natural, and some users have therefore difficulties to navigate through VR applications. This could lead to a higher cognitive load, which reduces the learning effect for the users. Furthermore, usability issues can break the illusion of a VR environment. Things like the cable of the headset, the limited field of view or gestures that wasn't recognized correctly decrease the immersion and hence disturb the learning process.

All mentioned issues can negatively influence the learning effect and lower the willingness of the users to use such learning applications. However, this will change in the near future (and has partly already taken place). Due to the technological progress, the quality and usability of the headsets are getting more and better. Another problem is the heavy price for the hardware, as many educational institutions cannot equip every student with a headset at the moment. However, with the technical advancement, the devices will not only get better, but cheaper and affordable – for universities as well.

4.4 Kinetosis

One challenge in VR applications in general is the danger of the occurrence of motion sickness (kinetosis), especially when using a head mounted display (where the eyes have no possibility to other look at thinks outside the projected view of inside the glasses). Often, in a virtual environment, there is a difference between the optokinetic stimulus (of the eye) and the vestibular stimulus of the organ of equilibrium. For example, the eye sees a locomotion, but the body recognizes no or another movement. In general, the causes of the occurrence of motion sickness are not yet fully understood, but there exist some explanatory attempts, for example the Sensor Conflict Theory [23], the Postural Instability Theory [24], the Poison Theory [21] and others. The symptoms of kinetosis are dizziness, blurred vision head ache, nausea, etc. The in this way induced indisposition of the users can lead to an aversion of VR application in general, which in particular is very inconvenient at training and learning environments.

In order to avoid this negative impact, several counteractions have to be considered, although mostly the occurrence of motion sickness decreases with increasing VR experience: One can accustom to be in a virtual 3D world – to a certain degree.

Some measures to minimize motion sickness are for example:

- The persons should be in a healthy constitution; fatigue or disease increase the possibility of motion sickness.
- An adequate frame rate is necessary: a minimum of 45 Hz for each eye is recommended. This only be achieved using a powerful hardware. The update method should be programmed in a way, that flickering is avoided.
- A fix point is helpful for orientation. This can be a stable horizon, the rim of a helmet or a virtual nose [10]. We have confirmed the consequences, if no fix point is available by applying the 'rest frame theory' [7].
- Rotations of the virtual camera are critical. Sometimes, black pictures are integrated in the running rotation (which means a kind of teleportation), or the rotation is done by successively changing the degree of the rotation: 15°, 30°, etc.

An automated horizontal movement of the virtual camera should be avoided. Instead, this kind of movement should be caused be the movement of the user's head.

5   Summary and Outlook

There are fascinating possibilities of 3D in visualization and collaboration. Information transfer by means of a three-dimensional representation corresponds to natural spatial vision. Objects can be viewed from all sides, in different sizes and with an adjustable level of detail. In addition, things can be represented that no longer or not yet exist. The entire working or learning environment can also be generated: a user can "immerse" in this, disconnected from the outside world; there is a reduction to what is essential for the respective training or learning setting.

The degree of immersion will be increased for example by force feedback, especially via gloves.

Meanwhile, there exist many groups for collaboration and exchanging in the context of XR learning: In the German-speaking area for example the expert groups *Human Computer Interaction* and *Virtual Reality and Augmented Reality* of the German Society for Computer Science and the interdisciplinary network group *3D for education* in Switzerland.

Actually, in the context of an interdisciplinary research project we will explore further possibilities for virtual 3D environments for teaching at universities and for professional education.

References

1. Abott, D., Jeffrey, S., Gouseti, A., Burden, K., Maxwell, M.: Development of cross-curricular skills using 3D immersive learning environment in schools. In: Communications in Computer Science and Information Science book series (CCIS), vol. 725 (2017)
2. Badets, A., Havard, V., Richard, K., Baudry, D.: Using collaborative VR technology for lean manufactoring training: a case study. In: Laval Virtual VRIC ConVRgence 2022 Proceedings, pp. 118–127 (2020)
3. Bodenlos, E., Lennex, L.: 3D technology in schools. In: Resta, P. (Ed.) Proceedings of SITE 2012 – Society for Information Technology & Teacher Education International Conference, pp. 4209–4211. Association for the Advancement of Computing in Education (AACE), Austin (2012)
4. Boekaerts, M.: Self-regulated learning at the junction of cognition and motivation. Eur. Pychologist **1**(2), 100–112 (1996)
5. Dalgarno, B.: The potential of 3D virtual learning environments: a constructivist analysis. Electron. J. Inst. Sci. Technol. **5**(2), 2–6 (2002)
6. Dembski, F., Wassner, U., Letzgus, M.: The digital twin – tacking urban challenges with models, spatial analysis and numerical simulations in immersive virtual environments. In: eCAADe + SIGraDI Conference - Architecture in the Age of the 4th Industrial (2019)
7. Deuser, F., Schieber, H., Lecon, C.: Kinetosis Analyzation of the symptoms occurrence in combination with eye tracking. In: 15th International Conference on Information Technology & Computer Science, Athens (Greece), 20–23 May 2019, ATINER Conference Paper Series, No. COM2019–2660 (2019)
8. Qi, Q., et al.: Enabling technologies and tools for digital twin. J. Manuf. Syst. **58**(B), 3–21 (2021)
9. Garau, M., Slater, M., Vinayagamoorthy, V., Brogni, A., Steed, A., Sasse, M.A.: The impact of avatar realism and eye gaze control on perceptual quality of commuication in shared immersive virtual environments. In: Conference on Human Factors in Computing Systems – Proeeding No. 5, pp. 529–536, 2003
10. Garrision, D.R., Heather, K.: Blended learning: uncovering its D. Whittinghall, B. Ziegler, T. Case, and B. Moore, Nasum Virtualis: a simple technique for reducing simulator sickness. In: Games Developers Conference (GDC) (2015)
11. Greenwald, S.W., et al.: Technology and applications for collaborative learning in virtual reality. In: Computer-Supported Collaborative Learning Conference, CSCL, vol. 2, pp. 719–726 (2017)
12. Gusteti, M.U., Rifandi, R., Manda, T.G., Putri, M.: The devolopment of 3D animated video for mathematics learning in elementary schools. In: Journal of Physics: Conference Series, Volume 1940, The 4th International Conference on Mathematics, Science, Education and Technology (ICOMSET) in Conjunction with the 2nd International Conference on Biology, Science and Eduction (ICoBioSE), Padang, Indonesia, 22–24 July 2022 (2022)
13. Jenova, Ch.: Flow in games (and everything else). Commun. ACM **50**(4), 31–34 (2007)
14. Kansanen, P., Meri, M.: The didactic relation in the teaching-studying-learning process. In: Hudson, B., Buchberger, F., Kansanen, P., Seel, H. (eds.): Didaktik/Fachdidaktik as Science(s) of the Teaching Profession, vol. 2, no. 1, pp. 107–116. TNTEE Publications (1999)
15. Lecon, C., Herkersdorf, M.: Virtual blended learning - virtual 3D worlds and their integration in teaching scenarios. In: 9th International Conference on Computer Science and Education (IEEE ICCSE 2014), Vancouver, Canada, pp. 153–158 (2014)
16. Lecon, C., Engel, B., Schneider, L.: VR live motion capture. In: 16th International Conference on Computer Science and Education (ICCSE 2021), 17–21 August 2021, Lancester, UK (2021)

17. Lorenzo-Alvarez, R., Rudolphi-Solero, T., Ruiz-Gomez, M.J., Sendra-Portero, F.: Medical student education for abdominal radiographs in a 3D virtual classroom versus traditional classroom: a randomized controlled trial. Am. J. Roentgenol. **212**, 644–650 (2019)
18. Lueckemeyer, G.: Virtual blended learning enriched by gamification and social aspects in programming education. In: 10th International Conference on Computer Science and Education (IEEE ICCSE 2015), Cambridge, UK, pp. 438–444 (2015)
19. Mantovani, F., Castelnuovo, G.: The sense of presence in virtual training skills – aquisation and transfer of knowledge through learning experience in virtual environments. In: Riva, G., Davide, F., Ijsselsteijn, W.A. (eds.): Being There: Concepts, Effects and Measurement of User Presence in Synthetic Environments. Ios Press, Amsterdam (2003)
20. McDonald, M., Gregory, S., Farley, H., Harlim, J., Sim, J., Newman, Ch.: Coming of the third wave: a move toward best practice, user defined tools and mainstream integration for virtual worlds in education. In: Hegarty, B., McDonald, J., Loke, S.-K. (eds.) Rhetoric and Reality: Critical Perspectives on Educational Technology, Dunedin, pp. 161–170 (2014)
21. Money, K.E., Lackner, J.R., Cheung, R.S.: The autonomic nervous system and motion sickness. In: Yates, B.J., Miller, A.D. (eds.) Vestibular Autonomic Regulation, pp. 147–173. CRC, Boca Ragon (1996)
22. Moskaliuk, J., Bertram, J., Cress, U.: Training in Virtual Enviroments: Putting theory in practice. Tayler & Francis (2013)
23. Previc, F.H.: Intravestibular balance and motion sickness. Aeros. Med. Human Perf. **89**(2) (2018)
24. Ricco, G., Stoffregen, T.: An ecological theory of motion sickness and postural instability. Ecol. Psychol. **3**(3), 195–240 (1991)
25. Riva, G., et al.: Affective interactions using virtual reality: the link between presence and emotions. Cyberpsychol. Behav. **10**(1), 45–56 (2007)
26. Scott, E., Soria, A., Campo, M.: Adaptive 3D virtual learning environments – a review of the literature. IEEE Trans. Learn. Technol. **10**(3), 262–276 (2017)
27. Souchet, A.D., et al.: Virtual classroom´s quality of experience: a collaborative VR Platform Testet *in situ*. In: Laval Virtual VRIC ConVRgence 2022 Proceedings, pp. 5–12 (2020)
28. Zielasko, D., et al.: Towards preservation and availabilty of heterogenous cultural heritage research via a virtual museum. In: Meyers, B., Luering, B., Zielasko, D. (eds.) GI VR/AR Workshop, German Society for Computer Science (GI) (2022)
29. Zinn, B., Guo, Q., Saga, D.: Entwickung von und Evaluierung der virtuellen Lern- und Arbeitsumgebung VILA. J. Tech. Educ. **4**(1), 89–117 (2016) [in German]

Clinical Intelligent Interactive System Based on Optimized Hidden Markov Model

Yuan Liu[1], Yi Wang[2], Junjun Tang[1], and Tao Tao[1(✉)]

[1] School of Computer Science and Technology, Anhui University of Technology, Ma'anshan 243002, China
taotao@ahut.edu.cn
[2] Ma'anshan Maternal and Child Health Care Hospital, Ma'anshan 243002, China

Abstract. In recent years, the relationship between doctors and patients in hospitals has been relatively tense. Doctors often comfort patients in hospital on the one hand, and manually record various information on the other hand. In order to facilitate the recording of nursing information and facilitate doctors' ward rounds, the hospital needs to establish a clinical intelligent interactive system. The system can use voice to input information in the case of inconvenient manual operation. For the speech recognition module in the system, the acoustic model for speech recognition based on Hidden Markov Model is used, and by combining the specific conditions of the hospital to collect the speech of all doctors, the interaction efficiency between doctors and patients is greatly improved.

Keywords: Hidden Markov Model · Speech recognition · Intelligent interaction

1 Introduction

At present, doctors in the Maternity and Children's Health Hospital go to the ward with medical records every day, and cannot view the patient's medical record information in real time and cannot issue medical orders for patients in real time.

In order to optimize the management of medical services and continuously improve the quality of medical services, promote the harmonious development of the doctor-patient relationship, and improve the efficiency of doctors' work and ward rounds, a set of optimization-based hidden Markov model clinical intelligent interaction system is designed.

Because it has a large vocabulary, the use and development of speech recognition using hidden Markov models can more effectively ensure that the answers to patients are accurate and reliable.

As a one-stop information service platform, the system fully integrates the hospital information system through the connection of software and hardware. The system adopts a voice recognition module, allowing the system to automatically translate and record the ward rounds records; realize the voice function. Further improve the combination of the Internet and medical care, optimize the medical service management process, and reform the mobile medical care model. Therefore, the goal of effectively improving the efficiency of medical staff and improving the quality of medical services is a step across the times [1].

2   System Voice Model Design

At present, the speech recognition system mainly adopts the Hidden Markov Model. The algorithm is evolved from Markov chain and mainly consists of four parameters: initial probability distribution, observation probability, observation sequence and identification sequence. It is a parametric probability model of statistical nature used to describe random processes that appear to be disordered but regular in practice [2].

A piece of speech is actually a given disordered random process. For each moment, it only has discrete state and time parameters, and any moment is only related to the previous moment, that is, X_{N+1} is only related to X_N, but before X_{N-1} (including X_{N-1}) and after X_{N+1} (including X_{N+1}) has nothing to do, that is, it satisfies the Markov property (no aftereffect), and it is called a Markov chain at this time. A random process is called a Markov process [3].

2.1 Introduction to Hidden Markov Models

The optimized hidden Markov model used in the speech recognition function of this system is developed on the basis of the Markov chain. Compared with the Markov model, it has one more state transition probability parameter. It is a double random process. is a Markov chain describing state transitions, in which state changes are implicit, hence the name "hidden" Markov model.

A model consists of several states. After a lot of experiments, it has been proved that dividing the model into several states has the best recognition effect. In order to reduce the amount of calculation, this paper divides the model into several states. Transitions can occur between each state, and can also reside within a state. For different states, each observation vector has its own output probability [4].

A Hidden Markov Model is a quintuple (S, A, V, B, π), where:

$S = \{s1,...,sN\}$, is the state set;

$V = \{v1,...,vM\}$, is the set of output symbols;

$\pi = \{\pi 1,...,\pi N\}$, $1 \leq i \leq N$, is the initial state probability distribution;

$A = (ai,j)N*N$, is the state transition probability distribution matrix;

$B = (bj,k)N*M$, is the probability distribution matrix of state symbol transmission [5].

2.2 Speech Unit Segmentation Optimization

According to the content of the ward records for one year, all possible dictionary words are extracted from them, and then they and all single words are used as nodes to construct an n-ary segmented word graph.

The word-based n-gram grammar model is a typical generative model. Its basic idea is: first, simply match the sentence according to the dictionary to find all possible dictionary words, and then use them and all single words as nodes to construct The n-gram segmentation word graph, the nodes in the graph represent possible word candidates, the edges represent paths, and the n-gram probability on the edges represents the cost. Finally, the relevant search algorithm is used to find the path with the least cost as the final word segmentation result [6].

We set the state value function set S = (B, M, E, S), the value in the function represents the position of each word in the phrase, where B represents the first word in the phrase, M represents the middle word in the phrase, E represents the end word in the phrase, and S represents a piece of speech to be recognized; the optimal sequence is estimated by the sequence predicted in the word segmentation learning stage [7].

Take a paragraph from the ward round record: prolong the use of antibiotics after surgery; the expected sequence in the word segmentation learning stage is: BEBEBMEBEBE.

Use the sequence predicted in the learning phase to perform word segmentation to obtain the optimal sequence: BE/BE/BME/BE/BE/.

Results from the final word segmentation executionstage: postoperative/extended/antibiotics/use/time [8].

3   Overall System Design

The whole system is based on the concept of platform, deeply carries out scene customization and functional specialization, develops and connects some new subsystems, and builds the core carrier of ward doctor-patient interaction in the era of intelligent medical care [9].

The purpose of the clinical intelligent interactive system is to build a medical-nursing-patient service platform and provide more convenient service access channels for doctors, nurses and patients. Taking the patient as the center allows patients to communicate with doctors more conveniently, and enables medical staff to provide medical services more effectively Fig. 1 [10].

The system plans to use the MVP (Model-View-Presenter) model for development. MVP is the abbreviation of Model View Presenter, which is a variant of MVC architecture, emphasizing the maximum decoupling and single responsibility principle of Model and View Fig. 2 [11].

The system is mainly composed of speech recognition interaction, information interaction, bedside information presentation and other modules Fig. 3 [12].

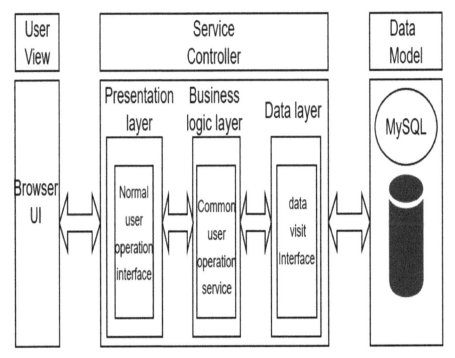

Fig. 1. Overall system architecture diagram

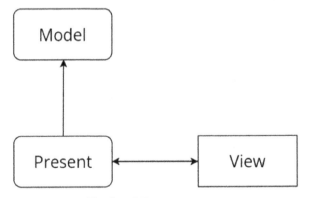

Fig. 2. MVP pattern concept

3.1 Speech Recognition Interaction Module

The bedside medical care module based on voice recognition includes two functions: doctor end and nurse end. Among them, the nurse side mainly collects body temperature, blood pressure and other signs, confirms the execution of medical orders at the bedside, and fills in forms; the doctor side mainly provides patient inspection and inspection information, medical record information, and the viewing and issuing of medical orders,

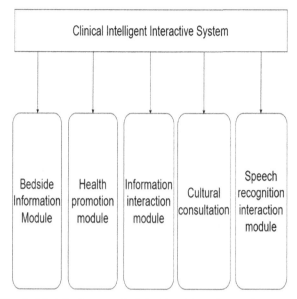

Fig. 3. Module diagram of clinical intelligent interactive system

and supports intelligent voice recognition for doctor rounds. Records are convenient for lower-level doctors to write disease course records Fig. 4 [13].

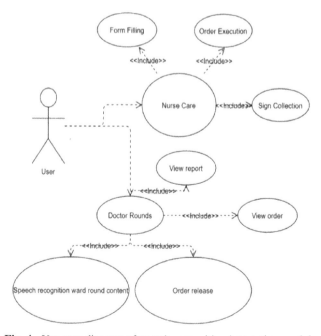

Fig. 4. Use case diagram of speech recognition interaction module

Doctors can retrieve various information of patients through the bedside rounds interface for doctors to consult, analyze and diagnose, realizing the transition from mobile rounds to bedside rounds. The bedside doctor's ward round module provides doctors with information from multiple angles, a wide field of view, and beyond the paper medical records, and becomes an effective tool for grasping the patient's condition, which is beneficial to the doctor's diagnosis and treatment of the patient. After the analysis and diagnosis, the records of the patient's condition are conveniently and quickly recorded into the memo by means of voice recognition, which reduces the errors of handwritten records and avoids unnecessary troubles Fig. 5 [14].

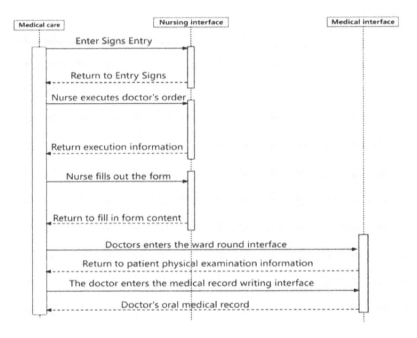

Fig. 5. Sequence diagram of speech recognition interaction module

3.2 Information Interaction Module

The information interaction module includes notification confirmation, service evaluation, message reminder, and payment and settlement. The payment and hospital system connection supports scanning code pre-payment and discharge settlement; provides a full range of message push functions, supports nurses' self-service sending, automatic payment reminders, and Check the inspection reminder function Fig. 6.

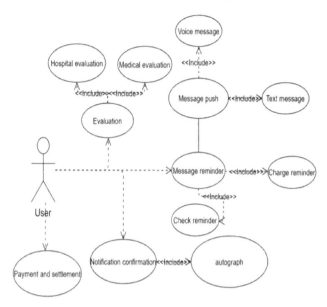

Fig. 6. Use case diagram of information interaction module

After connecting with the comprehensive payment function of the hospital's system, patients can conveniently pay and settle bills by themselves. The patient prepays the hospitalization fee by scanning the code on the mobile phone, realizing the function that the inpatient can complete the recharge function in the ward; when the patient is discharged from the hospital, the self-service settlement function is used to settle the expenses during the hospitalization, and the excess deposit will be automatically returned. To the Alipay or WeChat account of the patient's payment, the experience of the patient's hospitalization has been greatly improved [15] Fig. 7.

3.3   Bedside Information Presentation Module

The bedside information presentation module is directly connected to multiple systems in the hospital, and synchronizes various medical information such as patient identity information, medical staff information, and patient care in the ward in real time. List, inspection report and other convenient information query module. This function aims to fully implement the full sharing of medical information, enhance patients' understanding of various medical information, and reduce misunderstandings and even medical disputes caused by incomplete information acquisition Fig. 8 and Fig. 9.

The network adopts the Retrofit2 network framework, which simplifies the complexity of data access, provides synchronous and asynchronous data access methods, and improves the flexibility of network access Fig. 10.

In terms of data processing, the GreenDao data persistence framework is used to improve data access efficiency, reduce system resource overhead, and enhance the user experience of tablet operations.

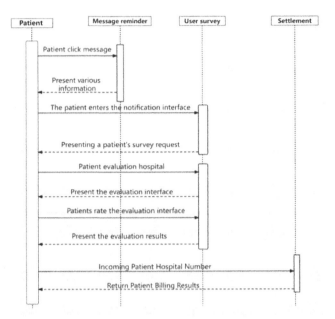

Fig. 7. Timing diagram of information interaction module

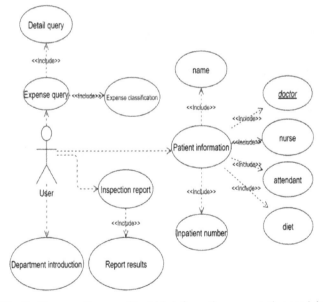

Fig. 8. Use case diagram of bedside information presentation module

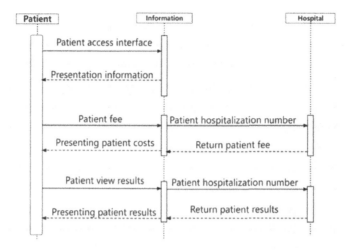

Fig. 9. Sequence diagram of bedside information presentation module

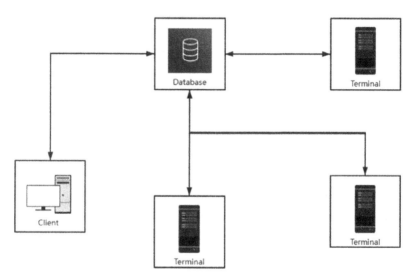

Fig. 10. Network topology

4 System Security Design

The security of the system is embodied in the security of the architecture and the security of the data.

The design of the system security architecture is based on the existing security architecture of the hospital, which realizes the security access control without destroying the protection of the existing security level of the hospital [16].

Data security is generally considered from three aspects: data integrity, confidentiality and recoverability. In terms of data integrity and confidentiality, each system adopts the HTTPS hypertext transmission security protocol in the data transmission process, and HTTPS uses SSL/TLS to process data packets. Encryption is performed, and the encryption is completed before transmission on the network, which ensures the privacy and integrity of the exchanged data. In terms of data recoverability, since the business data source of each system is the hospital business system, local synchronization is performed on a regular basis. Once the data is lost, it will be automatically recovered in the next synchronization cycle.

5 Conclusion

At present, the clinical intelligent interactive platform system has been used in a city hospital. Through the clinical intelligent interactive platform system, the patient information presentation module is connected with the hospital HIS and electronic medical record system, enabling doctors and patients to clearly understand patient information, reducing misunderstandings and even medical disputes caused by incomplete or inaccurate information.

The clinical intelligent interactive system introduced in this paper is based on tablet computer, which aims to provide services for doctors, nurses, and patients, and deeply connect with various business systems of the hospital. With the help of voice recognition technology and strict security management tools and identity authentication control, an efficient, accurate and harmonious communication interface between doctors and patients can be realized. Provide comprehensive ward information services for patients, family members, doctors, nurses, operation and maintenance personnel and hospital administrators.

In-depth understanding of the ward hospitalization model, through the construction of a future ward medical service system with the bedside intelligent interactive system as the core entrance, while providing various medical and living services for patients, we hope to strengthen the interaction between patients and medical staff to enhance patients' sense of participation in their own treatment process, so that patients can better cooperate with various medical arrangements and build a good doctor-patient relationship.

Acknowledgment. This research is supported by the Key Program of the Natural Science Foundation of the Educational Commission of Anhui Province of China (Grant No. 2022AH050319, 2022AH052740, 2022AH052713) and the Natural Science Foundation Project of Anhui Province of China (Grant No. 1908085MF212).

References

1. Cheng, P.: The application and development of AI technology in nursing. General Oral Med. Electron. J. **27**, 13 + 15 (2019)
2. Adams, S., Beling, P.A.: A survey of feature selection methods for Gaussian mixture models and hidden Markov models. Artif. Intell. Rev. **52**(3), 1739–1779 (2017). https://doi.org/10.1007/s10462-017-9581-3

3. Wu, S., Wu, W., Yang, X., Lu, Lu., Liu, K., Jeon, G.: Multifocus image fusion using random forest and hidden Markov model. Soft Comput. **23**(19), 9385–9396 (2019). https://doi.org/10.1007/s00500-019-03893-9

4. Calvo-Zaragoza, J., Toselli, A.H., Vidal, E.: Hybrid hidden Markov models and artificial neural networks for handwritten music recognition in mensural notation. Patt. Anal. Appl. **22**(4), 1573–1584 (2019). https://doi.org/10.1007/s10044-019-00807-1

5. Kordnoori, S., Mostafaei, H., Behzadi, M.H.: PSO Optimized Hidden Markov Model Performance Analysis for IEEE 802.16/WiMAX Standard. Wireless Pers. Commun. **108**(4), 2461–2476 (2019). https://doi.org/10.1007/s11277-019-06533-5

6. Yu, F.-H., Lu, J., Gu, J.-W., Ching, W.-K.: Modeling Credit Risk with Hidden Markov Default Intensity. Comput. Econ. **54**(3), 1213–1229 (2018). https://doi.org/10.1007/s10614-018-9869-7

7. Zehnder, T., Benner, P., Martin, V.: Predicting enhancers in mammalian genomes using supervised hidden Markov models. 20(1) (2019). https://doi.org/10.1186/s12859-019-2708-6

8. Rahman, M.S., Haffari, G.: Analyzing tumor heterogeneity by incorporating long-range mutational influences and multiple sample data into heterogeneity factorial hidden Markovmodel. J. Comput. Biol. 26(9) (2019)

9. Du, Y., Dong, D., Ma, F., Xue, Z., Yuan, L., Lv, Y.: Application progress of artificial intelligence in the field of nursing. PLA Nursing J. **36**(04), 58–61 (2019)

10. Zhao, Y., Ma, Y.: Research on the development of nursing career under the background of artificial intelligence and big data. Softw. **40**(06), 173–175+196 (2019)

11. Ting, C.: Design and implementation of future ward medical service system based on bedside intelligent interaction. China New Technol. New Products **05**, 30–34 (2019)

12. Lili, H.: Several attempts of basic experimental teaching of nursing based on intelligent cloud teaching. Guangdong Vocational Tech. Educ. Res. **01**, 165–166 (2019)

13. Jie, F., Wanqi, H., Aoxue, Z.: Analysis of the application of intelligent informatization in clinical nursing. Bohai Rim Economic Outlook **02**, 196 (2019)

14. Zhao, X., Zhang, Y.: A review of the construction of acoustic models for speech keyword recognition systems. J. Yanshan Univ. **41**(06), 471–481 (2017)

15. Liu, P., Yunan, S., Hong, L.: Research on speech recognition system based on deep learning. New Indust. **8**(05), 70–74 (2018)

16. Yang, Z., Sun, Li., De, M.: Research on speech recognition system based on HMM model. Internet Things Technol. **7**(10), 74–76 (2017)

Exploring Motivation in Oral English Learning Among Chinese English Majors Through Mobile-Assisted Service Learning

Hui Yan⬤, Yifan Chen⬤, Nan Wang⬤, Yuxin Zhao⬤, and Ying Lu$^{(\boxtimes)}$⬤

NingboTech University, No. 1 South Qianhu Road, Ningbo, China
luying@nbt.edu.cn

Abstract. This research examines Chinese English majors' motivation in oral English learning and the influence of WeChat and DingTalk in the light of Self-Determination Theory (SDT). A mobile-assisted service-learning project initiated by NingboTech University is reported. Two types of motivation including controlled motivation (external regulation and introjected regulation) and autonomous motivation (identified regulation and integrated regulation) are measured during three stages of the project. The results suggest that external regulation does not provide lasting motivation, while identified regulation and integrated regulation both play vital roles in students' oral English learning. Well-designed projects with more responsibility can activate and sustain students' autonomous motivation. The utilization of mobile technology also plays a significant role throughout the project.

Keywords: ESL Motivation · Oral English · Self-determination Theory · Mobile Learning · Service Learning

1 Introduction

In China, ESL students' wish to learn oral English well is common, but the wish is not always effectively translated into sustainable motivations because opportunities for real communication after class are relatively limited. Such limitations are more obvious during the COVID-19 epidemic starting from 2020, because cross-border exchange has shrunk and regular epidemic prevention in daily lives has led to reduced offline activities like English corners. For English majors, the chances of speaking English in authentic cross-cultural settings have also lessened due to the lack of foreign teachers on campus resulting from international travel restrictions. It is important for universities to provide their students with new modes of oral English learning. Fortunately, the popularity of mobile Internet applications has opened up many new possibilities.

A considerable amount of literature has already been published on ESL/EFL motivation, including the impact of service learning and mobile technology. Among various researches on motivation, Self-Determination Theory (SDT) is one of the most influential propositions. According to Ryan and Deci, there are controlled motivation and autonomous motivation [1]. Controlled motivation is activated by external incentives and comprises external regulation and introjected regulation, while autonomous motivation arises out of genuine interest and personal volition and consists of identified regulation, integrated regulation and intrinsic regulation, as shown in Fig. 1 [1].

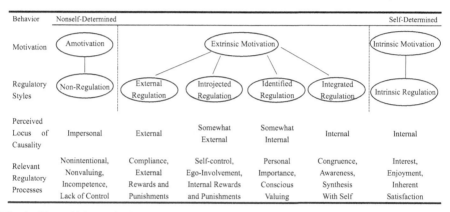

Fig. 1. The self-determination continuum showing types of motivation with their regulatory styles, loci of causality, and corresponding processes

1.1 Self-determination Theory in ESL/EFL

There have been a lot of researches on the relationship between second language learning and motivation. Promoting students' motivation is believed to be a key step towards improving classroom atmosphere and making learning more effective and persistent [2]. It is found that novel and different activities are more likely to develop intrinsic motivation among FL learners [3]. Studies also show that students' endorsement of autonomous type of motivation is linked to increased amount of engagement with the target language community [4].

Previous research has also shown that the use of mobile technology applications like WhatsApp in language learning settings contributes to the development of learners' autonomy, the reduction of their anxiety, and the enhancement of their language skills including reading, listening, writing, and speaking [5].

1.2 Self-determination Theory in Service Learning

Service learning is defined as a form of experiential education in which students participate in activities that meet the identified needs of human and community. It also features structured opportunities for reflection in such a way as to realize desired learning outcomes [6]. In recent decades, service learning pedagogy has been applied in plenty of higher education institutes to encourage active learning, by associating students' community service and classroom learning [7]. Based on self-determination theory (SDT), many studies examine students' perception of learning and level of motivation in service-learning courses. One study shows that service learning creates an autonomy-supportive learning environment, and therefore students gain benefits through this experience [8]. Moreover, various scholars have noted that service learning can also be combined with modern online learning [9, 10]. By integrating service learning with the online platform in oral English training course, Yu-Chih Sun & Fang-Ying Yang find that both the skills of students and their confidence in public speaking have been enhanced. The project also fosters a sense of accomplishment and increases students' motivation in L2 learning [11].

1.3 Self-determination Theory in Online Learning

Based on SDT, some researchers have analyzed student motivation and engagement in the online learning environment. Studies have found a relation between using WhatsApp, an instant messaging application, and students' autonomous motivation in the field of mobile-assisted language learning [5]. In addition, Chiu's research indicates that three basic psychological needs in SDT—autonomy (feeling self-governed and self-endorsed), competence (feeling competent and effective), and relatedness (feeling connected and loved)—have an influence on student engagement in online learning. Digital support strategies are also emphasized [12].

1.4 WeChat and DingTalk in Language Learning

In China, instant messaging applications like WeChat and DingTalk penetrate users' lives and provide them with a new form of communication and a new platform of language learning. WeChat and DingTalk both have the following merits for language learning [13].

Multi-functionality. Users can enjoy various messaging functions, including texts, photos, voice messages, video calls and conference calls, which to a great extent facilitate learners' study.

Individuality. Users can communicate online with each other freely in an informal way without trying to meet the task-specific requirements in the traditional classroom settings. This provides learners with a kind of personalized, relaxed, intimate, and private learning experience.

Accessibility. As of December 2021, the total number of mobile phone base stations had reached 9.96 million in China [14]. Mobile phone users have easy access to the Internet in both urban and rural areas. This provides people with new opportunities to learn language online in the post-pandemic era without the limitation of time and space.

Interactivity. Emojis, stickers and memes shared by users can help generate more interest in communication, which may consequently boost learners' motivation.

Affordability. Users can send and receive messages and make calls free of charge as long as they have an existing Internet data plan. Therefore, instant messaging applications allow learners to communicate with others at low cost.

Though researches on motivation in oral English learning abound, previous published studies are mostly limited to SDT and second language learning in general, or focus on one factor such as online technology or service learning. Reports on integrated projects are relatively scarce. Based on the mobile-assisted service-learning project at NingboTech University (NTU), we intend to explore the synergy of different methods in enhancing motivation for oral English learning.

2   The Project and Research Questions

2.1   The Service-Learning Project

With China's increasing exchange with the world in the medical field, many healthcare professionals in Ningbo wish to improve their oral English. In November 2021, the School of International Studies of NTU initiated an online volunteer program named "Days with Angels" to help the healthcare professionals to practice spoken English on a one-to-one basis. 29 healthcare professionals and 21 English major students were enrolled in the program. After a speaking test conducted by both NTU teachers and Ningbo-UCAS (University of Chinese Academy of Science) Clinical Teaching Center, 16 students were assigned to the oral communication group. Among them, 10 are in junior year, 5 in senior year and 1 in the freshman year. All the 15 juniors and seniors have won awards in English contests, including English speaking contest, interpretation competition, etc. 2 students have overseas study experience. Each volunteer is responsible for 1–3 doctor(s)/nurse(s). All the students followed the regulations for volunteering projects of NTU, and were credited with volunteering hours.

During the 10-week online program (from Jan. 22, 2022 to Apr. 10, 2022, with a break during Chinese Spring Festival), each student had English conversation with a doctor/nurse for about 1 h per week on average. The activity was conducted through synchronous video calls or voice calls in DingTalk and WeChat. Topics for the conversations are as listed in Table 1. In order to have sufficient preparation for the online conversations, 49 articles, 26 videos and 4 audios related to the topics were collected beforehand by both the teachers and the students. They were all shared in the DingTalk group. Students chose the materials that they perceived as helpful to share with their partners during the communication.

Table 1. Topic for each week during the project

Time	Topic
Week 1	English learning
Week 2	Gratitude
Week 3	Traditional Chinese festivals
Week 4	Sports and hobbies
Week 5	Health
Week 6	Charity and volunteering
Week 7	Comfort Zone
Week 8	Technology and human life
Week 9	Trust
Week 10	Pandemic

2.2 Research Questions

Though there have been plenty of researches on motivation in second language learning on the basis of SDT, there is still a gap regarding motivation driven by novel and unique designs of service learning empowered by mobile technology. Therefore, this study intends to analyze the specific and dynamic motivations derived from new incentives like technology, curiosity and sense of responsibility, etc. so as to explore new ways of oral English learning. Three research questions are raised as follows:

1) What specific motivations do students have in oral English learning in the service learning project?
2) How do English majors' controlled motivation and autonomous motivation evolve during the different stages of the project?
3) Would students' autonomous motivation in learning oral English be enhanced with the help of mobile technology applications like WeChat and DingTalk?

3 Methodology

3.1 Reflective Reports

As part of the requirement of volunteering programs of NTU, students were asked to write reflective reports about their work procedure, feelings, gains and reflections during the mobile-assisted service learning. The reports are also used to gain more insight into participants' feedback towards this activity and their learning strategies. Each student described his/her own feelings and thoughts during the project in Chinese. The researchers collected them and extracted keywords and themes from the reports. They help to have a comprehensive understanding of oral English learning motivation in this project.

3.2 Questionnaire

To survey participants' oral English learning motivation in this project, a questionnaire is designed according to 4 motivation categories based on the self-determination theory. The items aim at a better understanding of two motivation types: controlled motivation and autonomous motivation. The former includes external and introjected regulation, and the latter includes identified regulation and intrinsic motivation. Since different types of regulation constitute a continuum in SDT [1], integrated regulation is combined with intrinsic regulation in our research so that questions targeted at those internal factors would be more direct and comprehensible. The questionnaire consists of 3 parts. The first part is for the registration period, the second for speaking material preparation stage, and the last part for the session of online conversations.

The questionnaire is designed in Chinese to ensure accurate understanding by the participants. The participants choose the answer according to a 5-point scale: strongly disagree = 1, disagree = 2, uncertain or unsure = 3, agree = 4, strongly agree = 5. There are 29 questions in this questionnaire, and the specific items will be shown in Part IV. The students answered the questions through a popular online survey platform in China named "Wenjuanxing".

3.3 Interview

We interviewed sixteen students on a one-to-one basis via WeChat online voice calls. Each interview took about 20–30 min and was conducted in Chinese to ensure a thorough communication without misunderstanding. The interview questions were mainly centered around the impact of WeChat and DingTalk on their oral English learning motivation in the project. Students were encouraged to describe their feeling or give some advice for the project. The guiding questions of the interview include:

1) Are you interested in mobile-assisted service learning? How does the technology influence your extrinsic and intrinsic motivations?
2) How does mobile technology (e.g., WeChat & DingTalk) impact on your oral English learning motivations in the three stages of the service-learning project?
3) Which feature of mobile terminal technology do you think best facilitates your language learning during the ten-week project?

4 Results and Analysis

4.1 Reflective Reports

Among the 16 students, 15 reflective reports were collected. One student did not submit the report because his partner was too busy to continue learning after two weeks. Therefore, he was not required to submit the report. The reports show students' methods of oral English communication and their personal gains during the NTU project of mobile-assisted service learning, as well as their advice for future practice. The common features are as follows:

Communication Methods. All the students communicated with doctors/nurses on WeChat and DingTalk via voice calls, video calls and online conferences. Most of them communicate with each other in the form of free talk. Several participants also adopted Q&A, role play, etc. to better satisfy the learning need of the healthcare professionals. Besides, all students would share learning materials with their partners to help them improve oral English. They used the materials shared by the whole team and also add some tailored supplements according to the need of the speaking partners.

Gains and Areas to Be Improved. The gains mentioned by students include improvement in oral English, the joy of oral English communication, a broadened horizon and more confidence, etc.. Students also reflected on the areas to be further improved in their oral English learning, for example, the need to expand vocabulary.

We measured students' gains according to Bloom's taxonomy of educational objectives [15]. As shown in Table 2, 14 students mentioned cognitive enhancement (93.3%). Among them, 13 (86.7%) reported improvement in communication skills and oral English in terms of complexity, accuracy and fluency (CAF). 11 reported positive affective experiences (73.3%), including vision, confidence, self-development, friendship and enjoyment in communication.

Table 2. Gains perceived by students

Taxonomy	Number of students	Proportion
Cognitive domain	14	93.3%
Affective domain	11	73.3%

4.2 Questionnaire

According to the result of the questionnaire, at the very beginning of the volunteering project, namely the registration period, all the four dimensions of motivation—external regulation, introjected regulation, identified regulation, and intrinsic motivation had a relatively high score. With the progress of the project, external regulation (the motivation to participate in the activities in order to obtain instrumental results) weakened significantly. However, introjected regulation remained stable, and the rest two dimensions showed a little fluctuation but went back to the original level in the conversation period. Figure 2 depicts the four dimensions of motivation throughout the three periods.

Four Dimensions of Motivation Throughout Three Periods

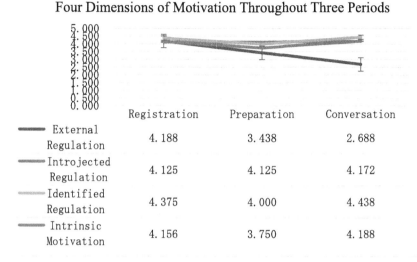

	Registration	Preparation	Conversation
▬ External Regulation	4.188	3.438	2.688
▬ Introjected Regulation	4.125	4.125	4.172
▬ Identified Regulation	4.375	4.000	4.438
▬ Intrinsic Motivation	4.156	3.750	4.188

Fig. 2. Four dimensions of motivation throughout three periods

During the Registration period, participants showed high motivation, especially in the field of identified regulation, which includes their aspiration to improve oral English, respect for doctors and sense of purpose by contributing what they could do as English-major students. Also, the participants admitted that they were interested in the service-learning project because it provided a new experience, and they were curious about the communication with doctors. They might feel regretful for missing the chance. Table 3 shows the four dimensions of motivation during the Registration Period.

Table 3. Four dimensions of motivation in registration period

Dimension	Mean	Std. Deviation	Variance
External Regulation			
1.1 Being Beneficial to my future career	4.188	0.882	0.777
Introjected Regulation			
2.1 Feeling regretful if missing the chance	4.125	0.927	0.859
Identified Regulation			
3.1 To improve oral English	4.375	0.899	0.809
3.2 To do as an English-majored student	4.438	0.704	0.496
3.3 To respect doctors	4.313	0.768	0.590
Intrinsic Motivation			
4.1 Desire of a new experience in serve learning	4.1864	0.784	0.614
4.2 Curiosity about communicating with doctors	4.125	0.927	0.859

When it came to the period of preparation, the external regulation (for instance, requirements for the project), and intrinsic motivation (for example, enjoying preparing for the oral communication) both declined a little bit, because there was no real communication at this stage. But motivations like "to learn new knowledge and broaden horizon", "to obtain a sense of achievement" and "to value the preparatory process" still had a high score above 4. Table 4 illustrates the four dimensions of motivation in Preparation Period.

Table 4. Four dimensions of motivation in preparation period

Dimension	Mean	Std. Deviation	Variance
External Regulation			
1.3 Requirements for the project	3.437	0.964	0.929
Introjected Regulation			
2.2 Self shame if not doing well	4.125	1.025	1.050
Identified Regulation			
3.4 To gain respect and admiration of doctors	3.563	0.964	0.929
3.5 To learn something new and broaden horizon	4.313	0.793	0.629
3.6 To obtain a sense of achievement	4.125	0.719	0.517
3.7 To value the preparatory process	4.000	0.632	0.400
Intrinsic Motivation			
4.3 Enjoying preparing for the oral communication	3.750	0.683	0.467

At the phase of conversation, participants had an overall increase in three dimensions of motivation. But the score for external regulation, i.e., to obtain the certification of volunteering project, went even lower. The service-learning project motivated participants to be a reliable partner capable of helping others, to meet doctors'/nurses' expectations and to enhance the sense of responsibility. They said they would feel regretful if not doing well, and they didn't want to affect the reputation of the school. Table 5 demonstrates the four dimensions of motivation in Conversation Period.

Table 5. Four dimensions of motivation in conversation period

Dimension	Mean	Std. Deviation	Variance
External Regulation			
1.3 Certification of voluntary project	2.688	1.250	1.563
Introjected Regulation			
2.3 Being a reliable partner capable of helping doctors	4.438	0.629	0.396
2.4 Affecting our reputation if not doing well	3.875	0.885	0.783
2.5 Feeling regretful if not doing well	4.000	0.894	0.800
2.6 To meet their expectations in oral communication	4.375	0.719	0.517
Identified Regulation			
3.8 Self obligation	4.375	0.957	0.917
3.9 To improve oral English through a successful communication	4.500	0.633	0.400
Intrinsic Motivation			
4.4 Enjoying a successful oral communication	4.188	0.834	0.696

4.3 Interview

According to the interview, despite the fact that every student had his or her own special motivation stimulated by technology, they also shared something in common. At the registration period, what motivated the students most was that technology (e.g., Wechat & Dingtalk) could provide a private, undisturbed and productive environment for oral English communication, which could ease the tension caused by face-to-face meeting, provide a flexible arrangement rather than fixed one and also save the time spent on commuting. During the period of preparation, technology played an important role in information search and material storage. For example, through DingTalk, students could share PowerPoints, videos and other documents with doctors, thus enriching the forms of oral English learning for both parties involved. At the phrase of conversation, it was the technology that rendered a better interaction between doctors and students by means of video calls, voice calls and exchange of short messages. Additionally, the mobile-assisted service learning did appeal to students a lot for the chance to serve others together with the specific aim to improve themselves, which in turn enhanced the efficiency of oral English practice. The following are excerpts from the students' answers towards the motivation brought by the technology.

Student 1: Conduced online, this project helps to avoid the nervousness in the communication process to a certain extent and draws the distance between me and doctors closer. Also, the abundant resources online are of great help for my oral English learning.

Student 6: It really helps to share PowerPoints and audios with them, which caters to their personalized needs.

5 Discussions and Conclusions

5.1 Discussions

This study focuses on Chinese English majors' specific motivations in oral English service learning and the impact of WeChat and Dingtalk, with a purpose of putting forward some suggestions for improving students' enthusiasm in speaking English.

Above all, it is found that the mean score of overall motivation in this project is about 4.21, which is a relatively high number compared with the previous studies. It indicates the effectiveness of the activity to a certain extent. The success of the project is also proved by the reflective reports of the participants. 13 of them report improvement in oral English (86.7%), including CAF and communication skills.

A closer look at the specific items in the questionnaire reveals that the high-score motivations (above 4.3) include improving oral English, self obligation, broadening horizons, respect for doctors and so on, which generally belong to autonomous motivation. The low-score items (below 3.5) include obtaining certification of volunteering project, project requirements, etc., which belong to external regulation and controlled motivation.

Through a further analysis, changes can be seen across different stages of the project. Controlled motivation fails to exert a long-term impact on students' oral English learning, while autonomous motivations, especially interest, self-obligation, self-worth and self-development, have stimulated students' enthusiasm in oral English learning to a great extent.

The dynamic picture of students' motivations, to some extent, indicates the effectiveness of real cooperative learning brought by the project. Students and healthcare professionals exchange ideas in English and capitalize on each other's resources, which not only improves the oral English competence of both parties, but also contributes to the enhancement of their autonomous motivations.

The high motivation of the participants in this study suggests the value of novel designs in service-learning activities. The present project introduces new communicators, namely healthcare professionals eager to improve oral English, and new communication platforms like WeChat and DingTalk. Stimulated by the new mode, students' motivation in learning oral English is greatly enhanced. Though the healthcare professionals have advanced education degrees and can perform well in medical English reading, most of them feel inadequate in oral English, because they don't have many chances to speak the language in their lives. Thus, English majors in universities have a "comparative advantage" in this respect. Through helping doctors/nurses, students are greatly motivated by self-obligation, self-worth and self-development. Therefore, some innovations can be made in traditional oral English communication activities. Teachers might incorporate more challenging tasks related to the real world and targeted at autonomous motivation. Meanwhile, sufficient support is very important so as to help students meet the challenges. It is also interesting to notice that the motivation related to collectivism in Chinese culture (e.g. sense of responsibility) contributes significantly to students' language learning. This provides schools and teachers with inspiration about the potential to make full use of culture-specific factors in activity design.

Furthermore, technology also contributes to the high motivation among students at different stages of the project. Mobile applications like Wechat & Dingtalk provide an ideal environment for students to practice oral English and serve doctors at the same time. The convenience and functional diversity of the mobile platforms cater to both students' and doctors' needs to engage in oral English communication in a more interesting and efficient way. Also, technology renders students a new and rare chance to improve oral English through real conversations with people outside school. In addition, thanks to the support from such platforms, exploration about new educational possibilities under the concept of "Internationalization at Home" is made possible during and after COVID-19 epidemic.

However, technology also has its own weakness. First of all, there must be a stable connection to the Internet, without which people involved couldn't achieve satisfactory communication and might feel a sense of frustration due to low efficiency. Secondly, online communication lacks the multidimensional interaction of face-to-face communication, an indispensable part of productive interpersonal relations. Therefore, in the future, we can combine the online and offline communication or arrange different ways according to the specific needs of students and doctors/nurses.

There are still some limitations in this project. The sample size of participants is small ($N = 16$). The specific motivations that Chinese English majors have in learning oral English in this project might not have universal significance. However, positive feedback from participants suggests that this project should continue and expand its scale to welcome more students from different major backgrounds, which will help to reduce the study limitations. Moreover, the present research is based on a ten-week project. It is not yet clear whether the motivation is sustainable for a longer time. But some participants have mentioned their plan to get involved in the project again because it has offered them opportunities to improve oral English and provided benefits for personal growth. Therefore, it is worthwhile to carry on the project, and further research from a long-term perspective will help us to better understand learners' motivation.

5.2 Conclusions

In conclusion, this study explores Chinese English majors' motivation in oral English learning through a mobile-assisted service-earning project. The mobile platforms (Wechat and Dingtalk) provide new environments for students to communicate with others and practice oral English by taking advantage of the diverse functions such as multimodal messages, voice calls, video calls and many others. These advantages, when combined with creative designs of oral English activities, can produce a strong synergy in enhancing students' motivation. As the findings demonstrate, the mobile-assisted service-learning project not only motivates the students greatly, but also promote their English-speaking skills (e.g., complexity, accuracy and fluency). In addition, the project helps students to develop oral English learning strategies and time management skills. Educational objectives in both the cognitive and affective domains are satisfactorily achieved.

As most educational institutions have to adjust their teaching modes during the COVID-19 epidemic and online learning becomes widespread, mobile-assisted service learning can be a new choice for colleges in designing curriculum in the digital age. Given more real-world opportunities and being engaged in well-designed projects, students can become more active in language learning and find both enjoyment and sense of achievement.

Acknowledgment. The authors gratefully acknowledge the research project "Language Service for 'Internationalization at Home' in Health-care System in the Post-COVID-19 Era" supported by China's National Program of Undergraduate Innovation and Entrepreneurship (No. 20700540605/008). Thanks to all the volunteer students for their participation in the questionnaire and interviews. Special thanks to the Deputy Dean of the School of International Studies of NTU, Professor Cai Liang, for his support throughout the project.

References

1. Ryan, R.M., Deci, E.L.: Self-determination theory and the facilitation of intrinsic motivation, social development, and well-being. Am. Psychol. **55**(1), 68–78 (2000). https://doi.org/10.1037//0003-066x.55.1.68
2. Alqurashi, F.A.: The effects of motivation on EFL college students' achievement. Stud. Engl. Lang. Teach. **7**(1), 83–98 (2019). https://doi.org/10.22158/selt.v7n1p83
3. Printer, L.: Student perceptions on the motivational pull of Teaching Proficiency through Reading and Storytelling (TPRS): a self-determination theory perspective. Lang. Learn. J. **49**(3), 288–301 (2021). https://doi.org/10.1080/09571736.2019.1566397
4. Noels, K.A., Clément, R., Pelletier, L.G.: Intrinsic, extrinsic, and integrative orientations of French Canadian learners of English. Can. Mod. Lang. Rev. **57**(3), 424–442 (2001). https://doi.org/10.3138/cmlr.57.3.424
5. Alamer, A., Al Khateeb, A.: Effects of using the WhatsApp application on language learners motivation: a controlled investigation using structural equation modelling. Comput. Assist. Lang. Learn. **36**(3), 1–27 (2021). https://doi.org/10.1080/09588221.2021.1903042
6. Jacoby, B., Howard, J.: Service-Learning Essentials: Questions, Answers, and Lessons Learned. Jossey-Bass, San Francisco (2015)
7. Bennett, D., Sunderland, N., Bartleet, B.L., Power, A.: Implementing and sustaining higher education service-learning initiatives: revisiting Young et al.'s organizational tactics. J. Exp. Educ. **39**(2), 145–163 (2016). https://doi.org/10.1177/1053825916629987
8. Levesque-Bristol, C., Stanek, L.R.: Examining self-determination in a service learning course. Teach. Psychol. **36**(4), 262–266 (2009). https://doi.org/10.1080/00986280903175707
9. Bourelle, T.: Adapting service-learning into the online technical communication classroom: a framework and model. Tech. Commun. Q. **23**(4), 247–264 (2014). https://doi.org/10.1080/10572252.2014.941782
10. Waldner, L.S., McGorry, S.Y., Widener, M.C.: E-service learning: the evolution of service-learning to engage a growing online student population. J. High. Educ. Outreach Engage. **16**(2), 123–150 (2012)
11. Sun, Y., Yang, F.: I help, therefore, I learn: service learning on Web 2.0 in an EFL speaking class. Comput. Assist. Lang. Learn. **28**(3), 202–219 (2015). https://doi.org/10.1080/09588221.2013.818555
12. Chiu, T.K.F.: Applying the Self-determination Theory (SDT) to explain student engagement in online learning during the COVID-19 pandemic. J. Res. Technol. Educ. **54**(sup1), S14–S30 (2021). https://doi.org/10.1080/15391523.2021.1891998
13. Shi, Z., Luo, G., He, L.: Mobile-assisted language learning using WeChat instant messaging. Int. J. Emerg. Technol. Learn. **12**(2), 16–26 (2017). https://doi.org/10.3991/ijet.v12i02.6681
14. CNNIC Homepage. https://www.cnnic.com.cn/IDR/ReportDownloads/. Accessed 24 Apr 2022
15. Bloom, B.S.: Taxonomy of educational objectives: the classification of educational goals: handbook I: cognitive domain. Longmans, Green and Company, Toronto (1956)

Intelligent Positioning Management System of Slag Tanks Based on RFID Technology

Junjun Tang, Xiaoyan Wang, Yuan Liu, and Tao Tao[✉]

School of Computer Science and Technology, Anhui University of Technology,
Ma'anshan 243002, China
taotao@ahut.edu.cn

Abstract. With the continuous development of Industry, the disadvantages of the traditional management methods of slag tanks in steel factory gradually appear, which resulting in the low management efficiency and the high management cost. Aimed to achieve digital management, the intelligent positioning management platform of slag tanks is designed, which implementing the positioning of the slag tanks by RFID technology, data collection and so on. The operation results show that the system greatly improves the production efficiency.

Keywords: Intelligent Positioning · Slag Tanks · RFID

1 Introduction

In the process of producing iron and water in steel companies, high temperature slag will be generated. Enterprises need to transport high temperature slag to the next production unit, and then cool with water. In this process, a container needs to be used, which is a slag tank.

With the continuous development of steel companies, the disadvantages of the production and management methods of traditional slag tank gradually appear. Traditional management methods cannot accurately understand the specific location of the slag tanks. Each slag tank cannot be corresponding to the position. This makes it impossible to understand the production data information at each position. Secondly, during the transportation process of the slag tanks, the position of the slag tanks cannot be understood. As a result, the manager cannot use the idle slag tanks for production and transportation, resulting in low management efficiency. Third, managers need to understand the number of available positions in real time in order to transport the slag tanks by transport personnel. Finally, because high -temperature furnaces may cause damage to the slag tanks, the demand for production after all slag tanks is also urgently needed to prevent waste of resources.

In order to solve these problems, we design this system, the goal is to realize the slag tank management remote centralized monitoring, establish information collection and analysis platform. To meet the needs of slag tank management and improve production efficiency.

2 Passive RFID Localization Algorithm Based on RSSI

Some areas of the steel plant need to know the location of the slag tanks. When the slag pot location exceeds the designated area or the personnel enter a specific dangerous area, the alarm event is triggered. Therefore, this system adopts the RSSI-based localization algorithm, which is low in cost and does not need additional equipment. It only needs to ensure the normal work of the reader to achieve localization.

2.1 Formula of Signal Attenuation

Based on RSSI localization algorithm, by measuring the RSSI value of the target node in the test environment, using the signal propagation attenuation model, the loss value caused by the path loss in the process of information propagation is calculated, and then the linear distance between the target node and the signal sending point is obtained. By selecting the appropriate algorithm, the coordinate information of the target node is obtained [1]. When the attenuation degree of the signal is correlated with the propagation distance, the logarithmic distance path loss model that ignores the accidental error ζ is often used, and the formula is:

$$P = P_0 - 10nlg\frac{d}{d_0} \tag{1}$$

where P_0 represents the energy intensity at d_0 meters from the signal source (empirical reference value); P is the energy intensity at d meters from the signal source (the signal receiving intensity of the reader), the unit is dbm; n Represents path loss index; d represents the distance between the reader and the label, the unit is m; d_0 is the reference distance, usually $1\ m$ [2].

2.2 Least-Square Method

The least square method is based on RSSI ranging and positioning principle, which is solved by likelihood estimation through simultaneous equations [3].

As shown in the diagram, assuming that n ($n \geq 3$) readers are deployed, the corresponding coordinates are: $(x_1, y_1), (x_2, y_2), (x_3, y_3), \cdots, (x_n, y_n)$.

When the system is running, according to the signal strength received by the reader, the distance between each reader coordinate and the measuring point is calculated by combining the signal energy attenuation model: $(d_1, d_2, d_3, \cdots, d_n)$ (see Fig. 1).

According to the reader coordinate and its distance vector with the measuring point, the equation set is established as follows:

$$\begin{cases} (x_1 - x)^2 + (y_1 - y)^2 = d_1{}^2 \\ \quad\quad\quad \vdots \\ (x_n - x)^2 + (y_n - y)^2 = d_n{}^2 \end{cases} \tag{2}$$

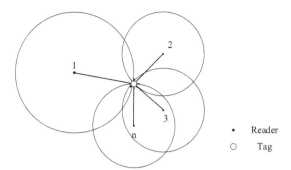

Fig. 1. Diagram of least square method

Each equation in equation group (2) minus the last equation shall:

$$\begin{cases} x_1{}^2 - x_n{}^2 - 2(x_1 - x)x + y_1{}^2 - y_n{}^2 - 2(y_1 - y_n)y = d_1{}^2 - d_n{}^2 \\ \vdots \\ x_{n-1}{}^2 - x_n{}^2 - 2(x_{n-1} - x)x + y_{n-1}{}^2 - y_n{}^2 - 2(y_{n-1} - y_n)y = d_{n-1}{}^2 - d_n{}^2 \end{cases} \tag{3}$$

According to the characteristics of Eq. (3), it can be denoted as $AX^T = b$, where A, X, b are all matrices, and X^T is the inversion of the matrix, respectively:

$$A = \begin{bmatrix} 2(x_1 - x_n) & 2(y_1 - y_n) \\ \vdots & \vdots \\ 2(y_{n-1} - y_n) & 2(x_{n-1} - x_n) \end{bmatrix} \tag{4}$$

$$b = \begin{bmatrix} x_1{}^2 - x_n{}^2 + y_1{}^2 - y_n{}^2 + d_n{}^2 - d_1{}^2 \\ \vdots \\ x_{n-1}{}^2 - x_n{}^2 + y_{n-1}{}^2 - y_n{}^2 + d_n{}^2 - d_{n-1}{}^2 \end{bmatrix} \tag{5}$$

$$X = \begin{bmatrix} x \ y \end{bmatrix} = (A^T A)^{-1} A^T b \tag{6}$$

3   Overall Design of the System

The system uses RFID radio frequency technology. RFID technology is a long -distance recognition of target information and data reading and writing [5]. The non-contact two-way data communication is carried out by radio frequency, and the recording media (electronic tags or radio cards) are read and written by radio frequency, so as to achieve the results of identification targets and data exchange [6]. RFID has the following advantages:

The first advantage: RFID's electronic label has a capacity of 16 to 64KB, and also supports reading and writing data at any time [7].

The second advantage: RFID label recognition is fast, the recognition distance is far, and multiple targets can be identified at the same time [8].

The third advantage: This technology is contaminated, covered with light, and direction is very small, which can resist the harsh environment [9].

In summary, RFID technology is easy to use and long life, which can realize the automated supervision and transportation of the slag tanks [10]. It not only saves the human and material resources in the production environment, but also simplifies the query and statistics of related production information.

Therefore, the functional framework of the positioning management system based on RFID technology is shown in Fig. 2:

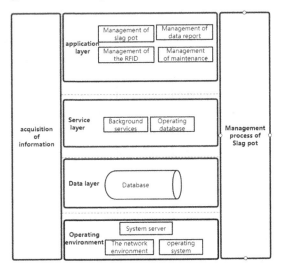

Fig. 2. Function framework of slag tanks management system

RFID hardware equipment, network and operating environment are the foundation of the system, and application layers and service layers and data collection are the main development directions. The hardware equipment collected by the data is composed of electronic tags, fixed readers, antennas, network devices, and servers of RFID. The hardware communication management program uses the C/S architecture, and the slag tank management system is developed by B/S architecture (see Fig. 3).

Based on the design of this system, the RFID reader needs to be installed at each station that needs to be collected, and each part is connected through the network cable to communicate with each other. The network connection model of the hardware designed this is shown in Fig. 4.

The entities of the database of this system include the slag tanks, RFID electronic labels, positions, etc. Therefore, the design of the data table includes the slag tab data table, position status table, production data table, and maintenance data table.

The slag tab data table is used to record all the slag tanks numbers and the information saved by the electronic label. The position status data table is used to record the position

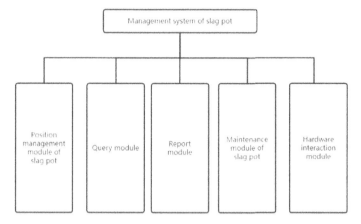

Fig. 3. Function module diagram of the system

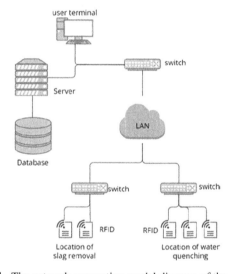

Fig. 4. The network connection model diagram of the device

and status information of the slag tanks. The production data table is used to record related production data for production data reports. The maintenance data table is used to record the quality of the slag after the water is cooling, and whether the slag tanks need to be maintained.

The relationship between them is shown in Fig. 5.

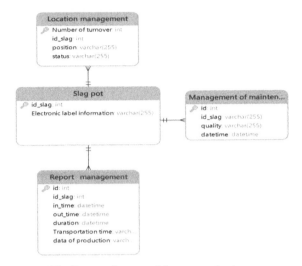

Fig. 5. E-R diagram of the system database

4   System Requirement Analysis

4.1   Hardware Function Module

According to the actual situation at the scene, we need to install the passive RFID label on the slag tank. The label needs to select the type of high temperature resistance, anti -metal interference, and anti -liquid interference [11].

RFID readers are fixed because we want to manage all stations, each station we need to install a reader and at least one antenna. Reader needs power supply and LAN connection. The reader communicates with the server through a physical network to ensure that it works properly(see Fig. 6).

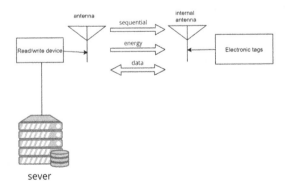

Fig. 6. Principle diagram of RFID work

4.2 Management Module of Slag Tanks

The first is the management and positioning management of the slag tank. The user can monitor the real -time location of each jar to understand. It can also query the state of the slag tank at this time. For example, whether the slag tank is loaded with slag and whether it is quenching the dregs with water. Users can query the information of the slag tanks in each station. From the beginning of the slag, the time to enter the slag stake station, the time to end the slag at the end of the station, the relevant information during the transportation process, and finally the entry and exit time of the quenching position, and the cooling time of the water, the entire process, the entire process, the entire process in the middle, the entry and exit management and location information of the slag can be queried in real time(see Fig. 7).

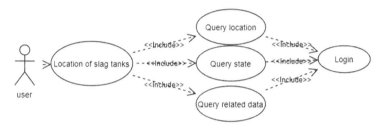

Fig. 7. Use case diagram of the position management of the slag tanks

4.3 Data Report Management Module

Related production data can also be bound in the process of slag tank entry and exit management. We can count and analyze these data. For example, the transport efficiency in the slag tank management process is analyzed by counting the average transport time of the slag tank; secondly, by analyzing the water quenching time to optimize the generation process and so on. There are also some relevant production data that need to be provided by iron and steel enterprises, such as the current slag weight and the number of slag-removing. These production data can be bound to the slag tank management system, which is more uniform and clearer. The final analysis of the data can generate reports, which can be visually displayed to the management personnel, and exported and downloaded in Excel format. The following diagram is shown in Fig. 8.

Fig. 8. Use case diagram of data report management

4.4 Maintenance Management of Slag Tanks

The slag in the slag tanks needs water cooling and water quenching. When the water quenching is completed, the user can fill in the quality of each water quenching in the system. If the slag tank is damaged, it needs maintenance, and also needs users to fill in the cause of maintenance and other information. The diagram is shown in Fig. 9.

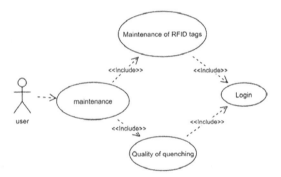

Fig. 9. Use case diagram of maintenance management

5 System Detailed Design Function Module

5.1 Hardware Function Module

The work flow of the reader is: the management software sends the instruction of the reading label to the RFID reader, and the antenna of the RFID reader starts to detect whether the label is read. If not, the software is notified; if the label is detected, the data of the label is returned to the label data. Essence The work flowchart is shown in Fig. 10.

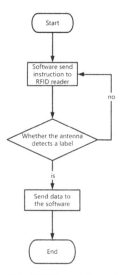

Fig. 10. RFID work flow chart

5.2 Management Module of Slag Tanks

When users use this function module, they need to login first. After the login is successful, they visit the slag tanks management page and query the position and state of the slag tanks. The page sends the request to the background service program. The background service program operates the database to obtain the corresponding data and put it back to the management page. The page displays the information to the user.

The corresponding sequence diagram is shown in Fig. 11.

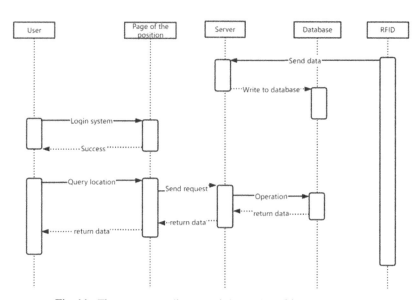

Fig. 11. Time sequence diagram of slag tank position management

5.3 Data Report Management Module

In the case of login, the user accesses the data report page, and requests to export the report data. The background service obtains the request, and operates the database to obtain the corresponding data, and returns the data to the front end. The front end provides the download of the report. As shown in the picture below(see Fig. 12).

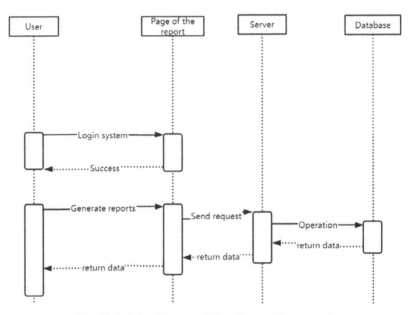

Fig. 12. Timing Diagram of Data Report Management

5.4 Maintenance Management of Slag Tanks

When users log in, they visit the maintenance page, fill in the quality of slag quenched with water, and whether the slag tanks need maintenance and other information. The page sends the data to the background server, and the background service program saves the data to the database. Finally, the results are returned to the user (see Fig. 13).

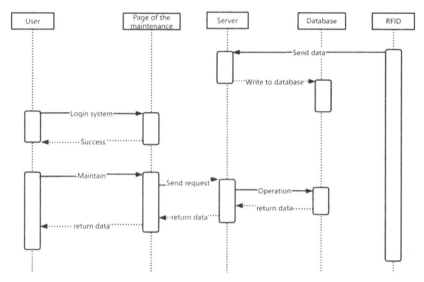

Fig. 13. Timing diagram for maintenance management

6   System Implementation

At present, the system has been officially operated, which mainly realizes the positioning of slag pot in the transportation process, the acquisition and analysis of relevant production data, the display and export of daily data, and the maintenance module of slag pot. The system has met the main needs of users, and its more accurate positioning will continue to be optimized in the future.

7   Conclusion

RFID technology can identify multiple targets at a long distance and quickly, with high safety and reliability, and has broad application prospects in slag tank management in iron and steel enterprises. In this paper, a slag tanks positioning management system based on RFID technology is designed. The hardware and software of the system are analyzed in detail, and the functional structure and business management process of the management system are designed. The application of the system can reduce the workload of managers and improve efficiency. The data related to the slag tanks position detection in the production, logistics and other business systems are integrated. Through visualization and timely centralized display, it can provide support for a comprehensive understanding of the on-site production situation and comprehensive collaborative command, improve the slag tanks control ability, and ensure stable production and smooth transportation.

Acknowledgements. This research is supported by the Key Program of the Natural Science Foundation of the Educational Commission of Anhui Province of China (Grant No. 2022AH050319, 2022AH052740, 2022AH052713) and the Natural Science Foundation Project of Anhui Province of China (Grant No. 1908085MF212).

References

1. Liu, Q.: Automated logistics management and distribution based on rfid positioning technology. Telecommun. Radio Eng. **79**(1), 17–27 (2020)
2. Kudelska, I., Pawłowski, G.: Influence of assortment allocation management in the warehouse on the human workload. CEJOR **28**(2), 779–795 (2019). https://doi.org/10.1007/s10100-019-00623-2
3. Qureshi, R.: The proposed implementation of RFID based attendance system. Int. J. Softw. Eng. Appli. **11**(3), 59–69 (2020)
4. Ilyina, T.A., Kirina D.N.: Logistic processes digitalization of Russian companies based on implementation of RFID technology. St. Petersburg State Polytech. Univ. J. Econ. 13(84), 36–45 (2020)
5. Robb, B.: Tailoring RFID technology for managing cotton modules. Southwest Farm Press (2018)
6. Mobile Asset Tracking with RFID and IoT Support. Material Handling & Logistics, (2018)
7. Sharing information on public transport with RFID and NFC technologies: an application proposal. Urbe: Revista Brasileira de Gestão Urbana **9**(2) (2017)
8. Su, N.M., Oo., M.M.: Automated multi-storied car parking system using RFID. Am. Sci. Res. J. Eng. Technol. Sci. (ASRJETS), **26**(3), 65–81 (2016)
9. Design and Development of a Clinical Risk Management Tool Using Radio Frequency Identification (RFID). Acta Informatica Medica **24**(2) (2016)
10. Amy, CY., Yip, M.H.: Strategic values of technology-driven innovation in inventory management: a case study of Zara's RFID implementation. Int. J. of Inventory Res. **3**(4) (2016)
11. Hwang, Y.-M., Rho, J.-J.: Strategic value of RFID for inter-firm supply chain networks. Inf. Developm. **32**(3) (2016)

FedHD: A Privacy-Preserving Recommendation System with Homomorphic Encryption and Differential Privacy

Wenxing Hong$^{(\boxtimes)}$, Hejia Zhang, and Jiacheng Zhu

School of Aerospace Engineering, Xiamen University, Xiamen, China
`hwx@xmu.edu.cn`

Abstract. To solve the problem of leakage of user privacy information in traditional recommendation systems, this paper proposes a federated learning recommendation system framework with homomorphic encryption and differential privacy, called FedHD. While protecting the privacy of users' personal information and interaction information, a personalized mask filling is designed, which ensure the performance of the overall recommendation system and keeps the balances between the privacy protection and time consumption of the overall system. Experiments on three real-world datasets show that FedHD can meet the real-time accuracy of the recommendation system while achieving privacy protection.

Keywords: Federated learning · differential privacy · privacy-preserving recommendation system

1 Introduction

Recommendation systems have become an important tool to help users discover useful information. In the recommendation process, it is necessary to collect the attribute information of users and items as well as their interaction records to model user preferences and achieve accurate recommendation. Traditional recommendation systems assume that the platform and users are completely trusted with each other. However, there is often a risk of privacy leakage in real scenarios. This risk is manifold, existing between users and platforms, users and users, as well as platforms and platforms. The main task of privacy-preserving recommendation system research is how to make accurate recommendations on the premise of protecting user privacy. Most of the existing privacy-preserving recommendation systems use federated learning as the basic framework. The scheme using federated learning can save the user's privacy data locally and only exchange gradients with the recommendation server, but the study [1] shows that the gradient content can restore some information containing personal privacy. Therefore, using homomorphic encryption as the encryption scheme can prevent gradients from leaking user privacy. At the same time, in the process of gradient transmission, the density of the gradient also leaks the user's privacy to a certain extent. Network attackers can judge whether the user interacts with a specific item by observing the existence of a certain value in the gradient matrix sent by the user to the server, thereby revealing the user's interaction privacy. Therefore, introducing perturbations into the differential privacy algorithm can effectively protect the privacy of interaction information.

Specifically, Homomorphic encryption can be used to encrypt user features or gradient results so that the recommendation system platform can perform recommendation operations without seeing decrypted user-specific information. Further, the fuzzification processing method is to use random perturbation technology to add random noise to user data and uses differential privacy technology to fill in the noise design, which is used to solve the problem of leakage of user privacy by the sparse matrix in recommendation. This research con-structs a framework of federated learning recommendation systems with homomorphic encryption and differential privacy, called FedHD. To solve the problem that the addition of noise in the fuzzy processing method may make the data inaccurate, we design a personalized mask filling which can better reflect the individual characteristics of different users and obtain more accurate recommendation results. Therefore, FedHD makes the performance of the recommendation algorithm unchanged or even improved, which satisfies the re-al-time accuracy of the recommendation system. In summary, the main contribution of paper are:

- We propose FedHD, a Federated learning-based recommendation system with Homomorphic encryption and Differential privacy. Base on this framework, we design a personalized mask filling part.
- Compare with existing methods which only protect the privacy of users' personal information, FedHD can protect both the privacy of users' personal in-formation and interaction information. Moreover, a personalized mask filling part is design to solve the problem that the addition of noise may decline the recommendation accuracy.
- To illustrate the effectiveness of the proposed framework, three real-world datasets are utilized to achieve more accurate performance of recommendation and moderate consumption of time as compared to the baseline model.

2 Related Work

2.1 Federated Learning

Federated learning is to realize the training of a common model without data sharing. The long-term goal of federated learning is to analyze and learn the data from multiple data sources without data exchange directly, to solve the problem of data silos. Horizontal federated learning is widely used in the field of privacy-preserving recommendation systems. The essence of horizontal federated learning is the union of samples. First, each participant downloads the latest model from the server, and then each participant uses local data to train the model and uploads the model gradient to the server. The server aggregates the gradients of each user to update the model parameters and returns the updated model to each participant to update their respective models. FCF in [2, 3] is a typical implicit feedback collaborative filtering framework based on a federated learning paradigm. In the framework of FCF, users use personal data to update their own user hidden vectors locally, and at the same time calculate the local item hidden vector gradients and upload them to the central server. The central server collects the gradients of the item hidden vector and averages them. The item hidden vector is updated and distributed to the user's local model. The federated learning recommendation system FCF directly transfers the gradient, but research [1] has proved that the user's private information can also be restored through the gradient. Therefore, based on horizontal federated learning, it is necessary to encrypt gradient using homomorphic encryption to protect the security of user privacy information.

2.2 Homomorphic Encryption

Homomorphic encryption (HE) is often used in federated learning to protect user privacy by providing parameter in-formation for cryptographic exchanges. Homomorphic encryption is a special encryption scheme that allows any third party to manipulate encrypted data without decrypting it in advance. The mathematical definition of homomorphic encryption is:

$$E(m_1) \odot E(m_2) = E(m_1 \odot m_2), \forall m_1, m_2 \in M \tag{1}$$

where E is the encryption algorithm and M is the set of all possible information. If the encryption algorithm E satisfies the above formula, then E conforms to the properties of homomorphic encryption in the $\odot$ operation. The current homomorphic encryption algorithm mainly supports two kinds of homomorphism in operations: addition and multi-plication.

The existing work of federated learning combined with cryptography methods generally uses additive homomorphism, which directly encrypts the gradient and then uploads it to the server [5, 6]. After that BGV-CF [7] is a privacy-preserving user-based CF protocol based on the BGV fully homomorphic encryption scheme. Fully homomorphic encryption can satisfy both additive homomorphism and multiplicative homomorphism. However, the computational cost and time overhead of full homomorphism is much larger than that of partial homomorphism. Since the homomorphic encryption algorithm has a rigorous theory and ideal accuracy, this method can ensure the performance of the model. Although homomorphic encryption can only solve the risk of gradient value leakage, homomorphic encryption cannot solve the problem of leakage of user interaction privacy in the case of a sparse gradient matrix. If user i has an interaction record with item j, the ij-th item of the gradient matrix is filled with value, otherwise it is null. An attacker can determine whether a user interacts with a sensitive item based on the sparsity of the gradient matrix. Therefore, it is necessary to introduce a fuzzing method with local differential privacy to protect the user's interaction privacy from being leaked.

2.3 Local Differential Privacy

Differential privacy (DP) is a method in cryptography that removes individual characteristics to protect user privacy while preserving the statistical characteristics of data. Differential privacy which was defined by [8] is a new definition of privacy for the privacy leakage problem of statistical databases. Therefore, the risk of privacy leakage caused by adding a record to the data set is controlled within a very small and acceptable range, and attackers cannot obtain accurate individual information by observing the calculation results [9, 10]. However, centralized differential privacy also involves the problem of untrusted entities, so local differential privacy techniques is proposed to solve this problem.

Define given n users, each user corresponds to a privacy algorithm M and its definition domain Dom(M) and value domain Ran(M). If the algorithm M is in any two records t and t' (t, t' $\in$ Dom (M)) to obtain the same output result t (t $\subseteq$ Ran(M)) satisfies the following inequality, then M satisfies ε-localized differential privacy:

$$\Pr\left[M(t) = t^*\right] \leq e^\varepsilon \times \Pr\left[M\left(t^{'}\right) = t^*\right] \tag{2}$$

where the parameter ε is called the privacy protection budget. The smaller the value of ε, the greater the degree of privacy protection, but it also means that the larger the amount of noise added, the lower the availability of data.

FMF [11] is a framework that uses the Local Differential Privacy (LDP) module to encrypt the item latent vector gradient matrix. FedRec [12, 13] is a framework which adds perturbation noise which satisfy the Local Differential Privacy to gradient matrix to protect privacy by preventing the server from inferring the user-interacted items through the gradient uploaded by the user. Although LDP-based federated algorithms are effective, they compromise model accuracy. Therefore, this study introduces LDP in the gradient matrix filling strategy, and the specific process is introduced in III.C.

3 Methodology

3.1 Framework of FedHD

The recommendation system framework FedHD with homomorphic encryption and differential privacy proposed in this study is composed of two parts: part of the server and part of multiple clients, which is shown as Fig. 1. The server side is responsible for aggregating user gradient information to update the item feature vector for clients to download. The client keeps personal data locally for calculation and update. The obtained gradient through a series of processing send to the server.

The specific process is as follows:

- The server-side initializes the item feature vector V and encrypts V with the public key.
- Client loads the encrypted feature vector Cv from the server, then use the private key sk to decrypt Cv to obtain the V.
- The client calculates and updates the local model according to V and local user data, and processes the gradient parameters through the LDP filling module.
- The processed gradient data is encrypted with the public key pk to obtain the encrypted gradient vector Cg.

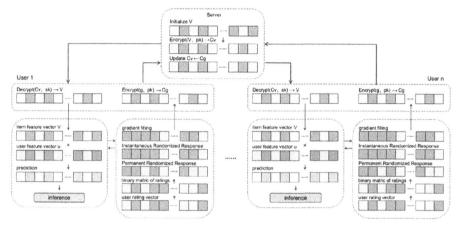

Fig. 1. Framework of FedHD

- The server obtains the encrypted gradient vector Cg of each round of each user and updates the Cv value using Cg to obtain the latest Cv value.

The training repeats the second to fifth steps until the model converges.

3.2 Federated Collaborative Filtering

Suppose there are a total of n users and m items. User ID = {0,1,2,...n-1}, Item ID = {0,1,2,...m-1}. Vector U and vector V represent the user and item features. The real rating value of user i to item j is rij, and the predicted rating value of user i to item j is calculated by the user feature vector and the item feature vector $< u_i, v_j >$, where $< u_i, v_j >$ is the dot product of the two value.

The recommendation algorithm for this paper inspire from the federated learning collaborative filtering framework [3]. In order to enable the server and client to be updated separately, we use a variant of the least alternating squares method,

$$\min_{U,V} \frac{1}{M} \left(r_{ij} - < u_i, v_j > \right)^2 + \lambda U^2 + \mu V^2 \tag{3}$$

where λ and μ are used as regularization coefficients to prevent overfitting.

In the way of stochastic gradient descent, the server-side and the user-side can update the item feature vector and user feature vector respectively:

$$\nabla u_i F\left(U^{t-1}, V^{t-1}\right) = -2 \sum_{j:(i,j)} v_i \left(r_{ij} - \langle u_i, v_j \rangle \right) + 2\lambda u_i \tag{4}$$

$$\nabla v_i F\left(U^{t-1}, V^{t-1}\right) = -2 \sum_{j:(i,j)} u_i \left(r_{ij} - \langle u_i, v_j \rangle \right) + 2\mu v_j \tag{5}$$

3.3 LDP-Filling

The LDP-filling module is divided into two parts: padding policy processing and padding value selection.

In the padding strategy processing stage, this study is inspired by the RAPPOR strategy to realize the selection of the pad-ding strategy for gradients. RAPPOR is divided into two stages: PRR (Permanent Randomized Response) and IRR (Instantaneous Randomized Response). Therefore, the pad-ding strategy of FedHD is processed by a two-stage random perturbation (Fig. 2).

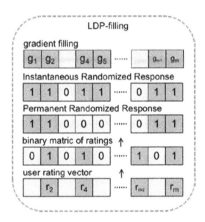

Fig. 2. Framework of LDP-filling

The process of padding strategy processing stage is as follows:

- Binarization. Set elements with values to 1 and elements without values to 0 in the rating matrix of users. B is a binary matrix that represents whether the user rated the item, where Bi indicates items from user i.
- Permanent randomized response (PRR). Sets the value of matrix B to 0 or 1 according to the following formula:

$$B'_i = \begin{cases} 1, & \text{with probability } \frac{1}{2}f \\ 0, & \text{with probability } \frac{1}{2}f \\ B_i, & \text{with probability } 1-f \end{cases} \tag{6}$$

where f is a user-tunable parameter controlling the level of privacy guarantee. B'_i is a binary matrix which is the result of PRR, as the input of IRR.

- Instantaneous randomized response (IRR). Allocate an array S and initialize to 0. Set each bit i in S with probabilities

$$P(S_i = 1) = \begin{cases} q, & \text{if } B'_i = 1 \\ p, & \text{if } B'_i = 0 \end{cases} \tag{7}$$

- Fill gradient matrix. The gradient matrix G is filled according to the binary matrix S using the padding value selection mechanism.

3.4 Personalize Mask

A personalization mask is designed in the padding value selection section. The personalized mask is set according to the personal characteristics and personal habits of each user. The personalized mask can better reflect the individual characteristics of different users and obtain more accurate recommendation results. There are two types of personalization masks: predicted value masks and average masks. Algorithm 1 shows the padding method. T_local defined as the iteration of local pre-training. T_predict is a round detection parameter value which decides the type of personalized mask. Si is the result of padding strategy processing stage of user i. The predicted mask is defined as using user i's predicted value r_ij^' which calculate by <ui, vj> for item j as the value r_ij in the gradient calculation. The predicted value is obtained by the local iterative update of the user feature vector of the current round. The average mask is defined as taking the average rating value r_ij^' = (r_i)- of the user for all rated items as the value r_ij in the gradient calculation.

Algorithm 1 Personalize mask Algorithm

Input: u
Parameter: T_local, T_predict, S_i
Output: $\nabla v'$
1: **for** t_local=1,2,...,T_local **do**
2:     Calculate ∇u via Eq.6
3:     Update u via u-$\gamma\nabla u$
4: **end for**
5: Assign r'_{ij} to each item j∈S_i=1
6: **if** t<T_predict **then**
7:     $r'_{ij}=\bar{r}_i$
8: **else**
9:     $r'_{ij}=u_i \cdot v_j$
10: Calculate $\nabla v'$ via Eq.7
11: **return** $\nabla v'$

3.5 Encryption Scheme

From (4) and (5), it can be known that using the stochastic gradient descent method to update the user feature vector and item feature vector only needs to perform addition and subtraction operations. Therefore, the gradient values are encrypted using additively homomorphic encryption. The specific homomorphic encryption process is as follows:

- KeyGen → (pk, sk): generating public and private keys.

- Enc (m, pk) → c: encrypt plaintext m with public key pk to generate ciphertext c.
- Dec (c, sk) → m: decrypt plaintext c with private key sk to generate plaintext m.
- Add (c1, c2) → ca: c1 and c2 correspond to the ciphertexts of m1 and m2 respectively, and the added value ca is obtained by adding c1 and c2.
- DecAdd (ca, sk) → ma: use the private key sk to decrypt ca get the plaintext ma, and ma corresponds to the value of the addition operation of m1 and m2.
- In this study, the classical homomorphic encryption algorithm paillier is chosen as the encryption scheme.

4 Experiments

4.1 Dataset

The experiments use three public datasets to verify the experimental results.

Movielens100K: MovieLens dataset was organized by the GroupLens research group at the University of Minnesota - University of Minnesota. MovieLens is a collection of movie ratings that is often used in empirical research on collaborative filtering algorithms. In the MovieLens dataset, users rate the movies they have watched, with a score ranging from 1 to 5. The experiment uses Movielens100K as the experimental data which includes 100,000 ratings of 1,682 movies from 943 users.

FilmTrust: FilmTrust is a small dataset scraped from the entire FilmTrust website in June 2011. It contains 1508 users' ratings of 2071 items, with a score ranging from 1 to 5.

Amazon-Books: This dataset is provided by the Amazon website and contains the shopping data of users in different categories from May 1996 to June 2014. This paper selects the classification of -books that is the most scoring samples in all shopping categories as another public dataset for the experiments in this paper. A total of 879 users' ratings of 2,000 books were selected as experimental data.

4.2 Evaluation Metrics

We use the following commonly used evaluation metrics to evaluate the performance.

Mean Absolute Error (MAE). MAE is the error measure between the predicted and true ratings in the test data. The specific definitions are as follows:

$$\text{MAE} = \frac{1}{m} \sum_{i=1}^{m} \left| \left(h(x^{(i)}) - y^{(i)} \right) \right| \tag{8}$$

Root Mean Square Error (RMSE). RMSE is the square root of the error between the predicted rating score in the test data and the true rating score. It is more sensitive to results with larger errors than to MAE, as shown in the following equation:

$$\text{RMSE} = \sqrt{\frac{1}{m} \sum_{i=1}^{m} (h(x^{(i)}) - y^{(i)})^2} \tag{9}$$

Area Under Curve (AUC). To further evaluate the performance of the recommendation algorithm in the experiment, the items with a rating greater than the average of the user's rating are labeled as positive samples, and the items less than the average of the user's rating are labeled as negative samples. By introducing the concept of confusion matrix, different statistical results of TP, FP, FN and TN are obtained, and the AUC value is used to measure their performance.

Time Cost. To balance the algorithm performance and time consumption, the sum of the average user-side update time and the server-side update time average is defined as the measurement time cost.

$$\text{TimeCost} = \overline{\text{user}_{\text{update}}} + \overline{\text{server}_{\text{update}}} \tag{10}$$

FedHD Implementation

Experimental environment: The operating system of the test experiment is Windows, and the programming language is Python. Use the gmpy8 module to speed up the homomorphic encryption part in Python, making it as fast as C++ implements homomorphic encryption.

Parameter settings: The fixed parameter settings are shown in Table 1.

Table 1. Parameter settings

Dataset	d	γ	Λ, μ	iteration
Movielens100K	10	0.01	0.01,0.01	40
FilmTrust	10	0.01	0.01,0.01	60
Amazon Books	10	0.01	0.01,0.01	40

Experimental setup: Overall the experiment is divided into three parts. The first part verifies that FedHD cannot degrade the performance of the recommendation algorithm after introducing privacy-preserving policies. The second part verifies that the FedHD filling strategy does not make time-consuming too much while protecting user privacy. The third part verifies the security of FedHD.

5 Result Evaluation

5.1 Performance Evaluation

The experiments use three public datasets to verify the experimental results.

We choose to compare two typical models in the federated learning recommendation system with FedHD to conduct a comparison experiment on the performance of the recommendation algorithm. One is FCF [3]. FCF is a classic model that applies federated learning to collaborative filtering recommendation without homomorphic encryption and differential privacy. The second is FedMF [4]. FedMF is a secure matrix factorization model based on federated learning. FedMF uses homomorphic encryption technology based on FCF.

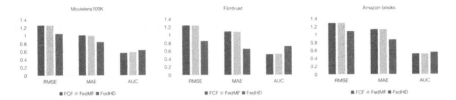

Fig. 3. The performance of FCF, FedMF, FedHD in Movielens100K, FilmTrust, Amazon-books

We experiment with three models on each of the three datasets. The experimental results are shown in Table 2 and Fig. 3.

The results can verify that after using homomorphic encryption and differential privacy in FedHD, the RMSE and MAE values are lower than other models, and the AUC values are higher than other models. This proves that our research not only protects the privacy of users' personal information and user interaction information but also the recommendation performance of the recommendation system remains un-changed and even improved by designing personalized mask padding.

Table 2. The performance of FCF, FedMF, FedHD in Mov-ielens100K, FilmTrust, Amazon-books

Dataset	Model	RMSE	MAE	AUC
Movielens100K	FCF	1.2624	1.0125	0.5596
	FedMF	1.2613	0.9998	0.5844
	FedHD	**1.0486**	**0.8433**	**0.6270**
FilmTrust	FCF	1.2431	1.0892	0.5113
	FedMF	1.2428	1.0873	0.5281
	FedHD	**0.8566**	**0.6519**	**0.7227**
Amazon Books	FCF	1.2919	1.1277	0.5124
	FedMF	1.2918	1.1274	0.5131
	FedHD	**1.0869**	**0.8739**	**0.5546**

5.2 The Strategy of Filling

Considering that FedMF also introduces the same homo-morphic encryption technology, the two filling strategies of FedMF are selected for comparison with the filling strategy in this paper. The parttext filling strategy is defined to only fill in gradient values for items that the user has rated or interacted with. The full-text padding strategy is defined as padding all items but unrated or not interacted items with 0 values.

The comparison of filling strategies is divided into two parts. The first part is to verify the impact of different filling strategies on the performance of the algorithm. The second part is to compare the time consumption of different filling strategies. The results are shown in Table 3.

Table 3. The performance of difference strategy of filling in Movielens100K, FilmTrust, Amazon-books

Dataset	Model	RMSE	MAE	AUC	TimeCost (second)
Movielens 100K	FedMF-parttext	1.2613	1.0001	0.5845	**65.2022**
	FedMF-fulltext	1.2613	0.9998	0.5844	155.7525
	FedHD	**1.0486**	**0.8433**	**0.6270**	98.6856
FilmTrust	FedMF-parttext	1.2429	1.0873	0.5281	**30.5682**
	FedMF-fulltext	1.2428	1.0873	0.5281	130.8197
	FedHD	**0.8566**	**0.6519**	**0.7227**	66.1267
Amazon Books	FedMF-parttext	1.2969	1.1309	0.5124	**41.2091**
	FedMF-fulltext	1.2969	1.1309	0.5124	116.6825
	FedHD	**1.0869**	**0.8739**	**0.5546**	73.5847

The results show that there is no difference in performance between the two filling strategies of part-text and full-text, but the cost value of part-text is much smaller than that of full-text. Comparing our proposed FedHD with other filling strategies, FedHD is significantly better than the other two filling strategies in performance by designing personalized mask padding. In terms of time-consuming, FedHD is between part-text and full-text. Our filling strategy solves the problem that part-text leaks the privacy of user interactions, while at the same time does not need to consume as much time as full-text. This verifies that FedHD can better balance the protection of user interaction privacy and time consumption.

5.3 Performance Evaluation

The security of FedHD is reflected in two aspects: homo-morphic encryption and local differential privacy.

Homomorphic encryption algorithm uses Paillier [14] scheme. The Paillier scheme satisfies the standard security definition of an encryption scheme: Semantic security, that is, the ciphertext is indistinguishable under a chosen-plaintext attack (IND-CPA), which means that the ciphertext does not reveal any information about the plaintext. The security of Paillier's scheme can be reduced to the Decisional Composite Residuosity Assumption (DCRA), that is, given a composite number n and an integer z, it is difficult to determine whether z is an n-th residual under n2. In nearly a decade of adequate research, there is still no polynomial-time algorithm that can break this assumption, thereby proving the security of Paillier's scheme.

The local differential privacy part is inspired by the two-stage random perturbation of the RAPPOR scheme. RAPPOR is a solution proposed by Google to solve the problem of privacy and data utility. RAPPOR based on random response mechanism is used to protect the privacy of statistics on client data. RAPPOR [15] has been shown to satisfy ε_p differential privacy in the Permanent Randomized Response

$$\varepsilon_p = 2hln\left(\frac{1 - \frac{1}{2}f}{\frac{1}{2}f}\right) \tag{14}$$

and satisfy ε_i differential privacy in Instantaneous Randomized Response.

$$\varepsilon_i = 2hlog\left(\frac{q^*(1 - p^*)}{p^*(1 - q^*)}\right) \tag{12}$$

It can be seen intuitively from Table 4 that the overall performance indicators remain unchanged, and only the time consumption Time Cost value increases as the privacy protection parameter decrease (the privacy protection strength increases). Therefore, in practical applications, users can freely choose the size of the privacy protection parameters for different scenarios.

Table 4. The performance of difference privacy protection parameter in Movielens100K, FilmTrust, Amazon-books

Dataset	$\varepsilon_p, \varepsilon_i$	RMSE	MAE	AUC	TimeCost
Movielens100K	4,8	1.0486	0.8433	0.6270	98.6856
	2,4	1.0486	0.8433	0.6270	100.4562
	1,2	1.0486	0.8433	0.6270	103.6512
FilmTrust	4,8	0.8566	0.6519	0.7227	66.1267
	2,4	0.8567	0.6521	0.7105	73.4392
	1,2	0.8566	0.6518	0.7201	79.9282
Amazon Books	4,8	1.0869	0.8739	0.5546	73.5847
	2,4	1.0871	0.8740	0.5532	77.4815
	1,2	1.0869	0.8739	0.5546	80.8030

6   Conclusion

This paper proposes a recommendation system framework FedHD with homomorphic encryption and differential privacy. Homomorphic encryption is used to encrypt user features or gradient results, etc. so that the recommendation system platform can perform recommendation operations without visible user-specific information. Differential privacy technology is used to fill the noise design to solve the problem of user interaction privacy leaked by the sparse matrix in collaborative filtering recommendation. The personalized mask is designed to combine user characteristics and achieve ac-curate recommendations to improve model accuracy. Experiments on three public datasets prove that FedHD cannot reduce the recommendation performance of the operation recommendation system and even can improve it while achieving privacy protection. Moreover, in the comparison of different filling strategies, FedHD can better achieve a trade-off between recommendation performance, privacy protection, and time consumption.

Homomorphic encryption algorithm has strict theory and ideal accuracy, but the computational cost is high. Future work should consider how to optimize the homomorphic encryption algorithm to reduce the time consumption and computational cost.

Acknowledgement. This work is partly supported by the first batch of joint project plans for innovation strategy research in Fujian Province in 2021, sponsored by the Fujian Provincial Department of Science and Technology and the Provincial Association for Science and Technology: "Digital Silk Road Innovation Service Platform" (Grant No. 2021R0166).

References

1. Zhu, L., Han, S.: Deep leakage from gradients. In: Yang, Q., Fan, L., Yu, H. (eds.) Federated Learning. LNCS (LNAI), vol. 12500, pp. 17–31. Springer, Cham (2020). https://doi.org/10.1007/978-3-030-63076-8_2
2. Shin, H., Kim, S., Shin, J., Xiao, X.: Privacy enhanced matrix factorization for recommendation with local differential privacy. IEEE Trans. Knowl. Data Eng. **30**(9), 1770–1782 (2018)
3. Ammad-ud-Din, M., Ivannikova, E., Khan, S.A., et al.: Federated Collaborative Filtering for Privacy-Preserving Personalized Recommendation System (2019). http://arxiv.org/abs/1901.09888
4. Chai, D., Wang, L., Chen, K., Yang, Q.: Secure federated matrix factorization. IEEE Intell. Syst. **36**(5), 11–20 (2021)
5. Fang, H., Qian, Q.: Privacy-preserving machine learning with homomorphic encryption and federated learning. Future Internet **13**(4), 94 (2021)
6. Yang, L., Tan, B., Liu, B., Zheng, V.W., Chen, K., Yang, Q.: Practical and secure federated recommendation with personalized masks (2021). http://arxiv.org/abs/2109.02464
7. Jumonji, S., Sakai, K., Sun, M.-T., Ku, W.-S.: Privacy-preserving collaborative filtering using fully homomorphic encryption. IEEE Trans. Knowl. Data Eng. **35**, 2961–2974 (2021)
8. Dwork, C., McSherry, F., Nissim, K., Smith, A.: Calibrating noise to sensitivity in private data analysis. In: Halevi, S., Rabin, T. (eds.) TCC 2006. LNCS, vol. 3876, pp. 265–284. Springer, Heidelberg (2006). https://doi.org/10.1007/11681878_14
9. Dwork, C.: Differential privacy: a survey of results. In: Agrawal, M., Du, D., Duan, Z., Li, A. (eds.) TAMC 2008. LNCS, vol. 4978, pp. 1–19. Springer, Heidelberg (2008). https://doi.org/10.1007/978-3-540-79228-4_1
10. Dwork, C.: A firm foundation for private data analysis. Commun. ACM **54**(1), 86–95 (2011)
11. Minto, L., Haller, M., Haddadi, H., Livshits, B.: Stronger privacy for federated collaborative filtering with implicit feedback (2021). http://arxiv.org/abs/2105.03941
12. Lin, G., Liang, F., Pan, W., et al.: Fedrec: federated recommendation with explicit feedback. IEEE Intell. Syst. **36**(5), 21–30 (2020)
13. Liang, F., Pan, W., Ming, Z.: Fedrec++: Lossless Federated Recommendation with explicit feedback. In: Proceedings of the AAAI Conference on Artificial Intelligence, vol. 35, no. 5, pp. 4224–4231 (2021)

14. Paillier, P.: Public-key cryptosystems based on composite degree residuosity classes. In: International Conference on the Theory and Applications of Cryptographic Techniques, pp. 223–238. Springer, Heidelberg (1999). https://doi.org/10.1007/3-540-48910-X_16
15. Erlingsson, Ú., Pihur, V., Korolova, A.: RAPPOR: randomized aggregatable privacy-preserving ordinal response. In: Proceedings of the 2014 ACM SIGSAC Conference on Computer and Communications Security, pp. 1054–1067. ACM (2014)

Deep Neural Networks with Cross-Charge Features

Enzhi Ren$^{(\boxtimes)}$ (ID), Yang Weng (ID), and Hao Wang (ID)

College of Mathematics, Sichuan University, Chengdu, China
enzhiren@163.com, {wengyang,wangh}@scu.edu.cn

Abstract. Sentencing bias and sentencing imbalance due to various factors is a worldwide problem at present, and many researches in recent years have applied deep learning to deal with the problem of charge prediction and sentence prediction to unify the process of conviction and sentencing in criminal trials, which has weakened the above problems to a certain extent and has positive significance to promote the scientific nature of legislation and judicial rationality. In this paper, we propose the common elements and individual elements of charges according to the criminal law and other legal norms, and design a deep neural network with cross-charge features(CCFDNN) based on warm-start, and the feature input constructed based on the elements of charges makes the CCFDNN have better interpretability. The original features are revisited using skip connections in the design of CCFDNN as a way to provide multi-scale semantic information to reduce training errors. In this paper, we conduct experiments on four common criminal charges for charge prediction and sentence prediction, and explain the experimental results in detail, aiming to make the trial results more reasonable.

Keywords: Charge prediction · Sentence prediction · Deep Neural Networks

1 Introduction

With the progress and transformation of society, various conflicts occur frequently, criminal cases become more diverse and complex, and the amount of data generated in the judicial field grows by leaps and bounds, providing data support for analyzing and predicting the results of judicial trials. Recent advances in artificial intelligence(AI), particularly natural language processing and machine learning, have provided tools to automatically analyze legal materials, and the resulting outcome prediction models can be used to reveal patterns that drive judicial decisions. This is a very useful judicial aid, both for judges and lawyers, to quickly identify cases and distill the behavioral logic that leads

This work was partly supported by National Key R&D Program of China under Grant 2020YFC0832400. This work was partly supported by Key R&D Program of Sichuan Province under Grant 2021YFS0397.

to certain decisions. The legal judgment prediction is a hot spot of attention of AI technology in recent years, and a novel and forward-looking application in the field of intelligent justice. The use of data mining and AI technology to quantitatively analyze massive judicial data, provide judges with references on case sentencing, and establish an intelligent sentencing assistance system is the current trend of judicial reform in China.

Legal experts tend to use mathematical and statistical methods to construct legal decision prediction models [1], including quantitative analysis methods, hierarchical analysis methods, mathematical modeling methods, which are highly interpretable, but lack important information such as case specifics, and thus the prediction results are often poor. Researchers in artificial intelligence techniques, on the other hand, prefer to tackle the problem using feature engineering and machine learning [2–4], which rely on a large number of manually labeled features for semantic representation of case specifics and thus improve the performance of the models to some extent. Most existing methods follow a text classification framework [5], as deep learning techniques have matured, some researchers have applied deep neural networks to legal decision prediction models [6–8], which no longer rely too much on manually annotated features, all of which have achieved good results but fail to explain the prediction results. End-to-end methods such as [5,9,10] are simpler in model design and can train models with lower inputs, but the prediction accuracy is often not high. Feature-based methods such as [6–9] are substantially better than other methods, although some effort is invested in designing and processing features in the early stage.

This paper focuses on the problem of charge prediction and sentence prediction in single person single charge cases. In this paper, we use the factual part of the case of the judgment document to propose the common elements and individual elements of charges according to the criminal law and other legal norms with the help of legal experts, and then use the data-driven and embedding methods to semantically represent the specific contents of the case. The Deep Neural Networks with cross-Charge Features(CCFDNN) designed on this basis identifies and extracts hidden features while automatically combining the charge features through the input layer, hidden layers and output layer, while using skip connections to re-input the original features. Training the neural network with multidimensional charge features allows the model to learn the sample data more effectively, giving the model better interpretability. By setting a reasonable activation function and optimization algorithm, CCFDNN can converge quickly when learning and improve the training speed of the model. Inspired by the idea of warm-start in meta-learning, this paper considers using the model parameter configuration that minimizes the generalization error on various tasks in the initial stage to accelerate the model optimization process and improve the generalization ability of the model.

2   Data

The dataset was selected from a total of 439665 judgments in criminal cases including robbery, snatching, traffic offense, and endangering public safety by dangerous manners in 31 provinces between 2000 and 2020 on China Judgment Online, considering only single person and single charge cases. These four counts were chosen for two reasons:

Reason 1. Robbery and traffic offense are the charges that account for a relatively large proportion of criminal cases, and the corresponding trial elements are more obviously easy to extract.

Reason 2. Snatching and endangering public safety by dangerous manners are highly similar to the case elements of the above two charges, respectively, and the features learned on the large data set can be experimented on the small.

Analysis of the data set yielded the longest average sentences for robbery and the shortest average sentences for traffic offenses, with 10.8% of robbery cases receiving 12-month sentences and 36.8% of endangering public safety by dangerous manners cases receiving 36-month sentences. The percentage of the number of cases for each charge is shown in Fig. 1.

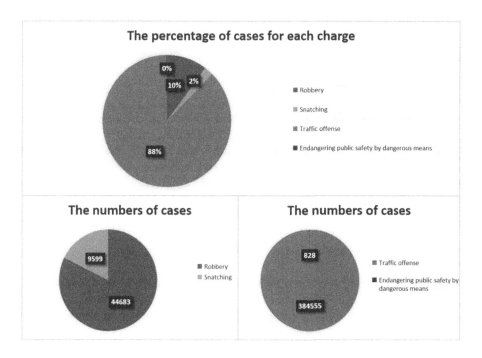

Fig. 1. The percentage of the number of cases.

Each case has certain constituent elements, and the process structure is basically the same, although the contents of the cases vary. Based on legal norms such as the Criminal Law of the People's Republic of China, judicial interpretations and sentencing guidelines promulgated by the Supreme Court, this paper proposes common elements that are shared by all seven types of arbitrary charges, which have an important impact on the verdict results of the charges and sentences; considering the specificity of different cases, we consider extracting the elements specific to the charges as a feature named individual elements to distinguish confusion. The Fig. 2 shows an example of element extraction for a traffic offense case.

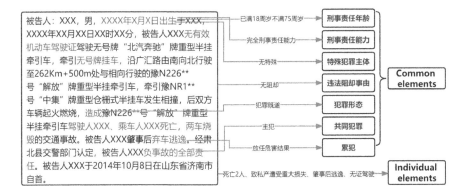

Fig. 2. An example of element extraction for a traffic offense case.

Compared with the lack of detailed features in most existing datasets, this paper combines legal knowledge to propose seven types of common elements and one individual elements for each charge, taking into account the overall and individual variability and diversity. In addition, this paper also introduces charge features and charge classification features into the sentence prediction task, and the addition of these two features makes it easier for the model to make sentence prediction under specific charges, i.e., adds deeper semantic information, which largely weakens sentencing bias and sentencing imbalance.

3   The CCFDNN Model

Deep neural networks are based on the simplest neural network, the multilayer perceptron (MLP), which usually consists of more than two layers of neural networks. Since deep neural networks have natural cross-combination characteristics for the input of samples, a reasonably designed deep neural network model with feature combination of common and individual charge elements can effectively extract the hidden information in the data and further enhance and optimize the performance of the model. The Deep Neural Networks with cross-Charge Features(CCFDNN) architecture designed in this paper is shown in Fig. 3.

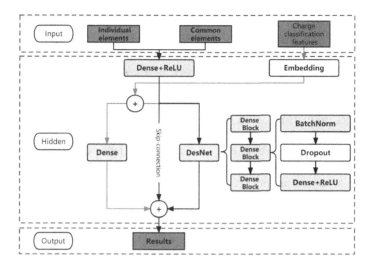

Fig. 3. Architecture of the CCFDNN. Layers with learnable parameters are marked as colored.

The deep neural network with cross-charge features further extracts the case element representation, and then performs charge prediction and sentence prediction by multiple hidden layers. The neural network structure for the charge prediction problem consists of the solid black line in Fig. 3, and the neural network for sentence prediction adds the charge classification features and the Dense layer after embedding, specifically the solid gray line in Fig. 3.

A neural network consists of many neurons, and the neurons of CCFDNN are the features of each charge of the input. Let x_i denote the input of the ith neuron, w_i be the corresponding connection weight, b_i be the bias term, f be the activation function, and y_i be the output of the neuron, then a linear relationship is learned between the input and output of each layer as follows:

$$y_i = f\left(\sum w_i x_i + b_i\right) \tag{1}$$

3.1 Input Layer

In this paper, we note that the model selection and hyperparameter optimization problems of most machine learning methods tend to start from a relatively large search space, and performing each search task is a more expensive process, so we consider providing a better initial search configuration at the initial stage to speed up this optimization process, and "warm-start" the new task by borrowing some existing optimization results from similar historical tasks.

CCFDNN sets the initial model parameters for the crime prediction task to the model with the lowest generalization error in the existing data set, and then sets the model parameters that perform well on this task to the initial model for the sentence prediction task, which provides a good warm-start for the above two tasks, solves the problem of too many parameters brought by self-supervised learning to a certain extent, and improves the accuracy and generalization ability of the model prediction, so as to adapt to the differences of different regions, generations, courts, judges, defendants' attitudes, etc.

For the charge prediction problem, the input layer consists of two charge features, the individual elements $X^{(1)}$ and the common elements $X^{(2)}$.

For the sentence prediction problem, a feature $X^{(3)}$ is added to the input layer, and the corresponding charge is treated in two special ways: first, the "charge" is encoded to add semantic information; second, the different types of charges are embedded, i.e., a feature is added to represent this classification attribute, and this embedding layer enables the neural network to understand each charge separately before the charge representation is mixed with other features.

3.2   Hidden Layers

The raw variables in the dataset correspond to the charge elements, each of which has its own meaning, so the raw features designed in this paper are both input to DesNet, which contains three layers of Dense blocks, and directly connected to the output through a skip-connection. Specifically, the full connection is first made through the Dense layer:

$$y = W * X_i \tag{2}$$

To make the neural network more robust, the features passing through the Dense layer are activated using the ReLU activation function:

$$f(x_{i,j}) = \max(0, x_{i,j}) \tag{3}$$

To mitigate the gradient disappearance and gradient explosion problems that may occur during the training process of the model, each Dense block of DesNet [11] consists of BatchNorm, dropout regularization and ReLU activation function, which is designed to improve the propagation rate and utilization of the guilty features and reduce the number of parameters of the network. Among them, BatchNorm refers to batch normalization of data and contains learnable parameters γ and β; dropout regularization stops the forward propagation process of a certain neuron with a certain probability p, as a way to avoid local dependency and enhance the generalization performance of the neural network. Down-sampling between each Dense block by convolution of 1×1 and pooling of 2×2 [11].

3.3 Output Layer

In order to improve the utilization of text features, the original features are fed in the output layer of CCFDNN using skip connections, which provide more scale information to the output layer of the neural network as a way to reduce the training error and further improve the accuracy, and to improve the quality of its prediction results through an improved gradient flow.

Finally the output of DesNet and the original features are feature-connected through a fully-connected layer and then fed into a prediction layer for the prediction of the charges. The loss function is the L_1 loss:

$$\mathcal{L} = \sum |Y_i - f(X_i)| \tag{4}$$

In this process, Adam algorithm [12] with weight decay penalty is used for optimization, which is based on the idea of "momentum" and combines the advantages of Adagrad algorithm for sparse data and RMSProp algorithm for non-stationary data. The CCFDNN is not tuned using general hyperparameter optimization, all settings are derived from the optimal network settings for the task in question, but the hidden layers are still scaled adaptively in a fixed manner (128 and 256).

4 Eeperiments and Analysis of Results

4.1 Setup

The dataset was randomly divided into training and test sets in the ratio of 8:2, and the model was trained using a 5-fold cross-validation method. The network is trained 1000 times (Epoch = 1000), after which all parameters are set to search randomly within the given range, the learning rate of Adam optimizer is $\{1e-6, 1e-7, 1e-8, 1e-9\}$, the hidden size is $\{20, 50, 100\}$, the exit rate of the hidden layer is $\{0.1, 0.2, 0.3, 0.4, 0.5\}$, and the input layer exit rates are $\{0.0, 0.05, 0.1, 0.15, 0.2\}$, and the optimization parameters are $\{0.9, 0.95, 0.99\}$.

4.2 Evaluation

Charge Prediction Task. In this paper, we use accuracy and AUC to evaluate the charge prediction task and logloss to reflect the precision of model prediction.

Sentence Prediction Task. In this paper, we use accuracy, macro-precision(MP) and macro-recall(MR) to evaluate the sentence prediction task.

Interpretability. In this paper, we use SHAP (SHapley Additive exPlanation) [13] to interpret the output of CCFDNN, which calculates an importance value, or Shapley value, for each feature relative to its prediction, and this method can distinguish the model output categories more effectively. The SHAP summary shows the contribution of each sample feature, which is used to describe and demonstrate the interpretability of the local features.

4.3   Charge Prediction

Because the elements of robbery and snatching are very similar, in particular, 46% of the individual elements of robbery were labeled the same as snatching; similarly, for the group of traffic offense and endangering public safety by dangerous means, the latter has 50% of the same individual element labels as the former. Therefore, the prediction tasks were divided into two groups: robbery and snatching, and traffic offense and endangering public safety by dangerous means (referred to as charge prediction 1 and 2, hereinafter). The following Table 1 shows the experimental results of these two tasks.

Table 1. Results of the charge prediction.

Task	Accuracy(%)	AUC(%)	logloss
charge prediction 1	99.96	99.98	0.0086
charge prediction 2	99.99	99.99	0.0002

Figure 4 shows the SHAP value of charge prediction 1. According to the variable importance diagram of charge prediction 1, it can be seen that the four individual elements of robbery/snatching amount, use of violent coercive methods, driving a (non-)motor vehicle and causing serious consequences such as suicide, have a large impact on the classification of the charges, and the common elements of elderly offenders, abettors and over-defense also have a large impact on the classification results. The results for charge prediction 2 are similar to 1, these important influences reflected by the model are consistent with the requirements of the Criminal Law of the People's Republic of China for the conviction of these two charges.

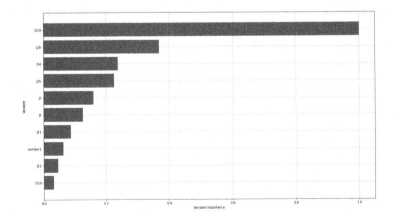

Fig. 4. Variable Importance of charge prediction 1.

4.4   Sentence Prediction

The sentence prediction tasks corresponding to each charge are initialized according to the model training results of the charge prediction tasks, and the sentence lengths of the four charges are predicted separately (referred to as sentence prediction 1, 2, 3, and 4, hereafter). The following Table 2 shows the experimental results of these four tasks.

Table 2. Results of the sentence prediction

Task	Accuracy(%)	MP(%)	MR(%)
sentence prediction 1	39.90	39.89	39.88
sentence prediction 2	39.89	39.89	39.65
sentence prediction 3	39.94	39.94	39.91
sentence prediction 4	41.57	40.36	39.76

Figure 5 (a) shows the SHAP aummary for sentence prediction 1. As can be seen from the fingure, the individual elements of multiple robberies, amount robbed, and necessity of life have important influences on the sentences imposed, and the common elements of recidivism and confession also have some influence on the sentences imposed. The influencing factors of snatching are very similar to those of robbery, and these important influencing factors reflected in the model are also consistent with the sentencing requirements of the Criminal Law for these two crimes.

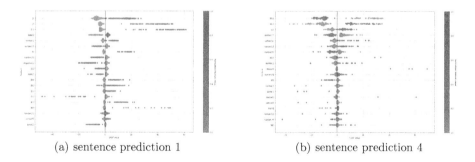

(a) sentence prediction 1   (b) sentence prediction 4

Fig. 5. SHAP summary of sentence prediction

Figure 5 (b) shows the SHAP aummary for sentence prediction 4. As can be seen from the fingure, whether or not serious consequences are caused has the greatest impact on sentence, followed by factors such as actively obtaining the victim's understanding, fleeing after the crime, and letting the harmful outcome go. The traffic offense influences factors very similar to it, which is the reason for using warm start initial training model parameters between the two charges here.

Comparing the results of the four tasks clearly shows that the charges feature elements extracted in this paper have a significant effect on the length of sentence and that this effect is consistent with the legal sentencing causality of each charge, further illustrating the interpretability of the model in this paper.

5   Conclusion

In this paper, after element extraction and feature processing of more than 430,000 judgment documents from China Judgment Online, we propose a deep neural network with cross-charge features (CCFDNN) based warm-start, while the original features are fed into the prediction layer via skip-connection, and feature processing such as these enhance the model's ability to handle classification problems. The feature input constructed based on the elements of the crime makes CCFDNN better interpretable, aiming to promote the uniformity of adjudication and sentencing, reduce the influence of human factors on the verdict outcome, and assist the verdict of criminal cases.

In this paper, charge prediction and sentence prediction experiments are conducted on four common criminal charges, namely robbery, snatching, traffic offense, and endangering public safety by dangerous manners. The significant factors influencing the conviction and sentencing of each crime were obtained experimentally, which is consistent with the legal realism theory that judicial decisions are significantly influenced by the facts and circumstances of the case, and with the focus and requirements of criminal law for the conviction and sentencing of these crimes. The influence of each factor on the final result is quantified by the SHAP framework, which further reflects the explanatory ability of the model for the corresponding tasks and problems.

The model in this paper still has much room for improvement: First, this paper deals with the problem of single person single crime charge prediction and sentence prediction, considering that there are single person multiple crimes and multiple people multiple crimes in real cases, further research on these cases can be considered subsequently. Second, considering that the case frequencies of different crimes are very unbalanced, the performance of existing methods on severely unbalanced data is still limited. Third, some methods take into account the dependencies among subtasks of the legal decision prediction problem, and in this paper, only the model training results of the charge prediction task are output to the sentence prediction task, and other methods to deal with the dependencies can be considered subsequently.

Acknowledgements. The authors would like to express their gratitude for the support from National Key R&D Program of China under Grant 2020YFC0832400 and Key R&D Program of Sichuan Province under Grant 2021YFS0397.

References

1. Ringquist, E.J., Emmert, C.E.: Judicial policymaking in published and unpublished decisions: the case of environmental civil ligaton. Polit. Res. Q. **52**(1), 7–37 (1999)
2. Liu, C.-L., Hsieh, C.-D.: Exploring phrase-based classification of judicial documents for criminal charges in Chinese. In: Esposito, F., Raś, Z.W., Malerba, D., Semeraro, G. (eds.) ISMIS 2006. LNCS (LNAI), vol. 4203, pp. 681–690. Springer, Heidelberg (2006). https://doi.org/10.1007/11875604_75
3. Lauderdale, B.E., Clark, T.S.: The Supreme Court's many median justices. Am. Polit. Sci. Rev. **106**(4), 847–866 (2012)
4. Lin, W.-C., et al.: Exploiting machine learning models for Chinese legal documents labeling, case classification, and sentencing prediction. Proc. ROCLING **17**(4), 140 (2012)
5. Sulea, O.-M., et al.: Exploring the use of text classification in the legal domain. arXiv preprint arXiv:1710.09306 (2017)
6. Chen, S., Wang, P., Fang, W., Deng, X., Zhang, F.: Learning to predict charges for judgment with legal graph. In: Tetko, I.V., Kůrková, V., Karpov, P., Theis, F. (eds.) ICANN 2019. LNCS, vol. 11730, pp. 240–252. Springer, Cham (2019). https://doi.org/10.1007/978-3-030-30490-4_20
7. Zhang, H., Wang, X., Tan, H., Li, R.: Applying data discretization to DPCNN for law article prediction. In: Tang, J., Kan, M.-Y., Zhao, D., Li, S., Zan, H. (eds.) NLPCC 2019. LNCS (LNAI), vol. 11838, pp. 459–470. Springer, Cham (2019). https://doi.org/10.1007/978-3-030-32233-5_36
8. Hu, Z., et al.: Few-shot charge prediction with discriminative legal attributes. In: Proceedings of the 27th International Conference on Computational Linguistics (2018)
9. Shen, Y., et al.: Legal article-aware end-to-end memory network for charge prediction. In: Proceedings of the 2nd International Conference on Computer Science and Application Engineering (2018)
10. Yang, X., et al.: Interpretable charge prediction with multi-perspective jointly learning model. In: 2019 IEEE 5th International Conference on Computer and Communications (ICCC). IEEE (2019)
11. Huang, G., et al.: Densely connected convolutional networks. In: Proceedings of the IEEE Conference on Computer Vision and Pattern Recognition (2017)
12. Kingma, D.P., Ba, J.: Adam: a method for stochastic optimization. arXiv preprint arXiv:1412.6980 (2014)
13. Lundberg, S.M., Lee, S.I.: A unified approach to interpreting model predictions. Adv. Neural Inf. Process. Syst. **30**, 1–10 (2017)

Community Detection Based on Graph Attention and Self-supervised Embedding

Yuwei Lu[✉], Guoyan Xu, and Qirui Zhang

Hohai University, Nanjing, China
670314725@qq.com

Abstract. In community detection, clustering method is usually applied. Because graph embedding is not designed for specific community detection tasks, which usually have a poor effect. In this paper, a graph-attention auto-encoder (GATE) is proposed, which uses the attention mechanism to capture the importance of adjacent nodes to the target nodes. For the over-smoothing problem of multi-layer attention network, the deep auto-encoder (DGAE) is integrated into GATE, which can enhance the accuracy of clustering. We also designed a selfsupervised module to train the GATE and DGAE encoding process in a unified framework, jointly optimize the training task, and guide the updating of the whole model. The experimental results on multiple datasets show the superiority of this method for community detection task.

Keywords: Community detection · Network embedding · Graph auto-encoder · Graph neural network · Self-supervised learning

1 Introduction

In real life, various entity mappings are constructed into complex networks. Vertices in the network represent solid objects, and edges represent the connection between vertices. Community detection divides nodes into a series of subgraphs according to the relationship between nodes in the network, which is community. The nodes in a community are densely connected, while nodes in different communities are sparsely connected, so as to clearly understand the structure of the network.

At present, the existing community detection algorithms, in addition to the general traditional methods, network embedding has attracted great attention in academia and industry in recent years. It refers to learning the representation of relevant nodes from a given network, and taking the obtained node representation as the feature input of subsequent application tasks. In 2014, Bryan perozzi proposed deepwalk algorithm [1]. Its core idea is to generate random path by random walk, use random path to simulate sentences in natural language processing, and then use word2vec method to generate low dimensional node representation of nodes. Line [2] considers both the first-order proximity and the second-order proximity of network nodes. The above embedding methods automatically sample the path of nodes through random walk strategy, and then obtain the representation of nodes through neural network model. In recent years, deep learning methods have made remarkable achievements in computer vision and other fields. The network embedding method based on deep learning has stronger node representation ability. The community detection algorithm based on deep neural networks (DNN) makes use of the advantages of DNN in learning feature representation to further improve the accuracy of clustering.

However, the existing methods get the node low-dimensional representation usually adopt the two-step strategy, the learned embedding may not be suitable for subsequent community detection tasks. In addition, in the process of network embedding, integrating the community structure of the network into the node embedding representation can also reveal the implicit relationship between nodes from a global perspective. This paper proposes a graph attention and self-supervised embedding model (GASE) for community detection, the model learns the node attributes and global topology at the same time, and uses the attention mechanism to capture the importance of adjacent nodes to the target node. For the over smoothing problem of multi-layer attention network, integrating the DAE into the GATE, which can enhance the accuracy of clustering. A self-supervised module designed to supervise the cluster loss of the DAE and GATE encoder, and guide the update of the whole model. The main work of this paper is as follows:

- Based on the DAE and GATE model, a graph attention and self-supervised community detection model GASE is proposed. It can learn the network's node attributes and topology at the same time, mapping the representation of nodes in the low dimensional feature space.
- The attention mechanism is used to capture the importance of adjacent nodes to target nodes, and the community similarity of nodes is integrated into the calculation of attention coefficient to further integrate the macro structure of network, so as to improve the accuracy of subsequent community detection tasks.
- Compared with the existing network embedding methods in classical datasets, the effectiveness of the proposed model GASE is verified in the community detection task.

2   Related Works

In this section, we will briefly introduce the representative methods of Network embedding based on graph auto-encoder and self-supervised network embedding, which are highly related to our model GASE.

2.1   Network Embedding Based on Graph Auto-Encoder

The method based on auto-encoder is one of the commonly used community detection methods based on deep learning. Auto-encoder (AE) is an unsupervised neural network, which compresses the original input data into low dimensional data, and then reconstructs the input data through the decoder to make it as close as possible to the original data. Graph auto-encoder is the most commonly used method in the scheme based on graph neural network. Graph auto-encoder (GAE) and Variational graph auto-encoder (VGAE) were proposed by Kipf et al. [3]. This framework encodes the network into a low-dimensional representation in latent space and reconstructs the network structure from the low-dimensional representation. SDNE [4] algorithm applies deep learning to the network embedding problem for the first time, maps the input data to a highly nonlinear space through the auto-encoder model to capture the network structure, and jointly optimizes the first-order and second-order proximity of nodes to maintain the network structure. ANRL [5] uses node attributes as input, what it reconstructs is not its own attributes, but the aggregation of neighbor nodes attributes. The aggregated features can contain local topology information. The deep neural network representation method DNGR [6] constructs the PPMI (positive pointwise mutual information) incidence matrix between nodes, and learns the low-dimensional representation of nodes through the deep noise reduction auto-encoder model.

2.2   Self-supervised Network Embedding

Xie et al. [7] designed KL divergence loss to make the representation learned by the auto-encoder closer to the cluster center to jointly optimize the feature representation and clustering allocation of data. Wang et al. [8] used the graph attention network to weight the importance of adjacent nodes and obtain a more accurate representation of each node, and then introduced the self-supervised module, which takes the clustering results as soft labels to guide the optimization process. Li et al. [9] combined the advantages of K-means and spectral clustering and embedded them into the graph auto-encoder to generate better data representation. Wu et al. [10] proposed using relaxd K-means to cluster the embedding features of graph auto-encoder. Bo et al. [11] introduced the embedded representation learned by the auto-encoder into the corresponding graph convolution auto-encoder, and proposed a dual self-supervise mechanism to unify these two different deep neural structures. These clustering algorithms based on graph auto-encoder are also suitable for commuity detection tasks.

3   Proposed Model

In this section, we will introduce our proposed graph attention self-supervised embedding model GASE, and its overall framework is shown in Fig. 1. Firstly, input the node adjacency matrix and node attributes into the deep auto-encoder and the graph attention auto-encoder respectively. We connect each layer of the deep auto-encoder with the corresponding graph attention auto-encoder layer, which can solve the over-smoothing problem in the multi-layer attention network, consider the topology and node features at the same time, and enhance the accuracy of community detection. In addition, we introduce a self-supervise mechanism to further supervise the embedding representation through the distribution function. We will describe each module of our model in detail below.

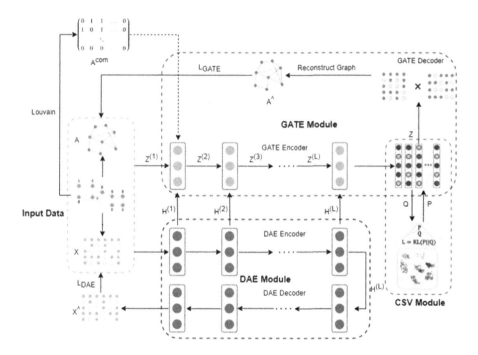

Fig. 1. Overall framework of GASE

3.1 Deep Auto-Encoder Module(DAE)

In community detection, learning effective representation is very important. This part introduces the deep auto-encoder module used in this algorithm. The input of this module is the feature matrix $X \in R^{n*m}$, where n is the number of nodes, m is the dimension of feature, x_i represents the feature of the i_{th} node. Suppose the encoder contains l layers, and the l_{th} layer representation $H^{(l)}$ can be expressed as (1):

$$H^{(l)} = \phi\left(W^{(l)}H^{(l-1)} + b^{(l)}\right) \tag{1}$$

where ϕ is the activation function of the full connection layer, $H^{(l-1)}$ represents the hidden representation of $(l-1)_{th}$ layer, and $B^{(l)}$ and $W^{(l)}$ represent the deviation and weight matrix of l_{th} layer of the encoder respectively. The original feature matrix X is used as the initial input layer $H^{(0)} = X$. The output of the encoder has two operations: one is for clustering and training the self-supervised model, and the other is decoding to obtain the reconstructed adjacency matrix. The decoder reconstructs the feature matrix X through the full connection layer, and the function of this part can be expressed as (2):

$$H^{*(l)} = \phi \left(W^{*(l)} H^{*(l-1)} + b^{*(l)} \right) \tag{2}$$

where $b^{*(l)}$ and $W^{*(l)}$ represent the deviation and weight matrix of the l_{th} layer of the encoder respectively. After the encoded data passes through the decoder, the original data can be reconstructed, that is, the final output result of the decoder $H^*(l) = \hat{\chi}$ is the reconstruction of the original data, which should have the minimum loss with the original data. The loss function is shown in (3):

$$L_{DAE} = \frac{1}{2N} \sum_{i=1}^{n} \|x_i - \hat{x}_i\|_2^2 \tag{3}$$

3.2 Graph Attention Auto-Encoder Module(GATE)

The GATE encoder uses the multi-attention network to encode the input network, and then attempts to reverse the encoding process to reconstruct the network information in the decoding process. l_{th} layer attention coefficient $\alpha_{ij}^{(l)}$ can be calculated as (4) and (5):

$$e_{ij}^{(l)} = W^{(l)} Z_i^{(l-1)} + W^{(l)} Z_j^{(l-1)} \tag{4}$$

$$\alpha_{ij}^{(l)} = \text{Softmax} \left(e_{ij}^{(l)} \right) = \frac{A_{ij}^{com*} \exp \left(e_{ij}^{(l)} \right)}{\sum_{k \in N_i} A_{ik}^{com*} \exp \left(e_{ik}^{(l)} \right)} \tag{5}$$

While the conventional GAT (Graph attention network) only considers the first-order neighbors of nodes, here we capture high-order neighborhood information in the encoder. In our model, we use Louvain [12] algorithm to obtain community structure. N_i represents the neighborhood of node i, $A^{com} \in R^{n*n}$ represents the community similarity between nodes, that is, if nodes i and j belong to the same community, $A_{ij}^{com} = 1$, otherwise $A_{ij}^{com} = 0$. In addition, in order to solve the transition smoothing problem in multi-layer attention networks, outputs of $(l-1)_{th}$ layer of DAE and GATE are taken as the input of GATE l_{th} layer. the input of GATE $(0)_{th}$ layer is the original node feature X, the representation $z_i^{\wedge(1)}, z_i^{\wedge(l)}$ are shown in (6) and (7):

$$z_i^{\wedge(1)} = \sum_{j \in N_i} \alpha_{ij}^{(1)} W^{(1)} X \tag{6}$$

$$z_i^{\wedge(l)} = \sum_{j \in N_i} \alpha_{ij}^{(l)} W^{(l)} \left(\theta * z_i^{(l-1)} + (1-\theta) * H_i^{(l-1)} \right) \tag{7}$$

Among them, is a trade-off parameter, we set it to 0.5 here. Assuming that there are k-layer (k > 1) encoders, we can finally get representation of the last layer as (8):

$$Z_i^{(k)} = \phi \left(\sum_{j \in N_i} \alpha_{ij}^{(k)} W^{(k)} Z_j^{\wedge}(k-1) \right) \tag{8}$$

ϕ is the activation function of the full connection layer, through (4)–(8), we connect the DAE and GATE layer by layer. The decoder reconstructs the network structure and node features by reversing the encoding process. Using the decoder with the same number of layers as the encoder, each decoder layer reconstructs the node features by using the representation of its neighbor nodes. Take the output of the encoder as the input of the decoder, that is, $Z^{\sim(1)} = Z^{(k)}$. In addition to the same data reconstruction as DAE, the loss function contains a simple inner product decoder, $A_{ij}^{\wedge} = \text{sigmoid} \left(Z_i^T Z_j \right)$, Z_i^T represents the transpose of the representation obtained by the last layer encoder. Thus, we can get the reconstruction loss function of GATE, as shown in (9):

$$L_{GATE} = \frac{1}{2N} \sum_{i=1}^{n} \| x_i - \hat{x}_i \|_2^2 - \sum_{i=1}^{n} \sum_{j=1}^{n} A_{ij} \log (A_{ij}) \tag{9}$$

3.3   Clustering Self-supervise Module(CSV)

At present, the network embedding based community detection method is mainly a two-step strategy, that is, learning the embedding and then performing it on the clustering algorithm. The main challenge is that there is no label guidance. The graph clustering task is naturally unsupervised, so it is impossible to obtain feedback on whether the learned embedding has been well optimized during training. To meet this challenge, we developed a self optimizing embedding algorithm as a solution. In addition to optimizing the reconstruction errors of DAE and GATE, we also input the hidden embedded information into the self optimizing clustering module to minimize (10):

$$L_{CLU} = KL \left(P \| Q \right) = \sum_{u=1}^{n} p_{iu} \log \frac{p_{iu}}{q_{iu}} \tag{10}$$

where, q_{iu} indicates the similarity between the node embedding Z_i and the cluster center embedding Z_u. Using the idea of [13] for reference, t-distribution of students is introduced as the allocation measure of soft clustering. Assuming that there are k clusters, as (11):

$$q_{iu} = \frac{\left(1 + \| z_i - z_u \|^2 \right)^{-1}}{\sum_{j=1}^{k} \left(1 + \| z_i - z_j \|^2 \right)^{-1}} \tag{11}$$

where, z_u is initialized by the parameters of K-means in the pretrained auto-encoder. The objective function p uses the following probability distribution as (12):

$$p_{iu} = \frac{q_{iu}^2 / \sum_{i=1}^{n} q_{iu}}{\sum_{j=1}^{k} \left(q_{ij}^2 / \sum_{i=1}^{n} q_{ij} \right)} \tag{12}$$

The soft assignment with high probability is considered credible in Q, and then the clustering loss forces the predicted distribution Q close to the target distribution P. By learning the node assignment with high confidence, reduce the distance between the predicted distribution Q and the target distribution P to train the model. Through this mechanism, GASE can directly combine two different objective functions into a loss function, that is, embedding task and clustering task, which can ensure meaningful embedding and more stable results. In addition, higher clustering accuracy can be obtained by combining the node features. Therefore, the overall loss function of GASE is (13):

$$L = \alpha L_{DAE} + \beta L_{GATE} + \gamma L_{CLU} \tag{13}$$

where, α, β, γ are trade-off parameters, which balances the proportion of DAE, GATE and CSV in loss function. After the training reaches the final stage, GASE will obtain stable results, then label the node. We choose the cluster assigned to the highest probability in the distribution Q as the community corresponding to the node:

$$r_i = \arg \max_j q_{ij} \tag{14}$$

4   Experiment

In the experiment, firstly analyzing the parameters of the proposed GASE to find the most suitable parameters for each network, so as to get the best result. The hardware environment of the experiment is as follows: CPU Intel (R) Xeon (R) CPU e5-2680 V4 @ 2.40 GHz, 16 GB ram, GPU NVIDIA Titan XP. The software environment uses Python 3.8, pytorch 1.7.0 and CUDA 11.0.221.

4.1   Datasets

- Cora: it is a data set to study the citation relationship between literatures.
- Citeseer: it is a paper citation network, which is also a dataset for studying the citation relationship of papers.
- ACM: a subset selected from the ACM paper collaborator network.
- DBLP: a subset selected from the DBLP collaborator network.

Please refer to Table 1 for details of datasets.

Table 1. Experimental datasets and its structure

Dataset	Nodes	Features	Clusters	Links
Cora	2708	1433	7	5429
Citeseer	3327	3703	6	4732
ACM	3025	1870	3	13128
DBLP	4058	334	4	3528

4.2 Baselines

In order to verify the effectiveness of gase, we compared it with several typical graph clustering methods, including:

- K-means [14]: the clustering algorithm based on the original data, using the K-means function in the sklearn.cluster package.
- GAE/VGAE [3]: an unsupervised graph auto-encoder algorithm, which uses graph convolution network (GCN) as an auto-encoder. VGAE combines variational inference algorithm on the basis of GAE.
- DEAGC [15]: it uses graph attention network to learn node representation, and uses clustering loss to supervise graph clustering process.
- SDCN [11]: use auto-encoder and GCN encoder to integrate structure and feature information, and use soft clustering for dual self-supervision.
- CaEGCN [16]: Based on SDCN, a deep clustering framework of end-to-end cross attention fusion is proposed, in which the cross attention fusion module connects the GCN auto-encoder and auto-encoder at multiple layers.

4.3 Parameter Setting and Metrics

- Parameter setting: in the experiment, we set the number of layers of GASE encoder to 3, and the dimensions of each layer are (500, 256, 16). α, β, γ in loss function are set to (1, 10, 10). For Cora and Citeseer, we set the learning rate to $5 * 10^{-3}$, and for ACM and DBLP, we set the learning rate to 10^{-3}. For the comparison method, we carefully set the parameters of each algorithm according to the steps in the paper.
- Metrics: We used four metrics to evaluate the results: accuracy (ACC), normalized mutual information (NMI), F-score and adjusted Rand index (ARI). A better clustering result should lead to higher values of all metrics.

4.4 Experimental Results and Analysis

We can see that for most metrics, our method is significantly better than all baseline methods. K-means algorithm only uses node attributes as input and cannot capture the direct correlation between nodes. Algorithms that consider node topology and attributes at the same time, such as GAE and VGAE, can

Table 2. Table captions should be placed above the tables.

Datasets	Metrics	k-means	GAE	VGAE	DAEGC	SDCN	CaEGCN	GASE
Citeseer	ACC	0.544	0.613	0.609	0.672	0.659	0.680	**0.715**
	NMI	0.312	0.346	0.326	0.397	0.387	0.400	**0.524**
	F-score	0.413	0.573	0.577	0.636	0.636	0.613	**0.702**
	ARI	0.285	0.335	0.331	0.410	0.404	0.424	**0.479**
Cora	ACC	0.500	0.530	0.592	0.704	0.596	0.632	**0.716**
	NMI	0.317	0.397	0.408	0.528	0.388	0.459	**0.538**
	F-score	0.376	0.415	0.456	0.682	0.619	0.650	**0.710**
	ARI	0.239	0.293	0.347	**0.496**	0.319	0.359	0.485
ACM	ACC	0.637	0.845	0.841	0.869	0.869	**0.901**	0.883
	NMI	0.326	0.553	0.532	0.561	0.589	0.670	**0.684**
	F-score	0.675	0.846	0.841	0.870	0.868	**0.900**	0.892
	ARI	0.306	0.594	0.577	0.593	0.652	0.730	**0.751**
DBLP	ACC	0.364	0.612	0.576	0.620	0.661	0.682	**0.705**
	NMI	0.088	0.308	0.218	0.324	0.324	0.338	**0.357**
	F-score	0.263	0.614	0.545	0.617	0.655	0.666	**0.713**
	ARI	0.065	0.220	0.234	0.210	0.333	0.361	**0.328**

better capture the relationship between nodes and node attribute information. However, vgae has the problem of over smoothing. SDCN and caegcn supplement the content information to the GCN module of each layer, which effectively alleviates the problem of over smoothing. However, the capture of node neighborhood by graph volume self encoder is limited to the first-order neighborhood and lacks the integration of high-order topology information. For example, on the citeseer dataset, our method achieved the relative growth of ACC and NMI of about 8.50% and 35.40% compared with SDCN. The reason is that we consider the community structure of the network and introduce it into the calculation of attention coefficient. After inputting the code obtained by DAE, our gate module focuses on weighting its upper layer code and DAE code, which effectively integrates the information of the two modules.

Analysis: The parameters of the GASE proposed in this paper mainly include trade-off parameters α, β, γ. In order to study the influence of different trade-off parameters on the experimental results, we carried out experiments on the different values of trade-off parameters. Considering that α, β are the trade-off parameters that control the clustering loss of DAE and GATE respectively. Therefore, we conduct a joint analysis of these two parameters, the change of clustering loss parameter γ is analyzed separately. Take $\gamma \in \{10^{-2}, 10^{-1}, 0, 1, 10, 10^2\}$ and carry out experiments on four datasets. Average the results of the 100_{th} to 200_{th} iterations in each case. The γ - histogram is drawn as shown in Fig. 2.

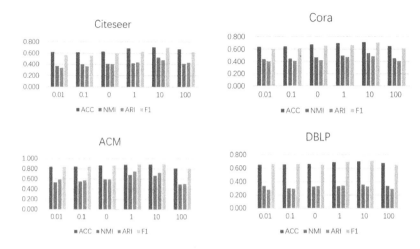

Fig. 2. Influence of γ on different datasets

As shown in Fig. 2, the results of parameter adjustment in four datasets are shown respectively. It can be seen that good accuracy is achieved when $\gamma = 10$, indicating the importance of clustering loss of self-supervise module. Next, setting $\frac{\alpha}{\beta} \in \left\{ 10^{-2}, 10^{-1}, 1, 10, 10^2 \right\}$, experiments were conducted on four datasets. The NMI values of the 100_{th} to 200_{th} iterations in each case were averaged and plotted $\frac{\alpha}{\beta} - NMI$ line chart is shown in Fig. 3.

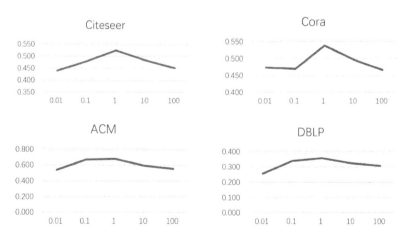

Fig. 3. $\frac{\alpha}{\beta} - NMI$ on different datasets

As shown in Fig. 3, it represents results when setting different value of $\frac{\alpha}{\beta}$. It can be seen that a good accuracy was obtained at $\frac{\alpha}{\beta} = 1$, so the ratio of (α, β) is finally determined to be 1.

Visualization: We applied T-SNE algorithm based on tensorboard on the citeseer, as shown in Fig. 4. The results of 100 times, 1000 times, 2000 times and 5000 times respectively from left to right and reaching the final stable state. Then, through self-training clustering, with the increase of iteration times, the overlap between different clusters becomes less and less, and the nodes in the same cluster gradually gather together.

Fig. 4. 2D visualization process of GASE iterative training on Citeseer

5   Conclusion

In this paper, we propose a community detection model GASE, which is composed of DAE module, GATE module and CSV module. Our model can effectively combine the auto-encoding structure of deep neural network with the auto-encoding structure based on graph attention network, and supervise the clustering process with the help of auxiliary distribution. In addition, we introduce community structure to consider the macro structural information of network topology, which is not considered by most methods at present. Compared with the existing typical methods, it is proved that the proposed model can obtain high accuracy.

References

1. Perozzi, B., Al-Rfou, R., Skiena, S.: Deep Walk: online learning of social Representations, pp. 701–710 (2014)
2. Tang, J., Qu, M., Wang, M., et al.: Line: Large-scale information network embedding. In: Proceedings of the 24th International Conference on World Wide Web, pp. 1067–1077 (2015)
3. Kipf, T.N., Welling, M.: Variational graph auto-encoders. arXiv preprint arXiv:1611.07308 (2016)
4. Wang, D., Cui, P., Zhu, W.: Structural deep network embedding. In: Proceedings of the 22nd ACM SIGKDD International Conference on Knowledge Discovery and Data Mining, pp. 1225–1234 (2016)
5. Zhang, Z., Yang, H., Bu, J., et al.: ANRL: attributed network representation learning via deep neural networks. In: IJCAI, vol. 18, pp. 3155–3161 (2018)
6. Cao, S., Lu, W., Xu, Q.: Deep neural networks for learning graph representations. In: Proceedings of the AAAI Conference on Artificial Intelligence, vol. 30, no. 1 (2016)

7. Xie, J., Girshick, R., Farhadi, A.: Unsupervised deep embedding for clustering analysis. In: International Conference on Machine Learning (2016)
8. Wang, C., Pan, S., Hu, R., Long, G., Jiang, J., Zhang, C.: Attributed graph clustering: a deep attentional embedding approach. In: International Joint Conference on Artificial Intelligence, pp. 3670–3676 (2019)
9. Li, X., Zhang, H., Zhang, R.: Embedding graph auto-encoder with joint clustering via adjacency sharing. arXiv:2002.08643 (2020)
10. Wu, J., Wang, Y., Wu, Z., et al.: Deep k-means: re-training and parameter sharing with harder cluster assignments for compressing deep convolutions. In: International Conference on Machine Learning, pp. 5363–5372. PMLR (2018)
11. Bo, D., Wang, X., Shi, C., Zhu, M., Lu, E., Cui, P.: Structural deep clustering network. In: The Web Conference (2020)
12. Blondel, V.D., Guillaume, J.-L., Lambiotte, R., Lefebvre, E.: Fast unfolding of community hierarchies in large networks. J. Stat. Mech. (2008). https://arxiv.org/abs/0803.0476
13. van der Maaten, L., Hinton, G.: Visualizing data using t-SNE. J. Mach. Learn. Res. **9**, 2579–2605 (2008)
14. Hartigan, J.A., Wong, M.A.: Algorithm AS 136: a k-means clustering algorithm. J. Roy. Stat. Soc. Ser. C (Appl. Stati.) **28**(1), 100–108 (1979)
15. Wang, C., Pan, S., Hu, R., Long, G., Jiang, J., Zhang, C.: Attributed graph clustering: a deep attentional embedding approach. In: IJCAI (2019)
16. Huo, G., Zhang, Y., Gao, J., et al.: CaEGCN: cross-attention fusion based enhanced graph convolutional network for clustering. IEEE Trans. Knowl. Data Eng. **35**, 3471–3483 (2021)

Research on Multimodal Rumor Detection Based on Hierarchical Attention Network

Guoyan Xu, Qirui Zhang[✉], Yuwei Lu, Yuwei Zhang, and Chunyan Wu

College of Computer and Information, Hohai University, Nanjing 211100, Jiangsu, China
`zqr971031@163.com`

Abstract. In recent years, the rise of the Internet has made it more and more convenient for people to obtain news, but it not only brings convenience to people, but also promotes the spread of rumors. Nowadays, many rumor detection methods are based only on textual content information. The traditional neural network model treats all the words and sentences of the text equally in text feature extraction, and can not pay attention to the important content in the news text. Therefore, it is impossible to capture the characteristics of the hierarchical structure of news documents. And under the trend of rich media of social media, false news gradually changes from a single text form to a multimodal form. In view of the above situation, a multimodal rumor detection method based on hierarchical attention network is proposed. For textual features, Glove pre-trained model is used, and it is able to capture the semantic features of the news document hierarchy by applying a two-level attention mechanism at the word and sentence levels respectively. For image features, we use the pre-trained VGG19 to obtain visual information, and finally combine the text and image features to comprehensively detect rumors. Experimental results of FakeNewsNet dataset from Twitter show that this method can effectively improve the performance of multimodal rumor detection.

Keywords: Social Media · Rumor Detection · Hierarchical Attention Network · Multi-mode

1 Introduction

Social media has revolutionized the way people access information. The portability and low cost of social media bring collective wisdom, but at the same time, it also breeds a variety of false rumors. Rumors in social media have the characteristics of fast propagation speed, wide influence range, high cost and low efficiency of manual rumor refutation. Rumors widely spread on social media not only hurt the audience and impacted the authority and credibility of the mainstream media, but also produced potential risks in many aspects such as economy and politics. Due to the huge online content, it is very time-consuming to expose rumors manually. Therefore, to build an effective and practical automatic rumor recognition system, it is very important to mine news information from different angles.

As the narrative subject of news events, the text contains rich information and provides clues at different levels for the determination of news credibility. Most of the existing methods use cyclic neural network to model the context information of the input text and capture the pattern of the text presentation layer. However, due to the lack of participation of corresponding factual knowledge in the feature extraction process, this kind of method has limited ability to understand the named entities in the news text, and it is difficult to fully capture the clues at the semantic level of false news.

In recent years, with the rich media trend of social media, news has gradually changed from a single text form to a multi-modal form. A single language pattern cannot be fully understood and rumor detection cannot be performed effectively. Today's news entities come in a variety of forms, presenting information not only through text, but also images, videos, and more. For pictures, rumor pictures mainly include tampering pictures and misuse pictures. Tampering with pictures refers to the use of tools to deliberately make pixel level changes or the non real pictures automatically generated by the algorithm, while misused pictures generally refer to the real pictures that are not deliberately modified, taken from other events or the contents of the pictures are misinterpreted. Therefore, image information now plays an equally important role as text in the task of rumor detection.

In order to solve the above challenges, we propose a multimodal rumor detection model based on hierarchical attention network. Firstly, we use the improved hierarchical attention model to extract text features. Firstly, the model uses the word2vec pre-training model from Glove [1], and applies two levels of attention mechanism at the word and sentence levels to extract features, so that it can distinguish the important and unimportant content when When extracting text features, so as to capture the characteristics of the news document hierarchy. According to the image features, the pre trained VGG19 [2] is used to obtain visual information, and finally combined with the text and image features to comprehensively detect rumors, so that the final detection results are more suitable for today's multimodal news and make a more comprehensive and accurate rumor prediction.

The main contributions of this paper include three aspects:

1. The improved Glove pretrained hierarchical attention model is adopted to capture the characteristics of the hierarchical structure of news documents and better understand the entity semantics in news, so as to mine the semantic clues of news more fully;
2. The image feature extraction model based on VGG19 is adopted to better obtain the information features of visual mode;
3. The proposed method is verified on the real-world twitter data set. Compared with the current better methods, our model can greatly improve the accuracy of false news detection.

2 Related Work

According to the different research objects, the rumor detection task can be to detect the news level news or the event level news. Event level detection uses the information of all tweets under the same event to jointly judge the credibility of the news event, but the formation of the event often takes a certain time. Some major rumors may have been widely spread on social media before the formation of the event, which will have a great negative impact in a very short time. Message level detection refers to judging the credibility of the content of a single news message. Compared with event level detection, this method can achieve real-time detection in practical application, so it has attracted extensive attention of researchers. This paper focuses on rumor detection at the message level.

Most existing studies use text content to detect rumors. Early rumor detection mainly used heuristic rules or statistical information to manually construct text features, such as clue keyword, language style, and then applied these features to machine learning algorithm for rumor detection, which has obvious defects in generality and expansibility. In recent years, researchers began to use deep learning methods to model text language, and achieved very good results. Ma et al. [3] used recurrent neural network (RNN) to learn implicit representation from text content for classification; Yu et al. [4] used convolutional neural network (CNN) to learn key features and their high-order features from text content for rumor detection. However, the traditional neural network model treats all the contents of the text equally, and can not pay attention to the important words and sentences in the news text, so it can not capture the characteristics of the hierarchical structure of news documents.

And in the trend of rich media of social media, false news has gradually changed from a single text form to a multi-modal form. False news pictures have the characteristics of low quality and strong visual impact. In contrast, real news is often more objective and rigorous, and the quality of pictures is higher. In works [5], the basic characteristics of additional images in news content are explored. However, these features are still handmade and difficult to represent the complex distribution of visual content.

Therefore, in the semantic feature extraction of news content, the traditional deep learning models such as GRU [6] and LSTM treat all the contents in the text equally when extracting text features, which can not pay attention to the important contents in the news text, and have the disadvantage of forgetting. Therefore, they can not capture the characteristics of the hierarchical structure of news documents and can not make full use of the characteristics of visual modal information. We propose a multimodal rumor detection model based on hierarchical attention network. It can not only capture the characteristics of the hierarchical structure of news documents, but also fully integrate the heterogeneous characteristics of different modes of text and vision.

3   Multimodal Rumor Detection Model Based on Hierarchical Attention Network

Let $P = \{p_1, p_2, ..., p_k\}$ be a rumor detection data set, where p_i represents the ith event. k is the number of news events the data set. $p_i = \{t_i, i_i\}$, where t_i is the text in event i and i_i is the picture in event i. Our task is to determine whether a given piece of multimodal news is a rumor or a non-rumor. The goal of the rumor detection task can be thought of as learning a function f: $f : f(p_i) \rightarrow y_i$, where the label value $y_i \in \{0, 1\}$.

Figure 1 shows our proposed multimodal rumor detection model based on hierarchical attention model, which is mainly consists of 4 parts: word2vec pre-trianing based on Glove, hierarchical attention model, image feature extraction based on VGG19 and classification.

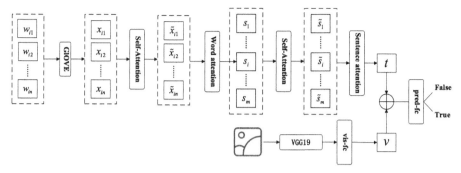

Fig. 1. Structure diagram of rumor detection model based on hierarchical attention network

3.1 Glove-Based Word2vec Pre-training

Glove is a commonly used unsupervised learning algorithm for obtaining word vector representations. Specifically, the learning of word vector requires the best prediction of the co-occurrence frequency of any two words. Therefore, a new weighted least square regression model is proposed, and the weighted function $f(X_{ij})$ is introduced into the cost function. The model is given below:

$$J = \sum_{i,j=1}^{V} f(X_{ij})(w_i^T \tilde{w}_j + b_i + \tilde{b}_j - \log X_{ij})^2 \tag{1}$$

where V is the size of vocabulary. Specifically, for the word sequence $W_i = \{w_{i1}, w_{i2}, ..., w_{im}\}$ in the ith sentence in a given news text, the word is embedded into the vector by Glove pre-training, and the word embedding representation $X_i = \{x_{i1}, x_{i2}, ..., x_{in}\}$ is obtained.

Different from random initialization of word vectors, Glove pre-trained language model can acquire effective semantic features and common sense knowledge through corpus learning in the early stage of modeling.

3.2 Hierarchical Attention Model

We use a hierarchical attention model to extract text features. This module applies two-level attention mechanisms at the word and sentence levels to extract features. When constructing the document representation, it can distinguish between the important content and the unimportant content, and can capture the characteristics of the interaction between words and words and between sentences in news documents. Thus, the characteristics of the hierarchical structure of news documents can be captured. The model mainly consists of four parts: GRU-based word encoder, word attention encoder, sentence encoder and text encoder. Below, we will show you how to use hierarchies to build document-level vectors step by step from word vectors.

Word Encoder Based on Self-Attention. Give a sentence s_i with words $x_{it}, t \in [0, T]$, The traditional hierarchical attention model [7] uses bidirectional GRU to obtain the context information of words by summarizing bidirectional information of words. This method has obvious defects, it can not distinguish the importance of each word in the sentence to the current word, and when the sentence is too long, it has the characteristic of forgetting. Therefore, we introduce the Self-Attention mechanism [8] to extract other words in sentences that are important to the current word, so as to obtain the context information of the word to represent the current word. Specifically, we introduce parameter matrixes W_Q, W_k, W_v. For each word x_t:

$$q_t = W_Q x_t \tag{2}$$

$$k_t = W_K x_t \tag{3}$$

$$v_t = W_V x_t \tag{4}$$

Then we measure the importance of words according to the similarity between q_t and all $k_{jt}, j \in [0, T]$, and get the normalized importance weight through the *softmax* function. Finally, we calculate the weighted sum of v_t as the final word vector $\tilde{x}_t$, that is:

$$a_{tj} = \frac{\exp(k_{jt}^T q_t)}{\sum_j \exp(k_{jt}^T q_t)} \tag{5}$$

$$\tilde{x}_t = \sum_j a_{tj} v_j \tag{6}$$

Word Attention. Not all words contribute equally to the expression of sentence meaning. Therefore, we introduce the attention mechanism to extract words that are important to sentence meaning, and aggregate the representation of these word information to form sentence vectors. Specifically,

$$u_{it} = \tanh(W_w \tilde{x}_{it} + b_w) \tag{7}$$

$$\alpha_{it} = \frac{\exp(u_{it}^T u_w)}{\sum_t \exp(u_{it}^T u_w)} \tag{8}$$

$$s_i = \sum_t a_{it} h_{it} \tag{9}$$

In other words, we first use linear transformation to transform the word representation h_{it}, and the hyperbolic tangent function is used to obtain the hidden representation u_{it} of h_{it}, Then measure the importance of words according to the similarity between u_{it} and word context vector u_w, and obtain the normalized importance weight through *softmax* function. Finally, we calculate the weighted sum of the word representation based on the weight as the sentence vector s_i. The word context vector can be regarded as a high-level representation of fixed query "what is the information word", which is randomly initialized and jointly learned in the training process.

Sentence Encoder Based on Self-Attention. Similarly, we use the self-attention mechanism instead of the traditional bidirectional GRU to obtain the context information of the sentence to represent the current sentence. Similarly, we introduce parameter matrixes $\tilde{W}_Q$, $\tilde{W}_k$, $\tilde{W}_v$. For each sentence s_l:

$$q_l = \tilde{W}_Q s_l \tag{10}$$

$$k_l = \tilde{W}_K s_l \tag{11}$$

$$v_l = \tilde{W}_V s_l \tag{12}$$

Similarly, after calculating the similarity between sentences and normalizing *softmax*, we calculate the weighted sum of v_l as the final sentence vector $\tilde{s}_l$, that is:

$$a_{lj} = \frac{\exp(k_{jl}^T q_l)}{\sum_j \exp(k_{jl}^T q_l)} \tag{13}$$

$$\tilde{s}_l = \sum_j a_{lj} v_l \tag{14}$$

Sentence Attention. In order to reward those sentences as clues to correctly classify documents, we use the attention mechanism again, introduce the sentence level context vector u_s, and use this vector to measure the importance of sentences, which leads to

$$u_i = \tanh(W_s \tilde{s}_i + b_s) \tag{15}$$

$$\alpha_i = \frac{\exp(u_i^T u_s)}{\sum_t \exp(u_i^T u_s)} \tag{16}$$

$$t = \sum_t a_i h_i \tag{17}$$

where t is the document vector that summarizes all sentence information in the document.

3.3 Image Feature Extraction Based on VGG19

In order to capture the image features of news data sets, we use VGG19. In order to extract visual features effectively, we first fine tune the VGG19 pre trained based on ImageNet. For any input picture i_i, we first adjust the size of the picture to 224×224 pixels, and add a fully connected layer on the last layer of the VGG19 network to adjust the dimension of the final visual feature representation to d_i. Therefore, the final image feature can be expressed as:

$$v = \{v_i | v_i \in R^{d_i}\} \tag{18}$$

where v_i is the final image feature of event i and $d_i = 32$ is the dimension of i_i.

3.4 Classification

After the above operations, we get the feature vector representation t_i of news text and the visual feature vector representation v_i of pictures. These features model the different levels of semantic information of the input multimodal news from different angles, which are complementary to each other. We splice these features together to obtain the final multimodal representation of the news:

$$x_i = t_i \oplus v_i \tag{19}$$

After obtaining the multimodal representation of the input news, we input it into the full connection layer, and the output of the full connection layer generates the distribution of classification labels through the *softmax* layer:

$$p = soft\max(W_C x + b_c) \tag{20}$$

where, W_C and b_C are the parameters of the model. We use cross entropy as the loss function of the model:

$$L = -\sum [y^f \log p^f + (1 - y^f) \log\left(1 - p^f\right)] \tag{21}$$

where, y^f is the true label of the sample, 1 indicates that the sample is a rumor, and 0 indicates that the sample is a non rumor; p^f represents the probability that the sample is predicted to be false news.

4 Experiment and Analysis

4.1 Dataset

We use the data set of FakeNewsNet [9], which is specially collected to detect rumors. FakeNewsNet contains labeled news from two websites: politifact.com and gossip-cop.com. The news content includes text and picture information. We crawled the text and picture information of each news through the crawler.

In order to ensure the quality of the data set, we preprocessed the FakeNewsNet data set crawled by the crawler, deleted the news samples with missing text and images, and divided the final training set and test set according to the ratio of 7:3. Relevant data indicators are shown in Table 1.

We compare our model with the rumor detection model using different information. Based on the single text mode, CSI [10] uses LSTM to encode news content information for rumor detection. SAFE [11] uses textCNN to encode news text information. We also apply MLP directly to news text embedding encoded by word2vec. Based on single vision mode, VGG19 is widely used as visual feature extractor. This paper uses the pre trained VGG19 model to fine tune the data set in this paper.

Table 1. Statistics of the dataset.

Dataset	Training set		Test set		Total
	T	F	T	F	
Politifact (POL)	110	110	47	47	314
Gossipcop (GOS)	1578	6108	637	2621	10944
Total	1660	6218	712	2668	11258

Similarly, we also compare the multimodal methods based on text and image in recent years. EANN [12] used TextCNN and pre-trained VGG19 to extract text and visual modal features for rumor detection. MVAE [13] performs feature extraction through Bidirectional LSTM and pre trained VGG19.

4.2   Result Analysis

Table 2 lists the results of the comparative experiment, and the conclusions can be drawn from the observation:

1. The method based on single text mode is better than that based on single visual mode, which shows that rumor detection mainly depends on text clues. The multimodal method is better than the single-mode method with the same sub network structure, which shows that the text and picture modes can provide complementary clues for the rumor detection task.
2. Among the methods based on single text mode, the pre-training language model is better than the traditional text modeling methods such as CNN and RNN, which shows that the pre-training language model effectively learns linguistic knowledge from a large number of pre-training corpus, and also shows the necessity of Glove pre-training.
3. The prediction results of all methods on POL data set have not been significantly improved. The main reason may be that there are too few samples in POL data set, so that all models can not obtain sufficient information for effective modeling. Because the number of samples in GOS data set is sufficient, and the accuracy of our method is significantly higher than that of other comparison methods, it shows that the multi-modal model based on hierarchical attention network proposed in this paper can effectively improve the performance of false news detection. It shows that our model can detect rumors missed by existing methods by fully mining multimodal semantic clues.

Table 2. Performance comparison of different methods

Classification	Method	POL		GOS	
		ACC	F1	ACC	F1
Single text	CSI	0.764	0.759	0.752	0.750
	SAFE	0.733	0.728	0.773	0.771
	Word2vec + MLP	0.764	0.743	0.826	0.815
Single vision	VGG19	0.688	0.675	0.713	0.698
Multi-mode	EANN	0.763	**0.762**	0.848	0.842
	MVAE	0.755	0.748	0.839	0.828
	Ours	**0.773**	0.758	**0.884**	0.876

4.3 Elimination Analysis

In order to verify the influence of different model components on the experimental results, we designed three variants of the model and analyzed the elimination of the model. And because the GOS data set has sufficient samples and can effectively judge the performance of the model, the experiment is only carried out on the GOS data set.

1. Remove the word2vec pre-training based on Glove: All word vectors in the news text are initialized randomly, and then sent to the hierarchical attention network.
2. Remove the hierarchical attention network: After Glove pre-training, all word vectors in the news text are only sent to the most basic bidirectional GRU to encode the text information.
3. Remove the image feature extraction based on VGG19: The text features are extracted only through Glove pre-training and hierarchical attention network, ignoring the picture information in the news samples.

Figure 2 lists the experimental results of elimination analysis, and two conclusions can be obtained:

1. If any part of the model is removed, the classification accuracy of the model will decline to a certain extent, which shows the effectiveness of each element of the model.
2. According to the decline of the classification accuracy of the model after removal, the importance of each model component can be sorted as follows: layered attention > Glove pre-training > VGG19. This shows that for the rumor detection task, text plays a more important role than pictures. And because hierarchical attention can distinguish the important and unimportant content when constructing document representation, it can capture the characteristics of news document hierarchy and play the greatest role in rumor detection task.

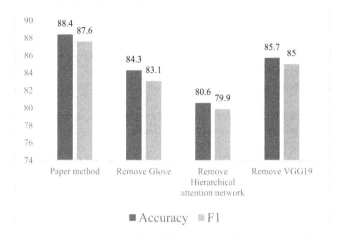

Fig. 2. Ablation study

5 Conclusion

For the rumor detection task, this paper proposes a multi-modal detection model based on hierarchical attention for text feature extraction. Firstly, the model uses the word2vec pre-training model from Glove, and applies two-level attention mechanism at the word and sentence levels to extract features, so as to capture the features of the hierarchical structure of news documents. According to the image features, the pre trained VGG-19 is used to obtain visual information, and finally combined with the text and image features to comprehensively detect rumors, so that the final detection results are more suitable for today's multimodal news and make a more comprehensive and accurate rumor prediction. The algorithm in this paper still has some shortcomings. After a period of time, news has the characteristics of effective and high-quality communication and more semantic information. In the following research, we will also consider mining rumor patterns through communication characteristics to solve the problem of rumor detection.

References

1. Pennington, J., Socher, R., Manning, C.: Glove: global vectors for word representation. In: Conference on Empirical Methods in Natural Language Processing, pp. 1532–1543 (2014)
2. Simonyan, K., Zisserman, A.: Very deep convolutional networks for large-scale image recognition. Computer Science (2016)
3. Ma, J., Gao, W., Mitra, P., et al.: Detecting rumors from microblogs with recurrent neural networks. In: Proceedings of the 25th International Joint Conference on Artificial Intelligence, pp. 3818–3824. AAAI, PaloAlto (2016)
4. Yu F., Liu Q., Wu S., et al.: A convolutional approach for misinformation identification. In: Twenty-Sixth International Joint Conference on Artificial Intelligence (2017)
5. Qian, S., Zhang, T., Xu, C., et al.: Social event classification via boosted multimodal supervised latent dirichlet allocation. ACM Trans. Multimedia Comput. Commun. Appl. (TOMM) **11**(2), 1–22 (2015)

6. Cho, K., Merrienboer, B., Gulcehre, C., et al.: Learning phrase representations using rnn encoder-decoder for statistical machine translation. Computer Science (2014)
7. Yang, Z., Yang, D., Dyer, C., et al.: Hierarchical attention networks for document classification. In: Proceedings of the 2016 Conference of the North American Chapter of the Association for Computational Linguistics: Human Language Technologies, pp. 1480–1489 (2016)
8. Vaswani, A., Shazeer, N., Parmar, N., et al.: Attention is all you need. Adv. Neural Inf. Process. Syst. **30** (2017)
9. Shu, K., Mahudeswaran, D., Wang, S., et al.: FakeNewsNet: a data repository with news content, social context, and spatiotemporal information for studying fake news on social media. Big Data **8**(3), 171–188 (2020)
10. Ruchansky N., Seo S., Yan L.: CSI: A Hybrid Deep Model for Fake News Detection. ACM (2017)
11. Zhou, X., Wu, J., Zafarani, R.: SAFE: similarity-aware multi-modal fake news detection. In Pacific-Asia Conference on Knowledge Discovery and Data Mining, pp. 354–367. Springer, Heidelberh (2020)
12. Wang, Y., Ma, F., Jin, Z., et al.: EANN: event adversarial neural networks for multi-modal fake news detection. In: Proceedings of the 24th ACM Sigkdd International Conference on Knowledge Discovery & Data Mining, pp. 849–857. ACM (2018)
13. Khattar, D., Goud, J.S., Gupta, M., et al.: MVAE: multimodal variational autoencoder for fake news detection. In: Proceedings of the Web Conference 2019, pp. 2915–2921. ACM, New York (2019)

Research on Workflow Model and Verification Method of Remote Sensing Data Processing

Baojun Qiao[1,2], Siyuan He[1,2], Ying Du[1,2(✉)], and Xianyu Zuo[1,2]

[1] Henan Key Laboratory of Big Data Analysis and Processing, Henan University, Kaifeng, China
280034662@qq.com

[2] School of Computer and Information Engineering, Henan University, Kaifeng, China

Abstract. To reduce the uncertainty factors in the remote sensing data processing process and the complexity of remote sensing data processing software, a remote sensing data processing workflow model is presented based on Petri net and UniNet theory. The model can not only describe the data, tasks and their logical relationships involved in remote sensing data processing workflow formally, but also analyze the logic of the process dynamically. Furthermore, the model can be effectively combined with workflow technology, which provide great help for solving remote sensing application needs.

Keywords: Remote sensing data processing process · Petri net · UniNet · Workflow model

1 Introduction

With the continuous improvement of the level of earth observation, remote sensing application technology has made remarkable contributions to the development of society and economy. At the same time, it also involves more and more complex remote sensing data processing, which are composed of a series of interconnected operational tasks and remote sensing data. There may be various structures, such as sequence, concurrency and selection between these tasks and data, making the process complicated and difficult to control. Remote sensing research units in various industries have made breakthroughs in their own fields and have developed a series of remote sensing data processing algorithms [1–3], but most of these algorithms are relatively independent, and there is no practical remote sensing data processing system. Therefore, modeling the remote sensing data processing process can help to rationally plan and manage the implementation of large-scale remote sensing applications in combination with workflow technology.

Workflow technology can support complex application process modeling, process execution and process management, and remote sensing data processing flow is very similar to workflow in form. Therefore, many researchers in the industry apply workflow technology to remote sensing data processing. References [4, 5] studied the application of workflow technology to remote sensing data processing, according to the characteristics of remote sensing product production process, the establishment of workflow model was described, which provided help for solving problems such as complex processing algorithms and lack of unified management of processes. Model construction is the basis for solving practical application problems, especially in the research of dynamic adaptive distributed collaborative workflow for remote sensing big data processing. Building a suitable model can abstract and generalize the remote sensing data processing process well. It can effectively reflect the all-round connection between states, activities and resources, which is the beginning of the construction of remote sensing data processing workflow.

In 1962, the German scholar Carl Adam Petri [6] first proposed the Petri net, which has been widely used in many fields such as computer and automation. Reference [7] describes the application of Petri net in computer science in detail by introducing state elements and transition rules, and believes that Petri net are a graphical modeling tool whose expressive ability is equivalent to Turing machine. Reference [8] extended the classical Petri net and proposed a new description tool UniNet, which avoids the absolute dynamic characteristics of the classical Petri net in the modeling process, while taking into account the relative static characteristics of the system. Reference [9] builds a spatial information workflow model based on UniNet and the background of GIS. PNML is a standard format for Petri net, in 2000, the Petri net standardization effort was initiated at the International Conference on Petri Net Applications and Theory, and PNML was proposed as one of several XML-based exchange formats [10].

In view of this, this paper combines the characteristics of remote sensing data processing flow, based on Petri net theory, constructs remote sensing data processing workflow model RSDPWfModel (Remote Sensing Data Processing Workflow Model) and its standardized expression. In addition, the verification method is researched, and a series of simplified rules are introduced to verify the smoothness of the process.

2 Construction of Workflow Model for Remote Sensing Data Processing

Remote sensing data processing not only requires a lot of computing resources and storage resources, but also the task itself involves multiple steps, and its logic is becoming more and more complex. Remote sensing data processing workflow is the application of workflow technology in remote sensing field, which is different from general workflow. The remote sensing data processing process usually has the characteristics of large amount of calculation, complex algorithm, data-centric process, data-dependent tasks and so on. Remote sensing data processing workflow model is a computerized process model used to describe the remote sensing data processing process, which can support remote sensing data flow and task flow.

2.1 Petri Net and UniNet

Petri net is a formal modeling tool with both graphics and powerful analytical capabilities. At the same time, Petri net has a solid mathematical foundation. The workflow process represented by Petri nets has a very clear and strict definition. Compared with many other informal block diagram techniques, it avoids ambiguity, uncertainty, and contradiction.

Petri net are composed of places, transitions and directed arcs. Places are a collection of states, transitions are a collection of actions, and directed arcs connect places and transitions, tokens are constantly flowing in the places and transitions.

Since the original Petri net modeling is absolutely dynamic, it can describe the control flow of the system well, but ignores the relatively static resources in the system model, which also ignores the data. As an improvement of the petri net, UniNet is originally used as a model to describe the program, it mainly improves the following four aspects:

1) The place is expanded into the control place and the variable place. The control place is similar to the place in the classical Petri net. The variable place is used to store variables, and the variable resources are non-flowing and non-consuming.

2) Extend the meaning of token to the original token and variable. The original token is consistent with the classic Petri net and used to describe the control flow level, while the variable are stored in the variable place and used to describe the data flow level.

3) In addition to the original transition, add the semantics of variable transition, variable transition can interact with both variable place and control place. When variable transition and variable place interact, only use but do not consume the resources, the relationship with the control place will consume the token.

4) Arc are extended into flow relation arc, read arc, write arc and read & write arc. Flow relation arc are equivalent to directed arc in classical Petri net, representing the flow direction and consuming or generating token. The read arc means that only the variables stored in the variable place are read, while the write arc means that the content in the variable place will be changed when the change occurs. The read & write arc is the synthesis of the read arc and write arc.

However, UniNet omitted the understanding of the weight in Petri net. The weight represents the token quantity in the place that needs to be consumed or generated when transition occur. Meanwhile, the weight also controls the branch structure (the default value is 1 if the weight is not marked), and the setting of weight can completely replace the logical control structure in WF-net. The semantic constraints of the model are not affected, and the use value replaces the logical control structure as shown in Fig. 1.

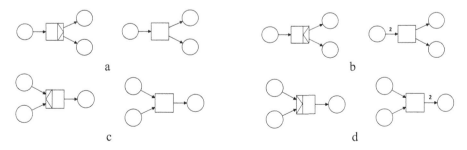

Fig. 1. Weights replace logical control structures.

The left side of Fig. 1-a, 1-b, 1-c and 1-d are OR branch, AND branch, OR connection and AND connection logic control structure, respectively, and the right side is the substitution of logic control using weights. For example, the OR branch on the left in Fig. 1-a indicates that the logic control can only activate one of the two subsequent places. When replacing with the right weight, just change the weight on the front arc to 1, indicates that the transition needs to get one token from the former set place, and the redundancy of tokens are not allowed in each node. One token in a transition can only activate one state of the two successor places; the AND branch on the left in Fig. 1-b represents the state where the logic control can activate two subsequent places at the same time, when replacing with the right weight, just change the weight on the front arc to 2, indicates that the transition needs to get two tokens in the former place, the weights on the two arcs after the transition are 1, only one token is required for the state activation of the two successor places. Therefore, the transition can activate the states of the two successor places at the same time. Similarly, the OR connection and the AND connection in Fig. 1-c and 1-d can also be replaced by weights.

2.2 Remote Sensing Data Processing Workflow Model RSDPWfModel

The weight on the arc in the original Petri net represents the number of tokens that need to be consumed or generated in the place for the transition to occur. However, since the description method of UniNet is to describe the program, The operation data and control coexist in the model, and the biggest characteristic of the variable place is non-flow and non-consumption. Therefore, UniNet omits the understanding of the weights in the Petri net. According to the research results in the related fields of Petri net, and referring to the idea of place and arc extension in UniNet, this paper proposes a remote sensing data processing workflow model RSDPWfModel based on Petri net.

RSDPWfMode consists of a 6-tuple $N = (Pc, Pd, T; R, W, F)$, and satisfy the following conditions:(1) $Pc \cup Pd \cup T \neq \varphi$; (2) $(Pc \cap Pd) \cap T = \varphi$; (3) $R \subseteq Pd \times T$, $W \subseteq Pd \times T$, $F \subseteq Pc \times T \cup T \times Pc$; (4) $Pc = Dom (F) \cup cod (F)$, $Pd = dom(R \cup W)$, $T \subseteq dom (F) \cup cod (F) \cup cod (R \cup W)$.

Pc, Pd, T are the control place, data place and transition, respectively. Control place has the same meaning as the place in the classic Petri net, the significance of control place to hold tokens to represent a certain state, the data place is used to express the data required in the process, among them, the data in the data place is characterized by flow and non-consumption. At the same time, the data place also stores tokens, which represent the state conditions, and together with the weights, determine the occurrence rights of subsequent transitions. Transition is similar to the classical Petri net, used to represent task operations, which can act on both the data place and the control place. R, W, and F are arcs, which represent the read relationship, write relationship and control flow relationship between the place and the transition, respectively. The read relationship means that the transition acquires the data stored in the data place and consumes the tokens in it. The write relationship means that the transition rewrites data in the data place and stores the tokens. The control flow relationship represents the flow direction of the process, and tokens are consumed during the process flow.

RSDPWfModel is shown in Fig. 2, the place is represented by a circle, and the transition is represented by a square. The control place, transition and the control flow relationship between them are shown in Fig. 2-a, the weight on the arc represents the number of tokens required for the transition to occur. The database and the transition and the read relationship between them are shown in Fig. 2-b, the transition gets the data in the data place, and consume the tokens in it. Figure 2-c shows the data place and the transition and the write relationship between them. After the transition occurs, the data in the data place will be rewritten and stored in tokens.

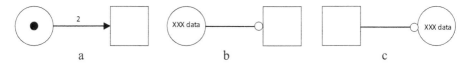

a   b   c

Fig. 2. Control flow, read and write relationship.

The read arc and write arc can also have weight, as shown in Fig. 3. The role of the weight here is not represents the number of times to obtain and rewrite data, instead, according to the process semantics, the number of tokens consumed and produced determines whether the structure here is concurrent or selective. The occurrence of transition T_1 causes the corresponding data written in the data place Pd_1 to store 2 tokens at the same time, when subsequent transitions T_2 and T_3 acquire Pd_1 data, the occurrence of T_2 and T_3 only needs to consume one token each. Therefore, T_2 and T_3 are concurrent. Similarly, the occurrence of T_4 makes Pd_2 have only one token, only one of these transitions can occur in T_5 and T_6. Similarly, the subsequent transitions of Pd_3 can only be T_8, T_9 or T_8, T_{10} two groups of transitions concurrent, T_9 and T_{10} cannot be concurrent. Although the concurrency conditions are met, there will be token redundancy in Pd_3, which is not allowed.

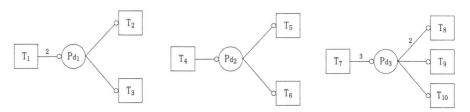

Fig. 3. Weight determination structure.

3   The Expression of RSDPWfModel

Since the RSDPWfModel proposed in this paper is based on Petri net, the types of Petri net and the diversification of tools make the file formats of Petri nets complex and numerous, and there are gaps between different types of Petri net files. This problem was solved in the International Conference on Petri Net Application and Theory in 2000. Petri net markup language PNML is taken as one of the schemes. In order to expand the use mode and scope of RSDPWfModel and improve the standardization of RSDPWfModel, this section studies the normalized structure file of Petri net markup language PNML of RSDPWfModel, and proposes the normalized expression of RSDPWfModel to the improved part of Petri net. The corresponding relationship is shown in Table 1, which is of great significance to solve the interoperability problem between different Petri net variants.

Table 1. PNML expression of RSDPWfModel file.

class	PNML elements	PNML properties
RSDPWfModel file	\<pnml\>	
RSDPWfModel net	\<net\>	id: unique identifier
place	\<place\>	id: unique identifier type: type
transition	\<transition\>	id: unique identifier
arc	\<arc\>	id: unique identifier Source: the starting element Target: the target element
graphical information	\<graphics\>	
name	\<name\>	
...	...	...

1) The place is represented by the label\<place\>, the attribute of label \<place\> in the original Petri net has only one id as the unique identification of the place. Because RSDPWfModel divides the place into data place and control place, a new attribute type is added in \<place\> to define the type of the place. The value of the attribute type is data or control, representing the data place and control place respectively. The label \<graphics\> describes the drawing information of the place, the label \<position\> describes the two-dimensional location information of the place, the label \<dimension\> represents the size of the place, the label \<name\> describes the information of the name of the place, the label \<initialmarking\> is the initial state of the place, and the conversion from the place to PNML in RSDPWfModel is shown in Fig. 4.

RSDPWfModel element	Representation of PNML
| | ```
<place id="P1" type="data">
    <graphics>
        <position x="" y=""/>
        <dimension x="" y=""/>
    </graphics>
    <name>
        <value>xxx data</value>
        <graphics>
            <offset x="" y=""/>
        </graphics>
    </name>
    <initialMarking>
        <value>1</value>
        <graphics>
            <offset x="" y=""/>
        </graphics>
    </initialMarking>
</place>
``` |

Fig. 4. PNML expression of place.

2) The arc is represented by the label <arc>, and the label <arc> in the original Petri net gives three attributes: id, source and target, which are used to represent the unique identification, starting node and target node of the arc respectively. The label <graphics> is the same as that defined in the place. It is used to describe drawing information, <start_position> is the start position of the arc, <end_position> is the end position of the arc. Tag <instruction> sub tag <value> represents the weight on the arc. Redefine the value attribute value of tag <type>, which can be read, write and control, representing the read relationship, write relationship and control flow relationship respectively. The conversion from arc to PNML in RSDPWfModel is shown in Fig. 5.

The improvement of RSDPWfModel on Petri net mainly lies in the extension of place and arc. Therefore, the PNML standardized format of other elements in the model should be basically consistent with that in the original Petri net. This paper will not describe other elements in detail. The PNML file fragment of RSDPWfModel is shown in Table 2.
```

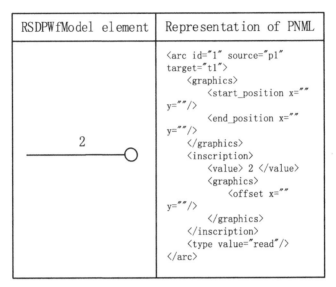

RSDPWfModel element	Representation of PNML

2 ──────○	`<arc id="1" source="p1" target="t1">`
	`    <graphics>`
	`        <start_position x="" y=""/>`
	`        <end_position x="" y=""/>`
	`    </graphics>`
	`    <inscription>`
	`        <value> 2 </value>`
	`        <graphics>`
	`            <offset x="" y=""/>`
	`        </graphics>`
	`    </inscription>`
	`    <type value="read"/>`
	`</arc>`

Fig. 5. PNML expression of arc.

Table 2. PNML file fragment of RSDPWfModel.

```
<?xml version="1.0" encoding="utf-8" ?>
<pnml>
    <net id="01" type="RSDPWfModel">
        < place id ="p1"> ... </place >
        < place id ="p2"> ... </place >
        < place id ="p3"> ... </place >
        ...
        < transition id ="t1"> ... </transition >
        ...
        < arc id ="a1" source ="p1" target ="t1"> ... </arc >
        < arc id ="a2" source ="p2" target ="t1"> ... </arc >
        < arc id ="a3" source ="t1" target ="p3"> ... </arc >
        ...
    </net>
</pnml >
```

4   Verification Method of RSDPWfModel

After the definition of remote sensing data processing workflow process is completed, it is necessary to verify its correctness first. Only after it is proved that the built workflow model has no deadlocks and no dead tasks, it is meaningful to perform performance analysis and simulation optimization on it. The correctness of RSDPWfModel directly determines the success of remote sensing data processing. There may be token redundancy, deadlock and other problems for manual or automatic construction processes. Therefore, the construction of remote sensing data processing process needs strict verification, so as to find the problems in the process. This paper introduces the concept of synchronizer and the corresponding simplification rules to RSDPWfModel for patency analysis to achieve the purpose of verification.

Definition of synchronizer: $T_1 = \{t_{11}, t_{12} \ldots t_{1n}\}$, $T_2 = \{t_{21}, t_{22} \ldots t_{2m}\}$ are two task sets, while a and b meet: $1 \leq a \leq n$, $1 \leq b \leq m$, place P is the connecting location of T_1 and T_2, $t_{1i} \in T_1$, $t_{2j} \in T_2$ meet the close neighbor relationship, then P is called synchronizer, represented by $P = (T_1, T_2, (a, b))$.

The synchronizer details are shown in Fig. 6. The weight on the back arc of P is a and the weight on the front arc is b. Because a transitions are selected to occur in T_1, after each transition occurs, information will be passed to the back. The transition in the second group has to wait for the information of a tasks to come in, so the weight of the subsequent transition to happen is a. The weight on the previous arc is b, after the tasks are completed, b tokens will be issued to the subsequent b tasks, and each task will be given to one. When the token number in P is the product of a and b, the b transitions in T_2 have the right of occurrence. These b transitions need to obtain the right of occurrence at the same time, because the weight a means that one token needs to be obtained from each of the a transitions. The physical meaning of synchronizer is that the previous transitions are concurrent. After it happened, all the tokens went into P, b transitions in T_2 simultaneously get the right to occur, so as to realize global synchronization by local synchronization.

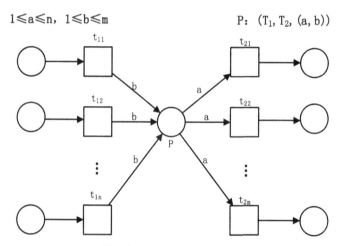

Fig. 6. Synchronizer details.

In principle, the model verification method based on graphical simplification is to continuously use simplification rules to simplify all process logic structures from the model. A workflow process model with structural conflicts cannot be completely simplified. If the final result after simplification is a single place, then the process is smooth and reasonable.

Simplification rule 1: Synchronizer $P = (\{t_1\}, \{t_2\}, (1,1))$, when $t_1 \bullet \cap \bullet t_2 = P$, P can be eliminated, and t_1, t_2 can be combined into t.

Simplification rule 2: If the transition t, the places P_1 and P_2 satisfy $t \in P_1 \bullet \wedge \{t\} = \bullet P_2$, and $P_2 \neq \emptyset \vee P_1 \bullet = \{t\}$, then P_1 and P_2 can be completely merged into P.

Simplification rule 3: Synchronizers $P_1 = (T_1, T, (a, u))$, $P_2 = (T, T_2, (v, b))$, when $a = b$, synchronizers P_1, P_2 can be combined into one synchronizer P, and $P = (T_1, T_2, (a, b))$, as shown in Fig. 7.

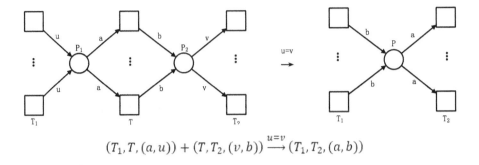

$$(T_1, T, (a, u)) + (T, T_2, (v, b)) \xrightarrow{u=v} (T_1, T_2, (a, b))$$

Fig. 7. Simplification rule 3.

Simplification rule 4: $\bullet t_1 = P$, $\bullet t_2 = P$, and t_1 and t_2 conflict, at this time, P can be split into P_1 and P_2, as shown in Fig. 8.

Fig. 8. Simplification rule 4.

5   Process Case of Extracting Vegetation Area from Remote Sensing Data

The process of extracting vegetation area from remote sensing data is represented by RSDPWfModel, as shown in Fig. 9. The remote sensing data processing flow is entered from a starting place, and read remote sensing data sources through start transition, establishes the interpretation mark and preprocesses the remote sensing data transition through the remote sensing data source. After these two transitions occur, the remote sensing image map is obtained. On the basis of remote sensing images, traditional manual classification methods or deep learning classification can be selected, and different changes can be selected according to different classification methods. After the classification result is obtained, the area is extracted using the result, and the process ends.

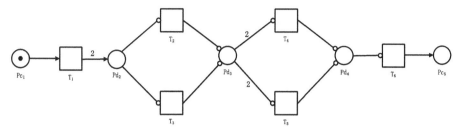

Fig. 9. RSDPWfModel representation of the process of extracting vegetation area from remote sensing data.

The corresponding relationship between the meanings of places and transitions in this process is shown in Table 3.

Table 3. Corresponding relationship between the meanings of places and transitions.

transition	meaning	place	meaning
T_1	Start	Pc_1	In
T_2	Create interpretation flags	Pd_2	Remote sensing data sources
T_3	Preprocessing remote sensing data	Pd_3	Remote sensing image map
T_4	Deep learning classification	Pd_4	Classification result
T_5	Traditional manual classification	Pc_5	Out
T_6	Area extraction		

The proof of the correctness of the process logic using the simplification rules is shown in Fig. 10. All places (including the control places and the data places) can be considered as synchronizers. The weight of the arc in front of the remote sensing data source is 2, which means that the two transitions of establishing the interpretation flag and preprocessing the remote sensing data are carried out simultaneously. The weight of the arc behind the remote sensing data source is 1, which means only waiting for the previous token, so the remote sensing data source is a kind of sequential and concurrent synchronization. The remote sensing image map is obtained after the establishment of the interpretation mark and the preprocessing of the remote sensing data. The weights of the two arcs behind the remote sensing image are both 2, indicating that the previous establishment of the interpretation mark and the preprocessing of the remote sensing data require concurrent, and the latter two classifications transition can happen. The weight of the arc in front of the remote sensing image map is 1, which means that the subsequent deep learning classification and traditional classification changes can only choose one of them to occur, so the remote sensing image map is a synchronization of concurrency and selection. According to the simplification rules mentioned above, the remote sensing data source and remote sensing image map can be regarded as a synchronizer. Ultimately, the process can be simplified into a repository, which means that the process is smooth and logical.

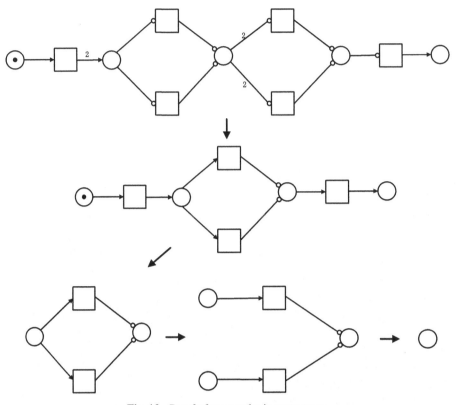

Fig. 10. Proof of process logic correctness.

6 Summary

By establishing a remote sensing data processing workflow model to analyze and verify it, it makes up for the lack of a unified workflow model in the current remote sensing data processing. The RSDPWfModel proposed in this paper can not only formally describe the data and tasks involved in the process of remote sensing data processing, but also the advantages of Petri net can be well reflected. For example, the strict semantics of Petri net can meet the rigor of remote sensing data processing procedures; The local determination principle of Petri net can effectively reflect the dynamics of remote sensing data processing flow and so on. Introducing the data place into the Petri net, which facilitates the management of data in the process. While retaining the advantages of Petri net in describing dynamic systems, it also solves the shortcomings of insufficient expression of data flow by Petri net. And enhances the advantages of Petri net modeling. The project is supported in partly by National Key Research and Development Program of China (2019YFE0126600), Major Project of Science and Technology of Henan Province (201400210300), Henan Province Key R&D and Promotion Special (Science and Technology) Project (212102210079), Henan Province Education Reform Project (2021SJGLX080), Henan University Teaching Reform Project (HDXJJG2021–010).

References

1. Sidorova, V.S.: Hierarchical cluster algorithm for remote sensing data of earth. Pattern Recogn. Image Anal. **22**(2), 373–379 (2012). https://doi.org/10.1134/S1054661812020149
2. Zhou, B., Guan-feng, W., Yong, X., Li, J., Liu, Y.: A visual dataflow model for the process flow of remote sensing products. In: Huang, D.-S., Bevilacqua, V., Figueroa, J.C., Premaratne, P. (eds.) ICIC 2013. LNCS, vol. 7995, pp. 482–489. Springer, Heidelberg (2013). https://doi.org/10.1007/978-3-642-39479-9_57
3. Yuan, J., et al.: A new classification algorithm for high spatial resolution remote sensing data. Int. Soc. Optics Photonics **7285**, 72850H (2008)
4. Sun, X., et al.: Workflow application in operation and control of remote sensing data processing. Comput. Eng. (2012)
5. Wang, Q., Li, X.: Research of visual customized production platform of remote sensing products based on workflow. Comput. Era (2) (2015)
6. Peter, R.: Petri net theory and the modeling of systems. Comput. J. (1), p. 1
7. Yuan, C.: Principle and Application of Petri Net. Publishing House of Electronics Industry (2005)
8. Zhou, G., Yuan, C.: Mapping PUNITY to UniNet. J. Comput. Sci. Technol. **18**(3), 378–387 (2003)
9. Gao, Y., Liu, Y., Wu, L.: Geo-workflow model based on petri nets. Comput. Eng. **31**(16), 3 (2005)
10. Bastide, R., et al.: Meeting on XML/SGML based interchange formats for petri nets. Unify. Petri Nets Lncs Adv. Petri Nets **13**(27), 47–52 (2000)

Relation-Aware Facial Expression Recognition Using Contextual Residual Network with Attention Mechanism

Xue Li[1,2,3] , Chunhua Zhu[1,2,3(✉)] , and Fei Zhou[1,2,3]

[1] Key Laboratory of Grain Information Processing and Control, Ministry of Education, Henan University of Technology, Zhengzhou, Henan, China
zhuchunhua@haut.edu.cn
[2] College of Information Science and Engineering, Henan University of Technology, Zhengzhou, Henan, China
[3] Henan Key Laboratory of Grain Photoelectric Detection and Control, Henan University of Technology, Zhengzhou, Henan, China

Abstract. With the existence of occlusion or posture changes, facial expression recognition (FER) under uncontrolled conditions is difficult. To obtain a discriminative representation for challenging expression recognition, we present a relation-aware FER model, referred to attention-coordinated contextual residual network (ACRN), which contains a contextual residual network (CRNet) and attention module (AM). Firstly, multi-level features of facial expression are extracted by CRNet. There are some contextual convolution (CoConv) blocks in CRNet to integrate expression information in facial space; then, AM is embedded into each stage of CRNet to coordinate contextual information from CoConv blocks across the channel and spatial location, weighting multi-level expression features to differentiate their importance; finally, to highlight expression-related facial areas, the output of CRNet will be fed into AM, which can focus on salient features. The experiments on Affectnet-7 and RAF_DB datasets have shown that ACRN can both explore the interaction of facial information and capture subtle features related to expression, thus obtaining a better recognition performance.

Keywords: Facial Expression Recognition (FER) · Contextual Residual Network (CRNet) · Expression Information · Attention Module (AM)

1 Introduction

During conveying human emotion, facial expression is important. Some studies have shown that more than fifty percent of human emotions are conveyed through their facial expressions [1]. Recently, the technology of facial expression recognition(FER) is extensively used in home automation, online education, health assessment, and other scenarios [2–4]. How distinguish different categories of expressions has been a challenging task, especially when there is occlusion or pose variation on face, which results in some invisible facial regions.

Overviewing the existing FER methods, they are mainly sorted into both types: hand-crafted patterns and deep neural calculation. The classical methods are driven by some feature operators such as HOG [5] LBP [6], and SIFT [7], which are developed to describe the different facial expressions to train classifiers. In [8], the features were extracted from eyes and mouth regions by the HOG descriptor. And the LBP feature extraction operator has the characteristics of computational simplicity and illumination in-variance, however, which is readily affected by the noise [9], and the SIFT can describe the facial images successfully and keep invariant for rotation and scaling [10], but there is also a part of needless information which is described by SIFT. Limited by these predefined patterns, the facial expression images from changing environments cannot be well represented. Lately, the DL technique, especially convolutional neural network (CNN), which performs strong generalization, is broadly adapted in FER. A patch-based attention network denoted as pACNN introduced a attention mechanism in CNN [11]. In [12], Li et al. designed a deep network named locality preserving convolutional neural network (DLP-CNN), which aimed to boost the discriminative ability of representation by maintaining local proximity and maximizing the difference between classes.

Although these methods are successfully under controlled conditions, they perform not well as transferred from controlled conditions to uncontrolled ones. Subsequently, some improved methods were proposed. Some methods improve FER performance by redesigning the network structure. A pairwise differential Siamese network (PDSN) in [13] is designed to implement facial expression recognition by modeling the relation between occluded patches of face and impaired features. Xie et al. [14] proposed a FER network with two branches, one of which acquired local features from each facial part, and the global features in the entire facial scope were perceived by the other branch. Specifically, the details were described by local features, while the semantic information was described by global features, which are eventually aggregated for facial expression classification. In [15], the facial expression information was regarded as a combination of general information across different categories and specific information for each category. So, the ways of decomposition and reconstruction learning were employed to extract advanced features to capture fine-grained differences between different expressions. A feature selection network (FSN) was presented in [16] that filters out irrelevant features automatically. Besides, attention mechanism is utilized to further refine features in some works. A new attention mechanism is introduced in [17], namely grid attention, where the former was used to extract low-level features to take the dependencies between regions of facial expression images, while the latter represented high-level semantic features, enhancing the ability of distance biased learning. For the FER task, Liu et al. [18] exploited a sparse self-attention approach to capture spatial context, so as to learn subtle expression-related features from regions of face. At the same time, the cascade structure in 18 is also used to improve FER. However, the potential relation cross facial patches are incompletely explored in these methods, which means not acquiring comprehensive information related to expression.

In our method, we produced a relation-aware network for FER under uncontrolled conditions, termed attention-coordinated contextual residual network (ACRN), in which a contextual residual network (CRNet) is built and attention modules (AM) are embedded. The proposed network can explore interactivity between local details in a global scope and capturing subtle information on facial expressions. Our work content can be generalized as follows:

1) By integrating contextual convolution (CoConv) blocks in ResNet, a contextual Residual network (CRNet) is constructed, which extracts features of facial expression from multiple levels.
2) To further refine features, the multi-level features are adaptively modulated by coordinate attention modules, encouraging the network to retain subtle information related to information.
3) The effectiveness of ACRN is verified on Affectnet-7 and RAF_DB datasets.

2   Proposed Method

The overall structure about our approach is displayed in Fig. 1, which contains a contextual residual network (CRNet) for extracting multi-level features and attention modules (AM) for enhancing features and emphasizing salient regions. More details are explained as follows.

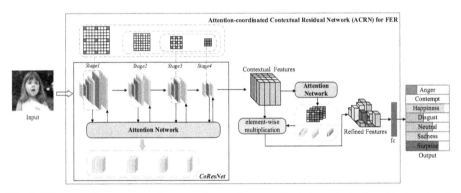

Fig. 1. The overall structure of proposed attention-coordinated contextual residual network (ACRN)

2.1   CRNet for Multi-level Feature Extraction

In deep facial expression recognition, multi-level features can describe global information while capturing local details. Inspired by [19], we introduce contextual convolution (CoConv) blocks in ResNet to construct contextual residual network (CRNet), obtaining multi-level features of facial expression. A contextual convolution (CoConv) block is illustrated in Fig. 2.

A CoConv block at level of $Level = \{1, 2, \ldots, n\}$ with kinds of dilation ratios $Dilation = \{d_1, d_2, \ldots, d_n\}$ receives a feature map M^{in}. At $level = i$, there are convolutional kernels with $d_i, \forall i \in L$. And the dilation ratio is gradually increased, which can explore the contextual information widely. The output feature maps are denoted as

M^{out_i}, the width of each of which is W^{out} and the height is H^{out}. The local details of face are captured by the contextual convolution kernels with lower dilation ratios, and the global information is incorporated by higher ones, to benefit FER.

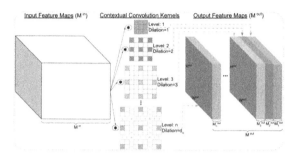

Fig. 2. A contextual convolution (CoConv) block. At each level, there are multiple kernels $d_1 = 1$, $d_2 = 2$ which are visual in this illustration. Generally, d_i should be equal to i.

Different from the way of cascaded networks, contextual convolution (CoConv) is directly integrated into each stage in CRNet, which contains a CoConv block at different level. The deeper the network layer is, the smaller the feature map size is. So, the level of CoConv blocks at each stage are set on the basis of their size. Table 1 shows the settings of parameters in stages of CRNet.

Table 1. Parameters of contextual residual network

Stage	Input	Level	Coconv block
1	56×56	$level = 4$	$\begin{bmatrix} 3 \times 3, 16, d_1 = 1 \\ 3 \times 3, 16, d_2 = 2 \\ 3 \times 3, 16, d_3 = 3 \\ 3 \times 3, 16, d_4 = 4 \end{bmatrix}$
2	28×28	$level = 3$	$\begin{bmatrix} 3 \times 3, 64, d_1 = 1 \\ 3 \times 3, 32, d_2 = 2 \\ 3 \times 3, 32, d_2 = 3 \end{bmatrix}$
3	14×14	$level = 2$	$\begin{bmatrix} 3 \times 3, 128, d_1 = 1 \\ 3 \times 3, 128, d_2 = 2 \end{bmatrix}$
4	7×7	$level = 1$	$[3 \times 3, 512, d_1 = 1]$

2.2 Attention Modules for Feature Enhancement

To enhance subtle features and emphasize salient regions of facial expression, as shown in Fig. 3, attention modules (AM) are embedded into CRNet to coordinate multi-level features in each stage of the network.

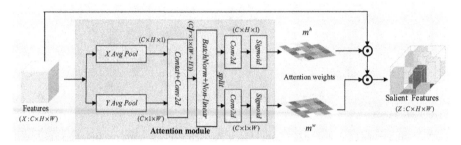

Fig. 3. A attention module (AM) for feature enhancement. Here, the global average pooling operations in horizontal and vertical directions is denoted as '*X Avg Pool*' and '*Y Avg Pool*'.

Feature encoding is carried out on each channel through horizontal and vertical global pooling operations in Eq. 1 and Eq. 2. The input is denoted as x, and the output is denoted as y.

$$y_c^w(w) = \frac{1}{H} \sum_{0 \leq i \leq H} x_c(j, w) \tag{1}$$

$$y_c^w(w) = \frac{1}{H} \sum_{0 \leq i \leq H} x_c(j, w) \tag{2}$$

where, x_c is the feature map of the c-th channel, while y_c^w and y_c^h are the corresponding output in two directions; h,w represents the size of the encoded output respectively.

Through the above two transformations, the feature maps are aggregated in two spatial directions respectively [20], which encourages the network to capture the correlation of facial expression information and retain the location of the salient facial region. Then, the transformation function F in Eq. 3 is executed on the merged feature maps.

$$g = \delta\left(F\left(\left[y^h, y^w\right]\right)\right) \tag{3}$$

where, $\left[y^h, y^w\right]$ refers to the merged feature maps; δ represents the *sigmoid* activation function; the middle feature maps is g, and $g \in R^{C/r \times (H+W)}$, where a reduction rate r is adopted to lessen channels. Next, the middle feature maps g is disentangled into g^h and g^w, which are employed F_h and F_w in Eq. 4 and Eq. 5.

$$m^h = \delta\left(F_h\left(g^h\right)\right) \tag{4}$$

$$m^w = \delta\left(F_w\left(g^w\right)\right) \tag{5}$$

Here, m^h and m^w are two attentive weights in different spatial directions, which are orderly multiplied with the input features in Eq. 6 to obtain the final output z.

$$z_c(k, l) = x_c(k, l) \times m_c^h(k) \times m_c^w(l) \tag{6}$$

3 Experiments

3.1 Datasets

Affectnet-7 [21] has 280K images of real facial expressions for training and 3500 images for testing, including six kinds of basic facial expressions and neutral expression.

DAF_DB [12, 22] is collected under uncontrolled condition. It is tagged based on crowd-sourcing technology. In our experiments, a subset with single-label containing seven kinds of basic emotions is used.

3.2 Implementation Details

We firstly align each facial expression image and then resize it to 256×256. The standard stochastic gradient descent (SGD) is as our optimizer during model training phase, whose momentum is 0.9. The random crops is our way of data augmentation. At test time, the central crops with the size of 224×224 are as input. There are 60 epochs for training. The learning rate is 0.01 at the beginning. After every 20 epochs, it is reduced to one tenth of the previous one. For Affectnet-7, the batch size is set to 32, and for DAF_DB, it is set to 16.

3.3 Quantitative Evaluation Results

By quantifying the recognition results, the performance on two facial expression datasets is evaluated respectively in Table 2. The ResNet was used as our baseline, and multiple levels of contextual convolution (CoConv) blocks were applied to construct the contextual residual network (CRNet). Then, the attention module(AM) is embedded into each stage of the CRNet, termed CRNet-AM-a, while the final output of the CRNet is fed into an attention module, which is termed CRNet-AM-b. The final model, namely Attention-coordinated Contextual Residual Network (ACRN), is combined the above two modes in Network.

Observing Table 2, we draw a conclusion that ACRN better than baseline and CRNet. The results verify the effectiveness of ACRN in discriminating subtle differences of facial expressions under uncontrolled conditions.

The performance of our method with comparable models are in Table 3 and Table 4, from which, the recognition accuracy of ACRN is 62.86% on AffectNet-7 and 83.60% on RAF_DB datasets respectively, which is higher than other models. And the results can be explained by the aggregation of facial information and the refinement of facial features in ACRN.

In Table 3 and Table 4, the metrics of recall is also used to evaluate our proposed model. The recall of ACRN on both datasets is higher than that of other models, specifically, which is 64.19% on AffectNet-7 and 75.34% on RAF_DB.

Table 2. The expression recognition performance about various models on two facial expression datasets

Model	Accuracy (%)	
	RAF-DB	AffectNet-7
ResNet(baseline)	80.96	60.28
CRNet	81.81	60.83
CRNet_AM-a	83.25	62.06
CRNet_AM-b	83.54	62.61
ACRN	**83.60**	**62.86**

Table 3. Performance Comparison on AffectNet

Method	Accuracy(%)	Recall(%)
FMPN [23]	61.25	–
OADN [24]	61.89	64.00
Ensemble CNN [25]	62.11	62.11
DDA-Loss [26]	62.34	62.34
ACRN	**62.86**	**64.19**

Table 4. Performance Comparison on RAF_DB

Method	Accuracy(%)	Recall(%)
FSN [16]	81.10	73.34
CNN [27]	82.69	–
DLP-CNN [22]	82.84	74.35
pACNN [11]	83.27	–
ACRN	**83.60**	**75.34**

3.4 Visual Evaluation Results

In order to further analyze the performance of ACRN, together with baseline, the feature distributions of RAF-DB under the proposed method are presented, which is as shown in Fig. 4. We used a widely used visualization method, namely t-SNE [28].

According to the visualization results, for FER task under uncontrolled conditions, the facial features under the baseline model are not sufficient to distinguish similar expressions, while features from our model (ACRN) tend to cluster in space for easy discrimination of different expressions, which benefits from extensive contextual information.

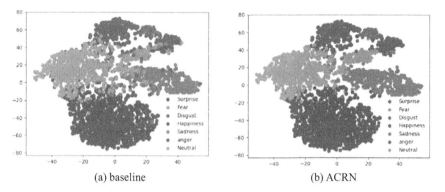

(a) baseline   (b) ACRN

Fig. 4. The feature distributions of RAF-DB under (a) baseline and (b) "ACRN".

4 Conclusion

By cooperating the contextual residual network (CRNet) with the attention modules (MA), a relation-aware FER model named attention-coordinated contextual residual network (ACRN) is presented. The contextual convolution (CoConv) blocks are employed in the CRNet to obtain the facial information in latent space, so as to extract expression features from multiple levels. Furthermore, there are attention modules (AM) for modulating features according to their importance for expression recognition. Finally, the experiments show that ACRN is effective for discriminating different expressions in the wild, which is better than others.

The recognition accuracy is improved by redesigning the network structure, making it beneficial to facial expression image classification that requires fine-grained information. In the proposed network, the contextual convolution and attention mechanisms work cooperatively with each other. However, the performance of the network is limited due to the unbalanced distribution of data in various expression categories, so we will define a suitable loss function in future research to administrate during model training on imbalanced data, so as to achieve better performance.

Acknowledgment. This work was supported in part by the National Science Foundation of China (Grant No. 61871176), applied research plan of key scientific research projects in Henan colleges and Universities (Grant No. 22A510013), the Scientific Research Foundation Natural Science Project in Henan University of Technology (Grant No. 2018RCJH18), and the Innovative Funds Plan of Henan University of Technology Plan (Grant No. 2020ZKCJ02).

References

1. Ramdani, C., Ogier, M., Coutrot, A.: Communicating and reading emotion with masked faces in the Covid era: a short review of the literature. Psychiat. Res. **316**, 114755 (2022)
2. Deng, S., Sun, Y., Galvan, E.: Neural architecture search using genetic algorithm for facial expression recognition. In: Genetic and Evolutionary Computation Conference Companion, pp. 423–426 (2022)

3. Seal, A., Saha, R., Kumar, R., et al.: facial emotion recognition in static and live streaming image dataset using CNN. In: International Conference on Computational Intelligence in Communications and Business Analytics, pp. 288–297 (2022)

4. Tuama, B.A., Shawkat, S.A., Askar, N.A.: Recognition and classification of facial expressions using artificial neural networks. In: 2022 International Congress on Human-Computer Interaction, Optimization and Robotic Applications, pp. 1–8 (2022)

5. Yan, R., Yang, M., Zheng, Q., et al.: Facial expression recognition based on hybrid geometry-appearance and dynamic-still feature fusion. Multimedia Tools. Appl. **82**, 1–26 (2022)

6. Lei, J., Liu, Z., Zou, Z., et al.: Mid-level representation enhancement and graph embedded uncertainty suppressing for facial expression recognition. arXiv preprint arXiv: 2207.13235 (2022)

7. Ramadhan, A.D., Usman, K., Pratiwi, N.K.C.: Comparative analysis of various optimizers on residual network architecture for facial expression identification. In: 2nd International Conference on Electronics, Biomedical Engineering, and Health Informatics, pp. 279–288 (2022)

8. Ahadit, A.B., Jatoth, R.K.: A novel multi-feature fusion deep neural network using HOG and VGG-Face for facial expression classification. Mach. Vision Appl. **33**(4), 1–23 (2022)

9. Kartheek, M.N., Prasad, M.V.N.K., Bhukya R.: Texture based feature extraction using symbol patterns for facial expression recognition. Cogn. Neurodyn., 1–19 (2022)

10. Du, Y., Wang, Q., Xiong, Y.: Adaptive graph-based feature normalization for facial expression recognition. arXiv preprint arXiv: 2207.11123 (2022)

11. Li, Y., Zeng, J., Shan, S., et al.: Patch-gated CNN for occlusion-aware facial expression recognition. In: 24th International Conference on Pattern Recognition, pp. 2209–2214 (2018)

12. Li, S., Deng, W., Du, J, P.: Reliable crowdsourcing and deep locality-preserving learning for expression recognition in the wild. In: IEEE Conference on Computer Vision and Pattern Recognition, pp. 2852–2861 (2017)

13. Song, L., Gong, D., Li, Z., et al.: Occlusion robust face recognition based on mask learning with pairwise differential siamese network. In: IEEE/CVF International Conference on Computer Vision, pp. 773–782 (2019)

14. Xie, S., Hu, H.: Facial expression recognition using hierarchical features with deep comprehensive multipatches aggregation convolutional neural networks. IEEE Trans. Multimedia. **21**(1), 211–220 (2018)

15. Ruan, D., Yan, Y., Lai, S., et al.: Feature decomposition and reconstruction learning for effective facial expression recognition. In: IEEE/CVF Conference on Computer Vision and Pattern Recognition, pp. 7660–7669 (2021)

16. Zhao, S., Cai, H., Liu, H., et al.: Feature selection mechanism in CNNs for facial expression recognition. In: British Machine Vision Conference, p. 317 (2018)

17. Huang, Q., Huang, C., Wang, X., et al.: Facial expression recognition with grid-wise attention and visual transformer. Inf. Sci. **580**, 35–54 (2021)

18. Liu, D., Ouyang, X., Xu, S., et al.: SAANet: siamese action-units attention network for improving dynamic facial expression recognition. Neurocomputing **413**, 145–157 (2020)

19. Duta, I.C., Georgescu, M.I., Ionescu, R.T.: Contextual convolutional neural networks. In: IEEE/CVF International Conference on Computer Vision, pp. 403–412 (2021)

20. Hou, Q., Zhou, D., Feng, J.: Coordinate attention for efficient mobile network design. In: IEEE/CVF Conference on Computer Vision and Pattern Recognition, pp. 13713–13722 (2021)

21. Mollahosseini, A., Hasani, B., Mahoor, M.H.: Affectnet: a database for facial expression, valence, and arousal computing in the wild. IEEE Trans. Affect. Comput. **10**(1), 18–31 (2017)

22. Li, S., Deng, W.: Reliable crowdsourcing and deep locality-preserving learning for unconstrained facial expression recognition. IEEE Trans. Image. Process. **28**(1), 356–370 (2018)

23. Chen, Y., Wang, J., Chen, S., et al.: Facial motion prior networks for facial expression recognition. In: IEEE Visual Communications and Image Processing (VCIP), pp. 1–4 (2019)
24. Ding, H., Zhou, P., Chellappa, R.: Occlusion-adaptive deep network for robust facial expression recognition. In: IEEE International Joint Conference on Biometrics (IJCB), pp. 1–9 (2020)
25. Hua, W., Dai, F., Huang, L., et al.: HERO: human emotions recognition for realizing intelligent Internet of Things. IEEE Access **7**, 24321–24332 (2019)
26. Farzaneh, A.H., Qi, X.: Discriminant distribution-agnostic loss for facial expression recognition in the wild. In: IEEE/CVF Conference on Computer Vision and Pattern Recognition Workshops, pp. 406–407 (2020)
27. Lian, Z., Li, Y., Tao, J.H., et al.: Expression analysis based on face regions in real-world conditions. Int. J. Autom. Comput. **17**(1), 96–107 (2020)
28. Skublov, S.G., Gavrilchik, A.K., Berezin, A.V.: Geochemistry of beryl varieties: comparative analysis and visualization of analytical data by principal component analysis (PCA) and t-distributed stochastic neighbor embedding (t-SNE). J. Min. Inst. **255**, 455–469 (2022)

An Edge-Cloud Collaborative Computing System for Real-Time Internet-of-Things Applications

Xing Liu[1]([✉]), Yongqi Yu[1], Mei Yu[2], Denghong Liao[2], Yaxin Li[1], and Zihan Ji[1]

[1] School of Computer Science and Artificial Intelligence, Wuhan University of Technology, Wuhan, China
liu.xing@whut.edu.cn
[2] Huawei Technology Co. Ltd., Chengdu, China
{yumei,liaodenghong}@huawei.com

Abstract. Edge-cloud collaborative computing system (ECCS) can combine the advantages of edge computing system's low computing latency and cloud computing system's high computing performance, which makes it widely applied in the real-time Internet of Things (IoT) applications. This paper presents an ECCS based on the open-source EdgeX and Huawei openLooKeng. To enable the ECCS to be low-latency, low-power and intelligent, the ECCS is integrated with a serial of enabling technologies such as lightweight k8s (k3s), heterogenous computing acceleration, edge intelligence, edge-cloud joint inference and federated learning. First, the EdgeX is built on k3s to make the ECCS have the functionalities of automating deployment, scaling, and management of containerized applications. Then, a set of algorithms such as AlexNet, YOLO and fast Fourier transform (FFT) are integrated into EdgeX to enhance the edge nodes' intelligence and functionalities. Following that, several FPGA and GPU accelerators are developed and deployed on the edge side to accelerate the computationally-intensive tasks which run on the edge nodes. Finally, the joint inference and federated learning mechanisms are implemented to improve the algorithm accuracy as well as protecting the data privacy. The proposed ECCS has been implemented on the Zynq SoC and Raspberry Pi boards, and the real-world experimental results show that this ECCS has low resource cost, intelligent data processing capability, and also high real-time response performance.

Keywords: Internet of Things · Edge computing · Collaborative computing · Heterogenous computing

1 Introduction

Many Internet of Things (IoT) applications involve the process of collecting data, analyzing the data, and then taking actions in terms of the analysis results.

Supported by the Ministry of Industry and Information Technology of China (Grant No. TC210804V-1), and also by the National Innovation and Entrepreneurship Training Program for College Students.

Traditional ways resort to the cloud computing to perform the data analysis. However, it suffers from the problems such as network congestion and high latency. To solve this problem, the edge computing has been widely applied in the IoT applications. With the edge computing technology, the data can be processed on the edge side closer to the device, thus reducing both the communication cost and data processing delay [10].

However, edge devices usually have constrained computing and storage resources, which makes them not suitable to run the computationally-intensive algorithms or processing large amounts of data in real time. To address this challenge, two mechanisms are implemented in this paper. On the one hand, the heterogeneous computing technology is applied to the edge computing system (ECS) to accelerate the computation of computationally-intensive tasks [6]. On the other hand, the edge-cloud collaborative computing technologies such as joint inference and federated learning are applied in the ECS to take advantages of both cloud computing's high performance and edge computing's low latency.

Therefore, this paper targets to build such an edge-cloud collaborative computing system (ECCS) for the real-time IoT applications. The system consists of two parts: ECS and cloud computing system (CCS). The ECS is built on the basis of EdgeX, which is an open source, vendor neutral, Edge IoT middleware platform, under the LF Edge umbrella [1]. The CCS is built on the basis of Huawei openLooKeng, which is a distributed, low latency, reliable data engine for all data, big or small, local or remote, which makes big data simplified [4]. Between the edge side and cloud side, the edge-cloud collaborative intelligent computing mechanisms are implemented, which includes joint inference and federated learning. Joint inference can improve the recognition accuracy of artificial intelligence (AI) algorithms. It enables the edge nodes to transfer the tasks to the cloud for recognition in case that the small models on the edge side cannot provide sufficient recognition accuracy. Moreover, it deploys the more complex recognition models in the cloud side, which enables higher recognition accuracy to be achieved. Federated learning can protect the data privacy by training the data on the edge side rather than the cloud side, and then uploading only the trained model parameters rather than the original data to the cloud for fusion. In this way, the data privacy can be protected.

In addition to the above mechanisms, the heterogenous computing technology [6] is also applied in the ECS. On the one hand, a set of FPGA accelerators are designed dedicated to the computationally-intensive algorithms. By offloading these algorithms to run on the FPGA accelerators, the time and energy cost of ECS can be optimized significantly. On the other hand, some embedded GPU processors are also integrated in the ECS. By taking advantage of the highly parallel computing features of GPUs, the computing process can be further accelerated.

The organization of this paper is as follows: In Sect. 2, the related work of using ECCS in the IoT applications are introduced. In Sect. 3, an edge cloud collaborative computing architecture is presented. In Sect. 4, the edge-cloud joint inference and federated learning mechanisms are discussed. In Sect. 5, the combination of edge computing technology and heterogenous computing technology is investigated. In Sect. 6, the real-world deployment work is presented. In Sect. 7, the experiments are conducted to evaluate the performance of ECCS. Finally, in Sect. 8, the conclusion is given.

2   Related Work

ECCS has played an important role in many IoT applications and has attracted widespread research interests.

Qiu et al. outline the research progress concerning edge computing in industrial IoT (IIoT). They discuss the concepts, research progress, future architecture, technical progress as well as the opportunities and challenges of edge computing in the IIoT [10]. Pan et al. investigate the key rationale, the state-of-the-art efforts, the key enabling technologies and research topics, and typical IoT applications benefiting from edge cloud [9]. Ghosh et al. aim to combine edge and cloud computing for IoT data analytics by taking advantage of edge nodes to reduce data transfer. They use deep learning to perform feature learning, and place the encoder part of the trained autoencoder on the edge while placing the decoder part on the cloud [5]. Song et al. propose a cloud edge collaborative intelligent method for object detection, and apply it to insulator string recognition defect detection in the power industrial IoT, for the purpose of reducing the computational load for intelligence computing of unmanned aerial vehicles (UAV) [11]. Wu proposes an edge-cloud orchestration mechanism which provides a crucial computing architecture for the IoT applications, and the AI technology is used to enable the intelligent orchestration in this architecture [12]. Kaur et al. present a competent controller, named Kubernetes-based energy and interference driven scheduler (KEIDS), for container management on edge-cloud nodes taking into account the emission of carbon footprints, interference, and energy consumption [7].

The above work has effectively promoted the development of edge-cloud collaboration technology in the IoT field. However, less consideration has been paid to the ways of enhancing the computing capability of ECS while maintaining the high energy efficiency of ECS. Since many IoT applications have large amounts of data to be processed and the algorithms to process these data can be highly computationally intensive, the integration of edge computing technologies with the other technologies such as heterogeneous computing acceleration and edge-cloud collaborative intelligent computing for the purpose of enabling the ECS to process the IoT data in an efficient, real-time and intelligent way is of great significance.

3   Edge-Cloud Collaborative Computing Architecture

The architecture of the ECCS is depicted in Fig. 1. It is composed of the ECS and CCS.

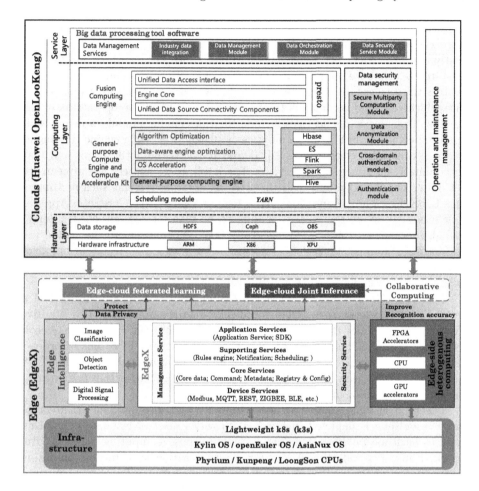

Fig. 1. The architecture of the edge-cloud collaborative computing system.

The ECS consists of four components, which are respectively the infrastructure, the EdgeX which provides the key edge computing services, the edge intelligence service, and the heterogenous computing system.

The infrastructure includes three layers. The lowest layer is the hardware such as Phytium CPUs, Kunpeng CPUs, and LoongSon CPUs. The middle layer is the operating system (OS) such as Kylin OS, openEuler OS, and AsiaNux OS. Upon the hardware and OS, the lightweight Kubernetes (k3s) is deployed. K3s is a fully compliant Kubernetes distribution which can make the ECS have the functionalities of automating deployment, scaling, and management of containerized applications [3].

The EdgeX mainly provides four kinds of services: device service, core service, supporting service and application service. The device service is in charge of connecting the devices to EdgeX and it supports a range of mainstream protocols including the modbus, MQTT, REST, ZigBee, Bluetooth and so on. The core services include the Redis data service which can be used to persistently store the collected device data, the meta-data service which can be used to store the attribute information of devices, the registry & config service which enables the services to be registered and discovered, and also the command service which can send commands to the devices to control the operations of the devices. The supporting services include the rules engine module which is built based on eKuiper, an IoT data analytics or stream processing engine running at resource constraint edge devices [2]. It also provides the notifications and task scheduling (e.g., timed task) services. The application services are a means to get data from the edge and send them to the external systems such as Huawei openLooKeng clouds, Azure IoT, AWS IoT, or Google IoT Core, etc. Application services provide the means for data to be transformed, enriched, filtered, and also formatted, compressed, encrypted, before being sent to the clouds.

The edge intelligence service is responsible for integrating the intelligent algorithms such as image classification and object detection to the edge side to enhance the ECS's intelligence and functionality.

The CPU/GPU/FPGA heterogenous computing system is composed of a set of FPGA accelerators designed specifically for the computationally-intensive tasks. It also includes the CPUs and GPUs. During the run-time, the ECS collects the data from the devices, and then use appropriate algorithms to process these data. For the algorithms which have high computational complexity, ECS dispatches them to run on the FPGA accelerators or GPUs, so that the processing speed of the data can be accelerated.

The CCS is built on the basis of Huawei openLooKeng. The architecture of openLooKeng is depicted in Fig. 1. It provides a set of clouding computing services such as YARN scheduling, general-purpose computing engine (Hive, Spark, Flink, ES and Hbase), computing acceleration kits, fusion computing engine, data management services and also data security mechanisms. Compared with the other CCS, openLooKeng has the following features:

- supports distributed resource pools across data centers; supports storage-computing integration and storage-computing separation.
- support openEuler, CentOS, Redhat and other Linux OS.
- support x86, Kunpeng, Phytium processors.
- support drag-and-drop operations, task scheduling and data management, so as to reduce development difficulty.
- support collaborative computing capabilities among ten or more data centers or clouds.
- support cross-source collaborative processing across different data sources (including HDFS, ElasticSearch, Kafka, HBase, MySQL, PostgreSQL, openGauss, etc.).
- support private computing; support federated learning and multi-party secure computing.
- enable the data service release time to be reduced from the traditional several days to several hours.

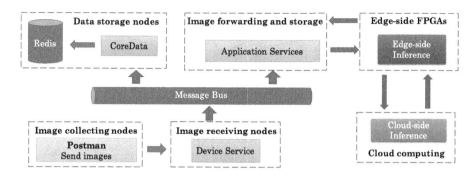

Fig. 2. The joint inference mechanism implemented on the basis of EdgeX.

4 Joint Inference and Federated Learning Based on EdgeX

To combine the advantages of ECS's low computing latency and CCS's high computing performance, the edge-cloud collaborative computing mechanisms, including the joint inference and federated learning, are implemented in the ECCS.

4.1 Joint Inference

The edge-side devices commonly have constrained computing and memory resources. Thus, only the models which have low resource cost are deployed at the edge. These models commonly have low recognition accuracy, and are more appropriate to process some simple tasks. In case the recognition accuracy of the edge-side models cannot satisfy the requirements, the inference tasks will be transferred to the clouds. The clouds have powerful computing capability with more complex inference models, so they can soundly meet the recognition accuracy requirements. Through the above joint inference mechanism, the inference accuracy can be improved, and the overall delay can be reduced. Moreover, the throughput can be increased.

The joint inference mechanism is implemented on the basis of EdgeX, as is depicted in Fig. 2. The models to process the images are deployed on the FPGA accelerators. After the images arrive at the edge nodes, they will be sent to the application service through message bus. Then, the application service invokes the edge-side FPGA accelerators to process these images. If the recognition accuracy of the FPGA accelerators cannot meet the requirements, the image tasks will be forwarded to the clouds for further processing.

4.2 Federated Learning

Many IoT applications need to process large amounts of data, and the data also needs privacy protection. If the data is sent to the cloud for training, it will suffer

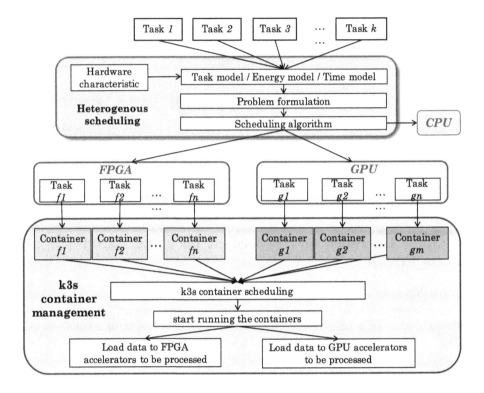

Fig. 3. The workflow of the heterogenous scheduling in the edge computing system.

from network congestion and privacy leak. To solve this problem, the edge-cloud collaborative federated learning is implemented to train the models on the edge side, and then aggregate the training parameters in the cloud side. In this way, the data privacy can be protected, the amount of data transferred to the cloud can be reduced. Moreover, the data island problem can be solved.

5   CPU/GPU/FPGA Heterogenous Computing System

Different processors have different architectures and are therefore good at performing different tasks. To improve the computing efficiency of ECS, the CPU/GPU/FPGA heterogenous computing technology is applied in ECS. This way can not only decrease the task execution time, but also optimize the energy cost of ECS.

In Fig. 3, the workflow of heterogenous scheduling system in ECS is depicted. A set of CPUs, GPUs and FPGA accelerators are deployed in ECS. First, the task model, energy model and time model of the CPU/GPU/FPGA heterogenous system are built. Then, the scheduling algorithm is applied to schedule each task to run on the most appropriate processor [8]. The task dispatching operation in ECS is realized by k3s. The programs running on the CPUs are compiled into containers. When the containers is started by k3s, they will load the data to be processed into GPUs or FPGA accelerators. After the data processing is complete, the GPUs or FPGA accelerators will send the processing results back to CPUs.

Since the ECS needs to run many computationally-intensive AI algorithms, it is of great significance to apply the above heterogeneous computing technologies in ECS.

6   Real-World Deployment

A real-world ECS for the IoT applications is built as is shown in Fig. 4. The k3s is used to build the ECS cluster, which connects all the agents, servers, cloud nodes and edge devices.

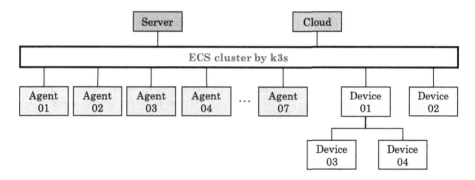

Fig. 4. The ECS cluster built on the basis of k3s and EdgeX.

In Table 1, the device list, working modes and functionalities of this ECS are depicted. The EdgeX computing systems are running on the servers and agents. The server, agent No. 01 and No. 02 are used as the primary working nodes, while the agents No. 04 to 07 are used as the backup working nodes. The backup nodes will start running when any primary working node fails, which enables the ECS to keep robust. And this failure recovery mechanism is managed by k3s.

The PYNQ FPGAs are working as the CPU/FPGA platforms, while the Raspberry Pi-4B boards are working as the CPU/GPU platforms. During the run-time, the image processing tasks are offloaded to the Raspberry broads, while the other computationally-intensive tasks such as YOLO object detection and FFT signal processing are offloaded to the PYNQ boards.

7   Experimental Results

The performance of ECCS is evaluated from three aspects: resource cost, edge-cloud collaborative computing functionality, and heterogeneous computing performance.

Table 1. The device name, working modes and functions in the ECS cluster.

Name	Device	Mode	Functions
Cloud	PC	cloud	Joint inference and federated learning in the cloud side
Server	Phytium Industrial computer	master	Monitor and manage K3s clusters
Agent 01	Phytium Industrial computer	agent	Federated Learning No. 1 edge node; Primary node of ECS
Agent 02	Phytium Industrial computer	agent	Federated Learning No. 2 edge node; Primary node of ECS
Agent 03	PYNQ FPGA	agent	CPU/FPGA heterogenous computing node
Agent 04	Raspberry Pi-4B	agent	Backup node of ECS; CPU/GPU heterogenous computing node
Agent 05	Raspberry Pi-4B	agent	Backup node of ECS; CPU/GPU heterogenous computing node
Agent 06	Raspberry Pi-4B	agent	Backup node of ECS; CPU/GPU heterogenous computing node
Agent 07	Raspberry Pi-4B	agent	Backup node of ECS; CPU/GPU heterogenous computing node
Device 01	MQTT gateway	MQTT	Modbus RTU Device Management
Device 02	Sensors	Modbus TCP	Collect environmental data
Device 03	Sensors	Modbus RTU	Collect environmental data
Device 04	Sensors	Modbus	Collect environmental data

7.1   Resource Cost

The container image size of the different components in ECS is as follows: core-command-arm64 (7.84 MB), core-data-arm64 (9.26 MB), core-metadata-arm64 (8.14 MB), consul (41.8 MB), redis (10.8 MB), device-rest-arm64 (9.58 MB), device-virtual-arm64 (11 MB), support-nontifications-arm64 (8.23 MB), support-scheduler-arm64 (7.86 MB), ekuiper (18.6 MB), app-service-configurable-arm64 (10.9 MB). The total image size is 144.01 MB.

The memory cost of the different components in ECS is as follows: core-command-arm64 (15.62 MB), core-data-arm64 (12.56 MB), core-metadata-arm64 (15.12 MB), consul (24.60 MB), device-rest-arm64 (17.64 MB), device-virtual-arm64 (19.46 MB), support-nontifications-arm64 (11.64 MB), support-scheduler-arm64 (14.75 MB), ekuiper (12.54 MB), app-service-configurable-arm64 (20.54 MB). The total image size is 164.47 MB.

Both the container image size and memory cost of ECS are small, which makes ECS appropriate to be deployed on the embedded devices such PYNQ and Raspberry Pi.

(a) Object detection by YOLO at the edge side

(b) Object detection by YOLO on the cloud side

Fig. 5. Joint inference for YOLO on the edge side and cloud side respectively.

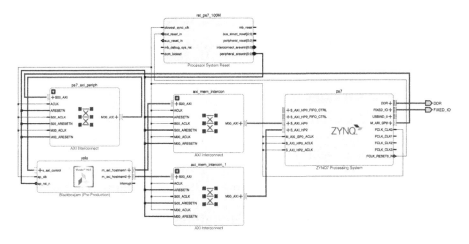

Fig. 6. The design of FFT accelerator based on FPGA.

7.2 Edge-Cloud Collaborative Computing System

Two edge-cloud collaborative computing mechanisms, joint inference and federated learning, are implemented in the ECCS. The joint inference has been applied to realize object detection and the model used is YOLO, as is shown in Fig. 5. In Fig. 5(a), the application has low requirements on the recognition accuracy, thus the recognition task is performed on the edge side. In Fig. 5(b), the application has high requirements for the recognition accuracy, thus the recognition task is transferred to the clouds for execution.

When the object detection task runs on the edge side, the average time cost is 1000 ms. When it is transferred to the clouds for joint execution, the average time increases greatly to 10000 ms, due to the network transmission delay.

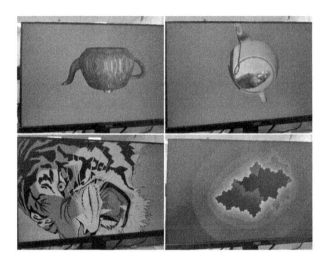

Fig. 7. Performance evaluation to edge-side CPU/GPU computing acceleration.

7.3 Heterogenous Computing System

In the ECCS, several FPGA accelerators have been developed, including the FPGA-based YOLO accelerator and the FPGA-based FFT accelerator.

The YOLO accelerator has been applied to perform object detection, as is shown in Fig. 5. And the results show that the inference time of running YOLO on ARM A9 CPU with working frequency 1 GHz is 70 s, whereas it is only 3 s on the FPGA-based YOLO accelerator.

The FFT accelerator has been used to detect the abnormal conditions of several IoT applications such as airport runway deformation detection and metro illegal construction detection. In Fig. 6, the RTL of FPGA-based FFT accelerator is depicted. The results show that the time of processing 1000 frames of data on ARM CPU is 118.48 ms, whereas it is only 0.368 ms on this FPGA-based FFT accelerator.

In addition to FPGA accelerators, the GPUs have also been used to accelerate the image processing tasks in ECS. In experiment, the GPUs on Raspberry Pi boards are used to perform image rendering and 2D/3D animation tasks, as is shown in Fig. 7. The results show that the GPU can accelerate the video converting tasks by 30% compared with the ARM A9 CPU. Note that the GPUs of Raspberry Pi is a rather low-end GPU.

8   Conclusion

This paper proposes an ECCS which integrates the technology of edge computing, edge-cloud collaborative computing (joint inference and federated learning), heterogenous computing, edge intelligence and also k3s. The ECCS is built on the basis of open-source EdgeX and Huawei openLooKeng. Experimental results validate that this ECCS has small resource consumption, intelligent data processing capability and can also support real-time data processing. These features make it appropriate to be applied in the real-time IoT applications.

References

1. Edgex - an open source, vendor neutral, edge iot middleware platform, under the lf edge umbrella (2022). https://www.edgexfoundry.org/
2. ekuiper - lightweight iot data streaming analytics engine for edge computing (2022). https://ekuiper.org/
3. k3s - lightweight kubernetes (2022). https://rancher.com/docs/k3s/latest/en/
4. Openlookeng - a distributed, low latency, reliable data engine for all data, big or small, local or remote, which makes big data simplified. (2022). https://openlookeng.io/en/
5. Ghosh, A.M., Grolinger, K.: Edge-cloud computing for internet of things data analytics: embedding intelligence in the edge with deep learning. IEEE Trans. Industr. Inf. **17**(3), 2191–2200 (2020)
6. Hennessy, J.L., Patterson, D.A.: A new golden age for computer architecture. Commun. ACM **62**(2), 48–60 (2019)
7. Kaur, K., Garg, S., Kaddoum, G., Ahmed, S.H., Atiquzzaman, M.: Keids: Kubernetes-based energy and interference driven scheduler for industrial iot in edge-cloud ecosystem. IEEE Internet Things J. **7**(5), 4228–4237 (2019)
8. Liu, X., Liu, P., Hu, L., Zou, C., Cheng, Z.: Energy-aware task scheduling with time constraint for heterogeneous cloud datacenters. Concurr. Comput.: Pract. Exp. **32**(18), e5437 (2020)
9. Pan, J., McElhannon, J.: Future edge cloud and edge computing for internet of things applications. IEEE Internet Things J. **5**(1), 439–449 (2017)
10. Qiu, T., Qiu, T., et al.: Edge computing in industrial internet of things: architecture, advances and challenges. IEEE Commun. Surv. Tutorials **22**(4), 2462–2488 (2020)
11. Song, C., Xu, W., Han, G., Zeng, P., Wang, Z., Yu, S.: A cloud edge collaborative intelligence method of insulator string defect detection for power iiot. IEEE Internet Things J. **8**(9), 7510–7520 (2020)
12. Wu, Y.: Cloud-edge orchestration for the internet of things: Architecture and ai-powered data processing. IEEE Internet Things J. **8**(16), 12792–12805 (2020)

Research on Post Epidemic Brand Co Branding Based on Big Data – Taking Liangpin Store as an Example

Ying Li[✉]

School of Art and Design, Hubei University of Technology, Wuhan, Hubei, China
2010248594@qq.com

Abstract. 2020 is destined to be a difficult year. The rapid spread of COVID-19 has brought great impact on public life, public health and even the whole industry. But at the same time, online has been rising. As the most active marketing method in the Internet era, Brand Co branding still plays a role during the epidemic. At present, China has achieved phased victory in the epidemic prevention campaign, and we have also ushered in the post epidemic era of small-scale outbreak of the epidemic. As a major victim city of the epidemic, many brands in the post epidemic era are also continuing to explore new methods of Brand Co branding. In this case, in order to find a new method of liangpin Store Brand Co branding suitable for Wuhan in the new era, the author will use the form of big data and questionnaire to analyze the factors affecting the development of liangpin store Regional Brand Co branding in the post epidemic era through data: first, analyze the factors affecting regional brands from three aspects of packaging, category and policy and put forward suggestions; Second, analyze the factors affecting regional brands from three aspects: purchase convenience, word-of-mouth and selectivity, and put forward suggestions; Third, analyze the factors affecting regional brands from three aspects: purchase price, brand and publicity methods, and put forward suggestions to find the form of Brand Co branding suitable for the post epidemic era.

Keywords: Big Data · Post Epidemic Era · Brand Co Branding · Regional Brand · Influence Factor

1 Introduction

Regional Brand Co branding consists of regional brand and co branding. As the name suggests, regional brand refers to the brand in a certain region, which can represent the extracted regional characteristics. Joint signature refers to the joint signature of multiple people or groups. Regional Brand Co branding in commodity cooperation refers to a product jointly designed by brand images or people in different regions, and then jointly released and sold in the name of both parties. This kind of cooperation focuses on creating new products or services and obtaining benefits from them on the premise of retaining the original characteristics of the brands of both parties.

W. Hong and Y. Weng (Eds.): ICCSE 2022, CCIS 1811, pp. 664–676, 2023.
https://doi.org/10.1007/978-981-99-2443-1_57

Nowadays, there are a lot of data on the Internet, but not all the data are useful, and the data is complex, which leads to the poor value density of many big data. Therefore, this paper combines big data with questionnaire survey to more effectively use and screen the data to obtain useful information big data [1]. Compared with traditional news communication and advertising, regional brand building in the era of big data will give better suggestions to brands and enterprises.

2 Opportunities and Challenges for Wuhan Brand in the Post Epidemic Era

Wang Zhuli explained the "post epidemic era". The so-called "post epidemic era" is not like what we think. After a period of time, the epidemic will completely disappear and everything will return to the previous state, but the epidemic may explode in a small scale and in a small range. This state will not disappear in a short time. This situation will have an impact on all aspects. In this case, Online marketing still dominates. With the advent of the post epidemic era, the changes of society, market and consumer psychology also require the joint names of Wuhan brands to make changes suitable for this era.

2.1 Offline Sales are Restricted and Brand Competition is More Intense

Under the epidemic, all walks of life have been affected, and offline brands such as shopping malls and restaurants have suffered heavy losses. The epidemic has been effectively suppressed due to the measures of home isolation and distance keeping, but many marketing activities can not be carried out. For example, some businesses have withdrawn from the market due to the impact of cash flow and market, and catering businesses have also decreased from more than 10 million in 2019 to more than 9 million. In addition to the serious damage to the catering industry, offline retail entertainment and other industries have suffered similar problems. At the same time, in the post epidemic era, with the gradual rejuvenation of the economy and market, many leading brands will concentrate in advance and seize the opportunity. The surviving enterprises will adopt more radical sales strategies and try their best to expand market share. The eliminated brands in the market will be gradually replaced by new ones, and the competition between brands will be more intense [2]. Local brands in Wuhan have also suffered a lot. Small business districts have closed down directly, and chain brands have also been greatly damaged. The epidemic is a double-edged sword. Although Wuhan suffered the most losses, it also welcomed the help of the state and enterprises. The reconstruction of Wuhan's urban image also brought all kinds of opportunities to Wuhan brand. According to the report on the development of snack industry in the context of consumption upgrading issued by the Ministry of Commerce, under the influence of the epidemic, the consumption environment, ability, content and mode are upgrading, and enterprises must develop with high quality. Liangpin store has determined the characteristics of "high quality", "high appearance" and "high experience" in the early stage, and Brand Co branding has become an urgent way of brand development under the epidemic [3].

2.2 After the Epidemic, Wuhan's Popularity Increased and Its Potential Market Expanded

The epidemic has certainly had a major impact on the life of Wuhan, but at the same time, the epidemic has also made more people see Wuhan, a heroic city, and the popularity of the city has increased sharply. During the outbreak of the epidemic, various social software broadcast the current epidemic information with high intensity and high speed, and the audience gained attention to Wuhan from the epidemic report, so as to deepen the image cognition of Wuhan. At the same time, the 818 million users of the short video platform make the story of Wuhan spread rapidly, which greatly helps the spread of Wuhan's urban image [4]. The spread of the "anti epidemic hero story" during the anti epidemic period has formed the general understanding of Wuhan's culture, history, economic development and urban level. The high-speed dissemination of Wuhan information and the expansion of popularity have brought huge market opportunities to Wuhan local brands. At the same time, Wuhan, as the initial outbreak of the epidemic, has also attracted the attention of the state. Since the epidemic gradually improved, the state has increased its support for Wuhan. Both economic support and infrastructure support have brought rare help to Wuhan, a damaged city [5]. Wuhan brands also take this opportunity to gain more exposure and cooperation opportunities, and the resulting market is gradually expanding.

2.3 After the Epidemic, Wuhan's Popularity Increased and Its Potential Market Expanded

In June 2020, the implementation report of Rural Revitalization Strategy prepared by the Ministry of agriculture and rural areas, the national development and Reform Commission and relevant departments was released. The role of enterprises in helping rural development and Supporting Rural Revitalization has been mentioned many times. The implementation of the Rural Revitalization Strategy is a necessary link for the party to promote common prosperity, and its importance is self-evident. The emergence of such a national policy has given enterprises more choice and provided a new direction for their development. Many enterprises began to actively transform and participate in the national strategy.

2.4 The Transformation of People's Ideas in the Post Epidemic Era

Under the rampant COVID-19, the change of the general environment has changed the consumer psychology. The outbreak of COVID-19 has magnified and stimulated the contradictions among the state, society and families. The emotional demands of trust, healing, health and gathering shown by brand products have become extremely important. Comforting consumers' hearts has become an important breakthrough for the brand [6]. At the same time, in the face of major disasters, the public morality and value responsibility displayed by the brand has become a major outlet to display the brand value.

3 Development Overview of Liangpin Brand

Headquartered in Wuhan, liangpin store is committed to providing consumers with high-end snacks, forming categories covering nut fried goods, meat snacks, candy cakes, snack gift boxes and so on. Relying on Wuhan cuisine, it sells leisure snacks. In the more than ten years after the establishment of the brand, liangpin stores have expanded continuously, and there are more than 2200 stores, covering 14 provinces and cities in Central China, South China, East China, northwest and southwest China. With the simultaneous development of online and offline, the company's revenue reached 7.7 billion in 2019, which has become the preferred brand of high-end snacks in the hearts of consumers and the leading enterprise in the snack industry. In the wave of joint marketing, liangpin store also seized the opportunity to try to sign joint names with many enterprises. It has signed joint names with xiahuang, fengxiangjia, Dunhuang Research Institute, Huangshanghuang and so on, and achieved good results. According to the big data of Baidu Index in Fig. 1 and Fig. 2, the sales volume of liangpin shop is the highest in Hubei and the highest in Wuhan. This not only shows that liangpin shop was founded in Wuhan, but also began to develop in Wuhan. Under the impact of the epidemic, it is also the first to develop by innovatively using Brand Co names in the post epidemic era.

1	hubei
2	guangdong
3	shanghai
4	jiangsu
5	sichuan
6	henan
7	zhejiang
8	hunan
9	beijing
10	jiangxi

Fig. 1. Ten provinces with the highest sales of liangpin stores under Baidu Index.

1	wuhan
2	shanghai
3	shenzhen
4	beijing
5	chendu
6	guangzhou
7	changsha
8	zhenzhou
9	hangzhou
10	nanchang

Fig. 2. Ten cities with the highest sales of liangpin stores under Baidu Index.

4 Development Overview of Liangpin Brand

Under the normal condition of the post epidemic era, online marketing has become the mainstream, and as a commonly used CO branding method, it has also changed with the trend of the times. Here, we will analyze the case of Brand Co branding of Wuhan local brand liangpin store in the post epidemic era through the combination of big data and questionnaire survey, and explore a new method of Brand Co branding suitable for Wuhan in the post epidemic era. Experimental data research and factor analysis on the impact of packaging, categories and policies on liangpin Store Brand Co branding under big data.

4.1 Experimental Data Research and Factor Analysis on the Impact of Purchase Packaging, Categories and Policies on Liangpin Store Brand Co Branding Under Big Data

This experiment adopts the combination of big data and questionnaire survey. Many useful information can be searched through data mining and questionnaire star. This data will be analyzed by SPSS to get the most accurate results as far as possible. This experiment focuses on three different age groups: 6–10 years old, 13–18 years old and 30–40 years old. Explore the factors affecting the Brand Co branding of the store from the three aspects of packaging, category and policy, and put forward adaptive suggestions for the brand.

dependent variable	mean square	F	P
packing	370.880	122.863	0.000
category	266.427	57.374	0.000
policy	356.287	166.394	0.000

Fig. 3. ANOVA analysis of packaging, categories and policies on liangpin Store Brand Co branding under big data.

It can be seen from the data in Fig. 3 that there are obvious differences in the significance of packaging, categories and policies ($P < 0.01$). Nowadays, liangpin Store Brand Co branding should pay attention to considering the differences in three aspects, so as to obtain good consumption results. It can be seen from the data in Fig. 4 that in terms of packaging, there are differences in the significance of packaging for 6–10 years old, 13–18 years old and 30–40 years old ($P < 0.05$). In terms of packaging design, targeted design should be carried out for each age stage. For category comparison between 6–10 years old and 30–40 years old, the significance of multiple comparison between 6–10 years old and 30–40 years old ($P < 0.05$) is different, but there is no difference between 6–10 years old and 13–18 years old ($P < 0.05$). In category design, enterprises should focus on the design of 6–10 years old and 30–40 years old. In terms of policies, there are significant differences ($P < 0.05$) between the ages of 6–10, 13–18

dependent variable	I	J	P
	6-10 years old	13-18 years old	0.000
packing	6-10 years old	30-40 years old	0.000
	13-18 years old	30-40 years old	0.000
	6-10 years old	13-18 years old	0.309
category	6-10 years old	30-40 years old	0.000
	13-18 years old	30-40 years old	0.000
	6-10 years old	13-18 years old	0.000
policy	6-10 years old	30-40 years old	0.000
	13-18 years old	30-40 years old	0.000

* The significance level of the mean difference was 0.05.

Fig. 4. Multiple comparative analysis of packaging, categories and policies on liangpin Store Brand Co branding under big data.

and 30–40. Nowadays, under the leadership of national policies, Brand Co branding will become the development point of the next enterprise.

Since the 21st century, the country is moving towards common prosperity, and issues such as helping agriculture, rural areas and farmers and Rural Revitalization have been put on the agenda. Seizing the national strategy, catering to the tide of rejuvenating the economy and helping the countryside, the rise of the country has shifted the demand of a new generation of young consumers for products from meeting food and clothing to pursuing novelty and health. Brand image has also become a factor for consumers to consider. Huangshanghuang and liangpin shop "think about Jiangxi and Hubei" - regional local specialties. Joint cooperation will seize the common points of products, meet national policies, create new products and establish a good corporate image for the brand.

Based in Jiangxi for 28 years, Huangshanghuang focuses on the research and development of sauce and brine products, cold dishes and rice products, adheres to the spirit of ingenuity, inherits the craftsmanship, and is committed to making good taste with ingenuity. These two kinds of products focus on food and are committed to spreading local cuisine. On this basis, Huangshanghuang and liangpin store seize the highlight of local specialties. In order to create a joint product of "exploring Jiangxi and Hubei", they take the best-selling single products of liangpin store and Huangshanghuang and the combination of local specialties as the sales and selling points, and integrate the sales of local specialties of both sides, build market exchanges and promote sales. The topic and attraction brought by the new products with joint brand names will spread rapidly under the operation of the Internet. The number of topics of the brand will grow rapidly on the original basis, bringing a win-win situation of benefits and brand awareness. Secondly, such Brand Co branding can make local specialties live, make remote villages go out, make more local specialties in the two places known and accepted by more people, and bring economic benefits to the countryside at the same time. The joint name of Huangshanghuang and liangpin shop conforms to the national strategy of helping rural development and supporting rural revitalization. Whether successful or not, the social responsibility of the two brands will be seen by the public, and the establishment of brand value will be deeply rooted in the hearts of the people.

4.2 Experimental Data Research and Factor Analysis on the Influence of Purchase Convenience, Reputation and Selectivity on Liangpin Store Brand Co Branding Under Big Data

This experiment also adopts the combination of big data and questionnaire survey. Many useful information can be searched through data mining and questionnaire star. This data will be analyzed by SPSS to get the most accurate results as far as possible. The subjects of this study were three groups aged from 13 to 30 years old. Explore the factors affecting the Brand Co branding of the store from the three aspects of convenience, word-of-mouth and selectivity, and put forward adaptive suggestions for the brand.

dependent variable	mean square	F	P
purchase convenience	189.14	116.841	0.000
word of mouth	60.247	23.423	0.000
selectivity	34.94	6.605	0.002

Fig. 5. ANOVA analysis of Brand Co branding of liangpin store based on purchase convenience, reputation and selectivity under big data.

It can be seen from the data in Fig. 5 that there are obvious differences in the significance of convenience, word-of-mouth and selectivity ($P < 0.01$). Nowadays, liangpin Store Brand Co branding should pay attention to considering the differences in three aspects, so as to obtain good consumption results. It can be seen from the data in Fig. 6 that there are significant differences ($P < 0.05$) in the multiple comparisons between 6–10 years old and 30–40 years old, 13–18 years old and 30–40 years old, but there is no difference ($P < 0.05$) in the comparison between 6–10 years old and 13–18 years old. It can be concluded that the younger the age, there is a demand for purchase convenience, but there is no difference for the higher age group, Liangpin Store Brand Co branding should consider the differences in this regard and make specific countermeasures. Word of mouth for 6–10 years old, 13–18 years old and 30–40 years old were significantly different ($P < 0.05$). In the Brand Co branding of liangpin shop, different word of mouth should be carried out for each age stage, and special distinction should be made for age groups. In terms of selectivity, the multiple comparison significance ($P < 0.05$) of 6–10 years old, 30–40 years old, 13–18 years old and 30–40 years old are different, but there is no difference in the comparison significance ($P < 0.05$) of 6–10 years old and 13–18 years old. Nowadays, liangpin Store Brand Co branding should pay attention to selectivity and achieve great success.

The sudden outbreak of the COVID-19 has brought people panic and anxiety. After the panic, people's mental health also need to be pacified and mobilized. Seize the

dependent variable	I	J	P
purchase convenience	6-10 years old	13-18 years old	0.273
	6-10 years old	30-40 years old	0.000
	13-18 years old	30-40 years old	0.000
word of mouth	6-10 years old	13-18 years old	0.000
	6-10 years old	30-40 years old	0.000
	13-18 years old	30-40 years old	0.022
selectivity	6-10 years old	13-18 years old	0.410
	6-10 years old	30-40 years old	0.001
	13-18 years old	30-40 years old	0.009

* The significance level of the mean difference was 0.05.

Fig. 6. Multiple comparative analysis of Brand Co branding of liangpin store by purchase convenience, reputation and selectivity under big data.

psychological comfort of the epidemic and jointly create a tribute food box. During the epidemic period, liangpin shop continued to cooperate with Dunhuang to create a "liangpin thank you gift" food box. The food box contains more than 40 classic snacks matched with each other, creating more than 30 classic gift boxes for different groups. Consumers can choose the package according to their needs. At the same time, we jointly created the Thanksgiving public welfare short film "listen to him, thank you" with Hubei TV station to pay tribute to the ordinary people who struggle in the front-line posts. This series of CO branded products of liangpin store well grasp the hearts of the people, pay attention to people's inner world, and meet the integration of demand and emotion. Liangpin Store Brand Co branding should pay attention to the differential design of consumers from the aspects of purchase convenience, reputation and selectivity, which will be a great success.

4.3 Experimental Data Research and Factor Analysis on the Influence of Purchase Price, Brand and Publicity Mode on Liangpin Store Brand Co Branding Under Big Data

This experiment also adopts the combination of big data and questionnaire survey. Many useful information can be searched through data mining and questionnaire star. This data will be analyzed by SPSS to get the most accurate results as far as possible. The subjects of this study were three groups aged from 13 to 30 years old. Explore the factors affecting the Brand Co branding of the store from three aspects: price, brand and publicity methods, and put forward adaptive suggestions for the brand.

dependent variable	mean square	F	P
price	74.207	67.228	0.000
brand	123.92	54.374	0.000
publicity methods	97.38	20.356	0.000

Fig. 7. ANOVA analysis of Brand Co branding of liangpin store based on purchase convenience, reputation and selectivity under big data.

dependent variable	I	J	P
price	6-10 years old	13-18 years old	0.924
	6-10 years old	30-40 years old	0.000
	13-18 years old	30-40 years old	0.000
brand	6-10 years old	13-18 years old	0.000
	6-10 years old	30-40 years old	0.147
	13-18 years old	30-40 years old	0.000
publicity methods	6-10 years old	13-18 years old	0.000
	6-10 years old	30-40 years old	0.000
	13-18 years old	30-40 years old	0.021

* The significance level of the mean difference was 0.05.

Fig. 8. Multiple comparative analysis of purchase price, brand and publicity methods on Brand Co branding of liangpin store under big data.

It can be seen from the multiple data obtained in Fig. 7 that there are obvious differences in the significance of purchase price, brand and publicity methods ($P < 0.01$). Nowadays, liangpin Store Brand Co branding should pay attention to considering the differences in three aspects, so as to obtain good consumption results. It can be seen from the data in Fig. 8 that there are significant differences ($P < 0.05$) in the multiple comparison of prices for 6–10 years old and 30–40 years old, 13–18 years old and 30–40 years old, but there is no difference (P < 0.05) in the comparison between 6–10 years old and 13–18 years old. It can be concluded that the younger the age, there is demand for purchase prices, but there is no difference for the higher age group, Liangpin Store Brand Co branding should consider the differences in this regard and make specific countermeasures. The multiple comparisons of brands between 6–10 years old and 13–18 years old, 13–18 years old and 30–40 years old have significant differences (P < 0.05), but there is no significant difference between 6–10 years old and 13–18 years old (P < 0.05). From this, it can be concluded that young people aged 13–18 pay special attention to brand effect, and liangpin store brand joint names should also make different joint names for young people. The publicity methods for 6–10 years old, 13–18 years old and 30–40 years old were significantly different (P < 0.05). Liangpin Store Brand Co branding should have great innovation in the publicity methods.

During the epidemic, the domestic implementation of prevention and control policies forced the suspension of commercial activities across the country, and all offline entertainment activities stalled. We should seize the emerging consumption mode of live broadcasting and enhance the sense of product interaction. However, according to the survey of Colliers International, since the outbreak of Xinguan, the passenger flow of offline catering industry has decreased by more than 80% year-on-year, and more than half of the impact of the epidemic has been suspended [7]. However, at the same time, the live broadcasting and goods brought by the development of the network rose rapidly during the epidemic, becoming a beautiful economic phenomenon during the epidemic. Liangpin shop was active in front of consumers through live broadcasting during the epidemic, which also brought a lot of economic benefits to the brand. Yang Hongchun, chairman of liangpin store, has participated in the anchor with goods for many times. These anchor with goods are different from other online celebrities or stars. They can better represent the corporate image and corporate culture. In addition to selling goods during the live broadcast, Yang Hongchun also repeatedly mentioned the measures taken by liangpin store during the epidemic, how to ensure food safety, ensure and promote liangpin store's commitment to excellent snacks and ensure conscientious enterprises. Take yourself as the guarantee of quality, establish good values and value needs for the brand, and let consumers feel at ease when buying and eating.

In the Brand Co branding of liangpin store, we should give more consideration to the factors such as price, brand and publicity methods, and put forward appropriate methods. In addition to this kind of internet live broadcast interaction, liangpin store also carries out message interactive display through various other ways, such as xiaohongshu and microblog, so as to obtain consumer feedback in time, continuously improve products, improve product image, improve consumer satisfaction with products, and achieve all-round improvement.

5 Optimization of Joint Innovation Strategy in the Post Epidemic Era

Brand Co branding has always been a "double high problem" - high risk and high return. The rapid sharing of Brand Co branded user groups and the mutual drainage of topics lead to high profits, but on the other hand, there is also the risk of collapse at the expense of both sides. At present, online promotion is developing rapidly, but generally speaking, online sales are the following: price reduction promotion, star online red belt goods, and new products are on sale within a limited time [8]. Price reduction promotion is a strategic plan with small profits and quick turnover. It attracts consumers to buy through direct price reduction, which has strong incitement. Stars bring goods is to invite popular traffic stars or online bloggers to use the fan effect to promote purchases. Limited sale generally means that when new products are launched in the brand live broadcasting room, relevant surrounding or other special products of stars are presented, and stars are used to attract shopping. In the wave of live broadcasting, the combined use of sales methods can bring double or even multiple returns. However, on the one hand, this sales method of price reduction makes the commodity value depreciate and the profit space becomes smaller. Blindly price reduction is detrimental to the brand value and image, and is more likely to bring vicious competition. At the same time, Brand Co branding is mostly based on fan economy and topic heat. The trend of CO branding in recent years has also reached a pattern. How to follow the trend of the times and expand the new consumer market remains to be considered. There are bound to be new problems in the way of emerging in the new era, but the author finds that there are traces to follow in solving these problems by studying some successful cases.

5.1 Establish Brand Responsibility Awareness

Brand responsibility awareness is a point that people gradually value in the post epidemic era. Brand trust is an important standard for the long-term development of a brand. This year's Henan disaster relief hongxingerke boss's "wild donation" has set a good example for other brands. Such wild behavior has won unanimous praise from netizens. Such a sense of responsibility has moved consumers, making this precarious brand instantly popular, and the sales volume of products has also doubled. This also confirms the importance of brand responsibility awareness, and choosing trusted enterprises in Brand Co branding also provides guarantee for the success of joint branding.

5.2 Pay Attention to Generation Z, Make Good Use of Private Domain Traffic and Strengthen the Relationship Between Brands and Consumers

According to the latest seventh census, there are more than 200 million people with college degrees in China, and quality education has been a great success. Similarly, the average quality of consumers is also greatly improved. Generation Z consumers love life more, pursue beauty, quality and value more and more strongly, and are willing to consume for the spirit. As the main force of consumption in recent years, in the context of the new era, their private desire flow is also a sales space to be developed.

The circle of friends is a small circle of its own. Receiving advertisements, private letters and discounts will not only disturb customers and make customers feel resentful, but also be easily hacked. This kind of personal information obtained through big data is easy to make consumers have rebellious psychology and even disgust. How to obtain such a marketing market is indeed a difficult problem, but Lin Qingxuan did it. The method is to publish some information set up by people through the circle of friends, and then chat with customers who like to leave messages, talk about home habits, do not take the initiative to sell, and introduce products at the right opportunity. Such friendly operation rarely causes people's disgust. In this silent chat, the brand has been deeply rooted in the hearts of the people. The brand and consumers are slowly connected in daily life and participate in consumption. This kind of imperceptible relationship of becoming friends enables consumers to speak for the brand in the process of sharing and communication. This new way of marketing also provides a new way for brands, and Brand Co branding and respecting customers must also be considered. This new way is worthy of reference for brands in market saturation.

6   Limitations of This Study

This experiment only aims at the influence investment of three age groups on Brand Co branding, which has limitations. In the subsequent research, it will be further expanded to the whole population of multiple age groups, and strive to make the experiment more accurate.

In all experiments, the influencing factors are less considered, and the relationship between products, advertising and co branding should be considered, so that the influencing factors of Brand Co branding can be analyzed in more detail.

7   Conclusion

The post epidemic era is an irreversible situation. In the new era, key and effective information data can be obtained by analyzing data in combination with big data. Wuhan Brand Co branding should seize the opportunities and characteristics of the new era, make rational use of current resources, carry out innovative design, seize opportunities, seize the changes of the times, find breakthroughs, and create a sales method suitable for Wuhan brand. Today's brands want not to be eliminated in the fierce and complex market in the post epidemic era, they must keep pace with the times and update their brand image at all times. The most popular way today is Brand Co branding and timely brand activity marketing planning. In today's Z era, consumers promote the confrontation and resonance between modern art and brands, and promote the joint development of brands to a higher level. Therefore, if you want to further improve the co branding effect of the brand and pay more attention to the product itself, you should further give play to the market channels, actively carry out the online channels of the brand, make up for the shortcomings of offline channels, and timely find the favorite traffic stars of today's teenagers for endorsement, which will make the brand more popular.

References

1. Lili, Y., Liu, J.: Research on clothing brand knowledge mining under the background of big data. West. Leather **JO3**, 69–71 (2022)
2. Xu, Y., Xia, M.: How to break the situation of brand marketing in the "post epidemic" era. In: China Convention and Exhibition (China Conference), vol. J16, pp. 40–43 (2021)

3. Wei, D.: How to build future oriented brand increment in the post epidemic Era. Zhongguancun **J06**, 35–37 (2020)
4. Sun, C., Zhou, W.: Discourse communication of Wuhan city image in the post epidemic Era. Shanghai Urban Manag. **J07**, 73–77 (2020)
5. Han, L., Zhu, J.: The path and method of Wuhan city image communication in the post epidemic Era. News Res. Guide **J12**, 85–89 (2021)
6. Tang, S.: On the embodiment of humanized packaging design in the post epidemic Era. Green Packa. **J04**, 71–74 (2021)
7. Jia, H., Chen, D.: Cold thoughts on "'live broadcasting with goods'" in the post epidemic Era. North. Media Res. **J04**, 78–84 (2021)
8. Song, Y.: On the way of advertising in the post epidemic era – Taking live online advertising and media combination advertising as an example". Sci. Technol. Commun. **J23**, 143–145 (2020)

Gene Variation Detection Approach Based on Multimodal Data Fusion

Yu Li, Yimin Cao, and Jingyang Gao[✉]

Department of Computer Science and Technolog, Beijing Univeristy of Chemical Technology, Beijing, China
gaojy@mail.buct.edu.cn

Abstract. Structural variations (SVs), related to human's health, are numerously common in human genes, hence, it's vital for human to detect the gene structural variation precisely. Traditional gene variation detection methods classify the type and position of gene variation mostly by extracting hand-crafted attributes, which has their limitations. As a well feature extractor, deep convolution neural network could be utilized in gene variation detection field. We present a combined model consisted of Inception-V3 and VGG resembling two-stream model, extracting feature of two different properties at the same time, fusing them and make predictions, achieving 2% improvement averagely in precise, recall and F1-score.

Keywords: Gene variation detection · Machine Learning · Computer Vision
First Section

1 Introduction

DNA contains the genetic information of organisms, and the invention of DNA sequencing technology enables people to discover that the causes of many diseases are related to genes. With the deepening of research, it has been found that there are a large number of variations in the genome, which can be divided into structural variations (SVs) and single nucleotide polymorphisms (SNPs) according to the length of the variation. Structural variation refers to the change in the length of gene variation of more than 1kb, and single nucleotide polymorphism refers to the DNA polymorphism caused by the change of only a single base. Structural variations include many types, such as deletions, duplications, inversions, insertions, etc., which have been confirmed to be associated with a variety of diseases, such as tumors [1–3]. Thus, accurate detection of gene variations plays an vital role in predicting disease and researching in treatment of disease.

With the development and wide application of deep learning [4], more and more studies have proved that it also has a good performance in the medical field, such as 3DUNet used for semantic segmentation of brain tumors [5]. However, at the level of biological genes, currently it has not been widely used yet. This paper proposes a method for gene variation detection based on convolutional neural networks (CNNs). The input data of the traditional convolutional neural network is generally a single image or multiple images stacked on the dimension of channels. For complex data such as genetic variation

W. Hong and Y. Weng (Eds.): ICCSE 2022, CCIS 1811, pp. 677–689, 2023.
https://doi.org/10.1007/978-981-99-2443-1_58

that needs to be considered from multiple sequencing fields, they cannot be well received by CNN. it is easy to miss detection to consider whether a gene is mutated or not in a single field, further resulting in the inability to handle problems such as diseases caused by gene mutation in time. Therefore, for gene variation detection, it is very important to ensure the recall rate.

Based on the convolutional neural network, the key to ensure the recall rate are receiving multiple input data and extracting the key information of the input data in the same time. Inspired by the two-stream network [6], this paper proposes a two-stream-like Inception-V3 [7] and VGG [8] fusion model. The two-stream network is a pioneering work in action recognition in videos. It inputs the original video frame image and the optical flow image into two different networks at the same time, solving the problem that the neural network is not able to extract the dynamically changing features in video frames. Inspired by this, we combines the features of the Cigar and SEQ fields in the gene sequencing file, which solves the multi-input problem well, and ensures that the neural network can extract the key information from the features of these two fields. The experimental results show that the method in this paper not only ensures a stable recall rate, but also improves other metrics of gene variation classification.

2   Data Preparation

The third-generation sequencing technology is known for its long read length. The SMRT sequencing technology of PacBio and the single-molecule nanopore sequencing technology of ONT (Oxford Nanopore Technologies) [9] are the representatives of the third-generation sequencing technology. Comparing with the previous two generations, the third-generation sequencing technology is single-molecule sequencing, which does not require PCR amplification during the sequencing process.

The data in this paper are the third-generation sequencing data, all from the Genome in a Bottle (GiaB) project. The Genome in a Bottle [10] project is a cooperative project between NIST, FDA, NCBI, academic sequencing team, sequencing technology developers and clinical laboratories, which is committed to the authoritative characterization of human benchmark genome.

The goal of this work is to enhance the generalization ability of the model through input visualization data to accurately predict structural variation in the gene sequences. The most commonly used approaches for structural variation detection based on the third-generation sequencing data are Cigar field analysis, sequencing fragment split alignment, and sequencing data coverage depth analysis. If we only focus on the Cigar field, although the comparison between the sequencing fragment and the reference genome ca n be obtained, doing so loses a lot of information contained in the base sequence itself because the SEQ field can intuitively show the positional relationship of the base sequence and the alignment of multiple gene sequences can also allow the model to correct individual base error during training. If only the SEQ field is considered, the alignment information between the sequencing segment and the reference genome will be lost, and the lost reference information will make the model more difficult to train, which further makes it difficult to have good classification performance.

Gene image refers to the algorithm that mapping gene sequencing text data into image data, which has been proved to be an effective gene data format in previous studies, such as DeepSV [11], Deepvariant [12] and so on. This work proposes a method to map the text data of the two fields into images while making the loss of sequencing information as few as possible, and utilize the images of the two fields as the input of the model.

2.1 Format of Gene Data

With the continuous progress of sequencing technology, the throughput is also increasing, and large-scale genetic data also requires efficient and effective storage methods. These data may be obtained directly from sequencing tools or analyzed by biological software. Therefore, well-recognized format of gene data is necessary.

Through the third-generation sequencing technology, FASTQ file or BAM file without alignment information can be obtained. Then through the third-generation sequencing data alignment tools NGMLR [13]/BWA [14], etc., comparing FASTQ file or BAM file without alignment information with the reference genome FASTA file to obtain the BAM file which containing the alignment information. Finally, the BAM file is analyzed by the structural variation detection tool, then the structural variation is identified and variation information is stored in the VCF [15] (Variant Call Format) file. VCF file records variant information such as sample individual, chromosome number, breakpoint location and alignment information such as variant type, quality assessment and other result information. The fields of the BAM file and the fields of the VCF file mainly used in this work are shown in Table 1 and Table 2 respectively.

2.2 Cigar

Cigar's full name is Compact Idiosyncratic Gapped Alignment, which uses a combination of numbers and letters to indicate the alignment results. The numbers indicate the length of the base, and the letters indicate the alignment results of a single base. The specific meaning of each operation is shown in Table 3. For example, 13M1D1I means that starting from the starting position POS of the sequenced fragment, the first 13 bases are matched with the reference sequence (13M), and the result of comparing the next base with the reference sequence is deletion (1D), the last base is an insertion (1I).

Visualizing the Cigar field can clearly display the comparison of each base of each sequenced fragment with the reference sequence, and the changes in the comparison of each sequence will also be presented by color changes. After visualization, not only the original information is kept well, but also the feature of contrast change is introduced in an intuitive way, and the rich features in the data can make the model more generalizable. Therefore, visualizing the Cigar field as an input will improve performance of the model.

2.3 SEQ

The meaning of the SEQ field is the base arrangement of the gene, which is an intuitive representation of the gene sequencing data. G (GUANINE, guanine) and empty position N constitute. It is mainly composed of four bases A (ADENINE), T (THYMINE), C (CYTOSINE), G (GUANINE) and the empty position N.

Cigar field analysis is a common method in gene variation detection, because the alignment information of the sequenced fragment and the reference sequence it contains

Table 1. Description of fields in BAM format file

Field	Description
RNAME	Reference sequence Name
POS	1-based leftmost mapping POSition
MAPQ	MAPping Quality
CIGAR	**Cigar String**
TLEN	Observed Template LENgth
SEQ	**Segment SEQuence**

Table 2. Description of fields in VCF format file

Field	Description
CHROM	An identifier from the reference genome
POS	The reference position
REF	Reference base(s)
ALT	alternate base(s)
QUAL	Quality

Table 3. Description of Cigar

Operation	Description
M(MATCH)	Matched compared to reference sequence
I(INDEL)	Indel compared to reference sequence
D(DEL)	Deletion compared to reference sequence
S (SOFT CLIP)	Soft Clip Fragment

is an important condition for judging whether the gene fragment is mutated. Nevertheless, if only the Cigar field is considered, the model will lack the understanding of the arrangement information of the base sequence and the ability to discriminate the position of the base. In order to present the original information of the sequencing data as completely as possible, we use the visualized SEQ field image as one of the inputs of the model. Due to the dependence of genetic variation detection on visualization, this article will visualize the SEQ field in a way similar to Cigar visualization, as shown below.

2.4 Mapping Text Data into Image Data

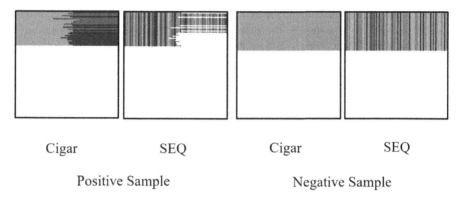

Cigar   SEQ   Cigar   SEQ

Positive Sample   Negative Sample

Fig. 1. Xxx

To express gene alignment information as completely as possible, we propose a method that mapping gene text data into image data. Since single-channel images could only represent grayscale images and have limited information expression capabilities, we select images with three RGB channels as mapping result. In the RGB color mode, R, G, and B represent red, green, and blue respectively, and each pixel of each channel is represented by an 8-bit integer, that is, 0–255, a total of 256 choices, and the three-channel superposition is enough to fully express information such as base type and alignment quality in gene sequencing files.

In this work, a single base is used as the basic unit, each text sequence as the ordinate, the gene sequence as the abscissa. The sliding window method with a size of (100, 100) and stride of (50, 1) is used to generate two key attributes, Cigar and SEQ, the image background base color is white (255, 255, 255).

For the SEQ field, it is set to the following four colors: (255, 128, 0), (128, 0, 255), (0, 128, 255), (0, 255, 128) represent four bases A, C, G, T. For the Cigar field, it is represented by four colors different from the SEQ field, and its four operations M, I, D, S are set to green (0,255,0), black (0,0,0), red (255, 0,0), blue (0,0,255). Two sets of images (as shown in Fig. 1) are randomly selected from the positive and negative samples for display.

3   Method

3.1   Inception-V3

Inception-V1 [16] (also known as GoogLeNet [16]) is a convolutional neural network proposed by Christian Szegedy in 2014, with a total of 22 layers, which won the championship in the 2014 ILSVRC [17] competition. At that time, deep neural networks generally achieved better results by increasing the depth and width of the network, but while expanding the scale of the model, it was hard to avoid side effects such as increased computation and overfitting, so GoogLeNet provided a method that can simultaneously reduce the amount of parameters and expands the scale of the model - the Inception module, whose structure is shown in the Fig. 2. In February 2015, Inception-V2 [18] was proposed, which borrowed the idea of VGG [8] which replaced one 5×5 convolution with two 3×3 convolutions. It is worth mentioning that this is also the first time for the famous Batch Normalization method being proposed. In December 2015, Inception-V3 continued to optimize on the basis of Inception-V2. The main improvements in the network structure (as shown in Fig. 3) are:

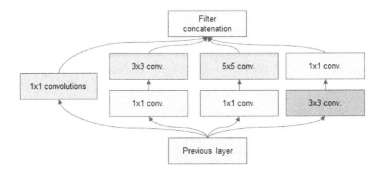

Fig. 2. Inception-v1 module

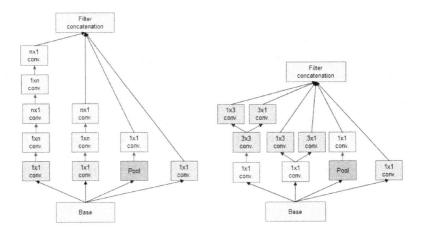

a) Series connected Asymmetrical conv   b) Parallel connected Asymmetrical conv

Fig. 3. Inception-v3 module

- Add more types of convolutions to the Inception module, such as 35×35, 17×17, 8×8, etc.

- Asymmetrically split the convolution kernel into two small convolution kernels, such as 3×3 split into 1×3 and 3×1, the series connection is used to better extract features, and the parallel is used to generate high-dimensional sparse features.
- In order to avoid representation bottleneck, that is, too much information is lost in the process of downsampling, the traditional series connected convolutional layer and pooling layer are changed into parallel convolutional layers and pooling layers with stride 2.

Such improvements are very helpful for the extraction of richer spatial features, while further reducing the amount of computation.

3.2 VGG

VGG [8] is a convolutional neural network proposed by Oxford's Visual Geometry Group, which won the second place in ILSVRC 2014, second only to GoogLeNet. Compared with the previous convolutional neural network, it replaces a convolutional layer with a large convolutional kernel with multiple convolutional layers with a small convolutional kernel, thereby reducing the number of parameters, deepening the network, and making the decision function more discriminative.

3.3 Model Choice for CIGAR and SEQ

Bases are the components of genes, and the meaning of the SEQ field is the sequence of bases in the gene sequencing file, which is an intuitive reflection of gene arrangement and the fundamental source of genetic structural variation. The SEQ field is composed of multiple reads, each of which contains a base sequence (including A, C, G, T). The length and position of the base deletion in each read may be different, for example, in a SEQ image, there may be multiple deletions of diverse lengths at different positions separated by multiple lines, or these deletions may all appear on the same line. This makes it difficult for us to extract these discrete distributed information with a fixed-size convolution kernel, however, Inception-V3 solve this perfectly. Inception-V3 not only has a variety of convolution kernels of different sizes, but also asymmetric convolution generated by decomposing the spatial convolution. This asymmetric convolution is more efficient and more effective than the symmetric convolution structure when it comes to complex spatial features and increasing feature diversity, so that it perfectly adapt to the complex arrangement information of bases in the SEQ field, amplifying every region that may cause variation. Thereby, Inception-V3 is more suitable for SEQ field as a feature extraction network.

The meaning of the Cigar field is the comparison between the bases of each read in the gene sequencing file and the reference sequence, which contains rich gene alignment information. For the image of the Cigar field, the comparison result of each read in the image with the reference sequence needs to be considered. Compared with the discrete information of the SEQ field, the Cigar field needs to be comprehensively considered. VGG replaces the large convolution kernel with multiple small convolution kernels, which deepens the model while maintaining the same receptive field size, brings more non-linear expressions to the model and enhances the fitting ability of the model. It is more suitable for deep meaning information extraction. Therefore, we choose VGG as the feature extraction network of the Cigar field.

3.4 Model Structure

Both Cigar and SEQ fields contain rich gene information. If the model is required to accurately predict whether the gene segment is mutated, the Cigar and SEQ fields need to be fused in an appropriate way. In order to fully extract and fuse the image information of the two fields, we propose a model fusion method based on the above characteristics of Inception-V3 and VGG, so that the information of the two fields of Cigar and SEQ can be fully extracted and utilized.

Since the difference between Inception-V3 and VGG is mainly in the convolutional layer part of feature extraction, and the final fully connected layer is not much diverse, we parallel the convolutional parts of the two, and each part is used as a sub-network of the fusion network, adjust the output size of the two sub-networks by fine-tuning the number of convolutional layers in the last layer, stack the two outputs to get the fused features, and feed them into the fully connected network for classification at last.

A single sub-network can only receive one of the fields, or two fields stacked as input, which lacks the comprehensiveness and independence of the two fields. The fusion model makes good use of the two fields. Two fields will not affect each other in the process of feature extraction and would only be intersected at the final fusion part. Doing so makes the final result more objective.

The overall structure of the model is shown in Fig. 4. The Cigar image and the Sequence image in the same area are fed into the network respectively. After the features are extracted by the convolutional layer, the two sub-networks output a one-dimensional tensor with a length of 4 respectively. Then we stack the two tensors and input it into the fully connected network for classification of variation or non-variation.

4 Experiment and Result Analysis

In the classification task of gene variation detection, we use precision rate, recall rate, and F1-score to evaluate the experiment. These three metrics of evaluation are further calculated from the confusion matrix of the experimental results. We define Precision as P, Recall as R. The following table is the definition of confusion matrix and there are three calculation methods of evaluation metrics (as shown in Table 4 and Eq. (1)(2)(3)):

$$P \ = \ TP \ / \ (TP \ + \ FP) \tag{1}$$

$$R = TP/(TP + FN) \tag{2}$$

$$F1 = 2 * P * R/(P + R) \tag{3}$$

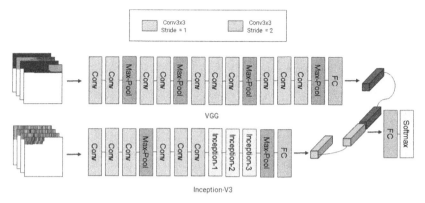

Fig. 4. Construction of Our Model

Table 4. Confusion Matrix

Prediciton\Label	Positive	Negative
True	TP	FP
False	FN	TN

4.1 Training

To train our model, we use Tensorflow framework to accelerate our GPU operation based on CUDA.

The training data is the PacBio whole genome sequencing data of three of a Jewish family, from the Genome in a Bottle (GiaB) project. The three sequencing individuals are HG002 (son), HG003 (father), and HG004 (mother). We made 20,000 positive samples (variation) and 20,000 negative samples (non-variation) to supervise our model. The training process iterated 64 epochs, with Adam [19] as the optimizer, 0.001 as the learning rate. The training process are shown in Fig. 5:

4.2 Inference

We evaluated the model with the lowest loss in the training process, tested it on the simulate dataset and compared it with traditional detection tools. The results are shown in Table 5 and Table 6.

As can be seen from Table 5 and Table 6, the method in this paper not only performs well on homozygous datasets, but also has little performance drop on more complex heterozygous datasets, indicating that the model has sufficient generalization ability to make judgments on visualized data. Compared with the low recall rate of other tools, the method in this paper maintains a good performance in terms of recall rate in both homozygous and heterozygous datasets, indicating that the multi-input solution proposed in this paper has achieved good results.

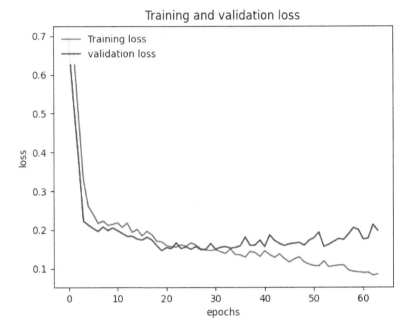

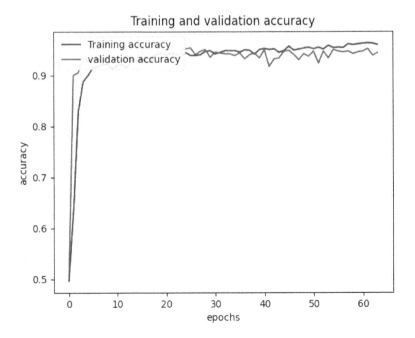

Fig. 5. The loss curve and accuracy curve of training process

Table 5. The performance comparison in homozygous data

Deletion Len	Tools	Precision	Recall	F1
50-1k	NextSV	99.19	95.05	97.07
	SVIM	98.83	96.25	97.52
	Picky	98.86	93.93	96.33
	Our Method	99.40	99.60	99.50
1k-5k	NextSV	98.31	63.64	77.26
	SVIM	98.18	92.43	95.21
	Picky	98.31	95.89	97.08
	Our Method	96.00	99.75	97.84

Table 6. The performance comparison in heterozygous data

Deletion Len	Tools	Precision	Recall	F1
50-1k	NextSV	97.34	95.67	96.49
	SVIM	97.61	97.29	97.44
	Picky	95.08	97.10	96.07
	Our Method	98.80	97.50	98.16
1k-5k	NextSV	95.77	53.90	68.97
	SVIM	92.48	97.15	94.75
	Picky	93.36	94.38	93.86
	Our Method	96.73	98.34	97.53

5   Conclusion

In this paper, in view of the instability of gene variation detection using traditional tools, we propose a deep learning detection method using two-stream-like network to improve the precision and recall rate of gene variation detection. The traditional gene variation detection method is to first manually extract the mutation characteristics, and then count its parameters to identify and predict. The high stability of the detection gene segment leads to a large deviation of the overall detection effect. Because the neural network can extract features invisible to the human eye according to the sample to be detected, it has high fault tolerance and strong generalization ability, and can further improve the index of gene mutation detection. The main work of this paper can be summarized into the following three aspects:

1) Present the sequencing fragment of the gene in the form of RGB three-channel images, to minimize the loss of information during the conversion of text sequencing

fragment to images, and provide effective input data for the neural network at the same time.

2) Design the overall structure of the two-stream-like convolutional neural network.
3) Compare the detection performance of the model in this work with traditional tools. The experimental results show that the deep learning gene variation detection method proposed in this paper is superior to other mainstream detection tools such as: NextSV [20], SVIM [21], Picky [22].

References

1. Bochukova, E.G., et al.: Large, rare chromosomal deletions associated with severe early-onset obesity. Nature **463**, 666–670 (2010)
2. Diskin, S.J., et al.: Copy number variation at 1q21.1 associated with neuroblastoma. Nature **459**, 987–991 (2009)
3. Edwards, P.A.: Fusion genes and chromosome translocations in the common epithelial cancers. J. Pathol. **220**, 244–254 (2010)
4. Esteva, A., Kuprel, B., Novoa, R.A., et al.: Dermatologist-level classification of skin cancer with deepneural networks. Nature **542**(7639), 115–118 (2017)
5. Qamar, S., Ahmad, P., Shen, L.: HI-Net: hyperdense inception 3D UNet for brain tumor segmentation. In: Crimi, A., Bakas, S. (eds.) Brainlesion: Glioma, Multiple Sclerosis, Stroke and Traumatic Brain Injuries: 6th International Workshop, BrainLes 2020, Held in Conjunction with MICCAI 2020, Lima, Peru, October 4, 2020, Revised Selected Papers, Part II, pp. 50–57. Springer International Publishing, Cham (2021). https://doi.org/10.1007/978-3-030-720 87-2_5
6. Simonyan, K., Zisserman, A.: Two-stream convolutional networks for action recognition in videos. Adv. Neural Inf. Process. Syst. **27**, 1–9 (2014)
7. Szegedy, C., Vanhoucke, V., Ioffe, S., et al.: Rethinking the inception architecture for computer vision. In: Proceedings of the IEEE Conference on Computer Vision and Pattern Recognition, pp. 2818–2826 (2016)
8. Simonyan, K., Zisserman, A.: Very deep convolutional networks for large-scale image recognition. arXiv preprint arXiv:1409.1556 (2014)
9. Rothberg, J.M., Hinz, W., Rearick, T.M., et al.: An integrated semiconductor device enabling non-optical genome sequencing. Nature **475**(7356), 348–352 (2011)
10. Xiao, C., Zook, J., Trask, S., et al.: Abstract 5328: GIAB: Genome reference material development resources for clinical sequencing. Can. Res. **74**(19 Supplement), 5328 (2014)
11. Cai, L., Wu, Y., Gao, J.: DeepSV: accurate calling of genomic deletions from high-throughput sequencing data using deep convolutional neural network. BMC Bioinf. **20**(1), 1–17 (2019)
12. Poplin, R., Chang, P.C., Alexander, D., et al.: A universal SNP and small-indel variant caller using deep neural networks. Nat. Biotechnol. **36**(10), 983–987 (2018)
13. Li, H.: Minimap2: pairwise alignment for nucleotide sequences. Bioinformatics **34**(18), 3094–3100 (2018)
14. Li, H., Durbin, R.: Fast and accurate short read alignment with Burrows-Wheeler transform. Bioinformatics **25**(14), 1754–1760 (2009)
15. Danecek, P., Auton, A., Abecasis, G., Albers, C.A., Banks, E., et al.: The variant call format and VCFtools. Bioinformatics **27**, 2156–2158 (2011). https://doi.org/10.1093/bioinformatics/btr330
16. Szegedy, C., Liu, W., Jia, Y., et al.: Going deeper with convolutions. In: Proceedings of the IEEE Conference on Computer Vision and Pattern Recognition, pp. 1–9 (2015)

17. Russakovsky, O., Deng, J., Su, H., et al.: ImageNet large scale visual recognition challenge. Int. J. Comput. Vision **115**(3), 211–252 (2015)

18. Ioffe, S., Szegedy, C.: Batch normalization: accelerating deep network training by reducing internal covariate shift. In: International Conference on Machine Learning. PMLR, pp. 448–456 (2015)

19. Kinma, D.P., Ba, J.: Adam: a method for stochastic optimization. arXiv preprint arXiv:1412.6980 (2014)

20. Fang, L., Hu, J., Wang, D., et al.: NextSV: a meta-caller for structural variants from low-coverage long-read sequencing data. BMC Bioinf. **19**(1), 1–11 (2018)

21. Heller, D., Vingron, M.: SVIM: structural variant. Bioinformatics **35**(17), 2907–2915 (2019)

22. Gong, L., Wong, C.H., Cheng, W.C., et al.: Picky comprehensively detects high-resolution structural variants in nanopore long reads. Nat. Methods **15**(6), 455–460 (2018)

Nonlinear Robust Control for Tilt Rotor UAV with Convex Polytopic Uncertainty

Yucheng Wang, Yanru Zhou$^{(\boxtimes)}$, and Jingyi Zheng

School of Electrical Engineering and Automation, Xiamen University of Technology, Xiamen 361024, China
zhouyr1986@126.com

Abstract. This paper focuses on the nonlinear robust control problem for the modal conversion of tilt rotor UAVs with parameter perturbation, external disturbance and input constraints. Based on the NPV model of the tilt rotor UAV with convex polytopic uncertainty, the corresponding nonlinear robust state feedback stabilization controller is designed using Lyapunov stability and polynomial sum of squares (SOS) theories. Furthermore, by using the generalised S-procedure, the solvable conditions of nonlinear robust control satisfying the input constraints is established, which can be effectively checked with the aid of convex optimization tools. The simulation results show that the obtained controller satisfies the saturation constraint, and can well suppress the external disturbance and adaptive parameter perturbation in the process of realizing the modal conversion of the tilt rotor UAV.

Keywords: convex polytopic · uncertainty · robust control · input constraint · sum of squares

1 Introduction

The tilt rotor UAV combines the advantages of helicopters and fixed wing aircraft. It can not only take off and land vertically and hover in the air like a helicopter, but also fly at high speed and long distance like a fixed wing aircraft, which has important application prospects in military and civil fields. Due to the serious aerodynamic interference between the rotor and the wing during the modal conversion progress of the tilt rotor UAV, its dynamic system has significant nonlinearity, time-varying, strong coupling and uncertainty, which brings great challenges to its flight control design.

PID is the simplest and most practical control algorithm in engineering practice and has been applied in tilt rotor UAV systems [1]. However, this type of UAV has significant nonlinearity and time-varying during the conversion flight, so the PID algorithm cannot fundamentally meet its control requirements. Gain scheduling is a popular control method for the conversion flight of the tilt rotor UAVs [2]. However, this method needs extensive scheduling with the tilt rotor nacelle angle. When the scheduling variable changes rapidly or it is difficult to capture the nonlinear characteristics of the object, the system performance and even stability are difficult to be guaranteed. Additionally, dynamic inversion control [3], model predictive control [4], and backstepping [5] etc. are also used for the flight control of tilt rotor UAVs. The main drawback of these methods is that they ignore the time-varying dynamics of the tilt rotor UAV during conversion flight.

In recent years, the linear parameter-varying (LPV) model has received a lot of attention for its modeling and control methods because it can well characterize the time-varying characteristics of the controlled objects [6]. Meanwhile, the breakthrough of sum of squares (SOS) convex optimization theory has strongly promoted the study of LPV system [6] and the Linear-like state-dependent nonlinear systems [7]. However, for nonlinear time-varying problems, although the research progress in these two aspects has its own advantages, both are still insufficient. The LPV method belongs to the category of segmented linear-like systems, which fails to faithfully reflect the nonlinear dynamics of the original controlled object, while the existing SOS-based polynomial systems research ignore the time-varying characteristics.

In this regard, some scholars begin to study nonlinear parameter-varying (NPV) system, which is a generalization of polynomial time-invariant system and LPV system, and can well characterize the nonlinear and time-varying characteristics of the controlled objects. Fu and Zeng et al. [8] take the lead in establishing an NPV model for the modal conversion of a tilt rotor UAV, and design an exponential stabilization control method. On this basis, a modal conversion control scheme of a tilt rotor aircraft based on disturbance observer is proposed in [9]. Zhu et al. [10, 11] Investigated the guaranteed cost control and Mixed H_2/H_∞ control of a tilt rotor aircraft. However, none of these works consider the parameter perturbation of the tilt rotor UAV during conversion flight.

Inspired by the above, in this paper, the dynamic parameter perturbation in the modal conversion of the tilt rotor UAV is limited to a convex polyhedron set, that is, it is expressed as the convex polyhedron uncertainty, and a new nonlinear robust control method is designed based on SOS. Furthermore, the generalised S-procedure is used to convexify the input constraints such that the resulting closed-loop system satisfies input constraints for any state starting from an admissible set. The proposed method can be solved by the SOS convex optimization tool, and the obtained controller is easy to implement in engineering because it is only the polynomial or rational functions of the states, the time-varying parameters and their time derivatives.

Notations. R^n is the set of n-dimensional real vectors, $R^{n \times m}$ is the set of $n \times m$ real matrices and I is an identity matrix; Φ_{sos} is the set of SOS polynomials; For $x \in R^n$, $\|x\|$ is its Euclidean norm; For a square matrix A, $He(A) = A + A^T$. $R[x]$ is the set of all real polynomial function of vector $x \in R^n$.

2   System Description and Problem Statement

Fig. 1. Body axes of tilt rotor UAV

This paper studies the tilt rotor UAV as shown in Fig. 1, which installs rotatable grids on both sides of the wings of conventional fixed wing aircraft, and embeds rotors on the grids. The direction of the rotor pull is changed by tilting the grid between horizontal and vertical positions, thereby changing its flight mode. The longitudinal dynamics equation of the UAV is as follows [8]:

$$
\begin{cases}
m\dot{V} = F_{xt}(\overline{x}, \delta, \tau) \cdot \cos\alpha - F_{yt}(\overline{x}, \delta, \tau) \cdot \sin\alpha \\
mV\dot{\alpha} = mVq - F_{xt}(\overline{x}, \delta, \tau) \cdot \sin\alpha - F_{yt}(\overline{x}, \delta, \tau) \cdot \cos\alpha \\
\dot{\vartheta} = q \\
I_z\dot{q} = M_z(\overline{x}, \delta, \tau) \\
\dot{H} = V\cos\alpha\sin\vartheta - V\sin\alpha\cos\vartheta
\end{cases}
\tag{1}
$$

where $V, \alpha, \vartheta, q, H$ are the velocity, the angle of attack, the angle of pitch, the pitch angle rate, the altitude, respectively; $\overline{x} = \begin{bmatrix} V \ \alpha \ \vartheta \ q \ H \end{bmatrix}^{\mathrm{T}}$ is the state of the UAV; τ is the tilt angle; δ is the longitudinal control surfaces; m is the mass of the aircraft; I_z is the moment of inertia about the pitch axis; F_{xt} and F_{yt} are components of the force along the body x and y axes; M_z is the pitching moment.

In order to transform the control problem in the modal conversion stage of the tilt rotor UAV into the tracking problem of the tilt rotor UAV, the corresponding longitudinal deviation model of the tilt rotor UAV needs to be established according to the generalized conversion corridor. The physical quantities of the generalised conversion corridor are: the reference velocity V^*, the reference angle of attack α^*, the reference pitch angle ϑ^*, the reference pitch angle rate q^*, the reference altitude H^*, the reference components F_{xt}^* and F_{yt}^* of the force along the body x and y axes, and reference pitch moment M_z^*. Let $\Delta V = V - V^*$, $\Delta\alpha = \alpha - \alpha^*$, $\Delta\vartheta = \vartheta - \vartheta^*$, $\Delta q = q - q^*$, $\Delta H = H - H^*$, $\Delta F_{xt} = F_{xt} - F_{xt}^*$, $\Delta F_{yt} = F_{yt} - F_{yt}^*$ and $\Delta M_z = M_z - M_z^*$, then the trajectory-tracking problem of the system (1) can be converted into the stabilization problem of the following error system

$$
\begin{cases}
\dfrac{d(\Delta V)}{dt} = \dfrac{-F_{yt}^*}{m}\Delta\alpha + \dfrac{F_{xt}^*}{m} - (\alpha^* + \Delta\alpha)\dfrac{\Delta F_{yt}}{m} \\[2mm]
\dfrac{d(\Delta\alpha)}{dt} = \Delta q + A_{21}\cdot\Delta V + A_{22}\cdot\Delta\alpha + B_{21}\cdot\Delta F_{xt} + B_{22}\cdot\Delta F_{yt} \\[2mm]
\dfrac{d(\Delta\vartheta)}{dt} = \Delta q \\[2mm]
\dfrac{d(\Delta q)}{dt} = \dfrac{\Delta M_z}{I_z} \\[2mm]
\dfrac{d(\Delta H)}{dt} = (\Delta\vartheta - \Delta\alpha)\Delta V + V^*\Delta\vartheta - V^*\Delta\alpha
\end{cases}
\tag{2}
$$

where $A_{21} = -m^{-1}\left(F_{xt}^*\alpha^* + F_{yt}^*\right)(a\Delta V + 2\alpha V^* + b), A_{22} = -F_{xt}^*m^{-1}\left[a(V^* + \Delta V)^2 +\right.$
$b(V^* + \Delta V) + c\left.\right], B_{21} = -m^{-1}(\alpha^* + \Delta\alpha)\left[a(V^* + \Delta V)^2 + b(V^* + \Delta V) + c\right], B_{22} = -m^{-1}$
$\left[a(V^* + \Delta V)^2 + b(V^* + \Delta V) + c\right].$

Further considering the external disturbance and parameter perturbation in the modal conversion stage of the tilt rotor UAV, the model (2) can be transformed into the following corresponding state-space description:

$$
\begin{aligned}
\dot{x} &= (A(x,\sigma) + \Delta A(x,\sigma))x + B_1 w + (B_2(x,\sigma) + \Delta B_2(x,\sigma))u \\
z &= Cx + Du
\end{aligned}
\tag{3}
$$

where $x = \begin{bmatrix} \Delta V & \Delta\alpha & \Delta\vartheta & \Delta q & \Delta H \end{bmatrix}^T \in R^5$ is the state, z is the controlled output, $u = \begin{bmatrix} \Delta F_{xt} & \Delta F_{yt} & \Delta M_z \end{bmatrix}^T \in R^3$ is the control input, w is the external disturbance assumed to satisfy $\int_0^\infty \|w(t)\|^2 dt < \infty$, $\sigma = \begin{bmatrix} \tau & \dot\tau \end{bmatrix}^T \in R^2$ is the time-varying parameter vector; $\Delta A(x,\sigma)$ and $\Delta B(x,\sigma)$ are uncertain matrices, $B_1 = \begin{bmatrix} 1 & 0 & 0 & 0 & 0 \end{bmatrix}^T$, $A(x,\sigma) =$

$$
\begin{bmatrix}
0 & -\frac{F_{yt}^*}{m} & 0 & 0 & 0 \\
A_{21} & A_{22} & 0 & 1 & 0 \\
0 & 0 & 0 & 1 & 0 \\
0 & 0 & 0 & 0 & 0 \\
\Delta\vartheta - \Delta\alpha & -V^* & V^* & 0 & 0
\end{bmatrix},
B_2(x,\sigma) =
\begin{bmatrix}
m^{-1} & \frac{-(\alpha^* + \Delta\alpha)}{m} & 0 \\
B_{21} & B_{22} & 0 \\
0 & 0 & 0 \\
0 & 0 & I_z^{-1} \\
0 & 0 & 0
\end{bmatrix},
C = \begin{bmatrix} 1 & 0 & 1 & 1 & 7 \end{bmatrix}^T,
$$

$D = \begin{bmatrix} 0 & 0 & 1 \end{bmatrix}.$

The following assumptions are given for the above system.

Assumption 1: Let u_i denote the i th row of u, the control input u satisfies the following constraints:

$$
|u_i| \le u_{i\max}, u_{i\max} \ge 0, i = 1, 2, 3
\tag{4}
$$

Assumption 2: Given the vectors $h^{(1)}$, $h^{(2)}$, ..., $h^{(p)} \in R^q$ and define the polyhedral set.

$$\alpha = co\{h^{(1)}, h^{(2)}, \cdots, h^{(p)}\} = \left\{ h(t) \in R^q | h(t) = \sum_{j=1}^{p} g_j h^{(j)}, \right.$$

$$\left. \sum_{j=1}^{p} g_j = 1, g_j \in [0,1], t \geq 0, \right\},$$

then for $h = h(t) := \begin{bmatrix} h_1 & h_2 & \cdots & h_q \end{bmatrix}^T \in \alpha$, we have

$$\Delta A(x, \sigma) = \sum_{i=1}^{q} h_i A^{(i)}(x, \sigma), \Delta B_2(x, \sigma) = \sum_{i=1}^{q} h_i B_2^{(i)}(x, \sigma) \tag{5}$$

where $A^{(i)}(x, \sigma) \in R^{5 \times 5}$ and $B_2^{(i)}(x, \sigma) \in R^{5 \times 3}$ are the given matrices.

Combining (3) and (5), the longitudinal NPV model of the tilt rotor UAV with convex polytopic uncertainty can be established as:

$$\dot{x} = \left(A(x, \sigma) + \sum_{i=1}^{q} h_i A^{(i)}(x, \sigma) \right) x + B_1 w + \left(B_2(x, \sigma) + \sum_{i=1}^{q} h_i B_2^{(i)}(x, \sigma) \right) u \tag{6}$$

$$z = Cx + Du$$

Remark 1: System (6) is a class of NPV system, when the system matrices do not depend on the state, it can degenerate into an LPV system; when the system matrix only depends on the state, it becomes a quasi-linear time-invariant system.

For the above system, design the following nonlinear state feedback controller

$$u = K(x, \sigma, \dot{\sigma})x \tag{7}$$

where $K(x, \sigma, \dot{\sigma}) \in R^{3 \times 5}$ is the controller gain matrix to be designed.

Substituting (7) into (6), we can obtain the corresponding closed-loop system

$$\dot{x} = \left(A_{cl}(x, \sigma, \dot{\sigma}) + \sum_{i=1}^{q} h_i A_{cl}^{(i)}(x, \sigma, \dot{\sigma}) \right) x + B_1 w \tag{8}$$

$$z = C_{cl}(x, \sigma, \dot{\sigma})x$$

where $A_{cl}(x, \sigma, \dot{\sigma}) = A(x, \sigma) + B_2(x, \sigma)K(x, \sigma, \dot{\sigma})$, $A_{cl}^{(i)}(x, \sigma, \dot{\sigma}) = A^{(i)}(x, \sigma) + B_2^{(i)}(x, \sigma)K(x, \sigma, \dot{\sigma})$, $C_{cl}(x, \sigma, \dot{\sigma}) = C + DK(x, \sigma, \dot{\sigma})$.

Problem1: For the system (6) without input saturation constraint, design a state-feedback controller (7) such that the closed-loop system (8) is uniformly asymptotically stable at the zero equilibrium point (UASZ) and has L_2- gain $\leq \gamma$.

Problem 2: For the system (6), design a state feedback controller (7) satisfying the constraint condition (4) such that the corresponding closed-loop system (8) is UASZ and has L_2- gain $\leq \gamma$.

3 Main Results

To start this section, we list some important lemmas for further use in the subsequent derivation.

Definition 1 [12]: A polynomial $f(x)$ in $x \in R^n$ is a sum of squares, if there exist polynomials $f_1(x), f_2(x), \cdots, f_m(x)$ such that $f(x) = \sum_{i=1}^{m} f_i^2(x)$.

Obviously, $f(x) \in \Phi_{sos}$ naturally implies $f(x) \geq 0$ for all $x \in R^n$, whereas the converse is generally not true. Although being SOS is a stricter condition than non-negativity, it's more tractable in computation. Besides, numerical experiments indicate that the gap between them is not significant and they are even equivalent under some circumstances, such as quadratic polynomials.

Definition 2 [13]: Consider the system $\Pi : \begin{cases} \dot{x} = A(x)x + B(x)w \\ z = C(x)x + D(x)w \end{cases}$, whose initial condition is $x(0) = 0$. Given a scalar $\gamma > 0$, if for all $T \geq 0$ and $w(t) \in L_2[0, T]$, there is $\int_0^T \|z(t)\|^2 dt \leq \gamma^2 \int_0^T \|w(t)\|^2 dt$, then the L_2- gain of the system $\leq \gamma$.

Lemma 1 [7]: For a symmetric polynomial matrix $P(x)$ that is nonsingular for all x, one has.

$$\frac{\partial P(x)}{\partial x_i} = -P(x)\frac{\partial P^{-1}(x)}{\partial x_i}P(x), i = 1, 2, \cdots, n$$

Lemma 2 [14]: Given $\{g_i(x)\}_{i=0}^{m} \in R[x]$, if there exist $\{s_i(x)\}_{i=1}^{m} \in \Phi_{sos}$ such that.

$$g_0(x) - \sum_{i=1}^{m} s_i(x)g_i(x) \in \Phi_{sos}$$

then

$$\{x \in R^n | g_1(x) \geq 0, \cdots, g_m(x) \geq 0\} \subset \{x \in R^n | g_0(x) \geq 0\}.$$

Theorem 1: For the tilt rotor UAV system (6) with convex polytopic uncertainty, given constants $\gamma > 0, 0 < \varepsilon_1 \leq \varepsilon_2$ and $\varepsilon_{3j} > 0(j = 1, 2, \cdots, p)$, if there exists a symmetric polynomial matrix $P(\sigma)$ and a polynomial matrix $Y(x, \sigma, \dot{\sigma})$ such that.

$$\tau_0^T (P(\sigma) - \varepsilon_1 I)\tau_0 \in \Phi_{sos} \tag{9}$$

$$\tau_1^T (\varepsilon_2 I - P(\sigma))\tau_1 \in \Phi_{sos} \tag{10}$$

$$-\delta_j^T \left(\begin{bmatrix} \Xi_{1j}(x,\sigma,\dot{\sigma}) & * & * \\ B_1^T & -\gamma^2 I & * \\ \Xi_2(x,\sigma,\dot{\sigma}) & 0 & -I \end{bmatrix} + \varepsilon_{3j} I \right) \delta_j \in \Phi_{sos}, j = 1, 2, \cdots, p \tag{11}$$

then Problem 1 is solvable, and the corresponding controller gain matrix $K(x, \sigma, \dot{\sigma}) = Y(x, \sigma, \dot{\sigma})P^{-1}(\sigma)$. Where $\tau_0 \in R^5$, $\tau_1 \in R^5$, $\delta_j \in R^7$, $\Xi_{1j}(x, \sigma, \dot{\sigma}) = \text{He}\big(\tilde{A}_j(x, \sigma)P(\sigma) + \tilde{B}_{2j}(x, \sigma)Y(x, \sigma, \dot{\sigma})\big) - \sum\limits_{k=1}^{s} \frac{\partial P(\sigma)}{\partial \sigma_k}\dot{\sigma}_k$, σ_k is the k th row of σ, $\Xi_2(x, \sigma, \dot{\sigma}) = CP(\sigma)+DY(x, \sigma, \dot{\sigma})$, $\tilde{A}_j(x, \sigma) = A(x, \sigma) + \sum\limits_{i=1}^{q} h_i^{(j)}A^{(i)}(x, \sigma)$, $h_i^{(j)}$ denote the element of the i th row of $h^{(j)}$, $\tilde{B}_{2j}(x, \sigma) = B_2(x, \sigma) + \sum\limits_{i=1}^{q} h_i^{(j)}B_2^{(i)}(x, \sigma)$.

Proof: Define the Lyapunov function as $V(x, t) = x^{\mathrm{T}}P^{-1}(\sigma)x$. According to Definition 1, it is clear that $0 < \varepsilon_2^{-1}I \leq P^{-1}(\sigma) \leq \varepsilon_1^{-1}I$ from (9) and (10), therefore, we know.

$$0 < \varepsilon_2^{-1}\|x\|^2 \leq V(x, t) \leq \varepsilon_1^{-1}\|x\|^2 \tag{12}$$

which means that $V(x, t)$ is positive definite and bounded.

Then, define $\dot{v}_j(x, t) = \dot{V}(x, t)\big|_{h=h^{(j)}}$, for the closed-loop system (8), one has

$$\dot{v}_j(x,t) = \Big(\dot{x}^{\mathrm{T}}P^{-1}(\sigma)x + x^{\mathrm{T}}P^{-1}(\sigma)\dot{x} + x^{\mathrm{T}}\dot{P}^{-1}(\sigma)x\Big)\big|_{h=h^{(j)}}$$

$$= x^{\mathrm{T}}\left(\text{He}\left(P^{-1}(\sigma)\left(A_{cl}(x,\sigma,\dot{\sigma}) + \sum_{i=1}^{q} h_i^{(j)}A_{cl}^{(i)}(x,\sigma,\dot{\sigma})\right)\right)\right.$$

$$\left. + \sum_{k=1}^{s} \frac{\partial P^{-1}(\sigma)}{\partial \sigma_k}\dot{\sigma}\right)x + \text{He}\Big(x^{\mathrm{T}}P^{-1}(\sigma)B_1 w\Big) \tag{13}$$

$$\dot{V}(x,t) = \Big(\dot{x}^{\mathrm{T}}P^{-1}(\sigma)x + x^{\mathrm{T}}P^{-1}(\sigma)\dot{x} + x^{\mathrm{T}}\dot{P}^{-1}(\sigma)x\Big)$$

$$= x^{\mathrm{T}}\left(\text{He}\Big(P^{-1}(\sigma)A_{cl}(x,\sigma,\dot{\sigma})\Big) + \sum_{k=1}^{s}\frac{\partial P^{-1}(\sigma)}{\partial \sigma_k}\dot{\sigma}\right)x + \text{He}\Big(x^{\mathrm{T}}P^{-1}(\sigma)B_1 w\Big)$$

$$+ x^{\mathrm{T}}\text{He}\left(P^{-1}(\sigma)\left(\sum_{i=1}^{q}(\sum_{j=1}^{p} g_j h_i^{(j)})A_{cl}^{(i)}(x,\sigma,\dot{\sigma})\right)\right)x \tag{14}$$

$$= x^{\mathrm{T}}\left(\text{He}\Big(P^{-1}(\sigma)A_{cl}(x,\sigma,\dot{\sigma})\Big) + \sum_{k=1}^{s}\frac{\partial P^{-1}(\sigma)}{\partial \sigma_k}\dot{\sigma}\right)x + \text{He}\Big(x^{\mathrm{T}}P^{-1}(\sigma)B_1 w\Big)$$

$$+ \sum_{j=1}^{p} g_j x^{\mathrm{T}}\text{He}\left(P^{-1}(\sigma)\left(\sum_{i=1}^{q} h_i^{(j)}A_{cl}^{(i)}(x,\sigma,\dot{\sigma})\right)\right)x$$

Since $\sum\limits_{j=1}^{p} g_j = 1$ and $g_j \geq 0$, combing (13) and (14), it is easy to know that

$$\dot{V}(x,t) = \sum_{j=1}^{p} g_j \dot{v}_j(x,t) \tag{15}$$

Next, from Definition 1 and condition (11), we have

$$\Xi_{1j}(x,\sigma,\dot{\sigma}) + \varepsilon_{3j}I \leq 0,$$

multiplying it from the left-hand and right-hand by $P^{-1}(\sigma)$ respectively, and denoting $K(x,\sigma,\dot{\sigma}) = Y(x,\sigma,\dot{\sigma})P^{-1}(\sigma)$, implies that (16) holds by Lemma 1.

$$\mathrm{He}\left(P^{-1}(\sigma)\left(A_{cl}(x,\sigma,\dot{\sigma}) + \sum_{i=1}^{q} h_i^{(j)} A_{cl}^{(i)}(x,\sigma,\dot{\sigma})\right)\right) + \sum_{k=1}^{s} \frac{\partial P^{-1}(\sigma)}{\partial \sigma_k}\dot{\sigma}_k \leq -\varepsilon_{3j}P^{-2}(\sigma)$$

(16)

When $w = 0$, from (13), (15) and (16), it can imply that

$$\dot{V}(x,t) \leq -\sum_{j=1}^{p} g_j x^{\mathrm{T}} \varepsilon_{3j} P^{-2}(\sigma)x$$

And since $0 < \varepsilon_2^{-1}I \leq P^{-1}(\sigma)$, therefore

$$\dot{V}(x,t) \leq -\sum_{j=1}^{p} g_j \varepsilon_{3j} \varepsilon_2^{-2} x^{\mathrm{T}} x$$

(17)

By (12) and (17) hold, it is obvious that the closed-loop system (8) is UASZ. Finally, when $w \neq 0$,

$$\dot{v}_j(x,t) + z^{\mathrm{T}}z - \gamma^2 w^{\mathrm{T}}w$$

$$= x^{\mathrm{T}}\left(\mathrm{He}\left(P^{-1}(\sigma)\left(\tilde{A}_j(x,\sigma) + \tilde{B}_{2j}(x,\sigma)K(x,\sigma,\dot{\sigma})\right)\right) + \sum_{k=1}^{s} \frac{\partial P^{-1}(\sigma)}{\partial \sigma_k}\dot{\sigma}\right.$$

$$+ C_{cl}^{\mathrm{T}}(x,\sigma,\dot{\sigma})C_{cl}(x,\sigma,\dot{\sigma})\Big)x + \mathrm{He}\left(x^{\mathrm{T}}P^{-1}(\sigma)B_1 w\right) - \gamma^2 w^{\mathrm{T}}w$$

(18)

$$= \begin{bmatrix} x \\ w \end{bmatrix}^{\mathrm{T}} \begin{bmatrix} \mathrm{He}\left(P^{-1}(\sigma)\left(\tilde{A}_j(x,\sigma) + \tilde{B}_{2j}(x,\sigma)K(x,\sigma,\dot{\sigma})\right)\right) + & * \\ C_{cl}^{\mathrm{T}}(x,\sigma,\dot{\sigma})C_{cl}(x,\sigma,\dot{\sigma}) + \sum_{k=1}^{s} \frac{\partial P^{-1}(\sigma)}{\partial \sigma_k}\dot{\sigma}_k & \\ B_1^{\mathrm{T}} P^{-1}(\sigma) & -\gamma^2 I \end{bmatrix} \begin{bmatrix} x \\ w \end{bmatrix}$$

Note that (11) implies

$$\begin{bmatrix} \Xi_{1j}(x,\sigma,\dot{\sigma}) & * & * \\ B_1^{\mathrm{T}} & -\gamma^2 I & * \\ \Xi_2(x,\sigma,\dot{\sigma}) & 0 & -I \end{bmatrix} < 0,$$

multiplying its matrix from the left-hand and right-hand by $\mathrm{diag}\left(P^{-1}(\sigma), I, I\right)$ respectively, and according to Lemma 1, Schur complement and (18), it follows that

$$\dot{v}_j(x,t) + z^{\mathrm{T}}z - \gamma^2 w^{\mathrm{T}}w < 0$$

Further, by formula (15) and $\sum\limits_{j=1}^{p} g_j = 1$, one has

$$\dot{V}(x,t) + z^\mathrm{T} z - \gamma^2 w^\mathrm{T} w < 0$$

Integrating the above equation from $t = 0$ to $t = T$ under the condition of $V(x(0), t(0)) = 0$, we have

$$\int_0^T \left(\|z(t)\|^2 - \gamma^2 \|w(t)\|^2 \right) dt \leq V(x(0), t(0)) - V(x(T), t(T)) \leq 0$$

According to Definition 2, it is known that the system (8) has L_2- gain $\leq \gamma$.

On the basis of the above theorem, the following results can be obtained with the help of the generalized S-procedure and the concept of invariant set by further considering the input constraints.

Theorem 2: For the system (6) with input saturation constraints (4), given constants $\gamma > 0$, $0 < \varepsilon_1 \leq \varepsilon_2$, $\eta_i > 0 (i = 1, 2, 3)$ and $\varepsilon_{3j} > 0 (j = 1, 2, \cdots, p)$, if there exists a symmetric polynomial matrix $P(\sigma)$ and a polynomial matrix $Y(x, \sigma, \dot{\sigma})$ such that conditions (9)–(11) and the following conditions hold.

$$\varsigma_i^\mathrm{T} \left(\begin{bmatrix} u_{i\max}^2 & Y_i \\ Y_i^\mathrm{T} & P(\sigma) \end{bmatrix} - \eta_i \begin{bmatrix} 1 & -x^\mathrm{T} \\ -x & P(\sigma) \end{bmatrix} \right) \varsigma_i \in \Phi_{sos}, i = 1, 2, \cdots 3 \tag{19}$$

then the Problem 2 can be solved for $\forall t \geq t_0$ when the initial state satisfies $x(t_0) \in \Omega :=$ $\left\{ x \in \mathrm{R}^n : x^\mathrm{T} P^{-1}(\sigma) x \leq 1 \right\}$, and the corresponding controller gain matrix $K(x, \sigma, \dot{\sigma}) = Y(x, \sigma, \dot{\sigma}) P^{-1}(\sigma)$. Where $\varsigma_i \in \mathrm{R}^6$, Y_i is the i th row of $Y(x, \sigma, \dot{\sigma})$.

Proof: According to the Theorem 1, from conditions (9)–(11), it can be seen that there exists a state-feedback controller (7) such that the corresponding closed-loop system (8) is UASZ and has L_2- gain $\leq \gamma$. Therefore, we just need to prove that when $x(t_0) \in \Omega$, the controller satisfies constraint condition (4) for $\forall t \geq 0$.

Since $\dot{V}(x, t) < 0$ for $\forall t \geq t_0$ and $\forall x \neq 0$, Ω is an invariant set of the resulting closed-loop system(8), that is, if $x(t) \in \Omega$, then $x(t) \in \Omega$ for $\forall t \geq t_0$.

Define the set

$$\Psi = \left\{ x \in \mathrm{R}^n : \left| Y_i P^{-1}(\sigma) x \right| \leq u_{i\max}, i = 1, \cdots, m \right\}.$$

Obviously, if $\Omega \subset \Psi$, one has $x(t_0) \in \Omega \Rightarrow x(t) \in \Psi$ for $\forall t \geq t_0$, that is, the control input satisfies the constraints in (4). Consequently, the problem amounts to verifying whether $\Omega \subset \Psi$ holds.

According to Lemma 2, the condition (19) is equivalent to the following statement:

$$\begin{bmatrix} u_{i\max}^2 & Y_i \\ Y_i^\mathrm{T} & P(\sigma) \end{bmatrix} \geq 0 \tag{20}$$

for all x such that

$$\begin{bmatrix} 1 & -x^{\mathrm{T}} \\ -x & P(\sigma) \end{bmatrix} \geq 0 \tag{21}$$

By Schur complement, (23) and (24) are respectively equivalent to

$$Y_i P^{-1}(\sigma) Y_i^{\mathrm{T}} \leq u_{i\max}^2 \tag{22}$$

and

$$x^{\mathrm{T}} P^{-1}(\sigma) x \leq 1 \tag{23}$$

Next, it is easy to know that $x(t) \in \Omega$ for $\forall t \geq t_0$ from (22). Finally, combining inequalities (22) and (23), we can get

$$\begin{aligned}
|u_i|^2 &= \left| Y_i P^{-1}(\sigma) x \right|^2 \\
&\leq \left\| Y_i P^{\frac{-1}{2}}(\sigma) \right\|^2 \left\| P^{\frac{-1}{2}}(\sigma) x \right\|^2 \\
&= Y_i P^{-1}(\sigma) Y_i^{\mathrm{T}} x^{\mathrm{T}} P^{-1}(\sigma) x \leq u_{i\max}^2
\end{aligned}$$

Therefore, the condition (19) means that $\Omega \subset \Psi$.

4 Numerical Examples

To illustrate the feasibility and effectiveness of the proposed approach, the tilt rotor UAV given in [8, 11] is used as a simulation example, whose relevant parameters are as follows:

$V^* = -2.797 \times 10^{-3} \tau^2 - 2.973 \times 10^{-2} \tau + 23.04, \alpha^* = \vartheta^*,$
$\vartheta^* = -9.59 \times 10^{-8} \tau^3 + 1.563 \times 10^{-5} \tau^2 - 8.149 \times 10^{-4} \tau + 3.981 \times 10^{-2},$
$q^* = \frac{d\vartheta^*}{dt} = \frac{\partial \vartheta^*}{\partial \tau} \dot{\tau} = \left(-2.877 \times 10^{-7} \tau^2 + 3.126 \times 10^{-5} \tau - 8.149 \times 10^{-4} \right) \dot{\tau},$
$H^* = 20, F_{xt}^* = \left(1.546 \times 10^{-8} \tau^2 - 1.118 \times 10^{-2} \tau - 5.935 \times 10^{-2} \right) \dot{\tau},$
$F_{yt}^* = \left(2.169 \times 10^{-7} \tau^2 + 2.596 \times 10^{-4} \tau + 2.753 \times 10^{-3} \right) \dot{\tau}, m = 2\text{kg},$
$M_z^* = \left(-1.479 \times 10^{-8} \tau^2 + 1.607 \times 10^{-6} \tau - 4.189 \times 10^{-5} \right) \ddot{\tau} + \left(-2.958 \times 10^{-8} \tau + 1.607 \times 10^{-6} \right) \dot{\tau}, a = 8.791 \times 10^{-4}, b = -0.03274, c = 0.3491, I_z = 0.0514\text{kg} \cdot \text{m}^2.$

It is assumed that the parameters a, b and c of the UAV have a wide range of perturbation under the influence of many factors, which can be expressed as convex polytopic uncertainty in the form of (5), and the related parameters are as below.

$$A^{(i)}(x, \sigma) = \begin{bmatrix} 0 & 0 & 0 & 0 & 0 \\ \Delta A_{21}^{(i)} & \Delta A_{22}^{(i)} & 0 & 0 & 0 \\ 0 & 0 & 0 & 0 & 0 \\ 0 & 0 & 0 & 0 & 0 \\ 0 & 0 & 0 & 0 & 0 \end{bmatrix}, B_2^{(i)}(x, \sigma) = 0(i = 1, 2, 3);$$

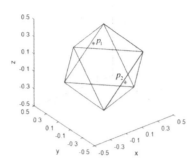

Fig. 2. Variation range of uncertain vector h

$$\Delta A_{21}^{(1)} = \frac{-(F_{xt}^*\alpha^* + F_{yt}^*)(a\cdot\Delta V + 2aV^*)}{2}, \ \Delta A_{22}^{(1)} = \frac{-F_{xt}^*a(V^* + \Delta V)^2}{2}, \ \Delta A_{21}^{(3)} = 0, \ \Delta A_{21}^{(2)} =$$
$$\frac{-(F_{xt}^*\alpha^* + F_{yt}^*)b}{2}, \ \Delta A_{22}^{(2)} = \frac{-F_{xt}^*b(V^* + \Delta V)}{2}, \ \Delta A_{22}^{(3)} = \frac{-F_{xt}^*c}{2}.$$

Furthermore, h is confined within a convex octahedron consisting of 6 vertices $h^{(j)}(j = 1, 2, \cdots, 6)$, as shown in Fig. 2.

In order to make the designed trajectory more systematic, the following tilt angle trajectory is planned using the 7-segment acceleration and deceleration algorithm commonly used in CNC systems [15].

$$\tau = \begin{cases} 78 - \frac{t^3}{60} & 0 \le t \le 3 \\ -0.15(t-3)^2 - 0.45(t-3) + 77.55 & 3 < t \le 10 \\ \frac{(t-10)^3}{60} - 0.15(t-10)^2 - 2.55(t-10) + 67.05 & 10 < t \le 13 \\ -3(t-13) + 58.5 & 13 < t \le 26 \\ \frac{(t-26)^3}{60} - 3(t-26) + 19.5 & 26 < t \le 29 \\ 0.15(t-29)^2 - 2.55(t-29) + 10.95 & 29 < t \le 36 \\ -\frac{(t-36)^3}{60} + 0.15(t-36)^2 - 0.45(t-36) + 0.45 & 36 < t \le 39 \\ 0 & t > 39 \end{cases}$$

According to Theorem 2, $P(\sigma)$ is aconstructed as a 2-degree polynomial matrices in σ, $Y(x, \sigma, \dot{\sigma})$ is constructed as a 2-degree polynomial matrices in x,σ and $\dot{\sigma}$, and other simulation parameters are chosen as $\varepsilon_1 = 10^{-8}$, $\varepsilon_2 = 1$, $\gamma = 0.9$, $\varepsilon_{3j} = 1 \times 10^{-5}(j = 1, 2, \cdots, 6)$, $\eta_i = 1 \times 10^{-5}(i = 1, 2, 3)$, $u_{1\max} = 400N$, $u_{2\max} = 200N$, $u_{3\max} = 100N \cdot m$, then we can obtained a non-linear robust controller (7) by using the Matlab toolbox SOSTOOLS. Next, in order to verify the feasibility and effectiveness of controller, the initial condition is set at $x(0) = \begin{bmatrix} 0.0001 \ 0.01 \ 0.01 \ 0.01 \ 0.1 \end{bmatrix}^T$, and the simulations are performed for the following three different situations, as shown in Fig. 3, 4, 5, 6, 7, 8, 9 and 10.

a. desired reference trajectory
b. disturbed and uncertain system 1 (DUS1)

$$h = p_1 = \begin{bmatrix} 0.1 \ 0.3 \ 0.1 \end{bmatrix}, w = \begin{cases} t, \ 0 < t \le 10 \\ 0, \ t > 10 \end{cases};$$

c. disturbed and uncertain system 2 (DUS2)

$$h = p_2 = \begin{bmatrix} 0.2 & -0.1 & -0.2 \end{bmatrix}, w = \begin{cases} 5 \sin t, & 0 < t \le 15 \\ 0, & t > 15 \end{cases};$$

As can be seen from the figures, with the increase of time, the influence of parameter uncertainty or disturbance on tilt rotor UAV system gradually disappears. In about 25 s, the system responses in the two disturbed and uncertain conditions are consistent with the desired reference trajectory, that is, the desired control objectives are achieved. Moreover, the forces and moment are always within the limited range, satisfying the control input saturation constraints. The simulation results show that the nonlinear robust controller designed in this paper satisfies the saturation constraint, which not only realizes the modal conversion control of the tilt rotor UAV, but also can well suppress external disturbances and adapt to a wide range of parameter perturbations.

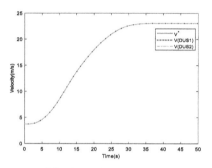

Fig. 3. Trajectories of V

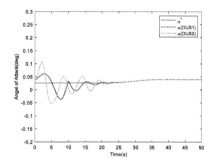

Fig. 4. Trajectories of α

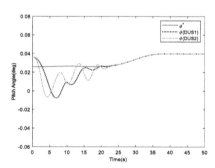

Fig. 5. Trajectories of ϑ

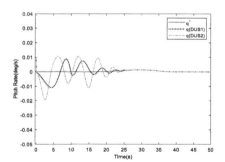

Fig. 6. Trajectories of q

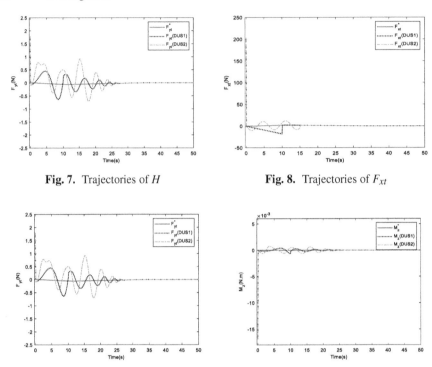

Fig. 7. Trajectories of H

Fig. 8. Trajectories of F_{xt}

Fig. 9. Trajectories of F_{yt}

Fig. 10. Trajectories of M_z

5 Conclusions

To solve the problems of external disturbances, dynamic parameter perturbation and control input saturations during the conversion flight of the tilt rotor UAV, a new nonlinear robust control method was designed under the SOS framework, combining Lyapunov stability theory and generalised S-procedure. This approach can be checked with the aid of an convex optimization tools, which can effectively avoid the computational difficulties commonly existing in nonlinear and time-varying control research. Simulation results show that the designed controller satisfies the saturation constraints, can accurately track the desired reference trajectory, and has good robustness to external disturbance and parameter uncertainties.

Acknowledgments. The work was supported in part by Natural Science Foundation of Fujian Province, China(No. 2020J01284), the Science and Research Project of Fujian Province, China (No. JAT200495); Science and Technology project of Xiamen (3502Z20203066) and Science and Technology Innovation Project for Graduate Students of Xiamen University of Technology (YKJCX2021–114).

References

1. Oner, K.T., Çetinsoy, E., Kandemir, I.: Mathematical modeling and vertical flight control of a tilt-wing UAV. Turkish Journal of Electrical Engineering & Computer Sciences **20**, 149–157 (2012). https://doi.org/10.3906/elk-1007-624
2. Cai, X.H., Fu, R., Zeng, J.P.: Robust H_∞ gain-sheduling control for mode conversion of tiltrotor aircrafts. J. Xiamen Univ. (Nat. Sci.) **55**, 382–389 (2016)
3. Chao, C., Lincheng, S., Daibing, Z., Jiyan, Z.: Mathematical modeling and control of a tiltrotor UAV. In: IEEE International Conference on Information and Automation 2016, ICIA, pp. 2016–2021. IEEE, Ningbo(2016). https://doi.org/10.1109/ICInfA.2016.7832150
4. Papachristos, C., Alexis, K., Nikolakopoulos, G., Tzes, A.: Model predictive attitude control of an unmanned Tilt-Rotor aircraft. In: IEEE International Symposium on Industrial Electronics, pp. 922–927. IEEE, Gdansk (2011). https://doi.org/10.1109/ISIE.2011.5984282
5. Kendoul, F., Fantoni, I., Lozano, R.: Modeling and control of a small autonomous aircraft having two tilting rotors. In: Proceedings of the 44th IEEE Conference on Decision and Control, pp. 8144–8149. IEEE, Seville (2005). https://doi.org/10.1109/CDC.2005.1583480
6. Zhou, Y.R., Zeng, J.P.: Observer-based robust stabilization for a class of uncertain polynomial systems. Trans. Inst. Meas. Control **39**, 675–687 (2017). https://doi.org/10.1177/0142331215618444
7. Prajna, S., Papachristodoulou, A., Wu, F.: Nonlinear control syn-thesis by sum of squares optimization: a Lyapunov-based approach. In: 2004 5th Asian Control Conference, vol. 78, pp. 600–611. IEEE, Melbourne (2016). https://doi.org/10.1109/ASCC.2004.184761
8. Fu, R., Sun, H.F., Zeng, J.P.: Exponential stabilization of nonlinear parameter-varying systems with applications to conversion flight control of a tilt rotor aircraft. Int. J. Control **92**, 2473–2483 (2019). https://doi.org/10.1080/00207179.2018.1442022
9. Rong, F., Zeng, J., Wang, Y., Zhang, D.: Conversion flight control for tilt rotor aircraft using nonlinear time-varying perspective. J. Aeros. Eng. **33**(5), 04020062 (2020). https://doi.org/10.1061/(ASCE)AS.1943-5525.0001179
10. Zhu, P.F., Wang, J.Y., Zeng, J.P.: The guaranteed cost controller for nonlinear systems with time-varying parameters and input saturation. Trans. Inst. Meas. Control **42**, 565–575 (2020). https://doi.org/10.1061/10.1177/0142331219878063
11. Zhu, P.F., Zhou, Y.R., Zeng, J.P: Mixed H_2/H_∞ control for non-linear parameter-varying systems. Control Theory Appl. **37**, 2231–2241, (2020). https://doi.org/10.7641/CTA.2020.90808
12. Wu, F., Prajna, S.: SOS-based solution approach to polynomial LPV system analysis and synthesis problems. Int. J. Control **78**, 600–611 (2006). https://doi.org/10.1080/00207170500114865
13. Lu, W.M., Doyle, J.C.: H∞ control of nonlinear systems via output feedback: controller parameterition. IEEE Trans. Autom. Control **39**(12), 2517–2521 (1995). https://doi.org/10.1109/9.362834
14. Jarvis-Wloszek, Z.W.: Lyapunov Based Analysis and Controller Synthesis for Polynomial Systems using Sum-of-Squares Optimization. wloszek (2003)
15. Tian, J.F., Lin, H., Yao, Z., Li, J.: Study on S-shape curve acceleration and deceleration control fast planning on CNC system. J. Chin. Comput. Syst. **34**, 168–172 (2013)

Detecting Medical Insurance Fraud Using a Heterogeneous Information Network with a Multi-behavior Pattern

Ke Shaojie⬤, Lin Kaibiao⬤, Zhu Shunzhi$^{(\boxtimes)}$⬤, and Chen Ruicong

Xiamen University of Technology, Xiamen, China
kblin@xmut.edu.cn, zhusz99@qq.com

Abstract. Medical insurance frauds impose huge losses on the medical insurance funds. Hence, efficient detection of medical insurance frauds is essential for sustainable medical insurance funds and affects the quality and affordability of health care. The existing detection methods determine fraudulent cases by statistical analyses of the patients' characteristics using graph neural network models. Nevertheless, such methods ignore the potential relationship between the graph nodes which represents the degree of similarity between the patients' characteristics. To address this issue, we propose a medical insurance fraud detection model based on a heterogeneous information network with a multi- behavior pattern, namely BPGAN. In our proposed approach, we analyze the characteristics of different behavior patterns among patients and design an attentional mechanism for embedded learning of patient nodes in the medical insurance data network. It enables capturing potential relationships between the patients' nodes and obtaining the corresponding weight coefficients of different behavior patterns in the process of embedded learning. Experimental results on real medical insurance data sets confirm that the proposed method effectively identifies medical insurance fraudsters and overperforms existing fraud detection methods.

Keywords: Medical insurance fraud · behavior pattern · fraud detection

1 Introduction

With the rapid development of medical services, the reform of China's medical insurance system has promoted the popularization of medical insurance. By 2020, the number of people participating in the national basic medical insurance (hereafter referred to as basic medical insurance) has reached 1,36 million, and the proportion of people covered by China's medical insurance system has stabilized at over 95% [1]. Nevertheless, with the expansion of the health care system coverage health care fraud has also increased. Only in 2020, China's medical insurance fund dealt with 26,100 illegal insurance participants in various regions with the equivalent loss of 22.31 billion Chinese Yuan [2]. Many other countries also face similar problems. For instance, in 2018, the UK lost more than 1 billion pounds to fraud in England alone [3]. Similarly, in the United States, the annual loss caused by medical insurance fraud is about 170 billion dollars [4]. Therefore, it is an immediate need to develop reliable systems to accurately detect cases of medical insurance fraud from complex medical data.

Medical insurance fraud often refers to a range of illegal actions taken by the doctors and patients using false and/or incomplete evidence or deliberate withholding important information to obtain illegal monetary gain. From the patients' point of view, it is mainly through faking diseases to obtain prescribed drugs or items for their or others' use. In the medicare records, such activities are often represented as abnormal use of medical items. Medical insurance fraud has greatly damaged the interests of policyholders, and significantly hindered the implementation and promotion of medical insurance policies. Therefore, it is of great significance to develop reliable methods to discover the fraudsters in the medical insurance systems.

(a) Distribution of medical insurance fraudsters' visits to the same department in different hospitals

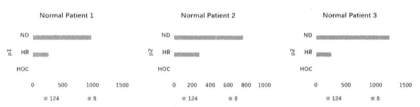

(b) Distribution of normal patients' visits

Fig. 1. Distribution of people's visits to the same department in a hospital

In the case of medical insurance fraud, there is usually a specific correlation between the fraudsters. Medicare fraudsters often carry large numbers of Medicare cards to falsely treat patients or obtain drugs at low prices. Such drugs are then sold at a much higher price. These medical insurance frauds are often organized. Therefore, there is always some sort of correlation between the location of the fraud, the medication involved, and the clinic/health care provider. Therefore such activities can be discovered through careful analysis of such correlative relationships. In this paper, we investigate the behavioral patterns of nephrotic patients and find out that normal patients show quite different behaviors when compared to fraudsters (Fig. 1). Figure 1 (a) shows the behavioral patterns amongst a handful of entities labeled as fraudsters. As it is seen, fraudsters often seek medical treatment in the same department of different hospitals, yet the proportion of their visits to the same department of different hospitals is very similar. From the bar chart comparison of Fig. 1 (a) and Fig. 1 (b), it can be seen that the normal patients generally do not go to the hemodialysis outpatient clinic (HOC) of other hospitals. Even though patients and fraudsters are treated in the same hospital departments, there are significant differences in the frequency of their visits. The frequency of patients receiving treatment in the nephrology department (ND) of the same hospital is higher than that of the hemodialysis room (HR). This indicates a substantial difference between these two behavioral patterns. This situation inspires us to carry out research on medical insurance fraud detection by studying the difference between patients' diagnosis and treatment trajectories.

In recent years, heterogeneous information networks have been able to characterize the objects and their inter-relationships in real scenarios. Thus, we use heterogeneous information networks to represent complex entities and relationships in real medical insurance scenarios.

Aiming at the specific task of medical insurance fraud detection, this paper introduces a multi-behavior pattern model with a single-layer attention mechanism to detect fraud by investigating the patients' behavioral patterns in a heterogeneous network framework. The basic idea of this model is to establish a medical trajectory amongst the patients through multiple behavioral patterns. The information on the patient's attribute characteristics is then fused with the information mined through behavioral patterns. Through a large number of experiments on real healthcare data sets, we then show that the performance of our proposed method is higher than other existing models. The main advantage of this model is to capture the similarity between patients through multiple behavioral patterns, learn different effects of various behavioral patterns on node representation, and obtain more semantic information.

The contributions of this paper are as the following:

- The proposed model makes full use of the potential semantic information in the heterogeneous information network of medical insurance and combines the characteristics of patients' behavior patterns with data characteristics. This improves the accuracy of the embedded representation learned by the model.
- We further design an attention mechanism based on behavioral patterns, and the impact of different behavioral patterns on the embedded representation learning is reflected through different weight coefficients. This further improves the interpretability of the proposed model.
- To improve the performance of medical insurance fraud detection, we also obtain the weights based on the similarity amongst the patients, fuse more information, and improve prediction accuracy.

2   Related Work

Fraud in daily life causes substantial harm to the interests of the country and its people. Thus a large number of researchers have carried out relevant studies on different types of fraud in various settings including credit cards, online transactions, and medical insurance. The existing fraud detection methods mainly include rule-based fraud detection, supervised and unsupervised learning, and graph-based fraud detection algorithms.

2.1 Rule-Based Fraud Detection Method

Early research works in this area were focused on using rule-based methods for fraud detection. These methods are often based on determining a set of rules related to fraud detection based on prior knowledge. Instances are a very high total price of a single prescription or taking multiple unrelated drugs [5]. These rules are very efficient in fraud detection because of their simple and interpretable nature. However, these methods are highly dependent on the prior knowledge of experts and cannot be flexibly changed with the diversification of fraudsters' methods. Once the rules are discovered by fraudsters, they can evade the detection of these rules by special means. In contrast, machine learning-based approaches are more flexible.

2.2 Fraud Detection Using Supervised Learning

Supervised learning has been widely used in fraud detection methods. It trains various classification models from labeled data and uses these models to classify unlabeled data to identify abnormalities.

In 2010, Maranzato et al. [6] compared the fraud detection model using the statistics feature with the models using logistic regression. They used stepwise regression to optimize the logistic regression model to improve the performance of the method. The results showed that the fraud detection method based on logistic regression has higher accuracy than that of methods based on statistical features. In 2013, Ekin et al. [7] proposed a method based on the bayesian copolymerization method of Markov chains to the datasets of doctor and patient pairs associated with access to the chain. Using the Bayesian clustering and link analysis method, Ekin then quantified uncertainty about fraud and identified potential fraud of doctors and patients to improve the accuracy of detection.

Supervised learning has been also widely used in the field of financial fraud detection. In 2015, Liu Chengwei [8] studied the application of random forest in financial fraud detection, conducting feature selection, importance measurement, and partial correlation analysis on financial data sets. The results showed that random forest has higher accuracy than the above methods. In 2018, Cao et al. [9] improved the TLSTM algorithm and took the sequence of patients' medical behavior as the input of the LSTM model to predict patients' medical behavior. By comparing the difference between the algorithm output and the current medical treatment behavior, the possibility of fraud can be judged. To improve the accuracy of the algorithm, Hancock et al. [10] used Catboost for fraud detection on unbalanced medical insurance claim data for the first time in 2020 and showed through experiments that Catboost's classification was superior to previous algorithms.

Supervised learning methods obtain an optimal classification model by training based on the existing training samples, but each model needs to train based on huge data sets which takes a long time.

2.3 Fraud Detection Using Unsupervised Learning

Compared with supervised learning, unsupervised learning does not involve a training process, the data is directly modeled and analyzed. The detection method of unsupervised learning is to learn the same characteristics from a large amount of data and divide the data set into different data groups to distinguish normal data from abnormal data.

In 2014, Stephen et al. [11] extracted some potential information from the medical insurance claim results provided by The Nigerian Medical Insurance Plan (NHIS). They then applied the inflection point K-means clustering method to detect cluster-based outliers. In addition, Zhang et al. [12] proposed an improved local anomaly factor algorithm in 2017. By analyzing the limitations of the LOF algorithm in the medical neighborhood, a robust regression model was used to model the variable relationship to detect potential fraud. With the application of random forest algorithms in the field of fraud detection, Bauder et al. [13] used algorithms to detect fraud in the data of the American medical insurance system involving originally isolated forest and unsupervised random forest in 2018.

Experimental results show that unsupervised random forest has better detection performance. In 2019, Ekin et al. [14] proposed the use of an unsupervised hierarchical Bayesian algorithm as a pre-screening tool to assist in the evaluation of medical insurance fraud, and the proposed hierarchical model is conducive to the detection of medical insurance fraud. In 2020, Naidoo et al. [15] proposed an unsupervised generative adversarial Network anomaly detection model (GAN-AD) to introduce adversarial networks into medicare fraud detection by training generators and discriminator models to identify anomalies from invisible data.

The methods based on unsupervised learning such as clustering-based outlier detection and clustering analysis can efficiently discover outlier objects without labeling data. Nevertheless, due to the few input parameters, only a small amount of information can be learned, and the accuracy of results obtained in complex medical insurance data sets often fails to meet the requirements of fraud detection.

2.4 Fraud Detection Based on Graphs

Most fraud detection methods based on machine learning only use the attribute characteristics of entities in the data set and thus do not consider the characteristics based on the relationship network between those entities. However, there are many different types of entities in a realistic medical treatment scene, and there are rich interactions among these entities. There is a lot of potentially important information in these interaction relationships, such as patients going to the hospital on a certain date, patients going to a certain department to pick up a certain drug, etc. Not only do healthcare fraudsters have unusual characteristics, but there are also unusual behaviors in these interactions. In recent years, it has become common to use graphs to imitate the real scenes and establish appropriate relationship networks to be used in fraud detection [11, 16, 17].

In 2019, Hu et al. [18] proposed a graph embedding method based on meta path for user cash out detection. This method learns the interactive relationship between users and user characteristics through meta paths and hierarchical attention mechanisms to learn the vector representation of entities. Similarly, Zhong et al. [19] proposed a heterogeneous information network for financial default detection. This method uses meta paths on different views to capture the structural characteristics of nodes and then obtains the user embedding in 2020 by calculating the importance between meta paths. Although the above methods and models consider the interaction between entities, the behavior patterns between different entities are different. Therefore their importance to the target entity is also different. In the same year, Chen et al. [20] proposed a graph-based method for joint fraud detection in health care. The algorithm uses the similarity of patients' medical behavior to find potential relationships and then detects suspicious fraud groups through a community detection algorithm. For example, if entity A and the known medical insurance fraudster went to the same hospital to see the same department on the same day, while entity B and the fraudster went to the same hospital, but not on the same day, and they didn't see the same department, there is a certain difference in the similarity of behavior patterns between them.

Patients have similar medical trajectories in a single behavior pattern. Inspired by this idea, maybe they also have similar medical trajectories in other different behavior patterns. In addition, different behavior patterns have different effects on the representation learning of target nodes. Therefore, this paper proposes a medical insurance fraud detection method based on behavior patterns to study the above problems.

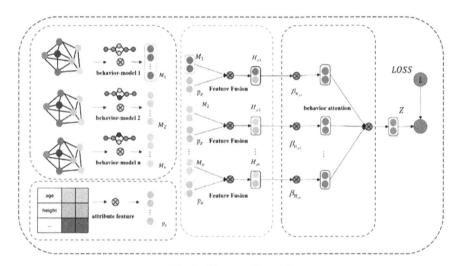

Fig. 2. The overall model

3   Fraud Detection Based on Behavioral Patterns

In this section, we propose a fraud detection method based on behavioral patterns by constructing the medical insurance heterogeneous information network. This network represents the patient attributes in a real medical treatment scene based on medical insurance data. The overall architecture of the model is presented in Fig. 2. Through common-sense reasoning and data analysis, a variety of special behavior patterns are selected from the heterogeneous information network. In this model, the similarity between patient trajectories is calculated by behavior patterns as the weight of the adjacency matrix. The characteristics of neighbor nodes obtained from different behavior patterns are then fused with the attribute characteristics of the target node itself. We also note that different behavior patterns have different effects on target nodes. Therefore, we introduce a behavior pattern level attention mechanism to calculate the importance of different behavior patterns. By aggregating the node representations in different behavior patterns we then obtain the final node embedded representation which is used for detecting medical insurance fraud.

3.1 Construction of Heterogeneous Medical Insurance Information Network

An information network is defined as one with object type mapping $\phi: V \to A$, link type mapping $\psi: E \to R$ and directed graph $G(V,E)$ of $e \in E$. Each object $v \in V$ belongs to a specific object type $\phi(v) \in A$, and each link $e \in E$ belongs to the relationship type set $R: \psi(e) \in R$ for a specific relationship type. In cases where the number of node types $L > 1$ or the number of edge types $L > 1$, the information network is a heterogeneous information network (HIN) [21, 22]. In a certain scenario, for patients going to a hospital to see a doctor and register at different nodes (e.g. in a certain hospital), there are different contact dates between different departments. This network, which is composed of multiple types of medical insurance entities and multiple types of edges connecting medical insurance entities, is a heterogeneous information network of medical insurance (see, Fig. 3).

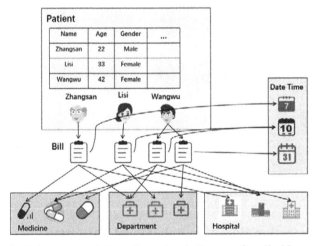

Fig. 3. Heterogeneous information network diagram of medical insurance

3.2 Behavior Pattern Similarity Calculation

Behavior pattern refers to the structure, content, and regular behavior series of people's daily activities with motivation, purpose, and characteristics. For instance, one can explore the same behavior pattern in two different hospitals as in Fig. 4 (a) and (b).

Therefore, we can analyze the similarity in the medical trajectory of patients going to the same hospital on the same date to get the special interaction between patients (Fig. 5 (a)). Fraudsters have highly similar behavior patterns, and they often go to the same hospital on the same date. Even though ordinary patients and fraudsters often go to the same hospital, only a few of them go to the hospital on the same date, as shown in Fig. 5 (b). It can be found that there are great differences between fraudsters and patients in some behavioral patterns. Therefore, selecting an appropriate behavior pattern for node representation learning can improve the accuracy of medical insurance fraud detection.

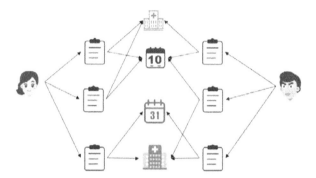

(a) Patients going to the same hospital on the same day.

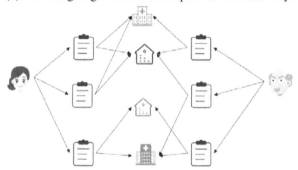

(b) Patients going to the same department at the same hospital.

Fig. 4. The same behavior pattern in two different hospitals

To obtain the similarity matrix $M = \begin{bmatrix} sr_{11} & \cdots & sr_{1m} \\ \vdots & \ddots & \vdots \\ sr_{m1} & \cdots & sr_{mm} \end{bmatrix}$ of each behavior pattern, We

calculate the similarity between the two diagnostic events and take the average value as the matrix coefficient sr_{ij}, , as shown in (2)

$$d_{p_x} = (\frac{S}{|d_{p_x}|} + \frac{S}{|d_{p_y}|})/2 \tag{1}$$

where p_x and p_y represent two patients, $d_{p_x} = \{d_{p_x1}, d_{p_x2}, d_{p_x3}, \ldots, d_{p_xn}\}$ is the set of diagnostic events, d_{p_xi} is the i_{th} diagnostic events of patient p_x and S represents the number of diagnostic events of p_x and p_y in the same behavior trajectories, as shown in (2).

$$S = Sum(\sum_{i=1}^{n}\sum_{j=1}^{n} S(d_{xi}, d_{yj}) \begin{cases} 1 \; n_{d_{pxi}} = n_{d_{pyj}} \\ 0 \; n_{d_{pxi}} \neq n_{d_{pyj}} \end{cases}) \tag{2}$$

In formula (2), $n_{d_{pxi}} = \{n_1, n_2\}$ indicates the collection of attribute nodes related to the diagnostic event. For example, in the behavior pattern of patients going to the same hospital on the same date, n_1 and n_2 represent the hospital and date nodes, respectively.

Since we use multiple behavior patterns, we use $N = \{M_1, M_2, \cdots, M_n\}$ to represent the set of similarity matrices.

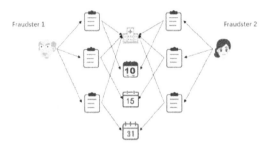

(a) The behavior patterns among fraudsters

(b) The behavior patterns of fraudsters and patients

Fig. 5. The medical trajectory of patients going to the same hospital on the same date

3.3 Feature Fusion

For each patient p_x we get its characteristics and its medical trajectory similarity matrix M_i based on multiple behavior patterns. To better represent the features of learning nodes, we establish a feature fusion module to fuse and transform the original features. Firstly, to aggregate the potential representation of medical trajectories among patients, we fuse the original attribute features of patients with the medical trajectories obtained through various behavior patterns. This is to obtain the embedded representation sets $\{H_1, H_2, \cdots, H_n\}$ of patients, as shown in (3).

$$H_i = g(h_u, M_i) \tag{3}$$

where $g(,)$ is the fusion function that can be connection or element product, h_u is the original attribute characteristics of the patient and M_i is characteristics of various behavior patterns of patients. To reduce the redundant information and computational complexity in the patient fusion features, we reduce the dimension of the feature representation and obtain the embedded representation set $\{H_{\rho 1}, H_{\rho 2}, \cdots, H_{\rho m}\}$ which fuses various behavior patterns, as shown in (4).

$$H_{\rho i} = W \cdot H_i \tag{4}$$

where $W \in R^{D \times d}$ is the transformation matrix, D is the dimension of feature space, and d is the dimension of potential representation.

3.4 The Attention Mechanism Between Behavior Patterns

Generally, each node and edge in each behavior pattern contains different types of semantic information. Previously, we learned that the node embedding representation set $\{H_{\rho 1}, H_{\rho 2}, \cdots, H_{\rho m}\}$ in each behavior pattern. Furthermore, the node embedding of a specific single behavior pattern can only reflect the node information from a single aspect. Therefore, to obtain a more comprehensive node embedding representation, we need to learn the influence of different behavior patterns on our final task.

The attentional mechanism has been shown as an efficient tool in heterogeneous graph learning for node embedding representation learning. Here, we propose an attention mechanism of behavior-level to automatically learn the importance of different behavior patterns, aggregate node embeddings among various behavior patterns, and generate specific node embeddings as shown in (5).

$$Z = \sum_{i=1}^{\rho} \beta_{\rho i} \cdot H_{\rho i} \tag{5}$$

where Z is an embedding specific to behavior patterns, $\rho = \{\rho_1, \rho_2, \cdots, \rho_i\}$ is the collection of behavior patterns in the medical insurance network. In formula (5) $\beta_{\rho i}$ can be seen as the degree of contribution of the behavior pattern $H_{\rho i}$.

To understand the impact of different behavior patterns on the final task in a heterogeneous information network, we use the attention mechanism to assign different weights to different behavior patterns. In this approach, we first measure the importance of mode-specific node embedding through the attention vector $\omega_{\rho i}$ of the transformed behavior pattern, as shown in (6).

$$\omega_{\rho i} = tanh\left(W_0 \cdot h_i^{\rho} + b_0\right) \tag{6}$$

where ω is the importance of the behavior pattern, W_0 is the weight matrix, and b_0 is the bias vector. For a meaningful comparison of the importance of behavioral patterns, all of the above parameters are shared among all nodes embedded in the healthcare network.

After obtaining the importance of embedding each behavior pattern in the medical insurance network, we normalize it by *Softmax* function, as shown in (7).

$$\beta_{\rho i} = softmax(\omega_{\rho i}) = \frac{exp(\omega_{\rho i})}{\sum_{i=1}^{\rho} exp(\omega_{\rho i})} \tag{7}$$

The weight of each behavior mode learned in the medical insurance network is taken as the coefficient, and the weighted sum of the specific embeddings of all behavior modes is carried out to obtain the final node embeddings representation Z. Given a set of node embeddings specific to behavior patterns as inputs, the contribution of each behavior pattern can be as shown in (8).

$$(\beta_{\rho 1}, \beta_{\rho 2}, \cdots, \beta_{\rho m}) = ATTN(H_{\rho 1}, H_{\rho 2}, \cdots, H_{\rho m}) \tag{8}$$

After obtaining the attention score of behavior patterns, we fuse the information contained in m behavior patterns and aggregate the node vectors of m behavior patterns to obtain the final node embedding Z.

3.5   Model Optimization

We use the cross-entropy as the loss function and optimize the model through the back-propagation minimization function. We then apply the final embedded Z to different downstream tasks. The CrossEntropy loss function as shown in (9).

$$L = -\sum_{k \in y_L} Y_L ln\left(W \cdot Z^l\right) \tag{9}$$

where y_L is the set of node indexes with labels, Z^l and Y_L are the embedding of label nodes and corresponding labels respectively. Furthermore, W is a parameter of the classifier. In this graph neural network model, these frameworks are used to learn weights and aggregate information layer by layer to obtain node embedding with rich information.

4   Experiment

We used some baseline model methods on real datasets as comparative experiments to evaluate the effectiveness of our model. The basic setup of the experiment is also briefly described, and the interpretability of our model is improved by the ablation experiment. We then analyze the influence of the parameters in the experiment on the final task.

4.1   Data Set

We used the real data of a city's Medical Insurance Bureau in 2018 (nephropathy_2018), see Table 1. The fraud samples in the data set are abnormal patients detected by abnormal kidney disease, repeated prescriptions, simultaneous outpatient hospitalization, and other methods. There are medical data of 440 patients, and all the following experiments are based on this dataset.

Table 1. Dataset: Number of Nodes and Their Types

	Nodes
Medical records	922784
Hospital	80
Medical	3963
Department	532
Date Time	365

4.2 Baseline Experiment

We consider the following representative neural network detection methods for detailed comparisons:

- GCV [21]: A GNN variant designed for isomorphic graphs, which is a semi-supervised graph convolution network. We test all behavior patterns and feedback on the best performance.
- Metapath2vec [23]: This is a heterogeneous graph embedding method based on a random walk that realizes the random walk guided by meta path which is embedded by the skip-gram model.
- GAT [24]: A GNN variant for isomorphic graph design is a semi-supervised neural network with an attention mechanism. Here, we test all paths and feedback on the best performance.
- HAN [25]: That is a heterogeneous graph neural network for graph embedding. The behavior pattern-specific node embedding is learned from different meta path based isomorphic graphs. It is then aggregated into a vector embedding to represent each node by using the double-layer attention mechanism.
- BPGAN: In this paper, we calculate the similarity of the patient's behavior pattern to the traditional Chinese medicine trajectory. It is then aggregated using the attention mechanism to generate a vector to represent the target node.
- $BPGAN_{am}$: The variant of BPGAN is associated with patients directly through behavior patterns, where the similarity of patients' medical trajectories is not calculated (Table 2).

For the random walk based methods such as Metapath2vec, we set the window size to 5, the walk length to 100, the walk length of each node to 40, and the number of negative samples to 5. For other graph neural networks, we use the same training, test, and verification sets. The learning rate is 0.01, the embedding dimension of the algorithm is set to 128, the regularization parameter is 0.001, and the number of multiple headers is set to 8. In addition, we set the patient stop in advance to 100. If the verification loss is not reduced by 100 iterations, the experiment is stopped.

By comparing metapath2vec's random walk-based method with other baseline methods, it is seen that there is potential semantic information in structural information. Hence aggregating the potential information in structural information can improve the detection

Table 2. Experimental Results of Node Classification on the Dataset

Train:Val:Test	Metrics	Metapath2vec	GAT	GCN	HAN	BPGAN
1:1:3	f1	0.5690	0.7749	0.7914	0.791	0.8351
	acc	0.6098	0.8222	0.8523	0.8598	0.8788
2:1:2	f1	0.6240	0.7500	0.7547	0.7455	0.8962
	acc	0.7330	0.8125	0.8523	0.8409	0.9280
3:1:1	f1	0.5231	0.7586	0.7772	0.7407	0.8958
	acc	0.6477	0.7727	0.8371	0.8409	0.9242

effect. GAT mainly uses the single-layer attention mechanism to calculate the impact of different neighbors on the target node before aggregation. HAN mainly calculates the influence of neighbors on the target node in the meta path as well as the influence of different meta paths on the target node. Compared with these two methods, it is seen that the fusion of more information through similarity in the medical insurance data set is effective in improving the performance. Comparing the experimental results of BPGAN variants and BPGAN, further indicates that BPGAN is better than BPGAN$_{am}$. This is because this variant turns the similarity of comparison through the behavior pattern into the adjacency matrix of contact input between the two. This further proves the importance of using similarity as the weight of patients' direct contact to represent learning for nodes.

4.3 Ablation Experiment

Here, the similarity weight matrix is substituted with the ordinary adjacency relationship. We then compare the impact of behavior pattern similarity weight on node prediction and use recall, F1, and accuracy as performance evaluation indicators. The results are shown in Fig. 6.

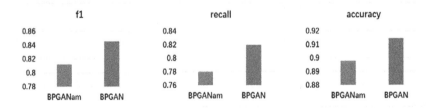

Fig. 6. Comparison between BPGAN and BPGAN$_{am}$ in terms of recall, F1, and accuracy

As it is seen in Fig. 6, the overall performance of BPGAN is higher than that of BPGAN$_{am}$. The results confirm that adding the patient interaction relationship and the similarity of patient behavior trajectory in the node embedding representation is

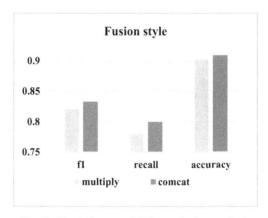

Fig. 7. The influence of different fusion methods

more efficient in mining the characteristics of patients, hence improving the prediction accuracy.

Different fusion methods also affect the performance of the model. This paper studies the connection between statistical features and similarity matrix, and the product of the two features as the embedded representation of users (Fig. 7). The comparison between the two shows that the overall effect of comcat is better than the product of features. This is because some structural feature information might be lost after multiplication.

4.4 Visual Representation

To further demonstrate the effectiveness of our proposed model, we carry out the visualization task on the medical insurance dataset. Specifically, we learn the node representation based on BPGAN and other baselines, and then we use T-SNE [26] to project the learned node representation into two-dimensional space.

The results in Fig. 8 are colored based on real labels. The visualization indicates that Metapath2vec has the most divergent representation of node learning compared with other models with an attention mechanism. Furthermore, there is a clear visual intra-class similarity in GAT, but the boundary between different classes is not clear enough. It is also seen that BPGAN obtains the best performance because the learned node representation has the highest intra-class similarity hence the clearest boundary between different classes.

4.5 Node Embedding Dimension Influence

In the parametric experiment, we also studied the impact of different dimensions of feature embedding on the final results. In the model experiment of this paper, the influence of feature embedding of {64, 128, 256} three different dimensions on the downstream experiment is studied. As is seen in Fig. 9, the proposed model performs best in terms of F1, recall, and accuracy when the feature embedding dimension is $d = 128$. Interestingly, the overall trend of dimension change versus performance is stable.

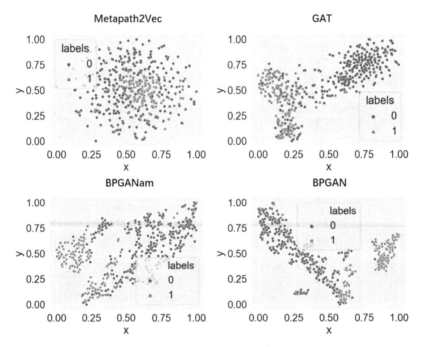

Fig. 8. Visualization of node representation using T-SNE

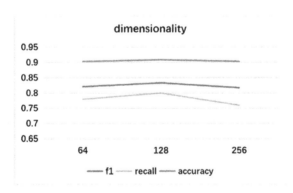

Fig. 9. Dimensional influence

5   Conclusion

This paper studies the problem of medical insurance fraud in the real medical insurance scene and proposes a medical insurance fraud detection model based on behavior patterns and a single-layer attention mechanism to improve the accuracy of medical insurance fraud detection. Incorporating the behavior pattern, we then weighted the information network based on the similarity of patients' medical trajectories and aggregated it in combination with the statistical characteristics of patients. In addition, we learn the effects of different behavior patterns on node embedding through the attention mechanism. Taking a real medical data set as an example, a large number of experiments are carried out on the medical insurance fraud detection task to verify the effectiveness of our model. In future works, we would study the integration of more heterogeneous information and extend our model to semi-supervised scenarios.

Acknowledgment. This research was funded by the Science Foundation of Fujian Province (No. 2021J011188, 2019Y0057), the Open Fund of Engineering Research Center of Big Data Application in Private Health Medicine, Fujian Provincial University (No. KF2020003), the Joint Funds of 5th Round of Health and Education Research Program of Fujian Province (No. 2019-WJ-41), and the XMUT Scientific Research Project (No. YKJCX2020117).

References

1. National Healthcare Security Administration of The People's Republic of China-2020. http://www.nhsa.gov.cn/art/2021/6/8/art_7_5232.html
2. National Healthcare Security Administration of The People's Republic of China-2019 National. http://www.nhsa.gov.cn/art/2020/6/24/art_7_3268.html
3. The United Kingdom: The Taxpayer. Cheat health & quot; More than 1 billion pounds was lost to the Treasury. Sichuan Labor Secur. (4),1 (2018)
4. Lin, Y.: An analysis of the research status of medical insurance fraud at home and abroad. Insurance Res. (12), 115–22 (2010)
5. Tang, J.Y.: Proactive detection of health care fraud. Coop. Econ. Sci. Technol. (16), 188–190 (2016)
6. Maranzato, R., Pereira, A., Neubert, M.: do Lago AP: fraud detection in reputation systems in e-markets using logistic regression and stepwise optimization. ACM SIGAPP Appl. Comput. Rev. **11**(1), 14–26 (2010)
7. Ekina, T., Leva, F., Ruggeri, F., Soyer, R.: Application of Bayesian methods in detection of healthcare fraud. Chem. Eng. Trans. **33**, 151–156 (2013)
8. Liu, C., Chan, Y., Alam Kazmi, S.H., Fu, H.: Financial fraud detection model: based on random forest. Int. J. Econ. Financ. **7**(7), 178–188 (2015)
9. Luhui, C.: Medical insurance fraud detection based on TLSTM. Comput. Eng. Appl. **56**(21), 237–241 (2020)
10. Hancock, J., Khoshgoftaar, T.M.: Medicare fraud detection using CatBoost. In: 2020 IEEE 21st International Conference on Information Reuse and Integration for Data Science (IRI), pp. 97–103 (2020)
11. Xie, J., Kelley, S., Szymanski, B.K.: Overlapping community detection in networks: the state-of-the-art and comparative study. ACM Comput. Surv. (CSUR) **45**(4), 1–35 (2013)
12. Zhang, W., He, X.: An anomaly detection method for medicare fraud detection. In: IEEE International Conference on Big Knowledge, pp. 309–314 (2017)
13. Bauder, R.A., Rosa, R., Khoshgoftaar, T.M.: Identifying medicare provider fraud with unsupervised machine learning. In: 2018 IEEE International Conference on Information Reuse and Integration for Data Science, pp. 285–292 (2018)
14. Ekin, T., Lakomski, G., Musal, R.M.: An unsupervised Bayesian hierarchical method for medical fraud assessment. Stat. Anal. Data Mining ASA Data Sci. J. **12**(2), 116–124 (2019)
15. Naidoo, K., Marivate, V.: Unsupervised anomaly detection of healthcare providers using generative adversarial networks. In: Hattingh, M., Matthee, M., Smuts, H., Pappas, I., Dwivedi, Y. K., Mäntymäki, M. (eds.) I3E 2020. LNCS, vol. 12066, pp. 419–430. Springer, Cham (2020). https://doi.org/10.1007/978-3-030-44999-5_35

16. Fortunato, S.: Community detection in graphs. Phys. Rep. **486**(3–5), 75–174 (2010)
17. Beutel, A., Akoglu, L., Faloutsos, C.: Graph-based user behavior modeling: from prediction to fraud detection. In: ACM SIGKDD International Conference on Knowledge Discovery & Data Mining, pp. 2309–2310 (2015)
18. Hu, B., Zhang, Z., Shi, C., Zhou, J., Li, X., Qi, Y.: Cash-out user detection based on attributed heterogeneous information network with a hierarchical attention mechanism. In: Proceedings of the AAAI Conference on Artificial Intelligence, pp. 946–953 (2019)
19. Zhong, Q., Liu, Y., Ao, X., Hu, B., He, Q.: Financial defaulter detection on online credit payment via multi-view attributed heterogeneous information network. In: WWW 2020: The Web Conference 2020, pp. 785–795 (2020)
20. Chen, R., Zhang, H., Lin, K.: A graph-based method for health care joint fraud detection. In: ICCPR 2020: 2020 9th International Conference on Computing and Pattern Recognition, pp. 122–129 (2020)
21. Defferrard, M., Bresson, X., Vandergheynst, P.: Convolutional neural networks on graphs with fast localized spectral filtering (2016)
22. Han, J.: Mining heterogeneous information networks: the next frontier. In: Proceedings of the 18th ACM SIGKDD International Conference on Knowledge Discovery and Data Mining, pp. 2–3 (2012)
23. Dong, Y., Chawla, N.V., Swami, A.: metapath2vec: Scalable representation learning for heterogeneous networks. In: Proceedings of the 23rd ACM SIGKDD International Conference on Knowledge Discovery and Data Mining, pp. 135–44. Association for Computing Machinery Halifax (2017)
24. Velikovi, P., Cucurull, G., Casanova, A., Romero, A., Liò, P., Bengio, Y.: Graph attention. Networks **1050**(20), 10–48550 (2017)
25. Yang, Z., Yang, D., Dyer, C., He, X., Hovy, E.: Hierarchical attention networks for document classification. In: Proceedings of the 2016 Conference of the North American Chapter of the Association for Computational Linguistics: Human Language Technologies, pp. 1480–1489 (2016)
26. Laurens, V.D.M., Hinton, G.: Visualizing data using t-SNE. J. Mach. Learn. Res. **9**(2605), 2579–2605 (2008)

Author Index